Advance Praise for

*The Persistence of Mysticism in Catholic Europe:
France, Italy, and Germany (1500–1675)*

"This volume, completing the account of Christian mysticism in the early modern period (1500–1675) with a special emphasis on the French School, has all the hallmarks of McGinn's work: readability, profound learning, and consistent methodology. This study is a worthy addition to what is already recognized as a monumental work of scholarship."

Lawrence S. Cunningham
The University of Notre Dame

"An astonishing achievement and gift to us all! There are times when one must simply be thankful that the rare scholar like Bernard McGinn is present in our midst, who not only commands a vastly enormous field of material, but can communicate its central features with excitement and seasoned discernment. Here one is treated not only to a careful study of the primary texts, but also to a dazzling conversation with the authorities in the field. Perhaps the reader will come away inspired as well, as was this reader."

William Thompson-Uberuaga
Emeritus Professor of Theology,
Duquesne University (Pittsburgh)
Editor, *Bérulle and the French School*,
Classics of Western Spirituality

"Bernard McGinn's magisterial exploration of the Christian mystical tradition reveals further riches in this volume on *The Persistence of Mysticism in Catholic Europe: 1500–1675*. One continues to appreciate the author's careful analysis of the historical and cultural context—the "socio-logic"—in which mysticism must take root. But, even more, one savors his penetrating discernment of the perennial "Christo-logic" which orients and governs every authentic witness to the mystical element of Christianity. This volume only increases our grateful debt to Professor McGinn for his splendid accomplishment."

Father Robert P. Imbelli
Boston College Emeritus
Author of *Rekindling the Christic Imagination*

THE PERSISTENCE OF MYSTICISM IN CATHOLIC EUROPE

A multi-volume series

**THE PRESENCE OF GOD:
A HISTORY OF WESTERN CHRISTIAN MYSTICISM**

I.	*The Foundations of Mysticism*
II.	*The Growth of Mysticism*
III.	*The Flowering of Mysticism*
IV.	*The Harvest of Mysticism in Medieval Germany*
V.	*Varieties of Vernacular Mysticism*
VI.1	*Mysticism in the Reformation*
VI.2	*Mysticism in the Golden Age of Spain*

THE PERSISTENCE OF MYSTICISM IN CATHOLIC EUROPE

France, Italy, and Germany (1500–1675)

Vol. VI, Part 3 of
The Presence of God:
A History of Western Christian Mysticism

by
Bernard McGinn

A Herder & Herder Book
The Crossroad Publishing Company
New York

A Herder & Herder Book
The Crossroad Publishing Company
www.crossroadpublishing.com

© 2020 by Bernard McGinn

Crossroad, Herder & Herder, and the crossed C logo/colophon are registered trademarks of The Crossroad Publishing Company.

All rights reserved. No part of this book may be copied, scanned, reproduced in any way, or stored in a retrieval system, or transmitted, in any form or by any means, electronic, mechanical, photocopying, recording, or otherwise, without the written permission of The Crossroad Publishing Company. For permission please write to rights@crossroadpublishing.com.

In continuation of our 200-year tradition of independent publishing, The Crossroad Publishing Company proudly offers a variety of books with strong, original voices and diverse perspectives. The viewpoints expressed in our books are not necessarily those of The Crossroad Publishing Company, any of its imprints or of its employees, executives, or owners. Although the author and publisher have made every effort to ensure that the information in this book was correct at press time, the author and publisher do not assume and hereby disclaim any liability to any party for any loss, damage, or disruption caused by errors or omissions, whether such errors or omissions result from negligence, accident, or any other cause. No claims are made or responsibility assumed for any health or other benefits.

Book design by The HK Scriptorium

Library of Congress Cataloging-in-Publication Data
available from the Library of Congress.

ISBN 978-0-8245-8900-4 cloth
ISBN 978-0-8245-0195-2 ePub
ISBN 978-0-8245-0196-9 mobi
ISBN 978-0-8245-9886-0 tradepaper

Books published by The Crossroad Publishing Company may be purchased at special quantity discount rates for classes and institutional use. For information, please e-mail sales@crossroadpublishing.com.

Dedicated to

*The Faculty, Students, and Staff
of
The Oblate School of Theology
San Antonio, Texas*

*For their personal, spiritual, and intellectual
hospitality and kindness
over the years*

Contents

Abbreviations	xi
Preface	xiii
Notes	xv
PART I. Mysticism in France	1

Chapter 1
Introduction: The Hegemony of France — 3
  A Sketch of Events — 4
  Religious Developments — 7
  The Surprise of French Mysticism — 14
    The Sources of French Mysticism — 16
    Schools and Nomenclature of French Mysticism — 20
  Some Themes and Issues of the Seventeenth-Century
      French Mystics — 22
  Notes — 29

Chapter 2
The Beginnings of French Mysticism — 36
  Louis de Blois — 37
  Barbe Acarie and Her Circle — 43
  Benet of Canfield and the Mysticism of Annihilation — 50
    Life — 50
    The Question of Sources — 53
    The Structure and Teaching of The Rule of Perfection — 54
  A Note on Some Other French Capuchin Mystics — 74
  Notes — 77

Chapter 3
Francis de Sales: Love and Holy Indifference   **89**

  Life and Times   90
  Writings and Sources   100
    Writings   100
    Sources   109
  Teaching   110
    The Starting Point: God as Love and the World as Participation in Love   111
    The Path to God: Progress through the Devout Life   123
    The Goal: Heart-to-Heart Union with God in the Life of Prayer   126
  Conclusion   155
  Appendix: Followers of Francis de Sales: Jane de Chantal   156
  Notes   163

Chapter 4
Pierre de Bérulle. Annihilation and Elevation   **181**

  Introduction: Bérulle's Theocentric Christocentrism   181
  Bérulle's Life and Writings   183
  Bérulle's Mystical Teaching   192
    The Mystery of God   194
    Creation and Humanity   201
    The Incarnation and Christology   204
    Bérulle's Mariology   218
    The Practice of the Annihilated Life   222
  Conclusion   239
  Appendix: In the Wake of Bérulle   239
  Notes   253

Chapter 5
Other French Mystics of Le Grand Siècle   **273**

  Jesuit Mystics   273
    Louis Lallemant   275
    Jean-Joseph Surin   282
  Carmelite Mysticism   293
    Jean de Saint-Samson   294
    Lawrence of the Resurrection   304
  Ursuline Mysticism and Marie de l'Incarnation   308

Appendix: Jansenism and Mysticism:
    The Case of Blaise Pascal   321
Notes   332

PART II. Mysticism in Other Catholic Areas   345

Chapter 6
English Recusant Mysticism   347
The Recusant Situation   347
Augustine Baker (1575–1641), Bakerism, and *Sancta Sophia*   349
  An Eccentric Monastic Life   350
  Baker's Writings   354
  The Teaching of "Sancta Sophia"   357
Baker's Disciples among the Benedictine Monks and Nuns   372
A Recusant Mystical Poet: Richard Crashaw   380
Notes   396

Chapter 7
Mysticism in Italy (1500–1675)   408
Introduction   408
Collaboration and Controversy: Isabella Berinzaga
    and Achille Gagliardi   414
A Selection of Women Mystics   429
  St. Caterina de'Ricci, O.P. (1522–1590)   431
  Maria Domitilla Galluzzi, O.F.M. Cap. (1595–1671)   432
  St. Maria Maddalena de'Pazzi, O. Carm. (1566–1607)   436
Early Modern Italian Male Mystics   451
  Blessed Paolo Giustiniani (1476–1528)   452
  Giovanni Bona (1609–1674)   454
Conclusion   458
Notes   459

Chapter 8
Mysticism in Catholic Germany and the Low Countries
    (1525–1675)   471
Introduction   471
The Jesuits   473
Johannes Scheffler (Angelus Silesius)   481
  Life and Works   481
  Sources, Style, and Perspective   483
  Johann Scheffler's Cherubic Mysticism   489

Mysticism in the Low Countries: Maria Petyt   507
    The Carmelite Maria Petyt (1623–1677)   509
  Notes   516

Conclusion   **532**

Bibliography   **535**

Index of Scripture References   **571**

Index of Names   **573**

Index of Subjects   **580**

Abbreviations

Bremond, *Histoire*
: Henri Bremond, *Histoire littéraire du sentiment religieux en France depuis la fin des guerres de religion jusqu'à nos jours*. 11 vols. Paris: Bloud & Gay, 1915–33. This has been reprinted with additions in 5 vols. Grenoble: Jérôme Millon, 2006. This is the edition cited here.

Bremond, *History*
: Henri Bremond, *A Literary History of Religious Thought in France from the Wars of Religion down to Our Own Times*. Translated by K. L. Montgomery. 3 vols. London: SPCK, 1928–36. Translation of the first three vols. of the original eleven-volume edition.

Cognet, *La spiritualité moderne*
: Louis Cognet, *La spiritualité moderne. I. Essor: 1500–1650*. Paris: Aubier, 1966.

Certeau, *Mystic Fable*
: Michel de Certeau, *The Mystic Fable: Volume One. The Sixteenth and Seventeenth Centuries*. Chicago: University of Chicago Press, 1992. *Volume Two, The Sixteenth and Seventeenth Centuries*. Chicago: University of Chicago Press, 2015.

DS
: *Dictionnaire de spiritualité: Ascétique et mystique, doctrine et histoire*. Edited by Marcel Viller et al. 17 vols. Paris: Beauchesne, 1937–1997.

Dionysian Corpus
　　　　　　　　The writings ascribed to Dionysius the Areopagite are found in the critical edition of Beate Regina Suchla, Günter Heil, and Martin Ritter, *Corpus Dionysiacum*, 2 vols. Berlin: Walter de Gruyter, 1990–91. The following abbreviations will be used:
　CH　　　　　*De coelesti hierarchia* (*The Celestial Hierarchy*)
　DN　　　　　*De divinis nominibus* (*The Divine Names*)
　EH　　　　　*De ecclesiastica hierarchia* (*The Ecclesiastical Hierarchy*)
　Ep　　　　　*Epistulae* (*Letters*)
　MT　　　　　*De mystica theologia* (*The Mystical Theology*)
McGinn　　　　Bernard McGinn, *The Presence of God: A History of Western Christian Mysticism*. New York: Crossroad Herder, 1991–. The previous volumes in the series will be abbreviated as follows:
　Foundations　*The Foundations of Mysticism: Origins to the Fifth Century* (1991)
　Growth　　　*The Growth of Mysticism: Gregory the Great through the Twelfth Century* (1994)
　Flowering　　*The Flowering of Mysticism: Men and Women in the New Mysticism (1200–1350)* (1998)
　Harvest　　　*The Harvest of Mysticism in Medieval Germany, 1300–1500* (2007)
　Varieties　　　*The Varieties of Vernacular Mysticism, 1350–1550* (2012)
　Reformation　*Mysticism in the Reformation, 1500–1650* (2016)
　Spain　　　　*Mysticism in the Golden Age of Spain (1500–1650)* (2017)

PL　　　　　　*Patrologia cursus completus. Series Latina*. Edited by J. P. Migne. 221 vols. Paris: J. P. Migne, 1844–64.
STh　　　　　Thomas Aquinas, *Summa theologiae* (cited by part, question, and article; e.g., Ia, q. 3, a. 1).
Vg　　　　　　*Biblia Vulgata* (*Vulgate Bible*)

Preface

This volume brings to a close a lengthy examination of mysticism in early modern Europe, a time of Reformation, religious wars, growing absolutist government, and the revival of Roman Catholicism associated with the Council of Trent and the Counter-Reformation. Volume V of *The Presence of God*, entitled *The Varieties of Vernacular Mysticism, 1350–1550*, was published in 2012. As I began the research and writing of Volume VI, it soon became clear to me that what was originally conceived of as a single volume would have to be divided, given the richness of the sources, the complexity of the developments, and the plethora of important mystics of the period roughly 1500–1650/75. A tripartite division of Volume VI soon emerged as the most reasonable way to deal with the issue.

Contrary to some commonly held beliefs, but much in accord with the latest findings of both Protestant and Catholic scholars, the Reformers of the sixteenth century and their seventeenth-century successors did not reject mysticism. There were, rather, important mystical currents and mystics in the Lutheran tradition, among the Radical Reformers, and in the English Reformation of the *via media*. I tried to present these in *Mysticism in the Reformation* (2016). From the perspective of Catholic mysticism, one of the high points of the entire mystical tradition occurred in Spain in the sixteenth century with some ramifications into the seventeenth century. I felt that this important period deserved a volume of its own—*Mysticism in the Golden Age of Spain* (2017). But Catholic mysticism of the early modern period cannot be restricted to Spain. Catholic Italy of the sixteenth and seventeenth centuries also had important mystics, especially women, as did the Catholic parts of Germany and the Low Countries, and even the English Catholic exiles, or "Recusants," who fled to the Continent to escape persecution. In the seventeenth century, however, it was above all France that witnessed a veritable explosion of mystical piety in the wake of terrible religious wars and the consolidation of the absolutist French monarchy. As Ronald Knox put it, speaking of France, "[T]he seventeenth century became a century of mystics. The doctrine of the interior life was far better publicized, was developed in far more detail than it had ever been in late-medieval Germany or late-medieval England."[1] The mysticism of France and these other parts of Catholic Europe is the subject of this volume, which I have decided to call *The Persistence of Mysticism (1500–1675)*. I have chosen "persistence" to characterize this part of Volume VI, because the word expresses a central theme of my argument—despite many developments and shifts in perspective, the early modern Catholic mystics presented here are best viewed in the context of mystical traditions that go back to the patristic past and that were decisively reshaped in the late Middle Ages.

A word about the chronological limits of the volume. Exact chronology is at best a crude marker for movements of the mind and the spirit. The year 1500 is a convenient date for the new situation that the mystical tradition had to face in light of the wave of religious reformations sweeping across Europe (both Protestant and Catholic). I have argued throughout Volume VI that the new situation did not lead so much to a break in the history of mysticism as to a series of adaptations of the mystical element of Christianity in the face of rapid change. The other end of the chronology of this book and its predecessors is more complicated. It is my contention that the movements of mystical piety that get perhaps artificially grouped under the rubric of "Quietism" and the reaction of the institutional church against them mark a real, indeed decisive, break in the story of Western Christian mysticism. A convenient date for the beginning of Quietism is 1675, the year of the publication of Miguel Molinos's international bestseller, *The Spiritual Guide* (*Guia espiritual*), which was to earn papal condemnation in 1687. By 1680, Madame Jeanne Guyon, another archetypal Quietist, had begun her daring apostolic preaching and teaching tours and was soon to flood the French world with the torrent of her mystical writings. To be sure, there had been eruptions of attacks and condemnations of those seen as dangerous mystics from the late thirteenth century on.[2] In sixteenth- and seventeenth-century Spain the *Alumbrados* ("Enlightened ones") were subject to condemnation and persecution by the Inquisition, and even in France the rapid proliferation of mysticism in the first third of the seventeenth century was followed by a period of suspicion and attack. It has become common practice in some circles to use the term "Pre-Quietism" to describe some mystical writers of the early seventeenth century who announce themes linked to the later Quietists. Although this is a retrospective label that may not do full justice to the situation and intentions of these figures, I have decided not to treat them in this volume but will take them up later as part of the background to Quietism. The struggle over Quietism that convulsed the Catholic religious world of Italy, Spain, and France after 1675 built on past tensions between mysticism and magisterium but was something different—and far more serious. That is the reason why Volume VI, Part 3, of *The Presence of God* ends with the third quarter of the 1600s.

The intellectual and personal debts I've incurred over the three decades of the writing of *The Presence of God* fill me with a sense of gratitude difficult to express. My teachers, my students, my readers, and my friends have all given me so much. As far as *The Persistence of Mysticism* is concerned, the several distinguished experts who read chapters, or parts of chapters, will be thanked at the appropriate places. I wish also to thank the Institute for Advanced Studies of the University of Notre Dame, where parts of this book were written, for its gracious hospitality during my Fellowship Semester there in 2017. That the long labor of Volume VI was able to see the light of day in three substantial volumes I owe to the ongoing encouragement of Gwendolin Herder, the publisher of Crossroad-Herder, and the very able assistance of Chris Myers, the Senior Editor at the Press. A great debt of gratitude is owed to Paul Kobelski and Maurya Horgan of The HK Scriptorium, who are responsible for the impeccable copyediting and composition of this book and many of its predecessors. My wife, Patricia Ferris McGinn, as ever, has seen the book through its gestation, proofread every page, made extensive suggestions, and put up with my obsession with finally getting it finished. But then, as William Butler Yeats once asked, "Why should not old men be mad?"[3]

Chicago
October 2019

Notes

1. Ronald Knox, *Enthusiasm: A Chapter in the History of Religion* (Oxford: Oxford University Press, 1950), 231–32.

2. I have given an earlier sketch of these in Bernard McGinn, "'Evil-Sounding, Rash, and Suspect of Heresy': Tensions between Mysticism and Magisterium in the History of the Church," *Catholic Historical Review* 90 (2004): 193–212.

3. *The Collected Poems of W. B. Yeats* (New York: Macmillan, 1973), 333.

PART I

Mysticism in France

Chapter 1

Introduction: The Hegemony of France

In the seventeenth century, France became the major Catholic power, the center of new religious reforms and intellectual contributions, political influence, and also, more problematically, the fountainhead of issues that were to affect modern Catholicism for centuries, such as Jansenism, Quietism, Gallicanism, and political Absolutism. Much of Catholic history over the years between 1600 and 1900, especially in the Francophone and Anglophone worlds, was shaped in part by events in early modern France.

Sixteenth-century Catholicism, in reaction to the shock of the Reformation and the split in Western Christianity, had to reinvent itself, while always claiming fidelity to the church's past. Theologically, the reassertion of Catholic fidelity was given doctrinal expression in the Council of Trent (1545–1563). Politically, the medieval papacy had to make a painful transition to a new world. During the fifteenth and sixteenth centuries both the papacy and the Holy Roman Empire, the twin pillars of the medieval world (at least in the ideal), experienced challenges and a diminishment of their effective authority as the nation-states gained power. In the fifteenth and sixteenth centuries the popes began to recognize the new situation by entering into special agreements ("concordats") with various national rulers. The shift in power eventually aided the success of the Reformation, as well as doing much to shape early modern Catholicism. With regard to Spain, as I have tried to show in *Mysticism in the Golden Age of Spain*, and now in the case of seventeenth-century France, new forms of church–state relations had a strong impact on how mysticism came to expression in distinctive linguistic and cultural forms.

A Sketch of Events

The kingdom of France during the period ca. 1500 to ca. 1650 underwent a series of upheavals in which political and religious dimensions were inextricably mixed.[1] Throughout much of the sixteenth century, the ruling house of the Valois fought with the Hapsburgs both in Central Europe and in Spain for European hegemony. Under Francis I (ruled 1515–47) royal power over the church was increased by the Concordat of Bologna (1516), which guaranteed the king rights over the nomination of bishops and abbots. In the 1520s, during Francis's reign, Protestantism began to make inroads in France, not the Protestantism of Luther and his followers but the more radical "Reformed" tradition initiated by the Swiss Ulrich Zwingli (1484–1531) and carried forward by the French preachers William Farel (1489–1565) and especially John Calvin (1509–1564).[2] Despite royal opposition, the Reformed Protestants (Huguenots in France), grew strong in the decades that followed, especially among sections of the nobility and in many cities and towns. By 1562, there may have been as many as two to three million Reformed believers in France out of a population of perhaps twenty million.

Under Francis's son, Henry II (ruled 1547–59), persecution of the Protestants intensified, and wars with both the emperor Charles V in 1552 and his successor in Spain, Philip II, in 1556–59 strained France's resources. Henry's son Francis II ruled briefly (ruled 1559–60) and was succeeded by his ten-year-old brother, Charles IX (1560–74), who was dominated by his Italian mother, Catherine de'Medici (1519–1589). The weakness of the House of Valois led to the growing influence of powerful noble families, such as the House of Guise (Catholic) and the House of Bourbon (Protestant), who vied for control of the kingdom. The situation was ripe for the outbreak of the worst religious wars of the sixteenth century.

The Wars of Religion or, perhaps better, Wars of More-than-Religion[3] raged for more than three decades (1562–98) and devastated the realm, as well as the French church.[4] The major cause was the standoff between the Catholic and Reformed parties, with the former convinced that loyalty to the true church was integral to French identity, and the latter eager to destroy the "idolatry, abominations, and perversions" of traditional Catholicism. This series of eight civil wars involved a maze of aristocratic rivalries and plots to gain power over a weak king under the domination of his unpopular foreign mother. The precipitating events were edicts issued by Catherine in Charles's name that rolled back the repression of the Huguenots. This was unacceptable to the intransigent Catholic party led by the Duke of Guise, and fighting broke out in 1562. The horrors of civil war, pitting faction against faction, city against city, family against family, descended on the land. The collection of taxes began to suffer, and the longer the wars continued, the worse the financial situation of the French crown became. Three wars followed the outbreak of hostilities until the Peace of St.-Germain in 1570 restored to the Huguenots the right to worship in selected locations. This arrangement, however, was again not acceptable to the Catholic party.

In August 1572, the nobles of the realm, both Catholic and Huguenot, gathered in Paris to celebrate the wedding of the Protestant Henry of Navarre to the king's sister, Marguerite (Margot) of Valois. The responsibility for what took place beginning on Saint Bartholomew's Day, August 24, remains murky, but King Charles was convinced (by his mother?, by his Guise councillors?) that the Protestant nobles were plotting against him, so he gave orders that a number of the leaders should be eliminated. The killing got out of hand, however, and both in Paris and in a number of cities enraged Catholics, often thinking they were acting with the king's approval, slaughtered Protestants (ten thousand may have died). A fourth war followed the Saint Bartholomew's Day massacre (1572–73), and then a fifth (1574–76). In the meantime, Charles died and was succeeded by his brother, Henry III (ruled 1574–89), who was also seen as dominated by his mother.

The peace that ended the fifth war was favorable to the Huguenot party, now led by Henry of Navarre. This angered many Catholic leaders, who proceeded to form the Holy League in 1576, a body that plotted to destroy the Protestants with the aid of Philip II of Spain and to make one of the Guises king of France. A split emerged in the Catholic camp between the intransigents, or Leaguers, and the *politiques*, who sought peace through compromise. The Huguenots were defeated in the sixth war of 1577, but a seventh followed in 1580, and then an uneasy period of exhaustion on both sides lasted from 1580 to 1585. The final chapter in these long civil wars was the War of the League, or the War of the Three Henries,[5] which raged between 1585 and 1589. During this period, natural disasters, such as famine and plague in 1586 and 1587, increased the misery of France. The new round of war began when Henry III felt compelled to capitulate to the Holy League and Henry of Guise by rolling back the concessions made to the Huguenots and ordering the Protestants to return to Catholicism. In the struggles that followed, the Leaguers grew stronger, not just militarily but also by sponsoring a popular piety featuring preaching, processions, the formation of confraternities, and other practices to advance their ultra-Catholicism. Fearing for his position, the unpopular Henry III ordered the assassination of Henry of Guise and his cardinal brother, Louis, in 1588, a move that backfired. Much of the Catholic realm rose in revolt fueled by popular apocalyptic preaching. Henry III, who had no children, was assassinated on August 1, 1589, by a fanatic Leaguer cleric, but not before naming Henry of Navarre, his twenty-first cousin, as his heir.

Henry IV (ruled 1589–1610) faced a difficult situation, but his military prowess and diplomatic skills eventually won out over the forces of the Catholic Leaguers, especially given the desire of the majority of French people to return to a strong and stable monarchy.[6] The War of the Bourbon Succession was long (1589–98) and highly destructive. After an unsuccessful siege of Paris in 1590, Henry abjured Protestantism in 1593 and was crowned at Chartres in 1594. Paris surrendered to him and he won favor by treating the Leaguers with clemency. War dragged on against some of the ultra-Catholics but was finally ended on April 15, 1598, when Henry issued the Edict of Nantes, which gave the Huguenots political rights and some restricted freedom of worship. Henry IV worked hard to restore the kingdom and recoup its finances. He was generally respected, but a core of ultra-Catholics continued to oppose him and he too was assassinated in 1610. Henry was succeeded by his nine-year-old son Louis XIII (ruled 1610–43), who was under the control of his mother, Marie de'Medici (1573–1642). Never a strong monarch, Louis continued to depend on others during the course of his reign, notably Armand-Jean du Plessis, Cardinal Richelieu (1585–1642), who pursued a policy of *Realpolitik* regarding French interests in Europe, even if that meant siding with Protestant powers against the Catholic Hapsburgs during the early stages of the Thirty Years' War in Central Europe (1631–48). Richelieu also crushed the political power of the Huguenots after another revolt (1625–28). Having strengthened France's position in Europe and reorganized the royal administration, Richelieu paved the way for the succession of Louis XIII's son, the five-year-old Louis XIV, in 1643. Louis was to reign down to 1715. Although under the control of Cardinal Mazarin during the early years, by the time his personal rule began in 1661, Louis was ready to take on the role of absolute king by divine right. By this time, the great age of French mysticism was over, although some mystical writing continued. The last two decades of the seventeenth century were to see the crisis of the Quietist controversy (to be treated in the next volume). Under Louis XIV the political and cultural preponderance of France was assured, despite the ruinous wars that he engaged in during his long rule. The king's revocation of the Edict of Nantes in 1685 and the subsequent flight of most Huguenots from the country were doubtless popular with the Catholic mass of the population but harmed France in many ways.

Religious Developments

The religious history of France during these years echoes the tumultuous character of the political events.[7] The crisis of the Reformation and the particularly bloody way in which it was resolved in France resulted in three decades of confusion, turmoil, and destruction during which ecclesiastical life, in both the higher and the lower clergy, suffered greatly. It has been estimated that fully a third of the French dioceses lacked a bishop by the end of the Wars of Religion.[8] The devotional life of the rural communities was often rendered impossible by fighting and marauding armies. Religious houses, many decayed and corrupt, were particular objects of the attacks of the Huguenots. The lugubrious state of French Catholicism during the Wars of Religion was evident on all sides.

The attitude of the French monarchy toward Rome and the papacy is also an important factor for understanding early modern French Catholicism. Despite French official respect for the papacy, the Gallicanism of the French church—that is, its insistence on its own prerogatives and independence—was deeply ingrained. Because the Council of Trent was held in areas under the Hapsburg Empire, French bishops did not attend, and the reforms of the council were not to be accepted in the realm until 1615, and then only partially. France only slowly became "Tridentine." French opposition to Rome's ideas about how to enforce Catholic belief extended to the Inquisition. Several times the French church rebuffed Rome's advice to set up an Inquisition in the kingdom. Politically, the popes were also sharply at odds with Richelieu's alliance with Protestant powers to curb the Hapsburgs during the Thirty Years' War. Louis XIV's high-handed treatment of a succession of popes also caused tensions. Nonetheless, the papacy's need for French political support generally moderated these problems.

The dawn of peace at the end of the sixteenth century ushered in an era of reform and rejuvenation in French Catholicism. Some of this religious force grew out of the intense ascetical and at times apocalyptic religiosity of the Leaguers, but even the more moderate *politiques* now realized that the time was ripe for a revival of faith and practice. Early seventeenth-century France witnessed the emerging power of the *dévots*, that is, groups of pious, generally aristocratic, laymen and women who spearheaded the religious revival of the time by their personal piety and above all by sponsoring the foundation of new religious houses. Their contribution to the religious creativity evident in the early decades of the seventeenth century was great, and continued on well into the century.[9] Henri Bremond summarized this era in French religious history thus: "France was then entering upon one of those periods I will not say of transition, for all periods are that, but of a religious fermentation in which the most unforeseen and audacious departures are taken, without surprising or even annoying anyone. . . . Christian France under Henri IV resembled a part of a mission-field in the first years of advance."[10] A later scholar, Jean Dagens, saw this revival as closely allied with mysticism: "It was the confidence in the illuminations of sanctity that made the first half of the seventeenth century a great age of mysticism."[11] The following brief impressionistic sketch of some of the aspects of this revival will help frame the story of the French mysticism of the time.

The French bishops enjoyed a degree of independence from Rome superior to that of other European episcopates, but they were not independent from the crown, although it was probably not until the time of Richelieu that the royal appointment of bishops was fully restored. While the majority of bishops came from the aristocracy and received their positions because of family connections, the Tridentine ideal of the reforming, pastoral bishop grew apace in the seventeenth century. Nonetheless, many bishops spent more time at court pursuing their political agendas than in their sees. The educational and pastoral situation of the secular clergy seems to have improved considerably during the seventeenth century. The numerous colleges established by the Jesuits and other orders helped raise the educational and spiritual level of the clergy, and, although the great wave of founding seminaries came in the middle of the seventeenth century, this Tridentine reform played a significant role. Many of the religious reformers of the early seventeenth century, such as Pierre de Bérulle, were concerned with elevating the role of the priest in church and society. Overall, there appears to have been a marked restoration of parish life after the destruction of the Wars of Religion.[12]

Another important aspect of the revival of religion was the missions, that is, preaching programs in rural areas designed to revitalize Christian observance. These were conducted by new groups of secular clergy, such as the Congregation of the Mission, called the Lazarists, founded by Vincent de Paul in 1625. Raymond Deville has claimed that this "missionary invasion" should be seen together with the "mystical invasion" (see below) as complementary aspects of the seventeenth-century renewal of French Catholicism.[13] Furthermore, if the new congregations of clergy were important for renewal, so too were the "confraternities," that is, voluntary associations of mostly urban lay Christians, who came together under a heavenly patron for purposes of mutual religious aid and assistance. Along with the thirteenth century, the seventeenth century, especially in France, was a golden age for confraternities, which performed a wide variety of good works. It is difficult to summarize the effect of this broad movement, but some measure of its importance can be seen from the calculation that, by the end of the century, there may have been as many as a million and a half confraternity members in France (ca. 8 percent of the population).[14]

In the sixteenth and seventeenth centuries, as in the late Middle Ages, the religious "professionals" were the orders of monks, nuns, and mendicant friars. Reforms of the Benedictines, Franciscans, Dominicans, and Carmelites had begun as early as the fourteenth century. Further reform movements, as well as foundations of new orders to meet rising apostolic needs, were vital to the French religious revival. The new orders and congregations were by no means a French phenomenon, but their manifestations in France were essential to the pastoral and spiritual life of the kingdom. Though our emphasis will be on their spiritual contributions, the religious orders also played a large role in the social, political, and financial fabric of the kingdom. In a survey made under Richelieu in 1625, it was calculated that fully a third of the material property of the kingdom belonged to the clergy, both secular and religious.[15]

With regard to the many monastic houses in France and their considerable wealth, the great enemy of reform was the *commendam* system, in which the king named powerful clerics, usually bishops, as abbots of monasteries to allow them to receive the financial proceeds of the houses as benefices without the necessity of residence or supervision. Though this practice was often decried, the reforms of the seventeenth century did little to change this engrained feature of early modern Catholicism. Cardinal Richelieu, for example, was the commendatory abbot of the venerable houses of Cluny and Cîteaux, and Cardinal Mazarin set the record by holding twenty-five abbeys *in commendam*. This sad situation did not block all reforms. For example, the worldly clerical courtier Armand Jean de Rancé (1626–1700), who had once held five commendatory abbeys, underwent a conversion in 1657 and gave up all his benefices, except the rigorous Cistercian house of La Trappe, whence he strove to further the reform of the Cistercian Order.

The reform of older orders and the proliferation of new apostolic congregations and groups were of central importance in early modern French Catholicism. The Capuchin reform of the Franciscans was begun in Italy in 1528 by Matteo da Bascio (ca. 1495–1552) out of a desire to return to the simplicity, poverty, and contemplative life of Saint Francis.[16] Capuchin severity of life, dedication to preaching, and missionary zeal made them, after the Jesuits, the most successful of the orders spearheading the Counter-Reformation reaction against Protestantism. Established in France by 1573, the Capuchins were powerful supporters of the Catholic League and produced a number of spiritual and mystical authors. The new apostolic reform of the Jesuits, founded by Ignatius Loyola, was approved by Pope Paul III in 1540. The spread of the order was remarkable. The Jesuit commitment to education was particularly important for their impact on France, where they appeared as early as 1556. The work of the Jesuits was vital, but the order was controversial. They were banned from the kingdom between 1595 and 1603 for the role of a Jesuit student in an attempt on the life of Henry IV, but the king later chose the Jesuit Pierre Coton (1564–1626) to be his confessor and spiritual adviser.[17] The Jesuits engaged in internal struggles over the importance of mystical writings in relation to the order's tradition of apostolic commitment.

The Carmelite reform was decisive for sixteenth-century Spanish Catholicism, and also became important in seventeenth-century France.[18] Even before her canonization, Teresa of Avila had emerged as miraculous proof of the divine support for Counter-Reformation Catholicism. In seventeenth-century France, Teresa's reputation for sanctity and the depth of her mystical teaching gave her a special status. Two Carmelite reform movements contributed to French religious life and spirituality in the seventeenth century. In 1601, three volumes of Teresa's *Works* were translated into French, as well as the Jesuit de

Ribera's *Life of Mother Teresa of Jesus*. The circle of devout clergy and laity that had been meeting at the house of the noblewoman Barbe Acarie (1566–1618) was especially taken with Teresa, and Acarie resolved to found a house of the Discalced Carmelite nuns in Paris.[19] The negotiations were delicate, not only due to the political opposition between France and Spain, but also because the Spanish nuns feared to go to France, thinking it a hotbed of heresy. In 1604, however, a group of Spanish nuns, including two of Teresa's closest disciples, Ana de Jesús (1549–1621) and Ana de San Bartolomé (1549–1626), arrived in Paris and set up the first French Carmel. The new house experienced difficulties, not only due to the differences in styles of prayer between the Spanish and the French nuns, but also because the Spanish nuns thought of themselves as still under the Spanish male Carmelites, while Pierre de Bérulle, who had been instrumental in bringing them to France, soon made it clear that they were subject to him and his view of reformed religious life. Nonetheless, the house attracted so many women that it soon began to expand. By 1644 there were no fewer than fifty-five reformed convents in France and the Low Countries, which produced a number of female mystics.

The other Carmelite reform was a homegrown affair, primarily of male houses, the "Reform of Touraine."[20] The currents of reform that had percolated through the Carmelite Order in the fifteenth and sixteenth centuries began to affect France, especially Brittany and Paris, around 1600. Desiring a more strict observance of the original Carmelite charism, Philippe Thibault (1572–1638) and some other friars introduced a reform stressing prayer, silence, and solitude into the monastery of Rennes in Brittany in 1602. This spread throughout the province of Touraine and to the other French Carmelite provinces. Unlike the Discalced reform, the Touraine reform did not seek to establish a separate order but rather to return the established Carmelites to something like their original vision. The Touraine reform attracted one of the premier mystics of seventeenth-century France, Jean de St. Samson (1571–1636). Other mystical authors from this branch of the Carmelites include Dominic de St. Albert (1596–1624).

There were other religious reforms that had an impact on seventeenth-century France, such as the congregation of the Feuillants, a breakaway from the Cistercians that began in 1577. A number of reforms of older Benedictine houses and congregations also proliferated.[21] It was the "experiments," however, that is, new ventures in the religious life, for both men and women, that had the greatest effect, at least with regard to spirituality and mysticism. Pierre de Bérulle's desire to revive and enhance the secular clergy led him to found the French Oratory in 1611, after the model of Philip Neri's Roman Oratory, but with special characteristics. The Oratorians were engaged in pastoral renewal, as well as in education, in both colleges and seminaries. By 1630 there were already seventy-three houses. The Oratorians gave rise to offshoots, that is, congregations founded by priests who had been associated with the Oratory but saw a need for new apostolates. In 1643 John Eudes (1601–1680) founded the Congregation of Jesus and Mary (Eudists) to engage in seminary work. Jean-Jacques Olier (1608–1657), a parish priest at Saint-Sulpice in Paris, was much influenced by Bérulle and other early Oratorians. He founded the Society of Saint-Sulpice in 1642, which was also primarily devoted to seminary education. All three of these founders were important mystical writers, and we will see more of them in what follows.

Among the most remarkable aspects of the religious revival in France in the first half of the seventeenth century was the new role of women, both those in established forms of religious life and the pious wealthy women (*dévotes*) who founded and supported religious houses and often led lives of deep sanctity.[22] We have already noted Barbe Acarie's role in bringing Teresa's Discalced reform to France, but Acarie was just one of a number of aristocratic women who channeled their religious zeal into the founding of convents during the seventeenth century.[23] Among the new orders that profited from the support of the *dévotes* were three groups that had a great impact on French religious life, both in the seventeenth century and after. The Company of Saint Ursula was founded by Angela Merici (1474–1540), a native of Brescia, who was for a time a Franciscan tertiary.[24] In 1535 she gathered a community of uncloistered women who took no vows and lived in their own houses while engaging in apostolic work among the poor and sick. Such groups spread in Northern Italy, but, under the influence of Tridentine prescriptions, many of them had to accept enclosure and full vows, thus becoming a religious order in the canonical sense of the word. The first French Ursuline house was opened in 1592 in Avignon, and by 1610 there were twenty-nine houses in Southern France. They soon spread north to Paris (1614) and other cities. Some houses kept full enclosure; others did not. Many communities engaged in an active apostolate, teaching girls and catechizing mixed groups.[25] This sometimes led to tensions, but the Ursulines were effective and widespread. It has been calculated that 320 Ursuline convents were founded in France in the seventeenth century, containing as many as twelve thousand religious women.[26] Their mixture of the active and contemplative lives produced at least one great mystic in Marie de l'Incarnation (1599–1672), who left France to catechize and educate the native children in far-off Quebec.

A similar initiative can be found in the Order of the Visitation (Visitandines) founded by Francis de Sales and an aristocratic widow from Dijon, Jane de Chantal, in 1610. As will be detailed in chapter 3, Francis, a model Tridentine bishop, first met Jane in 1604, and spent several years pondering how best to move ahead with her in founding a new style of religious life that would be contemplative but also unenclosed and open to apostolic efforts. As the Visitandines began to spread, however, they came under pressure to conform to Tridentine strictures regarding formal vows and strict enclosure, and Francis eventually acquiesced in these. The Visitandines, nonetheless, maintained an opening to apostolic work, and their "strict" enclosure was often more porous than might be imagined from its legal prescriptions. The Visitandines were another great success, counting 124 houses by the middle of the century. A third innovative option for women was the congregation of the Daughters of Charity, the product of the efforts of the secular priest Vincent de Paul (ca. 1580–1660), one of the few nonaristocrats who had real impact on seventeenth-century French Catholicism. With the help of Louise de Marillac (1591–1660), in 1633 he founded the unenclosed Ladies of Charity, a congregation of upper-class women, who, along with the assistance of the lower-class Daughters of Charity, engaged in apostolic work and educational endeavors.[27]

While it would be a mistake to think of early seventeenth-century France as an ideal world of religious revival and apostolic fervor, the age was quite remarkable for its piety, as well as for its innovations, both in the contemplative life and in the active apostolate. This contribution was especially true in the case of women, as shown by the fact that between 1600 and 1650 there were no fewer than forty-five female houses founded in Paris, as compared to twenty for men.[28] It has sometimes been said that the new female foundations were primarily an expression of women's desire to share in the apostolic life fostered by the Council of Trent and by the Catholic reaction against the Reformation.[29] There were, indeed, many new efforts on the part of women to undertake the apostolic work long denied them, but from the start of France's religious revival the traditional enclosed and contemplative life for women also remained powerful, and the number of new foundations of contemplative houses, such as those of the Carmelites, was impressive.[30] The historical record, as ever, displays a complexity that belies easy generalizations.

The Surprise of French Mysticism

The literature on seventeenth-century French mysticism produced over the past century is staggering and, to the outsider, can at times seem like an intensive in-house discussion. Nevertheless, the French chapter in the long story of mysticism is still but one chapter, however rich and interesting. The modern study of French mysticism of the seventeenth century began with a long, complex, and unfinished masterpiece, the eleven volumes of the *Histoire littéraire du sentiment religieux en France* . . . (1915–33), of the Abbé (and former Jesuit) Henri Bremond (1865–1933), a member of the Académie Française.[31] In these lengthy volumes, Bremond did not even manage to reach the end of the century (his original intention was to go from Francis de Sales to Fénelon), but he set up a mountain range that later researchers have explored, debated, and often sought to overcome. The history of the writing of the project and the debates it inspired has recently been well told by Peter Gorday, so, while I will often cite Bremond in what follows, I will not try to give further reflections on the monumental importance of these volumes.[32]

Among the numerous phrases pioneered by Bremond was that of *la invasion mystique* to describe the outburst of mystical writing in the first half of the seventeenth century in France.[33] It still has currency today.[34] The notion of "invasion" suggests an intrusion from outside, and, despite considerable influence from other and older mystical traditions, the French phenomenon was in many ways homegrown.[35] It may be more helpful to think of this chapter in the story of mysticism under the rubric of "surprise." It is not so much that mysticism was totally new to France (Bernard of Clairvaux, after all, was Burgundian French), but it is true that mysticism did not really have an important role in France in the later Middle Ages, despite occasional figures, such as Marguerite Porete in the fourteenth century and Jean Gerson in the fifteenth. The flood of mystical literature that appeared in French from about 1590 to 1650/60 was, indeed, *surprising*.[36] This massive corpus was produced by a host of figures. (Even a selective list of mystics and mystical authors of this period can approach a hundred names!) It is obvious, therefore, that any general account of French mysticism in the seventeenth century will necessarily have to be selective. The chapters that follow will investigate only a few of the most important contributors to this mystical surprise; in other words, it will supply a series of portraits, some short, others longer, of a rich field of study.

The French surprise, like the story of mysticism in the Golden Age of Spain, was not without tension, debate, and controversy. The mystical element in religion has often been seen as threatening, even dangerous, to the institutional structures of Christianity. So too, there have been some scholars who have viewed mysticism as inherently irrational and thus at odds with sound philosophy and theology. Do not claims to have some form of direct access to God involve at least a potential threat to orthodoxy and church discipline? Nevertheless, as Gershom Scholem once pointed out, mystical claims may be seen as involving more of a dialectical relation to other aspects of religion, rather than one of inherent opposition.[37] Some mystics have, indeed, announced a new message that conflicts with the sources of the tradition, but most have rather claimed to have found an access to God, the founder of the tradition, in a way that seeks not to supersede what went before but to revitalize it. Of course, the judgment about whether a particular mystic is trying to overturn tradition or rebuild it is often difficult to make—and is often made by his or her opponents. Therefore, the mystical tradition involves the possibility of misunderstanding, of disruption, conflict, and condemnation, and during the course of the history of Christianity there have been a number of conflicts between mystics and institutional leaders, especially since the thirteenth century.[38]

These conflicts are particularly evident in the religious turmoil of the early modern period, from those of the Spanish *alumbrados* in the early sixteenth century, through the teachings of the Radical Reformers, to the claims of the supremacy of the inner light made by the Quakers. Many of the major mystics of Spain, such as Ignatius of Loyola, Teresa of Avila, John of the Cross, and Luis de León, were investigated by the Spanish state-church system represented by the Inquisition. These tensions also became evident in seventeenth-century France, where they are seen as early as the 1620s, grew in strength toward the middle of the century, and reached an explosive conclusion in the condemnation of Quietism at the century's end. The perception of the dangers of mysticism, its subversive potential, in seventeenth-century France has been analyzed by a number of important, if controversial, studies.[39] The mystical surprise was encouraged by many, resisted by others. These conflicts will be part of the history set out below, but not its main focus, since I am leaving the Quietist controversy to the next volume.

Before taking up some individual figures in the story of French mysticism, three preliminary questions will be briefly examined: the sources of French mysticism; the question of the so-called Schools; and, finally, some of the crucial general themes shared by many of the mystics.

The Sources of French Mysticism

There has been considerable discussion about the sources for French mysticism of the seventeenth century, or more precisely about how to weigh the impact of three different types of sources: first, the tradition of patristic and medieval mysticism; second, Northern European mysticism of the Late Middle Ages (in French literature this is often called "Rhéno-Flamand," a misnomer); and, third, the role of contemporary mystics from Spain and Italy. What is clear is that the French mystics of the period had a wealth of spiritual and mystical texts available to them, both in Latin and in the vernacular.[40] As the Benedictine scholar Jacques Huijben, once put it, "The sixteenth century, especially in its second half, was in effect a century of translations."[41]

The traditional masters of mysticism from the patristic and medieval periods form the backbone of the resources of the French mystics, both men and women, although naturally the women were less likely to cite sources. Augustine's *Opera omnia* were published often in the sixteenth century, while the *Confessions* appeared frequently in Latin and in a French version in 1609. We should also remember that the most substantial theological quarrel of the seventeenth century, Jansenism, hinged on the interpretation of Augustine's views on grace and freedom. Along with the bishop of Hippo, a full array of patristic authors who touched on mystical themes was available.[42] A special case is the Dionysian corpus, which was used by many French mystical authors, although selectively. The Latin translations of Ambrogio Traversari and Marsilio Ficino had appeared in incunable editions in Strassburg and Venice and were often reprinted in the sixteenth and seventeenth centuries. A French translation of the corpus by the Feuillant monk Jean de Saint-François Goulu was published in 1608. The extent of Dionysian influence on French mysticism was widespread but needs to be determined author by author.[43]

The same general availability, sometimes also in the vernacular, was true for the major twelfth- and thirteenth-century mystical authors, such as the Cistercians, Victorines, and Franciscans. Bernard of Clairvaux's *Opera omnia* were often printed (1520, 1536, 1540, etc.), and some of his works were available in the vernacular. Probably no medieval mystic was more widely read and cited than the abbot of

Clairvaux.⁴⁴ The Victorines, both Hugh and Richard, were available, along with the commentaries of the "last Victorine," Thomas Gallus (*Vercellenensis*), on the Dionysian corpus, which appeared in some editions of the Areopagite. Bonaventure's writings and the popular Pseudo-Bonaventuran materials, such as the *Meditationes Vitae Christi*, were widespread. What may be surprising, however, is how many of the female mystics of the late Middle Ages were printed in the sixteenth and seventeenth centuries. These include Angela of Foligno, with Latin editions being published in the sixteenth century and a vernacular text in 1604. Among other important female mystics were the three Italian Catherines: Catherine of Siena, Catherine of Bologna, and Catherine of Genoa. Lefèvre d'Étaples's *Liber trium virorum et trium spiritualium virginum* of 1513 included excerpts from Hildegard of Bingen, Elisabeth of Schönau, and Mechthild of Hackeborn. Gertrude of Helfta also appeared in print (1536 in Latin; 1580 in the vernacular).

Building on the work of Jacques Huijben in the 1930s,⁴⁵ Jean Dagens, Louis Cognet, and others have made large claims for the influence of the late medieval Northern European mystics on seventeenth-century French mysticism. There is no question that many of the writings of these mystics were available in France and were read by French authors. Once again, however, it is important not to generalize or exaggerate, but to consider each author individually. For example, one can argue for far more use of the mystics of Germany and the Low Countries in Benet of Canfield and Pierre de Bérulle than in Francis de Sales. There were, of course, key themes and vocabulary that the French took over from the Northern mystics. One example of a direct borrowing can be found in the use of the term *superessentialis* to describe the highest stages of union with God. This language originated in Ruusbroec but was probably conveyed to French authors mostly through the writings of Hendrik Herp.⁴⁶ Other examples sometimes cited are more problematic. For example, both the French mystics and some previous Northern mystics spoke of the soul's annihilation as a prerequisite for union. This theme, however, occurs in different forms in many mystical traditions (e.g., Catherine of Genoa and Isabella Berinzaga in Italy), and it is hard to prove that mystical annihilation among the French has its direct source only in texts from German and Dutch mysticism.

The channels by which this material became available in Latin and French were many. Willem Jordaens of the Groenendaal community translated three of Ruusbroec's works into Latin, which enabled the Humanist Jacques Lefèvre d'Étaples to publish the first Latin edition of

Ruusbroec's *Spiritual Espousals* in Paris in 1512. The Dutch Observant Franciscan Hendrik Herp (Harphius, ca. 1400–1477) wrote his Ruusbroecian *Mirror of Perfection* in Dutch in the 1460s.[47] A Latin translation was prepared by the Cologne Carthusian Peter Blomeveen (1466–1536) and published in 1509 under the title the *Golden Directory of Contemplatives* (*Aureum directorum contemplativorum*).[48] Blomeveen was the prior of the Carthusian house of Saint Barbara at Cologne, which was the most important conduit for making late medieval, mostly Northern, mystical texts available to early modern Catholicism.

In his book *Bérulle et les origines de la restauration catholique (1575–1611)*, Jean Dagens claimed, "The Charterhouse of Cologne is no less important for religious history than the obscure brotherhood for whom Thomas à Kempis produced the *Imitation*."[49] This may be an exaggeration, but research has shown that the Cologne Carthusians were at the center of a Pre-Tridentine movement of Catholic reform that sought to counter the inroads of Protestantism by translating and disseminating medieval mystical literature and encouraging the production of new mystical texts by the nuns and beguines of the Eastern Netherlands.[50] A succession of monks under the leadership of Peter Blomeveen (prior 1507–36) and Gerard Kalckbrenner (prior 1536–62), carried on impressive publishing projects, including the printing of the voluminous writings of Denis the Carthusian (d. 1471), and making available in Latin the works of mystics like Henry Suso, Gertrude the Great, and Mechthild of Hackeborn. The greatest of these translators was Laurent Sauer (Laurentius Surius, ca. 1523–1578), who published Latin versions of John Tauler's *Opera omnia* in 1548, as well as Ruusbroec's *Opera omnia* (1552) and Henry Suso's *Opera omnia* (1555).[51] Among the important efforts of the Cologne Carthusians was the publication of a late gem of medieval Northern mysticism, the Dutch classic the *Evangelical Pearl*, the anonymous work of a pious woman from Gelderland in the Eastern Netherlands.[52] Through the efforts of Dirk Loher and Nicholas van Es a short form of the text appeared in 1537 and 1539, while the longer *Great Evangelical Pearl* came out in 1542. The first edition of the somewhat different Latin version, which may have been the work of Surius, appeared in 1545. In the 1590s, a group of Carthusians at Paris, probably under the leadership of Jacques Morice (d. 1595), translated the Latin text into French and had it published in 1602.[53] The work was read and praised by many of the seventeenth-century French mystics.

Surius's Tauler edition proved popular, being reprinted a dozen times between 1548 and 1697. Equally important was Pseudo-Tauler.

As Jean-Marie Gueullette has shown, Surius's Latin version of Tauler included the spurious *Institutiones spirituales* or *divinae*, often ascribed to Tauler.[54] The story of the transmission of Tauler's Middle High German writings, both authentic and pseudonymous, to early modern Europe is complicated. The leader of the early Jesuits in Northern Europe, Peter Canisius (1521–1597), had been close to the Cologne Carthusians before his entry into the Society of Jesus. In 1543, he put out a German text of Tauler's sermons (including a number by Eckhart), as well as treatises pseudonymously ascribed to the Dominican. Among these were the *Institutiones spirituales*, often referred to as the *Institutiones taulerianae*, a florilegium of mystical texts in thirty-nine chapters that included both the reworking of Eckhart's *Talks of Instruction* put together about 1380 by the Groenendaal canon Godeverd van Wevele under the title *The Twelve Virtues*, as well as large excerpts of Eckhart's original text of twenty-three chapters.[55] Surius made his Latin Tauler translation from his friend Canisius's German text, so the young Eckhart's views on radical obedience, poverty, detachment, interior and exterior work, and other topics were now accessible to early modern readers, although not under Eckhart's name. The work was soon translated into a variety of languages: Spanish (1551), Italian (1568), and French (1587).[56] Thus, as Gueullette puts it, "The spiritual Christians in France in the sixteenth and seventeenth centuries did not receive the teaching of a disciple of Eckhart, or of an inauthentic text distantly inspired by him, but from actual texts of the master of Rhineland mysticism, without knowing it."[57] The *Institutiones divinae* were even more popular than the Tauler *Opera omnia*, enjoying thirteen separate editions down to 1681. Finally, we can note that the *Theologia deutsch*, so favored by Luther and Reformation mystics, was also made available in Latin and French versions by Sebastian Castellio in 1558, but it appears to have been less read by Catholics. In sum, there was no dearth of German and Dutch mystical texts available to French readers of the sixteenth and seventeenth centuries.

The third body of sources for seventeenth-century French mysticism was that of contemporary, that is, sixteenth- and seventeenth-century mystics from Spain and Italy. French readers eagerly turned to the rich mystical literature produced in Spain. The Franciscan "recollection" (*recogimiento*) mystics of the first half of the century, such as Bernardino de Laredo and Francisco de Osuna, were not available in French, but a number of authors of the second half of the century were soon translated. The most important was Teresa of Avila.[58] A priest from Normandy with Spanish roots, Jean de Quintanadoine de Brétigny, collaborated with the Carthusian Dom du Chèvre to produce a translation of three of Teresa's major works in 1601: the *Life*, the *Way of Perfection*, and the *Interior Castle*. Sixty-five later translations appeared in the course of the seventeenth century. John of the Cross came somewhat later. René Gualtier (ca. 1560–1628) was a Franciscan tertiary, a member of the circle of Barbe Acarie, and a supporter of the early Carmelite reform in France. He put the works of John of the Cross into French in 1622, including the *Canticle of Divine Love*, which had not been included in the first Spanish edition of 1618. Gualtier did more, translating Peter de Alcántara (1602), the Jesuit Louis de la Puente (1611), and Pietro de Ribandeneyra (1605), among others.[59] The impact of both Teresa and John on French mysticism was powerful. Other Spanish mystics who became available in France include those still well known, such as Luis de Granada, and others who are mostly forgotten. Ignatius of Loyola was known, but through the *Spiritual Exercises*, not his mystical writings.

Among the Italian mystics, Catherine of Siena was probably the best known, although perhaps more as a figure of hagiography through the French translation of Raymond of Capua's *La vie de Madame Saincte Catherine* published in Lyon in 1520. The saint's own *Dialogues et oraisons* were put out in 1580 and again in 1587. Catherine of Genoa appears to have been known primarily through the 1597 translation of *La vie et les oeuvres spirituelles de sainte Catherine d'Adorni de Gênes*, produced by the Carthusians of Bourgfontaine, a book often reprinted. Although more of an ascetical than a mystical text, *Il combattimento spirituale* (*The Spiritual Combat*) of the Theatine Lorenzo Scupoli (ca. 1530–1610), first published in 1589, appeared in a French translation in 1595 and was widely read. A special case is the text of the *Breve compendio di perfezione cristiana* written by the Jesuit Achille Gagliardi (1537–1607), between 1584 and 1594, based on his conversations with the Milanese mystic Isabella Cristina Berinzaga (1551–1621).[60] This work circulated in manuscript and first appeared in an abbreviated French form, the *Bref discourse de l'abnégation intérieur* in 1597.[61] It did not appear in Italian until 1611, but the book was often printed and translated into many languages.

Schools and Nomenclature of French Mysticism

Anyone who reads about seventeenth-century French mysticism in the classic *History* of Henri Bremond and in subsequent writers will encounter the language of "Schools" of mysticism, such as the "French

School," the "Abstract School," and even the "Salesian School." This form of nomenclature was once widespread in speaking about mysticism, as terms like the "Cistercian School," "Franciscan School," "Dominican School," "Ignatian School" indicate. In recent years there has been movement away from such characterizations.[62] The term "School" often implies more direct continuity and coherence of themes than large religious orders with long histories have maintained. It is even more difficult to speak about Schools that are independent of religious orders. "Traditions," or "genealogies" are perhaps vague, but less misleading.

One could argue that in the case of France between 1590 and 1650 the more limited chronological framework and personal connections between many of the mystics encourage the language of Schools, but that does not address the issue of the meaning of what constitutes a school. A case might be made that the close dependence of Francis de Sales's followers, like Jane de Chantal and Jean-Pierre Camus, on his person and teaching does, indeed, make a school of some sort, but Camus's views are not always those of Francis, and Jane de Chantal is not just a repetitor of her spiritual director. Even more problematic is the terminology of the French School and the Abstract School; each term has serious shortcomings and will therefore not be used in the following chapters.

The immediate problem with the term "French School" is that it includes only some of the numerous French mystical writers of the seventeenth century, and that therefore one can wonder how "French" a French mystic has to be to belong to the "French School." This has led to some debate about who really should be listed as belonging to this School. The term itself is modern. It seems to have been created in nineteenth-century Sulpician circles and first used in print in 1873 by M. Hulst in a biography of François Courtade. Bremond adopted the term in his *History* and made it central to his early volumes, but he seems to have used it in different senses, at times restricting it to Pierre de Bérulle and those directly influenced by him; at other times employing it in a broader sense. Jean Dagens does not use it in his monograph on Bérulle, and Louis Cognet avoided the term in his *La spiritualité moderne*, preferring to speak of Bérulle's "synthesis" (chap. 9) and the Bérullian "current" (chap. 10). Writers on French spirituality during the second half of the twentieth century have also questioned the usefulness of the term. Jacques Le Brun, in his *Dictionnaire de spiritualité* article, "Le Grand Siècle de la spiritualitè française et ses lendemains," says, "[S]ome have spoken of the 'French School,' [but] the term is too vague, and it is better to speak of the 'Bérullian School' to clearly mark out that these spiritual authors rely on the teaching of the founder of the Oratory" (DS 5:934). The detailed treatment of Yves Krumenacker reviews the history of the term and opts for "Bérullianism" as a more adequate, if still complex and shifting, characterization.[63] François Marxer even critiques Bremond's argument that Bérulle belongs to something called the "French School."[64] Given these strictures, I will avoid referring to the "French School" in what follows.

The origin of the term "Abstract School," often used of Benet Canfield and other members of the Acarie circle, as well as of later authors such as Jean de St. Samson and François Malaval at the end of the seventeenth century, is more difficult to trace.[65] Bremond does not use the term in relation to Canfield or the Acarie circle. It seems to have come into popularity especially through the writings of Louis Cognet. According to Cognet, the Abstract School was derived from the Dionysian corpus, the Northern mystics, and Catherine of Genoa, and constituted "a synthesis [that] . . . laid great stress on the abstract side of this [Northern] mysticism of essences. In this trend, Christ is always the sole way of access to God, but the negative aspect of this way is emphasized, always seen under the aspect of annihilation." Such annihilation involves the rejection of all created things and the extinction of conscious activity in its quest for an unmediated union with the divine essence, "which involves a 'bypassing' of the humanity of Christ." The fusion of the human will in the divine results in "a sort of depersonalization."[66] There are many problems with this vague description. First of all, the "mysticism of essences" is a pseudo-category, not at all adequate to describe the various strands of Northern mysticism's teaching on the divine nature mentioned by Cognet. Second, it is unclear what Cognet means by "the abstract side" of the pseudo-category. Third, there are a variety of ways of understanding annihilation, and it is hard to think that all the members of the Abstract School share the same view. Fourth, it remains to be proven that these mystics "bypass" the humanity of Christ. In short, the Abstract School, at least in this presentation, is not a helpful tool for illuminating an important separate strand in seventeenth-century French mysticism.[67]

Some Themes and Issues of the Seventeenth-Century French Mystics

Trying to give a brief overall characterization of French mysticism of the seventeenth century is a difficult, perhaps impossible, task. It may be useful, nonetheless, to suggest some important aspects, both of the social context of this chapter in the story of Christian mysticism and of some of the dominant intellectual interests of the figures involved.

Sociologically, French mysticism was in general an elitist phenomenon, as was so much of the religious revival of the seventeenth century. The aristocracy, both of the old noble families and the new civil servants of the crown ("the aristocracy of the robe"), as well as the high bourgeoisie, made most of the contributions. This contrasts with Spain—an equally structured class society—where the important spiritual writers reflected a broader cross-section of society. A second social factor concerns gender. Both in Spain and in France, women had a major impact, often through collaborative conversations with male mystics and clerical advisors. Seventeenth-century France had many important female mystics, such as Barbe Acarie, Jane de Chantel, the Ursuline Marie de l'Incarnation, and later Madame Guyon. Many of these women left writings, although other noted female mystics, both nuns and lay women, are known to us primarily through the hagiographies composed by their clerical advisors.[68]

The role of the laity, both men and women, a phenomenon that began in the fourteenth century, increased greatly in the seventeenth. This is in part reflected in the fact that many of the French mystics, such as Francis de Sales, emphasized the universal call to the devout, and even the mystical life. The lay *dévots* provided not only the financial resources but also much of the audience for the outpouring of mystical writing, preaching, and teaching of the time. A number of mystics (e.g., Barbe Acarie for most of her life, René Gaultier, Michel de Marillac, Gaston de Renty, Jean de Bernières-Lovigny, François Malaval, Jeanne Guyon, etc.) were themselves lay.

Among the central themes of the French mystical authors, few were totally new, nor should we expect them to be. Nonetheless, seventeenth-century French mystics brought many nuances and distinctive adaptations to traditional mystical topics, and even some innovations.[69] A prime example of an old theme that saw new developments is the issue of interiority expressed in terms such as "the interior man,"[70] "introversion,"[71] and "inner experience."[72] Mino Bergamo hailed seventeenth-century France as "one of the summits" of the mysticism of interiority.[73] It is surely correct to say that seventeenth-century French mysticism is *among* the summits of mystical introversion, but it is certainly not the only one.[74] The seventeenth-century French were obsessed with interiority, both their own and that of Jesus. For them "interior space" was the true location of the infinity where the soul could encounter the infinite divine.[75] One of the distinctive ways in which the French mystics came to express interiority, both the interiority of Jesus and Mary, as well as the interiority of the mystical soul, was through the language of the "heart."[76] Again, devotion to the hearts of Jesus and Mary was not new, nor was the mystical motif of the exchange of hearts, but the French developed "heart-mysticism" to a new degree.

Closely related to the stress on interiority are modern claims about the psychological focus of the early modern French mystics. Detailed attention to the subject's interior states is evident among many of the French mystics, but such concerns did not begin in the seventeenth century. They were also found in Teresa and John of the Cross and were pioneered by the male and female mystics who began analyzing "the book of experience" (*liber experientiae*) as long ago as the twelfth century. What we witness in relation to interiority and the psychological investigation of interior states at this time is not so much a new departure as an intensification of long-term developments.

Recent discussion of French mysticism has also emphasized the role of mystical discourse, that is, the new modes of expression found among the seventeenth-century French mystics. The history of mysticism, as often emphasized in these volumes, is not the history of experience (to which we have no real access), but the history of texts and the different ways in which texts express what their authors confess to be inexpressible—a paradoxical but seemingly necessary task. Scholars like Michel de Certeau, Mino Bergamo, and Dominique Salin have made important contributions to our understanding of the new forms of discourse of the French mystics of the era. A strong current among some of the seventeenth-century French mystics emphasized the specialized nature of the vocabulary and modes of speaking of the "mystics" (as they were increasingly called). Francis de Sales, however, the most read of the mystics of the time, wrote for all and in what he insisted was everyday language. Nonetheless, much of the mystical discourse of the early modern period has a fluidity, brokenness, incompleteness, perhaps even impermanence, that seems new. Michel de Certeau tried to capture this aspect in his notion of the "mystic fable," that is, the evolution of what had once been spoken discourse into a suggestive story symbolizing a hidden reality and resisting final objective fixation.[77]

Beginning in the second decade of the seventeenth century, both in Spain and in France, the traditional qualifier "mystical" (*mysticus*) began to be used more and more about special supernatural experiences in the soul, rather than about the hidden depths of the Bible and Christian rituals and the whole way of life of the contemplative.[78] The spiritual teachers who had customarily been called "contemplatives" began to be increasingly referred to as "mystics." This, as well as the appearance of the substantive *la mystique* ("mystics," like mathematics), marked a major transition in the story of Christian mysticism in which "mysticism," often conceived of as "the science of the saints," took its place in the early modern reorganization of the theological disciplines. Rather than a description of a total mode of life and prayer, "mystical theology" became an academic category to be contrasted with "scholastic theology" and the "positive theology" that studied Christianity's historical development. This science of the saints (*scientia sanctorum*), although a biblical phrase,[79] took on new meaning as an organized form of knowledge, differing from the other theological disciplines in being based on personal experience, that is, the descriptions of their inner states by authoritative mystics like Teresa and John of the Cross.[80] As many of its proponents insisted, mystical theology had its own vocabulary and modes of organization not amenable to the logical methods of scholasticism. Michel de Certeau summarized: "Presented as an experience or as experimental knowledge, 'mystical theology' was frequently opposed to 'scholastic theology.' . . . [T]he 'mystical theologian' himself became a 'mystic.'"[81] Analyses of the mystical ways of speaking (*modus loquendi*) proliferated during the course of the seventeenth century down to the famous *Maxims of the Saints* (i.e., mystics) composed by Archbishop Fénelon to defend Madame Guyon and partially condemned by Innocent XII in 1699 in the papal brief *Cum alias*.[82]

Along with interiorization and mystical speech, three other themes that received much attention at the time were: (1) Christocentrism, that is, emphasis on the role of Jesus as both God and man; (2) abnegation/ annihilation (*abnégation/anéantissement*), namely, the self-denial and even self-destruction necessary to attain union with God; and (3) the issue of pure love, that is, whether it is possible (or desirable) that love can become so disinterested that it no longer even seeks salvation. The French mystics did not reach accord on these issues, but most of them found it important to deal with them.

Few, if any, Christian mystics are not Christocentric, at least in some way. The Dionysian corpus, for example, has been criticized for minimizing Christ's role; but on closer reading, it reveals a key function for the action of the God-man in the structure of the hierarchical system. There are, however, real differences among mystics in *how much* attention is given to Christ and the *ways* in which Jesus as both God and human enters into the mystic's path to contemplative union. Thus, Pierre de Bérulle's teaching on the necessity of sharing the "states of Jesus" is Christocentric in a more integral way than the references to the role of Christ found in many other mystics. Mystics like Benet of Canfield are sometimes judged to have abandoned the humanity of Christ in striving for superessential uniting with God, although whether that accusation is fair will be taken up in the next chapter. In any case, the seventeenth-century French mystics, especially Bérulle, pioneered new forms of Christocentrism that had a powerful influence both in its time and afterwards.

Abnegation, or denying the self and its desires, was a part of Christian tradition from the start, rooted in texts like Matthew 16:24: "If any want to become my followers, let them deny themselves and take up their cross and follow me." Abnegation can exist on many levels, from a moral annihilation of the sinful aspects of the will to deeper levels that at times seem to imply some form of the destruction of the self.[83] Strong forms of mystical annihilation (i.e., a letting go of the created self in order to let God be all) may seem bizarre, or merely metaphorical, but some mystics from the late Middle Ages on insisted on some kind of reduction to nothing.[84] Bernard of Clairvaux in his *De diligendo deo* appears to be the first to use the word (*annihilatio/annulare*) in relation to the union achieved in his fourth degree of love,[85] but the language of annihilation did not become widespread until the thirteenth century, where we find it in a number of mystics, especially Marguerite Porete.[86] Meister Eckhart and his followers also had a profound teaching about annihilation, though expressed in Germanic vocabulary (*vernichten, entwerden*, etc.). Among these authors annihilation language is used most often with regard to the will. While many mystics spoke about denying or annihilating the will *insofar as it is fallen* (we might call this a "soft," or ascetical-moral annihilation), a number of late medieval mystics began to talk about annihilating the will precisely *insofar as it is created and therefore distinct from God* (i.e., "strong" annihilation).[87] Strong forms of annihilation were often tied to a teaching on the need to return to the pre-created, ideal, or virtual "self," which is one with God and the divine will. Some of the late medieval mystics available to the seventeenth-century French, such Ruusbroec, Hendrik Herp, Catherine of Genoa, the *Evangelical Pearl*, Gagliardi's *Breve Compendio*, and the *Institutes* of the Pseudo-Tauler, have much teaching about annihilation of the will and/or self, expressed in a variety of forms.[88]

The seventeenth century might be called the Age of Annihilation. Most of the French mystics of this period have something, and often much, to say about annihilation. It is not always easy to tell if they are speaking about soft or hard annihilation, especially because they tend to use the word *anéantissement* in tandem with other terms, such as *abnégation*, *abaissement*, and even *exinanition*, developed from Paul's description of Christ's emptying himself and taking on the form of a slave (Phil. 2:7: *sed semetipsum exinanivit formam servi accipiens*). Jacques Le Brun notes two characteristics of early modern French mysticism: first, the analysis of interior states; and, second, the way in which, through "absolute stripping away" (*dépouillement absolus*), God expands himself in the soul that is empty of every reality, image, desire, and knowledge.[89] Annihilation is a central theme for Canfield, Bérulle, Olier, Marie de l'Incarnation, and others, as we shall see, although what form (or forms) of annihilation are being spoken about are by no means the same.

A third issue in seventeenth-century French mysticism is the problem of pure, or totally disinterested, love. This is an ancient theme, extending back to Plato, with rich developments in Augustine, as well as in medieval mystics such as Bernard of Clairvaux and Marguerite Porete.[90] Nonetheless, discussion about how pure love is necessary to attain God reached a crescendo in the seventeenth century, especially in the quarrel between Bossuet and Fénelon at the century's end. Peter Gorday has argued that the "idea of pure love" and its gradual unfolding over the century between Francis de Sales and Fénelon was the guiding principle behind Bremond's *Histoire*.[91] He also claims that Bremond eventually came to see the kind of loss of self found in the Bérullian notion of annihilation as subsumed in the Salesian and Fénelonian language of pure love, although this argument was not fully worked out because of the incompleteness of the *Histoire*.[92]

The issue of pure love was founded in the primary commandment of loving the Lord God above all things; the question was how far and how pure the love of God and the disregard of self should become. Bernard of Clairvaux's formula about loving God without hope of reward, but not without a reward (*De diligendo Deo* VII.17), was often cited, as were the passages from the *Sermon on the Song of Songs* 83, "Love does not need a cause outside itself, nor a fruit; its fruit is itself. I love because I love; I love that I may love"; and "Pure love is not mercenary [*Purus amor mercenarius non est*]."[93] Everyone could agree with these expressions, but what they meant in practice was another question. As the issues came to be more and more intricate in the course of the century, pure disinterested love began to involve questions not addressed by Bernard and earlier mystical authorities. In an age obsessed with the subject's interior states, pure love came to be seen as a love that should not involve any return of the subject to herself in order to examine how much she was delighting in the joy she was receiving from God. Also, pure love should not involve any sensual affectivity, but only the *fruitio dei* of the human fulfillment found in attaining inner union with God.[94] A particularly troubling issue concerning the disinterestedness of pure love involved what seventeenth-century authors called the "impossible supposition" (*suppositio impossibilis*), that is, *if* God so willed, was it legitimate to prefer damnation in accord with the divine will, rather than continue to hope for salvation? Various permutations of the question were pursued by seventeenth-century writers, and they became a major sticking point in the Quietist controversy. From one point of view, the focus on the impossible supposition was traditional, because for many centuries mystics had cited Paul's willingness to be lost in order to save his brethren (*resignatio ad infernum* of Rom. 9:3) as proof of the purity of their love for God. From another point of view, however, the obsessive concern over this issue says much about seventeenth-century mysticism and the theology of an era in which disputes over grace and freedom, as well as the universality of God's salvific will, came to the fore in new ways. These mystical quarrels took place against the background of the great struggle over sin, grace, and human freedom that we call the Jansenist controversy. While we will not enter into this directly in what follows, it is important to the context of the changing views of mysticism over the course of the seventeenth century.[95]

Seventeenth-century French mysticism was extraordinary on many counts—a true surprise in the history of Christian mystical traditions. Given the influence that seventeenth- and eighteenth-century French Catholicism had upon Anglophone Catholics in the nineteenth and early twentieth centuries, these French mystics, or at least some of them, were once more widely read than they are today. But they are still alive in many ways. Scholarly retrieval of early modern mysticism in France, beginning with the pioneering efforts of Henri Bremond, has uncovered much of the richness of this era, not just of a few familiar figures, but of the wider range of the mystics of the great era of French mysticism.

Notes

1. On the interaction of politics and religion during the long seventeenth century in France (ca. 1580-1730), see Joseph Bergin, *The Politics of Religion in Early Modern France* (New Haven: Yale University Press, 2014).
2. On early French Protestantism, see Lucien Febvre, "The Origins of the French Reformation: A Badly-Put Question?," in *A New Kind of History from the Writings of Lucien Febvre*, ed. Peter Burke (New York: Harper & Row, 1973), 44-107.
3. I owe this phrase to Brad S. Gregory of the University of Notre Dame.
4. For introductions, see Philip Benedict, "The wars of religion, 1562-1598," in *Renaissance and Reformation France, 1500-1648*, ed. Mack P. Holt, Short Oxford History of France (Oxford: Oxford University Press, 2002), 147-75; and Barbara B. Diefendorf, "The Religious Wars in France," in *A Companion to the Reformation World*, ed. R. Po-chia Hsia, Blackwell Companions to European History (Malden, MA: Blackwell, 2004), 150-68.
5. The three Henries were Henry III, the Valois king of France; the Bourbon Henry of Navarre; and Henry of Guise, the leader of the intransigent Catholic party.
6. For a discussion of the reasons for Henry IV's success over the Leaguers, see Benedict, "Wars of religion," 169-75.
7. A useful account of this period in French religious history is Joseph Bergin, *Church, Society, and Religious Change in France, 1580-1730* (New Haven: Yale University Press, 2009). Helpful for the seventeenth century are Louis Cognet, "The Leadership Position of France," part 1, in *The Church in the Age of Absolutism and Enlightenment*, ed. Wolfgang Müller et al., History of the Church 6 (New York: Crossroad, 1981), 3-106; and Jean Dagens, *Bérulle et les origines de la restauration catholique (1575-1611)* (Bruges: Desclée de Brouwer, 1962), especially books 2-3.
8. Bergin, *Church, Society, and Religious Change in France*, 157.
9. Ibid., chap. 15, "*Devots*: The Pious and the Militant" (366-93).
10. Bremond, *History*, 2:183-84.
11. Dagens, *Bérulle et les origines*, 131.
12. Bergin provides a survey of bishops, clergy, and parishes in this period (*Church, Society, and Religious Change in France*, part 3, "A New Clergy?" [153-226]).
13. Raymond Deville, *The French School of Spirituality: An Introduction and Reader* (Pittsburgh: Duquesne University Press, 1994), 109. For a treatment of the missions, see Bergin, *Church, Society, and Religious Change in France*, 283-96.
14. Bergin, *Church, Society, and Religious Change in France*, 361, whose chapter on the confraternities (339-65) is a useful summary.
15. See Cognet, "Ecclesiastical Life in France," in idem, "The Leadership Position of France," 4 (see n. 7 above).
16. On the Capuchins, see Father Cuthbert, O.S.F.C., *The Capuchins: A Contribution to the History of the Counter-Reformation*, 2 vols. (London: Sheed & Ward, 1928); and Melchiorre da Pobladura, "Cappucini," in *Dizionario degli Istituti di Perfezione*, ed. Guerrino Pelliccia and Giancarlo Rocca, 10 vols (Rome: Edizioni Paoline, 1973-2003), 2:203-52.

17. On Pierre Coton, see Dagens, *Bérulle et les origines*, 175–79; and Aloys Pottier and Michel-Jean Picard, "Coton (Pierre), jésuite (1564–1626)," DS 2:2422–32.

18. For an overview of Carmelite reform in France, see Henri Peltier, *Histoire du Carmel* (Paris: Éditions du Seuil, 1958), chap. 8, "Carmes et Carmélites en France et en Flandre" (163–97).

19. For an account of the foundation, see Barbara B. Diefendorf, *From Penitence to Charity: Pious Women and the Catholic Reformation in Paris* (Oxford: Oxford University Press, 2004), 102–18. There are many treatments of this initiative; see, e.g., Dagens, *Bérulle et les origines*, book 3, chap. 3 (191–204).

20. Canisius (P. W.) Janssen, *Les origines de la réforme des carmes en France au XVIIe siècle* (The Hague: M. Nijhoff, 1963).

21. Bergin, *Church, Society, and Religious Change in France*, chap. 4, "The Monastic Orders: Adjustment and Survival" (84–104).

22. There is a considerable literature on these pious women. For a survey, see Elizabeth Rapley, *The Dévotes: Women and Church in Seventeenth-Century France* (Montreal and Kingston: McGill-Queens University Press, 1990). A more recent overview of the larger picture of women's orders in the time of the Reformation is Amy E. Leonard, "Female Religious Orders," in Hsia, *Companion to the Reformation World*, 237–54.

23. Diefendorf, *From Penitence to Charity*; and eadem, "Contradictions of the Century of Saints: Aristocratic Patronage and the Convents of Counter-Reformation Paris," *French Historical Studies* 24.3 (2001): 469–99.

24. Querciolo Mazzonis, *Spirituality, Gender, and the Self in Renaissance Italy: Angela Merici and the Company of St. Ursula (1474–1540)* (Washington, DC: Catholic University of America Press, 2007).

25. See Linda Lierheimer, "Preaching or Teaching? Defining the Ursuline Mission in Seventeenth-Century France," in *Women Preachers and Prophets through Two Millennia of Christianity*, ed. Beverly Mayne Kienzle and Pamela J. Walker (Berkeley: University of California Press, 1998), 212–26, who summarizes, "Although most Ursulines did not overtly lay claim to the role of preacher, in practice their activities often amounted to the same thing" (213).

26. On the Ursuline contribution, see Rapley, *Dévotes*, 48–60; and Bergin, *Church, Society, and Religious Change in France*, 136–38.

27. For the role of the two in founding the various branches of what is now the Vincentian Order, see *Vincent de Paul and Louise de Marillac: Rules, Conferences, and Writings*, ed. Frances Ryan and John E. Rybolt, Classics of Western Spirituality (New York: Paulist Press, 1995).

28. See Bergin, *Church, Society, and Religious Change in France*, 146.

29. On the apostolic intent of a number of the female religious founders after Trent, see Ruth P. Liebowitz, "Virgins in the Service of Christ: The Dispute over an Active Apostolate for Women during the Counter-Reformation," in *Women of Spirit: Female Leadership in the Jewish and Christian Traditions*, ed. Rosemary Ruether and Eleanor McLaughlin (New York: Simon & Schuster, 1977), 131–52.

30. Diefendorf argues for the resurgence of the contemplative life in seventeenth-century France ("Contradictions of the Century of the Saints," 474–78).

31. Today these volumes need to be read in the revised version, with many additions that were cut out of the original, as well as a number of contemporary

critical essays, published in five massive volumes by Jérôme Millon in Grenoble in 2006.

32. Peter J. Gorday, *Pure Love, Pure Poetry, Pure Prayer: The Life and Work of Henri Bremond* (Eugene, OR: Wipf & Stock, 2018). Gorday follows the evolution of the *Histoire* (originally conceived of as three volumes) and the debates it fostered in clarifying detail. He sees a basic shift over the course of the eleven volumes from an early emphasis on theocentric Devout Humanism and the centrality of the French School to a later concentration on the equation of mysticism with the "Metaphysic of the Saints" understood as pure poetry–pure prayer–pure love (see, e.g., 9, 120, 126-28, 148-49, 210-11, 261, 281-82, and 381-84).

33. The title of the second volume of Bremond's original *Histoire*, was *L'Invasion mystique*. The English version by K. L. Montgomery fudged this by translating the title of volume 2 as *The Coming of Mysticism (1590-1620)*.

34. Dominique Salin, "'L'invasion mystique' en France au XVIIe S.," in *Dieu au XVIIe siècle: Crises et renouvellements du discours*, ed. Henri Laux and Dominique Salin (Paris: Facultés Jésuites de Paris, 2002), 241-66.

35. A point noted by both Salin ("'L'invasion mystique' en France," 243) and Bergin (*Church, Society, and Religious Change in France*, 316-18).

36. Studies of individual mystics and mystical traditions are many. General studies are few after Bremond; but see Jean Calvet, *La littérature religieuse de François de Sales à Fénelon*, Histoire de la littérature française 5 (Paris: Duca, 1956); and Louis Cognet, *La spiritualité moderne*, Histoire de la spiritualité chrétienne 3 (Paris: Aubier, 1966). On Cognet's book, see the review of Michel de Certeau, "La Spiritualité moderne," *Revue d'ascétique et de mystique* 44 (1968): 33-42. A short English book by Cognet, *Post-Reformation Spirituality* (New York: Hawthorn, 1959), devotes its brief chaps. 3 and 4 to seventeenth-century France. A good survey published in 1964 is Jacques Le Brun, "France, VI: Le Grand Siècle de la spiritualité française et ses lendemains," DS 5:917-53. Recent short introductions in English include David D. Thayer, "The French School," in *The Bloomsbury Guide to Christian Spirituality*, ed. Richard Woods and Peter Tyler (London: Bloomsbury, 2012), 171-83; and Wendy M. Wright, "Seventeenth-Century French Mysticism," in *The Wiley-Blackwell Companion to Christian Mysticism*, ed. Julia Lamm (Malden, MA: Wiley-Blackwell, 2013), 437-51.

37. Gershom Scholem, "Mysticism and Society," *Diogenes* 58 (1967): 1-24. A similar observation is made by Certeau, *Mystic Fable: Volume One*, 180-81, without citing Sholem.

38. Bernard McGinn, "'Evil-Sounding, Rash, and Suspect of Heresy': Tensions between Mysticism and Magisterium in the History of the Church," *Catholic Historical Review* 90 (2004): 193-212.

39. For example, Leszek Kołakowski, *Chrétiens sans église: La consience religieuse et le lien confessionnel au XVIIe siècle* (Paris: Gallimard, 1987); and Sophie Houdard, *Les invasions mystiques: Spiritualités, hétérodoxies et censures au début de l'époque moderne* (Paris: Belles Lettres, 2008).

40. This is evident from Jean Dagens, *Bibliographie chronologique de la littérature de spiritualité et des sources (1501-1610)* (Paris: Desclée de Brouwer, 1952).

41. Jacques Huijben, "Aux sources de la spiritualité française du XVIIe siècle," *Supplément à La Vie Spirituelle*, 25 (1930): [113-39]; 26 (1931): [17-46], [75-111]; 27 (1931): [20-42], [94-122], quotation from 25 (1930). Huijben's articles, published

first in Dutch and then in French more than eighty years ago, remain indispensable.

42. For example, Ambrose, Basil, Cassian (in French from 1504), Gregory the Great, Gregory Nazianzen, Gregory of Nyssa (*Oeuvres* in 1568), John Climacus, John Chrysostom, Jerome, Leo the Great, and Origen. Huijben calculates that about 110 editions of the Fathers appeared in the sixteenth century, with about thirty translations ("Aux sources," [125]).

43. See the multiauthor article, "Denys L'Aréopagite: En Occident. E. 17e et 18e Siècles," DS 3:410-29.

44. For an overview, see Bernard Jacqueline, "L'influence de S. Bernard au XVIIe siècle," *Collectanea Cisterciensia* 42 (1980): 22-35.

45. Huijben, "Aux sources"; see n. 41 above. Also useful is Jean-Pierre Van Schoote, "Les traducteurs français des mystiques rhéno-flamands et leur contribution à l'élaboration de la langue devote à l'aube du XVIIe siècle," *Revue d'ascétique et de mystique* 39 (1963): 319-37.

46. See Albert Deblaere, "Essentiel (superessentiel, suressentiel)," DS 4:1346-66; and Mariel Mazzocco, "'Suressential': Aux sources d'un langage mystique," *Revue de l'histoire des religions* 4 (2013): 609-27.

47. On Herp, see McGinn, *Varieties*, 130-36.

48. In 1538, the Cologne Carthusians also published an anthology of Herp's works under the title *De mystica theologia*, which includes the *Aureum directorum* as book 2.

49. Dagens, *Bérulle et les origines*, 79.

50. Gérald Chaix, *Réforme et contre-réforme catholiques: Recherche sur la Chartreuse de Cologne au XVIe siècle*, 3 vols., Analecta Cartusiana 80 (Salzburg: Universität Salzburg, 1981).

51. Augustine Devaux, "Surius (Sauer, Laurent)," DS 14:1325-29.

52. For an introduction to the history and teaching of the *Evangelical Pearl*, see McGinn, *Varieties*, 143-59.

53. This French version has been reissued. See *La perle évangélique–traduction française–(1602)*, ed. Daniel Vidal (Grenoble: Jérôme Millon, 1997). On this translation, see J. P. Van Schoote, "La Perle Évangélique," *Revue d'ascétique et de mystique* 37 (1961): 79-92, 291-313.

54. Jean-Marie Gueullette, *Eckhart en France: La lecture des "Institutions spirituelles" attribuées à Tauler, 1548-1699* (Grenoble: Jérôme Millon, 2012). The book includes a modern French version of the *Institutions spirituelles* (181-343), with a helpful identification of the sources. For a list of the early printings, see the chart on 171.

55. The Pseudo-Tauler *Institutiones* originated among the Cologne Carthusians. Gueullette (*Eckhart en France*, 66-69) speculates that it might be the work of the prior Gerhard Kalckbrenner (d. 1562). For more on the *Institutiones spirituales (Taulerianae)*, see Louis Cognet, *Introduction aux mystiques rhéno-flamands* (Paris: Desclée de Brouwer, 1968), 332-36.

56. Albert Ampe, "Een kritisch onderzoek van de 'Institutiones Taulerianae,'" *Ons Geestelike Erf* 40 (1966): 167-240.

57. Guelluette, *Eckhart en France*, 69.

58. Alphonse Vermeylen, *Sainte Thérèse en France au XVIIe Siècle, 1600-1660*, Recueil de travaux d'histoire et de philologie 4/15 (Louvain: Publications Universitaires de Louvain, 1958).

59. André Rayez, "Gaultier (René), traducteur," DS 6:144–47; and Certeau, *Mystic Fable: Volume One*, 130.

60. See below, chap. 7 (414–29).

61. Marcel Viller, "Autour de 'l'Abrégé de la perfection': L'influence," *Revue d'ascétique et de mystique* 13 (1932): 34–59, 257–93.

62. See, e.g., Jean-Marie Gueullette, "L'usage périlleux de la notion d'école de la spiritualité," in *Les écoles de pensée religieuse à l'époque moderne: Actes de la Journée d'Études de Lyon (14 janvier 2006)*, ed. Yves Krumenacker and Laurent Thirouin, Chrétiens et sociétés, Documents et memoires 5 (Lyon: Université Jean Moulin, 2006), 185–201.

63. Yves Krumenacker, *L'école française de spiritualité: Des mystiques, des fondateurs, des courants et leurs interprètes*, Histoire (Paris: Éditions du Cerf, 1999), especially chap. 1 (15–43), 408–21, 615–20.

64. François Marxer, "L'École Française: Le théologie entre éblouissement théocentrique et faille Christologique," in Bremond, *Histoire*, 1:875–905. See the summary of the debate in Gorday, *Pure Love, Pure Poetry, Pure Prayer*, 153–59, 164.

65. The term seems to have been created in the mid-twentieth century on the basis of the complaint that the Spanish Carmelite nun Ana de Jesús made about the prayer of the first French nuns, as quoted by Bremond: "I am careful that they [the French novices] meditate on and imitate Our Lord Jesus Christ, for he is often forgotten. All devotion is concentrated on the abstract idea of God: I do not know how it is done" (*History*, 2:229). Dagens (*Bérulle et les origines*, book 4, chap. 3, "L'Humanité de Jésus" [308–16]) includes a discussion of a key point of disagreement among early seventeenth-century French mystics on the role of the humanity of Christ in the higher stages of the mystical life, but he speaks of "abstract spiritualité" (306), not an Abstract School.

66. Cognet, *Post-Reformation Spirituality*, 60; see also idem, *La spiritualité moderne*, chap. 7.

67. See, e.g., Diefendorf, who criticizes the so-called passive nature of "abstract mysticism" and therefore also questions the usefulness of the term (*From Penitence to Charity*, 24).

68. Jacques Le Brun, *Soeur et amante: Les biographies spirituelles feminins du XVIIe siècle* (Geneva: Droz, 2013).

69. A helpful survey of some of these themes can be found in Salin, "'L'invasion mystique.'"

70. For remarks on the history of the term in this period, see André Derville, "Homme intérieur. 4: Le 17e siècle français," DS 7:669–74. Derville sees the seventeenth-century authors as stressing the "spiritual" meaning of the term, that is, its use for indicating the inner moral and spiritual conscience, rather than a more metaphysical sense of the inner structure of the soul, as was common in the Middle Ages.

71. On introversion, see Michel Dupuy, "Introversion," DS 7:1904–18, who distinguishes "Neoplatonic introversion," which sees introversion as the characteristic act of spiritual beings, from introversion as a method of recollection and interior prayer. He claims (c. 1917) that the seventeenth century saw an enlargement of the term "to designate every effort of the spiritual life, without keeping the Neoplatonic taste." Dupuy also notes that introversion in the traditional sense differs from introspection, because it deals not so much with consciousness of the self as with "the spiritual dimension of the whole being."

72. Aspects of inner experience as a method of interiorization are treated by Maurice Nédoncelle, "Intériorité. II: Intériorité et vie spirituelle," DS 7:1889–1903.

73. See Mino Bergamo, *L'anatomie de l'âme: De François de Sales à Fénelon* (Grenoble: Jérôme Millon, 1994), 7: "Je dirai dès à present que l'intérêt pour l'intériorité, l'interrogation sur les mouvements et les états de la vie intérieur, a atteint dans la culture française du XVIIe siècle un des sommets de son développement."

74. For some aspects of the history of inner experience, see Bernard McGinn, "The Language of Inner Experience in Christian Mysticism," *Spiritus* 1 (2001): 156–71.

75. Salin, "'L'invasion mystique,'" 256–58. Salin points out that the interiorization of mysticism also represents a protest against the new order of rationalism, utilitarianism, and absolutism gaining ground in French society (262–64).

76. For an overview, see Wendy M. Wright, "Captured Yet Free: The Rich Symbolism of the Heart in French Spirituality," in *Surrender to Christ for Mission: French Spiritual Traditions*, ed. Philip Sheldrake (Collegeville, MN: Liturgical Press, 2018), 71–89. Seventeenth-century France also saw the creation of the Feast of the Sacred Heart, on which see Auguste Hamon, "Coeur (Sacré)," DS 3:1023–46.

77. Certeau, *Mystic Fable: Volume One*, "Introduction," especially 12–13.

78. These shifts in the meaning of *mysticus* were first analyzed by Michel de Certeau, "'Mystique' au XVIIe siècle: Le problème de langage 'mystique,'" in *L'homme devant Dieu: Mélanges offerts au père Henri de Lubac*, 3 vols. (Paris: Aubier, 1963–64) 2:267–91. See also *Mystic Fable: Volume One*, chap. 3, "The New Science," especially 94–112.

79. *Scientia sanctorum* is based on Wisdom 10:10, Proverbs 9:10 and 30:3, and especially Ephesians 3:18–19, and occurs in Bernard of Clairvaux's *De consideratione* II.7 (*S. Bernardi Opera* 3:422): "Haec scientia sanctorum, haec longe ab illa quae inflat." For notes on its development and use, see Dagens, *Bérulle et les origines*, 250–52.

80. For a summary, see Salin, "'L'invasion mystique,'" 259–61.

81. Certeau, "'Mystique' au XVIIe siècle," 278–79.

82. Certeau, *Mystic Fable: Volume One*, chap. 4, "Manners of Speaking" (113–50). See also Salin, "'L'invasion mystique,'" 261–64.

83. *Annihilatio/adnullatio* is not a Classical term but was created in the fifth century (Jerome is the earliest witness) on the basis of biblical texts, especially in the Psalms, where God is described as reducing his enemies to nothing (e.g., Pss 14:4; 58:9; 72:20; 88:39).

84. For an overview of some medieval uses, see Sylvain Piron, "Adnichilatio," in *Mots médiévaux offerts à Reudi Imbach*, ed. I. Atucha et al. (Oporto, Portugal: Féderation Internationale des Instituts d'Études Médiévales, 2011), 23–33. For a comparative study, see David Bell, "A Doctrine of Ignorance: The Annihilation of Individuality in Christian and Muslim Mysticism," in *Benedictus: Studies in Honor of Benedict of Nursia*, ed. E. Rozanne Elder (Kalamazoo: Cistercian Publications, 1981), 30–52.

85. Bernard of Clairvaux, *De diligendo deo* X.27 (*S. Bernardi Opera* 3:142): "Te enim quodammodo perdere, tamquam qui non sis, et omnino non sentire seipsum, et a temetipso exinaniri, et paene annulare."

86. Joanne Maguire Robinson, *Nobility and Annihilation in Marguerite Porete's "Mirror of Simple Souls,"* SUNY Series in Western Esoteric Traditions (Albany: State University of New York Press, 2001); Juan Marin, "Annihilation and Deification in Beguine Theology and Marguerite Porete's *Mirror of Simple Souls*," *Harvard Theological Review* 103 (2010): 89-109; and Barbara Newman, "Annihilation and Authorship: Three Women Mystics of the 1290s," *Speculum* 91 (2013): 591-630.

87. The article by R. Daeschler ("Anéantissement," DS 1:560-65) assembles a number of texts, especially from the seventeenth century, and approves of a "moral"—or what I am calling weak—annihilation but attacks strong forms.

88. A sense of how widespread mystical annihilation language was can be seen by consulting the entries for "Annihilation" in the Index of Subjects in McGinn, *Flowering* (519); *Harvest* (715); and *Varieties* (713). The French version of the Pseudo-Tauler *Institutiones spirituales* (not indexed in these volumes) entitled its chap. XII, "De la suprême resignation et du ravissement en Dieu qui fait que l'esprit se plunge tout entier en Dieu et ne fait qu'un avec lui, dans la vraie pauvreté et l'anéantissement de soi-même" (see the text in Gueullette, *Eckhart en France*, 230-36).

89. Jacques Le Brun, "Le Dieu des mystiques au XVIIe S.," in Laux and Salin, *Dieu au XVIIe siècle*, 265-76, here 271.

90. For an overview concentrating on the modern period, see Jacques Le Brun, *La pur amour de Platon à Lacan* (Paris: Éditions du Seuil, 2001). An old, but useful, discussion is John Burnaby, *Amor Dei: A Study of the Religion of St. Augustine* (London: Hodder & Stoughton, 1938), chap. 9, "Pure Love" (253-97). See also Henri Sanson, *Saint Jean de la Croix entre Bossuet et Fénelon: Contribution à l'étude de la querelle du Pur Amour* (Paris: Presses Universitaires de France, 1953). Some material related to the issue can be found in the article of R. Daeschler, "Amour-Propre," DS 1:533-44.

91. Gorday, *Pure Love, Pure Poetry, Pure Prayer,* 126: "This development [of the *Histoire*] would start with an 'idea' [in the sense of Newman] that unfolds over time, namely, that of 'pure love' from Francis de Sales to Fénelon, gathering richness from varying witnesses but not changing in essence, through interplay with a changing historical context" (see also 381).

92. Ibid., 164.

93. The quotations are from Bernard's *Sermo super Cantica* 83 (S. Bernardi Opera 2:300-301).

94. On these issues, see Le Brun, "Le Dieu des mystiques au XVIIe S.," 273-76.

95. For a brief introduction stressing the relation of Jansenism to spirituality, see Louis Dupré, "Jansenism and Quietism," in *Christian Spirituality: Post-Reformation and Modern*, ed. Louis Dupré and Don E. Saliers, World Spirituality 18 (New York: Crossroad, 1989), 121-42.

CHAPTER 2

The Beginnings of French Mysticism

This chapter will investigate the first stages of early modern French mysticism in four sections. The first deals with the reforming Benedictine abbot Louis de Blois (1506–1566), the only major French mystic of the first half of the sixteenth century. Blosius, to give him his Latin name, was widely read for three centuries but has been somewhat neglected in the modern study of French mysticism, perhaps because he wrote in Latin. The second section will deal with what has been traditionally recognized as the starting point of the French mysticism that flourished between ca. 1590 and 1650, that is, the group of mystics and mystical sympathizers connected to the wealthy and pious Parisian noblewoman Barbe Acarie during the period from the late 1590s to about 1610. While the participants in the Acarie circle had their own backgrounds and concerns, their respect for this spiritually gifted woman, as well as their mutual contacts and interests, was the impetus for much that was to come, not only in French mysticism but also in the religious reform of the time. The third section of the chapter will concentrate on a key member of the Acarie circle, the English Capuchin Benet of Canfield. Born into a Puritan family, William Fitch fled to the Continent after his conversion to Catholicism and wrote his most influential mystical text in French, *La règle de perfection* (*The Rule of Perfection*). Canfield was an important, as well as controversial, mystical author, whose main work (at least in an Italian version) was put on the Index of Forbidden Books in 1689 during the

Quietist Controversy. Finally, the last part of the chapter will take a brief look at some of the other Capuchin mystical authors of the early decades of the seventeenth century.

Louis de Blois

Many treatments of French mysticism commence in the last decade of the sixteenth century as the Wars of Religion were winding down and France was beginning to undergo a revival of Catholic faith and piety. Despite the caesura represented by the religious conflicts, such an abrupt start does not do justice to what had gone on in the spiritual life of France in the first half of the sixteenth century during the early days of the Reformation. In France the main opposition to Catholicism came from the Reformed tradition established by thinkers like William Farel and John Calvin. The early French Catholic reaction to the Reformation was political and doctrinal, but also involved spirituality and mysticism. This initial reaction might be best described as a traditional late medieval attempt to address a new situation, rather than a creative new effort in response to a changed situation.

The primary example of an early sixteenth-century Catholic mystical reaction to the Reformation is the Benedictine abbot and monastic reformer Louis de Blois (Ludovicus Blosius, 1506–1566). Louis was born into a noble family at Donstienne near Liège in 1506.[1] He died in 1566, thus making him almost an exact contemporary of John Calvin (1509–1564). At a young age, Louis was sent to be a page at the court of the future emperor Charles V, with whom he maintained a friendship throughout his life. In 1520, he entered the Benedictine house of Liessies in Hainaut in what was then the Spanish Netherlands. Between 1524 and 1530, he studied arts and theology at Louvain but was recalled to Liessies, where he became abbot on July 12, 1530. For the next thirty-six years, Louis de Blois was one of the most important figures in the Spanish Netherlands, on both the religious and civic levels. His reforming activities began in earnest in his own house in 1537 and soon spread more widely. In 1545, Paul III approved his reforming *Statuta Monastica*. The abbot had close connections with the Northern European movements of Catholic reform in the early decades of the struggle against Lutheranism. He was a strong supporter of the Jesuits and facilitated their installation at the University of Louvain in 1552. In 1556, he even wrote to Ignatius, encouraging him to send more of his followers north.[2] Louis was also connected with the Cologne

Charterhouse of St. Barbara, the major center for the publication of vernacular mystical works and their translation into Latin as a way of countering Reformation attacks on Catholicism.[3] The most important of the Cologne translators, Laurent Sauer (Laurentius Surius, d. 1578), dedicated his edition of the *Opera omnia* of Henry Suso to Blosius in 1555. In his second edition of the works of Tauler published in 1553, Surius also cited Blosius's defense of John Tauler (*Apologia pro Thaulero*) against the Catholic theologian John Eck (d. 1543), who had accused the Dominican of being a forerunner of Luther. Louis de Blois thus had a good knowledge of the late-medieval mysticism of Germany and the Low Countries, including Tauler, Suso, Ruusbroec, Gertrude the Great, and even Meister Eckhart (if anonymously) through the popular *Institutiones spirituales* (*Institutiones Taulerianae*).[4] This did not make him any less a traditional Benedictine.[5] His first publication was the *Speculum monachorum*, which appeared in 1538. Louis's devotion to Augustine and Gregory the Great, for example, is evident in his *Psychogogia, or Recreation of the Soul*, a treatise of the 1540s on contemplation and union with God, consisting of long extracts from these two fathers.

Much of Louis de Blois's extensive oeuvre (thirty-one works are known) is taken up with monastic reform and ascetical piety, but a number of his treatises can be described as mystical.[6] The most important of these works, the *Spiritual Institution, or Instruction (Institutio spiritualis)*, was first published in 1553. The work was very successful, counting forty-seven later editions and translations, independent of its appearance in the *Opera omnia*, before the end of the eighteenth century. It was translated into French (1553), Italian (1562), Spanish (1587), German (1652), and Dutch (1696).[7] Cardinal Wiseman (1802–1865), the first archbishop of Westminster after the restoration of Catholicism to England in 1850, appears to have been the initiator of English interest in Blosius. In 1859, he wrote an elegant Latin preface to the edition of Blosius's works published in London,[8] and a number of translations of the abbot's writing into English followed in subsequent decades.[9]

Blosius's *Spiritual Instruction* has several advantages over the usual late medieval and early modern spiritual handbooks. First, it is better organized and contains a progressive account of the mystical life, whereas many of the earlier handbooks were digressive and poorly structured. Second, despite the author's wide reading, the book is not just an anthology and does not depend on extended quotations from mystical sources.[10] (In the appendices he did include two long series of quotations drawn from the writings of John Tauler.)[11] Blosius had absorbed a great deal of traditional mystical teaching, but he appropriated it and transformed it. In many ways he can be described as an independent mystical teacher, despite his grounding both in traditional Benedictine mysticism and in the late medieval thought of Suso, Tauler, Eckhart, Harphius (Hendrik Herp), and Jan van Ruusbroec, whose writings would have been available to him in Latin translation.[12] One reason why Blosius's treatise proved to be a best-seller is the tone of moderation that characterizes the work, an unusual achievement in the troubled times of the sixteenth century. Blosius's positive and balanced view of mysticism is reminiscent of a better-known French figure born the year after he died, Francis de Sales.

A brief look at the structure of the twelve chapters of the *Spiritual Instruction* will provide a sense of the abbot's organizing abilities before turning to a consideration of some central aspects of Blosius's teaching, especially about "mystical union" (*unio mystica*), a term we take for granted but that was something of an innovation in the sixteenth century.[13] Louis's theological training at Louvain equipped him for thinking in the doctrinally precise categories that were becoming increasingly prevalent in sixteenth-century Second Scholasticism. The pastoral and pedagogical purpose of his manual of mystical teaching meant that it could no longer be a meandering exercise in *lectio divina* but had to have a careful structure that would make it an apt teaching tool for those within and without the monastery.[14] It is obvious from the preface that the abbot organized his material to help the beginner (*Tyro*) to take on the role of what he calls the *Asceta*, or practitioner, in order to embark on the road to mystical union, the state of the *Sponsa Verbi*, as set forth in chap. XII.

The preface sets out a brief anthropological teaching about the soul and its powers. Louis says that sacred writers divide the soul into three aspects: the *anima*, which refers to the inferior and sensitive powers; the *spiritus*, which consists of "the three superior, rational, and intellectual powers" (memory, understanding, and will); and the *mens vel apex spiritus*, which is "the naked and God-formed depth of the soul, that is, the simple essence of the soul marked with the image of God."[15] He continues, "According to this depth [*fundus*] we speak of the superessential life [*vita superessentialis*] through which both the spiritual life and the active life are perfected." The use of the term *superessentialis* links the Benedictine abbot to Ruusbroec and his followers, such as Harphius and the *Evangelical Pearl*, which had been translated into Latin in 1545 and which Blosius may have read.[16] In traditional fashion, Louis describes the three powers of memory, intellect, and will as having a likeness to the three persons of the Trinity: "And so like the very Persons of the Divinity, these three powers work in an inseparable way."[17]

The Trinitarian dimension of the soul's powers recurs in several places in the course of the *Instruction*.[18] This was a theological commonplace, but Louis's version of this seems Ruusbroecian, as is his insistence throughout that the supreme union with God takes place in the "naked depth of the soul" (*nudus fundus animae*).[19] In his discussion in chapter XII.iv of what he calls the *vertex voluntatis/apex mentis/ fundus animae*, it is interesting to note that, like Francis de Sales after him, Blosius insists that both the intellect and the will have supreme points that are directly touched by God. At the beginning of chapter VIII he speaks of the fixed and steadfast prayer that takes place when the *Asceta* has arrived at a state "[w]here God is in him and he has been rooted and made firm in God through intimate union, where, I say, he is free of all multiplicity and reaches as far as the simple naked depth of the soul in which the original fountain of Divinity is found."[20] Blosius's teaching on the *fundus/abyssus* of the soul, deeper and closer to God than the three higher powers, reaches a climax in an impassioned hymn of praise at the end of chapter XII: "O noble Depth and divine temple, from which God never departs! O most splendid Depth in which dwells the Holy Trinity, and in which eternity itself is tasted. . . ." In accents close to those of Tauler, the Benedictine says that the abyss of God invites the soul's depth or abyss back into itself: "God, the uncreated Abyss, calls our spirit, the created abyss, back into himself, that it may be worthy to be made one with him so that our spirit itself, immersed in the deepest sea of Divinity, may joyfully lose itself in God's spirit."[21]

Like Ruusbroec, as well as Eckhart, Tauler, and Suso, Blosius insists that in its deepest reality the soul is uncreated and eternal. In an important passage in chapter VIII he says, "Hence, according to our ideal reality [*ideam*] we have been in God from eternity. In him, I say, we have been and are uncreated. . . . The exemplars of all things are in God's essence and that same divine essence is the Exemplar of all things and a single *idea*. All the multiplicity of things is reduced to unity in the totally simple and superessential essence of God. All things are one in God."[22] Whether Blosius knew Ruusbroec directly, or absorbed the Flemish mystic through an intermediary such as Hendrik Herp, is difficult to determine.[23] He certainly was familiar with Herp, as well as with Tauler and Suso, from the translations of his friend Surius.

Blosius organizes his treatise by dividing the discussion of aspects of mystical union in the preparatory chapters from the treatments of the exercises preparing for God's final gift of union, which, he says, may be realized initially in this life but will be fully attained only in heaven. Thus, chapter I discusses why all Christians should aspire to union and gives the broad lines of how it is to be pursued. The concrete details of the journey occupy chapters II through XI, beginning with ascetic practice (chap. II), interior recollection (chap. III), and the use of ejaculative prayer, or aspirations (chaps. IV-V). Blosius's description of the mystical path is Christocentric, often speaking of the importance of meditation on Christ's Passion, especially in chapter VI.[24] Chapter VII treats of the role of dryness, suffering, and desolation in the path to union, without, however, touching on the extreme forms of abandonment by God found in some late medieval and early modern authors. The monastic character of the *Spiritual Instruction* appears in the long chapter VIII, which provides advice about many of the standard exercises of the conventual life, such as the necessity of obedience, praying the daily office, reception of the Eucharist,[25] as well as dealing with temptation and sin, and the need for examination of conscience. Blosius counsels freedom with regard to all these practices—"The essential way to God is one, but the exercises are diverse."[26] Chapter IX provides encouragement for the struggling *Asceta* to continue on the path, no matter how difficult it is and how conscious he is of his failings. Chapters X-XI contain a series of examples and model prayers for striving toward union with God.

The goal of Louis de Blois's mystical teaching is found in the final chapter XII, a doctrine reprised in chapter XI of his *Spiritual Mirror* (*Speculum spirituale*), published in 1558. *Unio mystica*, which Louis de Blois also says is the *sapientia mysticae theologiae*, "wisdom of mystical theology" (thus using both new and old terms),[27] is described in a variety of ways in chapter XII. Like the German mystics and Ruusbroec, Louis emphasizes how the final stage goes beyond the soul's highest powers and all forms of thinking: "With its higher powers lifted up, illumined, and adorned by divine grace, the soul attains the unity and nakedness of the spirit, and acquires pure and untainted love and simple knowledge that is without any thoughts." This is contemplating the divine Abyss "with a peaceful, simple and delightful act of intuition, without imagination, or any admixture of intellect."[28] The passing beyond the higher operations of the soul is described not only in terms of transformation into God,[29] but sometimes even as a quasi-annihilation, although Blosius chooses his language carefully, never actually using the word *annihilatio* itself. In chapter XII.ii, for example, he says, "The loving soul, I say, flows away and leaves itself, and is, as it were, reduced to nothing, gathered into the abyss of eternal love, where, dead to itself, it lives to God, knowing nothing, sensing nothing, beyond the love it tastes."[30] In three places in the *Spiritual Instruction* he describes such union in Ruusbroecian terms as "without any intermediary,"[31] though it is significant that he never uses the controversial language of "union without difference, or distinction." Rather, in a number of texts Louis explicitly speaks of the continued distinction between God and the soul even in the most advanced stages of union.[32]

Louis de Blois's understanding of mystical union shows affinities with the sometimes suspect views of union in Eckhart and his followers, as well as those of Jan van Ruusbroec, who was attacked by Jean Gerson in the first decade of the fourteenth century for a false understanding of union.[33] In the final section of chapter XII, two aspects of the abbot's presentation make this clear. The first is the appeal to a final level of union that goes beyond even uniting with the three Persons in order to be merged into the simple unity of the divine essence.[34] At the very least, this suggests errors of the kind of which both Eckhart and Ruusbroec had been accused. The second aspect is the admittedly rare reference to the birth of the Word in the interior depth (*fundus*) of the soul that takes place in the process of becoming one spirit with God.[35] Despite these adaptations of some of the more daring aspects of the late medieval mysticism of Northern Europe, Louis de Blois was also essentially traditional in his teaching, as is evident in his frequent appeals to the language of *unitas spiritus*, or "union of spirits," based on 1 Corinthians 6:17, a text long favored by monastic mystics, to characterize the way in which the soul becomes one with God in love, but not in substance. Louis was also worried about false understandings of mystical union (not unlike Ruusbroec), views that would absolve contemplatives from concern for performing good works.[36]

Blosius's teaching on *unio mystica* is a mixture of the old and the new—old in accord with the long tradition of Benedictine "Western Mysticism,"[37] and new in using the distinctive, though sometimes controversial, mystical trends of Northern Europe that began in the fourteenth century.[38] A full analysis of chapter XII of the *Spiritual Instruction* and chapter XI of the *Spiritual Mirror* would be helpful in sorting out what Louis owed to each of these strands. The treatment here is designed only to indicate the richness of the teaching of this Benedictine abbot of the mid-sixteenth century and to demonstrate his links with some of the subsequent debated issues in French mysticism of the seventeenth century.

Barbe Acarie and Her Circle

The story of Barbe Acarie and her circle serves as a kind of foundation myth for seventeenth-century French mysticism, as is evident from Henri Bremond's perhaps surprising statement in volume 2 of his *History* (originally entitled *L'invasion mystique [1590–1620]*), that "Madame Acarie . . . is assuredly the most important person with whom this volume deals." And "[t]he activity of this woman, an invalid and ecstatic, who died at fifty-two, was miraculous."[39] We have only fragments of Acarie's own thought, the brief collection of *Écrits spirituels* (*Spiritual Writings*).[40] According to Jean Dagens, "The writings of Madame Acarie give only a weak idea of her life, and similarly, without doubt, of her profound spiritual thought."[41] What we know about her depends mainly on the 1621 *Life* written by the Sorbonne theologian André Duval (1564–1638), who was one of her circle.[42] She was born Barbe Avrillot on February 1, 1566, to a wealthy Parisian family.[43] Although she was attracted to the religious life, her family married her off to another wealthy aristocrat, Pierre Acarie, in 1582. She soon began to bear children (six between 1584 and 1592). According to the *Life*, the young mother took the opportunity to read romances while watching over the children, something that disturbed the pious Pierre, who asked a local priest to provide him with better reading for his wife. It was probably in 1588 that the young wife read a phrase that converted her to a deeper spiritual life—*Trop est avare à qui Dieu ne suffit* ("One is indeed a miser to whom God is not enough"). The phrase goes back to a sermon of Augustine, but Acarie was not reading the bishop of Hippo. The sentence is also found in chapter XX of the *Institutiones spirituales* of the Pseudo-Tauler, which had been translated into French in 1587.[44] Madame Acarie's entry into a life of mystical prayer and rapture was tied to this important witness to Northern mysticism, as well as to French versions of the writings of Louis de Blois, which we know she also read.[45]

Madame Acarie soon began experiencing lengthy ecstasies both at home and while attending Mass at her parish church. This led to considerable tension with her husband, who, though pious, was not ready for a mystic in the house. Where husband and wife did not disagree was in their politics, since Pierre Acarie was one of the foremost Parisian adherents of the Catholic League, and Barbe Acarie was also a strong supporter. During Henry IV's siege of Paris with its attendant famine in mid-1590, Madame Acarie served valiantly in succoring the wounded and helping feed the starving. As is often the case with ecstatic women, the problems regarding Barbe Acarie's raptures mounted. Many attacked her, and she herself had doubts about the source of her raptures. It was not until 1592 that the Capuchin friar Benet of Canfield became her spiritual advisor and freed her from doubt, convincing her that these special experiences came from God. She was even said to have received the stigmata in 1593. The changing political situation soon affected the Acarie family. Henry IV eventually defeated the League, converted to Catholicism, and entered Paris as king in March 1594. Henry adopted a policy of restraint toward most Leaguers, except for those who had engaged in assassinations and other forms of extreme violence. Pierre Acarie had not, but he had been too important in the League to escape all punishment, so the king exiled him from Paris in 1594. Madame Acarie had to manage the household and restore the family fortune, which had been destroyed in the Wars of Religion. She finally convinced the king to allow Pierre to return in 1599.

It was in the late 1590s, as peace returned to battered France, that Madame Acarie, whose reputation as a mystic had already spread, began to use her mansion on the rue des Juifs as a gathering place for a group of clerics and laity interested in spiritual literature and mystical piety.[46] Acarie's apostolic work, however, was considerably more than just with the restricted spiritual aficionados of her circle. She kept a kind of open house for the poor and sick, serving the needs of many and even allowing some unfortunates to take up residence. Madame Acarie also became famous for her skill in "discernment of spirits," that is, as a guide and spiritual advisor.[47] The Acarie circle was also a major source for the reform of the religious life in France in the early seventeenth century. The introduction of Teresa's reformed Carmelites in France, the spread of the Ursulines to northern France, the reform of female Benedictine convents, and the establishment of the Oratorians all had roots in or connections with the apostolic action of Madame Acarie and her friends. The fact that this "mystical circle" was centered on a married laywoman is remarkable, although it has a prototype in the community of followers, again both lay and clerical, who gathered around the mystic Angela of Foligno in the first decade of fourteenth-century Umbria.

The circle remained active down to about 1613, when Pierre Acarie died, thus leaving Madame Acarie free to embrace the cloistered life of the Carmelite Order she had helped establish in France in 1604. In February 1614, she entered the Carmel at Amiens as a lay sister, not a choir nun (her three daughters had already entered Carmel).

She transferred to the Carmel at Pontoise on December 7, 1616, and there she died on April 18, 1618. Under her religious name, Marie de l'Incarnation, Barbe Acarie was beatified in 1791.

A closer look at some of the major figures involved in the Acarie circle will provide a sense of the impact of this early chapter in the story of French mysticism. As already noted, the English Capuchin Benet of Canfield met Acarie in 1592 and served as her spiritual director for a number of years. Since he was imprisoned in England from 1599 to 1602, it is hard to know how much direct contact he had with Acarie after his return to France in 1603 until his death in 1610. Although Canfield's *Rule of Perfection* was not officially published until 1610, it circulated in manuscript from at least 1592. Its mysticism of obedience, radical abnegation, and annihilation doubtless had an influence on Acarie. Barbara Diefendorf notes that, while Canfield was a major force in the spirituality of the Acarie circle, there was a similar outlook in most of these *dévots*. "The important thing," according to Diefendorf, "is that all drew on a common intellectual heritage dominated by the concepts of conformity to God's will, pure love, and the allness of God and the nothingness of humankind. . . . [T]he *dévots* shared a belief that spiritual progress depended on emptying oneself of all that was human and therefore base so as to effect union with the divine by the unique power of God's pure love as manifest in Christ's sacrifice on the cross."[48] The resulting spirituality was Christocentric, mystical, as well as being devoted to apostolic action.

It may have been in 1599 when Canfield left for England that the Carthusian Richard Beaucousin (1561-1610) took over as Acarie's confessor.[49] Beaucousin wrote nothing himself, but, in good Carthusian fashion, encouraged the production and translation of mystical literature.[50] Born in Paris of a noble family, Beaucousin entered the Charterhouse of Vauvert at Paris in 1591. He soon acquired so great a reputation as a mystic and spiritual director that many pious folk, such as Acarie and her friends, flocked to his cell. The noise and confusion troubled the Carthusian community, so he was removed from Paris in 1602 to become the prior at Cahors, where he died in 1610. Another priest who was friendly with Barbe Acarie and served as her confessor was the Jesuit Pierre Coton (1563-1626), confessor and advisor to Henry IV. Coton wrote a number of spiritual works, including *The Interior Occupation of the Devout Soul* (1608), and he served as the confessor of the beguine Marie de Valence Teyssonier (1575-1648), whose credentials as a mystic were advanced by Louis de la Rivière's *History of the Life and Customs of Marie Tessioner* (1650).[51] Among the other close clerical associates of Madame Acarie were two professors at the Sorbonne, Jacques Gallemant, a noted ecstatic, and André Duval. Both theologians worked closely with Acarie in setting up the Carmelite reform in France and served as early superiors of the French Carmels. Duval, as noted above, went on to write the first life of the saint.

Another priest, Jean Quintanadoine de Bretigny (1555–1634), not only translated Teresa of Avila into French (1601) but was also one of Acarie's collaborators in the effort to bring the Carmelites to Paris.[52] There were also many lay *dévots*, both men and women, who frequented Madame Acarie's house. Among these was the Franciscan tertiary, René Gualtier (ca. 1560–1628), who translated the works of John of the Cross into French (1622), as well as those of a number of other Spanish mystics. Another layman was Michel de Marillac, the superintendent of the royal finances. There were also aristocratic and upper bourgeoisie women whose donations helped finance the many new houses of religious women springing up in Paris and elsewhere. These include Marguerite de Gondi, Charlotte de Hardy de Sancy, Marie de Tudert, and Claire d'Abra de Raconis, a convert from the Huguenots.

The most famous members of Acarie's circle were the two major French mystics of the first half of the seventeenth century, Francis de Sales (1567–1622) and Pierre de Bérulle (1575–1629). Francis de Sales's participation was fairly short, but still memorable both for him and Acarie. It was during his nine-month stay in Paris in 1602 on a diplomatic mission to Henry IV that he came into contact with Acarie and her friends. He was impressed with the mystic, as she with him. Francis de Sales often heard her confession, although he declined taking the role of becoming her official confessor. The discussions about mysticism and mystical literature among the group must have influenced Francis's developing thoughts about putting his own spiritual teaching in writing.

Pierre de Bérulle's life and thought were more decisively marked by Madame Acarie.[53] The two were related, and Acarie first met Pierre Bérulle as a student about 1594, when she was staying with her cousin, his mother. The young theology candidate soon began visiting the *maison Acarie*. As soon as he was ordained in 1599, he became one of Acarie's confessors and spiritual directors. Especially during the negotiations involved in setting up the Paris Carmel in 1604, he is said to have met with Acarie almost daily. He and Duval and Gallemant were established as the three clerical directors of the new French branch of the Discalced, though the arrangement was subsequently to create difficulties. Madame Acarie had long encouraged Bérulle to set up an order or congregation of secular priests modeled on that of Philip Neri in Italy. After considerable hesitation, Bérulle finally established the French Oratory, and Madame Acarie was present at the first Mass to celebrate the foundation on November 11, 1611. The close bonds between Acarie and Bérulle came to an unfortunate end. As noted above, Barbe became a Carmelite lay sister at Amiens in 1614. The Carmelite houses were under the general control of the three secular priests who had aided in their foundation. Bérulle, however, who had been appointed perpetual Visitor in 1614, had more power than Duval and Gallement and sought to introduce changes into the Carmelite practices, especially his controversial vows of servitude to Jesus Christ and to Mary, characteristics of the spirituality that Bérulle had been developing for more than a decade. These new vows did not sit well with most of the Carmelite nuns, including Marie de l'Incarnation, who had by now become fully imbued with the spirit of Teresa. Bérulle called at Pontoise in early 1618, a few months before Marie's death, and upbraided her in a long interview. According to an account in the chronicle of the convent, Bérulle reproached her with many words, "among others that hers was a petty mind, that she was mistaken and that she had bungled everything she had undertaken."[54] Sister Marie accepted all this in humility and died soon thereafter.

The full story of establishing the Carmelites in Paris cannot be told here,[55] but a review of a few highlights will reveal something of the inner dynamics of the Acarie circle, since this was the group's most notable institutional endeavor. Jean de Quintanadoine de Bretigny, with his Spanish background and contacts, had been endeavoring to bring the Carmelites to France for a decade or more without success. His translations of Teresa's writings (1601) had a profound effect on Barbe Acarie, who had the books read to her. She soon had a vision of the saint telling her to begin working to bring the Discalced nuns to France.[56] Acarie and her Carthusian confessor Beaucousin invited Fr. Gallemant and Fr. de Bretigny to come to Paris for a meeting. They met in Beaucousin's cell along with Bérulle and Duval. The group judged the project impossible, given the current political tensions between France and Spain. Teresa and Madame Acarie, however, did not give up. Duval tells us that Madame Acarie "was quite calm and determined not to think any more on the matter. But, seven or eight months later [1602], the Holy Mother [Teresa] appeared to her the second time, commanding her, more imperatively and forcefully, to bring the matter again under consideration and assuring her that . . . she would succeed."[57] So the same group, this time with the participation of Francis de Sales, assembled at the Carthusian monastery for several days and decided not only to proceed with the endeavor, but to begin thinking about the means for bringing it to pass. After many twists and turns, the first Carmelite house in France opened in Paris in 1604.

The true depth of Barbe Acarie's mystical life and teaching is hidden from us. At one time she did write down an account of her mystical experiences, but she told Duval that she burned it. Duval also says that she wrote "an infinite number" of letters, but only fifteen survive. The fragments of her spiritual exercises that we possess allow us but brief flashes into her inner life. As mentioned above, Acarie was noted for her frequent raptures, some of considerable length. She had to give up reading mystical texts, we are told, because they frequently induced raptures, although she apparently was able to have such books read to her. Duval records the testimony of the Jesuit Etienne Binet, who said, "I have never known anyone in whom was more clearly to be seen what S. Denis calls *divina patiens*, that is to say, she was passive rather than active, . . . being continually illuminated with much light and abundant heavenly favors and having God so present to her soul, that had she not practiced some distraction, she would have often fallen into ecstasy and been transported out of herself."[58] These raptures seem not to have ordinarily involved visions of Christ or other heavenly figures, but to have been forms of direct consciousness of God's presence, and, indeed, "presence" is a term that occurs fairly frequently in Acarie's sparse writings. Many witnesses speak of the radiance that came over her face during these raptures. Duval records a time he witnessed her at the Carmel of Amiens after she became a sister. Passing through the convent, he at first did not notice her, but his companion drew his attention to her. Duval says, "I turned round, but did not at first recognize her, so radiant and absolutely dazzling did her face appear to me."[59] Where Acarie was unusual among ecstatics was in her reticence to talk or write about her inner experiences.[60]

There is one letter, however, that does speak of the inner graces she received during a rapture. This letter, written to Bérulle probably in 1615, reflects events of a decade or more earlier.[61] Acarie says that on Holy Saturday, as she thought about how little she had appreciated Christ's sufferings for humanity on the preceding days of Holy Week, she glanced at a crucifix, and "the soul was so immediately and so sharply touched that I could no longer even look on it outwardly, but beheld it interiorly. I was amazed to see the Second Person of the Most Holy Trinity served in this wise for my sins and those of mankind." Acarie invokes the usual mystical topos of saying it is impossible to describe what took place in her interior regarding this presence of the Second Person of the Trinity, especially about the mystery of redemption on the cross. God comforted her during this anguish of sharing in Christ's Passion, otherwise she could not have borne it longer. This comfort was an inner enlightenment and conviction of Christ's presence. She goes on: "What is inwardly experienced cannot be spoken or expressed. I remember well that the soul admired his Wisdom, his Goodness, and particularly the excess of his Love for mankind. Joy and sorrow together made different effects and rendered the soul fertile in conceptions." These conceptions were the responses and prayers she then made: "What did she not say to the Lord so surely present within her? What needs did she forget? What desires and hopes? What thanksgivings where she made use of all heaven and especially the Most Holy Trinity?" Sister Marie concludes this part of the letter by saying, "Briefly, I cannot say how it was with me; it lasted during the morning prayer, about four or five hours."[62] She also notes how the experience aided her prayer life, especially after taking communion.

A text like this gives us a sense of why Barbe Acarie became a model for mystical rapture to her contemporaries. As Henri Bremond put it: "One thing alone is clear and should be sufficient for us: the contemporaries of Mme Acarie found in her a living type of the sublime life towards which so many souls felt themselves vaguely drawn." We may well ask why so many other mystics took this married woman as their paragon. Bremond's answer is in terms of her "utmost simplicity," her "horror of all subtlety, over-refining, and, still more, affectation in these matters."[63] A perusal of Acarie's brief surviving writings supports this judgment. They are, indeed, both simple and powerful. Passages are found about devotion to Jesus and the humanity of Christ, about the importance of the Eucharist, about total offering of self to God, about the desire to attain union with God, and even about the wish to plunge into God and be annihilated—all major themes of French mysticism. There are even texts that express an apophaticism doubtless influenced by her reading of late medieval mystics. In one passage, for example, she addresses God as her "Well-Beloved," and asks him to look upon her in "His Holy Spirit," because she is unworthy to be in his presence. She goes on: "This is why I hold myself here with profound reverence and a very great recognition of my own nothingness. I am nothing; I can do nothing; I know nothing."[64] For the most part, however, Madame Acarie was content to enjoy her deep relationship with God, not to speak or write about it, unless pushed. In her total humility, as well as her conviction that contemplative gifts were given for the sake of a more intense practice of love of others, this married mystic offers a challenge to all who study the history of mysticism.

Benet of Canfield and the Mysticism of Annihilation

Life

Henri Bremond described Benet of Canfield, as the "master of a whole generation of mystics," although he treats him only briefly in his *History*.[65] Given the importance and influence of Canfield's thought, it is surprising that there is not a larger literature devoted to him.[66] Born William Fitch into a Puritan gentry family at Canfield in Essex in 1562, the young William was sent to London to study law at the Inns of Court, where he began to wrestle over his spiritual life and religious affiliation. William's struggles are available to us in a fascinating spiritual account (obviously modeled on Augustine's *Confessions*) included in the Baroque hagiography composed about him by Jacques Brousse, *The Miraculous Life: Conversion and Conversation of The Reverend Father Benet of Canfield*.[67] William describes his spiritual problems in vivid detail: his evil life and many temptations; his religious perplexities over the true form of Christianity (Christ's real presence in the Eucharist was central for him); and his temptation to despair over the devil's suggestion that he is predestined to hell (the young Francis de Sales was experiencing a similar temptation at almost the same time in Paris).[68] William converted to Catholicism in 1587 and deemed it best to leave England for France, where he debated about joining the Conventual Franciscans (the "Cordeliers") or the more austere Capuchins. At this point, his spiritual *confessio* presents an account of a "spiritual ravishment" that revealed to him what he should do. After having three Masses said for his intentions, he tells us:

> For about midnight, being all alone in my chamber and lifting up my spirit towards Thee in this affair, I felt myself drawn by Thee and my spirit so filled with a sudden supernatural light, and was so surprised with so great a fire of charity. That being out of myself and being transported into Thee, I rested like one that had lost all feeling of myself and the world, in which ravishment and alienation of sense I knew after an unspeakable manner thy holy will touching my vocation, so that if an angel had appeared visibly to me to have declared it, I could not have better known it, nor more certainly believed it.

He concludes, "I passed the night in great sweetness and spiritual delight."[69] It is interesting to note that Barbe Acarie, the Parisian aristocrat, and William Fitch, the convert, were beginning new lives marked by what were reported as almost constant ecstatic experiences at about the same time. Whatever the truth of these hagiographical topoi, there can be no doubt that Benet of Canfield became a noted ecstatic. A later text from the *Life*, coming from Jacques Brousse, says, "I should not say that he had extasies or ravishments, but that his whole life from three-and-twenty years of age that he became a Capuchin was a continual rapt and perpetual extasy."[70] There seems to have been a kind of "ecstatic imperative" among some of these late sixteenth-century and seventeenth-century French mystics, that is, a need to prove one's mystical credentials by frequent states of alienation from the senses.

In 1587, William Fitch entered the Capuchins and was professed in 1588 with the name Benet of Canfield (his place of birth). His year of novitiate was marked with frequent raptures, including a two-day ecstasy that took place after beholding a representation of Christ on the cross.[71] Shortly after being professed, Friar Benet left France to pursue doctoral studies in Venice, where he remained from 1588 to 1591. Here he seems to have come into contact with the Capuchin polymath and eventual Doctor of the Church, Lawrence of Brindisi (1559–1619), who was teaching at Venice at the time. Friar Benet was a quick study and absorbed an impressive degree of doctrinal and mystical literature in the brief years after his conversion. It was during his stay in Venice that Benet began writing his major mystical work, *The Rule of Perfection*. According to Brousse's *Life*, the basic content of the book had been revealed to Friar Benet in one of the ecstasies he received during his novitiate.[72] The stages in the composition of the book are obscure. Much of its three books was probably written between 1589 and 1593, and the work circulated in manuscript for a number of years. During this period there were disputes about aspects of the last of the three books of the *Rule*, centering on its teaching on passive annihilation, which to some seemed to advance a kind of "pre-Quietist" indifference to ascetical practice and active charity. Several pirated copies and imperfect forms of the first two books and even the full three books appeared in print in the first decade of the sixteenth century. Canfield's own English translation of the first two books was printed at Rouen in 1608 and 1609. Shortly before his death in 1610 the Capuchin authorities ordered Friar Benet to put out an official edition of all three books, in both French and Latin. These editions deleted a number of earlier passages on passive annihilation and introduced a number of qualifications and additions designed to forestall criticism.[73] The work proved quite popular, with almost fifty printings in many languages during the seventeenth century.[74]

Friar Benet's short life had its share of drama. From his return to France in 1591 until 1599 he was active in the confused religious scene subsequent to the victory of Henry IV. He was connected with Barbe Acarie, as we have seen, and with other members of her circle. In 1599, he participated in a controversial case of a young woman, Marthe Brossier, suspected of diabolical possession. Since Brossier's devil was spouting anti-Huguenot revelations, the case pitted the Capuchins and other intransigent Catholic Leaguers against the seculars of the Parisian *Parlement*, who sought religious accommodation through acceptance of the Edict of Nantes. Friar Benet and other Capuchins were censured by the *Parlement*, and this may have had much to do with Benet's superiors accepting his offer to return to England to work for the restoration of the Catholic faith in the country at the risk of martyrdom.[75] He and another Capuchin set sail in July 1599, landed, and were promptly arrested. Friar Benet spent three years in English jails before being released in 1603 through the intercession of Henry IV and sent back to France. Between this time and his death on November 21, 1610, Benet of Canfield served in a number of leadership roles among the Capuchins, kept in contact with spiritual circles in France, and was occupied with revising his *Rule of Perfection*.[76]

Not much read today, *The Rule of Perfection* is a classic expression of a form of early modern mysticism that had considerable influence for more than a century. As Louis Cognet put it, "[T]he Capuchin's thought represents a powerful and original mystical synthesis."[77] The book can be seen in part as a late expression of the medieval tradition of handbooks of mystical theology, although Canfield's use of the strategies of Renaissance rhetorical and dialectical argumentation, based in the theories of Peter Ramus (d. 1572), give the treatise a different character from the medieval examples.[78] The use of topics (i.e., the discovery of themes for ordering knowledge), the juxtaposition of opposites to bring out deeper understanding of the terms in question, and the employment of rules or maxims, especially "the rule of rectitude" by which particular cases are to be measured, are just some of the rhetorical methods Canfield uses in the book. Above all, the Capuchin was interested in a form of *reduction*, that is, bringing the complexity of spiritual teachings back to their deepest point of origin. As the title of the book declares, "The Rule of Perfection, containing a brief and perspicuous abridgement of the whole spiritual life, reduced to the single point of the will of God; divided into three parts. . . ."[79]

The Question of Sources

When dealing with an academically trained theologian/mystic, it is easy to get lost in the question of sources. Canfield was learned and widely read, and he cites sources often. The notes in Orcibal's edition and Emery's translation make it clear how frequently the Capuchin utilized the riches of the theological and mystical traditions. Nevertheless, the basic source was the friar's own inner life. In the English translation of the *Rule* published at Rouen in 1609, Canfield included a dedicatory letter to the English Brigittine nuns at Lisbon in which he says of the *Rule*, "I have squared [it] out according to my own interior practice since my calling to Religion (though truly, with great negligence)."[80] Despite his use of many sources, it is important to take him at his word.[81]

What were Canfield's sources? His training gave him knowledge of many patristic and medieval theological writers, such as Augustine and especially Thomas Aquinas, whom he cites often. He knew major twelfth-century mystics, like Bernard of Clairvaux and Richard of St. Victor. Friar Benet was a Franciscan, so Bonaventure was a major resource for him, both authentic Bonaventuran writings, such as the *Itinerarium mentis in Deum*, as well as the Pseudo-Bonaventuran mystical writings included in the late sixteenth-century *Opera omnia* of the Seraphic Doctor.[82] There is no question that what is often referred to as the "affective Dionysianism" of Bonaventure and his followers, that is, the insistence that it is only through the "supreme point of affectivity" (*apex affectus*) that union with God can be realized, was a major component in Canfield's background. The threefold structure of the Capuchin's work (exterior life/interior life/supereminent life) is based ultimately on Ruusbroec, whose writings were available in the Latin translations of Laurentius Surius, but much of the Ruusbroecian foundation of his mysticism came from the writings of Hendrik Herp, or Harphius (another reformed Franciscan), which were widely available at the end of the sixteenth century.[83] Among Canfield's other important sources from late medieval Northern mysticism was the Dutch *Evangelical Pearl*, which the Capuchin could have read in either its Latin or French versions.[84]

How much Benet of Canfield used German mysticism of the late Middle Ages is unclear. Kent Emery argues for a considerable influence from Nicholas of Cusa.[85] Latin versions of Suso and Tauler were available to the Capuchin, with the latter including the *Institutiones spirituales*, or *Taulerianae*, which contained Eckhartian material. Optat de Veghel tried to show that Canfield employed this text, but the more careful investigation of Jean-Marie Gueullette concludes that it is difficult to establish any direct links.[86] Nonetheless, Canfield's mysticism was strongly influenced by the wave of interest in Northern European mysticism, both Dutch and German, that swept over France in the early seventeenth century.

There was more in Canfield's reading, however, than these "usual suspects." As an Englishman, Friar Benet possessed a copy of that masterpiece of English mysticism, the *Cloud of Unknowing*. How much he may have used it has been little investigated. Some have claimed he also knew Walter Hilton's *Ladder of Perfection* and Julian of Norwich's *Showings*, but this remains to be demonstrated. The Capuchin friar was familiar with a number of Italian spiritual and mystical works from his studies in Venice. Among these were certainly Lorenzo Scupoli's *Combattimento spirituale* (a text everyone read), the writings and life of Catherine of Genoa, as well as the popular *Breve compendio* that resulted from the collaboration of the Jesuit Achille Gagliardi and his protégé, the Milanese mystic Isabella Berinzaga (see chapter 7 below). Canfield's humanistic background seems to have given him an interest in the writings of Marsilio Ficino and his attempt to revive ancient Neoplatonic mysticism.[87] Finally, we may ask how far the English Capuchin was aware of sixteenth-century Spanish mysticism. One work that he did know was that of the Franciscan Alfonso of Madrid, the *Art of Serving God* (*Arte de servir a Dios*), first published in 1521 and translated into French in 1587. Canfield wrote the *Rule of Perfection* before the French translation of Teresa of Avila's works appeared, and he was dead before John of the Cross was available in either Spanish or French. He did, however, include two references to Teresa in chapter 20 of book III of the *Rule*, when speaking of the necessity of never giving up contemplation of Christ's Passion. Nonetheless, the *Rule of Perfection* appears to be fairly independent of the Spanish mystical wave.

The Structure and Teaching of The Rule of Perfection

Given the meticulously structured nature of Benet of Canfield's treatise, it needs to be studied as an architectonic whole. The work is essentially an *ars*, a teaching manual about how to attain God. The audience that the Capuchin has in mind, however, is not just that of friars, clerics, and spiritual directors but all Christians seriously seeking God. Like Francis de Sales, whom he probably met, Friar Benet wanted everyone to aspire to fulfill the will of God in this life and thus attain union. Once again, we can return to the title of the *Rule*, which lays out the threefold structure. This "brief abridgement of the whole spiritual life, reduced to the single point of the will of God" is divided into three parts. "The first, treating the exterior will of God, comprehending the active life; the second, treating the interior will, containing the contemplative life; the third, treating the essential will, speaking of the supereminent life" (*vie superéminente*). This division goes back to Jan van Ruusbroec,[88] but Canfield's source is likely Harphius, whose *Mirror of Perfection* (*Spieghel der volcomenheit*), Latinized as the *Aureum directorum contemplativorum* (*Golden Directory of Contemplatives*), had spoken of the active life, the contemplative spiritual life, and the superessential contemplative life.[89] This treatise formed book 2 of the collection of Harphius's works put out by the Cologne Carthusians in 1538 under the title *De mystica theologia*. The volume was put on the Index of Forbidden Books in 1559 for a number of theological errors, one of which was the use of the term *superessentialis*, so when a corrected version was published in 1586 this word was replaced with *supereminens*. *Superessentialis*, of course, had deep roots in tradition, all the way back to Dionysius's *hyperousios*, but in the midst of Counter-Reformation fears about theological error, especially about the theology of grace, it became suspect to some.[90] Canfield originally used *superessentialis* but corrected this to *supereminens* (sometimes *supernaturalis*) in the 1610 edition. Although the structure of the three lives was inherited, neither Ruusbroec nor Herp had linked the triple division precisely to the forms of the divine will, the nodal point for Canfield's system. Books I and II dealing with the exterior and interior will of God concern the accidental aspects of the spiritual life, while book III on the essential/superessential life deals with its essence, that is, with God in himself. Nonetheless, the spiritual life is a single whole consisting of both accidents (our experiences and actions treated in parts I and II) and our essential union with God in part III. This is the ground for Canfield's insistence on the union of action and contemplation.[91]

Another key aspect of the book is revealed in the picture inserted after the title page in which the divine will appears as the sun in the midst of three concentric circles of faces representing the souls in the three forms of life. "All these figures or faces," he says in explanation, "have their eyes fixed on this will of God, signifying the pure intention of souls, who in all things ought to look on the divine," which is "one continuous splendor." Significantly, however, the lower part of the page has an image of Christ in Gethsemane with the caption, "Not my will but your will be done" (Luke 22:42), thus indicating that imitation of Christ in the Passion is one and the same as the practice of the three lives.

Part I

The exterior will of God in the active life is treated in part I of twenty chapters.[92] Canfield begins (chap. 1) by emphasizing how "the exercise and point of the will of God" reveals and summarizes all other spiritual exercises in eight ways (brevity; meritoriousness; finality; universality, that is, being fit for all; freedom from multiplicity; freedom from deceptions; means and ends; and permanence). Of particular importance is the Capuchin's exposition on "means and ends," where he says, "This point of the will of God excels all others in that it serves as a rule and as an end for our actions, whereas other exercises serve only one or the other. It is (I say) the rule of our exterior and interior actions, revealing by its rectitude the obliquity of both." The notion of *rectitude* is central for Canfield, both the rectitude of exterior acts (what to do, what not to do, and how and when to do it), as well as of interior acts (how to will and not will, and the like).[93] In the course of his exposition, the Capuchin appeals to one of his most favored images for the divine will, namely, the sun shining on all things, as seen in the initial figure. Canfield says that the other apposite image for the divine will is the ocean or sea: "In this exercise ... one must begin, proceed, and end, since the will of God is a spiritual sea, on which each one may sail according to the capability of his vessel."[94]

Chapter 2 is of special importance, because here Canfield lists the eleven other forms of practice that the exercise of the will of God contains, most of which will appear later in the book in relation to the overarching theme of the divine will.[95] Citing a number of theological authorities on the supremacy and centrality of the divine will, Canfield notes, "Although the will of God in itself is incomprehensible, nevertheless when it dwells in our spirit it becomes comprehensible, and although in itself it is hidden, nevertheless when joined to our soul it is revealed."[96] After another summary of the three kinds of will, chapter 5 begins the real work of part I with a description of the exterior will as "the divine pleasure [*le divin plaisir*] known by the law and reason, which is the rule of all our thoughts, words, and deeds in the active life."[97] Canfield then explains nine different senses of law that command us to perform or to avoid certain actions. With regard to things that are indifferent, reason, that is, "discretion, piety, and counsel," must decide how to act. Canfield expands on this in the sixth chapter by discriminating among things commanded and things forbidden, on the one hand, where we act only because God wills it, and things indifferent, on the other hand, where detailed rules for determining the right course of action are required. According to our constant need for abnegation, indifferent things that please sensuality should be avoided, and those repugnant to sensuality chosen. Above all, even with regard to totally indifferent things, Canfield emphasizes the need for the right intention in all action, that is, that things must be done *only* for the sake of God.[98] Right intention is examined in more detail in chapter 8, where the Capuchin lists six degrees, or perfections, of right intention, illustrating these by the biblical image of Solomon's throne (3 Kgdms 10:18-20). The six degrees of right intention (actually, uniquely, willingly, assuredly, clearly, and promptly) are the topics for the following chapters 9-13. These early chapters from part I provide us with a good example of Canfield's at times tedious enumerations of topics and points.

The second section of part I begins with a discussion of how to preserve the requisite purity of intention. The first means is through a series of inner acts, including filial fear of God and reverence, joy, resignation, abnegation, and annihilation. The second, and most important, means of preservation of intention is "dispossession of the work [*expropriation de l'oeuvre*]; that is to say, that when one has rectified his intention according to these degrees, he must divest himself of the work, . . . as not being his own, and know that in truth after such rectification it is not his will that does the work, but the will of God."[99] In itself our work is something—that is, a reality—but viewed from the divine perspective it is nothing; rather, it has been transformed into God's will. Once again, the Capuchin provides a biblical image for the six degrees of right intention, namely, the "six mystical steps" of the Song of Songs. This mini-commentary on the Song takes six texts (actually many more) from the biblical song of love to illustrate each of the degrees of right intention. In chapter 16, the Capuchin shows how in all the mortifications and virtues, as well as in the true imitation of the life and Passion of Christ, are found the perfect practice of this rule and exercise of the will of God. He provides a number of examples of how acts of virtue and self-abnegation conform to events in Christ's passion, drawing out the general rule: "When one practices this exercise or rule of life, he also perfectly practices mortification, virtue, and the imitation of the life and Passion of our Savior, who in all things did the will of his Father." The object is not so much to imitate the exterior acts by which Christ suffered, but to fulfill Christ's interior will to suffer only for the will of the Father. "In this manner," he continues, "the Head suffers in its member and the member in the Head, in the divine will, who undergoes 'the selfsame sufferings that we also suffer' (1 Cor. 2:6). . . . Note that the clothing of one's self in the Passion is nothing other than the will of God."[100] Here Canfield seems to be commenting on the book's opening illustration in which the concentric circles around the divine sun (i.e., God's will) are pictured together with a passion scene. Thus, Franciscan passion-piety is not an intrusion or secondary theme for the Capuchin; it is the inner meaning of what may at first seem to be an abstract and purely theocentric exercise.

Chapter 17 becomes practical, somewhat in the manner of Ignatius's *Spiritual Exercises.* Beginners especially need to commit themselves to a certain number of times each day (three, five, or ten, Canfield says) when they will deliberately deny the body and the five senses by doing or suffering what is contrary to them, as, for example, not eating tasty dishes, or not touching delicate things. He also gives advice about mortifying the three inner powers of understanding, memory, and will. Chapter 18 continues in this practical vein by showing how to overcome two major errors concerning the exercise of the active life. The first is thinking that advancing to the higher forms of the life of contemplation allows a person to dispense with the practices of the active life. No, says Canfield, a person "must not proceed so far in it [the contemplative life] that he abandons the active life as if he had no more need of it." The second error is being so far given over to Martha (i.e., the active life) that we do not even wish to pass on to Mary and the contemplative life. There are those, he says, who are sometimes drawn outside the active life and their usual acts of meditation and aspirations into a state where they are forced "to fix all the strength of their spirit in the will of God alone and adhere to it (wherein consists pure and supereminent contemplation)," with the result that they become confused and reject contemplation.[101] There are two sources of this error of rejection of contemplation, and Canfield's analysis of these is significant. The first source of error is in the understanding. Canfield's answer turns to the Dionysian tradition, particularly to the affective reading of Dionysius, according to which speculation as a human exercise can never grasp God. Rather, we must employ the will, which "by love proportions itself, in some degree, to the immensity, infinity, and omnipotence of God." Thus, "the love of the will is a divine thing, lifting us up and drawing us outside ourselves, and transforming us into God."[102] The second source of the error of rejecting contemplation is in the will, specifically a will that becomes so busy in pouring out "aspirations, fervors, and interior acts" that it hinders the interior action of God. Fervor itself can never be too great, but it can be ill-governed and thus form a block to the supernatural operation of God. Canfield concludes, "Remaining in tranquility and profound silence the soul ought not so much to work as to be worked upon [see DN 2.9], not so much to act herself as suffer the gentle operation of God, and finally, not so much speak as listen to God." He finishes his advice by appealing to the incommunicable nature of mystical experience: "those who have not experienced it will not easily believe it."[103] Canfield ends part I on God's exterior will by showing how this teaching relates to four forms of prayer (chap. 19)[104] and then provides a summary of the first part in chapter 20.

Part II

Part II of the *Rule of Perfection*, on the interior will and its contemplative life, is shorter (eight chapters).[105] Once again, the Capuchin uses a carefully articulated structure to advance his argument, this time about the "five manifestations" that reveal God's interior will and thus form the foundation of the contemplative life. Canfield defines God's interior will as "the good pleasure of God known by a perfect, manifest, and experiential interior knowledge, which illumines the soul in the interior or contemplative life."[106] Hence, it is no longer a question of finding God's will in external commands or in law and human reason, but by way of inner supernatural and experiential knowledge. As Canfield describes it, this state results from God making use of the human will from within, through the light of inner "inspirations, illuminations, elevations, and drawings of God," not the exterior light of the commandments and laws of the church. The result of such conformity of the divine and human wills is that "the man in this interior will neither tastes nor feels any more his own will and his human satisfaction, but only the divine will and satisfaction, since his own is swallowed up and transformed into God's."[107] God's will is always one and the same, but we have to distinguish differing levels in it to make sense of our progress in the spiritual life. "Hence," says Friar Benet, "the same interior will does not show itself to us in the same way, but rather in diverse ways and by degrees." He says that there are many of these, but he will only discuss five, "manifestation, admiration, humiliation, exaltation, and elevation."[108]

The five degrees provide the content for the following chapters. Chapter 2 discusses the "manifestation" of the interior will, which the Capuchin says immediately flows from the pure intention of the exterior will; that is, if we perform an act only for God, we will inevitably feel and taste the will of God within. Canfield calls this "the key of the contemplative life," explaining that one must not depart from this interior feeling of God, but rather "one must carefully attend to its secret working and internal touch, and withdrawing within himself, one must endeavor to augment such spiritual feelings by cutting off all superfluous exterior and interior activities." The Capuchin describes this inner experience in the language of erotic mysticism, such as "hearing his sweet voice, gentle proposal, and mellifluous words, ... rejoicing in his loving and alluring glances, sweet kisses, chaste embraces, ... feeling the efficacious inworking [*efficace inaction*] and the living touch of his good pleasure."[109] The erotic dimension is enhanced by the numerous quotations from the Song of Songs and the Psalms that Canfield uses to explain the degree of "manifestation." The second degree is that of "wonder" (Fr.: *admiration*), a term associated with contemplation since the time of Richard of St. Victor (see *Mystical Ark* I.4). This wonder proceeds from three principal causes: the greatness of God, one's own nothingness, and God's amazing familiarity with the soul. One of the main ideas Canfield employs in the *Rule of Perfection* is that "opposites contrasted are more clearly seen," which he illustrates here by showing that we never know the greatness of God better than when it is contrasted with our own nothingness.[110] The third cause, God's amazing familiarity with the soul, allows him to introduce a passage on the burning wound of love that the Divine Archer shoots into the heart (Isa. 49:2; Vg) in interior contemplation.

Chapter 4 treats the third degree, namely, humiliation. Humble reverence is a necessary result of the great familiarity God has shown to the soul by becoming the soul's Spouse and by even letting the soul spiritually conceive him within, like Mary. If the soul is allowed to dwell only on herself, she proportions God to the soul and thus creates a wall between the Creator and the creature. Rather, she must behave with profound reverence toward God, "raising above herself to the greatness of God, and accommodating herself to this greatness." Thus, "the soul is proportioned to God," not vice versa.[111] The fourth degree of contemplation is exultation. Canfield says that "the same causes that humble also exult the soul, ... for the soul's nothingness that shows her what she is in herself also reveals to her how she is all in God, and how, in putting off her finite being, she unites with an infinite being." He goes on, "Finally, another more essential cause that produces this extreme exultation is the marvelous inseparable union with God," already discussed in part I.2.[112] The final degree, that of elevation, is taken up in chapter 6. Here Canfield analyzes the gradual lifting up of the soul that occurs in the four previous degrees seen as a process of divine illumination which he compares to the rising of the sun illuminating the world.

Chapter 7 provides advice about the exercise of God's interior will. First of all, Friar Benet emphasizes that these distinctions are not actual topics for meditation but are the objective effects of divine action within us. Souls who remain in God's exterior will have no knowledge of them, while souls in the second degree have begun to make what is exterior into what is interior. Those who "have attained perfection in the supereminent will [*la volunté Superéminente*] . . . see neither the exterior nor interior will, for they have made both the supereminent will."[113] Even those who have reached the supereminent will, however, are still bound to the practices of the two lower wills. (Slightly later on, Canfield refers to the three kinds of souls by the traditional distinction of beginners, advanced, and perfect.) Toward the end of part II Canfield notes that, while one must "feel and taste the divine will and the good pleasure of God within himself," it would be a mistake to abide in this feeling in a kind of spiritual self-enjoyment. In self-abnegation there are two elements, renunciation and contentment—"One must rest in the first and not in the second."[114] The same is true of resignation to the divine will. We must abide in the resignation but not cling to the savor that comes from it. The second part of the *Rule of Perfection* closes with a self-examination concerning the points taught, in which the Capuchin reminds the reader that these five degrees are not the soul's own operations but are the effects and operations of the divine spirit within. In other words, using the language being developed by the post-Teresian Spanish mystics, they are examples of infused contemplation.

Part III

Part III of the *Rule of Perfection* proved controversial, especially for its teaching regarding passive annihilation and the "supereminent" life in general. It is obvious that, in the version finally printed in 1610, Canfield went to some trouble to fend off attacks by excisions, additions, and qualifications. There are twenty-one chapters in this part divided into three sections.[115] The first two sections concern the two means of attaining the divine essence. The first of these, "a means without means that is passive and not active," takes up chapters 3 through 7, while the second means, "the will of God manifested in annihilation," is found in chapters 8 through 15. These two sections constituted the original form of part III; but when he published the book, Canfield added a third section (chaps. 16-21) on the necessity and manner of contemplating Christ's Passion. Some have seen this addition as an awkward addendum designed to forestall criticism, but it is difficult to think that this section does not represent the Capuchin's own teaching, however successful or unsuccessful we judge its placement and integration with the rest of the treatise.[116]

Benet of Canfield prefaces part III with "A Letter Necessary for the Reader," in which he says that his superiors persuaded him to publish this part due to the fact that an imperfect copy had already appeared and was causing controversy. He seems to be referring, at least in part, to the attack of Teresa of Avila's disciple Jéronimo Gracián (1545-1614), now resident in the Low Countries, on those whom he accused of "setting perfection in total annihilation."[117] In response, Canfield admits that this part of his book "exceeds the capacity of common persons," but notes that it is not right to deprive advanced souls of solid food because beginners can only drink milk (1 Cor. 3:2). No one, however, should try to read this section who has not been judged capable of it by a religious superior, confessor, or director. Because there are propositions and terms used here that those not versed in mystical theology might not understand, Canfield provides a list of nine such terms with citations to the mystical masters who use them.[118]

The first two chapters of part III are introductory. Canfield begins with a definition of his main theme, God's essential will: "The essential will, then, is purely spirit and life, totally abstract [*totalement abstraite*], pure in itself and stripped bare of all forms and images of created things, corporal or spiritual, temporal or eternal."[119] The essential will of God is God himself, beyond all forms and images, as well as all human knowing. The difference between the interior will (part II) and the essential will (part III) is laid out in terms of the absolute simplicity and finality of the essential will. In the interior will there are still some images and some activity on the soul's part; in the essential will the soul is without images and totally passive to the "inworking or intimate operation of her Spouse."[120] As the interior will is born of the exterior will, the essential will is born of the interior will, even though in reality all three wills are one.[121] Chapter 2 explains how there can be no human means of attaining God's essential will, because, "[s]ince this essence is wholly supernatural, our sense and judgment cannot comprehend it." The soul attains this essence only when she is passive, not active. In line with the tradition of affective Dionysianism, Canfield says, "Speculative contemplation cannot transform; only love can transform." Therefore, "every act and intellectual operation ought to be cut off."[122] Everything is in God's hands.

If there is no *human* means of attaining the essential will, this does not rule out divine means, of which there are two. Chapter 3 begins to explain the first of these, namely, "a means without means [*un moyen sans moyen*] which is passive and not active, and which is wholly divine above all understanding, and not human or made by acts of the spirit; this means is of two kinds."[123] This is described as a "means without means" because it is totally caused by God without any human cooperation and, thus, shows how "the whole spiritual life," from the beginnings in the exterior will to the sublimity of the supereminent life, is "contained in the single point of the will of God." Canfield speaks of this means as "abstract," that is, as devoid of images, and the fairly frequent use of this qualifier in part III may well be where the characterization of the Capuchin as the leader of an "Abstract School" of mysticism began.[124] Canfield, however, does not go on to analyze what he means by "abstract" in detail; it is just one term among many. Furthermore, a reading of the whole of part III shows that abstraction is part of the process, not the goal.

Canfield begins to describe how this first unitive means, or process, is achieved in two ways. The first is the intimate inworking of the divine will that "annihilates all the acts of the soul," while the second is more general, directed at all those who have set out on the spiritual way to God, even if they have not practiced Canfield's method. This is a useful distinction by which the Capuchin, in admitting that both means resemble each other and lead to the same object, shows himself willing to allow that many spiritual exercises come to the same goal (see *Rule* I.2). What follows, however, concentrates on Canfield's favored exercise, in which the attraction to the divine essence is accomplished by means of the essential will alone. In the topical style to which his reader has by now become accustomed, the Capuchin sets out four points regarding the explanation of this first means of attaining the essential divine will: (1) the very subtle knowledge of the imperfection of the soul's contemplation; (2) the flowing of her fervent desires into God; (3) a perfect denuding of the spirit; and (4) a close vision of this object and the final end.[125] Chapter 4 takes up the first point, while chapters 5–7 feature explorations of the following three.

Chapter 5, dealing with the "excessive surging of fervent desires," is a good example of Canfield's method of argument by articulation. The basic point is that the active and impetuous desires that often overcome the soul in these higher stages must be resisted as pertaining too much to our own efforts and depending less on peaceful openness to divine action. God can be experienced as flowing into us, but it is more important that we flow into God. "This flowing of burning desires into God is a transforming of working love into enjoying love,"[126] although we shall see that in the end both types of love are necessary. Canfield undertakes a lengthy analysis of the nature of this "flowing" (*écoulement*), structured around three topics: the changing of the place or subject of the desires, the transformation of the desires themselves, and the means of such transformation.[127] The desires first of all change their place, moving from being in the soul to being in God. Thus, the desires are no longer subjectively felt, because "abstraction hinders seeing concrete things in such a way that it is impossible for the perfectly abstract spirit to comprehend concrete things."[128] Canfield illustrates this ecstatic abstraction by the examples of the raptures of several saints. The desires are also transformed as the cause changes into the effect, that is, the longing becomes the thing longed for. The Capuchin explains this by turning to the erotic language of the Song of Songs, which he cites nine times in this section. Finally, the means of the transformation is also interpreted in a highly erotic way (with numerous quotations from the Song of Songs) as a process in which the Divine Lover appears more and more clearly to the soul in an intimate union "which cannot be explained any better than in comparison with that act between two lovers wherein there is actual cleaving, . . . where, as Scripture says, 'of two is made one flesh'" (Gen. 2:24).[129] Thus, not only are desires fulfilled, but they also vanish, because they have gained their goal of union with God. The desires have lost their own form, although their essence remains in God. The friar closes his analysis with another burst of erotic imagery, especially regarding the nakedness of God and the soul necessary for the embrace and penetration of God into the soul's innermost part.[130]

Chapter 6, on the "perfect denuding of spirit," carries the language of nakedness and abstraction further. "Denuding of spirit," Canfield says, "is a divine working purifying the soul, stripping her entirely of all forms and images of things both created and uncreated, making her thus wholly simple and naked, and enabling her to contemplate without form."[131] It is necessary for the soul to cease all her activity and allow God to work in her. Canfield distinguishes between pure natural abstraction, in which a person ceases acting and remains in false idleness, and the true denudation, abstraction, annihilation, in which we are inactive but passive to God's action. This denuding process both purges the soul and illuminates it. All images, including the "very secret image of the will of God" that the soul retained in the interior life, are let go of, although he notes that "one ought never to leave the object of the humanity and Passion of our sweet Redeemer." The illumination the soul receives is explained in terms of union, that is, becoming one with the divine light itself. Canfield expands on this in language that echoes mystics like Marguerite Porete about the coincidence of opposites, that is, the simultaneity of our absolute abasement and God's supreme majesty. He says:

> Indeed, having known perfectly that he is All and she is nothing, and that in him there is all beauty, goodness, and sweetness, and that in her there is nothing but the bitterness of malice, she dwells, resides, and lives uniquely in him and not at all in herself. Whence it follows that she is all in God, all God's, all for God, and all God, and nothing in herself, nothing of herself, nothing for herself, nothing herself.[132]

Finally, the fourth point of the "means without a means," namely, "the close vision and presence of the blessed end," is taken up in chapter 7. This highest degree is different from the third degree of denudation because it is the habit and continuation of the simple fleeting union of denudation. Canfield explores it in terms of the perfect mutual loving union of God and the soul in which the soul "is lodged so firmly in the abyss of her nothingness and knows it so well that by the same means she sees that all other things are likewise nothing. . . . This vast solitude of nothingness [*Cette vaste solitude de nihilaité*] is the solitude in which the Bridegroom says, 'I shall lead her into solitude, and I shall speak to her heart' (Hos. 2:14)."[133] Once the soul has "experientially tasted" (*expérimentalement goûté*) that God is more within her than she herself is, "the darkness will not be dark" (Ps. 131:12); that is, "the night of the active life will be as illumined as the day of the contemplative life." It is important to note that this union in which God gives the soul the vision and presence of the end includes both light and love, illumination and affectivity, thus indicating that the Capuchin goes beyond simplistic contrasts between affective and intellectual mysticism.[134] Union is transcendent to ordinary human categories. This is what enables Canfield to break with those thinkers who suppose that the active and the contemplative lives must be divided. Rather, "the active life of such a person is also contemplative."[135] The two are one.

Thus, Friar Benet joins the long line of mystics going back to Meister Eckhart and well represented in his own days by Teresa of Avila, who taught that at the summit of the mystical path there was no real distinction between action and contemplation.

Chapter 8 begins the second divine means by which the soul attains the essential will of God, the means described as "nothing but the will of God, manifested by annihilation and having two points, knowledge and practice."[136] Chapters 8 through 15 constitute a treatise on annihilation, one of the most interesting in a period in the history of mysticism that might be called "the age of annihilation." Canfield contrasts the two "means" in terms of the difference between the abstract soul, that is, one drawn out of herself by the strong drawing of God, and the non-abstract, that is, when the drawing of God's will is not so much actual as virtual. This means, therefore, is "spiritualized, denuded, supernaturalized, and exstaticized" even when "one is encumbered with images and occupied with business."[137] So, we are where we left off at the end of the previous chapter with the soul who is so advanced that it makes exterior things interior. The means of annihilation proceeds according to the most radical of the contrasts between opposites—the contrast between the All that is the will of God and the nothingness of the self.[138] Recognition that there is nothing else but God's essential will is taught in multiple ways: reason and philosophy, doctors and theologians, scripture and natural examples. An objector then asks, "What is the creature?" "A pure dependency on God," is the answer, like the dependence of the rays of light on the sun, or heat on a fire. Does that mean a creature is a "something." The answer is "yes and no." Yes, when viewed in itself, but no, when viewed from the perspective of God. "The Creator assumes and appropriates the creature as some spark gone out from him, and when he recalls it to himself as to its center and origin, in his infinity he annihilates and reduces it to nothing."[139]

More important than knowing the truth of annihilation is the practice of annihilation to which the next two chapters are devoted. Fundamentally, the practice of annihilation does not involve *doing* something, but rather refraining from doing, passively allowing God to work in the soul, not interfering with his action by worries, exercises, or even seeking God. This insistence on passivity leads to some expressions, especially in chapter 10, that might seem Quietist and were probably noted when this third part was put on the Index toward the end of the seventeenth century. Nevertheless, when we look at the whole of the Capuchin's teaching on annihilation, especially the superiority of active over passive annihilation, it is far from Quietistic (see *Rule* III.13–15). Canfield advises the reader to remain always in the divine abyss and to annihilate the things that separate us from God, that is, sin, darkness, and ignorance. "Therefore, one must not kill or annihilate the body, the soul, or any other thing, . . . but rather the sin, darkness and ignorance." We ourselves cannot do this, but God's essential will can, provided that we remain open to the divine will acting within us.

What this means in concrete terms is shown in chapter 10, where Canfield lists ten "most subtle and unknown imperfections" of the merely contemplative life that hinder the "supereminent life." For example, it is a mistake to struggle against superfluous thoughts and distractions. Rather, one must just have contempt for these and remain quietly in the "abyss of light and life" until they pass. Similarly, there should be no exercises and no forms or images in this practice, excepting always the image of the sacred Passion of Jesus Christ. (Canfield will explain later how active annihilation allows the presence of the image of the Passion.) Seeking sensible feeling of union is also wrong: "To remedy this, one should change this sensibility into a naked love, which is emptied of all feeling, stable, long lasting, and always the same, knowing that God is not at all sensible, not at all comprehended by sense, but is pure spirit."[140] Seeking experiential assurance from God, lifting up the spirit to God, seeking God, desiring God, thinking upon God, and casting a look upon God, are all equally wrong, because they treat God as though he were absent, whereas "contemplation in the supereminent life presupposes possession of God." Finally, it is even a mistake to observe these imperfections too much, since they concentrate the soul's attention on itself when it should be attending only to God. These are examples of the "Being" (*l'Etre*) that must be cured very subtly by the contrary cause of "non-Being" (*non Etre*). Canfield concludes, "For as all imperfection arises when a man is something, so all perfection is born when he is annihilated, for then God alone lives and reigns."[141]

Chapters 11 to 14 deal with the most distinctive feature of the Capuchin's teaching on annihilation, the distinction between passive and active annihilation.[142] He begins by noting that his treatment thus far has concentrated on getting rid of all acts, images, and exercises; but that still leaves the question of how annihilation relates to these things. The solution, he says, resides in a deeper double sense of annihilation: "In the former annihilation [i.e., what was investigated so far], he has simply annihilated all things, but here he must do so doubly.

For whereas previously he has annihilated them when they have vanished, here he must do so even when they remain."[143] What does this mean? The answer is in terms of the distinction between passive and active annihilation. Passive annihilation is what has been spoken of thus far, while active annihilation is when "the person and all things are not thus annihilated passively, but rather actively, that is, by a light as much natural as supernatural of the understanding, by which one discovers and knows assuredly that he and all things are nothing."[144] No image remains in passive annihilation, while in active annihilation images and feelings do remain, but the person *knows* that they are really nothing; God is all there is. Thus, active annihilation consists in intellectual, not experiential, knowledge and is paradoxically both active and passive. In active annihilation the spirit is just as passive as in passive annihilation. Active annihilation is therefore more perfect than passive, because it can coexist with mental and physical work that God performs in and through us. It is also more persevering. "These two annihilations," says Canfield, "serve two loves which comprehend the whole spiritual life, namely an enjoying love [*l'amour fruitive*] and a working love [*l'amour pratique*]."[145] The two loves, which reprise a major theme of Ruusbroec's mysticism, are constitutive of the friar's view of the height of mystical union.

In chapter 12, Canfield tells us that the perfection of active annihilation consists in making itself equal to passive annihilation, which is to say that the annihilation of the senses and mental activities realized in passive annihilation is now also present, but not "real" in the case of a human person sensing and thinking in active annihilation. As he puts it, "By this means when one sees, he does not see; when he hears, he does not hear; when he tastes, smells, and touches, he does none of them; when his concupiscible power desires, his irascible power hates, and reasonable power chooses something; they do none of them."[146] The key word in the description of this strange state (which Canfield insists can be understood only by those who have experienced it) is "he." The "he" being referenced, is no longer the created "he"; it is the divine "He" of God's essential will as the true agent of all these actions. We might say that the core contention of the English Capuchin is not new—God has taken over the soul's normal operations—but his manner of expression is novel.

The remainder of this important chapter presents the practice of active annihilation under two headings: light and remembrance. "Light" describes what is permanent in this state, that is, "pure, simple, naked and habitual faith, aided by reason, ratified and confirmed by experience."[147] In a way similar to what we find a bit later in Francis de Sales's *Treatise on the Love of God*, Canfield says that this light can be found only "in the summit and highest part of the soul."[148] This faith and light are contrary to the senses, he insists, because the senses say that such or such a thing exists, "and contrariwise this faith is saying that it is not, in respect to the presence of God." Thus, active annihilation is about learning to look from the perspective of God's essential will and see that creatures *are nothing in themselves*. The second component of active annihilation, which appears only from time to time when the soul may become distracted, is what Canfield calls *ressouvenance*, or remembrance, which he describes as "an inspiration or flash of light, a touching or darting of the divine light, . . . which strikes and awakens the soul, making her see where she is, namely, swallowed up in this All."[149]

In chapter 13, Canfield follows his usual pattern by exploring active annihilation in terms of ten hindrances or imperfections to its practice. Many of these may be described as standard (e.g., to doubt it, to trust the senses, to delay conversion, acts of the self, dissatisfaction, lack of perseverance, etc.). Others are important for revealing the Capuchin's special view of annihilation. The fourth hindrance, for example, is to flee exterior work. Although some of Canfield's earlier expressions may have seemed to have a Quietist flavor, this hindrance shows that his view of active annihilation is anti-Quietist. He says that a person should not flee any necessary interior or exterior work for fear it will distract them from their annihilated state: "To one who judges such a work something, it truly is something, and therefore to be feared; but if his annihilation were perfect, it would be nothing and therefore not to be feared at all."[150] Murmuring or grumbling about being commanded to do some work because of a desire for inner spiritual enjoyment is to flee God, not gain him. Similarly, it is a "very secret imperfection" to turn inward, as if God were not present to the annihilated soul both inwardly and outwardly. It is also a mistake to distinguish between feeling and not feeling, because one should be equally annihilated when one sees and experiences that God is All and things are nothing, as when "he is left in dryness without any taste." Toward the end of this chapter Canfield aptly summarizes the two forms of annihilation whose practice brings the soul to perfection of life in the divine supereminent will:

> [B]y passive annihilation the soul remains stripped of all images in a great denuding and repose of spirit and acts, and she is raised up

and carried with all her powers into God; by active annihilation she likewise remains fixed in him while among these acts and images, although not according to sense. One should practice both these annihilations by the simple remembrance explained in the twelfth chapter.[151]

Chapter 14 of part III carries on this theme with its teaching on the relation of the two forms of annihilation. One must practice each annihilation in its proper time and place, not out of order. The key here is that the two annihilations serve two loves, "passive annihilation serves an enjoying love [*amour fruitive*], or naked contemplation, union, and delight in God, and active annihilation serves a working love [*amour pratique*], or a vigorous turning outward and faithful working, either corporal or spiritual."[152] The proper *place* of passive annihilation is where we are enjoying God, while the proper *place* of active annihilation is where we are striving after God. The truly annihilated soul will, therefore, be able to combine action and contemplation—"going out without going out, working without working, existing without leaving one's nothingness, living and yet dead, one makes a working love an enjoying love, the active life the contemplative life, and he enjoys God as much, according to naked faith, in working and activity as he does in repose and idleness."[153] If one gets the order mixed up the result is either a "false idleness" or a "harmful activity."

The Capuchin next embarks on a lengthy analysis of the proper *time* for the practice of the two forms of annihilation. He begins with the distinction of three kinds of working found in active annihilation: exterior working; interior, or mental, working; and the intimate working that concerns the renewal of acts in contemplation. Concerning exterior works, he says they must be performed according to the rules set down in part I of the *Rule of Perfection*. Interior works like studying and reasoning are to be performed as necessity dictates, without doing anything superfluously. In the case of the intimate working of contemplation and enjoyment of union with God, Canfield gives a long account of the nature and joys of passive annihilation, the unitive state that establishes a person "in a perfect abstraction and denuding of spirit wherein the soul drives far away all vices and impurities, and practices all virtues and perfections, although in an essential manner without multiplicity of particular acts,"[154] even speaking of it as the practice whereby "man is made divine" (*l'homme est rendu divin*).[155] The Capuchin counsels that the soul in this state of passive annihilation must not leave it to go out by acts of active annihilation and working love without good cause. It is important to distinguish "true idleness" (*oisiveté*) from "false idleness," that is, a repose in self and not in God. "The good idleness," says Canfield, "is a total annihilation, wholly consuming a man. The one [the false] is turned from God and back upon self, the other is turned from self and turned back and directed to God." In sum, with all three kinds of working there are two extremes and a correct mean—"working too soon, which is false liberty; working too late, which is false idleness; working at the right time, which is holy activity."[156]

The final chapter in Benet of Canfield's treatise on annihilation summarizes how one achieves the three kinds of working, the reduction of the active and contemplative lives to the supereminent life, and the reduction of the first two divine wills into the essential will. Canfield says that all this concerns the "manner of working" in each will. The manner of working in the essential will is remote from the manner of working in the exterior will, so that "[i]n this third and supereminent life one must perform the operations of the first life, without, nevertheless, descending or returning again to the first will."[157] In reducing exterior and interior working to essential working, the key is that a person no longer works from the intention of fulfilling God's will as something outside us, "but rather, he must perform these works with the object of the essential will, that is, the divine essence, or because God is, or that God may be."[158] The friar insists that the correct intention is "that God will be," because God abstracts from the here and now, and thus is wholly everywhere. The practice of the essential life consists in the opposition between "All and nothing," that is, the person only takes notice of the All that is God and not the "nothing" of creation. Canfield closes his treatment with remarks on the nature of the intimate working in God's essential will that "casts the soul into the essence of God, removes her from herself and lifts her above nature." Ever conscious of the two errors of false idleness and harmful activity, he returns to the theme of remembrance: "The most perfect simple remembrance [*simple ressouvenance*] is the remedy against false idleness and harmful activity. The most pure, intimate, genuine, and perfect working in this case is a pure and simple remembrance of God, made and practiced by a pure and naked faith."[159] Canfield's continued stress on pure and naked faith is reminiscent of John of the Cross, though the foundations of his mystical theory are different.

The last six chapters of part III of the *Rule of Perfection* switch gears to the practice of contemplating the Passion of our Lord, something that the Capuchin insists is totally compatible with and, indeed, the inner meaning of the union of passive and active annihilation. He was convinced of this; not all his interpreters have thought that the inner coherence was so obvious. We can present his arguments briefly. This section is deeply Franciscan, making considerable use of Bonaventure, both authentic and pseudonymous works, as well as the Spanish Franciscan Peter of Alcántara. Chapter 16 opens by countering the arguments of those who think that the practice and contemplation of the passion are only for beginners. No, says Canfield, the practice of contemplating the Passion is necessary even for those in the supereminent life. According to an ancient typological reading of Exodus 25:40, the passion was the exemplar shown to Moses on the mountain to be contemplated and imitated by all. (Here, and in the following chapters, the Capuchin makes use of many Old Testament types for Christ's Passion.) Also traditional is his insistence that "if we wish God to speak to us and teach us high perfection and contemplation, we must not climb up to his divinity alone, but we must descend to his humanity and his Passion."[160] This practice, he says, is fittingly modeled by "our seraphic father, St. Francis." Chapter 17 speaks more directly about the manner of contemplating God and humanity in Christ's Passion, which must not be by looking at one first and then at the other, but we must look at both humanity and divinity "in one and the same simple sight," although this calls for great skill, because contemplating the humanity uses images, while contemplating the divinity does not. This double view is not possible for reason to attain on its own. To resolve the dilemma, says Canfield, "one must rise above reason to faith, which beholding this man recognizes him for God, who is without form or image. And although the imagination represents the form of a man, nevertheless faith, transcending all sense and imagination, does not see any form, since it sees God."[161] The merely representational aspect of the crucifix is thus annihilated by faith.

The long chapter 18 argues that it is better to practice and contemplate the Passion in ourselves, that is, by joining our sufferings and afflictions to Christ's, than by imagining it as far off in time or in space. We can perform this kind of contemplation both because of our personal union with Christ and also because we are joined with him in the Mystical Body. Since we contemplate the Passion to make us conform to it, it is better to contemplate nothing but sorrows and afflictions, both Christ's and our own, and not to seek any sensible consolations. Chapter 19 concerns what image of the Passion should be used in this contemplation. If we imagine the sufferings of Christ himself, we need to make use of an image of some particular point; but "if we contemplate the Passion as in us, we must not imagine it, but apprehend it such as we really feel it."[162] What this phrase entails is expounded later in the chapter. Attention to the "sharp point" of the sufferings of Christ in us is the key that opens the door to the true mysteries of the Passion. Seeing God in his lowliness allows the soul to discover the sublimity of the mystery: "She should not produce any intellectual act except a simple sight and lively remembrance of this great All, who is crucified, as we said in chapters ten and thirteen.... [O]ne must arrest every natural and intellectual working, in order to give place to affection."[163] In other words, the practice of the Passion is governed by the same rules as the practice of annihilation and is threatened by the same imperfections.

Chapter 20 picks up another constant theme found in the practice of annihilation, namely, that one should not forsake the Passion for the contemplation of divinity alone, just as the soul should never abandon the practice of God's exterior will to become totally lost in interior and supereminent contemplation. Here, Canfield relies on the authority of the Franciscan tradition of passion piety, especially in Francis himself and Bonaventure, as well as Teresa of Avila, who taught that consideration of the Passion was never to be abandoned. Since our life in this world must always be both active and contemplative, we always are in need of Christ on the cross, whose divinity illuminates us in contemplation and whose humanity shows us how to work. One of the issues that becomes clear as the chapter proceeds is that the knowledge of divinity alone through abstraction is not as good as the knowledge of divinity and humanity together through the Passion.[164] The development of this chapter is not a little repetitious, apparently because Canfield was convinced of the dangers of attempting to arrive at contemplation of the naked divinity alone, something he saw as "a benumbing of nature and repose in the human spirit instead of the divine." This critique echoes that which Ruusbroec directed against the false mystics of his era.[165] In the active life we act or suffer so that the will of God may be done, and in the supereminent life we act and suffer so that God may be. "Therefore," concludes the friar, "as in the active life we must behold the will of God and the affliction or cross without any multiplicity, so in the supereminent life we must contemplate God and his cross with a single glance."[166] The final short chapter of the *Rule of Perfection* is a summary of the two means for practicing the essential will of God and the hindrances that may affect them. In it Canfield insists once more on making active annihilation equal to passive annihilation and on contemplating Jesus in his Passion as both divine and human as the highest form of contemplation.

Benet of Canfield, although not much read today, is a potent name in the history of Christian mysticism, not only because he was widely influential for over a century but also because of the depth and consistency of his focus on a mysticism of the divine will. His meticulous description of how to practice this "mystical art," as well as his ability to synthesize so much of the mystical wisdom and themes that were to be important in the seventeenth century, help explain his former popularity, as well perhaps as his present neglect.

A Note on Some Other French Capuchin Mystics

The Capuchins and the Jesuits were in the forefront of the Counter-Reformation forces in early modern France, both great supporters of the Catholic League, which combated not only Protestants but also the moderates who won Henry IV over to Catholicism and accepted his Edict of Nantes granting limited toleration to the Huguenots. The Capuchins, at least, were not punished by temporary banishment under Henry IV, as were the Jesuits. Another difference was that these austere Reformed Franciscans produced a significant mystical literature between ca. 1590 and 1620, rather before the French Jesuits. Benet of Canfield is the major Capuchin mystic, but several other Capuchins are worth noting and were influential in their day. Today most of their works are difficult of access, and therefore they are little known.

Lawrence of Paris (1563–1631) was a contemporary of Canfield and, like him, studied philosophy, theology, and languages in Italy from 1584 to 1591. His modern interpreter, Madeleine Dubois-Quinard, describes him as "a theologian, a philosopher, a spiritual person, and a humanist."[167] After Lawrence's return to France, he taught at St. Honoré, the Capuchin convent in Paris, and served in a number of administrative posts. Friar Lawrence, like Canfield, wanted to reduce the whole of the spiritual life to a single practice, but he differed from his confrere by insisting that this practice was that of the love of God, not the exercise of the divine will. Friar Lawrence planned to write five books on the practice of divine love, but only two were ever published. The first was the *Palace of Divine Love* (*Palais d'amour divin*), which was in circulation in manuscript from about 1599 and was published in 1602. It had a modest success, going through four later printings. What was to have been the third volume, the *Tapestries of Divine Love* (*Tapiesseries de l'amour divin*), which added a passion-centered aspect to his view of union with God, appeared in 1631 but had limited readership.

Since Lawrence's *Palace of Divine Love* is largely inaccessible (only a few copies are known even in France), I mention only a few aspects of the work, based on the account of Dubois-Quinard. First of all, it is clear that Lawrence, like Canfield, was dependent on late medieval Northern mysticism, especially that of Harphius, although the basic orientation of his thought was the diffused Neoplatonism shared by many late medieval and early modern mystics. Second, Lawrence, again like Canfield, was interested in constructing a methodical and accessible road map for the path to perfection designed for all sincere Christians, a path later undertaken with greater success by Francis de Sales. Lawrence's single exercise of the perfection of love, according to Dubois-Quinard, consisted of three aspects or parts: the practice of the presence of God; the practice of the will of God; and the practice of the glory of God, which "would bring the soul to the annihilation of love of self through the removal of interest in the self, so that the soul would no longer will and no longer have any goal but God in its life."[168] Thus, annihilation for Lawrence, as for Canfield, was essential on the journey to God.[169] The Capuchin's teaching on annihilation, on pure love, as well as on the "summit, or center, of the soul," obviously fits well with major mystical themes that were developing in early seventeenth-century French mysticism.

A second Capuchin mystical author of the time is somewhat better known. Constantin de Barbanson (1582–1632) was a friar from the Spanish Netherlands, whose *Secret Paths of Divine Love* (*Les secrets sentiers de l'amour divin*) first appeared in 1623 but was written at least a decade earlier.[170] It went though several French editions and in modern times has been made available in Dutch and English.[171] Friar Constantine entered the Capuchins at Brussels, not Paris. He spent his career in Germany at Cologne and Münster. This may explain why this mystical handbook is rather different from the works of Benet of Canfield and Lawrence of Paris, although, like Lawrence, he focuses on the centrality of the practice of divine love. Constantine's treatise is fairly traditional, with its part I of six chapters consisting of discussions of standard spiritual instruction in the practice of the virtues as a way of leading to attaining experimental knowledge of God. Part II outlines a course in the practice of mental prayer from beginning meditation, through the progressive exercise of stirring the mind up in love, to the stage of spiritual elevation in which infusions of grace aid the exercise of the theological virtues of faith, hope, and charity. Beyond this intermediate state there are three higher stages. The first is the practice of the presence of God, in which infused knowledge and love take over the soul as its passivity increases in response to God's action.[172] Next comes a stage of desolation and privation, not unlike what can be found in mystics going back to Tauler, and also present among more recent mystics, like John of the Cross.[173] Finally, Friar Constantine speaks of perfect, stable, and permanent union in the center of the soul, where action and contemplation, Martha and Mary, become one—another major theme of early modern mysticism. This stage of fruitive union is described in some detail [174] In keeping with another contemporary concern, Barbanson closes by analyzing the difference between the way that Scholastic and mystical theologians approach the issue of union with God.[175] At a later stage (1631) Friar Constantine added a further book, the *Anatomy of the Soul and the Divine Operations in It* (*Anatomie de l'âme et des operations divines en icelle*), designed to show the agreement between the mystical life and Scholastic theology. The work was also intended to correct false readings of Canfield's *Rule of Perfection*.[176]

Another Capuchin, famous (or infamous) for his political activities as Cardinal Richelieu's right-hand man from 1614 until 1638, was the nobleman François Leclerc du Tremblay (1577–1638), Baron of Maffliers, known in religion as Père Joseph de Paris, and sometimes as "the Grey Eminence" (*l'Eminence grise*).[177] Aldous Huxley, who had considerable interest in mysticism, was fascinated with Friar Joseph and especially with his ability to combine a career as a mystical author with the practice of power politics. Huxley's *Grey Eminence: A Study in Religion and Politics* is the best account in English: well-informed, witty, and entertaining, as well as useful for getting a general picture of the Capuchin's mystical writings.[178] Joseph of Paris wrote a number of spiritual and mystical treatises but published only a few. His *Introduction to the Spiritual Life* (*Introduction à la vie spirituelle*), written for Capuchin novices and put out in 1616, was his most complete account of the mystical life, one in which he laid great stress on the importance of ecstasies and special revelations.[179] Joseph of Paris's spiritual writings are of more interest for their possible insight into his bifurcated personality than for the study of mysticism.

Connected with Joseph of Paris is the surprising question of Cardinal Richelieu himself as a possible spiritual, even mystical, author. Richelieu (1585–1642) was, of course, a priest and bishop, though one who famously was said to have adhered to the principle "To be a good [i.e., successful] man according to God is one thing; to be a successful man according to men is another." Richelieu was eminently successful in the latter task by furthering the political interests of France in ways that were harmful to the general cause of Catholicism in the seventeenth century. This ultimate French political prelate, nonetheless, was said to have written a work on the traditional three ways of the spiritual life (beginners, proficient, perfect), a book published only after his death. This was the *Treatise on Christian Perfection* (*Traité de la perfection chrétienne*), put out in 1646.[180] Given Richelieu's eminence in the history of France, this rather banal work has been given some attention,[181] although recent research suggests it was not from his pen but may have been the work of another Capuchin, Jean Desmarets de Saint-Sorlin (1595-1676). By the time the book appeared, the great age of French Capuchin mysticism was over.

Notes

1. A full, if old, biography exists; see Georges de Blois, *Louis de Blois: Un Bénédictin au xvi siècle* (Paris: Victor Palmé, 1875). For theological treatments, see P. de Puniet, "Blois (Louis de) ou Blosius," DS 1:1730-38; and Cognet, *La spiritualité moderne*, 48-52, as well as Cognet's more extensive treatment in his *Introduction aux mystiques rhéno-flamands*, 336-43. For bibliography, see Lambert (Henri) Vos, *Louis de Blois, Abbé de Liessies (1506-1566): Recherches bibliographiques sur son oeuvre* (Turnhout: Brepols, 1992). The best recent study (with a list of the many printings of Blosius's works from 1538 to 1697) is J. T. Rhodes, "Blosius and Baker," in *Dom Augustine Baker, 1573-1641*, ed. Geoffrey Scott (Leominster: Gracewing, 2011), 133-52.

2. The letter can be found in G. de Blois, *Louis de Blois*, 336-38.

3. See Gérald Chaix, *Réforme et contre-réforme catholiques*.

4. On this collection of mystical texts, containing material from Eckhart and other Northern mystics, though not from Tauler himself, see Gueullette, *Eckhart en France*, who discusses their influence on Blosius on 118-21.

5. Vos, *Louis de Blois*, 38: "Louis de Blois appartient tout entier à la tradition bénédictine."

6. No fewer than forty-two editions of Blosius's *Opera* were published before 1800, the most important being that put together by the abbot and monks of Liessies: *Opera omnia* (Antwerp: Balthazar Moretus, 1632). On these editions, see Vos, *Louis de Blois*, 255-65.

7. For a listing of the editions, see Vos, *Louis de Blois*, 191-200.

8. *Manuale vitae spiritualis continens Ludovici Blosii Opera Spiritualia quaedam selecta*, cura et studio Caroli Newsham cum praefatione Emi. et Rmi. Card. Wiseman (London: Thomas Richardson & Sons, 1859). The book contains the *Canon vitae spiritualis*, the *Speculum spirituale*, the *Institutio spiritualis* with its various appendices, and the *Monile spiritualis*. I will use this edition in what follows.

9. These include *The Spiritual Works of Louis de Blois Abbot of Liesse*, ed. John Edward Bowden, 3rd ed. (London: Washbourne, 1876); *A Book of Spiritual Instruction (Institutio Spiritualis) by Ludovicus Blosius*, trans. Bertrand A. Wilberforce (London, 1900); and *Ludovicus Blosius, Comfort for the Faint-Hearted*, trans. Father

Jerome Bertram (London: Art & Book Co., 1902). Wilberforce's translation of the *Institutio spiritualis* is generally accurate, but I will make my own versions.

10. An exception to this is in cap. XII.ii (ed., 245-46), where Louis's discussion of mystical union contains two long quotations from Dionysius (MT 1; Ep. 5).

11. The first "appendix" (ed., 257-66) is a summation of some of Tauler's main ideas on the path to union; the second (ed., 267-71) is in praise of the Virgin Mary.

12. The Latin versions of Ruusbroec that would have been known to Blosius include Willem Jordaens's translation of *The Spiritual Espousals*, which was published in Paris in 1516 as *De ornatu spiritualium nuptiarum*, and Laurentius Surius's version of Ruusbroec's *Opera Omnia* published in Cologne in 1552.

13. Although "mystical union" (*henōsis mystikē*) appeared several times in the Dionysian corpus, it was rare in the Christian mystical tradition for the next thousand years. Louis de Blois is one of the first authors to use it extensively (nine times in the *Institutio spiritualis* and three times in the *Speculum spirituale*). Another contemporary who used it, though sparingly, was John Calvin; see McGinn, *Reformation*, 53-54.

14. Louis de Blois states that even the *simplices* are called to mystical union: "Atqui etiam simplices et idiotae possunt ad ipsam Theologiae mysticae sapientiam et unionem pertingere" (ed., 204).

15. Blosius, *Institutio spiritualis, Praefatio* (ed., 178). Blosius's teaching on the structure of the soul has been examined by Bergamo, *L'anatomie de l'âme*, 48-52.

16. On the *Evangelical Pearl*, see McGinn, *Varieties*, 143-59.

17. *Praefatio* (ed., 178-79): "Mens vel apex spiritus est nudus et Deiformis animae fundus. Id est, simplex animae essentia imagine Dei insignita. Secundum hunc fundum dicitur vita superessentialis, per quam perficitur tam spiritualis quam activa vita.... Itemque sicut ipsae Divinitatis personae, sic et tres illae vires inseperabiliter operantur." For more on the *superessentialis vita*, see cap. XII (ed., 246-47). The term *superessentialis*, whose roots go back to Dionysius, entered into general use through the writings of Ruusbroec and his follower Hendrik Herp and became important in seventeenth-century French mysticism; see Deblaere, "Essentiel (Superessential, suressentiel)," DS 4:1346-66; and Mazzocco, "'Suressential,'" 609-27. (Neither Deblaere nor Mazzocco mentions Blosius.)

18. The teaching about the Trinitarian dimension of the *imago Dei* to be realized in union set out here (ed., 178-79) returns in cap. V (ed., 205); in the prayer to the Trinity in cap. XI (ed., 240-41); and in cap. XII.ii and iv (ed., 246, 251). The Trinitarian aspect of union is also found in Blosius's *Speculum spirituale* XI (ed., 159).

19. Blosius's notion of the *fundus animae*, which is the equivalent of the *essentia* and *apex*, bears comparison with a number of his predecessors; see Bergamo, *L'anatomie de l'âme*, 142-43.

20. Cap. VIII.i (ed., 213). For other references to the *nudus fundus animae* as the location of the deepest union, see caps. III (ed., 197-98); V (ed., 203); VI (ed., 208); VIII.ii (ed., 214) and iii (ed., 215); XI (ed., 239); and XII.i, iii, and iv (ed., 242, 249, 251).

21. Cap. XII.iv (ed., 254-55): "O nobilem fundum, divinumque templum, a quo Deus numquam recedit! O fundum praeclarissimum, in quo sancta Trinitas habitat, et in quo est ipsa aeternitas gustatur! . . . Deus, increata abyssus, spiritum nostrum, abyssum creatum, in se vocare, secumque unum facere dignetur, ut ipse

spiritus noster profundissimo Divinitatis mari immerses, feliciter in spiritu Dei se perdat." Tauler speaks of the uncreated Abyss calling the created abyss into itself in Sermon 41 (*Die Predigten Taulers*, ed. Fernand Vetter [repr., Zurich: Weidmann, 1968], 176).

22. Cap. VIII.ii (ed., 218): "Unde et nos in Deo secundum ideam ab aeterno fuimus; in eo, inquam, fuimus et sumus increati.... In essentia ergo Dei rerum omnium exemplaria sunt: et ipsa eadem divina essentia unum omnium rerum exemplar et una idea est. Nam omnis rerum multiplicitas in simplicissima superessentialique Dei essentia ad unitatem redigitur: et omnia in Deo unum sunt." In the highest form of union the soul "revolvat in ideam suam et principium suum Deum" (cap. XII.iv [ed., 252]).

23. Hendrik Herp's popular Dutch handbook, written in the 1460s and deeply influenced by Ruusbroec, was the *Spieghel der Volcomenheit* (*Mirror of Perfection*). See McGinn, *Varieties*, 130-36. Peter Bloomeven (d. 1536), the prior of St. Barbara's in Cologne, translated it into Latin in 1509 under the title *Directoreum aureum contemplativorum*. French versions of the first and second parts of the *Directoreum* appeared in 1549 and 1552. The Cologne Carthusians also published an anthology of Herp's writings under the title *De mystica theologia* in 1538.

24. Cap. VI (ed., 206-9) has the title "Fundamentum contemplationis mysticae, recordatio et meditatio vitae atque passionis, ac vulnerum Domini Jesu." There are also passages on meditation on the life and especially the Passion of Christ in cap. III (ed., 199); VIII.i (ed., 215); IX (ed., 232); and XI (ed., 113-14, and especially 115-16). In addition, cap. IX (ed., 230-34) is devoted to describing how our own merits need to be conformed to those of Christ. The christological dimension remains even in the deepest stages of union, as we are told in cap. VI (ed., 208). On the importance of Christology in the *Institutio*, see Cognet, *Introduction aux mystiques rhéno-flamands*, 338-39.

25. The Eucharist is singled out for its principal role in helping transform us into Christ in cap. VIII.i (ed., 215-16).

26. Cap. VIII.ii (ed., 218): "Essentialis ad Deum via est uniformis, sed exercitia sunt diversa."

27. See cap. V (ed., 203-4), and cap. XII.ii (ed., 243-44). *Unio* occurs dozens of times in the *Institutio spiritualis*, and the term *unio divina* is also frequent. The *terminus technicus* of *unio mystica* is used nine times; see cap. I (ed., 182 and 184); III (ed., 195); VIII.ii (ed., 219); and XII (ed., 241, 242, 244, 248, 251).

28. Cap. XII.11 (ed., 243; trans., 123-24): "Tandem vero superioribus ejus viribus divina gratia sublevatis, clarificatis, exornatis, unitatem nuditatemque spiritus obtinet, et purum atque indepictum amorem simplicemque cogitationem (quae cogitationum expers est), adipiscitur.... [A]d contemplandum Divinitatis abyssum sereno, simplici et jucundo intuitu, absque imaginatione, et sine aliqua intellectus admixtione."

29. The language of transformation into God is frequent and sometimes expressed in strong terms, e.g., cap. VIII.i (ed., 216): "...jamque puriori et excellentiori vita ornatus, transformatur atque transmutatur in Deum, et omni gratia gloriossimae Trinitatis impletur."

30. Cap. XII.ii (ed., 244)): Defluit (inquam) amans anima, deficitque a seipsa; et velut ad nihilum redacta, in abyssum aeterni amoris collabitur, ubi sibi mortua vivit in Deo, nihil sciens, nihil sentiens praeter amorem quem gustat. Perdit enim

se in vastissima Divinitatis solitudine atque caligine; sed sic perdere, potius se invenire est." The language of annihilation and losing the self became popular with the seventeenth-century French mystics; see Mariel Mazzocco, "Perdersi per ritrovarsi: L'avventura del desiderio nella letteratura mistica," *Rivista di Storia e Letteratura Religiosa* 48 (2012): 65–98.

31. On *unio absque medio*, see cap. I, XI, and XII.i (ed., 183, 239, 243). Cap. XII.iii (ed., 248) describes how every image or thought, even of Christ's Passion, impedes true mystical union. *Speculum spirituale* XI also speaks of being *sine medio conjungitur Deo* (ed., 159 and 161). The term *unio sine medio* appears in both Ruusbroec and in Tauler.

32. E.g, *Speculum spirituale* XI (ed., 159), where, after using the traditional image of iron being heated and transformed into fire, he says of the soul: "Fit unum cum Deo, non tamen ita ut sit ejusdem substantiae et naturae cum Deo." See also *Institutio spiritualis*, cap. XII.ii (ed., 244).

33. On this chapter in the history of late medieval mysticism, see McGinn, *Varieties*, 77–86.

34. Cap. XII.iv (ed., 252): ". . . inclinatque se in divinam essentiam usque ad supremam illam unitatem, ubi Pater et Filius et Spiritus Sanctus in ipsius divinae essentiae simplicitate unum sunt." This unity beyond the three Persons in the divine essence is typical of Ruusbroec and his followers.

35. For example, cap. XII.iv (ed., 251): ". . . atque [anima] in Deo profluens, unus cum eo spiritus in intimo fundo suo efficitur, et cum aeterno Dei Verbo (quod ibi Pater caelestis profert) generata, nobiliter renovata, aptaque ad omne bonum opus seu exercitium redditur."

36. See the attack on "the followers of false quiet" (*falsae quietis sectatores*) in *Speculum spirituale* XI (ed., 161).

37. See Cuthbert Butler, *Western Mysticism: The Teaching of SS. Augustine, Gregory, and Bernard on Contemplation and the Contemplative Life* (New York: E. P. Dutton, 1923).

38. An aspect of Blosius's teaching on mystical union that cannot be taken up here is its duration. He often emphasizes that the heights of union are brief and that the mystic must be ready to come back to the world of charitable action when this is called for. Nevertheless, a passage in cap. VIII.v (ed., 228; trans., 95) speaks of the necessity always to keep watch on the self even for a person who has attained such perfect control that "[l]icet in omnibus locis, et apud quoscumque homines Dei praesentiam attendere, atque cum Deo possit." The emphasis on becoming and remaining aware of God's presence (not necessarily mystical) is one of the constant themes of the *Institutio spiritualis*; e.g., cap. I (ed., 181 and 183); cap. III (ed., 196–98); cap. V (ed., 202); cap. VII (ed., 211); cap. VIII.i (ed., 214); and cap. XII.i (ed., 242).

39. Bremond, *History*, 2:145. Bremond devotes chapter 4 of volume 2 to "Madame Acarie and the Carmelites" (145–267, with 145–94 on Acarie herself).

40. The sources purporting to be her own writings (interpolations cannot be excluded) have been collected by Bernard Sesé in *Madame Acarie, Écrits spirituels* (Mesnil-sur-l'Estrée: Arfuyen, 2004). These include: (1) *Les Vrais Exercices de bienheureuse soeur Marie de l'Incarnation, composés par elle-même, très propres à tout Âmes qui désirent ensuivre sa bonne vie*, first published in 1622 and based on the *Exercises* of Louis de Blois; (2) fifteen *Lettres* preserved in the Carmel of Pontoise, where

she died; (3) the brief sayings in *Autres écrits* from J. B. Boucher, *Vie admirable de la bienheureuse soeur Marie de l'Incarnation* (Paris, 1800); and (4) an *Annexe* drawn from Duval's *Vie.* The whole amounts to 150 brief pages.

41. Dagens, *Bérulle et les origines,* 128.

42. André Duval, *La vie admirable de la bienheureuse soeur Marie de l'Incarnation, religieuse converse en l'ordre de Notre-Dame du Carmel et fondatrice de cet ordre en France, appelée dans le monde Mademoiselle Acarie* (Paris, 1621). On Duval, see André Dodin, "Duval (André), théologien française, 1564–1638," DS 3:1857–62.

43. The fullest modern account, though one much criticized, is Fr. Bruno de Jésus-Marie (O.C.D.), *La Belle Acarie, bienheureuse Marie de l'Incarnation* (Paris, 1942). Along with the treatment of Bremond mentioned above, see Dagens, *Bérulle et les origines,* book 2, chap. 2 (110–32), as well as the brief treatments in Cognet, *La spiritualité moderne,* 241–43; and Marie-Thérèse de Saint-Joseph, "Marie de l'Incarnation (bienheureuse)," DS 10:486–87. In English the best study is Lancelot C. Sheppard, *Barbe Acarie: Wife and Mystic* (New York: David McKay, 1953).

44. On the influence of the *Institutions spirituels* on Acarie, see Gueullette, *Eckhart en France,* 145–47, who quotes the text from chap. XX of the 1587 French version: "Certainement celuy-là est bien avaricieux que Dieu ne peut contenter auquel sont contenus tous les biens que l'homme peut desirer, car les richesses de Dieu sont inestimables." This is based on Augustine, *Sermo* 105 (PL 38:620): "Avare, quid aliud quaerebas? Aut si aliud petas, quid tibi sufficit, cui Deus non sufficit?"

45. On the influence of Blosius on Madame Acarie, see Dagens, *Bérulle et les origines,* 120–28.

46. On Acarie's circle, besides the literature cited above, see Barbara B. Diefendorf, chap. 3, "Mademoiselle Acarie's Circle," in *From Penitence to Charity,* 77–100.

47. For remarks about Acarie as a spiritual guide, mostly based on Duval's *Vie,* see Bremond, *History,* 2:179–82, 188–90.

48. Diefendorf, "Mademoiselle Acarie's Circle," 86.

49. Marcel Viller, "Beaucousin (Richard)," DS 1:1314–15; and Dagens, *Bérulle et les origines,* 115–18.

50. Beaucousin encouraged the young Pierre de Bérulle in his translation of the *Brief Discours sur l'Abnégation intérieur* (1597) and may have had a hand in the French translation of Ruusbroec's *Noces Spirituelles.* It is often said that the Carthusian translation of the *Perle Evangelique* published in Paris in 1602 was due to him, but this is not the case. As Daniel Vidal has shown ("Le coup terrible du néant," in *La perle evangélique–traduction française (1602)* [Grenoble: Jérôme Millon, 1997], 73–76), the preface of the French *Pearl* says it is the work of an unnamed deceased Carthusian, not the still living Beaucousin. Vidal argues that this person was Jacques Morice (d. 1595), who probably was the director of a team of Carthusian translators who made the French version in the 1590s.

51. There is an account of Coton in Bremond, *History,* 2:54–99, who also treats Marie de Valence in 2:27–54.

52. On Jean de Quintanadoine de Bretigny and his role in the creation of the French Carmels, see Bremond, *History,* 2:195–238.

53. On the relations between Acarie and Bérulle, see Sheppard, *Barbe Acarie,* 57–64.

54. I follow the account in Sheppard, *Barbe Acarie*, 176-92 (quotation from 190).

55. There is an account, although told from the French point of view, in Bremond, *History*, 2:208-38; see also Dagens, *Bérulle et les origines*, book 3, chaps. 3 and 4 (191-228). Sheppard (*Barbe Acarie*, chaps. 5-7 [86-135]) gives a more evenhanded approach, especially regarding Bérulle's controversial actions.

56. Sheppard (*Barbe Acarie*, 91-92) says that this was Acarie's first vision, because she was generally suspicious of visions, given the many false visionaries who proliferated at the time. Acarie's many raptures appear to have been mostly without visual content.

57. See the account of these two meetings in Bremond, *History*, 2:208-10, with quotations from Duval. See also Sheppard, *Barbe Acarie*, 88-96.

58. Duval's text is cited by Bremond, *History*, 2:170. The reference to *divina patiens* is to the story of Hierotheus in DN 2.9 (648B).

59. Translated in Bremond, *History*, 2:178.

60. Examples of this reticence taken from Duval are given by Bremond, *History*, 2:174-78.

61. The letter can be found in *Écrits spirituels*, 105-10. There are partial translations and comments in both Bremond, *History*, 2:172-73; and Sheppard, *Barbe Acarie*, 110-12. I have adapted Bremond's rendering.

62. *Écrits spirituels*, 106-8.

63. Both quotations are from Bremond, *History*, 2:193.

64. *Écrits spirituels*, 140: "C'est pourquoi je me tiens ici avec une profonde reverence et une très grande reconnaissance de mon néant. Je ne suis rien, je ne puis rien, je ne sais rien." This last triple insistence on nothingness is probably taken from the *Perle evangelique*, book I, chap. XL: ". . . nous devons toujours nous étendre en la consideration de notre néant, comme celui qui n'a rien, ne peut rien, ne sait rien et ne se peut prévaloir de rien: car c'est en ce néant que consiste tout notre salut" (ed. Vidal, 291).

65. The phrase comes from Bremond, *History*, 2:114. Bremond treats Canfield in 2:112-25.

66. The fundamental book is Optat de Veghel, *Benoît de Canfield (1561-1610): Sa vie, sa doctrine et son influence* (Rome: Institutum Historicum Ord. Fr. Min. Cap., 1949). In English there is a good study and translation of the *Rule of Perfection* by Kent Emery Jr., *Renaissance Dialectic and Renaissance Piety: Benet of Canfield's "Rule of Perfection." A Translation and Study* (Binghamton, NY: Medieval & Renaissance Texts & Studies, 1987). Among other treatments, see Daniel Vidal, *Critique de la raison mystique: Benoît de Canfield. Possession et dépossession au XVIIe siècle* (Grenoble: Jérôme Millon, 1990); Cognet, *La spiritualité moderne*, 244-58; and Paul Mommaers, "Benoît de Canfield: Sa terminologie 'essentielle,'" *Revue d'histoire de spiritualité* 47 (1971): 421-54; 48 (1972): 37-68; as well as the same author's "Benoît de Canfield et ses sources flamandes," *Revue d'histoire de spiritualité* 48 (1972): 401-34; 49 (1973): 37-66.

67. This work, originally published in French in 1621, along with the life of Benet's friend and fellow Capuchin Ange de Joyeuse, was translated into English in 1623 by the priest Robert Rockwood. I will use the slightly emended modern version of T. A. Birrell, *The Lives of Ange de Joyeuse and Benet Canfield* (London and New York: Sheed & Ward, 1959). The Augustinian model for William's account is

most evident in the thirteenth chapter, entitled "A brief repetition of the foresaid principal parts by way of thanksgiving" (Birrell, 125-29).

68. Birrell, *Lives of Ange de Joyeuse and Benet Canfield*, "The Life of Benet Canfield," chap. 4 (98-102).

69. Ibid., chap. 11 (121-22).

70. Ibid., chap. 21 (167).

71. Ibid., chap. 15 (136).

72. Ibid., chap. 17 (145).

73. For a brief history of the text, see Emery, "Introduction," in *Renaissance Dialectic and Renaissance Piety*, 21-25.

74. For a listing of the editions, see de Veghel, *Benoît Canfield*, 400-412, who counts nineteen French editions, twelve Latin, four English, four Italian, four Dutch, five German, and a possible Spanish edition.

75. For a treatment of the Brossier affair, see Birrell, "Introduction," in *Lives of Ange de Joyeuse and Benet Canfield*, xviii-xx. Bérulle also became involved in the affair of Marthe Brossier; see Dagens, *Bérulle et les origines*, book 2, chap. 4 (159-65).

76. Canfield's other major work, *Le chevalier chrétien*, was published in 1609; see Cognet, *La spiritualité moderne*, 247.

77. Cognet, *La spiritualité moderne*, 257.

78. On the role of Renaissance rhetoric and dialectic in the *Rule of Perfection*, see Emery, "Introduction," in *Renaissance Dialectic and Renaissance Piety*, 26-44.

79. The modern edition of the *Rule of Perfection* used here is that of Jean Orcibal, *Benoît de Canfield: La Règle de Perfection, The Rule of Perfection* (Paris: Presses Universitaires de France, 1982), containing both the French and English texts. The translation used will be that of Kent Emery Jr., *Renaissance Dialectic and Renaissance Piety*, 87-258. I will generally not cite the French text, unless the vocabulary requires particular notice.

80. This text is cited several times in de Veghel, *Benoît de Canfield*, e.g., 100.

81. On Canfield's sources, see the summaries in de Veghel, *Benoît de Canfield*, 358-73; and Emery, *Renaissance Dialectic and Renaissance Piety*, 35-36, 62-70, etc.; as well as Mommaers, "Benoît de Canfield et ses sources flamandes" (see n. 66 above).

82. The Pseudo-Bonaventuran works include (1) Rudolph of Biberach, *De septem itineribus aeternitatis*; (2) James of Milan, *Stimulus amoris*; and (3) Hugh of Balma, *De mystica theologia*. On these works and their influence, see McGinn, *Flowering*, 117-18; and *Harvest*, 366-67.

83. On Herp's role in Canfield, see de Veghel, *Benoît de Canfield*, 360-62, and especially Mommaers, "Benoît de Canfield et ses sources flamandes," 48 (1972): 402-23.

84. On the role of the *Evangelical Pearl* in Canfield, see Mommaers, "Benoît de Canfield et ses sources flamandes," 48 (1972): 423-34.

85. On Canfield and Cusa, see Emery, *Renaissance Dialectic and Renaissance Piety*, 35-38, 78.

86. Contrast the arguments in de Veghel, *Benoît de Canfield*, 369-73, with Gueullette, *Eckhart en France*, 134-37.

87. On Ficino as mystic, see McGinn, *Varieties*, 258-70.

88. Ruusbroec's threefold division, as found in the *Spiritual Espousals*, for example, was into the active life, the interior life, and the contemplative life, but

he spoke of the last in terms of "superessential contemplation" (*overweselijcken scouwene*), thus laying the ground for later adjustments by Herp and Canfield. For an account of Ruusbroec's three stages, see McGinn, *Varieties*, 37–47.

89. The *Mirror of Perfection* is divided into four parts: (1) Introduction (chaps. 1-12); (2) The Active Life (chaps. 13-26); (3) The Contemplative Spiritual Life (chaps. 27-58); and (4) The Superessential Contemplative Life (*dat ouerweselic scouwende leuen* in chaps. 59-65). See McGinn, *Varieties*, 130–36.

90. For a history of the term, see Deblaere, "Essentiel (Superessentiel, suressentiel)," DS 4:1346-66, who treats Canfield on 1362-64; see also Mazzocco, who treats both Harphius and Canfield ("'Suressentiel': Aux sources d'un langage mystique"); and Mommaers, "Benoît de Canfield: Sa terminologie 'essentielle'").

91. On this point, see Emery, *Renaissance Dialectic and Renaissance Piety*, 69, 74.

92. For an analysis, see de Veghel, *Benoît Canfield*, chap. 5 (212-38).

93. *Rule* I.1 (ed., 102; trans., 97). On the importance of the rule of rectitude in Canfield, see Emery, *Renaissance Dialectic and Renaissance Piety*, 52–55. In book I rectitude is established in the memory; in book II, in the intellect; and in book III, in the will.

94. *Rule* I.1 (ed., 98-108; trans., 95-98). Images of both the sun and the sea appear frequently in the work.

95. The eleven themes of chap. 2 (ed., 110-25; trans., 99-103) are (1) renouncing of the self, (2) resignation, (3) purity, (4) presence of God, (5) self-knowledge, (6) knowledge of God, (7) annihilation, (8) union with God, (9) contemplation, (10) love of God, and (11) transformation. The Capuchin puts particular emphasis on annihilation here, though not yet using his distinctive language of passive and active annihilation.

96. *Rule* I.2 (ed., 122; trans., 102).

97. *Rule* I.5 (ed., 142; trans., 109). Canfield's exterior will of God is not unlike Francis de Sales's notion of God's signified will and our need to be conformed to it (see the *Treatise on the Love of God* VIII.3-14, and chap. 3, 108, 140-42, 145, 147 below).

98. On right intention in the *Rule*, see Emery, *Renaissance Dialectic and Renaissance Piety*, 69–72.

99. *Rule* I.14 (ed., 216; trans., 135).

100. *Rule* I.16 (ed., 234-36; trans., 141-42).

101. *Rule* I.18 (ed., 250; trans., 146). It is interesting to note that the 1610 French text here has *la pure et suréminent contemplation*, while the earlier 1609 English has *the pure and essential contemplation*.

102. *Rule* I.18 (ed., 252; trans., 147). Canfield cites Dionysian texts here, MT 1, and Ep. 3.

103. *Rule* I.18 (ed., 258; trans., 149).

104. The four kinds of prayer discussed in I.19 (ed., 260-67; trans., 149-52) are vocal prayer; mental prayer/meditation, especially on the Passion; the prayer of aspirations; and finally, "prayer made in the will of God alone," without either words or meditation.

105. For a more detailed analysis, see de Veghel, *Benoît de Canfield*, chap. 6 (239-70).

106. *Rule* II.1 (ed., 274; trans., 155).

107. *Rule* II.1 (ed., 276; trans., 156).

108. *Rule* II.1 (ed., 280; trans., 157). These five degrees are based on Bonaventure's *Itinerarium mentis in Deum*, Prol. 4, and 4.3, 7.2.

109. *Rule* II.2 (ed., 284-86; trans., 158). The *efficace inaction* is the French equivalent of the Dutch *inwercken*, a common term in Ruusbroec and Harphius. For the history of this mystical term, see Jean-Pierre Van Schoote, "Inaction," DS 7:1630-39, who shows how the French form began with the positive sense of "God's action in the soul," but how during the course of the seventeenth century it flipped to the reverse "in-action," or the soul's own lack of any activity. Sometimes authors seem to use both meanings, but Canfield is resolute in following the positive sense of God's action. See also Mommaers, "Benoît de Canfield: Sa terminologie 'essentielle,'" 47 (1971): 431 n. 33.

110. *Rule* II.3 (ed., 294; trans., 161). The principle, cited in Latin (*Contaria inter se opposita magis elucescunt*), originates in Aristotle, *Metaphysics* 8.4 (306D) and is also cited by Thomas Aquinas, STh IaIIae, q. 48, a. 3, obj. 3.

111. *Rule* II.4 (ed., 306; trans., 165).

112. *Rule* II.5 (ed., 308; trans., 166).

113. *Rule* II.7 (ed., 318; trans., 169).

114. *Rule* II.7 (ed., 320; trans., 170).

115. On part III, see de Veghel, *Benoît de Canfield*, chap. 7 (271-344).

116. See the discussion in Emery, *Renaissance Dialectic and Renaissance Piety*, 59-60 and 79-82.

117. On this dispute, reflected in Gracián's 1609 treatise *The Life of the Soul in Christ*, see Cognet, *La spiritualité moderne*, 265-67, and the brief notice in McGinn, *Spain*, 369.

118. *Rule*, III: "Epître nécessaire au lecture" (ed., 327-32, with valuable notes on the sources; trans., 173-75). The phrases are: (1) "to be united to God without any means"; (2) "to contemplate the divine essence without forms and images"; (3) "to see God"; (4) "to contemplate God without images"; (5) "to cease working"; (6) "not thinking about God with images"; (7) "the denuding of spirit"; (8) "the inworking of God"; and (9) "annihilation." It is interesting that the only authority who is cited under all nine points is Harphius, *De mystica theologia*. Such lists and explanations and/or defenses of the special character of mystical discourse were becoming a feature of mystical writing in early seventeenth-century Spain and France. See, for example, the expositions of the Carmelites Diego de Jesús (Salablanca) and Nicholás de Jesús María (Centurioni) appearing in 1618 and 1631, discussed in McGinn, *Spain*, 370-71.

119. *Rule* III.1 (ed., 333; trans., 176).

120. *Rule* III.1 (ed., 338): ". . . patissante l'inaction, ou intime operation de l'Epoux." *Inaction* is also found in III.3 (ed., 344).

121. *Rule* III.1 (ed., 333-38; trans., 176-78).

122. *Rule* III.2 (ed., 341-42; trans, 179-80).

123. *Rule* III.3 (ed., 343-46; trans., 180-82).

124. *Rule* III.4 (ed., 347): "Touchant le premier il est à savoir qu'il n'ay a si haute contemplation qui ne puisse être plus haute, ni pensée si abstraite, que ne puisse être plus abstraite." According to Cognet (*La spiritualité moderne*, 244), Canfield is the "incarnation de l'école abstraite."

125. *Rule* III.4 (ed., 347-50; trans., 182-84).

126. *Rule* III.5 (ed., 353; trans., 186). Enjoying love and working love, an inheritance from medieval Dutch mysticism, are found frequently in the *Rule*.

127. For this discussion, see *Rule* III.5 (ed., 353–64; trans., 186–92).

128. *Rule* III.5 (ed., 354; trans., 187): ". . . ainsi au contraire l'abstraction empêche de voir les choses concrètes, en telle sorte qu'il est impossible que l'esprit parfaitement abstrait puisse comprendre les choses concrètes." This section features considerable use of *abstrait*.

129. *Rule* III.5 (ed., 359; trans., 189–90).

130. *Rule* III.5 (ed., 362–64; trans., 191–92). Francis de Sales and Jane de Chantal, as we shall see (chap. 3, 98–99 below), also emphasized the theme of the mutual nakedness of the soul and God.

131. *Rule* III.6 (ed., 365; trans., 192).

132. *Rule* III.6 (ed., 368–69; trans., 194–95).

133. *Rule* III.7 (ed., 373–74; trans., 196–97).

134. This point is emphasized by Mommaers, "Benoît de Canfield: Sa terminologie 'essentielle,'" 47 (1971): 429–33, especially in dependence on *Rule* III.7 (ed., 335, 337).

135. *Rule* III.7 (ed., 375; trans., 197–98).

136. The relation between Canfield's teaching on annihilation and that of the *Evangelical Pearl* has been studied by Mommaers, "Benoît de Canfield: Sa terminologie 'essentielle,'" 48 (1972): especially 430–34.

137. *Rule* III.8 (ed., 376). My own translation of the odd qualifiers "spiritualisée, dénuée, supernaturalisée, et extatiquée." Canfield does not use the terms "abstract" and "non-abstract" here, but that seems to be a legitimate interpretation.

138. Emery makes the following observation: "In the mystical life, God is known through the pair of the most extreme opposition, all and nothing, which is perceived either experientially (passive annihilation), reasonably (active annihilation), or imaginatively (contemplation of the Passion)" ("Introduction," in *Renaissance Dialectic and Renaissance Piety*, 42).

139. *Rule* III.8 (ed., 383; trans., 201).

140. *Rule* III.10 (ed., 392; trans., 205). This is one of the places where one wonders if Canfield may have been influenced by the *Cloud of Unknowing*.

141. *Rule* III.10 (ed., 398; trans., 208).

142. For more on annihilation as passive and active, see Emery, *Renaissance Dialectic and Renaissance Piety*, 58–59, 68–70, and 74–79, as well as de Veghel, *Benoît de Canfield*, 307–28. There is also a discussion in Mommaers, "Benoît de Canfield et ses sources flamandes," 49 (1973): 37–49, on the relation of these annihilations to the *Evangelical Pearl*.

143. *Rule* III.11 (ed., 400; trans., 209).

144. *Rule* III.11 (ed., 400; trans., 210).

145. *Rule* III.11 (ed., 401; trans., 211).

146. *Rule* III.12 (ed., 403; trans., 212). Cognet (*La spiritualité moderne*, 256) calls Canfield "un théoricien très absolu du non-voir et du non-agir."

147. *Rule* III.12 (ed., 404; trans., 212).

148. *Rule* III.12 (ed., 404 and 406). Canfield uses the expression twice in chap. 12, first only in Latin (*in apice animae*), citing Bonaventura, or actually Hugh of Balma's *Theologia mystica*, part 4, chap. 3; and the second time in both Latin and French (*in apice animae*) *en la plus haute partie de l'âme*. On the summit of the

soul in Canfield, see Mommaers, "Benoît de Canfield et ses sources flamandes," 49 (1973): 49-59.

149. *Rule* III.12 (ed., 406; trans., 213-14). Emery translates *ressouvenance* as "recollection," but this is potentially misleading, since it might suggest the Spanish notion of *recogimiento*.

150. *Rule* III.13 (ed., 408-9; trans., 215).

151. *Rule* III.13 (ed., 411; trans., 217).

152. *Rule* III.14 (ed., 413; trans., 218).

153. *Rule* III.14 (ed., 413-14; trans., 218 adapted). This is what Mommaers ("Benoît de Canfield et ses sources flamandes," 49 [1973]: 60-66) calls "La vie activo-contemplative." Canfield's notion of the union of contemplation and action is different from Ruusbroec's conception of the "common life," especially because it lacks a direct Trinitarian dimension.

154. *Rule* III.14 (ed., 417; trans., 221).

155. Divinization is an important theme in Canfield, although the term is not often used. See Jean Orcibal, "Divinisation. V. Au 17e siècle," DS 3:1445-52.

156. *Rule* III.14 (ed., 420-21; trans., 222-23).

157. *Rule* III.15 (ed., 422; trans., 224).

158. *Rule* III.15 (ed., 423; trans., 224).

159. *Rule* III.15 (ed., 426; trans., 226).

160. *Rule* III.16 (ed., 433; trans., 230).

161. *Rule* III.17 (ed., 444; trans., 235).

162. *Rule* III.19 (ed., 456; trans., 243).

163. *Rule* III.19 (ed., 458; trans., 245).

164. *Rule* III.20 (ed., 463, 470; trans., 248, 253). This is another strong argument why speaking of Canfield as a member of the Abstract School misses his message.

165. On Ruusbroec and the false mystics, see McGinn, *Varieties*, 29-34.

166. *Rule* III.20 (ed., 470; trans., 253).

167. Madeleine Dubois-Quinard, "Laurent de Paris, capuchin, d. 1631," DS 9:406-15; quotation from 407. Duboise-Quinard is also the author of the major modern monograph on Lawrence, *Laurent de Paris: Une doctrine du pur amour* (Rome: Institute for Capuchin Studies, 1959), which I have not seen.

168. Dubois-Quinard, "Laurent de Paris," 410.

169. For more on annihilation in Lawrence, see M. Dubois-Quinard, "L'humanisme mystique de Laurent de Paris: L'anéantissement de l'âme," *Études Franciscaines* n.s. 14 (1964): 31-57.

170. For a summary, see Candide de Nant, "Constantin de Barbanson," DS 2:1634-41.

171. Since I am unable to consult the French original, I will use the English translation, *The Secret Paths of Divine Love by Father Constantine Barbanson* (London: Burns, Oates & Washbourne, 1928). This modern edition is based on the 1657 version of Dom Anselm Touchet, whose version, in turn, was based on the translation of the English Benedictine mystic Dom Augustine Baker, who was much influenced by Barbanson (see chap. 6 below).

172. On this stage, see *Secret Paths*, part II, chap. 9 (trans., 158-76).

173. *Secret Paths*, part II, chaps. 10-11 (trans., 177-95).

174. *Secret Paths*, part II, chaps. 12-14 (trans., 196-224).

175. *Secret Paths*, part II, chap. 15 (trans., 224-37).

176. On the *Anatomy of the Soul*, see Paul Mommaers, "Pays-Bas IV: Les XVIe et XVIIe siècles," DS 12:730–50, here 741–42.

177. Raoul de Sceaux and André Rayez, "Joseph de Paris, capuchin, 1588–1638," DS 8:1372–88. See also Bremond, *History*, 2:125–44, for a rich, if idiosyncratic, account with many quotations, as well as Cognet, *La spiritualité moderne*, 271–73.

178. Aldous Huxley, *Grey Eminence* (New York and London: Harper & Brothers, 1941). Many of the figures seen in this chapter (Barbe Acarie, Ange de Joyeuse, Benet of Canfield, Bérulle, etc.) make an appearance in Huxley's book. Chapters 6 and 10 are where Huxley deals with the paradoxical combination of Friar Joseph's ascetical and mystical writings and his Machiavellian politics (also 286–87.) Huxley emphasizes the influence of Canfield on Joseph (chaps. 3–4), as does Bremond.

179. At least according to Huxley, *Grey Eminence*, 95, 120–21.

180. For a brief account of Richelieu's writings, see Willibrord Christian van Dijk, "Richelieu (Armand Jean du Plessis), cardinal, 1585–1642," DS 13:656–59.

181. There is an account, for example, in Pierre Pourret, *La Spiritualité Chrétienne*, vol. 3, *Les Temps Modernes* (Paris: Gabalda, 1927), 486–91.

CHAPTER 3

*Francis de Sales: Love and Holy Indifference**

*Je dis donc: qu'il ne faut rien demander ni rien refuser,
mais se laisser entre le bras de la Providence divine,
sans s'amuser à aucun desir, sinon à vouloir ce que Dieu veut
de nous.*

I say then that we must neither ask for anything nor refuse
    anything,
  but leave ourselves in the arms of Divine Providence,
  without entertaining ourselves with a single desire,
  save to will what God wills of us.[1]

Neither to ask for anything nor to refuse anything sent us by God's providential love aptly summarizes the teaching of Francis de Sales (1567–1622) on the "holy indifference" that unites the soul to God. Such indifference is not Stoic *apatheia*, but is rather the expression of supreme love symbolized in the image of "heart-to-heart" union with God, another phrase typical of Francis.

Francis de Sales is the only seventeenth-century mystic writing in French to have achieved a worldwide readership. Without detracting from the contributions and insights of the other

---

* I would like to extend special thanks to Prof. Wendy M. Wright, professor emerita of Creighton University, a noted expert on Francis de Sales, Jane de Chantal, and the Salesian tradition, who read this chapter and made many useful suggestions and corrections. Any problems that remain are solely my own.

French mystics, Francis's eminence is understandable. As a major force in Catholic reform, as a theologian and Doctor of the Church, as a spiritual director and religious founder, as a man of balanced character, sound judgment, warm amiability, and selfless compassion toward others, Francis stands above his contemporaries. The accessibility and modesty of the saint and Doctor of the Church are immediately evident to anyone who picks up his treatises, and more so his letters. As he once put it in a letter to his dear friend Jane de Chantal, "I am as human as anyone could possibly be" (*Je suis tant homme que rien plus*).[2] Francis's humaneness and his universal sympathy, so evident in both his life and his writings, led Henri Bremond to see him as the ideal representative of what he called "Devout Humanism," that is, the movement that, building on Renaissance Humanism and its confidence in the fundamental goodness of human nature, applied this outlook to the inner life of those seeking to live devoutly.[3] Devout Humanism, however, has been criticized as vague and may not be a helpful category today.[4]

Francis de Sales was a prodigious writer (his collected works number twenty-seven volumes), although he is most famous for two related treatises that constitute a classic summary of Christian spirituality: *The Introduction to the Devout Life* (1608) and *The Treatise on the Love of God* (1616). The first, a book treasured by generations of readers, lays out the fundamental themes and practices for Christian living, while the second is a detailed treatment of the nature and progress of the love of God (both as objective and subjective genitive) that leads to union with God in the here and hereafter.

Life and Times

Francis was not French, but Savoyard, a citizen of the Duchy of Savoy, an area in the Southeast of France that embraced parts of current-day France, Switzerland, and Italy. To be sure, he was Francophone (though also speaking Italian) and spent a good deal of time in France, but his life was shaped by many issues current in Savoy, especially the fact that some portions of the Duchy, notably the city of Geneva, were bastions of Reformed Protestantism. The split in Western Christendom that was a distant concern for the Spanish mystics, was for Francis a matter of everyday reality, and sometimes even personal danger. This is evident in the fact that, although Francis was the bishop of Geneva from 1602 until his death, he was able to set foot in the city only in clandestine fashion a few times. He presided over the Catholic parts of the diocese from the small city of Annecy some fifty miles south of Geneva. Francis has sometimes been seen as an ecumenist *avant la lettre*, but this is not the case. He was firm in his opposition to "Protestant heresy" and expended great effort to convert Protestants, both by his pen and his work as a missionary. He did not, however, believe in forced conversion as did so many of his contemporaries, but rather tried to win over Protestants with patience and compassion.[5] He held that current political circumstances might allow a certain measure of toleration, but the ideal to be aimed at was the return of all to the unity of faith.

Born on August 21, 1567, to a pious Catholic aristocratic family in service to the Duke of Savoy, Francis was the eldest of many children, of whom eight survived into adulthood.[6] His childhood was a happy one. Francis's father, Francis de Boisy, had high hopes for his gifted child and enrolled him in the Jesuit College of Clermont at Paris in 1578, where he spent ten years receiving a sound humanistic and spiritual education. Francis's lifelong love for the Song of Songs was inspired by the lectures on the biblical book of love given in Paris by the learned Benedictine Gilbert Génébrard in 1584. In person Francis was small and inclined to put on weight, especially in his later years, but there was a quality about him that seemed to attract everyone.

It was during this time in Paris that one of the most noted events in Francis's life occurred. The issue of predestination, that is, God's determination of the fate of both the saved and the damned without reference to their merits or demerits, had emerged as a key question in Reformation theology, with both Luther and Calvin adhering to strict double predestination. Post-Tridentine Catholic theology avoided double predestination, but advanced different ways of reconciling God's predestinating will with human freedom. In late 1586, young Francis experienced a spiritual crisis concerning the possibility of his salvation: If God had decided from all eternity who shall be saved, how can one ever have any confidence of attaining heaven?[7]

There are a number of accounts of this personal trial, which Francis said lasted about six weeks and reduced him to something close to despair. The most detailed witness is that which Jane de Chantal gave in her 1627 *Testimony* at the first inquiry for Francis's canonization. After describing Francis's inner turmoil; she tells us:

> One day [probably in January 1587], however, divine providence mercifully delivered him. He was on his way home from a visit to the

royal court, and coming to a certain church [St. Etienne des Grès] ... he went in to say his prayers. He knelt down in front of an altar of Our Lady where he found a little wooden board on which was mounted a copy of the prayer beginning: "Remember, O Most loving Virgin Mary. . . ." He said it right through, rose from his knees and at that very moment felt entirely healed; his troubles, so it seemed to him, had fallen about his feet like a leper's scales.[8]

Later, in an undated letter, Francis tried to console a gentleman who was suffering from a similar "dark mood" brought on by his "fear of sudden death and the judgment of God." Francis tells him, "That is, alas, a unique kind of anguish! My own soul, which once endured it for six weeks is in a position to feel compassion for those who experience it." His advice is that "anyone who has a true desire to serve our Lord and flee from sin should not torment himself with the thought of death or divine judgment." To be sure, these things are matters of concern, but not by a debilitating "natural fear," but rather by "a fear that is so full of confidence in the goodness of God that in the end it grows calm."[9] This incident is telling for underlining Francis's total resignation to the saving mercy of God, something that was at the heart of his mystical teaching.

Francis's father had plans for him to become a lawyer and to take a role in the government of Savoy, so the young student was sent to Padua from 1588 to 1591, where he did, indeed, pursue legal studies but also engaged in theological training under the Jesuit Antonio Possevino (1534–1611), whom he took as his confessor.[10] It was at this time that he seems to have come into contact with the recently published work of the Italian Theatine Lorenzo Scupoli, *The Spiritual Combat*.[11] Francis loved the book and carried it with him wherever he went for many years. An avid student, Francis took to theology, especially to Thomas Aquinas. Although he never completed formal course work, Francis became one of the major theologians of his era. It was apparently during his stay at Padua that Francis's reading and thinking led him to break with both Augustine, who otherwise remained a major influence on his life, and Thomas Aquinas (or at least what he thought was Aquinas's position) on the role of grace and freedom in salvation. Following the lead of the Jesuit Luis de Molina (1535–1600), whose view of God's "middle knowledge" (*scientia media*), that is, divine foreknowledge of what humans will do in specific future situations, allowed for an important, though not decisive, role for freedom in the process of salvation,[12] Francis argued that God's salvific will was universal and that the attraction to God innate in human nature was injured, but not destroyed, by Adam's Fall. Hence, while salvation comes from divine grace, human freedom has a subordinate role to play. In adapting this view, Francis took a nuanced but firm position in the great debates over the relation of grace and freedom that roiled the Catholic world between ca. 1590 and 1610, siding with the Jesuits and "Molinism" against the stricter predestinarian view of the Dominicans led by Domingo Bañez (1528-1604). These vituperative quarrels (called the "De auxiliis" controversy, because it focused on what kinds of gracious help God gives to humans so that they may be saved) were ended by the decree of Paul V in 1607 that deferred papal judgment, allowed both views to be taught, and told the Jesuits and Dominicans to refrain from calling each other heretics. Without going into these issues in detail, it is important to note that Francis de Sales rejected the rigorist positions on grace and freedom that he found in contemporary Reformed Protestantism and Banezianism. The quarrels, however, were to continue after his death in French Jansenism.

When he returned to Savoy in 1592, Francis was convinced that he did not want to follow the law but felt called to the priesthood. With his mother's support, he eventually won over his father and was ordained on December 18, 1593. Shortly before his ordination, Francis became friends with another Savoyard who had studied at Clermont College and Padua, the lawyer Antoine Favre (1557-1624), who was becoming a major figure in the government of Savoy. This close friendship was to last for the rest of Francis's life, as the many letters they exchanged demonstrate. Francis had a special gift for making friends.[13]

For the next four years (1594-98) the young priest served in the Chablais area in Savoy, which had largely gone over to the Reformed party. Francis's efforts to win the district back to Catholicism were revelatory of his character—energetic, innovative, doctrinally firm, but conducted without the savage polemics that marked so many Protestant-Catholic encounters of the age. Francis's success was aided by the political support of the Catholic ruler of Savoy, Duke Charles-Emmanuel I, but can be largely put down to his missionary efforts, especially his preaching and the apologetic pamphlets he wrote explaining the Catholic faith and its biblical authenticity.[14] The Catholic bishop-in-exile of Geneva, Claude de Granier, was aged and ailing and thus asked Clement VIII to appoint Francis as his coadjutor. Francis traveled to Rome in 1598-99, where he underwent a successful canonical examination for his candidacy as bishop on March 22, 1599. Three days later, while assisting at the papal Mass, Francis testifies in a later letter that he received great "interior lights" concerning the fundamental mysteries of the faith.[15] Upon his return to Savoy, Francis continued his work of preaching, reforming, and aiding Bishop de Granier.

In early 1602, Francis went back to Paris at the behest of de Granier to execute a delicate diplomatic mission to convince Henry IV to provide financial support for the clergy in the re-Catholicized district of Gex, which belonged to the diocese of Geneva but was actually in France. Francis's nine-month stay in Paris was not only a return to his student days but also a turning point in his life. He became a favorite of the court, even of the king himself, not only for his preaching (he delivered more than a hundred sermons) but also for his amiable demeanor and sanctity. In Paris he came into contact with the clergy and pious nobles of the circle around Barbe Acarie, who were working for the spiritual renewal of France. Francis greatly admired Acarie, though he declined to become her confessor. His contact with the young Pierre Bérulle, Benet of Canfield, Richard Beaucousin, and others not only brought him familiarity with the mystical themes and literature circulating in the Acarie circle but also may have stimulated his thinking about composing his own works of mystical teaching.

Upon de Granier's death in late 1602, Francis succeeded him, being consecrated bishop-in-exile on December 8, 1602. According to several testimonies, during the rite he received a mystical vision of some sort. Francis himself did not write about this, but, once again, Jane de Chantal is a witness for what he once told her. During the 1627 hearing she testified,

> While it [the consecration] was going on, he said he felt, quite simply, that the most adorable Trinity was imprinting inwardly on his soul what the bishops were enacting outwardly on his person, and that he seemed to see God's most holy Mother taking him under her protection, while the Apostles Peter and Paul were close beside him, watching over him.

Francis was absorbed in interior prayer for six weeks after the consecration, feeling that God had taken away his old self and given him a new self that existed only for the sake of his people.[16] Francis de Sales was to spend twenty years as bishop of Geneva. His tireless efforts for the reform of the clergy and the religious orders, as well as his work for pastoral renewal, were to make him, like his hero Charles Borromeo (bishop of Milan 1560–84), a model of the Counter-Reformation bishop. The details of Francis's rule of his diocese cannot delay us here, but in order to understand the development of his mysticism, it is necessary to consider some important events of these two decades.

While preaching a series of Lenten sermons in Dijon in 1604, Francis met the pious young widow Jeanne-Françoise Frémyot, Baroness de Chantal. This was a life-changing event for both. Jane de Chantal was born into a family of the "nobility of the robe" (i.e., royal functionaries) in 1572 and married in 1592 to Christophe, Baron de Chantal, who died in a hunting accident in 1601, leaving Jane with several young children. Deeply religious and given to interior prayer, Jane struggled on in the midst of difficulties, both material and spiritual. Her meeting with Francis was a striking example of spiritual friendship at first sight—she being immediately attracted to him as a spiritual guide and he finding in her a devoted searcher for God.[17] The history of Christian mysticism displays a number of examples of profound love between male and female mystics, a love that binds them not only to themselves but also to God. In the case of Francis and Jane, their lives were soon deeply intertwined, as can be seen in the story of the new religious order for women (the Order of the Visitation) they founded and nurtured together, as well as by the hundreds of letters they exchanged.[18] While Francis's influence on Jane as her spiritual director and the ecclesiastical authority for the foundation of the Visitation has been stressed in the past, the work of Wendy M. Wright and others has shown that their friendship was not a one-way street. Jane's struggles and the mystical graces she received helped to shape Francis's teaching in many ways, and what has come to be called "the Salesian tradition" is the product of the collaboration of the two saints.[19]

The depth of the spiritual love shared by Francis de Sales and Jane de Chantal is evident from even a cursory glance at their correspondence. Their letters began soon after their meeting on March 5, 1604, in Dijon. As early as June 24, Francis was writing to Jane about the "bond of perfection" (Col. 3:14) that existed between them. In this letter he gives Jane advice about the need for considering the interior troubles she is facing as a "spiritual childbirth" whose pains are no less than those of the physical childbirth she knew so well. In a rare appeal to the mystical motif of the birth of Jesus in the soul, he goes on: "Our souls should give birth, not outside themselves, but within, to the dearest and most charming and handsome male child one could wish for. It is Jesus whom we must form and bring to birth in ourselves."[20]

Francis and Jane agreed to meet again at the shrine of Saint Claude in the Jura mountains in the summer. Jane was accompanied by several friends, and Francis by his mother and his sister Jane. Here, during August 24–25, the two had the opportunity for long talks about spiritual matters, and he agreed to become her spiritual director. From then on Francis's letters began to be more direct about the deep love between the two. Writing on October 14, he says:

> As you became more and more open with me, a marvelous obligation arose for my soul to love yours more and more; that's why I was prompted to write you that God had given me to you. I didn't believe that anything could be added to the affection I felt for you, especially when I was praying for you. But now, my dear daughter, a new quality has been added—I don't know what to call it. All I can say is that its effect is a great inner delight which I feel whenever I wish you perfect love of God and other spiritual blessings.

The letter contains a subtle analysis of their mutual love, as well as advice about devotional practices and how to resist the severe inner temptations against faith that Jane was experiencing. Against these diabolical assaults Francis tells Jane that she must "strike back with the heart and not with our reason, with intense feelings and not arguments." One of the repeated themes of this extraordinary letter was to become a constant in all his writings—its emphasis on attaining the spirit of liberty (*l'esprit de liberté*): "I want you to have the spirit of liberty, not the kind that excludes obedience (this is freedom of the flesh), but the liberty that excludes constraint, scruples and anxiety." Liberty of spirit demands detachment, but also the practice of what Francis later called "the little virtues," the daily exercises of gentleness, humility, and patience for which Jesus is the model (see Matt. 11:28–30).[21] Toward the end of this letter-treatise in which Francis responds to a number of questions Jane sent him in a lost letter, he returns to the theme of their union in God. "I received the copy of your vows," he says, "which I will deeply treasure, looking upon it as a fit instrument of our union, which is totally rooted in God and which will last for all eternity, by the mercy of Him who is its author."[22]

Among the crucial issues in the relation of Francis and Jane were the gradually developing plans for the foundation of a new religious congregation of women. As we have seen in Chapter 1, reform of the religious life, both the reform of old orders that had fallen into decline and the founding of new orders to meet pressing apostolic needs, were the order of the day in early seventeenth-century France. Francis at one time had contemplated founding an order of dedicated priests after the model of Philip Neri's Oratorians. Pierre de Bérulle's foundation of the French Oratory in Paris in 1611 made that initiative unnecessary. It was different in the case of his new mode of religious life for women. Francis was not sure what his goal was at first, and he spent several years in prayerful discernment. What he did realize was that the link that God had established between him and Jane meant that these plans would center on her. Jane had vowed absolute obedience to his counsel, and Francis tested that obedience several times in their meetings between 1605 and 1606. Finally, during the second long visit the baroness made to Annecy in May–June 1607, he revealed to her the project that had been gestating in his mind. He wished to found a new kind of religious congregation (not *entirely* new, however, because it shared some characteristics with the Italian Ursulines founded by Angela Merici). Recognizing that many women, especially widows, were too old or too weak for the rigors of highly ascetic and contemplative orders like Teresa's Discalced Carmelites, which were already proliferating in France, he wanted to have Jane and other like-minded women form a small community, or Institute, under simple vows and with a less rigorous lifestyle. This community would be devoted to living together in deep heart-to-heart love after the example of the heart of the crucified Savior, as reflected in its motto, "Live Jesus!"[23] Devoted to interior prayer, these women would not be bound by full cloister but would be able to go out into society to perform apostolic work, such as nursing the sick and assisting the poor. Jane agreed at once, though both she and Francis recognized the many difficulties such a project would entail, especially due to her obligations for her small children. The difficulties were slowly overcome, however, so that by 1610 Francis told Jane to come to Annecy so that they could initiate the new Institute.[24]

The baroness's departure from Dijon and her family on March 29 was painful, especially because her eldest son, Celse-Benigne, made a terrible scene. Jane was deeply troubled but resolved to pursue her vocation.[25] Despite last minute financial difficulties, the new house was inaugurated on June 6, 1610, with four sisters who called themselves "Religious of the Visitation of Holy Mary"—the Visitation Order, or Visitandines. It was later in 1610 that Jane experienced a "ravishment" during Mass that inspired her to take a vow that she would do whatever was most perfect and agreeable to God.

Francis gave the sisters some initial constitutions and guided them during their year of probation. The full constitutions Francis wrote for the sisters in 1613 and the surviving "Spiritual Conferences" that he delivered to the community represent the Salesian spirit of humility, moderation, and charity that so characterized both the bishop and the baroness. The new foundation began to grow rapidly. In 1613, the archbishop of Lyons, Monsignor Denis de Marquement, requested a similar house for his city and one opened in 1615. The archbishop, however, had difficulties with Francis's model. Mindful of the Tridentine decree that all houses of religious women should have strict enclosure and solemn vows, he pressured Francis to change the character of the new Institute. Francis at first resisted, but he finally submitted to the archbishop's demands with his customary tranquility, convinced that the major purpose of his plan could still be realized. He did, nonetheless, make three exceptions. The first was that the sisters were not required to say the Divine Office in Latin, but only the vernacular "Hours of Our Lady" (Francis explained this by noting how French women were unable to pronounce Latin correctly); second, that widows still be allowed to enter the community; and, third, that lay women be allowed to live with the community to make retreats. A pontifical letter of 1618 made the Annecy Institute into a formal religious "Order" in the Tridentine sense. Francis's acquiescence to his ecclesiastic superior's request has been variously judged, with some thinking that he surrendered his original vision to the forces of episcopal meddling, while others support his willingness to compromise. In any case, the change in the nature of the Visitandines did not hinder their success. There were thirteen houses by the time of Francis's death in 1622.

One other aspect of the relation between Francis de Sales and Jane de Chantal is worth noting before returning to a survey of the bishop's life. The close association between the bishop and the now much-harassed head of the new order lasted until the end of their lives, but its character underwent a deepening in 1616.[26] In the last books of his *Treatise on the Love of God*, Francis had come to a more profound awareness of the importance of indifference/disinterestedness to all things, the total surrender to God following the model of the naked Christ on the cross. During the retreat that Mother de Chantal made in May of 1616, a remarkable exchange of letters shows that, at his prodding, Jane became increasingly aware that she had depended on her friend too much and needed to leave everything in the hands of God. Francis wrote her, "You must become indifferent to everything that it pleases God to give you, without considering whether it is I who serve as your nurse." Jane responded: "I have a great desire and, it seems to me, a firm resolution to remain in my nakedness, by the grace of God— and I hope that he will help me." Francis answered with a long letter on the theme of the nakedness necessary for pure love of God, and Jane then sent another letter praising God for having denuded and stripped her of all that was most precious to her. Francis's final letter praises her nakedness and thanks God for his own: "I also find myself naked, thanks to Him who died naked for us in order that we might live naked. O my Mother, how happy Adam and Eve were when they did not have clothes!" The emphatic repetition of nakedness in these letters may seem strange to the modern reader, but the point being made is important. As Wendy M. Wright put it, Jane had undergone a shift "from dependence on François to dependence on God alone [that] signaled a new perception of their relationship."[27] It is not that their friendship cooled, but it had taken on a deeper meaning, which Jane expressed when she said: "It seems to me that I see the two portions of our spirit [the inferior and the superior] as only one abandoned and surrendered to God." This detachment was not a rejection of the human love between Francis and Jane, but an ecstatic movement of their mutual love into the mystery of divine love itself.[28]

Francis's concerns with founding and guiding the new order of the Visitation was only one part of his many activities during the decade from 1606 to 1616. The initiatives he was involved in, some successful, others not, cannot delay us here. We do, however, need to consider his activity as a writer. It seems evident that Francis planned his two major works as integral parts of a single spiritual program, especially because the *Treatise on the Love of God* refers back so often to its foundation in the *Introduction to the Devout Life*. The *Introduction* grew out of the bishop's spiritual guidance given both in person and also in the form of letters. Among the many recipients of this advice was his cousin, the young noblewoman Louise de Charmoisy, who lived diagonally across the street from the bishop in Annecy, but was soon to join her husband in the unedifying circles of the court. Like Jane, Louise had a desire for a deeper spiritual life, and appealed to Francis to guide her. The verbal and epistolary advice he gave her grew into the *Introduction to the Devout Life*, first published in August of 1608.[29] Francis, however, was already at work in the planning and probably even the writing of the larger volume that would complement this introduction, what became the *Treatise on the Love of God*. He worked at this over the coming years, until the first edition appeared in August 1616.[30] These works, especially the latter, will be treated in detail below.

At the time of this latter publication Francis had only a little over six years to live. His eminence continued to grow. In 1618-19 he returned to Paris for another extended stay, dealing initially with negotiations over a delicate dynastic marriage. As in previous visits, the bishop was asked to preach everywhere, was feted and dined, and even pressed to become coadjutor to the see of Paris, an advancement he typically refused. In 1619, he oversaw the foundation of the first Visitation house in the city.[31] During this stay, Francis once again came into contact with the spiritual elite of France, such as Pierre de Bérulle, the young Bishop Richelieu, Vincent de Paul, and the gifted but mercurial nun Angelique Arnauld (1591–1661), the young abbess of the Cistercian house of Port Royal that was to play such a large part in the history of Jansenism. Francis's letters to her, like those to Jane, are revelatory for understanding his discernment and spiritual insight.[32] By early 1621 Francis began to realize that his many labors had exhausted his physical frame. He expressed the hope of retiring to a hermitage overlooking Lake Annecy where he might pursue his writing. The end came quickly. A trip to Avignon, Valence, and Lyons in November 1622, for the reception of Louis XIII in Lyons exhausted him. While in Lyons he faded rapidly. On December 11, he was able to see Jane de Chantal for the last time. After celebrating Christmas, he suffered a stroke on December 27 and died the morning of December 28 at the age of fifty-five.

After his body was carried back to Annecy, proceedings for his canonization moved forward rapidly, with the first inquiry being conducted in 1627. As so often happens, accidental events slowed the process down. Francis, however, was canonized by Alexander VII in 1665 and declared a Doctor of the Church by Pius IX in 1877. His real monument is to be found in the generations of readers who continue to find in him one of the premier voices in the history of Christian spirituality, elucidating its progress from the beginning stages up to the most exalted levels of mystical consciousness.

Writings and Sources

Writings

Francis left a massive oeuvre. His early works, as mentioned above, are apologetical writings directed against Protestants, a genre he abandoned after 1600 to concentrate on writing letters of spiritual advice, sermons, and, of course, his spiritual treatises. The massive corpus of letters reveals his mastery as a spiritual director.[33] (We are told that he used to spend an hour or two every morning writing letters.) André Ravier aptly summarizes the character of Francis's spiritual letters:

> [W]hat makes the original charm of this spiritual correspondence has to be the images and sentiments that rush forth so freely. Humor is mixed with the most profound thoughts; it goes from anecdote to the intimate confidence. This is so true that his correspondence is for the biographer the best and most sincere *Spiritual Journal* that Francis de Sales has left us.[34]

Francis was a prodigious preacher. Four volumes of the critical edition contain hundreds of sermons, which often repeat, or sometimes expand upon, thoughts and images found in his two main treatises.[35] Francis was also a theorist and teacher of preaching, as is shown in the letter-treatise he sent to Jane de Chantal's brother, André, the archbishop of Bourges, in 1604.[36] In dealing with the style to be adopted by the preacher, Francis provides a motto that characterizes all his works: "The sovereign artifice is to have no artifice" (*Le souverain artifice c'est n'avoir pointe d'artifice*).

Francis also left some *opuscula*, including his brief *Mystical Exposition of the Canticle of Canticles*.[37] In this probably early work (ca. 1600–1602), Francis interprets the biblical song of love as revealing the soul's progress to God through the life of interior prayer, "the secret colloquy which only the lovers themselves understand." Finally, a collection of considerable importance for understanding Francis's conception of the life of the Order of the Visitation, as well as for other aspects of his spiritual teaching, is the twenty-two *Spiritual Conferences* (*Les Vrays Entretiens spirituels*), which he delivered to the Visitandine nuns between 1610–12 and 1618–20.[38]

Francis's style is accessible and engaging. His audience was not one of academic theologians, but of individuals, lay, religious, and clerical. Francis was the heir of the Renaissance Humanists, who rejected medieval Scholasticism in favor of a rhetorical style that sought to move the reader to assent and action. A text in the preface to the *Treatise on the Love of God* is revealing about the bishop's mode of writing. Francis says, "I have in fact thought solely of presenting in a simple, natural way, without art and still more without dissimulation [*simplement et naifvement, sans art et encore plus sans fard*], an account of the birth, progress, decay, operations, properties, benefits, and excellences of divine love."[39] The passage is noteworthy not only for its insistence on the simplicity of his style but also for the clear and comprehensive way he lays out the plan of the work. A word the bishop himself often used has long been a favorite of French literary critics in describing his style—*douceur*. This term is difficult to render into English, because "sweetness" (*suavité* is another favored word) today often connotes something cloying, perhaps even superficial, while for Francis and his audience *douceur* would have had more overtones of dearness, gentleness, and lovableness, as well as gracefulness and goodness.[40] So too, Francis's description of his style as *simple* is not meant to suggest that he gives only rudimentary or watered-down ideas, but rather that he tries to convey his message in a direct and engaging way. As Hélène Michon has pointed out, part of the originality of Francis's conception of mystical theology is not only its new content but also the direct and nontechnical language he employed to convey his message to a broad audience, especially of laity.[41]

This is not to say that Francis was always a model of unambiguous exposition. Mino Bergamo has drawn attention to aspects of Francis's texts, especially in the *Treatise*, that are ambiguous, whether by accident or intent. Francis uses many terms in different ways (e.g., *raison* and *sens*), although the context usually helps determine the particular meaning. In some cases, however, ambiguity still remains. For example, in trying to express aspects of knowing that go beyond rational discursivity in *Treatise* I.12, Bergamo finds a variety of forms of ambiguity in "the pluri-vocal language of the Salesian text."[42] While this is an important point, it would be a mistake to push it too far as a total characterization of Francis's writings.

One of Francis's techniques for making his message accessible is his use of analogies or examples from scripture, from the natural world, and from human activity. His scriptural analogies are quite diverse. Some are drawn from the traditions of allegorical, and especially tropological, interpretation.[43] Nonetheless, many of the images and stories taken from the Bible that Francis uses are exempla of moral action, or analogies and comparisons that do not depend on allegorization.[44] Francis's appeals to the natural world are often drawn from his own observations, as in the case of his frequent use of flowers, or to the effect of the magnet on iron. A special case is his many references to bees, creatures for whom Francis seems to have had a great love, given how often he employs them for comparison to aspects of the Christian life.[45] One pleasing use is found in *Conference* XVI, where he says, "A Religious Community is a mystic hive occupied by celestial bees, gathered together there to store up the honey of heavenly virtues."[46] The bishop also draws on accounts of creatures, even fanciful creatures, from ancient writers, such as Aristotle and Pliny. An example can be found in his use of the birds called *apodes* (i.e., without feet) mentioned by Aristotle. These imaginary birds can fly, but without feet their wings are not strong enough to take off, so they need the aid of a strong wind. Whether or not they ever existed, Francis finds in them an analogy for humans, who, when they fall into sin, can fly again only when lifted up by grace.[47] Francis also makes use of contemporary analogies. For example, he uses the example of God as the great "clock-maker" of the universe, although he obviously does not understand this image in the same way that later Enlightenment thinkers would (*Treatise* IV.8). Another example is his comparison of human making with an artist laboriously painting a picture as contrasted to God's action as a celestial print maker who creates an entire scene with one act (*Treatise* II.2).

These characteristics (and many more) are amply evident in the bishop's most famous work, the *Introduction to the Devout Life*. A bestseller since its publication, the *Introduction* ranks with the *De imitatione Christi* as one of the most read and most influential of spiritual classics. Francis had taken his neighbor Louise de Charmoisy under his direction in Lent of 1607 and had begun to write her notes (*mémoires*) about the devout life, addressed to "Philothea" ("Lover of God"). She showed some of these to the Jesuit Fr. Fourier of the seminary at Chambery, who immediately importuned Francis to have them published. Francis agreed and the first edition came out in 1608. So great was the demand that the book was reprinted and augmented in 1609, but in an imperfect way, so that it was not until 1619 that a fully adequate edition appeared.[48] Some forty editions appeared in Francis's lifetime, and the book was soon translated into most European languages. Countless editions and translations have appeared over the past four centuries.[49]

The remarkable success of the *Introduction* depended on many factors. Perhaps most important was the broad and intense desire in contemporary French Catholicism for a deeper appropriation of faith. Although early seventeenth-century France was on fire with the proliferation of houses of contemplative prayer, the patrons of this movement were mostly aristocrats and other wealthy folk, who often hungered for a deeper spiritual life without being able to flee the world for the cloister.[50] These were the people Francis wrote for, and the instant success of his work showed his genius for discerning the spiritual needs of his audience. A second ground for the success of the work was its intimate, conversational style, as well as its comprehensive order. Francis did not compose in the tired logical genres of contemporary "Second

Scholasticism," but he had absorbed its commitment to the logical ordering of material. Francis was an innovator, but one who learned from the past to strike out in new ways.

The *Introduction* consists of five books. The "Dedicatory Prayer" ends with the fervent exclamation often found in Francis's writings: "*Vive Jésus, Vive Jésus!*" In the preface, the bishop emphasizes the originality of his endeavor. Whereas previous writers on devotion had written for religious men and women who had withdrawn from the world, his aim is "to instruct those who live in towns, in families, or at court." Many will say that such folk cannot really practice devotion; but Francis gives three natural examples of what seems impossible (e.g., the firefly passing through flames without burning its wings), to bring home the message: "[A] vigorous and resolute soul may live in the world without being infected by any of its moods, . . . and fly through the flames of earthly lusts without burning the wings of the holy desires of a devout life."[51] Francis then briefly describes the purpose of the five parts of the book and issues an apologia—he himself lacks true devotion, but not the desire for it.

The first part of the *Introduction* contains instructions and exercises needed for embracing the devout life in twenty-four brief chapters. The first four lay the necessary groundwork;[52] the actual work of purifying the soul stretches from chapter 5 to chapter 24. Purification entails five purgations. The first is purgation from mortal sin (chap. 6); the second purgation is from the affection for sin (chaps. 7-8). This purgation, which is crucial to further progress, centers on attaining perfect contrition. In order to gain this, Francis instructs Philothea on how to make ten meditations (chaps. 9-18) leading to an election and choice of the devout life—a clear reminiscence of the Ignatian spiritual method he had absorbed in his school days in Paris.[53] The election bears fruit in making a general confession (chap. 19), and then (something peculiar to the lawyer in Francis) in the signing of an "authentic protestation," that is, a legal resolution to serve God (chap. 20). The three last purgations are designed to strengthen the first two: (3) purgation from affection for venial sin (chap. 22); (4) purgation from affection for useless and dangerous things (chap. 23); and (5) purgation from all evil inclinations (chap. 24). Francis says that we can never get rid of all our evil inclinations in this life, but we must work to overcome them as best we can, primarily by the practices found in the succeeding parts of the *Introduction*.

Part II contains twenty-one chapters on how the soul is elevated to God by prayer and the sacraments. Prayer, that is, mental prayer, is absolutely necessary (chap. 1). Francis advises an hour a day. The bishop provides a mini-treatise on meditation in chapters 2 through 9, explaining the four parts of the exercise in detail and giving considerable practical advice. He then notes five other short forms of prayer that can be used throughout the day (chaps. 10–13). The rest of part II is a digressive consideration of the role of the sacraments (Eucharist in chaps. 14 and 20–21; Penance in chap. 19) and other pious practices for the progress of the devout soul.

Part III is a handbook on the virtues, the moral aspect of the life of devotion. Charity alone brings us to perfection, but the virtues are a necessary means to attain it (see chap. 11). Here the bishop's balance and moderation come to the fore. He insists that "[e]very condition of life has need to practice some particular virtue," and he advises Philothea, "Choose the best virtues, not the most esteemed; the most noble, not the most apparent; those that are actually the best, not those that make the most show."[54] This shows Francis's emphasis on "the little virtues," that is, virtues like humility, obedience, meekness, gentleness, compassion, and the like, that everyone can practice every day.[55] Francis makes the related point that special spiritual gifts like ecstasies, unions, and elevations are not virtues but rewards given by God to some souls for reasons of his own. Although good in themselves as foretastes of heavenly bliss, Francis advises Philothea, "We must not aspire to such graces, since they are by no means necessary to love and serve God well, which should be our only intention."[56] Francis then treats a number of key virtues separately: patience (chap. 3), humility (chaps. 4–7), meekness (chaps. 8–9), diligence (chap. 10), and the trio of obedience (chap. 11), chastity (chaps 11–12), and poverty (chaps. 14–16). Of particular importance for Francis, as for almost all Christian teachers, is the virtue of humility, which has a special relation to saving charity. In *Conference* VIII, he summarizes, "Charity is an ascending humility and humility is a descending charity."[57] Finally, the long part III of the *Introduction* ends with a potpourri of topics related to the devout life.[58]

Part IV has fifteen chapters on the negative side of the devout life, that is, temptations and how to overcome them. With regard to temptations, Francis wants Philothea to understand the difference between delight and consent. There are three steps to sin: temptation itself, the delight it often arouses in us, and the consent to delight that causes sin. He notes that many saints were sorely tempted but did not consent. In chapter 3 he says, "[I]t is not always in the soul's power not to feel temptation, though it is always in her power not to consent to it." Hence, when it comes to the delights that please the outer man but displease the inner, "we see that such delight is involuntary, and as such it cannot be sinful."[59] Francis also uses this fourth part to consider a variety of related topics, such as anxiety (chap. 11), sadness (chap. 12), the difference between spiritual and sensible consolations (chap. 13), and spiritual dryness and sterility (chaps. 14–15).

Part V concludes the *Introduction* with eighteen chapters on "Exercises and Instructions Calculated to Renew the Soul and Confirm Her in Devotion." Francis advises Philothea to renew her good resolutions every year by making meditations on the benefit that God affords us by calling us to his service (chap. 2), and our advancement or lack of it in the devout life (chap. 3). To this end he gives much advice about a four-part examination of conscience to be made over several days (chaps. 4–7), as well as a series of five considerations for renewing our good intentions (chaps. 9–15). The fourth and fifth considerations, on the love that Jesus Christ bears for us (chap. 13) and the eternal love of God for us (chap. 14) are strong expressions of the role of love and the heart in his spiritual teaching. This emphasis also appears in the three final counsels that close the *Introduction to the Devout Life* (chap. 18). For Francis, the key is desire. We must confess openly that we *desire* to be devout in order to live devoutly. He goes on:

> In conclusion, my dearest Philothea, I entreat you by all that is sacred in heaven and on earth, by the baptism which you have received, by the breasts by which Jesus Christ was nourished, by the loving Heart with which He loved you, and by the bowels of the mercy in which you hope, continue and persevere in this blessed enterprise of the devout life.[60]

Francis's greatest work, the *Treatise on the Love of God*, can be described as the last great classical summary of mystical theology. Later works entitled *Mystical Theology* were written in the seventeenth century, and, after the condemnation of Quietism, school theologians of the eighteenth and nineteenth centuries composed many weighty tomes on "Ascetic and Mystical Theology." Not all these works are devoid of value, but none come close to summarizing and analyzing the mystical tradition in the way that Francis's *Treatise* did. The genesis of this substantial book was protracted, going through several manuscript forms.[61] When it was finally published in 1616, the *Treatise* did not create the sensation of the *Introduction*, nor has it over the centuries, perhaps due to its length. Nonetheless, the work has been often reprinted and translated.[62] Addressed to "Theotimus" ("The One who Fears God"), despite the male name, Francis's exploration of mystical love was directed to a wide audience, including the Visitandine nuns. Aspects of its teaching about the mystical life certainly owe much to what he learned from his spiritual friendship with Jane de Chantal.

The *Treatise* comprises twelve books. In this context I will give only a brief outline of these, since the heart of the content will be discussed at more length in section III below. In treating of the love of God, both the love with which God loves us and the love we return to him, Francis was inspired by the whole of scripture, but especially by the Song of Songs. Some have seen the work as a kind of commentary on the Song, which is true in the broad sense.[63] In the preface, written under the motto *Vive Jésus!*, Francis explains the purpose of the book and gives a long list of the authorities, both men and women, who have written about the love of God. Testifying to his wide reading and his desire to represent the whole mystical tradition, he claims, "I have said nothing that I have not learned from others." But this is not really true, either of the structure of the work, or of many aspects of its presentation. Building on the message given to Philothea in the *Introduction*, Francis says the Theotimus to whom the work is addressed is any soul that has advanced in the devout life, man or woman. He also notes that there are many obscure things in the depths of this science on which he hopes to introduce "a light that is good and pleasant." He also expresses a cautious attitude toward the mysticism of Benet of Canfield and his peers: "In fact, just as I have not wished to follow those who despise certain books that treat of a way of life that is supereminent in perfection, so also I have not wished to speak of such supereminence. I can neither condemn those authors nor give approval to critics of a doctrine that I do not understand."[64]

Book I with eighteen chapters concerns the preparation for the love of God and lays out the fundamentals of Francis's theology of love, to be treated in detail below. The next three books are a kind of biography of divine love. The bishop treats its generation and birth (book II), especially through the action of the three theological virtues of charity, faith, and hope. Book III deals with the progress and perfection of divine love, while book IV concerns its decay and ruin, that is, the soul's ability to lose charity through sin. Book V closes off the first part of the *Treatise* by considering the two main exercises of love: the love of *complacency*, that is, the pleasure, or the loving contentment we take in God's goodness (chaps. 1–5), and the love of *benevolence*, that is, our desire to praise and thank God (chaps. 6–12) for his goodness. Books VI through IX present two models of the path to union with God. Books VI-VII are a consideration of mystical theology as growth in interior prayer and represent Francis's adaptation of Teresa of Avila's teaching found in her *Life* and *Interior Castle*. In these books, Francis not only uses Teresa on the kinds of prayer (meditation, contemplation, passive recollection, the prayer of union, rapture) but also incorporates into the Teresian model other methods of prayer, both from older authorities and from his own thinking. Book VI introduces the basic distinction between the affective love that makes us pleased to be in God, as well as the effective love that helps us please God, especially through prayer (chap. 1). The book goes on to talk about the initial stages of mystical prayer: meditation, recollection, and the prayer of quiet. Book VII analyzes the various modes of the soul's union with God in prayer, especially through a consideration of "the summit of the spirit" (chap. 1). It considers the degrees of union (chaps. 2-3) and gives a detailed treatment of the kinds of rapture (chaps. 4-6). The book concludes with a discussion of death (chaps. 9-14), both metaphorical and actual.

Book VIII treats the first part of the second model for the ascent to God, that of love as conformity with the will of God. The love of conformity springs from our complacency in God (see book V), but gradually transforms us into God through the interaction of the complacency that draws him into our hearts, and the conformity of submission, by which we cast our hearts into God, dedicating everything to him (chaps. 1-2). Conformity to God's "signified will" (i.e., what he manifests in history and our lives) is explained in terms of four different modes: God's will to save us in general, and our conformity to the three particular ways he makes his will known—commandments, counsels, and inspirations (chaps. 4-13). Book IX discusses the second mode of love, the love of submission, a form of what Francis called the "ecstasy or rapture of action" (see the three kinds of rapture in VII.4-6). This book represents the culmination of Francis's mystical teaching as a form of practical apophaticism. The union of our will with the will of God's good pleasure, according to Francis, is realized not in mystical gifts and consolations but chiefly in the trials and tribulations that teach the soul "holy indifference," that is, the necessity for loving nothing save that "God's will be done." We should love the God of consolations, not the consolations of God, as Francis often said—love God himself, rather than *our* love of God (*Treatise* IX.9). This is the meaning of "To ask for nothing and to refuse nothing." The archetype for this highest state of union with God is Jesus on the cross, the one who, in the midst of suffering and dereliction, totally surrendered his will to the divine will.

The final three books of the *Treatise* are a kind of add-on, addenda in which the bishop of Geneva took up issues relevant, but not central, to the main sections of the work. Book X treats of the commandment to love God above all things, while book XI features a return to the theme explored in part III of the *Introduction to the Devout Life*, namely, the relation of love and the virtues. In conclusion, book XII deals with progress in holy love, arguing that this depends on God's action in the "supreme point of the soul," not on our own efforts. Francis concludes with a series of maxims on living divine love and a meditation on Calvary as the academy of love, a fitting summation of his insistence that Christ on the cross is the source and the model of how we learn to live in divine love.

Sources

This survey of Francis's works has already suggested how deeply his teaching was rooted in traditional theological and mystical literature. A considerable literature has been devoted to the bishop's sources,[65] so a full account is not needed here. The bishop of Geneva was among the most widely read mystical authors of his time, but he was no slave to tradition. His is an independent voice.[66] Francis's use of his predecessors includes all three of the bodies of mystical literature mentioned in chapter 1 above. He was deeply influenced by the masters of Western mysticism, such as Augustine, Bernard, Bonaventure, and Dionysius.[67] He was also familiar with some of the late medieval Northern mystics in their Latin and French versions. These include John Tauler,[68] Jean Gerson, Hendrik Herp (Harphius), and the *Evangelical Pearl*.[69] Francis seems to have appreciated the *Pearl* but thought that its message could be dangerous to all but the most advanced souls.[70] Francis also praised women mystics, such as Gertrude the Great, Mechthild of Hackeborn, Angela of Foligno, Catherine of Siena, Catherine of Genoa, and, of course, Teresa of Avila.[71] He used and recommended a number of recent and contemporary spiritual and mystical authors from France, Italy, and Spain.[72] Francis appears not to have known the writings of John of the Cross.[73] Theologically, he was well-grounded in Thomas Aquinas, to whom he often refers,[74] despite his break with the Dominican on the issue of grace and freedom. We might summarize by saying that Francis was *informed*, but not decisively *formed*, by past theological and mystical writers.

Francis's major source was the Bible. Like many other early modern mystics, the bishop was a biblical theologian, something that tends to be neglected by those who overemphasize an early modern shift to personal experience and psychological investigation. The study of Antanas Liuima on the sources for the *Treatise* gives us some sense of how much the bishop's writings were shaped and pervaded by the Bible, although Liuima, alas, lacked any appreciation for Francis's spiritual hermeneutic.[75] Mere numbers, of course, do not reveal the whole story, because it was Francis's biblical "imagination" that decisively formed his thought, that is, his presentation of the message of salvation through and in the stories and images of the sacred text. This aspect of his theology has been explored by Hélène Michon, who shows the relation between the language of the Bible and Francis's manner of preaching—and, we might say, his whole mode of instruction as seen especially in the two great treatises.[76]

Teaching[77]

Francis de Sales has been much written about, although there are surprisingly few works that try to survey his theological and mystical teaching as a whole.[78] The bishop's basic message begins, proceeds, and terminates in love, the essential attribute of God and the gift that he shares with humans made in his image and likeness (Gen. 1:26).[79] In the preface to the *Treatise on the Love of God*, he says that the church is adorned with many wonderful works of devotion by a variety of authors. He continues, "Everywhere amid all that colorful variety in the doctrine the Church puts forth we discern the beautiful gold of holy love [*sainte dilection*], displaying itself in an excellent way; gilding all the science of the saints, it raises it above every science. All is from love, in love, for love and of love in Holy Church [*Tout est a l'amour, en l'amour, pour l'amour, et d'amour en la sainte Eglise*]."[80] More succinctly, in *Treatise* VIII.1 he says, "Love is the abridgment of all theology" (*Oeuvres* V:62). But love is not just a subject of academic study; it is the meaning of life, because "Love is the life of our heart" (XI.20; *Oeuvres* V:309). Love is the glue that ties together all aspects of the universe. The beginning of book X proclaims, "Man is the perfection of the universe; the spirit is the perfection of man; love, that of the spirit; and charity, that of love. Therefore, the love of God is the end, the perfection and excellence of the universe."[81] Although the centrality of love is emphasized by all Christian mystics, Francis de Sales's exposition of this fundamental theme has unique characteristics.[82] I will present these according to the following threefold exposition:

A. *Where do we start?* In God as loving goodness and in the love he shows to humans both in their creation and their redemption through Christ's absolute predestination.
B. *How do we progress?* Through the devout life lived out of love and desire for God.
C. *What is the goal?* Heart-to-heart union with God achieved by mystical theology (union) understood as the goal of the life of prayer.

The Starting Point: God as Love and the World as Participation in Love

God, Creation, and Redemption

Francis de Sales was a practical thinker. His treatises are designed to teach his audience how to love God, not to speculate about the divine nature. Nevertheless, there is a deep theological underpinning to his writings, that is, a doctrine of God.[83] At the beginning of the second book of the *Treatise*, Francis provides a summary of his doctrine of God in the first two chapters. Just as the sun takes on different colors depending on the air and the time of day, so too when we speak of God we do not talk so much about what God is in Godself, but according to how he is seen in his works. Thus, we use many attributes to describe God, but "He is himself one most sole, most simple, and most uniquely unique perfection, because everything that is in him is just himself."[84] Hence, only God is a true theologian, since he alone has perfect knowledge of his infinite greatness. In God there is nothing but "one sole very unique and very pure act" (*qu'un seul tres unique et tres pure acte*; II.2). This one act, which is nothing other than divinity itself, is able to produce all that exists, the way a printmaker creates a print by a single action. All the diversity of creation is brought together in proportion, order, and unity. All created things, visible and invisible, "are called the universe, perhaps because all their diversity is reduced to unity as though one said 'uni-diverse,' that is, one and diverse, one with diversity and diverse with unity."[85]

God's control over the *uni-diverse* is exercised through his providence, which is the subject of chapters 3 to 7 of book II. Of great importance in this exposition is chapter 4, where Francis explains that God's desire to communicate himself to the world necessarily involves his intention to unite himself to some created nature, so that "the creature might be engrafted and implanted in the divinity, and become one single person with it."[86] Francis, like Duns Scotus and others, but unlike Thomas Aquinas, held to what is often called the absolute predestination of Christ—the Word would have become human even if Adam had not sinned. Just as there is essential communication in God by which the Father gives his infinite divinity to the Son, and the two in consort communicate divinity to the Holy Spirit,[87] "this sovereign sweetness" (*cette souveraine Douceur*) was communicated outside itself into a creature in a way that united the properties of both the uncreated and created natures into one person. Thus, Christ, the God-man, is the purpose and goal of the whole creative process. Everything was made for him. Humans and angels were created to serve him and share in his glory. In his loving benevolence God determined that intellectual creatures should be given the freedom to love voluntarily, even though he foresaw that this would involve Adam's fall. Nevertheless, so that, "[t]he sweetness of his mercy might be adorned with the beauty of his justice, he determined to save humanity by way of a rigorous redemption, which could take place rightly only through his Son."[88] The eternal predestination of Jesus Christ is one pillar of Francis's doctrine of redemption; the other is God's universal salvific will. The two teachings are brought together in a passage from the opening of book VIII.4:

> God has signified to us by so many ways and means that we should all be saved, that no one can be ignorant of it. To this purpose he made us to his own image and likeness by creation, and made himself to our image and likeness by his Incarnation, after which he suffered death to ransom and save all mankind.[89]

Unable to comprehend the infinity of the one divine act in itself, we must talk about God on the basis of what we see in the created *unidiverse*. In this harmonious unity in diversity we discern the attributes that help us express something of the nature of the one divine act—especially Love, and the related predicates of Goodness and Beauty. The *Treatise* begins with a consideration of the relation of beauty and goodness in creation, following the teaching of Thomas Aquinas and Pseudo-Dionysius.[90] The good pleases the appetite and the will, while beauty pleases understanding and knowledge, according to Francis. In the "Sovereign Beauty" of God, which is one and the same as "the pure divine act," we acknowledge the unity of essence in the distinction of Persons, as well as the divine intention to make all things both good and beautiful. God gives order and unity to the multitude of distinct things by means of the principle of "Monarchy," that is, bringing everything under him as the "sovereign Monarch," and, in a participated way, the other forms of monarchy in the universe, including the "natural monarchy in the will, which rules and commands all that is found in this little world [i.e., humanity as microcosm]." If beauty is the attribute stressed in this opening chapter, other passages in the *Treatise* emphasize the other transcendental attributes. Book V, chapter 3, for example, says that the soul in love "cries continually in her sacred silence: 'It suffices me that God is God, that his goodness is infinite, that his perfection is immense; whether I die or whether I live matters little to me, since my dear well-beloved lives eternally an all-triumphant life.'"[91]

The divine Good reveals itself to us as benevolence—all we are and have is the gift of the loving God. Francis does not spend much time discussing Love as an attribute of God in Godself; his frequent analyses of love (*l'amour*), charity (*charité*), dilection (*dilection*), and friendship (*amitie*) are relational; that is, they begin with how we are to love God, which reveals, to be sure, how God loves us. We will see below how Francis understands the nature of love as comprising both complacency and benevolence (e.g., *Treatise* V). Francis constructs his theology of love by way of an analysis of the function of the two forms of human loving, that is, complacency and benevolence; but this presentation implies that both aspects exist in an infinite way in God as identical with the single divine act. Such an approach is in harmony with the practical character of the bishop's treatises. Chapter 22 of book II, the "Brief Description of Charity" is a summary of the relation of divine and human love. Francis says that by his "ineffable sweetness" (*suavité ineffable*) God leads the soul from the Egypt of sin into the mansions of his love, "the land of promise," which is nothing other than "most holy charity, which, to put it in a word, is a friendship, or disinterested love, for through charity we love God for his own sake, by reason of his most sovereignly lovable goodness." This true friendship is reciprocal, because "God has eternally loved all who have loved him." God cannot be ignorant of our love for him, because he bestows it on us, just as we cannot be ignorant of his love for us seen in the constant gifts of his benevolence. As the bishop puts it somewhat later in the chapter: "The charity which gives life to our hearts has not her origin from our hearts, but is poured into them as a heavenly liquor by the supernatural providence of the Divine Majesty."[92]

Human Nature: Francis's Theological Anthropology

Among the most studied aspects of Francis's teaching is his doctrine on human nature.[93] Although the saint rarely cites Genesis 1:26 explicitly, he often states that the foundation of his anthropology is that man is made in the image and likeness of God.[94] But what does this mean for Francis? In a revealing way, the bishop connects image and likeness to the double love command. In discussing the affinity (*convenience*) between God and man in *Treatise* I.15, he says that even a little attention to God brings with it "a certain delightful emotion of the heart that testifies that God is the God of the human heart" (*Oeuvres* IV:74). This great but secret affinity exists because we are created in the image and likeness of God. A later chapter (X.11) deepens this by showing that, "[a]s God created man in his own image and likeness, so did he appoint for man a love after the image and resemblance of the love which is due to his own divinity." Citing Bernard of Clairvaux on God alone as the reason we love God (*De diligendo Deo* 1), Francis argues that our image-nature means that we have the obligation not only to return love to God above all things, but also to love ourselves and to love our neighbors because all humans are made in the divine image and likeness. Thus, "the sacred love of man towards man is the true image of the heavenly love of man towards God." The highest love of the divine goodness of the Father is nothing else but "the perfection of the love of our brothers and companions."[95]

This central anthropological insight that to be an image and likeness of God is to be created to love God, ourselves, and other humans is the foundation for a teaching on human nature that can be characterized under three headings. First, Francis's anthropology is *optimistic*, because, despite the damages due to sin, humans retain the natural inclination to love God. Second, the bishop's view of humanity is *voluntaristic*, that is, the will is the supreme power of the soul and love dominates over the will. Finally, Francis's analysis of human nature is *psychological-mystical* in the sense that his understanding of the soul and its powers is directed to attaining union with God both here and hereafter.[96] Thus, there is a strong continuity between Francis's view of human nature and its powers and the higher activation of these in the mystical life.

The optimism of Francis in the *Treatise on the Love of God* raises the question of his understanding of the nature of sin and the role of freedom. Unlike Augustine, and especially the seventeenth-century extreme Augustinians, such as the Reformers, Banezians, and subsequent Jansenists, Francis took a moderate view of the Fall of Adam and its effect on humanity. In the discussion of the Fall in the *Treatise*, book II.5, Francis concentrates on the *felix culpa* understanding of original sin. Christ "died for all because all were dead and his mercy was more salutary to buy back the race of men than Adam's misery was to ruin it." Citing Paul on grace superabounding where sin abounded (Col. 1:16), as well as the Exultet passage, "O truly necessary sin of Adam," Francis boldly says that "in effect human nature has received more graces by its Savior redeeming than ever it would have received by Adam's innocence, if he had persevered therein."[97] Francis never denied the fact of original sin and its effects. Sin is the great obstacle to overcome in leading the life of devotion and pure love, as can be seen from the detailed analysis in the *Introduction to the Devout Life* about the need to purify the soul from mortal sin, venial sin, and all affections for sin (part I, chaps. 5–22). Nevertheless, the bishop of Geneva does not dwell, as did so many, on self-knowledge as the knowledge of our sinfulness and fallen misery, but rather he stresses God's superabundant mercy and goodness.

Francis's restricted attention to the state of man before and after the Fall has led some to accuse him of presenting an "a-historical" anthropology.[98] It might be rather called a "presentist" anthropology, in the sense that the bishop concentrates on the present situation of his readers—Where do they stand? How can they progress? The key is in harnessing desire. We should never desire evil things, or even good things that are not suitable to our place in life (*Introduction*, part V, chap. 18), but if we desire to be devout and to openly confess to this, half the battle is already won: "We must profess ourselves to desire devotion in order that we may be allowed to live devoutly."[99]

According to Francis, after the Fall we continue to have the *natural* inclination to love God above all things (*Treatise* I.16). From the time of his creation God gave man "a special natural inclination" (*une speciale inclination naturelle*), not only to love good things but to love Divine Goodness above all things. However, Francis did not hold, as many of his contemporaries did, that man was created in a state of pure nature. Rather, "the sweetness of his sovereign providence required that He should contribute to these blessed ones . . . as much help as should be necessary to practice and effectuate that inclination." This help is both *natural* as congruent with human nature and *supernatural* as coming from a special favor of God.[100] Although this natural inclination remains, it does not give us an inherent *power* to love God above all things (I.17). The inclination allows for a mere wish ("a will without will," *velleitas* for the Scholastics), not an effective desire.[101] Sin makes true and effective desire for God impossible. Thus, original sin affects the will more than the intellect. Therefore, grace is necessary for salvation: "But to advance as far as loving him above all things, which is the true maturity of love owed to such supreme goodness, belongs only to hearts animated and assisted by heavenly grace and in the state of holy charity."[102] The natural inclination to love God, while not sufficient in itself, is not useless, because it enables us to turn ourselves to God and ask his assistance (I.18). Francis's view here might seem Semi-Pelagian, but it actually is not, because we do not turn to God on our own power. Rather, our turning to God, our "doing what is in us to do" (Francis quotes the famous Scholastic dictum, *facere quod in se est*), is a result of a cooperation between God and the human agent, which affords us "some assistance" out of divine benevolence. The bishop uses another of his comparisons here: the natural inclination to love God is like the handle on the jug God gives us, which he then uses to draw us up to him.[103]

Thus, it is clear that Francis de Sales allows a measure of freedom to remain in fallen humanity.[104] How much freedom? Francis's theology of liberty is neither Semi-Pelagian nor Jansenist/Reformed. He does give a greater weight to human cooperation with grace than Augustine did, and, as we have already noticed above, he agreed with the Jesuit Molina that God's predestination operates *post praevisa merita*, that is, on the basis of having foreseen the merits that the just will gain by their response to God's love. This, plus Francis's insistence on the true universality of the divine will to save all people, is what accounts for the decidedly optimistic character of his anthropology. His emphasis on the cooperation between God and man in the process of redemption is perhaps reminiscent of some of the Greek Fathers, if expressed in a different key. As he once put it: "Grace is so gracious and so graciously seizes our hearts to draw them that she in no way offends the liberty of our will . . . , although the consent to grace depends much more on grace than on the will, while the resistance to grace depends on the will only."[105] If God always gives us the freedom to cooperate, this cooperation is meant to lead to the surrender of all our self-love in the radical "holy indifference" and "true freedom of spirit" that are the goal of the whole Salesian program.[106] Toward the conclusion of the *Treatise* in book XII.10, he summarizes in paradoxical fashion: "Theotimus, our free will is never so free as when it is a slave to the will of God, nor ever so much a slave as when it serves its own will. It never has so much life as when it dies to itself, nor ever so much death as when it lives to itself."[107]

What I am calling the voluntaristic and psychological-mystical aspects of Francis's anthropology are revealed through his teaching on the faculties and operations of the soul. A number of investigators have hailed his doctrine as original and even "modern" in the sense that it breaks with many medieval and early modern theories of the soul.[108] There is a measure of truth in this, although the point can be exaggerated, since Francis de Sales's views reflect his wide reading of a number of mystics and should not be judged against a few perhaps artificial general "models."

Francis's anthropology is most fully laid out in the dense chapters 11 and 12 of book I of the *Treatise*, which must, however, be viewed in the perspective of the whole of the first book. Chapter 1 of book I, as we have seen, deals with the relation of beauty and goodness and concludes that the will is the "monarch" of all the actions, feelings, inclinations, habits, passions, and faculties in human nature. Chapter 2 discusses how the will governs the outer and inner motions and powers, using the Augustinian triad of higher powers (memory, understanding, will), while chapter 3 deals with the relation between the will and the sensitive appetite and its motions, or passions.[109] Francis's treatment on the nature of the passions has been seen as an important part of his contribution to seventeenth-century thought.[110] Chapter 4 takes up the relation between the will and love. Since "love is the first complacency that we take in the good" (*l'amour estant la premiere complaisance que nous avons au bien*), it precedes all the other affections and passions. Thus, from one perspective, love rules over the will, because the will is moved by its affections, and, "Among them, as the first mover and first affection, love gives impetus to all the rest and causes all other movements in the soul."[111] From another perspective, however, the will rules over love, "since the will only loves while it wills to love," and the will decides what object to pursue. In chapter 5, Francis broadens his picture of the movements of the human mind by showing that the will, as intellectual and reasonable appetite, also has its movements, which are called "appetites" (*appetites*) to distinguish them from the "passions" (*passions*) of the sensitive part.[112]

Chapters 6–10 of book I constitute a short treatise on love as the most important of the appetites. Chapter 6 demonstrates that, just as the will governs all the other faculties, so too the love of God, although the last begotten of the affections, commands all other loves. In this chapter, two of the fundamental themes of Francis's mystical psychology first enter: the three theological virtues of faith, hope, and charity, which grant us salvation; and the "most high and sublime region of the spirit [*la plus haute et relevee region de l'esprit*], which is where divine love dwells." Chapter 7 contains one of Francis's central expositions of the general nature of love.[113] Francis says that the will has such a great agreement or affinity (*convenance*) with the good that, as soon as she perceives it, she turns to it to take delight in it. The sudden delight and complacency cause the will to move toward the object of delight in order to unite with it and receive a full enjoyment or "second complacency." Thus, there are five elements in love, which Francis compares to the five parts of a beautiful tree: (1) the root, which is like the innate affinity between the will and the good; (2) the foot of the tree, which is the initial complacency; (3) the trunk, which is like the movement toward the good object; (4) the branches, which are the "searches, pursuits, and other elements" the will employs in its movement toward the good; and (5) the fruits, which are the union and enjoyment, the second complacency that comes from gaining the beloved object. On this basis, despite those who argue that complacency is fundamental to love (Francis may have Thomas Aquinas in mind), he argues, "To put it clearly and precisely, love is simply the movement, outpouring, and progress of the heart towards the good."[114] Although love is born of complacency, maintained by complacency, and tends toward complacency, it is fundamentally a movement, "a true passion of the soul" (*une vraye passion de l'ame*).[115]

The final three chapters in this initial treatment of the nature of love analyze further aspects of this fivefold view of love. Chapter 8 explains that the "affinity" that first arouses love consists in both resemblance between the will and the object loved, but can also involve the "proportion, relation, or correspondence" between the lover and the thing loved, in which opposites may attract each other to form a new perfection. Chapters 9 and 10 round out the treatment of love by an analysis of union and its different types. Chapter 9 describes union by explaining the nature of the "chaste kiss," or union of hearts, of Song of Songs 1:1. Chapter 10 distinguishes two basic forms of union—first, natural unions, such as those in families; and then voluntary unions, which come in three forms: sense union of the body; reasonable union, such as takes place in knowing, and finally spiritual union, the highest form, which is realized in the reciprocal communication of souls.[116] This last is well manifested in the spiritual friendships that Francis cultivated throughout his life.

At this point, Francis seems to have felt the need to become more explicit about the powers and activities of the soul. What he lays out in chapters 11 and 12, however, is not without ambiguity, and some, like Bergamo, have seen a tension between the two chapters.[117] Chapter 11 addresses the why, or purpose, and the how (mode of operation) of the two portions of the soul.[118] The soul, although one, has three degrees of perfection: life, sense, and reason. Each of these has a particular property or inclination by which it is moved to accept or avoid things. The soul as living has "an occult or secret quality" that attracts or repels external things that are like or unlike it. As sensitive, the soul has the appetites of sensation, and as reasonable the soul has a rational will that Francis, following Augustine,[119] distinguishes into the *inferior* part that reasons and draws conclusions based on sense experience, and the *superior* part that depends on intellectual knowledge. In turn, the superior reason uses two sources of knowing: the *natural light* of science, and the *supernatural light* of faith, as well as of "particular illustrations, inspirations, and heavenly motions."[120] The reasonable aspect of the soul contains both the reason itself and the rational appetite, that is, the will, so Francis next analyzes the inferior and superior wills on the basis of examples taken from scripture (e.g., Jacob, Abraham, Christ). The inferior will is tied to the senses and the pleasure or pain they experience with regard to physical objects, while the superior will is directed to doing God's will and is therefore often in conflict with the inferior will, as we see from the example of Christ in the Garden of Gethsemane. Thus far, this all seems relatively clear; but the situation gets more complex when we turn to chapter 12.[121]

In this chapter Francis still insists that there are two portions of the soul, but he then introduces four degrees of reason that complicate the picture. Thus, as Bergamo puts it, "The interior space [of the soul] does not present itself in the Salesian model as an edifice of two stages, composed of a sensitive level and a rational level, but as an edifice with many stages, composed of a sensitive level and shifting set of levels in which the rational level subdivides each time."[122] The bishop illustrates the new fourfold model with two comparisons. The first is Solomon's "mystical temple" with its three courts and inner sanctum. The court of the gentiles signifies reasoning according to the experience of sense, while the court of the Israelites is the reasoning that follows the human sciences. The third court, the court of the priests, is reasoning according to faith. There remains the inner sanctuary. "Finally," says Francis, "beyond this there is a certain eminence or supreme point of reason and the spiritual faculty [*une certain eminence et supreme pointe de la rayson et faculté spirituelle*], which is not guided by the light of reason or of discourse, but by a simple intuition [*une simple veüe*] of the understanding and a simple movement of the will, by means of which the spirit acquiesces in and submits itself to the truth and to God's will" (IV.67). This is the first mention in the *Treatise* of the crowning element of Francis's mystical psychology, what he calls later in the chapter, *extremité et cime de nostre ame*, and *supreme pointe de l'ame*.[123]

In explaining the function of this supreme point Francis sets out a comparison between five aspects of the Old Testament description of the sanctuary, the high priest's once-yearly activity in it, and the objects it contains, with what takes place in the supreme point. First, the darkness of the temple sanctuary due to its lack of windows illustrates the fact that the light of reason does not operate in the supreme point. Second, in the sanctuary all the light enters by the door, which Francis equates with faith producing the sight of God's beauty and goodness. Third, the fact that only the high priest enters the sanctuary means that reason does not come into the supreme point, "but only the great, universal and supreme feeling [*sentiment*] that the divine will ought to be supremely loved, approved, and embraced." Fourth, the smoke of the incense used by the high priest indicates that "all the seeing [*veüe*] made in the supreme point of the soul is in some way obscured and veiled by the renunciations and resignations the soul makes." Here Francis takes an apophatic turn, saying that the soul wishes to close its eyes to all seeing of "the goodness of the truth and the truth of the goodness offered to her" in order to "more powerfully and perfectly accept it and by an absolute complacency [*complaisance absolue*] unite with it and submit herself to it." Finally, the last comparison links the three objects in the sanctuary (the tables of the law, the jar of manna, and Aaron's flowering rod) with the virtues of faith, hope, and charity, whose natural dwelling place is in the supreme region, whence they flow down to the inferior faculties.[124]

Two questions can be addressed to this summary of Francis's teaching on human nature. The first is whether there is a different position presented in chapter 11 with its bipolar model from that found in chapter 12, which is tripolar or even quadripolar, due to the introduction of the supreme point of the soul.[125] There is certainly a difference, but it may be thought that in chapter 12 we are dealing with an enriched perspective on the basic teaching of chapter 11, rather than a major change. The other question concerns the novelty or originality of Francis's anthropology. Is it the first modern theological anthropology?[126] Francis might seem to be taking an Augustinian direction in *Treatise* I.3, and, while he also uses Augustinian elements in I.11–12, his views are scarcely those of the bishop of Hippo. Bergamo contrasts Francis's model with the Aristotelian-Thomistic model and that of the Northern mystics. Francis's model is not that of Thomas, to be sure, but, since there is no single "*modèle rhéno-flamande*," the second comparison does not hold water. Francis's three levels of knowing (sense, reason, and faith—divine illumination) show a parallel with the tripartite structure of the soul found in some medieval monastics, such as William of St.-Thierry, but there is no proof that Francis actually took his triple view from the *Epistola aurea* written by William[127] but circulating under Bernard's name. There is a real newness to Francis's mystical anthropology, although the case of John of the Cross shows that many early modern Catholic mystics were creating new anthropologies to fit their mystical programs.

Two other interrelated issues need to be addressed before finishing this review of Francis's theological anthropology. The first concerns the sources, nature, and function of the "supreme point of the soul/spirit." The second deals with the "heart" (*coeur*), which Francis often mentions as the privileged place of communication with God (e.g., I.15-17). Is the heart a separate faculty or power of the soul? What is its relation to the "supreme point"? Is it merely a metaphor?

Francis discusses the *supreme pointe* often in the *Treatise*, as well as in his letters, although there are only a few occurrences of the term in the *Introduction*.[128] The frequent appeals to the "fine point" are not easy to reduce to any system, especially because Francis also employs terms like *fond, centre,* and *milieu*.[129] Are these to be seen as synonyms? How do they relate to terms like the Augustinian *acies mentis*, Scholastic discussion of the *synderesis*, the language of the *grunt* in Eckhart and other Northern mystics, and Teresa and John of the Cross on the *centro del alma*? The detailed study of Tullio Poli, as well as the treatments found in other Francis scholars, provides some answers to some of these questions, but by no means all.[130] Poli argues that Francis de Sales's notion of the *fine pointe* is not merely a transposing of earlier mystical views of the core of the self into a new French idiom, however much Francis may have been familiar with some of these mystical texts and their terminology.[131] Francis's view of the *fine pointe* is certainly not that of the *grunt* of Eckhart and his followers, because it cannot be ascribed to God, but only to a place in the soul where God enters. It is likely, as Poli argues, that Francis's attempts to understand how Jane de Chantal was able to maintain union with God while undergoing severe temptations against faith helped him to understand that there was an inmost dimension, or *fine pointe*, to the soul that could remain fixed on God no matter what trials of separation, and even despair, the other faculties were experiencing.[132] As noted above, biblical prototypes, especially Christ on the cross with his cry of despair, supported this view of the supreme point that could always remain in union with God.

The *supreme pointe de l'ame* has a central function in Francis's thought, as we will see below. Although related to terms like *fond* and *centre*, it differs from them insofar as they seem to be used primarily to describe that dimension of the soul where God is understood as communicating his gifts to humans, whereas the *supreme pointe* indicates that same dimension insofar as the soul cooperates with the divine action in attaining union.[133] Like many attempts to speak of the deepest, highest, most essential realm of the spirit, the *supreme pointe* is nondiscursive or, perhaps better, superdiscursive, an intuitive gaze and pure *sentiment*. Unlike the *apex affectus* of Bonaventure and the tradition of affective Dionysianism, however, Francis's *supreme pointe* pertains to both the intellect and the will. It is the seat of the three theological virtues, as we have seen in I.12. It also has an important role in the bishop's teaching on prayer, especially contemplative prayer.[134] Finally, the supreme point is the "place" where the human person accepts God and adheres to him in the love of complacency that involves total holy indifference.

The term "heart" (*coeur*) is one of the most ambiguous words in Francis's vocabulary, meeting us everywhere in the *Introduction to the Devout Life*, the *Treatise on the Love of God*, as well as the other writings.[135] As with the biblical use of the "heart," the general stress of the term is clear, although the many uses bring out different nuances. Preparing the heart, or using the heart in the pursuit of God, is one of the common themes of Francis's letters of direction. Therefore, the heart is the place where one can communicate with God. In the *Introduction*, part II, chapter 12, speaking of the importance of recollection, Francis says, "Remember, Philothea, to retire occasionally into the solitude of your heart, while you are outwardly engaged in business or association with others . . . [so that] your heart may remain in the presence of God alone. . . . Withdraw your thoughts from time to time into your heart. There, separated from all persons, you may treat heart to heart with God on the affairs of your soul."[136] Discussing the inner delight that transforms us into the God we love in *Treatise* VIII.1, Francis says, "Now this transformation is made insensibly by complacency, which having got entry into our heart brings forth another complacency, to give to him of whom we have enjoyed it."[137] It would be easy to give scores of examples of such heart-texts, but it is not always easy to say exactly what Francis means by "heart," because it has such a variety of meanings. Poli finds at least four primary senses of "heart." He summarizes his findings as follows: "Heart signifies rather the whole complex of affectivity, which includes dispositions, deep attachments, fundamental options that remain in the background, constituting such as a constant affective horizon. It has in large part a receptive sense, and has the aspect of an 'interior space.'"[138] Heart can also have more active dimensions, as when it is taken as the affective fullness that goes out from the self toward God. Obviously, there is no single meaning to "heart," but a wide range of possible uses to be determined by context. Nonetheless, it seems that "heart" primarily indicates the lower levels of the soul's affective relation to God, not the supradiscursive affectivity of the *supreme pointe*.

The Path to God: Progress through the Devout Life

Francis de Sales is a holistic thinker, so it is difficult and perhaps even artificial to separate the path of progress from the goal it seeks. Thus, what is presented in this section overlaps with what will be treated in the final section. Nonetheless, there is a pedagogical advantage to treating the material in two parts. This follows Francis's own practice in the writing of his two treatises. It has sometimes been thought that the *Introduction* is a devotional book for beginners, while the *Treatise* is for advanced mystics. But the devout life *is* the mystical life. All the practices taught in the *Introduction* are necessary for those who wish to reach union with God. But Francis did decide to write two books. The *Treatise* has more to say about the dynamics of the higher stages of the love relation to God, but its teaching is implied in the earlier work. This is because mystical union is not for the few—it is the goal of all, though naturally people will realize it in different degrees depending on the graces they receive. Francis de Sales is a mystical universalist.

Francis's notion of the soul's progress to God centers on two fundamental activities: devotion and prayer. Although he does not explicitly cite Thomas Aquinas in discussing the two, it is interesting to note that *devotio* and *oratio* are the two interior acts of *religio* in the *Summa theologiae* IIaIIae, questions 82–83. It is difficult not to think that the bishop was influenced by the Dominican in this connection. Francis's description of *la vie devote* is found in the first three chapters of the *Introduction*, as we have seen.[139] False devotions abound. Many think that the virtue they prefer constitutes the whole devout life, while they actually offend against many other virtues. True devotion is simple and comprehensive: "True, living devotion, Philothea, presupposes the love of God, and hence is nothing else but the love of God. But it is not always love as such." Divine love is the grace that adorns the soul, and it is also the charity that enables us to do the good. Francis continues, "When it [divine love] has arrived at that degree of perfection by which it not only makes us do well but also to do this diligently, frequently, and readily, then it is called devotion." He concludes, "In short, devotion is nothing else than that spiritual agility and vivacity by which charity works in us, or we work by her aid with alacrity and affection."[140] Francis's friend Jean-Pierre Camus summarized his teacher's view in his *The Spirit of St. François de Sales* when he recalled Francis saying, "[C]harity and devotion differ no more from each other than does the flame from the fire, for charity is a spiritual fire, which, when enflamed, is called devotion."[141] Henri Bremond also described Francis's view of devotion: "'devotion' is synonymous with 'perfection,' and 'perfection' with 'pure love,' in the crucifying sense given the term by the highest mystics."[142]

Chapter 2 describes the propriety and excellence of devotion, noting that it is not peevish and melancholy but is "a life gentle, happy, and amiable" (*une vie douce, heureuse et amiable*). What is perhaps most important about Francis's view of the devout life, however, comes in chapter 3, where he insists that all Christians should bring forth the fruits of devotion, not just people in religious life. What this means is that there are many forms of devotion fitted to the different vocations in the church. "So every vocation becomes more agreeable when united with devotion." As he says at the end of the chapter, "Wheresoever we are, we can and should aspire to the perfect life."[143] This universal appeal, especially when framed in terms of the different vocations of real people in early modern Europe, was extraordinary for the time.[144]

The mention of perfection in this text is significant. Many mystics had sketched out itineraries of the stages to perfection. Francis has a number of such discussions in both the *Introduction to the Devout Life* and the *Treatise on the Love of God*,[145] and it is noteworthy that the invitation to aim for perfection is present from the beginning of the *Introduction*. Two things must be remembered with regard to Francis's discussions of perfection. The first is that "[p]erfection of Christian life consists in conforming our wills to that of the good God. . . . So in order to acquire perfection we must always consider and recognize what God's will is in everything that concerns us."[146] The second is that, in considering the path to the more perfect life, Francis always treated those he advised with his customary discretion, moderation, and good sense. In *Conference IV* on "Cordiality and the Spirit of Humility," he advises the Visitandine nuns: "When we aim at perfection, we must aim at the center, but we must not be troubled if we do not always hit it."[147]

The bishop does not focus on any single model of progress to perfection; rather, he uses one or the other discussion of the stages as he sees fit within the development of his treatises. Still, we can say that even the earliest beginnings of the devout life sketched out in the five purgations discussed in part I.5–24 of the *Introduction* (see the discussion above) are integrally related to the higher stages of perfection detailed in the *Treatise*. This extends to other aspects of the relation of the two works. For example, the treatment of prayer in the *Introduction* deals primarily with meditation (II.1–9), while in the *Treatise* meditation appears as the first stage in a map of the ascending types of mental prayer. The use of the sacraments, so important in the *Introduction*, is for the most part presupposed in the *Treatise*. The practice of the virtues takes up the whole of part III of the *Introduction*, and Francis returned to the issue of the virtues in book XI of the *Treatise*.

Francis's view of the path to perfection is not a static or univocal—one might even say "perfectionist"—model. The wisdom and discernment of the bishop come through especially in his advocating for a process of continual betterment *on the road to perfection*. Francis wants his readers to have the *desire* for perfection and also the recognition of their own continuing imperfections and need to work for the goals that are possible for them. This attitude is reflected in many places in his letters. In a "Letter to a Young Lady on Perfection," he says:

> Our imperfection must accompany us to our coffin, we cannot move without touching earth. . . . We are dying little by little, so we are to make our imperfections die with us day by day; dear imperfections, which make us acknowledge our misery, exercise us in humility, contempt of self, patience, diligence, and in spite of which God regards the preparation of our hearts, which is perfect.[148]

Thus, the bishop counsels patience with the self, as well as patience with others. He advises his charges to be true to themselves and to their vocations, not always yearning for another self or way of life that they think might be better. In this connection he once asked Madame Brûlart, a friend of Jane de Chantal, "What is the use of building castles in Spain when we have to live in France?"[149] He advises another correspondent not to get discouraged by failures but to begin anew each day.[150] He cautions others not to worry about their worries, to realize that infirmity is not infidelity, and to correct immoderation moderately.[151] Camus notes that Francis thought that excessive eagerness was the mortal enemy of true devotion, and that he often said, "It is far better to do a few things well than to undertake many good things and leave them undone." One of his favorite sayings, also noted by Camus, was, "Soon enough, well enough."[152] The bishop gives the same message toward the end of the *Treatise* when he says, "God preserve us from those imaginary fervors that very often breed a vain and secret self-esteem in the bottom of our hearts. Great works lie not always in our way, but every moment we may do little ones with excellence, that is, with a great love."[153] Francis's view of the devout, that is, mystical life, is universal and also humane—Do the best you can, and always strive to do better.

The Goal: Heart-to-Heart Union with God in the Life of Prayer

Francis issued a universal call to devotion and perfection, that is, to the mystical life. In order to understand why the universal call is properly mystical we need to look at the saint's understanding of the adjective *mystique*. (Francis did not know the noun form, *la mystique*, which came into use shortly after his death.) Francis takes *mystique* in the inherited sense of "hidden, secret," that is, as a qualifier to be used of the deep meaning of many aspects, practices, and objects pertaining to the Christian life. He speaks of the "mystical sense" of scripture (e.g., *Introduction* II.12), albeit rarely. In the *Treatise on the Love of God* he describes many things as mystical[154] but also uses the term adverbially, such as to imitate mystically (I.10), and to describe mystically (VI.6).

The most important use of "mystical" in Francis is what he has to say about the time-honored term *théologie mystique*. Chapter 1 of book VI of the *Treatise* bears the title "Description of Mystical Theology Which Is Nothing Else but Prayer."[155] No one previously had brought out the equality of the two terms quite so directly, but Francis assumes that this was the meaning of tradition, as he shows by quoting liberally from established mystical authorities (Bernard, Basil, Bonaventure, Chrysostom, Augustine, John of Damascus, Teresa, etc.). It is obvious that Francis is using the term "prayer" in the widest possible sense as the comprehensive activity of loving God. In order to please God we must have a love that is affective (the love of complacency), as well as a love that is effective (the love of benevolence).[156] The first exercise, that of affectivity, consists principally in prayer, prayer understood not just as petition, but as Bonaventure and many other Fathers grasped, "all the acts of contemplation." Since all the discourse of prayer concerns God, Francis draws the conclusion: "Therefore prayer and mystical theology are one same thing. It is called theology, because, as speculative theology had God for its object, so this also treats only of God." Francis acknowledges three differences between the two theologies: (1) speculative theology concerns God as God; mystical theology treats God as lovable; (2) speculative theology speaks of God's interaction with humans, while mystical theology speaks of God in Godself; and (3) speculative theology tends to the knowledge of God, mystical theology to the love of God. Mystical theology is properly "mystical," because "its conversation is altogether secret, and there is nothing said in it between God and the soul save only from heart to heart by a communication incommunicable to all but those who make it." In conclusion, he gives the following definition: "Prayer and mystical theology are nothing else but a conversation in which the soul amorously entertains herself with God concerning his most amiable goodness to unite and join herself thereto." This is an apt summary of Francis's entire message.[157]

Mystical theology is prayer, and prayer is nothing else than loving conversation between God and the soul. Before considering Francis's account of the ascent to God by the degrees of prayer (books VI–VII), it will be helpful to step back a bit to look in more detail at two features of his expositions in books II–V: first, the role of the three theological virtues of faith, hope, and charity in bringing divine love to birth in us; and, second, how the two main exercises of love, that is, complacency and benevolence, are related.

Book II, chapters 13–22 contain an analysis of how love becomes active in faith, hope, and charity. These chapters sketch the process of conversion from its first beginnings to the true friendship of dilection with God. The journey starts with the action of prevenient grace on the natural inclination that even the sinful will maintains toward the good (II.13). The soul is compared to the mythic "apodes" (footless) birds, whose wings (i.e., natural inclination to love God) cannot function without the wind, or inspiration of grace, by which God works within us without us. These motions of love, a beginning and still imperfect love, are forerunners of the act of faith. Francis compares them to the first buds on the "mystic tree" that will someday be capable of producing true fruit. The second stage is the gift of faith when God proposes to the *understanding* the obscure mysteries of belief and gives complacency or delight to the *will* so that it moves the understanding to consent to these truths (II.14).[158] The soul's natural inclination to the Highest Good, but inability to love it effectively, leaves the soul anxious and uneasy before the gift of faith. When faith gives knowledge of God, the object of the inclination, our will immediately feels "the holy heat of heavenly love" (II.15). This is the beginning of the desire to unite forever with this Lovable Goodness—"Let him kiss me with the kiss of the mouth" (Song of Songs 1:1). Such a desire is the expression of the theological virtue of hope, which "is nothing else but the loving complacency we take in the expecting and seeking of our Sovereign Good" (II.16). The love that is in hope is good but imperfect, because it is a love of cupidity (i.e., we love God for ourselves, desiring that God should be *ours*). It is, however, a well-ordered cupidity in that we love God as our final felicity (II.17).

The highest form of love is found in charity, which loves God's infinite Goodness *in itself*, not just because it is our good. General love is present from the time of the soul's conversion, but it needs to be "drawn" deeper and deeper into complacency with the divine will by the soul's cooperation with grace (II.21). Finally, "God, by a progress full of ineffable sweetness, conducts the soul . . . from love to love, as from mansion to mansion, till he has made her enter into the land of promise, I mean into the most holy charity, which to say it in a word, is a friendship, a disinterested love, for by charity we love God for his own sake."[159] This love of friendship with God allows for continual communication with him, both interiorly and through the sacraments, especially the Eucharist. It is not just a simple friendship, but a friendship of dilection by which we make a choice to love God in a special way. Together with faith and hope, charity makes its abode in "the point and summit of the spirit" (*la pointe et cime de l'esprit*), where it reigns as queen seated on the will as on a throne. Francis de Sales, like John of the Cross and many other mystics, puts the three theological virtues at the center of progress towards God, although his distinction between the general love of God and the love of charity is unusual.

Loving God by having complacency in him implies the question of how we may be said to love God by benevolence. This issue, also important for understanding our progress to union, is taken up in book V, Francis's most detailed treatment of the two exercises of love mentioned so often in the *Treatise*. As usual, he begins from the anthropological perspective, saying, "Love is nothing else but the movement and outflowing of the heart towards the good by means of the complacency we take in it."[160] Complacency is the motive of love and love is the movement of complacency. Complacency toward God is born through the faith that tells us of God's incomprehensible perfection; it is nourished by meditating on him and is brought to action by the will using its freedom to perform acts of approbation and rejoicing. The treatment of complacency that follows (V.2–5) emphasizes the mutuality of the interaction between God and creature in the exercise. Francis says, "Our complacency is augmented in perceiving that God is pleased to see us pleased in him." Here the bishop makes use of one of his most frequent and appealing examples of the cooperation involved in the love between God and the soul, comparing it to the act of nursing by which a mother feeds the infant at her breast: "The bosom and breasts of the mother are the storehouses of the little infant's treasures: he has no other riches than those, which are more precious than gold and silver, more beloved than all the rest of the world." The mother is the chief cause of the feeding, but the infant takes delight in this nourishment "and makes little movements towards his mother's breast and dances with joy to see them uncovered."[161] Once again, Francis distinguishes between the "first complacency" that results from what the heart feels when it begins to delight in God and the "second complacency" that comes from growing union. Second complacency is reciprocal, which Francis illustrates by citing Song of Songs 2:16: "My beloved to me," which indicates our enjoyment of God's goods as though they were our own, and "I to him," which means that God is not only ours but that we are in him. "Complacency makes us possessors of God, drawing into us his perfections, but it also makes us possessed of God, applying and fastening us to his perfections." This movement of satiation and hunger is unceasing, a form of what Gregory of Nyssa called *epektasis*: "Now in this complacency we satiate our soul with delights in such a manner that we do not yet cease to desire to be satiated; and relishing the divine goodness we desire yet to relish it; while satiating ourselves we would still eat, as while eating we feel ourselves satiated."[162] In the second complacency the soul no longer seeks God in order to find him, but as ever "dilating" itself in the enjoyment it already possesses.

Such a love of second complacency also involves compassion; that is, it is like the love of the Blessed Virgin Mary that "draws all the pains, all the torments, travails, sufferings, grief, wounds, passion, cross and death" of Jesus into her body. Mary is the model for how we must focus our full complacency not on our own delight in God but in sharing the sufferings of the God-man. Francis employs examples of natural condolence with the sufferings of others (V.4) to heighten the importance of the condolence and complacency we should find in Christ's Passion, as mystics like Francis of Assisi and Catherine of Siena demonstrated (V.5). Compassion, which is mentioned in the *Introduction* part III, chapter 2, among the "little virtues," was an important practice for Francis.[163] His friend Jean-Pierre Camus describes the bishop as a model for his compassion for both human beings and animals.[164]

What does this exploration of the nature of the love of complacency mean for love as benevolence? The crucial point here is that our love of complacency in God cannot be selfish—a delight in our delight. Rather, "we desire not the complacency for the pleasure it yields us, but purely because this pleasure is in God."[165] A crucial distinction noted here is that we can never give true love of benevolence to God, because benevolence depends on our love supplying something to the beloved and God lacks for nothing. Hence, our love of benevolence toward God is always conditional; that is, *if* God could ever have an increase in his life, felicity, and so on, we would desire this with all our hearts. God's will toward us begins in benevolence, the good he gives us in which he then finds his delight or complacency. In reverse, our love toward God starts from our complacent delight in God to move on to the "quasi-benevolence" we direct to him (the first commandment of love of God), whose true meaning and measure are found in the real benevolence we direct to our neighbor (the second commandment). Aspects of this Salesian insight are explored in the second part of book V (chaps. 6–12), but the full exposition must be gleaned from the whole exposition of the two exercises of love found throughout the *Treatise*. The reciprocity of the love of complacency and the love of benevolence is a major feature of this part of book V.[166] Once again, the teaching is christologically grounded, as is evident in the "Hymn to the Wounded Savior's Heart" found in book V.11.[167] Francis de Sales's devotion to the suffering Christ as the essential paradigm for the meaning of love of God is striking here and elsewhere in the *Treatise*.[168]

We are now in a position to approach the two major forms of mystical ascent to God set forth in the *Treatise on the Love of God*. The first is the ascent by the degrees of prayer (books VI–VII), where the bishop not only describes the various types of prayer but also analyzes the mystical gifts given in contemplation.[169] The second form of mystical ascent centers on the modes of agreement with the divine will—the love of conformity and the love of submission (books VIII–IX). The final three books, which many authorities see as addenda, form a reconsideration of key aspects of the love of God.[170]

Ascent I: The Degrees of Prayer (Books VI–VII)
In this section, which we may say deals with *amour affective*, Francis was influenced by reading Teresa of Avila, adopting many aspects of her teaching, though within the parameters of his own thought. Chapter 1 of book VI, as we have seen, sets the stage by arguing for the equivalence of prayer and mystical theology. Chapter 2 takes up meditation, which Francis sees as already a part of mystical theology and not just as a preparation or propaedeutic.[171] For Francis, meditation is a general term for all focused thinking, that is, "simply an attentive and reit-

erated thought proper to produce good or evil affections," although "the word meditation is ordinarily applied to the attention we have to divine things to stir us up to love them."[172] Therefore, meditation proper is not just any kind of attentive thinking, but is a consideration of divine things directed to "excite the will to holy and salutary affections and responses," as Francis had done in the model meditations he gave in the *Introduction to the Devout Life* I.8-13. Meditation takes place in the mind but is directed to the affections, as Francis shows in a long exegesis of the ideal meditator, "the mystical bee," who is the bride of the Song of Songs.

The second stage of prayer is contemplation, which Francis defines as "a loving, simple and permanent attention of the spirit to divine things" (*une amoureuse, simple et permanent attention de l'esprit aux choses divines*; VI.3). The first difference between meditation and contemplation is that contemplation enjoys the fruits of the honey of devotion that the mystical bee gathers by her meditations. Both interdependent exercises are aimed at love and affectivity, meditation in a discursive way, contemplation by a simple regard. Contemplation has a reciprocal relation to love: "Love having excited in us contemplative attention, that attention breeds reciprocally a greater and more fervent love, which at last is crowned with perfection when it enjoys what it loves."[173] Hence, there is a dialectical movement from the sight of divine beauty to the love of divine goodness and back again. In chapter 4, Francis continues this analysis of the relation of sight, that is, the knowledge in the understanding, to the love it produces in the will, noting that "the great Saint Thomas" teaches that love can go far beyond the knowledge of God found in the intellect.[174] In proving the superiority of love over understanding (which is not actually Thomas's view), Francis cites a series of theological authorities and saints.[175]

The second difference between meditation and contemplation appears in chapter 5. Meditation deals with the details of the objects calculated to move us, while contemplation takes a simple and collected view of its object. Francis speaks of it as "a single steady regard of the spirit" (*un seul trait arresté de nostre esprit*).[176] The bishop illustrates this by passages from the Song of Songs, natural examples, and citations from mystical authorities. Chapter 6 presents the third difference between the two forms of prayer—contemplation demands no labor.[177] Francis explains this by distinguishing three modes of contemplating. First, we can contemplate a single divine perfection, such as goodness. At other times, we can contemplate several of God's infinite perfections at the same time but with a simple view and without distinction. Finally, we can contemplate a divine action, such as creation or redemption. "But take which of these three ways you will," he says, "contemplation still has this excellence that it is made with delight, for it supposes that we have found God and his holy love, that we enjoy it and delight in it saying, 'I found him whom my soul loves; I held him and I will not let him go' (Song 3:4)." On the basis of a quotation from Song 5:1, the bishop distinguishes between the work of eating, which is like meditation, and the ease of drinking, which is compared to contemplation, and can extend even to inebriation. The ancient mystical topos of *sacra ebrietas* makes its appearance here in an important passage:

> To be inebriated means to contemplate so frequently and so ardently that one may be out of oneself so as to be wholly with God—a holy, sacred inebriation [*sainte et sacree ivresse*], which unlike bodily inebriation, does not alienate us from spiritual sense but only from bodily senses, one which does not stupefy or brutalize us, but angelizes and as it were divinizes us [*ains nous angelise et, par maniere de dire, divinize*].[178]

Francis does not speak of divinization often,[179] but it is obvious he thought that divinizing, or coming to participate in the divine nature, was the goal of the contemplative life.

Both meditation and contemplation had been discussed by many mystical authors, including Teresa of Avila. When Francis turns to the next level of prayer in chapter 7, "loving recollection" (*recueillement amoureux*), the influence of Teresa, who is actually cited, becomes evident. Like the Carmelite, Francis distinguishes between two forms of recollection: the active recollection by which we place ourselves in God's general presence when we begin to pray, and "the recollection that is not made by [our] love's command, but by Love itself, that is, we do not make it by free choice, . . . but God at his pleasure works it in us by his most holy grace."[180] This passive recollection (Francis does not use the term) takes place through God's action alone and is the result of a new form of divine presence: "It happens then that sometimes our Lord imperceptibly infuses into the depths of our hearts a certain agreeable sweetness, which testifies to his presence [*qui tesmoigne sa presence*]." Then, all the powers of the soul, and even the exterior senses, turn within to the "most interior part," that is, the fine point. This whole chapter, with its many examples and citation of authorities from scripture and the Fathers, returns to the theme of presence again and again, even citing the reception of Christ really present in the Eucharist as an example.[181] It is obvious that God is present to us in many ways, but that the prayer of passive recollection is the result of a special form of presence, whose action Francis describes by saying, "[A]t the simple presence of God, or the simple feeling that he sees us, either from heaven or from any other place outside us, . . . our powers and faculties assemble and gather together within us out of respect for his divine Majesty."[182] The presence of God is a common theme across Francis's writings, although he nowhere provides an explicit discussion of the various forms of presence.[183]

In the *Interior Castle* IV.2-3, Teresa discussed both the "prayer of quiet" and the "prayer of recollection," which she seems to have understood as distinct, if overlapping, states of prayer. Francis de Sales follows her in this in chapters 8-11 of book VI, although he draws the prayer of quiet close to the "sleep of the faculties," or "spiritual sleep," which Teresa discusses in *Interior Castle* V.1.3-4.[184] The repose of the soul set out in chapter 8 sometimes goes so deep that the soul and all its powers "fall asleep," save for the will which "does no more than receive the delight and satisfaction that the presence of the Well-Beloved affords." In this repose, the soul is not conscious of herself or of the enjoyment itself—all is lost as in the sleep of a baby.[185] The prayer of repose seems to be the same as the "simple wordless prayer" that Francis spoke of in a number of his letters.[186] In describing this prayer in chapter 9, Francis turns to his favored image of the child asleep on the mother's breast to illustrate this and says that he found this fit comparison in the "Blessed Mother Teresa."[187] In this repose of presence, the soul does not need to exercise the understanding, the memory, or the imagination: "It is the will alone that softly, and as it were tenderly sucking, draws the milk of this sweet presence."[188] In chapter 10, Francis further explores the quality of this repose in God, arguing that it must remain direct and simple and not become the subject of reflexive acts—doubling and bending back on itself. Some people always want to scrutinize their progress; others "feel, see, and relish their contentment." Francis goes on: "There is a great difference, Theotimus, between being occupied with God who gives us contentments and being busied with the contentment God gives us."[189] Above all, he advises, avoid anxiety and also recognize, as Teresa said, that sacred repose need not be disturbed by necessary actions of the body, or by involuntary distractions.

The final part of the discussion of "Holy Quiet" comes in chapter 11, where Francis describes its degrees. He says that it is sometimes in all the powers united with the will; sometimes in the will alone, both sensibly and at other times not. Francis seems to be trying to create a loose taxonomy of the higher stages of prayer, involving the spiritual senses of perceiving the pleasure of God's presence (touching?), and speaking, hearing, and so on, but again the dominant intention is not to make a careful discrimination of the spiritual senses, but rather to emphasize the powerful interior conviction of the presence of God. To place oneself in the presence of God and there remain is the essence of this stage of prayer. Francis also appeals to another favorite analogy comparing the soul to the piece of sculpture placed in a niche of some great prince in his honor. If the statue could be given life and asked why it is stationed there without anything to do, Francis says it would respond that it is perfectly content just to be where its master wishes it. At this point, the bishop brings in for the first time the ultimate aspect of his view of the mystical path, holy indifference: "Now this quiet, in which the will acts solely by a most simple acquiescence in God's good pleasure, since it wills to be in prayer without any aim but to be in God's sight as it shall please him, is a supremely excellent quiet." The will no longer has any self-interest. He says the will, now in its highest point, "is content to have no further contentment but that of being without contentment out of love for the contentment and good pleasure of its God in whom it rests."[190] Contentment without contentment, or holy indifference, the highest stage of Salesian mysticism, will appear often in his later discussions of the mystical path. It is, as he puts it here, "the climax of loving ecstasy" (*le comble de l'amoureuse extase*).

The remaining chapters of book VI tease out some aspects of mystical repose and do not constitute a new stage in the progress of mystical theology/prayer. Francis is less interested than Teresa and John of the Cross in providing a clear road map of the stages of prayer,[191] but rather wants to explore different dimensions of the prayer of repose and the prayer of union to be discussed in book VII. The ecstasy mentioned at the end of chapter 11 seems to provide a launching place for the following discussions, which concentrate on the different modes of *ex-stasis*, or "standing outside the self." Thus, chapter 12 explores the "flowing out or liquefaction of the soul in God" (*l'escoulement ou liquefaction de l'ame en Dieu*).[192] The theme was an ancient one, and the Northern mystics had developed a rich theology of flowing out and back into God. Francis appeals not to this tradition but rather to biblical precedents like the Song of Songs, as well as to contemporary saints, for example, Teresa of Avila, Philip Neri, and Francis Xavier. Flowing out into God is the characteristic of the total complacency of the beloved into the lover, a "true ecstasy" in which the soul transcends her natural existence. It implies a kind of annihilation of self. When souls who have attained such excesses of holy love return to themselves, according to

Francis, they "find nothing on earth that can content them, and living in an extreme annihilation of themselves, remain much weakened in all that belongs to the senses."[193] Francis's willingness to use the language of annihilation here is important. Some scholars have claimed that Francis de Sales has no place for mystical "annihilation," meaning by this the annihilation we find in Benet of Canfield, Pierre de Bérulle, Jean-Jacques Olier, and later Madame Guyon. This is true, but the bishop of Geneva was perfectly willing to talk about annihilation, at least in the sense of the reduction to nothing of the natural operation of the will and the other faculties.[194] Annihilation language was common coin in early modern France, and it would have been remarkable if Francis had not used it.[195]

In chapter 13, Francis turns to another common topos of mystical discourse, the wound of love (*blesseure d'amour*).[196] All the affections and passions of the mind are based on the penetrating power of love that pierces the heart and makes a passageway for them. Love is indeed a complacency, but it can also wound, either when the beloved object is absent, or when we are not able to love God as much as we desire. Here Francis again turns to the notion of love as epektasis, or unfulfilled fulfillment: "This desire which can never be fulfilled is like a dart in the side of a generous spirit. Yet it is a welcome pain that issues from it, because whoever has an earnest desire to love also has an earnest love to desire. . . . He desires to love, and therefore receives pain; but he loves to desire, and therefore receives a sweet reward."[197] Chapter 14 continues the discussion by speaking of other ways in which holy love wounds the heart, particularly the reciprocal wound of love referred to in Song of Songs 4:9, a text often cited by mystics. Francis, like many others, refers this to Christ's Passion as arousing our compassion: "We, seeing the Savior of our souls wounded to death by love of us, 'even to the death of the cross' (Phil. 2:8), how can we but be wounded for him, but wounded with a wound as much more dolorously amorous as his was amorously dolorous, and a wound as great as is our inability to love him as much as his love and death require?"[198] Another form of the wounding of love happens when a soul truly loves God, but God treats her as if he is distrustful of her love. Then, says Francis, "the soul is put into an extreme anguish, as it is unsupportable for her to see and feel even the mere pretence God makes of distrusting her."[199] (This is the first mention of mystical dereliction in the bishop of Geneva.) Other forms of the wound of love are the memory that there was a time when we did not love God and the thought that there are still many people who do not love him. Citing the examples of Teresa of Avila's "Transverberation" and Catherine of Genoa's conversion, Francis concludes, "However it may be, it is a marvelous thing that the pain of wounds received from divine love is an agreeable pain. All who experience such pain accept it and would not change it for all the world's pleasures."[200]

The final chapter of book VI continues the consideration of the wound of love, this time under the rubric of the "loving languishing" (*langueur amoreuse*), or sickness of love. Citing Plato's picture of the poverty and neediness of love from *Symposium* 203cd, Francis says that the same properties are found in divine love, as a host of Christian examples of those who have been sick with love demonstrate (e.g., Paul, Francis of Assisi, the bride of the Song of Songs, and many women mystics). Much of this long chapter is devoted to a treatment of the stigmata of St. Francis as a perfect example of suffering for love both in mind and in body: "Love then drove the interior torment of this great lover St. Francis to the exterior, and wounded the body with the same dart of pain with which it had wounded the heart."[201]

Book VII of the *Treatise on the Love of God* takes up what Teresa called "the prayer of union," although Francis does not use that term, speaking instead of "The Union of the Soul with God that is Perfected in Prayer."[202] This book deals with the higher stages of mystical union that the Carmelite nun treated in her *Life* 18–20 and also in the last two Dwelling Places of the *Interior Castle*, though it recasts Teresa's material in particularly Salesian ways. Chapter 1 begins by saying that this book will not deal with the general union of the heart with God, but with the particular acts and movements that bring us to become more and more united with God in the manner of two physical objects being pressed together so closely that they interpenetrate. Once again, the bishop turns to the example of the baby nursing at the mother's breast to indicate how the union is really caused by God, although we cooperate with our feeble efforts. Francis notes two forms of this pressing together to deeper and deeper union—the first by way of frequent movements of the will expressing the desire for loving union; the second "by way of a continued insensible pressing and advancing of the heart in the divine goodness." Francis gives several examples of the latter, such as that of the tree whose roots are always slowly growing deeper though they cannot be seen. He closes by returning to the theme of the special divine presence that brings about all the higher forms of union: "When I speak here of the sacred perception of the presence of God, I do not mean to speak of a sensible perception [*sentiment sensible*], but that which resides in the summit and supreme point of the spirit where divine love reigns and carries out its principal exercises."[203]

Chapters 2 and 3 set out the different kinds of union in summary fashion. Francis specifies five forms. The first two are general: (1) union without cooperation where we simply follow God's action drawing us; (2) union where we cooperate, being drawn willingly. The next three seem to be modalities of cooperative union. The first is the union where we seem to begin the process and only later become conscious of God, although it was God who was effecting the union from the start. The second is when the union is made so insensibly that we are neither aware of God's operation or our own cooperation. The third is when we feel the embraces of union by sensible actions on God's side as well as our own. These can be (a) in the will only; (b) in will and understanding; and (c) sometimes in all the faculties of the soul gathered around the will. Francis illustrates these by appealing to examples from the lives of the saints and passages from the Song of Songs, but there is a hint of artificiality about this complicated taxonomy.[204] Chapter 3 turns to the highest type of union, "union by suspension and ravishment" (*par la suspension et ravissement*). Such a union is pure and strong, because it seeks God only for Godself. When it is most especially strict and close, "it is called by the theologians inhesion or adhesion, because by it the soul is caught up, fastened, glued, and affixed to the divine majesty, so that she cannot easily loose or draw herself back."[205] Citing Teresa of Avila (*Life* 18.7, 12; 20.1-21), Francis says that when such a union is short, it is called mere union, trance, or suspension (*union, ou suspension, ou pendement*); but when it is long, it is called ecstasy or rapture (*extase ou ravissement*). Francis closes by noting that he is speaking here of the union made by conscious exercises of love and charity, such as ejaculatory prayer, not the permanent union of the great saints who are not *being* united but are already permanently united to God. Thus, we have three forms of the highest union of suspension and ravishment: short, long, and permanent.[206]

The following three chapters (VII.4-6) carry the analysis of ravishment further by distinguishing three kinds: rapture of the intellect, rapture of the will, and rapture of act and life.[207] This distinction is not in Teresa, and, although Francis uses some elements from Richard of St. Victor's teaching on *raptus/alienatio mentis* (*Mystical Ark* V.5-19), the tripartite structure is his original contribution. The first rapture/ravishment is termed an ecstasy because "we go out of, and remain out of, and above, ourselves, to be united to God." Francis says that the first kind is by way of understanding and admiration, that is, encountering a new truth about God accompanied by beauty and goodness (VII.4).

The second species of ravishment is that of the fruition of affection as it is drawn to God as beautiful and good (DN IV is cited here). This rapture happens in the will when "God touches it with the attractions of his sweetness, . . . so the will touched with heavenly love moves forward and advances towards God, . . . leaving all its earthly inclinations, and by this means enters into a rapture, not of knowledge, but of fruition." These two forms of ecstasy can exist together, mutually encouraging each other, but they also can be experienced separately. Both forms of ecstasy, however, are capable of being imitated by the devil and are therefore potentially dangerous. This is not so in the case of the third form of ecstasy (VII.6), that is, the "ecstasy of work and life" (*l'extase de l'oeuvre et de la vie*).

In *Treatise* VII.6, Francis gives two marks for determining when an ecstasy comes from God as against one caused by natural means or the devil.[208] First of all, divinely sent ecstasy affects the will more than the intellect, so, although God may send illuminations to the intellect, if they are not accompanied by more fervent love of God, they are dangerous. Second, true ecstasies are always directed to the third form of rapture, that is, to more effective living of the Christian life. These are the heavenly inspirations that raise us up above the ordinary Christian life toward "a supernatural, spiritual, devout and ecstatic life, that is, a life that is in every way beyond and above our natural condition." What does this mean in practice? Francis goes on to illustrate. "Ecstasy of life" is nothing more than the life of true, heroic, Christian virtue—forsaking all one's own possessions; accepting reproaches, attacks, and even martyrdom; living in absolute chastity. "This," he says, "is not to live in ourselves, but out of and above ourselves, and because no one is able to go out of himself in this manner above himself unless the eternal Father draw him, hence it is that this kind of life is a perpetual rapture and a continual ecstasy of action and operation."[209] This is a good example of Francis's universal democratized view of mystical union. The height of contemplative union has been redefined as action. To be sure, Francis had predecessors in this redefining process. In his *Four Degrees of Violent Charity*, Richard of St. Victor, whose writings Francis knew, had said that the ecstatic union of love of the bride yields to the active and "insane" love of the busy mother. In the Seventh Dwelling Place of the *Interior Castle*, Teresa of Avila, in distinction from the mystical itinerary laid out in her earlier *Life*, taught that it was in the uniting of action and contemplation, of Martha and Mary, that the height of union was attained. Francis, however, seems to be saying something slightly different. First of all, he is not clear whether the individual soul needs to have experienced the first two ecstasies in order to attain the third. Second, the third ecstasy is not described as fusing action and contemplation, but solely in terms of action. Francis may have intended something closer to what we find in his predecessors, but his fruitful ambiguity here is telling.

The subsequent chapters in book VII do not remove this ambiguity. In chapter 7, the bishop returns to the dangers involved in "raptures of admiration," saying that ravishment in prayer can be dangerous, a diabolical deceit: "Blessed are they who live a superhuman and ecstatic life, raised above themselves, though they may not be ravished above themselves in prayer. But there are many saints in heaven who were never in ecstasy or rapture of contemplation."[210] Thus, one can become a saint without enjoying the first two forms of ecstasy, but no one ever became a saint without the third form. Here Francis's suspicion (not rejection) of ecstatic states of consciousness comes to the fore. Similarly, in chapter 8 the bishop reads Paul's exhortation to the ecstatic life in 2 Corinthians 5:14 ("The charity of Christ presses us, judging this") as an invitation to living a life of total dedication to God even to the point of death. Again, the model and inspiration are Christ on the cross. The chapter closes with a passionate invocation of dying along with Jesus, so that one can partake of "the holy ecstasy of true love, when we live not according to human reason and inclinations, but above them, following the inspirations and instincts of the divine Savior in our souls."[211]

The mention of Christ's death on the cross as the model and inspiration for the third form of ecstasy sets the agenda for the remainder of book VII, which centers on *mors mystica*, that is, the death that is always involved in total abandonment to the love of Christ.[212] In chapter 9, Francis says that the supreme effect of affective love is the death of the lovers, which in terms of divine love he says can be caused by "a holy love so violent that it sometimes causes a separation between body and soul that makes the lovers die a most happy death, better than a hundred lives."[213] This and the following chapters are filled with examples of saints whose loving dedication Francis was eager to celebrate. Most of the examples are hagiographical, though some, like the story of the knight who went on pilgrimage to the Holy Land and died of love on the Mount of Olives (VII.12), are anecdotal.[214] Francis concludes the book with two chapters (VII.13-14) on the death of Mary, who died a "sweet and tranquil death" for the love of her Son.

Ascent II: Love of Conformity and Love of Submission

The second model of the mystical life that Francis presents in the *Treatise on the Love of God* is that of the relation of the love of conformity (book VIII) and the love of submission (book IX), what we might call the road of *amour effective*. This is not so much an entirely new model as a further exploration of the third form of ecstasy, ecstasy of action. How are we to understand the love that enabled the saints to live lives of ecstatic goodness and service, even to the point of accepting death? For the bishop of Geneva the answer lies in perfect conformity to God's will leading to submission to God's "good pleasure" in pursuit of the end of attaining the holy indifference that enables us to ask for nothing and to refuse nothing. These two forms of love are our responses to the two ways in which the divine will is understood by us—the love of conformity is directed to God's expressed, or signified, will (*voluntas signi*) and the love of submission answers to God's will of benevolence (*voluntas beneplaciti*).

We conform our wills to the will of God as it is made known to us by his commandments, counsels, and inspirations (VIII.1). The initial complacency and pleasure we take in God's goodness to us gives birth to a second complacency by which we are pleased to give something back to him: "So, by often delighting in God, we become conformed to God, and our will is transformed into that of the Divine Majesty, by the complacency it takes in it." The affinity that exists between God and the soul grows into a mutual complacency that transforms us more and more into God. "My heart," says Francis, "feeds on the pleasure it takes in him, and his on my taking pleasure in him for his own sake."[215] However, it is not just the love of complacency that conforms us to God's will but also the love of benevolence (VIII.2). "The love of complacency draws God into our hearts, but the love of benevolence casts our hearts into God."[216] Such benevolence desires that all glory, honor, and adoration be given to God. Even on the "impossible supposition" that there were no hell or heaven, or even no obligation or duty to God in justice—the love of benevolence itself would demand this return to God.

Francis then moves on to a more detailed consideration of God's will.[217] In chapter 3, he says that, although God's will is in reality one, there are two ways of conceiving of it: God's will as it is in itself, and "God's will in the particular effects of it, as in the events that touch us, and accidents that befall us, and finally in the declaration and manifestations of his intentions." This last aspect of God's particular will is what Francis, following theological tradition,[218] calls "God's signified will" (*volonté signifiee de Dieu*), "because he has signified and made manifest onto us that it is his will and intention that all this should be believed, hoped for, feared, loved and practiced." The signified will expresses God's desire that we do good and avoid evil, but it leaves us our freedom to obey or disobey. The fact that we have the power to resist depends on our natural liberty. If we do actually resist God's desire, it proceeds from our own malice, but if we obey, God contributes "his assistance, his inspiration, and his grace." He concludes, "God's signified will remains the true will of God even if it be resisted, though it has not the effects it would have if it were seconded."[219] The Gospel as read in and taught by the church is the fundamental source for God's signified will.

The remainder of the short book VIII spells out the differing ways of conforming ourselves to God's signified will. The three modes that Francis discusses are (1) conformity to the commandments, (2) conformity to the counsels, and (3) conformity to the inspirations.[220] The starting point is to realize the essential meaning of the signified will—God's will that all be saved as shown in his death on the cross: "Our sanctification is the true will of God, and our salvation is his good pleasure, nor is there any difference at all between good-pleasure and delight, and, consequently between the divine delight and the divine good will."[221] The first mode of our conformity with God's signified will is by way of obedience to, and even love of, the commandments (VIII.5). The second mode consists of our conformity to the counsels of perfection, on which Francis spends some time (VIII.6-9). The commandments oblige us, while the counsels only invite us. Nonetheless, if we really wish to please God, the counsels have great utility: "Hence it is that the love of complacency, which obliges us to please the Beloved, consequently urges us to follow his counsels, and the love of benevolence, which desires that all wills and affections should be subjected to him, causes that we not only will what he ordains, but also what he counsels and exhorts to."[222] Nevertheless, the law of charity sometimes limits the applicability of the counsels for particular people. For example, charity may require a person to give aid to his aging parents, rather than giving away all his goods and entering a monastery. This is because "[t]he counsels are all given for the perfection of the Christian people, but not that of each Christian in particular" (VIII.6). The counsels are of great importance for the transforming effect of the love of God. Francis says, "The soul that loves God is so transformed into the divine will that it merits rather to be called God's will, than to be called obedient and subject to his will."[223] No one is bound to practice all the evangelical counsels, but each should do what he is able to do (VIII.9).

Francis next turns to the conformity to be given to inspirations sent from God (VIII.10–13). "Inspiration," Francis says, "is a heavenly ray which brings into our hearts a light full of heat by which it makes us see the good and inflames us with a desire to pursue it."[224] Examples given include the word of the preacher, the sight of good examples, the effect of tribulation, reading the lives of the saints, and so on. With regard to the inspirations, we might say that our conformity involves a process of discernment by which we come to see what is God's will for us through many circumstances of our everyday life.[225] The chapters that follow are filled with uplifting stories about the saints and quotations from spiritual writers to illustrate the nature and variety of inspirations. Many inspirations are ordinary, but Francis also gives advice about extraordinary inspirations, that is, those that go beyond the usual and sometimes are even in conflict with common laws and observances of Holy Church (e.g., hermits who go out into the desert where they cannot hear Mass). These, he says, are more admirable than imitable (VIII.12). In conclusion, Francis provides three assured marks of lawful inspirations: perseverance, peace and gentleness of heart, and humble obedience.

Francis de Sales closes off his treatment of the love of conformity with a chapter (VIII.13) discussing what he calls "A Short Method to Know God's Will." The bishop says that one should not be anxious about little issues, such as whether we should hear Mass in one church rather than another. Only matters of real moment, such as the choice of a vocation, should be seriously pondered to see what is God's will. Even in matters of moment, we should use humility, consulting with a director or other spiritual people to discern what is God's will. Once having made a choice, we should not second-guess the decision: "The resolution being taken in a holy fashion, we should not doubt the holiness of the execution."[226]

Book IX shifts attention to the other form of the ecstasy of action, the love of submission.[227] God's absolute will, or the will of good pleasure (*volonté de bon playsir/voluntas beneplaciti*), is the cause of everything that happens, save sin (IX.1). It is known to us by events; that is, if something happens, it is because God willed or permitted it. Everything that is, was, or will be reveals the wisdom, power, and goodness of God. Therefore, we must take complacency not only in the benefits God gives us in his mercy, but also in the tribulations he bestows on us through his justice, although these too are really for our benefit. Everything should be welcomed with the hymn of eternal acquiescence—"Thy will be done on earth as it is in heaven" (Matt. 6:10). Our union with God in the will of good pleasure, then, will primarily be through how we learn to deal with tribulation and suffering in this life, as chapter 2 begins to lay out. The first thing to learn is the correct perspective: "Look at tribulations in themselves and they are dreadful; behold them in the will of God, and they are loves and delights."[228] We should love God's good pleasure not only in consolations but even more in tribulations, because "the principal effect of love is to make the lover suffer for the thing beloved." Christian doctrine, the only true philosophy, has three principles on which it bases its exercises: abnegation of self; carrying the cross; and following our Lord, both in self-renunciation and in doing good works. The danger found in loving God in consolation is that we may easily come to love the consolation more than God. Hence, there are three degrees of the ascent of the love of good pleasure: (1) loving God's will in consolation; (2) loving God's will in his commandments, counsels, and inspirations, which lead us to renounce our own will and abstain from some pleasures; and (3) loving sufferings and afflictions for the love of God (IX.2). In chapter 3, Francis reflects on what we can call mystical dereliction, that is, the paradoxical way in which God may remain present while the mystic undergoes the severest affliction, citing the case of Angela of Foligno.[229] Probably reflecting on his spiritual direction of Jane de Chantal, who had experienced severe temptations against faith and a "Dark Night" period, Francis says that it is possible for the whole heart to be in trouble, moaning, and lamentation, while "sacred acquiescence is still preserved in the depths of the heart, in the highest and most delicate point of the spirit."[230] Here "it seems to retreat to the very end of the spirit as in the dungeon of the fortress, where it remains courageous."[231] Francis closes the chapter by introducing the two ways in which the love of submission works: either by "holy resignation," in which we still want to live, for example, but are willing to die if that be God's will; and by the higher act of "holy indifference," which goes beyond resignation.

Chapters 4 through 9 of book IX are a thorough exploration of holy indifference, a key issue in Francis's mysticism.[232] "Indifference goes beyond resignation," says Francis, "for it loves nothing except for love of God's will so that nothing touches the indifferent heart in the presence of God's will."[233] If we seek only God's will, then it does not matter to us whether it comes to us through consolation or through tribulation, although tribulation offers the stronger proof of our dedication, as demonstrated in the case of Job. The indifferent heart is like a ball of wax in God's hands, ready to take any form he wishes. Francis so emphasizes the need for total surrender to God's will that he supports "the impossible supposition," as it has been called, that is, the willingness to be consigned to hell, *if* that would be God's wish:

> God's Will is the sovereign object of the indifferent soul. . . . She is conducted by the Divine will, as by a beloved chain, which way soever it goes, she follows it. She would prize hell more with God's will than heaven without it, . . . so that if by supposition of an impossible thing she should know that her damnation would be more agreeable to God than her salvation, she would quit her salvation and run to her damnation.[234]

This was to become an issue in the Quietist controversy.

Indifference is not particular but is meant to extend to all things, in both the natural and the spiritual life (IX.5). Francis's primary model for holy indifference is Christ on the cross, beset by all manner of affliction and so swallowed up in grief as to cry out, "My God, my God, why have you forsaken me?" (Matt. 27:46). Yet in the "point of his spirit" he was still enjoying eternal glory. The analogy that Francis suggests here between Christ's cry of dereliction on the cross and the sufferings of mystics who have felt abandoned by God was scarcely new and is still found in modern mystics, as in figures such as Thérèse de Lisieux and Mother Teresa of Calcutta. Francis extends his treatment of indifference into other realms that were later to prove contentious. In chapter 6, for example, he praises Abraham for his total indifference as to whether or not Isaac would die, calling on the examples of the saints (e.g., Francis of Assisi, Ignatius Loyola, John of Avila) to defend his case. In chapter 7, he goes further, asking how far it is possible to be indifferent to our own progress in virtue, an issue that again was to be discussed in the Quietist Controversies at the end of the seventeenth century. Noting that it is God alone who crowns the fruits of our endeavors with success, he recommends that we do what we can to acquire virtue, but we should remain tranquil, realizing that God alone gives success: "Let us not be troubled at finding ourselves always novices in the exercise of the virtues, for in the monastery of the devout life everyone considers himself always a novice."[235] Thus, we must be sorry for our faults, but with a firm and not troubled sorrow. Rebellions in the sensual appetite, and other failings, such as anger, are given us by God so that we might strengthen our resolve and virtue by fighting against them. Once again, Francis's wisdom and pastoral moderation come to the fore. Perfect deliverance from the troublesome passions is not possible in this life: "God wills us to have enemies and it is also his will that we should repulse them. Let us then behave ourselves courageously between the one and the other will of God . . . ," that is, by submitting to the trials sent us by the divine will of good pleasure, while also resisting our assailants by conforming to God's expressed will.[236] Thus, we live between the two expressions of the one divine will in a spirit of active discipleship.

Chapter 8 takes on another delicate topic, that is, how it is possible to unite our wills with God's permission of evil? God does not will evil but permits it. What then should be our attitude? We should adore the holy will by which God permits sin but always detest sin itself, imitating Christ, who throughout his life exhorted sinners to repentance and who died to redeem them. Above all, Francis insists that we should not abandon sinners: "However obstinate sinners may be, let us never desist from aiding and assisting them. How do we know but that they may do penance and be saved?"[237] In good Augustinian fashion, however, Francis says that, at the end of time, the blessed will approve both the sentence of damnation of the reprobate and the salvation of the elect.

Chapter 9 deals with the purity of indifference, which Francis illustrates by his famous example of the deaf musician, a lute player who, although he had lost his hearing and took no pleasure in his playing and singing, still was happy to perform at the ruler's command, even if the ruler was not there. Francis contrasts this with those misled souls who started out by loving God for God's sake, but imperceptibly came to delight more in their own act of love than in God, thus "loving the love instead of the Beloved" (*aymant l'amour en lieu d'aymer le Bien-aymé*). Chapter 10 continues to explore this theme, obviously one of importance to Francis as a spiritual director. He insists that God is best served in the vocation and place to which we have each been called, and the key thing is to seek God's satisfaction, not our own. He admits that it is very hard to love God without also loving the pleasure we take in loving God; but still, "Our task must be to seek in God only the love of his beauty, not the pleasure which is in the beauty of his love."[238] A similar message is true of prayer. We should pray directly and immediately to God and not reflect back on ourselves to see how well we are praying. Do not think of the prayer you are making, but of the God you are praying to. Those who pray only to enjoy its subjective sweetness will soon abandon prayer in times of dryness and trouble. Chapter 11 returns to the story of the deaf musician to illustrate the nature of holy indifference. There is great pleasure in truly pleasing God and knowing that God himself is pleased with this love, but when God turns his face from us, the faithful soul is left in torment. The soul in the state of indifference, however, "ceases not, for all that, to love You faithfully, or continually to sing the hymn of its dilection, not for any delight it finds in it, for it finds none at all, but for the pure love of Your will."[239]

Chapter 11 closes with a strong passage on mystical dereliction that is in many ways comparable to what John of the Cross says about the Dark Night. When we have lost all consolation in the exercises of holy love, we enter into a situation of "extreme distress" (*un extreme ennui*). Here even the spirit and the "highest point of reason" can provide no relief. The soul is deprived of the usual consolation of thinking that "this too will end," but rather is unable to think that these troubles will ever cease. Faith alone is the rock of courage: "Faith, which resides in the supreme point of the spirit assures us that this trouble will have an end, and that one day we shall enjoy a true repose."[240] The rest of the soul, however, can scarcely hear faith's encouragement. Once again, Francis turns to Jesus on the cross and the compassion that Mary and John had with his sufferings. They remained constant in love even when the Savior "withdrew all his holy joy into the very summit of his soul and left no joy or consolation at all in his Divine Countenance."[241] A long Good Friday Sermon of March 1622, "On the Passion of the Lord and What It Means," addressed to the Visitandine nuns, deals with Jesus's seven last words, stressing the final word recorded in Luke 23:46, "Father, into your hands I entrust my spirit." For the bishop, this is the perfect expression of the Christ-like abandonment and indifference that are the height of the mystical life. We too must entrust our spirit to the Father. Francis asks his hearers to address God as follows:

> Do you wish me to be in dryness or in consolation? Into your hands I entrust my spirit. Do you wish me to be contradicted, to experience repugnances and difficulties, to be loved or not, to obey this one or that one, and in whatever it may be, in great things or small? Then into your hands I entrust my spirit.... If we act thus, we will indeed be able to say at the hour of our death, as did our dear Master: "All is consummated, O God."[242]

The final chapters of Book IX of the *Treatise* pick up on this theme of mystical death realized in the state of indifference. In chapter 12, Francis says that the soul overcome with interior anguish has the power to believe, trust, and love God, but the soul cannot see whether she really is doing so. "Hence," he continues, "she thinks that she has no faith, nor hope, nor charity, but only the shadows and fruitless impressions of these virtues, which she feels in a manner without feeling them."[243]

Nevertheless, these "spiritual anguishes" purify and refine the soul so that it is more immediately united, "heart to heart," with God than ever, because it is united without the medium of satisfaction or desire. Seemingly abandoned by love, the soul seeks love in vain in the exterior senses, in the imagination, and in the will. He goes on: "At length she finds it in the top and supreme region of the spirit where it resides, yet the soul does not recognize it and thinks it is not love, because the greatness of the distress and darkness hinders her from perceiving its sweetness. She sees it without seeing it, meets it but does not know it, as though all passed in a dream and imagination."[244] At that stage all the soul can do is surrender herself, following the model of Christ on the cross and saying, "Father, into your hands I commit my spirit."

This is mystical death, which Francis explicitly takes up in chapter 13 as he explores how, when the human will dies to itself, it is capable of living purely in God's will. He finds a particular fittingness in the French word for death, *trespas*, that is, a "passing over" (Latin *transitus*). Of course, this is not a literal death, because "our will can no more die than our soul, yet it does sometimes go out of the limits of its ordinary life to live wholly in the Divine Will." The will is annihilated, since it no longer wills anything, "but gives itself ever totally and without reserve to the good pleasure of the Divine Providence," to such a degree "that itself is seen no more, but all is hidden with Jesus Christ in God, where it lives, not it, but the will of God in it."[245] This hint of the language of Galatians 2:20 ("I live now, not I . . .") confirms that Francis de Sales has a place for the mystical annihilation that was to take on such a large role in seventeenth-century French mysticism, but it also makes clear that the annihilation or death of the will is in terms not of its substance but of its operation. The will no longer works as a human will; its operation has been absorbed into God's will. The will no longer says, "Your will be done, not mine" (Luke 22:43), but rather, "Lord, I commend my will into your hands" (Luke 23:46).

Book IX.14 returns to the theme of the two wills of God, the *voluntas signi* and the *voluntas beneplaciti*. There are two ways of walking with God, says Francis. The first way is walking with the steps of our own will by which we conform ourselves to God's signified will as expressed in his commands, counsels, and inspirations. The second way is when we walk with the Savior without any will of our own, "letting ourselves be simply carried at his divine good pleasure, as a little child in its mother's arms, by a certain kind of consent which may be termed union of unity of our heart with God's."[246] Here we simply acquiesce with everything that God sends us, for good or ill. After attaining indifference and the death of the will, according to chapter 15, we will be able to perform what Francis calls "a still higher exercise" (*un exercise beaucoup plus eminent*), which is to apply our attention fully to the Divine Goodness and bless it not in its effects but in itself and in its own excellence. Francis says that it is difficult to express "this extreme indifference of the will." It is not right to call it mere "acquiescence" (*acquiescement*), because acquiescence is an act of the will. Nor should we say that the will "accepts or receives," or even "permits," since these too involve actions, at least passive actions. Rather, "[i]t seems to me the soul which is in this indifference, and which wills nothing, but lets God will what pleases him, should be said to have its will in a simple and general state of waiting [*doit estre ditte avoir sa volonté en une simple et generale attente*], since waiting is not a doing or acting, but only the remaining prepared for some event."[247] Such waiting is voluntary but is not an activity; it is a "simple disposition to receive whatever will happen." Again Francis turns to Christ on the cross, who expressed his indifference in two ways: first, in the anguish and bitterness of his soul even in the midst of indifference when he said, "My God, my God, why have you forsaken me?"; and then in his direct and final word of indifference, "Father into your hands I commend my spirit." The soul who imitates Christ in this holy indifference has learned to strip away its affection for consolation, virtues, and spiritual exercises so as to "care for nothing but the divine Majesty's good pleasure" (IX.16). This stripping leaves the soul naked, but only to be reclothed by the risen Christ with the various affections and gifts of God it had before, but not now as things agreeable *to us*, but "because they are agreeable to God, profitable to his honor, and destined to his glory."[248] This is the true meaning of holy indifference.

Further Issues on the Love of God
It seems that with book IX Francis de Sales had completed his original intention for the *Treatise*, providing a biography of divine love (books I–V) and laying out two interrelated models of the exercise of love to attain union with God—first by the ascent of prayer (books VI–VII) and then by the practice of love of conformity and love of submission (books VIII–IX). The final three books of the *Treatise* take up ancillary issues that may have occurred to the bishop as he was writing the main treatise. Book X addresses the commandment to love God above all things. Book XI shows how love organizes the virtues, actions, and perfections of the soul, an issue addressed in part III of the *Introduction* but expanded upon here. Book XII provides counsels on the progress of love. We will look at these final books in brief fashion.[249]

"Since the love of God is the end, the perfection, and the excellence of the universe," the commandment to love God above all things is the first and greatest of the commandments.[250] Book X unpacks the meaning of this command by considering the commandment in itself, as well as its relation to other forms of love. The love of God that is the subject of command on earth will be a matter of pure contentment in heaven (X.2). The supremacy of the love of God, however, does not rule out other obligations of love (love of family, love of country, love of friends), as long as love of God is given the sovereign place—"The Divine Goodness is not offended by seeing in us other loves, so long as we preserve for him the reverence and submission due him."[251] Just as in heaven there will be different degrees of glory among the blessed, so too on earth, even among those who love God with all their hearts, there will be some who love more and some less. "All true lovers," says Francis, "are equal in this, that they all give their heart to God and with all their strength, but they are unequal in this, that they give it diversely and in different manners."[252] There is also the issue of the progress of love, which the bishop takes up in X.4-5 by introducing a new itinerary of the degrees of perfection, making use of the Song of Songs.

Francis notes that Solomon, the composer of the Song, had many women in his court. He uses four groups of women mentioned in Song 6:7-8 as figures of the various perfections of souls who love and serve Jesus. First, there are "the young maidens without number," who are types of the beginners who have recently turned from sin. They love the divine sweetness, but with a mixture of other affections (X.4). The second group is "the fourscore concubines," whom Francis identifies with those who "have progressed to some extent in the love of God and have cut away whatever love they had for sinful things, but still entertain dangerous and superfluous loves."[253] They love Divine Goodness "above all things, but not yet in all things." Hence, while they are entitled to some of the favors mentioned in books V and VI, such as the prayer of recollection and prayer of repose, they do not yet enjoy "divine unions with the Spouse." The two final groups are described in chapter 5. "The threescore queens" are the souls who do not love superfluities "but love only that which God wills and as he wills." They have "so great a union with the Spouse that they share his rank and are queens, just as he is King." In the final position is the one and only bride, the dove, the Shulamite. She is "the queen of queens, the most loving, the most lovely, and the most beloved of all the friends of the Divine Beloved, who not only loves God beyond all things and in all things, but also loves only God in all things, so that she loves not many things, but only one thing, which is God himself."²⁵⁴ Following a number of earlier commentators on the Song of Songs, Francis gives a Marian interpretation to the praise of the one dove (Song 6:7-8; 7:10), identifying her with "the Blessed Virgin our Lady, who has perfectly arrived at this height of excellence in the love of her Dearly Beloved."²⁵⁵ This new fourfold description of the stages of progress to union is a kind of supplement to the two major itineraries set out earlier in the *Treatise*.

In chapters 6-7 Francis explores the question of how we know that we love God above all things. The bishop notes that in the Vulgate text of Matthew 22:23 (*Diliges Dominum Deum tuum ex toto corde tuo*) the word "dilection" is used rather than just "love," because dilection (*dilectio*), as Thomas Aquinas says, is a love of choice (STh IaIIae, q. 26, a. 3). Hence, although there are many forms of love, the love of God must be the supreme object of choice as his goodness is the most excellent (X.6). Although we can never know with certainty if we love God beyond all things, there are signs of this, especially when a love of creature opposes love of God and we still choose to follow God and his will. In the following chapters (X.8-9) Francis gives examples from scripture and tradition to illustrate how God is to be loved above all things. In relating the love of God to our other loves, two stand out: love of ourselves and love of the neighbor. In chapter 10, Francis says that both natural knowledge of our dependence on God and the gift of grace move us to love God above ourselves. In chapter 11, as already noted, he argues that, because humans are created in the image and likeness of God, we love in charity both ourselves and all other human beings.

Two final issues considered in book X concern the relation of love and zeal (X.12-16) and the life of Christ as a model for all the forms of love. Love desires the good of the beloved and has hatred for everything contrary to the object loved. This explains the origin of zeal: "When love is ardent and has reached the point of wanting to take away, remove, and divert anything opposed to the beloved object, it is called zeal."²⁵⁶ Zeal for a good object is good; for a bad object bad. Francis includes jealousy under zeal—zeal looks to the complete good of the beloved object, whereas jealousy looks to a particular good. When we are zealous for worldly and temporal things, we often fall into envy because we do not want other people to possess these goods. Francis engages in some moral reflection in X.12, but his main intent in discussing zeal is revealed in what follows: an account of how God can be said to be "jealous" of us (X.13); a treatment of the zeal or jealousy we should have for God (X.14); advice for the direction of holy zeal (X.15); and an account of how certain saints were able to exercise their zeal with anger (X.15).

In the course of chapter 13, Francis touches on the question of "pure love," which was such an important issue throughout the seventeenth century and became so controversial in the Quietist Controversy.[257] God is jealous of us (Deut. 5:9; Exod. 24:14), because he wants us to be only his in a jealousy not of cupidity but of supreme friendship. In truth, our love of God is useless to him who possesses total felicity but is of supreme advantage to us. Hence, he wants our love for him to be "invariable, quite pure, quite solely his" (*invariable, toute pure, toute unique pour luy*). "Jealous love," says Francis, "tolerates no mixture of another affection, willing that all be for the Well-Beloved." Francis goes on to cite the teaching of Catherine of Genoa on the properties of pure love. "Perfect love," he says, "namely love that has gone as far as zeal, cannot suffer any mediation, intervention, or mingling with anything else, not even with God's gifts. It even becomes so rigorous that it permits love of paradise only with the intention of a more perfect love for the goodness of him who gives it."[258] This last phrase, raising the issue of the legitimacy of the soul's desire for the reward of heaven, was to become an item of controversy decades later.

In the final chapter of book X, Francis shows how Christ is the model of all the "sacred acts of divine love" that he has been describing, listing twelve motivations Christ "exercised in the whole work of our Redemption."[259] Christ loved us with both the love of complacency and the love of benevolence. Third, he united himself to us in an "incomprehensible union." He also "flowed out into us" as the source of living water (Jer. 2:13) and loved us to ecstasy, as St. Denis says in *Divine Names* IV. Christ emptied himself, indeed, annihilated himself to stoop down to our humanity and fill it with his divinity: "So has the love of man ravished God and drawn him into an ecstasy" (*tant l'amour de l'homme a ravi Dieu et la tiré a l'extase*; V:231). The following five marks of Christ's love toward humanity are other themes that Francis had discussed in relation to love earlier in the *Treatise*: admiration, contemplation, loving quiet, tenderness, and zeal. In the eleventh place, Christ had also suffered "a thousand thousand languors of love," especially in his Passion. Finally, "This Divine Lover dies amongst the flames and ardors of love, by means of the infinite charity which he had towards us, and by the force and virtue of love, that is, he died in love, by love, for love, and of love. . . . Love was not content to have only made him subject to death for us unless it had made him dead."[260]

Book XI, with twenty-one chapters, is the longest of Francis's *Treatise on the Love of God*, perhaps surprisingly so, since it treats of the virtues, a topic already taken up at length in the *Introduction*. The bishop's purpose here, however, is more expansive and systematic. He wishes to show how all the virtues are contained in charity as the form of the virtues (*caritas forma virtutum*), a teaching that goes back to Augustine and is found also in Thomas Aquinas.[261] He also wants to show how love embraces the seven gifts and twelve fruits of the Holy Spirit, as well as the eight beatitudes. A few of the more important chapters of this long book will be noted here.

The pagans practiced human and moral virtues, but the fruits that came from these were small and received only temporal rewards (XI.1). These natural virtues, however, are raised to a supernatural level by the love of the heart that has received grace (XI.2). The supernatural virtues of faith, hope, and charity, as well as the virtues employed in God's service (religion, penitence, and devotion), "not only receive the impression of divine love whereby they are raised to a great value, but they wholly incline towards it, associating themselves with it, following and serving it on all occasions."[262] In book XI.4, Francis returns to his earlier theme of the necessity of employing both effective love and affective love, that is, both the "Joseph" who organizes all the soul's powers to serve God and the "Benjamin" who gains his life in sweetness. Francis's penchant for extensive examples from nature, human activity, and the Bible come to fore in the following chapters—lengthy texts that were probably more appreciated in the seventeenth century than today. He insists that, although the virtues are not acquired altogether in one instant, "virtues cannot have their true integrity and sufficiency unless they be all together, as all philosophy and dignity assure us" (XI.7); hence, as chapter 8 teaches, "Charity Comprehends All the Virtues," both the four cardinal virtues now raised to a supernatural level and the strictly supernatural virtues of faith, hope, and charity (XI.8). The chapters that follow (XI.9–14), important for Francis's moral theology, are not directly relevant to his mysticism.

Toward the end of this book, Francis takes up some issues long involved with mystical theory. Since the time of Gregory the Great, the seven gifts of the Holy Spirit (Isa. 7:9) had been seen as integral to the soul's path to union with God. The bishop devotes a chapter to explaining how these gifts (wisdom, understanding, science, counsel, fortitude, piety, fear of the Lord) are all modalities of love. He says, "Charity, therefore, comprehends the seven gifts, and is like a fair lily that has six flowers whiter than snow and in the midst of a beautiful little garden golden hammers of wisdom, which beat into our hearts the taste and loving relish of the goodness of the Father our Creator, of the mercy of the Son our Redeemer, and of the Holy Spirit our Sanctifier."[263] This is a reminder that, although Francis is less overtly Trinitarian than some other Christian mystics, the action of the Triune God is always present in his thinking. The mention of fear among the gifts of the Spirit seems to have inspired the three following chapters (XI.16–18), in which Francis explores how love can coexist with fear. The answer depends on a distinction of the kind that the bishop of Geneva learned from his reading of the Scholastic theologians, especially Thomas Aquinas. He distinguishes three kinds of fear: servile and mercenary fear, filial fear, and the fear of spouses (XI.16). Servile fear is always necessary and will remain as long as we are in this life (XI.17–18), but the transition to filial fear is needed for true progress toward union (XI.18). Francis presumes he has said enough about spousal "fear" already, so he does not dwell on it here. In this long addition, Francis also treats how love contains the twelve fruits of the Holy Spirit (Gal. 5:22), and the eight beatitudes of Matthew 5:3–12 (XI.19), before concluding with a typically Salesian reflection on how three kinds of sadness (*tristesse*) are inimical to holy love (XI.21).

Francis's digressive additions come to a conclusion with book XII, on practical counsels for the soul in its progress toward union with God. The book reminds us that Francis was a pastor and spiritual director, as well as a contemplative. He never exercised an academic position but was a devoted bishop in the post-Tridentine mode. Although theologically astute, Francis was a preacher and teacher in a Renaissance Humanist mode, always ready to pile up fitting examples in pleasing language to drive home his point.

Book XII is an apt summary of much that went before, as well as a practical addendum. The subject of his book, says Francis, is not the natural temperament for loving, but "the supernatural love that God out of his goodness pours into our hearts and whose residence is in the supreme point of the spirit, a point which is above all the rest of the soul and independent of all natural disposition."[264] A natural temperament inclined to love may make the exercise of supernatural loving easier, but a more difficult temperament ("peevish, harsh, melancholy, churlish") may win a greater victory in loving on the supernatural level. The most important condition for loving, as Francis says in chapter 2, is having the desire to love: "The desire to love and love itself depend on the same will. For this reason, as soon as we have formed a true desire to love, we begin to have love. In proportion as this desire grows, love also is increased. One who ardently desires love will quickly love with ardor."[265] This is the true and good spiritual avarice. In its pursuit a person should avoid all distractions and keep fixed to the intention of loving God (XII.3). Nonetheless, lawful occupations do not hinder us from the love of God, as the example of saints like Bernard, King Louis, and Charles Borromeo show (XII.4). The truly devout soul finds no conflict between prayer and action: "The devout heart has no less love when it turns to external duties than when it prays. In such hearts their silence and their speech, their action and their contemplation, their work and their rest, equally sing the canticle of their dilection."[266] Action and contemplation are one for the devout soul.

A series of short chapters on the practice of divine love follows these introductory comments. Francis's teaching, as ever, is balanced and moderate, with an emphasis on the little virtues. Rather than planning great projects and imagining great crosses to come, it is better to do little works of charity and love as they present themselves every day, such as giving a cup of water to a thirsty traveler. If heavenly love is present, all the small daily victories are more profitable to our souls than we can imagine—condescension to others; bearing with troublesome neighbors; acknowledging our own imperfections; loving our abjection; keeping our souls in balance; and the like (XII.6). "Charity gives weight to all that we do" (*Charité qui donne le poids a tout ce que nous faysons*), so that "[t]o do little actions with a great purity of intention and with a strong will to please God is to do them excellently and then they greatly sanctify us."[267] The bishop of Geneva cites Thomas Aquinas (STh IaIIae, q. 88, a. 1, ad 2) in holding that, when we have the habit of charity, all our actions will glorify God, even if we do not make an explicit intention to serve God in doing each of them (XII.8).[268] Francis advises Theotimus to make use of the spiritual practices he had taught Philothea in the *Introduction to the Devout Life*, such as the yearly renewal of good resolutions, morning prayer of offering all to God, and daily use of ejaculations (XII.9).

Using the example of Abraham's willingness to sacrifice Isaac and Isaac's acquiescence, Francis invites the reader to the sacrifice of his or her free will in a holocaust to God: "Let us renounce this miserable liberty, and let us forever subject our free will to the rule of heavenly love. . . . For God's sake, let us sacrifice our free will and make it die to itself so that it may live to God!"[269] Chapter 11 sets out five key motives already discussed in the *Treatise* for making this sacrifice: God's goodness; natural Providence; supernatural Providence; salvation; and eternal glory. Chapter 12 provides three practices for bringing these motives to mind in daily life, the most important being the consideration of the divine benefits brought by Jesus our Redeemer. "Benefits do not inflame us," says Francis, "unless we behold the eternal will which destines them for us, and the heart of Our Savior who has merited them for us by so many pains especially in his death and Passion."[270] Fittingly, then, the *Treatise on the Love of God* concludes with a short chapter on "Mount Calvary as the Academy of Love." Here the bishop grows eloquent in hymning the paradoxes of this most powerful motive for the love of God:

> Theotimus, Mount Calvary is the mount of lovers. All love that does not take its origin from the Savior's Passion is foolish and perilous. Unhappy is death without the Savior's love; unhappy is love without the Savior's death. Love and death are so mingled in the Savior's Passion that we cannot have the one in our hearts without the other. Upon Calvary we cannot have life without love, or love without the Redeemer's death.[271]

Conclusion

Francis de Sales is the most important French-language mystic of the seventeenth century. Today he is not as widely read as the great Spanish mystics of the preceding century—Ignatius Loyola, Teresa of Avila, and John of the Cross, if only to judge by the number of recent editions and translations. Nonetheless, the writings of all four of these mystics have been studied over the centuries. Contemporary readers may find the bishop's prolix and fervid prose at times trying; some have also criticized his anthropocentric perspective as lacking the objective emphasis on saving mysteries found in earlier mystics.[272] But we should not use one standard to determine the success or failure of mystical classics. Francis the bishop wrote from a pastoral and practical perspective centered on the human subject whom he wished to bring to saving self-surrender of will, holy indifference as he called it, following the example of the Savior who laid down his life for humans. Francis does not engage in speculation for the sake of speculation, nor does he construct a full theological basis for his teaching on the path to union with God. Nonetheless, his writings are founded on the deepest mystery of all Christian belief—God's love as manifested in Jesus on the cross. Francis de Sales presents that mystery and its implication for life, not just to a select group of spiritual adepts who have fled the world but to all believers in his conviction that union with God, both here and hereafter, is the vocation of everyone.

Appendix
Followers of Francis de Sales: Jane de Chantal

One may say that the followers of Francis de Sales are multitude, since so many later spiritual writers and thinkers were influenced by the *Introduction* and the *Treatise on the Love of God*. Nonetheless, for the story of French seventeenth-century mysticism, it is important to look at some of the bishop of Geneva's friends and collaborators to get a sense of the immediate impact he had. There are a number of figures traditionally included among the close disciples of Francis, notably his biographer, Jean-Pierre Camus (1583–1652), the bishop of Belley.[273] Camus published a treatise in 1640 entitled *The Mystical Theology* (*La théologie mystique*), a title that was something of a misnomer. Francis de Sales, as we have seen, was hesitant about the status of special mystical experiences, although his association with Jane de Chantal gradually made him more aware of the value of special infused states, as we see in the *Treatise on the Love of God*. Camus's peculiar book is an antimystical "mystical theology," presaging the reaction against the "mystical invasion" that grew strong in France around the middle of the seventeenth century. Camus expressed deep devotion to the writings of Dionysius but used a peculiar understanding of the Dionysian corpus to attack the Northern mystics (Tauler, Ruusbroec, Harphius, etc.), who, in his view had encouraged a false passivity that endangered the true "[a]ctive prayer in which we can properly say consists the true and most certain Mystical Theology."[274] Camus was apparently drawn to this confused opinion by his reflections on Thomas Aquinas's view that, since special graces (*gratiae gratis datae*) do not require sanctifying grace (dubious in itself, as Hans Urs von Balthasar has pointed out), all such graces are dangerous to the active pursuit of virtue. Passive, or infused, contemplation is thus questionable for Camus, so that the mystical dimension of religion, at least as conceived of by Teresa, John of the Cross, and even Francis de Sales, needs to be suspected, perhaps even rejected.

The most significant figure among Francis de Sales's followers, one who reinforced and disseminated his teaching among the Visitandine nuns, was Jane de Chantal (1572–1641), at once a disciple, a collaborator, and also an inspiration to the bishop of Geneva.[275] This remarkable woman, a deep mystic, as well as a religious founder and skilled guide of souls, deserves independent notice. Her close association with Francis makes her one of the primary examples of the kinds of collaboration between men and women ("mystical conversations") that have marked

Christian history since at least the thirteenth century (e.g., Francis and Clare, Henry Suso and Elizabeth Stagel, Teresa and John of the Cross). Some would even see Jane as the co-founder of the Salesian tradition.[276]

With Jane de Chantal we not only have considerable biographical data, but also extensive writings mostly in the form of letters and conferences.[277] We have already looked at the essential facts of her biography above, as well as aspects of her relationship with Francis from when they first met in 1604 down to his death in 1622. Here I will concentrate on her teaching and not her later life (1622–41) as leader of the Visitandines.

Three aspects of Jane's spiritual life should be noted at the start. The first is her passive form of contemplative prayer, what she called *simple regard* (simple gaze or attentiveness), or *simple remise en Dieu* (simple entrustment to God). This was the key to her mystical teaching. The second is her ongoing inner trials, especially temptations against faith, which reached a culmination from about 1612 to 1615 but were to recur throughout her later years. The third, perhaps paradoxical, aspect was how, despite her devotion to contemplation and her inner trials, she showed such energy and organizing skills in helping grow and govern the Visitandine order both before and after Francis's death. There were no fewer than eighty-seven Visitandine houses by the time of her death in December 1641. Most of Jane's prose writings (short treatises, exhortations, conferences, responses, etc.) were written for her nuns. Her many letters of spiritual direction were composed both for her fellow religious and for a wide circle of other correspondents. She was not a natural writer, but her position as leader of the community led her to produce a considerable body of work.

Jane de Chantal did not leave a formal spiritual or mystical teaching, but a look at some of her letters,[278] as well as a study of some of her treatises on prayer,[279] can give us some sense of her teaching.[280] The close relationship between Jane and Francis has always been recognized, but Jane's role as a mystical teacher has not always received sufficient recognition. She is much more than a carbon copy of Francis. It is true that they shared much, and Jane constantly refers to Francis and his teaching in her letters and treatises; but, as Wendy M. Wright has shown, the agreement between the two on the major themes of Salesian spirituality does not preclude some differences and nuances in presenting their shared concerns.[281] It is not possible to enter into a full consideration of all these issues here, but a look at a few areas where Jane learned from Francis, but also took her own path, will be helpful.

With regard to areas of general agreement, it is clear that both Francis and Jane had a generally optimistic view of human nature. For them, the Fall did not totally vitiate humanity, as Calvin thought, and as the Jansenists held. Humans, of course, have to depend on God's grace for salvation, but they maintain a freedom of choice that allows them to cooperate with the gracious God in the process of redemption. Second, this means that Francis and Jane agreed that the call to salvation, and even to holiness, is universal, not restricted to the predestined few. Third, salvation as the gift of the loving God is symbolized in the Heart of Jesus. Human reception of God's gift necessitates an inner conversion of the heart to the divine offer extended in Jesus Christ. Although some believers expressed their response to God's love in heroic fashion (think of the martyrs), the path for most believers involves the practice of mutual love and cultivating the "little virtues," such as humility, simplicity, meekness, and *doceur* ("gentleness," or "gracefulness"). Finally, the path to God demands total abandonment of the selfish ego (*abandon-abjection-anéantissement*), as well as a concomitant reorientation toward a holy disinterestedness (*indifference*) by which one comes to accept both God's "signified will," which tells us what must be done (e.g., the commandments), and God's "will of good pleasure," that is, everything that happens to us in everyday life. A letter to her brother André Frémyot, the archbishop of Bourges, puts the point as follows:

> As for the will of God's pleasure, which we know only through events as they occur, if these events benefit us, we must bless God and unite ourselves to the divine will which sends them. If something occurs which is disagreeable, physically or mentally, let us lovingly unite our will in obedience to the divine good pleasure, despite our natural aversion. We must pay no attention to these feelings, so long as at the fine point of our will we acquiesce very simply to God's will.[282]

Every situation in which we find ourselves provides us with the opportunity to learn what God has determined for us and what must be accepted as his will. In *Conference* XXVI, given to her Visitandine nuns, Jane discusses the determination the soul needs in order to make progress in the spiritual life, noting how afflictions and sorrow are an excellent means of practicing the virtues. She tells them, "Abide, therefore, in this holy indifference and resignation to all it shall please His loving kindness to do with you, and reserve nothing for yourselves but the care of keeping your soul in purity."[283] Jane expressed this "holy indifference" by repeating Francis's formula, "Ask for nothing and refuse nothing."[284] Such *indifference* produces the "freedom of spirit" mentioned by Paul (2 Cor. 3:17), a freedom not of arbitrary choice or license but of generous service to others. Writing to Mother Péronne-Marie de Châtel, superior of the convent at Grenoble, she says, "And just as we must, with prudence and discernment, make use of the holy liberty that is given us, so we must guard it carefully and jealously, but always with humility." She goes on with a practical implication, "We show these confessors due respect, yet we explain to them very frankly our liberty of action."[285] The model for this freedom lived in obedience to God's will of good pleasure is always Jesus. Hence, "Live Jesus!," the motto that Francis wanted to have engraved on his heart, was also proclaimed by Jane de Chantal. As she put it in a letter of greeting she wrote from Paris to the Annecy community in 1619, "Allow me, my dearest Sisters, to greet you all. . . . But what a greeting it is! The very one that our great and worthy Father taught us: LIVE JESUS! . . . Yes, my beloved Sisters and daughters, I say the words with intense delight: LIVE JESUS in our memory, our will, and in all our actions!"[286]

The Salesian mode of life is solid rather than heroic, modest rather than extreme, moderate rather than excessive in penance and mortification. Nevertheless, the new order pioneered by Francis and Jane was founded on a deep commitment to contemplative prayer leading to union with God. Both Francis and Jane intended the Order as one of contemplation, along with, of course, the practice of the public prayer of the religious life. Jane thought the members of the Order of the Visitation were called to the highest form of prayer she calls *simple regard*, although she recognizes that this does not mean that the sisters who cannot advance beyond simple meditation are any less to be praised, especially if they live in the mutual charity of community life.

The bond of love, both the love between God and the soul and the love that is the glue of the community, is central for Jane de Chantal. The concrete embodiment of that love is the image of the heart, that key symbol of seventeenth-century French mysticism. Writing to her brother André Frémyot, she says, "What I mean is that we must want, above all, to adorn our souls with the virtues of our Savior, Jesus Christ, and also with that secret intimate union of our hearts with Jesus, which causes us to long for him everywhere, as you are doing."[287] It is not only the union of our hearts with the heart of Jesus but also the deep union, or marriage, of hearts that existed between Francis and Jane, Jane and her brother, and within the community of the Visitation, that concerned the Mother Superior. This union was delightful and consoling, but it also demanded a total commitment that Jane spoke of as a martyrdom of love. Her biographer records a conversation she had with a few sisters in 1632 about why some of the great figures of the early church, such as St. Basil, had not received the crown of martyrdom. She said, "For myself, I believe that there is a martyrdom of love in which God preserves the lives of his servants so that they might work for his glory. This makes them martyrs and confessors at the same time. I know that this is the martyrdom to which the Daughters of the Visitation are called." When asked how this martyrdom is realized, she answered by referring to the wound of love: "Give your absolute consent to God and you experience it. What happens is that divine love thrusts its sword into the most intimate and secret parts of the soul and separates us from our very selves." Jane says she knew a sister who had had this experience, and the biographer says she was speaking of herself.[288]

Jane de Chantal often spoke about prayer in her letters and conferences, and she even wrote a few short treatises summarizing her views. *Conferences* XXXII and XXXIII can form a starting point. *Conference* XXXII, "On Three Ways of Praying and On Simplicity," begins by setting out the three ways. "The first way," she says, "is by using our imagination, as when we picture the divine Jesus in the crib, in the arms of his Holy Mother and the great St. Joseph." This, of course, is traditional meditation. "The second way is by using consideration, recalling to our minds the virtues the Lord practiced." This way is intended to stir the will to produce strong affection within and resolutions for daily life without. "The third way," she says, "is to keep ourselves simply in God's presence, gazing on him in some mystery with eyes of faith and conversing with him by words full of confidence, heart to heart, yet so secretly as if we would not even have our guardian angel know of it." The third way is a divine gift. Jane says, "We should on no account take to it of our own accord if God does not draw us to it."[289] *Conference* XXXIII discusses "Prayer and Mortification," which for Jane always go together. Here she gives more detail on the practice and some of the dangers involved in each mode of prayer. In the souls who practice the second mode, that of affective prayer, she cautions against those who get so "inflamed in their speaking" that they cry out to be melted and annihilated before him. "We should not do that," she says, "but pray very calmly and gently [*avec beaucoup de tranquillité et douceur*]." She is also opposed to prayer that gets overly concerned with useless theological speculations. Her advice is: "My dear daughters, I strongly advise to you the prayer of the heart [*l'oraison cordiale*], that is, one that does not make use of the intellect, but the heart."[290]

The *Short Treatise on Prayer* provides an abbreviated but comprehensive view of Jane's teaching.[291] It begins by setting out two modes of preparation for prayer: the distant preparation, which is peace of conscience, guarding of the senses, and the like; and the proximate preparation, which entails getting rid of everything that troubles the spirit so that we can attain recollection and interior freedom. Jane describes mortification and prayer as the two wings of the soul that raise it to conversation with God. The great method for prayer, she says, is not to have a method but to allow the Holy Spirit to be our master and deal with us as he wishes: "Going to prayer one should render oneself a pure capacity for receiving the Spirit of God and that suffices for all method; prayer should be made through grace, not through artifice. Enter into prayer through faith, remain in it through hope, and do not leave it save through the charity that demands either acting or suffering."[292] To begin to pray we should put ourselves in the presence of God conceived of as pervading the universe, so that we are in him "as the fish in the sea and the bird in the air." After giving some rules for meditation, Jane talks about the transition to the higher stages: "If in prayer the soul feels certain touches of God, by which he shows that he wishes to communicate himself to it, it should then cease all working and stop short, . . . and dispose itself to receive him with interior silence and deep respect."[293] Such infused prayer is described in language reminiscent of the Song of Songs: "Just as God is infinitely elevated, it is necessary that the soul elevates itself infinitely to reach him. The heavenly Bridegroom speaks to his spouse, while she is engaged in prayer, comparing her to 'a wisp of smoke that mounts towards heaven' (Song 3:6) without finding anywhere to stop" (III:263; my trans.).

Jane emphasizes the role of the heart in this ascent of prayer, as well as the need for silence: "The soul exercises mystical silence [*le silence mystique*] when it speaks with no creature, not even with God, but listens with great attention in its interior: this silence honors God in a very elevated way" (III:264; my trans.). Such prayer leads to union: "God communicates himself spiritually, touching the deepest depth of the heart with his inspirations, uniting them so gently to the soul that she is not able to express them; and everything leads to the point where whoever is joined to God 'becomes one spirit with him' (1 Cor. 6:17)" (ibid.). Jane continues the short work by outlining four kinds of prayer (prayer of tranquillity, of application, of fidelity, and of poverty), before turning to further advice about prayer practice. We must remember that God is both light and darkness, so either of these aspects may be communicated to us in prayer. "Faith," she says, "is the light of this new world, which is the science of the saints. In prayer one should listen more than talk; it is for us to listen to the Son of God and not to speak;

we are not worthy to speak to him, leaving to God the choice of the discourse" (III:266; my trans.). Our proper disposition should be one of perfect annihilation in the face of the presence of God, like a candle consumed before the Blessed Sacrament. God will come to our support when he sees us not only deprived of all things, but even deprived of himself. This total stripping off of God for love of God will allow us finally to say: "What is there for me in heaven, and what should I search for on earth aside from my God?" The message of this treatise is to strive for total passivity to the divine initiative in the higher stages of unitive prayer.

Several other of Jane de Chantal's treatises fill in aspects of this general picture of prayer. For example, in the *Rules for Discerning Whether It Is the Spirit of God at Work in the Soul When It Is Not Able to Act in Prayer*, Jane, like John of the Cross and Francis de Sales, provides guidelines for discerning when ordinary prayer is to be left behind and the prayer of simple regard can be awaited.[294] The same short work also contains reflections on the role of the soul's three powers in prayerful union. Every human affection must be "liquefied in itself," so that the soul's understanding can attain "perfect union with Divine Wisdom." The perfection of the memory will be attained through being absorbed in God and "forgetting everything and itself, and reposing sweetly in God alone."[295]

Jane de Chantal was quite familiar with the paradoxes of the prayer of simple regard. In her *Counsels to a Superior* she tells the addressee that the perfect union with God found in prayer "is essential for our small Congregation." Nonetheless, the souls whom God leads "through this way of simplicity" are deprived of all satisfaction, desire, and feeling, so that they cannot express themselves about what is going on within them "in the final point of the spirit" (*l'extrême point de l'esprit*). Religious superiors should avoid interfering with such souls, but should suggest that they read the writings of Teresa of Avila, and, of course, Francis de Sales.[296] Finally, Jane de Chantal, as mentioned above, experienced not only periods of aridity in her prayer life but also the terrible darkness of temptations against faith and hope. She spoke of these to some extent in her letters to Francis, and in her treatises for her nuns on prayer she gives advice on how to deal with the suffering involved in the higher stages of prayer. For example, in her *Consoling Words* (*Paroles Consolantes*) she says, "States of aridity [*sécheresses*], which beginners in the spiritual life can call dull and hidden grace, are much more precious than the greatest consolations, because experience teaches us that all the virtues grow in the midst of aridities and trials."[297]

This brief look at Jane de Chantal's teaching on prayer shows that it is through prayer that the soul can attain union with God in this life. "The essence of true prayer," she says, "is nothing else but being always ready to receive all kinds of duties [*obeissances*], and to hold our soul united to God's will as much as possible: this is what is true prayer."[298] Union is not a discrete category in Jane's writings, but, as the goal of the spiritual life she and Francis instituted, it appears throughout her letters, conferences, and treatises, so that it would be artificial to try to create a distinctive theology of union in the Mother of the Visitandine order. She herself was happy to repeat the language of tradition regarding union, as when she says in a letter to a sister: "To feel God's presence so intimately and powerfully in oneself that one is no longer aware of the self is to have that little drop of water, self, dissolve in the Ocean of Divinity. How blessed are the souls who are so lost in God, for they can truly say with all the ardor of St. Paul: 'I live now, no longer I, but Jesus Christ lives in me' (Gal. 2:21)."[299] Jane de Chantal and Francis de Sales were in total agreement about the goal of the spiritual life.

Notes

1. Francis repeats this dictum often. This formulation is taken from *Entretien spiritual* XXI, as found in the critical edition of Francis's writings, *Oeuvres de Saint François de Sales . . . Édition complète*, 27 vols. (Annecy: J. Niérat et al., 1892–1964), VI:384. I will generally use this edition, citing as *Oeuvres* with volume and page number. I will generally not cite the French originals, save in a few places where it seems helpful for determining the precise meaning.

2. See *Oeuvres* XIII:330.

3. Bremond, *History*, vol. 1, especially the first part, "S. François de Sales: The Origins and Tendencies of Devout Humanism" (3–147). Bremond discusses the meaning of the term on 3–4, 8–11, 15, 100, and 255–56. Some of what Bremond put forth in vol. 1, however, seems to be qualified in his later treatment of Francis in the *Histoire*, vol. 3, part 1, chaps. 1–4, which deal with Francis's doctrine of prayer (35–137 in new ed.; originally vol. 7). On Bremond's use of the term, see Gorday, *Pure Love, Pure Poetry, Pure Prayer*, 132–38.

4. For a critique of Devout Humanism, see Ferdinand Cavallera, "Spiritualité en France au XVII siècle: Reforme de la Nomenclature," *Revue d'ascetique et de mystique* 29 (1953): 58–64. Others have preferred the term "Christian Humanism," on which see Julien-Eymard d'Angers, *L'humanisme chrétien au XVIIe siècle: St. François de Sales et Yves de Paris* (The Hague: M. Nijhoff, 1970), especially the introduction (VII–XXII) for his disagreement with Bremond, and all whom he judges to have fallen into the "Bremondian" trap (e.g., J. Orcibal, L. Cognet, J. Le Brun). A balanced view of the contributions, but eventual failure, of the term can be found in Jacques Le Brun, "Humanisme et spiritualité. VII: L'Humanisme dévot," DS 7:1028–33.

5. On Francis's attitude toward Protestantism, see Ruth Kleinman, *Saint François de Sales and the Protestants* (Geneva: Droz, 1962).

6. There are a number of biographies. The most detailed is E.-M. Lajeunie, *Saint François de Sales: L'homme, la pensée, l'action*, 2 vols. (Paris: Guy Victor, 1964). In English, see André Ravier, *Francis de Sales: Sage and Saint* (San Francisco: Ignatius Press, 1988). Although somewhat imaginative, the illustrated *Francis de Sales* by Dirk Koster (AZ Norden, The Netherlands: Bert Post, 2000) is valuable for the historical context it provides.

7. It has recently been argued that another factor in Francis's spiritual crisis was his reaction to the picture of the vengeful God put forth by the extreme Catholics of the Holy League during the French Wars of Religion in the 1580s; see Joseph F. Chorpenning, "*Lectio Divina* and Francis de Sales's Picturing of the Interconnection of Divine and Human Hearts," in *Imago Exegetica: Visual Images as Exegetical Instruments, 1400–1700*, ed. Walter S. Mellon, James Clifton, and Michael Weemans, Intersections 33 (Leiden: Brill, 2014), 453–56.

8. I cite from the translation by Elisabeth Stopp, *St. Francis de Sales: A Testimony by St. Chantal* (London: Faber & Faber, 1967), [45].

9. I use the translation of Péronne Marie Thibert in *Francis de Sales, Jane de Chantal: Letters of Spiritual Direction*, ed. Wendy M. Wright and Joseph F. Power, Classics of Western Spirituality (New York: Paulist Press, 1988), 180. The Letter is MCMLXXIV in *Oeuvres* XXI:11–14.

10. On the role of Possevino in Francis's life, see Elisabeth Stopp, "Saint Francis de Sales: Attitudes to Friendship," *Downside Review* 113 (1995): 175–92, here 181–82.

11. For a translation and study of Scupoli's *Spiritual Combat*, see William V. Hudon, ed. and trans., *Theatine Spirituality: Selected Writings*, Classics of Western Spirituality (New York: Paulist Press, 1996).

12. Molina's views were set forth most directly in his *Concordia liberi arbitrii cum gratiae donis* published in 1588. For a translation, see *Luis de Molina: On Divine Foreknowledge. Part IV of the "Concordia,"* trans., with an introduction and notes, by Alfred J. Freddoso (Ithaca, NY: Cornell University Press, 1988). For a recent account, see Kirk R. MacGregor, *Luis de Molina: The Life and Theology of the Founder of Middle Knowledge* (Grand Rapids: Zondervan, 2015).

13. On Francis and Favre, see Stopp, "Saint Francis de Sales," 182–90.

14. These apologetic pamphlets were published as *Les Controverses* (*Oeuvres* I). Francis also wrote a defense of images of the cross against Protestant iconoclasts (*Defense de l'Estendart de la sainte Croix* in *Oeuvres* II). It is interesting to note that, at the behest of Pope Clement VIII in 1597, Francis even arranged to have three meetings with the leader of the Geneva Reform, Theodore Beza (1519–1605). These encounters were polite but came to nothing.

15. See the text in Ravier, *Francis de Sales*, 99–100.

16. *St. Francis de Sales: A Testimony by St. Chantal*, [54–55].

17. For a good account of this example of spiritual friendship, see Wendy M. Wright, *Bond of Perfection: Jeanne de Chantal and François de Sales* (New York: Paulist Press, 1985).

18. Both Francis and Jane were prodigious letter writers, with over two thousand letters surviving from each. Although she destroyed most of the letters she wrote to him, forty-six survive. The over four hundred of Francis's surviving

letters to her are a rich witness to his spiritual teaching and the bond they shared. These letters have recently been re-edited in *François de Sales et Jeanne de Chantal: Correspondance*, edited by David Laurent with an Introduction by Max Huot de Longchamp (Paris/Perpignan: Desclée de Brouwer, 2016).

19. Wendy M. Wright, *Heart Speaks to Heart: The Salesian Tradition* (Maryknoll, NY: Orbis Books, 2004).

20. Letter CCXXIII (*Correspondance*, 63–68, text at 67). I use the translation in *Letters of Spiritual Direction*, 129.

21. I owe this suggestion, with thanks, to Wendy M. Wright.

22. Letter CCXXXIV (*Correspondance*, 69–87). For the translated sections, see *Letters of Spiritual Direction*, 131, 133, 134, 142.

23. Another formulation for which I thank Wendy M. Wright.

24. A helpful summary of what follows can be found in Ravier, *Francis de Sales*, chap. 11, "The Annecy Visitation," 185–97.

25. The scene has been rather overplayed in much literature. Celse-Bénigne was already an adolescent and no longer living at home.

26. The shift is discussed by Wright, *Bond of Perfection*, 159–73, with ample citation of the letters of Francis and Jane, which I will use in what follows. The letters themselves can be found in *Correspondance*, 583–94. See also Koster, *Francis de Sales*, 193–99.

27. Wright, *Bond of Perfection*, 168.

28. I thank Wendy M. Wright for this observation.

29. *Introduction à la vie devote* is found in *Oeuvres* III. I will use the translation of John K. Ryan, *Introduction to the Devout Life by St. Francis de Sales* (Garden City, NY: Doubleday, 1955).

30. *Traité de l'amour de Dieu* is found in *Oeuvres* IV and V. The most recent translation is by John K. Ryan, *Treatise on the Love of God by St. Francis de Sales*, 2 vols. (Garden City, NY: Doubleday, 1963; repr., Rockford, IL: Tan Books, 1975). The old translation by Canon Henry Benedict Mackey, the Benedictine editor of the Annecy edition, although criticized by Ryan, is still quite serviceable, and I will cite it often here, though sometimes updating the Victorian idiom. I use the 1953 edition: *Treatise on the Love of God by St. Francis de Sales* (Westminster, MD: Newman Press, 1953).

31. On the first Paris house of the Visitandines, see Diefendorf, *From Penitence to Charity*, 174–83.

32. Some of Francis's letters to Angelique Arnauld are available in *Letters of Spiritual Direction*, 168–77.

33. The letters are edited in *Oeuvres* XI–XXI. There are several partial translations in English. Along with *The Letters of Spiritual Direction* mentioned above, see the following nineteenth-century translations: *A Selection of the Spiritual Letters of S. Francis de Sales* (London: Rivingtons, 1871), of 159 letters; and the versions of Henry Benedict Mackey, *St. Francis de Sales. I: Letters to Persons in the World* (London: Burns & Oates, n.d.), with 186 letters; and *St. Francis de Sales: Letters to Persons in Religion* (Westminster, MD: Newman Bookshop, 1943), containing 181 letters.

34. Ravier, *Francis de Sales*, 147.

35. *Oeuvres* VII–X. There are four volumes of partial translations of the sermons by the Nuns of the Visitation published between ca. 1982 and 1987 in Rockford, IL, by Tan Books: *The Sermons of St. Francis de Sales on Prayer*; *The Sermons of*

St. Francis de Sales on Our Lady; The Sermons of St. Francis de Sales for Lent Given in 1622; The Sermons of St. Francis de Sales for Advent and Christmas.

36. Letter CCXXIX can be found in *Oeuvres* XII:299–325. There is a translation by John K. Ryan, *On the Preacher and Preaching: A Letter by Francis de Sales* (Chicago: Regnery, 1964).

37. The *opuscula* are found in *Oeuvres* XXVI–XXVII. Canon Mackey also translated the Song of Songs commentary, *The Mystical Explanation of the Canticle of Canticles: Composed by the Blessed Francis de Sales* (London: Burns & Oates, 1908). The text is to be found *Oeuvres* XXVI:10–19. On this brief work, see Thomas F. Dailey, "A Song of Prayer: Reading the Canticle of Canticles with St. Francis de Sales," *Studia Mystica* 15.4 (1992): 65–82.

38. *Oeuvres* VI. Again, there is a translation by Mackey, *The Spiritual Conferences of St. Francis de Sales* (London: Burns, Oates & Washbourne, 1906).

39. *Treatise*, preface (*Oeuvres* IV:8; trans., Ryan, 40).

40. On the difficulty of translating *douceur*, see Ryan, "Translator's Introduction," in *Treatise on the Love of God* 1:25–27; and Wright and Power, "Introduction," *Letters of Spiritual Direction*, 63–65. For a study, see Thomas A. Donlan, "Oasis of Gentleness in Desert of Militancy: François de Sales's Contribution to French Catholicism," in *Surrender to Christ for Mission: French Spiritual Traditions*, ed. Philip Sheldrake (Collegeville, MN: Liturgical Press, 2018), 90–108.

41. Hélène Michon, *Saint François de Sales: Une nouvelle mystique* (Paris: Éditions du Cerf, 2008), 34–51.

42. Bergamo, *L'anatomie de l'âme*, 98–103, 119–21.

43. Francis has a discussion of the traditional four senses of scripture in Letter CCXXIX to Bishop Frémyot (*Oeuvres* XII:308–11), in which he favors the literal sense but gives five rules for the proper use of the allegorical, anagogical, and tropological senses.

44. Letter CCXXIX (XII:309–10) gives an illustration of the difference between a comparison and an allegory. Francis notes that many interpreters read the juniper tree under which the prophet Elijah rested (3 Kgdms. 19:4–5) as an allegory of the cross. "But I would rather like to say that just as Elijah slept under the juniper, we ought also to repose under the Cross of Our Savior in the sleep of holy meditation, and not more. I do not want to assert that the one signifies the other, but I rather prefer to compare one to the other [*mays je voudrois bien comparer l'un a l'autre*]" (my trans.).

45. I count twenty-four references to bees in the *Introduction* and at least fifteen uses of bees in the *Treatise*.

46. *Conference* XVI (*Oeuvres* VI:300; trans. Mackey, *Spiritual Conferences*, 311).

47. The *apodes* are found in Aristotle's *De historia animalium* 1.1. Francis uses them in *Treatise* II.9, II.13, and II.21.

48. On the early history of the book, see Ravier, *Francis de Sales*, 166–69; and Koster, *Francis de Sales*, 135–45.

49. The first English translation of the *Introduction*, by the English Benedictine John Yaworth, appeared in 1613 and was reprinted a number of times. A second, improved, edition by a group of English priests came out in 1648 and was often reprinted and revised.

50. See Diefendorf, *From Penitence to Charity*.

51. *Introduction*, preface (*Oeuvres* III:6; trans., 30).

52. The first four chapters treat: (1) the description of true devotion, (2) its propriety and excellence, (3) its compatibility with every vocation and profession, and (4) the need for a guide in beginning and progressing.

53. The structure of Salesian meditation, laid down in chap. 9 consists in preparation, considerations, affections and resolutions, and conclusion. The relation between the Ignatian and the Salesian spiritualities is complicated, but it would be a mistake to draw them too close, as does, for example, François Charmot, *Ignatius Loyola and Francis de Sales: Two Masters–One Spirituality* (St. Louis and London: Herder, 1966). The Salesian meditation does not emphasize Ignatius's "composition of place" and is less interested in logical structure and intellectual operations than the Jesuit is.

54. *Introduction* III.1 (*Oeuvres* III:125–26; trans., 118–19).

55. In his summary of Francis's teaching, his friend Jean-Pierre Camus includes a whole chapter on "The True [i.e., little] Virtues"; see *The Spirit of St. François de Sales by Jean Pierre Camus (Bishop of Belley)*, trans. C. F. Kelley (New York: Harper & Brothers, 1952), chap. 11 (115–28).

56. *Introduction* III.2 (*Oeuvres* III:131; trans., 123): "Mais pour tout cela, il ne faut pas pretender a telles graces, puisqu'elles ne sont nullement necessaries pour bien server et aymer Dieu, qui doit estre nostre unique pretention." Somewhat later, he goes on: "Laissons volontier les sureminences aux ames surelevees: nous ne meritons pas un rang si haut au service de Dieu" (132). Francis's reserve about special mystical gifts will continue in the *Treatise*.

57. *Conference* VIII (*Oeuvres* VI:130; trans. in *The Spiritual Conferences*, 136).

58. The topics at the end of part III include: (a) a treatise on friendship (chaps. 17–22); (b) exterior mortification (chap. 23, Francis advises moderation); (c) treatment of society and solitude (chap. 24) and decency in attire (chap. 25); (d) a treatise on discourse, that is, how to speak to God and to other people (chaps. 26–30); (e) lawful and commendable recreations (chap. 31); (f) prohibited games and recreations (chaps. 32–34); and, finally, (g) a series instructions: for all the devout (chaps. 35–37), for the married (chaps. 38–39), for widows (chap. 40), and for virgins (chap. 41).

59. *Introduction* IV.3 (*Oeuvres* III:296–97; trans., 234–35).

60. *Introduction* V.18 (*Oeuvres* III:366; trans., 286).

61. For the process of composition and publication, see Ravier, *Francis de Sales*, chap. 12 (202–12); and Koster, *Francis de Sales*, 201–15.

62. The earliest English translation of the *Treatise* by Fr. Miles Carr of the English College at Douai appeared in 1630 and was often reissued. There are two modern English versions: Canon Mackey's (making use of Carr) was first published in 1884 and has been often reprinted; and Ryan's translation, *Treatise on the Love of God by St. Francis de Sales*.

63. On the *Treatise* as a commentary on the Song of Songs, see Ravier, *Francis de Sales*, 204, 212. By my count, the Song of Songs is cited approximately 115 times in the *Treatise*. Another listing can be found in Antanas Liuima, *Aux sources du Traité de l'Amour de Dieu de Saint François de Sales*, 2 vols., Collectanea spiritualia (Rome: Librairie Editrice de l'Université Gregorienne, 1959–60), 2:685–86, which contains 164 references to the Song, although some are indirect.

64. *Treatise*, preface (*Oeuvres* V:13; trans., Ryan, 1:44): "Et certes, comme je n'ay pas voulu suivre ceux qui mesprisent quelques livres qui traittent d'une certaine

vie sureminente en perfection, aussi n'ay-je pas voulu parler de cette sureminence; car ni je puis censurer les autheurs, ni authorizer les censeurs d'une doctrine que je n'entens pas." Francis also expresses a veiled critique of Canfield and some other mystical writers in *Introduction* III.2 (*Oeuvres* III:131–32), as well as in a letter of June 1620 (*Oeuvres* XIX:253).

65. The most detailed study, despite its restriction to the *Treatise*, is the two volumes of Liuima, *Aux sources du Traité de l'Amour de Dieu*.

66. Francis himself gives a helpful, if not exhaustive, survey of his authorities in the preface to the *Treatise* (*Oeuvres* IV:4–7).

67. Liuima, *Aux sources du Traité de l'Amour de Dieu*, provides the following figures for citations from these authorities in the *Treatise*: Augustine (95x), Bernard (17x), and Bonaventure (5x). Other frequently named patristic sources include Ambrose (8x), Basil (9x), Gregory the Great (7x), Gregory Nazianzenus (8x), Jerome (12x), and John Chrysostom (4x). Dionysius is cited seventeen times in the *Treatise*, but only three texts are used: DN IV (12x), CH VII (once), and Letter 8 (4x).

68. In a letter to Jane de Chantal of October 14, 1604, Francis recommends the Pseudo-Taulerian *Institutiones* published in 1548 (*Oeuvres* XII:359).

69. On the relation of Francis to late medieval Northern mysticism, there are contrasting positions. Cognet, as noted in the Introduction, argues for a strong influence, in what seems to me an exaggerated fashion. This is not to deny that there was a real connection, but a study of Francis's texts suggests a more cautious view. The treatment of Francis's relation to the Low Countries in Antoine Daniels, *Les rapports entre Saint François de Sales et Les Pays-Bas 1550–1700* (Nijmegen: Centrale Drukkerij, 1932), includes a chapter on "Saint François de Sales et la mystique néerlandaise" (44–69), which argues for considerable influence of the *Pearl* text on the bishop, although this also seems doubtful to me.

70. In a 1607 letter to President Brulart about spiritual books, Francis mentions the *Evangelical Pearl* (*Oeuvres* XIII:334–35).

71. Teresa of Avila is cited eleven times in the *Treatise* (Liuima, *Aux sources du Traité de l'Amour de Dieu*, 2:704). On the influence of Teresa on Francis, see Vermeylen, *Sainte Thérèse en France au xvii siècle*, IIère Partie (92–180).

72. Francis cites a wide range of contemporary writers on moral theology and prayer, some famous in their day but now scarcely known. He used the writings of Louis de Blois (see chap. 1). Among the Spanish writers he references Ignatius of Loyola, Alonso de Madrid, Luis de Granada, Luis de la Puente, Pedro Ribadeneira, Pedro de Alcántara, and Juan de Avila. Among the Italians, Lorenzo Scupoli holds pride of place, but Francis also knew Angela of Foligno, Catherine of Genoa, and the *Breve Compendio* of Achille Gagliardi. On Francis's use of Italian spiritual writers, see Benedetta Papàsogli, *Gli Spirituali Italiani e Il "Grand Siècle"* (Rome: Edizioni di Storia e Letteratura, 1983), 45–58. For Spanish influence on Francis, see Mother Mary Majella Rivet, *The Influence of the Spanish Mystics on the Works of Saint Francis de Sales* (Washington, DC: Catholic University of America Press, 1941).

73. I say this despite the attempt of André Bord to demonstrate an influence of John of the Cross on Francis, which I find unconvincing; see his "L'influence de Jean de la Croix sur François de Sales et Jeanne de Chantal," in *L'Unidivers Salésien: Saint François de Sales hier et aujourd'hui; Actes du Colloque international*

de Metz, 17-19 septembre 1992, ed. Hélène Bordes and Jacques Hennequin (Paris: Université de Metz, 1994), 51-56.

74. Liuima lists fourteen citations of Thomas in the *Treatise* (*Aux sources du Traité de l'Amour de Dieu*, 2:704).

75. Liuima has an exhaustive list of the biblical sources in the *Treatise* (*Aux sources du Traité de l'Amour de Dieu*, 2:681-92.

76. Michon, *Saint François de Sales*, part 1, chap. 2, "Le modèle biblique" (53-71).

77. In this section I will make use primarily of the *Treatise on the Love of God* and to a lesser extent the *Introduction to the Devout Life*. I will also utilize *The Spiritual Conferences* and the *Mystical Explanation of the Canticle of Canticles* when needed, as well as some *Letters* and *Sermons*.

78. The best general account is that of Michon, *Saint François de Sales*, already mentioned several times. A classic treatment is Bremond, *History*, vol. 1, part 1 (English version 1:3-147); and (only in the French), vol. 3, part 1 (new ed., originally vol. 7). See also Cognet, *La spiritualité moderne*, chap. 8, "Saint François de Sales et le Salesianisme" (274-309); and Pierre Serout, "François de Sales (saint)," DS 5:1057-97. In English, perhaps the only attempt at a general survey is that of C. F. Kelley, *The Spirit of Love Based on the Teaching of St. François de Sales* (New York: Harper & Brothers, 1951). For a short account, see Michael J. Buckley, "Seventeenth-Century French Spirituality: Three Figures," in *Christian Spirituality: Post-Reformation and Modern*, ed. Louis Dupré and Don E. Saliers, World Spirituality 18 (New York: Crossroad, 1989), 32-41. Wendy M. Wright has a number of treatments of Francis concentrating on the relation between Francis and Jane de Chantal.

79. Almost everyone who has written on Francis has recognized the centrality of love in his thought. Pierre Serouet says, "L'amour est l'alpha et l'oméga de la spiritualité salésienne" ("François de Sales [saint]," DS 5:1083). See also Michon, *Saint François de Sales*, 47-48. A fine summary of Francis's view of love can be found in Burnaby, *Amor Dei*, chap. 9, "Pure Love" (277-86). For a comparative treatment of Francis and Hindu mystics on love and surrender to God, see Francis X. Clooney, *Beyond Compare: St. Francis de Sales and Śrī Vedānta Deśika on Loving Surrender to God* (Washington, DC: Georgetown University Press, 2008).

80. *Treatise*, preface (*Ouevres* IV:4; my trans.).

81. *Treatise* X.1 (*Oeuvres* V:167; trans., Mackey, 410).

82. Burnaby goes so far as to say, "Here [i.e., in Francis] once more are Eros and Agape—man's need met by God's abundance, the potency of the human soul and the divine Act. But neither Augustine nor Thomas dared to bring Eros and Agape so near together, to bind them in so organic a unity" (*Amor Dei*, 282).

83. For a survey, see Michon, *Saint François de Sales*, 273-86.

84. *Treatise* II.1 (*Oeuvres* IV:88; my trans.).

85. *Treatise* II.2 (*Oeuvres* IV:93; trans., Mackey, 68).

86. *Treatise* II.4 (*Oeuvres* IV:99; trans., Mackey, 73). See also II.5 (trans., Mackey, 77).

87. Francis expresses this typically "Augustinian-Thomist" doctrine of the Trinity from time to time in his writings (e.g., *Treatise* I.15). For a more detailed treatment of the Trinity, emphasizing our coming heavenly union with God through our seeing the eternal generation of the Son and through the action of

the Holy Spirit as the mutual love of Father and Son, see *Treatise* III.12–13 (*Oeuvres* IV:203–8).

88. *Treatise* II.4 (*Oeuvres* IV:102; my trans.). Book II.5–7 analyzes the nature of redemption more closely.

89. *Treatise* VIII.4 (*Oeuvres* V:68; trans., Mackey, 332).

90. *Treatise* I.1 (*Oeuvres* IV:23–25), using Thomas Aquinas, STh IaIIae, q. 27, art. 1; and Dionysius DN IV.10. For another consideration of the relation of Goodness and Beauty as divine attributes, see *Treatise* X.1.

91. *Treatise* V.3 (*Oeuvres* IV:267; trans., Mackey, 206).

92. *Treatise* II.22 (*Oeuvres* IV:163–65; trans., Mackey, 124–25).

93. Important studies of Francis's anthropology include Bremond, *History*, vol. 3, part 1, chap. 2 (new ed., 63–105); Bergamo, *L'anatomie de l'âme*, part 1 (23–136); Michon, *Saint François de Sales*, part 2 (95–177); and Tullio Poli, *Punta suprema dell'anima: Virtù teologali, preghiera semplice e adesione alla volontà divina secondo S. Francesco di Sales*, Analecta Gregoriana B.76 (Rome: Gregorian University Press, 1982). In addition, there are many articles, some to be cited in what follows.

94. Noting man as made to the image and likeness appears in many places in the *Treatise*; e.g., I.6, II.18, III.2, III.8, VIII.4, etc. It is also found in other works, such as the Sermon for the Third Sunday of Lent (see *Lenten Sermons*, 86–91). On this topic, see James S. Langelaan, "Man, the Image and Likeness of God: Nature and Supernature according to St. Francis de Sales," *Downside Review* 95 (1977): 35–48.

95. *Treatise* X.11 (*Oeuvres* V:204–6; trans., Mackey, 440, 442).

96. On this point, see Michon, *Saint François de Sales*, 177.

97. *Treatise* II.5 (*Oeuvre* IV:104; trans., Mackey, 77).

98. Michon, *Saint François de Sales*, 177.

99. *Introduction*, part V, chap. 18 (*Oeuvres* III:365; trans., 286).

100. *Treatise* I.16 (*Oeuvres* IV:77; trans., Mackey, 57). On this view and its agreement with Thomas Aquinas, see Langelaan, "Man, the Image and Likeness," 43–48.

101. At this point in *Treatise* I.17 Francis has a discussion of the failure of even the good pagan philosophers, who came to know God through their natural inclination but who were unable to truly love God. On the difference between a true desire and a mere *velleitas*, see I.7 (*Oeuvres* IV:44–46; trans., Mackey, 33–35).

102. *Treatise* I.17 (*Oeuvres* IV:82; trans., Ryan 1:97).

103. Langelaan, "Man, the Image and Likeness," 48: "For St. Francis de Sales the natural inclination to love God above all things, which is constitutive of human nature, is the point of contact man has with God. It is the preamble to charity, it is the slight and imperfect love to be perfected by perfect love, poured out into our hearts by the Holy Spirit."

104. On Francis's teaching on freedom, see Eunan McDonnell, *The Concept of Freedom in the Writings of Francis de Sales* (Bern: Peter Lang, 2009); Michel Terestchenko, *Amour et désespoir de François de Sales à Fénelon* (Paris: Éditions du Seuil, 2000), 42–45; and Michon, *Saint François de Sales*, 286–98.

105. *Treatise* II.12 (*Oeuvres* IV:127; trans., Mackey, 96).

106. Freedom of spirit (2 Cor. 3:17) has been a major theme in the history of Christian mysticism, though at times under suspicion due to exaggerated claims.

Francis does not seem to use this phrase in the *Treatise*, but the theme of freedom appears often. The phrase "freedom of spirit" does appear in his letters and in the *Spiritual Conferences*; for example, *Letters of Spiritual Direction*, 138-40, 144, 146, 239, 265; *Letters to Persons in Religion*, 125, 151, 283, 320-21, 339; and *Letters to Persons in the World*, 138, 165-74 (an important letter to Jane de Chantal from 1604), and 261-62; and *Conference* XVIII (trans., Mackey, 363). For a discussion of the "spirit of freedom" in Francis, see Bremond, *History*, 1:98-99.

107. *Treatise* XII.10 (*Oeuvres* V:341; trans., Mackey, 550).

108. On the modern character of Francis's teaching on the powers of the soul, see Bergamo, *L'anatomie de l'âme*, 34-35, 58-59, 71-72, 132-36; Michon, *Saint François de Sales*, 164, 328-34; and Anthony Levi, *French Moralists: The Theory of the Passions, 1585 to 1649* (Oxford: Clarendon, 1964), 118-20.

109. *Treatise* I.3 (*Oeuvres* IV:28-32). Following Augustine (*De civitate dei* 14.8), Francis lists twelve movements, called passions, because they disturb the body: love, desire, hope, despair, joy, hate, flight, fear, courage, grief, anger, satisfaction. Both here and in I.5, Francis attacks the Stoic theory of *apatheia*, arguing that humans cannot exist without passions, although they need to control them by the rational will.

110. On Francis on the passions, see Michon, *Saint François de Sales*, 150-63; and Levi, *French Moralists*, 115-26.

111. *Treatise* I.4 (*Oeuvres* IV:33; trans., Ryan 1:61).

112. *Treatise* I.5 (*Oeuvres* IV:35-37). Toward the end of this chapter Francis distinguishes four kinds of affections in the reasonable part of the soul: (1) natural affections, like desiring health; (2) affections based on reason, such as seeking moral virtues; (3) Christian affections, like voluntary poverty; and finally (4) supernatural affections that come from "the simple sentiment of the truth of God."

113. *Treatise* I.7 (*Oeuvres* IV:40-46).

114. Ibid. (*Oeuvres* IV:43; trans., Ryan 1:68): "L'amour donques, a parler distintement et precisement, n'est autre chose que le mouvement, escoulement, et advancement du Coeur envers le bien."

115. At this point (*Oeuvres* IV:44) Francis introduces a distinction, saying that love that tends toward an object that is distant, absent, or future is properly called "desire."

116. *Treatise* I.10 (*Oeuvres* IV:55-62) also contains a long account of the two opposed forms of ecstasy: the sensitive, that is, sexual, ecstasy that degrades the self, and the spiritual ecstasy that raises the soul above itself (IV:57-62).

117. For discussions of *Treatise* I.11-12, see Bergamo, *L'anatomie de l'âme*, 59-136; Michon, *Saint François de Sales*, 117-41; and Poli, *Punta suprema dell' anima*, 26-31 (with a helpful chart), and 205-8.

118. *Treatise* I.11 (*Oeuvres* IV:62-66; trans., Mackey, 45-48).

119. Augustine's distinction between inferior and superior reason occurs in a number of places in his writings. The critical edition of the *Treatise* references *Enarratio in Psalmum* 145.5 (*Oeuvres* IV:63-64). It has also been pointed out that Francis's distinction of the inferior and superior aspects of reason and will may have been influenced by Lorenzo Scupoli in his *Spiritual Combat* 12 (Hudon, *Theatine Spirituality*, 129-30).

120. The distinction between the superior and inferior parts of the soul is

essential for Francis and is often appealed to in his letters and other writings, such as the *Spiritual Conferences* XII and XIV (Mackey, *Spiritual Conferences*, 216, 273).

121. *Treatise* I.12 (*Oeuvres* IV:67-70). There are translations in Mackey, 48-51; and Ryan, 1:85-87; but I will make my own versions from this chapter.

122. Bergamo, *L'anatomie de l'âme*, 131.

123. For a detailed discussion of the use of the term *fine pointe de l'âme* and related terms in the *Treatise*, see Poli, *Punta suprema dell'anima*, 43-60.

124. At the end of the chapter Francis turns to a second analogy, a legal one, in which reasoning represents the lower activity of lawyers arguing cases before a court, while the high court, or parliament, settles the strife by peremptory decision representing divine action in the supreme point that makes the final decision.

125. This case has been argued in detail by Bergamo, *L'anatomie de l'âme*, 114-36.

126. On the originality of Francis's anthropology, see Bergamo, *L'anatomie de l'âme*, 34-35, 58-59; and Michon, *Saint François de Sales*, 164.

127. In the *Epistola aurea*, William distinguishes the *homo animalis*, whose knowing is based on sense, from the *homo rationalis*, who knows from reason, and finally from the *homo spiritualis* based on the love that is a higher mode of knowing (*amor ipse intelligentia est*). See McGinn, *Growth*, 234-36.

128. For some other appearances of the "supreme point" in the *Treatise*, see VII.1; IX.3, 5, 6, 11, and 12; and XII.1 (Poli counts fifty-five uses of the term and its cognates). The "fine point of the will, heart, and spirit" occurs three times in the *Introduction* (especially part IV, chap. 15; *Oeuvres* III:336). The point is also found in the letters of both Francis and Jane de Chantal; see, e.g., *Letters of Spiritual Direction*, 173, 202, 238. In a letter to Jane of February 18, 1605, Francis writes, "[F]ree will, which, quite naked before God, resides in the supreme and most spiritual part of the soul, depends on no other than its God and itself; and when all the other faculties of the soul are lost and subject to the enemy, it alone remains mistress of itself so as not to consent" (*Letters to Persons in the World*, 264; see also 443).

129. See the list of terms and the discussion of their relation in Poli, *Punta suprema dell'anima*, 70-73.

130. Ibid. See also Michon, *Saint François de Sales*, 129-36; and Bergamo, *L'anatomie de l'âme*, 94-97, 110-14, 123-24, 166-67, and 191-92.

131. To give just one example of an argument that Francis derives his teaching on the *fine pointe* from an earlier mystic, see Daniels, *Les rapports entre Saint François de Sales et les Pays-Bas*, 60-64, who contends that the bishop took this notion from the *Evangelical Pearl*.

132. Poli discusses the origin of the term and four views of its meaning (*Punta suprema dell'anima*, 33-43).

133. This is the conclusion of Poli, who states, "si può dire in una frase che il 'centro' e il 'fondo' significano dove Dio è nell'uomo e si communica a lui, mentre la 'punta' ciò per cui e con cui l'uomo aderisce e accetta Dio" (*Punta suprema dell'anima*, 198; see also 201).

134. See the texts and discussion in Poli, *Punta suprema dell'anima*, 122-32.

135. See the entries under "Heart" in Mary Loyola Lynn and Mary Grace Flynn, *Index to the Writings of Saint Francis de Sales* (Philadelphia: Visitation Monasteries in the United States, 1968), 51-52. For a study of Francis's teaching on the heart within the history of Augustinian views of the heart, see Hélène Michon, "Le

Coeur dans la tradition augustinienne," in *Augustin au XVIIe siècle*, ed. Laurence Devillairs (Florence: Leo S. Olschki, 2007), 203–20 (210–13 on Francis). See also Wright, "Captured Yet Free," 71–89.

136. *Introduction* II.12 (*Oeuvres* III:92; trans., 92–93). The interior "Examinations" advised in part V, chaps. 4–10 are all directed to the heart.

137. *Treatise* VIII.1 (*Oeuvres* V:60; trans., Mackey, 325–26).

138. Poli, *Punta suprema dell'anima*, 27.

139. The bishop also treats devotion in a number of his letters: e.g., *Letters to Persons in the World*, 52–53, 56; and *Letters to Persons in Religion*, 33, where devotion is defined as "the promptitude, fervor, affection and agility which we have in the service of God." In addition, the summary of Francis's teaching compiled by Jean-Pierre Camus contains a chapter on devotion; see *The Spirit of St. François de Sales*, chap. 4 (28–36). Michael Buckley aptly calls devotion "magnanimity in love" ("Seventeenth-Century French Spirituality: Three Figures," 36).

140. *Introduction*, I.1 (*Oeuvres* III:14–15; trans., 36).

141. Camus, *Spirit of St. Françoise de Sales*, 31.

142. Bremond, *History*, 1:82.

143. *Introduction* I.3 (*Oeuvres* III:20–21; trans., 40).

144. The universality of the vocation to perfection has been studied by Vytautas Balciunas, *La vocation universelle à la perfection chrétienne selon Saint François de Sales* (Annecy: Académie salésienne, 1952).

145. For a discussion of the various models, see Julien-Eymard d'Angers, "Les degrees de perfection d'après saint François de Sales," *Revue d'ascétique et de mystique* 44 (1968): 11–31.

146. This comes from a "Memo on Christian Perfection" of uncertain date that Francis left among his papers (*Oeuvres* XXVI:185–87; translated in *Letters of Spiritual Direction*, 105–6).

147. *Conference IV*, part I (*Oeuvres* VI:70; trans., Mackey, *Spiritual Conferences*, 70).

148. *Letters to Persons in the World*, 10. Similar advice about using our imperfections to progress in humility is found in *Letters to Persons in Religion*, 23–25 and 257–58.

149. *Letters of Spiritual Direction*, 112.

150. *Letters to Persons in Religion*, 120.

151. These pieces of advice can be found in the *Letters to Persons in the World*, at 282, 383, and 184.

152. Camus, *Spirit of St. François de Sales*, 121. The same section gives the bishop's three rules for spiritual progress: (1) spiritual progress depends not on doing much but on acting in the spirit of love; (2) one good work done out of love is better than many done out of laziness; and (3) the worth of any good work depends on the purity of intention it is done with.

153. *Treatise* XII.6 (*Oeuvres* V:329; trans., Mackey, 541).

154. See, for example, the references to the soul as mystic dove (preface), mystical temple (I.12), mystical tree (II.13), mystical ladder (III.5), mystical and imaginary vision (III.12), mystical victim (V.8), mystical circle (V.8), mystical sleep (VI.8), mystical nightingale (IX.10), and mystical bees (XII.4).

155. *Treatise* VI.1 (*Oeuvres* IV:301–11; trans., Mackey, 231–35). See Terence O'Reilly, "The Mystical Theology of Saint Francis de Sales in the *Traité de l'amour*

de Dieu," in *Mysticism in the French Tradition: Eruptions from France*, ed. Louise Nelstrop and Bradley B. Onishi (Burlington, VT: Ashgate, 2015), 207-20.

156. Francis roots his customary complacency-benevolence understanding of love in Bernard of Clairvaux's discussion of love as *actus* and *affectus* in *Sermo super Cantica* 50.2.

157. Mystical theology is taken up elsewhere in the *Treatise* (e.g., V.2, VI.4, VII.4), but these discussions do not add anything substantially new. The fundamentals remain the same: mystical theology is affective; it is incommunicable; and it describes the whole ascent of prayer (see Michon, *Saint François de Sales*, 40-42).

158. Like John of the Cross, Francis emphasizes the obscurity of faith to rational understanding, illustrating this by quoting Song of Songs 1:4: "I am black but beautiful."

159. *Treatise* II.22 (*Oeuvres* IV:163; trans., Mackey, 124).

160. *Treatise* V.1 (*Oeuvres* IV:255; trans., Mackey, 196).

161. *Treatise* V.2 (*Oeuvres* IV:260-62; trans., Mackey, 200-201). For a study of this motif in Francis, see Suzanne Toczysky, "'Blessed the Breasts at Which You Nursed': Mother-Child Intimacy in St. Francis de Sales' *Treatise on the Love of God*," *Spiritus* 15 (2005): 191-213. For other uses, see III.10, VI.9-10, VII.1-2, IX.14, etc. Toczysky notes three aspects to the motif: (1) milk as love; (2) nursing as contemplative practice; and (3) the goal of union with God.

162. All these passages are from *Treatise* V.3 (*Oeuvres* IV:263-67; trans., Mackey, 203-4). It is interesting to compare this passage with Meister Eckhart's consideration of the dialectic of hungering and satiation in his comment on Ecclesiasticus 24:29 ("They that eat me shall yet hunger"). This passage from the Dominican's *Sermones et Lectiones super Ecclesiastici c. 24* is translated in Bernard McGinn, *Meister Eckhart Teacher and Preacher*, Classics of Western Spirituality (New York: Paulist Press, 1986), 174-81. A passage from the end of VI.13 (*Oeuvres* IV:350-51; trans., Mackey, 271) also emphasizes epektetic love on earth but denies that such can exist in heaven, where the divine will gives the soul a total quiet that brings an end to the thirst for greater love.

163. *Introduction* III.2 (*Oeuvres* III:132): *la tendreté envers le prochain*. See also IV.14, as well as several letters (e.g., *Letters to Persons in the World*, 298; *Letters of Spiritual Direction*, 180).

164. Camus, *Spirit of St. François de Sales*, chaps. 7, 9, 11, and 19-20.

165. *Treatise* V.6 (*Oeuvres* IV:277; trans., Mackey, 214).

166. See *Treatise* V.8, 10, and 12.

167. *Treatise* V.11 (*Oeuvres* IV:294-95; trans., Mackey, 226-27).

168. Major passages on Christ's Passion can be found in *Treatise* V.4 and 5, VI.12 and 14, VII.8, IX.12 and 15, X.17, and XII.13.

169. For an important analysis, see Bremond, chap. 2, "François de Sales et la Philosophie de la Prière," in Bremond, *Histoire*, vol. 3 (new ed., 63-104). Bremond sees Francis's teaching on prayer as having three stages: (1) an initial passivity through the gift of sanctifying grace; (2) human activity in prayer up to the level of acquiescence and adhesion; and (3) a final passivity of annihilation and indifference.

170. For a consideration of these books, see Michon, *Saint François de Sales*, part 3 (181-265).

171. On meditation in Francis, see Clooney, *Beyond Compare*, 90-94.

172. *Treatise* VI.2 (*Oeuvres* IV:306; trans., Mackey, 235).
173. *Treatise* VI.3 (*Oeuvres* IV:313–14; trans., Mackey, 241).
174. Francis seems to have in mind a passage from STh IIaIIae, q. 82, a. 3, ad 3.
175. Francis begins by referring to the Dionysian commentaries of Thomas Gallus and goes on to note a story about the Franciscan Brother Giles of Assisi, a passage from Augustine's *Confessions*, and the witness of Catherine of Genoa, before closing with a list of other theological authorities.
176. The extent to which this "simple steady regard" may approach Quietist views of the "one simple act" cannot be taken up here.
177. *Treatise* VI.6 (*Oeuvres* IV:322–25; trans., Mackey, 247–50).
178. Ibid. (*Oeuvres* IV:325; trans., Ryan, 1:285).
179. For other appearances of the divinization theme, e.g., X.11 (*Oeuvres* V:206), which speaks of the love of God working in us as "par consequent rendu capable de participer à sa bonté en la grace et en la gloire"; and X.17 (*Oeuvres* V:230), which says, "Il nous ayma d'amour de bienveuillance, jettant sa proper Divinité en l'homme, en sorte que l'homme fut Dieu."
180. *Treatise* VI.7 (*Oeuvres* IV:326; trans., Mackey, 251). At this point Francis quotes a passage from Teresa's *Interior Castle* IV.3.
181. The term "presence" occurs a dozen times in the chapter. Special divine presence as a trigger to recollection also occurs in the following chaps. 8–11, and in VII.1.
182. *Treatise* VI.7 (*Oeuvres* IV:329; trans., Mackey, 254): ". . . car la seule presence de Dieu, au seul sentiment que nous avons qu'il nous regarde, ou des le Ciel ou de quelqu'autre lieu hors de nous, . . . nos facultés et puissances se ramassent et assemblent en nous mesmes pour la reverence de sa Majesté." Francis closes by giving an example of someone he knows (Jane de Chantal?), who goes into ecstasy whenever mention of something about God puts her in mind of this presence.
183. The letters frequently speak about being in God's presence; see, e.g., *Letters of Spiritual Direction*, 151–53, 199, 218, 257–58; and *Letters to Persons in the World*, 31–32, 136–37, 332–33. There are also considerations of God's presence in *Conference* XI, and Camus, *Spirit of Saint François de Sales*, 40–41.
184. On the prayer of quiet repose in Francis, see Kelley, *Spirit of Love*, 167–74.
185. *Treatise* VI.8 (*Oeuvres* IV:330–31; trans., Mackey, 255). This is reminiscent of a passage in IX.10, where Francis says that a person who is really praying should not even notice that she is praying.
186. See *Letters of Spiritual Direction*, 84–86, 167. The same type of prayer is also mentioned by Jane de Chantal.
187. Teresa used the image in the *Way of Perfection*, chap. 31.9.
188. *Treatise* VI.9 (*Oeuvres* IV:335; trans., Mackey, 258).
189. *Treatise* VI.10 (*Oeuvres* IV:336–37; trans., Mackey, 259). The reference to Teresa is again to the *Way of Perfection*, chap. 31. Francis also makes another reference to a person of his acquaintance (Jane de Chantal?), who could remain in spiritual tranquillity so that she could understand what was said around her but not respond to it.
190. *Treatise* VI.11 (*Oeuvres* IV:342–43; trans., Mackey, 264).
191. Francis's freedom from strict adherence to any single method of prayer is evident from *Conference* XVIII (*Spiritual Conferences*, 359).

192. Thomas Aquinas discussed liquefaction as one of the effects of *amor* in STh IaIIae, q. 28, a. 5, ad 1. On this chapter, see Clooney, *Beyond Compare*, 94–98.

193. *Treatise* VI.12 (*Oeuvres* IV:346; trans., Mackey, 267): ". . . ne voyent rien en la terre qui les contente, et vivans en un extreme aneantissement d'eux mesmes demeurent fort alangouris en tout ce qui appartient aux sens."

194. A stronger passage is found in IX.13 (*Oeuvres* V:151; trans., Mackey, 399–400), where Francis says, "Mais la volunté qui est morte a soy mesmes pour vivre en celle de Dieu, elle est sans aucun vouloir particulier, demeurant non seulement conforme et sujette, mais toute aneantie en elle mesmes et convertie en celle de Dieu." For some other uses of annihilation language, see II.16, VII.6, IX.2, IX.17, and XI.19. Annihilation is found also in the letters; see, e.g., *Letters to Persons in Religion*, 93, 240, 297–98, 366, and 379, as well as the *Spiritual Conferences* IV and XX (trans., Mackey, 73, 387 and 395).

195. The "indices" to Francis's vocabulary are notable examples of this blindness, since neither the French nor the English has entries under "annihilation."

196. For the wound of love in Francis, see Kelley, *Spirit of Love*, 174–83.

197. *Treatise* VI.13 (*Oeuvres* IV:350; trans., Ryan 1:305).

198. *Treatise* VI.14 (*Oeuvres* IV:352; trans., Mackey, 272).

199. *Treatise* VI.14 (*Oeuvres* IV:353; trans. Mackey, 272).

200. *Treatise* VI.14 (*Oeuvres* IV:355; trans., Ryan 1:309).

201. *Treatise* VI.15 (*Oeuvres* IV:360; trans., Mackey, 278).

202. Book VII is the central treatment of union in the *Treatise*, although the theme comes up in many places. Other important texts include I.7, 9, 10, 12, 15; II.15; III.6, 9–15 (union enjoyed in heaven); V.5–6; VI.2, 4, 10–11; VIII.13; IX.1–4, and 12; X.10, 17; and XI.16. There is a brief discussion in *Introduction* III.5. On Francis's teaching on union, see Bergamo, *L'anatomie de l'âme*, 169–80, though I do not share all his conclusions.

203. *Treatise* VII.1 (*Oeuvres* V:10; trans., Ryan 2:17).

204. At the conclusion of the chapter, Francis discusses the three forms of union found in Christ the God-man (*Oeuvres* V:14).

205. *Treatise* VII.3 (*Oeuvres* V:16; trans., Mackey, 291).

206. Francis also talks about union in his sermons; see especially the "Sermon for the Third Sunday of Lent," of February 27, 1622, in *Sermons of St. Francis de Sales for Lent*, 83–98. Citing John 17:20, Jesus's prayer that we might be made one with the Trinity, Francis cautions, "Thus we cannot really hope to reach an identical union, for it is impossible, as all the ancient Fathers point out" (83). But later in the sermon, again quoting John 17:11–12 and 21–22, he says that loving union that makes us "one same thing with God" (95–96).

207. Ecstasy and ravishment/rapture are frequent topics in the *Treatise*. Along with the extended discussion in VII.3–8, see I.10, III.8, VI.3–4, 11–12, and X.10, 17.

208. Francis also warns about the dangers of some ravishments in Letter LVII in *Letters to Persons in the World*, 399–400.

209. *Treatise* VII.6 (*Oeuvres* V:28; trans. Mackey, 300).

210. *Treatise* VII.7 (*Oeuvres* V:30–31; trans., Mackey, 302).

211. *Treatise* VII.8 (*Oeuvres* V:35; trans., Mackey, 306).

212. On this motif in Christian mysticism, see Alois M. Haas, "Mors mystica—Ein mystologisches Motiv," in Haas, *Sermo mysticus: Studien zu Theologie und*

Sprache in der deutschen Mystik, Dokimion 4 (Freiburg, Switzerland: Universitätsverlag, 1979), 392–480.

213. *Treatise* VII.9 (*Oeuvres* V:36; trans., Mackey, 307).

214. On Francis's use of exemplary lives to illustrate love, see Clooney, *Beyond Compare*, 113–19.

215. Both quotations from *Treatise* VIII.1 (*Oeuvres* V:60–62; trans., Mackey, 326–27).

216. *Treatise* VIII.2 (*Oeuvres* V:63; trans., Mackey, 328).

217. On the divine will in Francis, see Joseph F. Power, "Entre l'une et l'autre volonté divine," in *L'Unidivers salésien: Saint François de Sales hier et aujourd'hui*, ed. Hélène Bordes and Jacques Hennequin (Paris: Université de Metz, 1994), 265–75.

218. The distinction between God's *voluntas beneplaciti* and *voluntas signi* seems to first appear in Peter Lombard's *Libri Sententiarum* I, dist. 45, cap. 5–6., and is found also in Thomas Aquinas, STh Ia, q. 19, aa. 11–12.

219. All quotations are from *Treatise* VIII.3 (*Oeuvres* V:65–67; trans., Mackey, 330–31).

220. Michon (*Saint François de Sales*, 215–18) suggests that the inspiration for this triple pattern came from Benet of Canfield.

221. *Treatise* VIII.4 (*Oeuvres* V:69; trans., Mackey, 332).

222. *Treatise* VIII.6 (*Oeuvres* V:74; trans., Mackey, 337).

223. *Treatise* VIII.7 (*Oeuvres* V:78; trans., Mackey, 340).

224. *Treatise* VIII.10 (*Oeuvres* V:89; trans., Mackey, 349).

225. My thanks to Wendy M. Wright for emphasizing the role of discernment.

226. *Treatise* VIII.14 (*Oeuvres* V:107; my trans.).

227. On loving surrender to God, see Clooney, *Beyond Compare*, chap. 4.

228. *Treatise* IX.2 (*Oeuvres* V:112; my trans.).

229. The reference to Angela of Foligno in IX.3 shows knowledge of her *Memoriale*, especially the sixth supplemental *passus* on dereliction; see Ludger Their and Abele Calufetti, eds., *Il libro della Beata Angela da Foligno* (Rome: Editiones Collegii S. Bonaventurae, 1985), 330–44. On mystical dereliction, see Bernard McGinn, "Suffering, Dereliction, and Affliction in Christian Mysticism," in *Suffering and the Christian Life*, ed. Karen Kilby and Rachel Davies (London: T&T Clark, 2019), 55–70.

230. Jane de Chantal's dereliction in the midst of temptations against faith are evident in a number of the surviving letters of her correspondence with Francis. For English versions, see *Letters of Spiritual Direction*, 153–55; and *Letters to Persons in Religion*, 100–103, 169–70.

231. *Treatise* IX.3 (*Oeuvres* V:118; my trans.): ". . . mais a la charge que tousjours le sacré acquiescement se fasse dans le fond de l'ame, en la supreme et plus delicate pointe de l'esprit. . . . [E]t semble qu'il soit retiré au fin bout de l'esprit, comme dans le dungeon de la forteresse, ou il demeure courageux."

232. The importance of indifference has been recognized by almost all who have written on Francis de Sales. The best treatment is in Mino Bergamo, *La science des saints: Le discours mystique au XVIIe siècle en France* (Grenoble: Jérôme Millon, 1992), 46–59, who shows how Francis transformed Ignatius Loyola's ascetic view of indifference into a mystical category. See also Kelley, *Spirit of Love*, 205–18; and Michon, *Saint François de Sales*, 230–38. There is also an important

general survey by André Rayez, "Indifference," DS 7:1688-1708, who treats "Indifference Salesienne" on 1701-4.

233. *Treatise* IX.4 (*Oeuvres* V:119; trans., Ryan 2:105).
234. *Treatise* IX.4 (*Oeuvres* V:122; trans., Mackey, 375).
235. *Treatise* IX.7 (*Oeuvres* V:130; trans., Mackey, 382).
236. *Treatise* IX.7 (*Oeuvres* V:133; trans., Mackey, 385).
237. *Treatise* IX.8 (*Oeuvres* V:135; trans., Mackey, 386).
238. *Treatise* IX.10 (*Oeuvres* V:141; trans., Mackey, 391).
239. *Treatise* IX.11 (*Oeuvres* V:143; trans., Mackey, 393).
240. *Treatise* IX.11 (*Oeuvres* V:145; trans., Mackey, 394).
241. *Treatise* IX.11 (*Oeuvres* V:144; trans., Mackey, 394).
242. This Good Friday Sermon has been translated in *Sermons of St. Francis de Sales for Lent*, 177-207. The seven last words are treated on 189-207, with the passage cited at 206.
243. *Treatise* IX.12 (*Oeuvres* V:147; trans., Mackey, 396).
244. *Treatise* IX.12 (*Oeuvres* V:148; trans., Mackey, 396-97; partly corrected with Ryan 2:128).
245. *Treatise* IX.13 (*Oeuvres* V:149; trans., Mackey, 398).
246. *Treatise* IX.14 (*Oeuvres* V:152-53; trans., Mackey, 401).
247. *Treatise* IX.15 (*Oeuvres* V:158; trans., Mackey, 405).
248. *Treatise* IX.16 (*Oeuvres* V:162; trans., Mackey, 408).
249. For a treatment of books X-XII as summarizing the life of loving surrender, see Clooney, *Beyond Compare*, 196-202.
250. *Treatise* X.1 (*Oeuvres* V:165; my trans.).
251. *Treatise* X.3 (*Oeuvres* V:171; trans., Mackey, 415).
252. *Treatise* X.3 (*Oeuvres* V:174; trans., Mackey, 417).
253. *Treatise* X.4 (*Oeuvres* V:179; trans., Ryan 2: 150).
254. *Treatise* X.5 (*Oeuvres* V:182; trans., Mackey, 422).
255. *Treatise* X.5 (*Oeuvres* V:184; trans., Mackey, 423). In the Sixth Discourse of the *Mystical Explanation of the Canticle of Canticles,* Francis identifies the bride with any soul who has reached the perfection of devotion (*Mystical Explanation*, 36-41).
256. *Treatise* X.12 (*Oeuvres* V:207; trans., Ryan 2:173).
257. Pure love is also discussed in some of the bishop's letters; see, e.g., *Letters of Spiritual Direction*, 96, 108, 257.
258. Both quotations from *Treatise* X.13 (*Oeuvres* V:212; trans., Ryan 2:177). According to the Annecy edition, the source in Catherine of Genoa is in her *Vita*, chaps. 18 and 37. Use of Catherine of Genoa by Francis and other French mystics often centered on her doctrine of pure love; see Papàsogli, *Gli Spirituali Italiani e il "Grand Siècle,"* 9-21, 46.
259. *Treatise* X.17 (*Oeuvres* V:229-33; trans., Mackey, 460-63).
260. *Treatise* X.17 (*Oeuvres* V:232; trans., Mackey, 462).
261. Aquinas, STh IaIIae, q. 62, a. 4; IIaIIae, q. 23, aa. 7, 8.
262. *Treatise* XI.3 (*Oeuvres* V:243; trans., Mackey, 471).
263. *Treatise* XI.16 (*Oeuvres* V:293-94; trans., Mackey, 511).
264. *Treatise* XII.1 (*Oeuvres* V:319; trans., Mackey, 533).
265. *Treatise* XII.2 (*Oeuvres* V:321; trans., Ryan 2:263).
266. *Treatise* XII.5 (*Oeuvres* V:328; trans., Ryan 2:268).
267. *Treatise* XII.7 (*Oeuvres* V:331; trans., Mackey, 542).

268. Francis recognizes that not everyone agrees with this teaching, so he also cites Bonaventure in its support (*In II Sent.*, d. 41, a. 1, concl.). In this chapter, Francis praises Ignatius Loyola and his work in popularizing retreats and the use of spiritual exercises.

269. *Treatise* XII.10 (*Oeuvres* V:341; trans., Mackey, 550-51).

270. *Treatise* XII.12 (*Oeuvres* V:344-45; trans., Mackey, 553).

271. *Treatise* XII.13 (*Oeuvres* V:346; trans., Ryan 2:281).

272. This is the gist of the critique of Hans Urs von Balthasar, despite his appreciation for many aspects of Francis's theology. After briefly summarizing the contents of the *Treatise*, he writes, "This means that the most important thing of all—the whole objective history of salvation, Incarnation, Redemption, Justification, the Church and Christian life in the world (obviously because it belongs to dogmatic theology)—is excluded, and so all that this 'spiritual theology' is left with is the anthropocentric point of view. This naively unintentional anthropocentricism of a spirituality that imagines itself to be totally theocentric, and indeed excessively presents itself as such, characterizes many of the systems of the seventeenth century and at least infects several others" (*The Glory of the Lord: A Theological Aesthetics*, vol. 5, *The Realm of Metaphysics in the Modern Age* [San Francisco: Ignatius Press, 1991], 116).

273. Camus is treated in Bremond, *History*, 1:118-47, mostly from a literary point of view. Cognet (*La spiritualité moderne*, 304-9) summarizes the problems of Camus's thought thus: ". . . les incohérences de Camus ne l'ont jamais éloigné du maître dont il n'a point cessé de vénérer la mémoire" (309).

274. Jean-Pierre Camus, *La théologie mystique 1640* (Grenoble: Jérôme Millon, 2003), 71. Camus's idiosyncratic view of mysticism is evident throughout chap. 1, "Pourfil de la Théologie Mystique" (37-72).

275. For an introduction, see Roger Devos, "Jeanne-Françoise de Chantal (sainte)," DS 8:859-69. See also Cognet, *La spiritualité moderne*, 399-404. In English, see Elisabeth Stopp, *Madame de Chantal: Portrait of a Saint* (Westminster, MD: Newman Press, 1963); and *Hidden in God: Essays and Talks on St. Jane Frances de Chantal* (Philadelphia: St. Joseph's University Press, 1999). Bremond's chap. 7, "François de Sales and Jeanne de Chantal" (*History*, 2:394-429) remains one of the most sensitive treatments of the relationship of the two figures. Bremond's book on Jane, *Sainte Chantal (1572-1641)*, was published to much acclaim in 1912 and was put on the Index in 1913 for "Modernist" tendencies. See the account in Gorday, *Pure Love, Pure Poetry, Pure Prayer*, 119-24.

276. See the writings of Wendy M. Wright referred to above: *Francis de Sales and Jane de Chantal: Letters of Spiritual Direction* (1988); and *Heart Speaks to Heart: The Salesian Tradition* (2004).

277. Jane de Chantal's writings were edited (poorly) twice in the nineteenth century: first in two volumes by the Abbé Migne (1862), and second by the nuns of Annecy. That edition will be used here, *Sainte Jeanne-Françoise Frémyot de Chantal: Sa vie et ses Oeuvres*, 8 vols. (Paris: E. Plon, 1874-79). Volume 1 contains the life of Jane by her last secretary, Françoise-Madeleine de Chaugy; vols. 2-3 are her prose works; vols. 4-8 contain her two thousand letters.

278. Translations of fifty-five of Jane's letters by Péronne Marie Thibert can be found in Wright, *Francis de Sales, Jane de Chantal: Letters of Spiritual Direction*, 183-266, with helpful introductions about the recipients.

279. The most useful of the treatises seem to be the seven *Opuscules* found in the Plon edition, 3:259–96, especially the first, the *Short Treatise on Prayer* (*Petit Traité sur l'Oraison*) (259–68). There is an English translation of most of vol. 2 of the Plon edition, which contains Jane's exhortations, conferences, and instructions given to the nuns; see *Saint Jane Frances Frémyot de Chantal: Her Exhortations, Conferences and Instructions* (Westminster, MD: Newman Bookshop, 1947).

280. There is a helpful book in English that summarizes her teaching on prayer: Auguste Saudreau, *Mystical Prayer according to St. Jane de Chantal* (London: Sheed & Ward, 1929). The work translates many passages from her writings.

281. Wright, *Letters of Spiritual Direction*, especially 34–90.

282. "Letter to André Frémyot" of 1625 (Wright, *Letters of Spiritual Direction*, 202). See also 188, 216, and many passages in the *Exhortations, Conferences and Instructions*, e.g., 203, 246–47, 343, 447, etc.

283. Conference XXVI in *Exhortations, Conferences and Instructions*, 230; see also 270 and 293.

284. See, e.g., the "Letter to a Visitandine," in Wright, *Letters of Spiritual Direction*, 266; and various texts in the *Exhortations, Conferences and Instructions*, e.g., 292–93, 448, 472, etc.

285. Wright, *Letters of Spiritual Direction*, 239.

286. Ibid. The slogan occurs throughout Jane's works.

287. Ibid., 205.

288. For a translation of this text, see Wright, *Heart Speaks to Heart*, 64.

289. *Entretien* XXXII, in *Sa vie et ses Oeuvres*, 2:331–33 (trans. Saudreau, 17–19).

290. *Entretien* XXXIII, 2:335–37 (my trans.).

291. *Petit Traité sur l'Oraison*, in *Sa vie et ses Oeuvres*, 3:259–68.

292. *Petit Traité* (3:260; my trans.).

293. *Petit Traité* (3:262; trans. Saudreau, 74).

294. The first rule is the inability to meditate; the second is when the heart has no attraction for fixing itself on any object that might help it in the practice of virtue; and the third is when the soul "takes pleasure in being alone in loving attention to God, without any special consideration" (3:276–77).

295. *Règles Données* (3:280; my trans.).

296. *Conseils de Direction à Une Supèrieure* (3:338; my trans.).

297. *Paroles Consolantes* No. 19 (3:461; my trans.). Saudreau collects a number of texts on how to deal with aridity and desolation in prayer (*Mystical Prayer*, 82–90).

298. *Paroles Consolantes* No. 26 (3:463; my trans.).

299. "Letter to a Visitandine," in Wright, *Letters of Spiritual Direction*, 257.

CHAPTER 4

Pierre de Bérulle
*Annihilation and Elevation**

Introduction: Bérulle's Theocentric Christocentrism

Pierre Cardinal de Bérulle (1575–1629) is central to the story of French seventeenth-century mysticism. Pope Urban VIII is said to have called him "the Apostle of the Incarnate Word."[1] What sets off Bérulle's particular form of mystical Christocentrism from others is the way in which he integrates the economy of the Incarnate Word into a powerful theocentric Trinitarianism. Henri Bremond, the modern rediscoverer of Bérulle, begins his account of the cardinal's thought by highlighting its theocentric nature,[2] but Bremond and later twentieth-century interpreters of Bérulle also stressed the importance of the ontological mediation of Jesus, the God-man, in his writings. In his brief discussion of Bérulle, Hans Urs von Balthasar says, "In the concrete order of the world, as the supreme miracle of divine grace, the God-Man Jesus Christ is like the bridge between the infinite and the finite, between absolute glory and absolute adoration, the mediator of the religious act."[3] One way to express this mediatorial function is to

---

* I want to thank Prof. William Thompson-Uberuaga, noted expert on Bérulle and his followers, who kindly agreed to read this chapter and made many valuable suggestions for changes. Errors that may remain are entirely the responsibility of the author.

speak of Bérulle's *christocentrisme théocentrique*, a term used by the editors of the modern critical edition.[4] What the phrase also brings out is that, for Cardinal Bérulle, as for his predecessor Cardinal Bonaventure, it is impossible to separate the Trinitarian from the Christological dimensions of the mystical path. As William M. Thompson noted, "Bérulle's originality consists in the consistent manner in which he drew spiritual consequences from his theology of the Incarnation."[5] For Bérulle, we never attain the Trinitarian God directly, "on our own," so to speak. We find God in the humanity and the humanity in the divinity of the Person of Jesus Christ, who is the only way to God, because he is both God and man. Through our union with Christ we come to share in the Son's relation to the Father, the relation by which he is one with the Father in essence and distinct from him in Person by mutual relationality.

Bérulle's integration of the activity of the Trinity, both within God and in creation, with the Incarnation of the Word as the focus of cosmos and history—his theocentric Christocentrism—involves a series of doctrinal themes to be discussed below. Three that are of particular significance can be set out here in preliminary fashion: *anéantissement, adhérence,* and *adoration.*[6] *Anéantissement* (annihilation), being reduced to nothing, is used along with a number of related terms, such as *abnégation, abaissement* (abasement), and the Latinate *exinanition* (emptying),[7] to express the act of radical self-dispossession by which the Word of God takes on human nature and conceals his divine status and glory in the nothingness of created humanity. As Vincent Carraud puts it, "The notion of nothing [*néant*] is without doubt the most operative notion of Bérullian theology."[8] Many late medieval and early modern mystics had developed doctrines of annihilation, as we have seen with Benet of Canfield, but their teaching generally dealt with human annihilation, that is, the necessity of the mystic to let go of self, sometimes conceived of in a primarily moral fashion, sometimes with a more ontological valence. Bérulle was unique in rooting the need for human *anéantissement/abnégation* in the exemplary act of emptying found in the Incarnation. To paraphrase the formula going back to Irenaeus: "The Word annihilated himself, so that humans too might be annihilated."

The language of *adhérence*, also frequent in Bérulle's writings, expresses another central aspect of the cardinal's thought. *Adhérence* is also linked to a number of synonymous terms to express the way in which humans willingly bind themselves to God and the Incarnate Word (*apartenance, liaison, application*). Henri Bremond insisted that *adhérence* is the "more expressive and exact" of these words, because,

"To adhere, whether to God himself or to the God-Man, is 'to unite ourselves' actively to God or to the God-Man, dwelling and acting in us; to present ourselves, to open our hearts, to surrender ourselves . . . , to subject ourselves to this Divine presence and action."[9] Here too there is a Pauline root, the union text in 1 Corinthians 6:17: "The person who adheres to God, is one spirit [with him] [*qui autem adhaeret Deo, unus spiritus est*]." *Adhérence* is the way in which we come to participate in what Bérulle famously calls the "states" (*états*) of Jesus, that is, the distinctive modes of being of the God-man. The notion of being bound to God through sharing in the states of the life of Jesus has affinity with another key theme of Bérulle's thought: *servitude*, the voluntary recognition of our own nothingness and acceptance of our total dependence on God.[10]

Adherence/adhesion is connected to the fundamental religious attitude of both the God-man and those who are one with him, namely *adoration*, returning to God the praise and love due to him as Creator and Redeemer. The created universe exists to adore its Creator, but all such adoration is finite. Only the God-man can give truly adequate adoration to God. Addressing Jesus, Bérulle says, "You alone adore him with an infinite adoration, as he is infinitely worthy of being served and adored. . . . From all eternity there had been a God infinitely adorable, but there still had not been an infinite adorer. . . . You are now, O Jesus, this adorer. . . . From now on we have a God served and adored without any defect in this adoration, and a God who adores, without detraction from his divinity!"[11] Although humans on their own cannot offer such perfect adoration, by adhering to Jesus and participating in his state of adoration, they too are caught up into ecstatic adoration, as Bérulle tries to express in the numerous *élévations*, the rhetorical prayers of praise and adoration, that fill his writings.[12] Another way of characterizing Bérulle's thought, therefore, is to call it a mysticism of adoration. Annihilation, adherence, and adoration are different modes of expressing the objective union with God we are given through the saving action of the God-man.

Bérulle's Life and Writings

The importance of Bérulle's thought and his efforts toward the reform of the church in early seventeenth-century France are not in question. Nonetheless, these contributions have not precluded ongoing criticism, both in his day and afterwards. For all his influence in France,

Bérulle is not well known outside the Francophone world. Even in France, his message seems to have been largely disseminated through his followers until the revival of interest that started about a century ago. As a result of this revival, we are now in possession of an excellent critical edition,[13] along with a number of general surveys,[14] as well as studies on specific issues.[15] In English there is relatively little. Only a few excerpts of Bérulle's lengthy writings are available,[16] as well as a handful of monographs and some helpful essays.[17]

Theoretically and stylistically, Bérulle broke new ground in the history of mysticism, but the Baroque form of epideictic rhetoric he used, while suited to the era of French Absolutism, is often difficult for modern readers to appreciate.[18] His outbursts of praise and devotion (no mystic was more devoted to the exclamation point!), as well as the repetitive character of his writings, especially of his central work, the *Discourses on the State and Grandeurs of Jesus* (hereafter *Grandeurs*), often make reading Bérulle a strain.[19] His speculative expositions are frequently dense and difficult to follow. While Bérulle's rhetoric may be a barrier for some contemporary readers, students of the history of the French language have praised his style and its contribution to the development of French prose. The following sketch of Bérulle's life will briefly locate his writings in the context of his often contentious career.

Like most of the seventeenth-century French mystics, Pierre de Bérulle was born into an aristocratic family, "nobles of the robe," that is, legal functionaries of the monarchy. The year was 1575. In the confusion of the Wars of Religion, his father, Claude de Bérulle, counselor of the *Parlement*, died when he was only seven, so his mother took him to Paris to be raised in her aristocratic family, the Séguiers. We know little about his early years, save that he was pious and given to study. His education was mostly under Jesuit auspices, especially at the College de Clermont (1592–94). He later took a theology degree at the Sorbonne.

Bérulle had received a good theological education, but he never formally taught theology, nor are his writings technical theological treatises. He was deeply influenced by a number of the great mystics and theologians of the patristic and medieval traditions. Jean Dagens emphasized Augustine as the major influence in his thinking, and Bérulle cites the bishop often.[20] The influence of the Pseudo-Dionysius is a special case, to be taken up below. Bérulle refers to a number of medieval mystics, such as Bernard of Clairvaux, and his theocentric Christocentrism bears interesting comparison with Bonaventure, as noted above. Bérulle knew the Latin and French translations of some of the late medieval Northern mystics, especially Hendrik Herp (Harphius) and the author of the *Evangelical Pearl*, but how influential they actually were on his thinking is not easy to evaluate.[21] When Bérulle was a student at the Sorbonne, Thomas Aquinas's two *summae* were part of the curriculum, and Bérulle often later referred to Thomas. In a letter from 1624, he says that his Christology is that found "in the school of Saint Thomas, whom we follow in this and in the matter of grace and in all the rest, as much as we are able."[22] Bérulle does generally adhere to Thomas and the Chalcedonian tradition in his Christology, but his manner of expressing this and the spirituality he draws from it is distinctly "Bérullian." The cardinal's knowledge of other patristic and scholastic authors has been studied by Dagens in some detail.[23]

In the middle-1590s the young Pierre became a part of the mystical salon of Madame Acarie, his cousin, and took the Carthusian Richard Beaucousin as his spiritual director. Bérulle was a frequent visitor to Acarie's house for many years. Here he would have come into contact with Benet of Canfield and also met Francis de Sales in 1602. It appears to have been at Beaucousin's urging that Bérulle produced his first work, the *Brief Discourse on Interior Abnegation* (*Bref discours de l'abnégation interieure*), published in 1597, an adaptation of the *Breve Compendio* of the Italian Jesuit Achille Gagliardi, based on his conversations with the Milanese mystic Isabella Berinzaga.[24] This treatise was a concentrated presentation of a theocentric mysticism based on the need to negate and annihilate all created things to attain a union with God beyond images and created means. A key problem concerning this text was the role of Christ in the path to God, something that the *Bref discours* does not deny, but also (rather significantly) never mentions. The young Bérulle, ordained in 1599, was soon to change his mind dramatically on this issue. This juvenile work, then, is an initial presentation of the theocentric aspect of Bérulle's developing mysticism, such as the importance of annihilation, but it completely neglects the central Christocentric dimension.[25]

In 1599, Bérulle became embroiled in the first of many controversies in his life: the affair of Marthe Brossier. Marthe was a young woman who was declared a demoniac and exorcised by the Capuchins, but the debate over whether she was really possessed took on a political dimension due to her anti-Huguenot proclamations, which served the interests of the intransigent Catholic Leaguers against the policy of Henry IV and the Paris *Parlement*, who had recently issued the Edict of Nantes (1598). Bérulle's contribution to the affair was more theological than polemical, a short work of 1599, the *Treatise on the Possessed* (*Traité des Energumènes*), in which he defends the exorcism and argues that the devil often tries to caricature mystical states. Some of the Capuchins were silenced; others exiled. Bérulle did not lose the king's favor, but he did show his allegiance to the strict Catholic party.

A turning point in Bérulle's life came in August 1602, when he made the Ignatian exercises at Verdun under the direction of the Jesuit Lorenzo Maggio. The young priest seems to have been engaged in a discernment process about his future: should he join a religious order (possibly the Jesuits), or continue as a diocesan priest? We are fortunate to possess the notes that he made during this retreat, which reveal a strong Christocentric turn in his thinking.[26] The nineteen points of the account are based on Ignatian headings, but what is fascinating are the places where Bérulle speaks about his own inner experiences (quite rare in his later writings), as well as his reflections on Christ as the center.[27] In Article V on the "Mystery of the Incarnation," he says, "Just as the Incarnation is the foundation of our salvation, I have also thought very profoundly how there ought to be a very great annihilation of the self through which one who is resolved to work for the salvation of his soul ought begin, until the Son of God has deigned to come to work in that mystery by way of the humiliation and abasement of the divine and eternal Person."[28] This appears to be the earliest text that testifies to one of the distinctive aspects of Bérullian mysticism: the linking of the annihilation of the Word and our own self-annihilation. It also speaks of the two forms of annihilation—that by our own efforts, and the higher form completed by Christ—a paradigm that will reappear in his later thought. In describing his desire to reach an Ignatian "election," Bérulle talks about his inner states during the thirty days. For example, in recounting the "Conclusion of the Election" in Article XII, he speaks of "an interior effect of an entirely extraordinary nature" (*un effet intérieur entièrement extraordinaire*) that he received during Mass, and in Article XIII he reflects on the inner gifts he received that confirmed his decision not to abandon his present state of life to enter the religious life.[29]

The 1602 "Retreat Account" is one of the earliest of the *Works of Piety* (*Oeuvres de piété*) that constitute the largest surviving part of Bérulle's writing, save for his letters. Numbering 385 pieces and taking up 1,155 pages in the critical edition, these occasional writings, some short, others fairly long, are a treasure trove of Bérulle's thinking on spiritual matters from early on down to his last days.[30] In the pieces that were written for himself, Bérulle often used a mixture of Latin and French, switching back and forth in a manner that would have been familiar to theologians up to about 1950, but that is lost today. It is difficult to give a general survey of this rich material, but all students of Bérulle have made ample use of these often remarkable writings.

Beginning in 1602, Bérulle became involved in the efforts to bring Teresa's Reformed Carmelite nuns to Paris, a project spearheaded by Madame Acarie, but one that would never have achieved success without the efforts of many, not least Bérulle.[31] His trip to Spain in 1604 broke the impasse over the possibility of the venture, but his promises to the nuns about their status in France, especially their relation to the Spanish male superiors, seem to have been disingenuous at best.[32] On September 15, 1604, seven Carmelite nuns finally entered Paris, among them two of Teresa's favored daughters, Ana de Jesús and Ana de San Bartolomé. A number of postulants prepared by Madame Acarie were waiting for them. Tensions grew between the Spanish nuns with their Teresian devotion to Christ's humanity and the French nuns who strove to attain the pure divine essence in their prayers. The original Spanish contingent split when it became obvious that Bérulle had no intention to allow the Spanish friars any control over the nuns, but wished to incorporate them into his own vision of French spiritual reform. Despite these crises, Carmel flourished in France. Bérulle's control over the French Carmelite nuns grew stronger, especially after he was named their permanent ecclesiastical Visitor in 1614. Although Bérulle was the papally appointed Visitor, he had to share governance of the French Carmelites with two Sorbonne theologians, André Duval and Jacques Gallement, a situation that often led to disagreements.

Bérulle's program of reform was larger than just Carmel. He took an active role in the reformation of many religious houses. During the first decade of the seventeenth century he also engaged in controversy with the Protestants (*Discours de controverse* of 1609) and continued to develop his Christological thinking, which was furthered by a mystical illumination he received in 1607. Bérulle's most noted reforming endeavor came in 1611 with the foundation of the French Oratory. In chapter 1, I have already discussed the decline of the parish clergy during the Wars of Religion. The reformers of early modern French Catholicism, such as Bérulle, recognized that a renewal of the parochial priesthood was imperative for a restoration of solid religious practice. Bérulle's successors in this endeavor (Vincent de Paul, Charles de Condren, Jean-Jacques Olier, Jean Eudes, and others) may have done more for the actual work of revitalizing diocesan priests; but Bérulle provided the theological rationale, and his foundation of an elite group of non-order priests, the French Oratory, was a beacon for inspiration and imitation. The "Oratory model" had been created in sixteenth-century Italy by Philip Neri (1515-1595). Beginning in the 1550s, Philip had attracted priests to a renewed apostolic life, forming houses of clerics living without the usual religious vows but dedicated to both contemplative prayer and apostolic life. The form of life was approved by Gregory XIII in 1575. Bérulle was inspired by Philip Neri's model, but he had something rather different in mind. Although the French Oratorians remained secular priests, Bérulle wanted a more organized structure under a central leadership and a dedication to working under the local bishops and providing resources to improve the quality of the clergy.[33] Bérulle's plans for the life and spirituality of the Oratory can be seen in another collection of his writings, the *Collationes*, the Latin conferences on the feasts of the liturgical year he gave to the early Oratorians during the years 1611 to 1615.[34]

In the second decade of the seventeenth century, Bérulle's developing Christology led him to the conviction that those aspiring to true sanctity should make a "vow of servitude" to both Mary and Jesus. Bérulle's insistence on these vows, the most controversial aspect of his ecclesiastical career, has been the subject of much study and continuing disagreement.[35] Vows of servitude to Mary were not new, having been used in Spain for centuries,[36] but Bérulle's initial insistence on making a private spiritual devotion into a public ecclesiastical act was unwise and widely criticized for a decade (1615-23). Bérulle seems to have developed his view on the vows of servitude at least partly on the basis of the Dionysian hierarchies, that is, the idea that each order (angels, humans, religious) was headed by a "Hierarch," or sacred leader (Bérulle himself in the case of the Oratorians and Carmelite nuns), who communicated divine grace to those belonging to this order.[37] But the foundations of the vows of servitude go even deeper in Bérulle's thought—into his view of the relation of creaturely nothingness to the fullness of divine life revealed to the world through the Incarnation.[38] Bérulle's personal recognition of this ontological reality is evident in the earliest copy of the vow, an autograph that may be as early as 1612. It begins:

> I make to God the vow of perpetual servitude to Jesus Christ; to his divinized humanity and to his humanized divinity, according to the intention of our Reverend Father Superior [Bérulle]. Thus, by this way, in honor of the *unity* of the Son with the Father and the Holy Spirit, and of the *union* of this same Son with this human nature

which he took and joined to his own Person, I bind my being to Jesus and to his divinized humanity by the bond of perpetual servitude.

Later in the text, typical notes of Bérullian Christology emerge: "I reverence and adore the life and the annihilation of the divinity in the humanity, and the life, the subsistence, and the divinization of this humanity in the divinity." It concludes by begging "the holy soul of Jesus" to take control over the self: "And I plead with this holy soul to keep me and treat me on earth as its slave who has surrendered all its desires and all its possessions to the sovereign rule over all that belongs to it."[39]

On September 8, 1614, Bérulle imposed the vow of servitude to Mary on the priests of the Oratory, and on February 28, 1615, the vow of servitude to Jesus. Bérulle was the sole and undisputed head of the Oratory, but he shared authority over the Carmelite nuns with Duval and Gallement. When he tried to extend the vows to some of the houses of Carmelite nuns beginning in June 1615, resistance developed. Duval and Gallement were against the innovation, and the nuns soon split. Why, some asked, add another obligatory vow to the traditional three religious vows of poverty, chastity, and obedience? What exactly were the import and obligations of the new vows? This controversy often shows Bérulle in a bad light—imperious, obstinate, and perhaps theologically suspect (there are various forms of the "vow" and some seem theologically questionable). In 1618, Bérulle even berated his old friend and patron Barbe Acarie, now the Carmelite nun Marie de l'Incarnation, who resisted the vow. The vow-of-servitude controversy was the beginning of years of disagreement and turmoil among the Carmelite nuns over their mode of government. In 1616, the Jesuit theologian Robert Bellarmine condemned the vow of servitude, and in the same year the vow, as well as other aspects of Bérulle's theology, was strongly criticized in an anonymous pamphlet written by the Carmelite Denis de la Mère de Dieu. In 1620, Fr. Denis obtained a defective copy of the vow and had it condemned by the theological faculties of Louvain and Douai, as well as the Jesuit theologian Leonard Lessius (1554-1623), although Lessius later retracted his condemnation when he studied an authentic text.

In the theologically polemical world of the seventeenth century, Bérulle hit back—and with great profit for the history of Western mysticism. His twelve *Discourses on the States and Grandeurs of Jesus* were designed to answer his critics' objections to the vows and their doubts about his Christology, but not in the tiresome polemical way so characteristic of the times. Rather, Bérulle took the opportunity to set out a full account of his theocentric Christocentrism to demonstrate the grounding of his new and controversial practice.[40] He also responded to accusations by Father Denis and others that his Christology had Nestorian or Monophysite leanings.[41] Although the vows are taken up explicitly only a few times in the *Grandeurs* (and several forms are given),[42] they form the background to the work, but fortunately the book is much greater than the controversy.[43] This ongoing dispute changed Bérulle's notion of the vows of servitude in several ways. He began to argue that vows were not "new vows" for the members of religious orders but were extensions of the promise made by all Christians at baptism to renounce Satan and dedicate their lives to Jesus.[44] He also gave greater stress to servitude as an "oblation of the self," rather than a juridical act. The *Account* (*Narré*) he wrote of the "Vows Controversy" makes it clear that Bérulle founded his view of servitude in the *exinanition* of Jesus and our free imitation of his surrender in self-annihilation and abasement.[45] In sum, while the affair of the vows caused major difficulties for Bérulle, which a more judicious man might have avoided, the vows were in full accord with his notion of the necessity of *anéantissement* and recognizing our dependence on God.[46]

During these years of controversy, Bérulle was also politically active.[47] He had filled various governmental positions under Henry IV, and his service to the crown continued under Louis XIII. Bérulle came to know Richelieu, then bishop of Luçon, as early as 1612. They were able to collaborate in a number of ways, such as in their support for having the Tridentine decrees finally received in France, but the two had fundamentally different personalities and agendas, and the differences led to conflicts in the 1620s. Bérulle was committed primarily to the good of the church; Richelieu to that of the kingdom of France. The split became most evident during the early stages of the Thirty Years' War when Richelieu's *Realpolitik* alliance with the German Protestants to weaken the Hapsburgs horrified Bérulle. Bérulle proved himself an able negotiator in a number of contentious issues, but his commitment to the good of the Roman Church did not allow him to compromise on certain points. Perhaps the Oratorian's most important political achievement in the 1620s was to assist in the negotiations leading up to the marriage between Charles I of England and Henrietta Maria of France in November 1624, the same year that Richelieu gained full power as the head of the King's Council. Bérulle's success in convincing Urban VIII to approve the English marriage was one of the factors in Louis XIII's nominating him for the red hat, which was awarded by

Pope Urban in 1627. In 1629, however, Richelieu was able to orchestrate Bérulle's downfall and exile from court. He died two weeks later on October 2, 1629, while celebrating Mass.

Bérulle's last years saw the publication of several important works. In 1625, he issued *A Memorial for the Direction of Superiors* (i.e., of the Oratory).[48] More important was the 1627 publication of the *Elevations on Saint Magdalene* (*Élevations sur Sainte Madeleine*). Mary Magdalene was extremely popular in Baroque Catholicism, as can be seen in a multitude of artistic and poetic renderings, as well as in religious devotion and literature. As a converted sinner, someone able to combine contemplation and apostolic action, and above all, as a model lover of Jesus, the Magdalene was a perfect representative of Bérulle's mystical ideal. He already had written a number of meditations and elevations on her in the *Collations*, *Works of Piety*, and the *Grandeurs*. The twenty chapters of these final elevations, addressed to Queen Henrietta of England, are the summit of his devotion to the Magdalene.[49] In 1629 Bérulle began a *Life of Jesus* (*Vie de Jésus*), in which he sought to summarize his Christocentric mystical outlook, but he was not able to finish the work.[50] Three further "Elevations" expressing Bérulle's theocentric Christocentrism have a complicated relation to these publications, appearing in some editions but not in others.[51] Despite the polemical aspects of the *Grandeurs*, they still form the heart of the cardinal's mysticism.[52]

What kind of a person was Pierre de Bérulle? A small man, but energetic, we have numerous portraits of him but apparently none from life. He was above all serious and committed. An observation made by his modern biographer Auguste Molien, may be telling. According to Molien, Bérulle seemed incapable of smiling.[53] Admired by many (including Francis de Sales), he was talented, single-minded, and tenacious in his endeavors. He was also a major mystical thinker, one who was able to put his mental gifts in the service of a Christ-centered mysticism, which incorporated new forms of devotional piety with deep theological speculation.[54] On the reverse side, Bérulle often appears insensitive to others, as well as to the wider implications of his projects. He was dogged by controversies and misunderstandings throughout his life, conflicts that might have been ameliorated by a less intransigent person. One of his most sensitive modern interpreters, Paul Cochois, summarizes the contradictory aspects of his personality in a comment on his political actions: "Despite their grandeur and evident correctness, Bérulle's political plans were affected by the same weakness as his designs as a mystical master: a kind of incapacity to see the world and people as they really are obstructed him from choosing the means to achieve them with the same lucidity he had regarding the definition of the goal."[55] One can admire Bérulle without necessarily liking him.[56]

Bérulle's Mystical Teaching

Bérulle never wrote a summary mystical text in the manner of his predecessor Bonaventure, but there is consistent vision behind his collected pieces, such as the *Works of Piety* and the *Collations*, as well as the more developed writings, such as the *Grandeurs*. What follows will sketch out Bérulle's mystical thought under five headings: (A) The Mystery of God; (B) Creation and Humanity; (C) The Centrality of the Incarnation; (D) The Mother of the Incarnate Word; and (E) The Practice of the Annihilated Life. By way of introduction, however, it will be useful to say something about how Bérulle conceived of knowledge of God, especially what he called "the science of the saints."

The phrase "science of the saints," or "science of Christians," as noted in chapter 1, was frequently used by seventeenth-century French mystics to indicate the distinctive form of knowing that grounds a believer's life and actions.[57] Bérulle and his contemporaries, like Francis de Sales, did not scorn reason and all forms of philosophy,[58] but they insisted that human science was insufficient and even misleading for attaining salvation. Only the knowledge brought by Christ was capable of that. The same conviction is reflected in Bérulle's attitude toward Renaissance Humanism. The cardinal knew and used both fifteenth- and sixteenth-century Humanist thinkers, such as Pico della Mirandola,[59] but his Christocentrism put him at odds with any form of Humanism that stressed the independence and self-sufficiency of the human person.

Henri Bremond spoke of Bérulle's theocentrism as a "Copernican revolution" in seventeenth-century mysticism.[60] Bérulle's reference to Copernicus's heliocentric view comes in the midst of a discussion of the role of Christ as the Sun of the believer's universe, the source of the "science of Christians." He says, "Jesus is the object of the science of salvation, the science of Christians. The teacher and the Apostle of the world proclaimed openly that his science was to know Jesus (1 Cor. 2:2). Should not Christians then be touched by the love and desire to see and contemplate the principal object of their belief, their science, their religion?" Bérulle then turns to the Copernican model:

> An excellent mind of this age claimed that the sun and not the earth is the center of the world. He maintained that it is stationary and that the earth, in conformity with its round shape, moves in relation to the sun. . . . This new opinion . . . is useful and should be followed in the science of salvation. For Jesus is the Sun that is immovable in his greatness and that moves all things. . . . Jesus is the Sun of our souls and from him we receive every grace, every light, and every effect of his power.[61]

The science of the saints, or *philosophie chrétienne*, based on the illumination received from Jesus the true Sun,[62] is what is taught in "the school of the Son of God, or "the school of love" (*l'école d'amour*). The *Elevations on Saint Magdalene* speak of her as the foremost student of the school of love.[63]

The importance of the science of the saints taught in the school of love raises two important issues in the history of mysticism: the relation of reason and faith, and the role of knowledge and love. Bérulle did not spend much time analyzing these issues, but his position is clear and important for understanding his thought. He contrasts reason and faith, because reason deals with the truth of what is said and faith depends on the authority of the speaker. Nevertheless, in the case of divine faith (not mere faith in a human speaker) the truths believed are more solidly established than the truths that mere human reason can discern.[64] The way of faith is a dark way, as in John of the Cross. In his *Collations*, Bérulle has several passages where he speaks of *fides obscura*. Noting that the devil often transforms himself into an angel of light to deceive those who seek after deep thoughts, he says, "When a soul serves God by adhering to him without light through the love and reverence from the truth of faith, although it is dark [*obscura*], the devil finds nothing in him in which to act."[65] In a later *Collation* he notes that, while in heaven the Seraphim serve God through love and the Cherubim through light and knowledge, "In this life we tend towards God through the way by which we are drawn, that is, with ignorance and a cloud. The state of this life is mixed with darkness; it is the state of faith by which we believe what we have not seen."[66]

The Ninth Discourse of the *Grandeurs* contains an important discussion of the relation of love and knowledge. Bérulle says, "We notice that one of the ways in which understanding [*entendement*] is superior to the will is that understanding transforms the object into itself, whereas the will transforms itself into the object." Knowledge does not lower the subject to the thing but elevates objects into the dignity of the human mind. Love, on the other hand, "transports the soul into the object it loves." This situation is reversed when we speak of the knowledge and love of God. In this life, we can possess God by knowledge, though "not as he is in himself, but as he is in the soul." But through love "the soul possesses God on earth, as he is in himself and not in the soul." He continues: "For love transports us out of ourselves into him, and what is more, it makes us such as he is in himself, by divinizing us and transforming us into God." Bérulle expresses puzzlement why there are so many schools of theology that train students in the "obscure, uncertain, and imperfect knowledge" of God, and so few people who attend and study "in the school of the love of God" (*l'école de l'amour de Dieu*). It is the intensity of our love of God on earth that will determine how much we will know of him in heaven. "However," he concludes, "let us leave until later this fundamental point of mystical theology [*ce point fundamentale en la théologie mystique*]. Let us save this secret for the school of love and all its disciples."[67] Although Bérulle only rarely used the term "mystical theology," it is clear that he adhered to the Dionysian view of *theologia mystica* as a life of contemplative love, not the new manner of conceiving mystical theology as an academic discipline. Thus, at the outset of No. 12 of the *Works of Piety* he says, "Mystical theology tends to draw us, to unite us, and to 'abyss' us in God. . . . His unity receives us and unites us with him, and his plenitude destroys us, annihilates us, and abysses us in the immense ocean of his perfections, as we see that the ocean destroys and abysses a drop of water."[68] Here the link between mystical theology and annihilation is clear.[69] In line with this Dionysian outlook, Bérulle asserts the superiority of negative to positive theology.[70] Therefore, we can conclude that the "science of the saints," the form of theology practiced by Bérulle, was a mystical theology—one that makes use of understanding and even speculation, but that is fundamentally taught in the school of loving annihilation.

The Mystery of God[71]

In discussing the mystery of God, Bérulle uses traditional language about the divine essence/being and its various attributes, especially unity and love. He is aware of the paradoxes involved in all speaking about God, as a passage in the "Preamble" to the *Life of Jesus* shows. In rich Dionysian rhetoric, the cardinal contrasts "the God of gods which the Christian religion adores" with the false gods of pagan antiquity:

> We understand that he surpasses our understanding, our spirit, and our words; . . . that his excellence is inestimable, his grandeur beyond

speech, his majesty adorable. [We know] that he ought to be revered with a sacred silence, and not profaned with rash human discourse. He is without name and better than every name. He is everything and beyond everything. . . . He is inaccessible and yet intimate to all. He is invisible, but sees everything. He is unmovable, but moves all. He is incomprehensible, but comprehends all.[72]

The cardinal's thinking is deeply theocentric, as this and many other passages demonstrate;[73] but his concentration on the role of the Incarnate Word means that much of what he has to say about the divine nature, its attributes, and the Trinity occurs in the context of treatments of Christology. Bérulle was especially focused on the divine unity as the source of all unities found in the created world.[74] Although God as Unity seems more important than God as *esse* to Bérulle, he never denied that God is also Supreme Being.[75]

Much of what Bérulle has to say about God deals not with the divine nature considered in itself but with the specifically Christian teaching about the one God as a Trinity of Persons. Since the Second Person of the Trinity was destined from all eternity to take on human nature in Jesus Christ, the mysteries of the Trinity and the Incarnation of the Son can never be separated. Hence, Bérulle rarely talks about the Trinity without invoking the Incarnation of the Word, as can be seen in a number of the *Works of Piety*.[76] One way in which he talks about the Trinity and the role of the Word is political in origin, that is, the distinction between the divine inner *cabinet*, that is, the secret discussions of the three Persons within God (*ad intra*), and the public deliberations of the divine *council*, evident in creation (*ad extra*).[77] The former is hidden from us; the latter reveals something of the divine plan.

The thoroughgoing Trinitarianism of Bérulle's thought is evident in his many enumerations in threes. One of the most important of these triads is the exposition of the three central mysteries of the Christian faith found in *Grandeurs* VI:

> There are three mysteries that serve as the principal object and exercise of our faith. . . . The first is the mystery of the most holy Trinity, through whose power we have been created and fashioned. . . . The second is that of the Incarnation, in which human nature has been singularly exalted and united with its original source, being joined to it in a new, admirable and holy way. . . . The third is the Eucharist, in which God gives to us and returns to us the very nature he deigned to take from us, like a sacred deposit.[78]

In *Grandeurs* VII we are told that each of these mysteries is the imitation and extension of the mystery superior to it by way of exemplarity: "That original and eternal communication of the Divinity [*communication primitive et éternelle de la Divinité*], fruitful in himself, is the cause and exemplar [*cause et l'exemplaire*] of the temporal communication which God makes from himself to our humanity in the mystery of the Incarnation." Also, "the Eucharist is like an imitation of the mystery of the Incarnation and an application and extension of it to each of the Christians and faithful."[79] Like many mystics influenced by Platonism, the notion of exemplarism, the way in which lower realities are dependent and imitate the higher realities from which they emanate, is important for Bérulle.[80] The root of exemplarism, the fact that all created realities preexist in the Ideas in the mind of God, is something Bérulle shares with most Christian mystics. His particular form of exemplarism is evident, for example, in how he links the three births of the Word in the last three Discourses of the *Grandeurs*.[81]

The three basic mysteries open up a series of other triadic structures that demonstrate that Bérulle's mysticism always involves both Trinity and Christology. The Trinity expresses three divine unities: of essence in the divinity itself, of unity of love in the Three Persons, and finally of unity of subsistence in the God-man taking on flesh.[82] Bérulle also speaks of the three fecundities involved in the intra- and extra-divine dynamism: the fecundity by which the Father produces the Son; the fecundity of the Father and Son emanating the Holy Spirit; and the fecundity by which the Virgin Mary bears Jesus.[83] There is another triad connected with the three essential mysteries: first, the divinity enclosed in the unity of essence in the Trinity; second, the mystery in the property of the Person found in the Incarnation; and, third, the unity in the concomitance in the Eucharist (i.e., the presence of the whole divine essence along with the Son). Further, the three mysteries reveal three ways of looking at the Son: as unique Son in the Trinity; as "Father" in the Incarnation, because Isaiah speaks of him as "Father of the age to come";[84] and as Spouse of humans in the Eucharist. There are also three forms of "indwelling" (*residence*): the substantial and essential indwelling of the divinity of the Father in the Son; the substantial and personal indwelling of the divinity of the Son in his humanity; and finally, "a substantial and bodily indwelling of the living and glorious body of the Son of God in our earthly and mortal bodies through the Eucharist."[85] Other triads can be found in *Grandeurs* VII, where Bérulle speaks of three secret and intimate communications, "indescribable in themselves and incomprehensible to humans and angels":

the eternal communication of the Father to the Son giving him the Father's own essence; the coeternal communication of the Son and the Father giving their common essence to the Holy Spirit; and the loving communication of the Word to the sacred humanity. Bérulle says that the three essential mysteries reveal one and the same Jesus Christ as the subject of contemplation and adoration, because the same Son of God is comprised and contained in all three mysteries: in the Trinity in the unity of the essence; in the Incarnation in the unity of his Person; and in the Eucharist in the unity of his body.[86] Bérulle's devotion to triads recalls the constant invocation of threefold patterns in the thought of Bonaventure.

These multiple triadic formulae show the basis of the "excellent communication" human beings have with the Divinity. "In this low world," says Bérulle, "we are united by certain degrees and steps substantially with God."[87] To buttress his claim to substantial union, Bérulle cites Christ's prayer in John 17:21–23, the premier scriptural text for deep union with God. For Bérulle these words indicate the chain of love by which the three mysteries bind us to God. The "inexpressible and incomprehensible love, which joined God and men, brings about a real and veritable abasement [*abaissement*] of the Son of God, who is God himself, and makes him human in order to make us gods [*et fait homme pour nous faire dieux*]."[88] Deification, as we shall see, is a central motif in Bérulle's thought.

The three mysteries and their connection with other aspects of Bérulle's theology provide an entry point into the doctrinal basis of his mysticism, though we must remember that the cardinal was not a systematic theologian in the Scholastic mode. Rather, as Miklos Vetö puts it, Bérulle created a form of "theology of adoration" based on a distinct "Christo-logic."[89] Bérulle reasserts the traditional link between doctrine and devotion, paying less attention to the inner psychological states of the mystical self than did the Spanish mystics or Francis de Sales.

Bérulle uses the traditional Neoplatonic model of emanation (*exitus*) and return (*reditus*) for expressing the relation of God and world, but with distinctive twists. The circular motion of emanation and return, common to many Christian theologians, receives a strongly Christological focus in Bérulle's interpretation of this dynamic process that takes place in three stages: (1) within the Trinity, (2) in creation and return through the Incarnation, and (3) in the Eucharist.[90] The Christological emphasis is evident in the passage at the end of *Grandeurs* IV, where Bérulle adopts the image of God as the "admirable sphere"

(*sphere admirable*), noting that "in his essence, in his knowledge and in his providence, he has his repose in his own center and has no movement save in himself." From the perspective of the self-knowledge that is the emanation of the Son, as well as from the perspective of his knowledge of creatures through providence, God is a "circle worthy of admiration." The movement of this circle/sphere terminates in the Incarnation: "God's councils, just as they proceed from God, also return to him in the deliberation he holds concerning the union of a created essence to an uncreated Person and the establishment in the world of the admirable unity that is the center and the final stopping point that brings to conclusion all his councils according to the Scriptures. . . ."[91]

With regard to the inner-Trinitarian emanations, Bérulle, in dependence on Dionysius (and in line with Bonaventure), speaks of the Father as *deitas fontalis*. In *Grandeurs* VI.i, for example, he says: "In the Trinity the Father is considered as the 'fontal deity' (to speak with the one who is called the Apostle of France), as the sole subsistent through himself, the only one without principle and origin, and the only 'principle without principle' of the other two divine Persons."[92] Citing the authority of Hermes Trismegistus, Orpheus, and Augustine, in one text Bérulle says that the Father engenders the Son as *expers Matri-Patri*, that is, as "being both Father and Mother together."[93] Similar descriptions of the dynamic process originating in the Father are found in a number of Christian theologians, but Bérulle gives the doctrine a Christological focus, because for him the mystery of the Trinity is revealed in our contemplation of the Word, as a passage in *Grandeurs* V shows: "In contemplating the Divine Word, whether in his emanation, or in his Person, or in his eternal production, in other words, in all the ways we can contemplate him in the Divinity, we see that he is uniquely expressed and vividly presented by the state and the qualities of this divine mystery [i.e., of the Trinity]."[94]

Bérulle extended the perspective of the Trinitarian equality of Persons, in a certain fashion at least, to the production, or emanation (*exitus*), of creation. As in the case of a number of other mystical theologians (e.g., Bonaventure, Eckhart), Bérulle says that the production of the Son in the Trinity is the "principle and model" for the production of the universe.[95] Because the motive of creation is the Incarnation of the God-man (more on this below), the universe does not consist so much as a graded series of levels of being, but rather as the unity-in-difference found in the one incarnate Person, who unites the natures of God and humanity as the universal microcosm. The intra-Trinitarian divine emanation of the Son from the Father and the Holy Spirit from Father and Son as the loving bond of their oneness necessarily includes the relation of humanity to its divine source. Edward Howells puts this point as follows: "For Bérulle, emanation does not have its Neoplatonic form. It does not move from divinity to humanity in stages. Rather, as centered on the Incarnation, it proceeds only from the unity of humanity and divinity [in Christ] and thence to us."[96]

Bérulle's treatments of the Trinity show that his technical theology of the processions, relations, and attributes of the three Persons was basically formed by the Western tradition of Augustine and Aquinas.[97] Although much of his discussion concerns the relation of the Father and the Son, he also speaks of the role of the Holy Spirit as the mutual bond of love of the Father and the Son.[98] Because the Spirit has this role in the inner life of the three Persons, the third Person is also crucial in our return to God. The fourth Discourse of the *Grandeurs* meditates on the role of the Spirit within God and in creation through the Incarnation, beginning with a citation from Pseudo-Dionysius: "And so, according to the great author who is named the Areopagite, 'Love is the heavenly power divinely uniting things that are most distant,' so the Holy Spirit, who is love in the divinity, is the one who unites uncreated being with created being, and who effects that great work according to the word the angel announced to the Virgin, 'The Holy Spirit will overshadow you.'"[99] Bérulle daringly says that the Spirit is in a sense "sterile" in the Trinity, since the Spirit does not produce a divine Person, as do the Father and the Son. In relation to the divine work *ad extra*, however, fecundity is especially appropriated to the Holy Spirit, and in a twofold way. The Spirit is the source of all creation (Gen. 1:2); but, even more, "the fertility of the Holy Spirit, outside itself, leads to the production of a God, preexisting (O strange wonder!) and from now on existing in a new nature." He summarizes: "Thus, the sacred mystery of the Incarnation is a work, a state and a mystery of love and unity. It is a masterpiece of the Holy Spirit."[100]

Bérulle's thinking takes a distinctive turn in what he has to say about "relation," both in the Trinity and in the human bond with God. Relation had been a central philosophical and theological category for centuries, but Bérulle elevated the meaning of *relation* to a new level, one in a sense higher than *being/essence*. If there is such a thing as a Bérullian metaphysics, it might be best spoken of as one of relation, as some Bérulle scholars have suggested.[101] The common teaching of Western theologians was that the Persons in the Trinity are constituted by their mutual relations—the Father is Father in his relation to the Son, and the Son is Son in relation to the Father, while the Spirit is Spirit as the relational love bond between Father and Son. Where Bérulle innovates is in extending Trinitarian relationality into our bond with God through the action of the God-man. A passage in *Grandeurs* X puts it as follows:

> Jesus is God, Son of God, for these things are distinct seeing that the Father is God and is not the Son of God, and the Son is God and is not the Father.... As he [the Son] holds everything from the Father (John 16:15), he refers everything to the Father, and his personal life is a kind of life that is totally relative to the Father; in his eternity he exists in referring to the Father, and, by his proper character, he is the relation to his Father itself [*il est même rélation à son Père*]. ... Just as the relation of the Son is the life and subsistence of the Son, so too, the relation we have to him will be our life and our subsistence forever, and will happily establish us within his eternity.[102]

As Howells points out, relationality is the way in which Bérulle deals with opposed terms by showing their mutual interdependence. In the Trinity, the Father is not the Son and vice versa, but Father and Son are constituted by their mutual relations. This is also true in a participated way with regard to the ontological opposites of human and divine, created and uncreated, historical and eternal. The key is Christology, which enables Bérulle to draw out "the way that 'humanity' and 'divinity' function as relational terms, since they both come already made for each other in the Incarnation."[103]

With regard to the created world and human nature, relation has a varied range of meanings. Taking relation in a neutral sense as an ontological and existential disposition toward anything, Bérulle implies a double sense of the term. The first aspect can be termed natural in the sense that being a creature is defined not so much in terms of being (*être*), since the creature in itself is really nothing (*néant*), but by its relation of reference to and dependence on God. In the address to the Trinity in the "Oblation to the Holy Trinity," Bérulle says, "I refer myself to You ... through the power and eminence of your Being and through the proper condition my own being which is nothing but an inseparable shadow of your Being and a simple relation to You." He continues: "You are my substance and I am nothing but a simple relation to You. You are the foundation and intimacy of my being, and I am but a simple dependence on You. My blessedness is to be in You and to be a pure capacity for You, filled with You."[104] Only God has real and independent Being; our being is participated and is totally unlike the Infinite First Cause. Hence, we are fundamentally constituted by our relation to God, "a relation not accidental, but substantial; not particular, but universal and absolute . . . ; an essential, perpetual and necessary relation toward God."[105] This created relationship, however, is not only a neediness, an emptiness, a capacity for God; but also, due to the Fall, it has been perverted from its goal. Nevertheless, the fact that we were created as a "need for God" provides us with an "obediential potency," a real ontological direction, toward the new and higher form of relationality we gain by the grace of Christ, which allows us to share in his own transcendental relation to the Father and the Holy Spirit.[106] This is what Bérulle calls "the perfect and absolute relation" (*relation parfaite et absolue*)—our share in the life of the Trinity. As he puts it, "As the Only Son of God has a continual rapport in all that he is toward his Father, and his being and his life consist in that rapport . . . , so too, the purpose [*usage*] of our being and our life ought to be totally employed in the service of a perfect and absolute relation of all that we are, in the order of nature and of grace, through his eternal mercies."[107]

Creation and Humanity

Bérulle was less concerned with setting out a theology of creation, that is, how God made the universe, than with an analysis of creatureliness, what it means to be dependent on God.[108] Nevertheless, the "Preamble" to the *Life of Jesus* provides a summary of his teaching on creation and fall, as well as the four thousand years of the Old Testament, the time of prophecy and preparation for the coming of the Redeemer.[109] After a brief consideration of the divine nature, Bérulle turns to God's action in making all things from nothing, emphasizing his goodness, freedom, and power (Pre. 6-7). In the midst of his divine repose, "God wishes to work and to produce outside himself a shadow of his being, an image of his life, and, what is more excellent, an expression of his love and emanation of his holiness" (Pre. 8). God began the work of creation with the light that is closely related to his speaking; he finished it with humanity, "the chief work of his hands and a living and intelligent light." Creating heaven and earth, God also made two natures "capable of his grandeur and his grace," the angels to fill the heavens and humans to fill the earth (Pre. 8). Some angels fell from the First Source and were thrown into hell; on earth things were even worse. The first man "rebelled against his Ruler, rather than give him fealty and homage." By his disobedience and offense, Adam "has condemned us to death by the iniquity he communicates to us, and when we die renders us capable of eternal damnation" (Pre. 9). Nevertheless, all is not lost: "This evil would be without remedy, if the same God who created the world with his power had not looked on it with his goodness and provided a relief for its evil through a rare and new providence" (Pre. 9).

Bérulle goes on to emphasize that the evil and nothingness of sin are far worse than the "simple nothingness of being where we were before creation" (Pre. 10). Only God is powerful enough to save us and overcome the disorder into which Adam's sin plunged the world. God's new plan leads him "to make a new Adam, more holy, more steady, more strong than the first; he wishes to form a new man, man and God together" (Pre. 11). From the start (Gen. 3:15), then, God announced his new plan of salvation—the mystery of Jesus and Mary—"the Lamb of God who is both alive and slain from the beginning of the world" (Pre. 12).

Creation is the secondary, participatory, emanation of the divine inner activity; its circular motion of *exitus* and *reditus* is a reflection of the transcendent interior life of the three Persons of the Trinity. Although the act of creation is the work of the whole Trinity, Bérulle attributes it primarily to the Person of the Son and sees its finality as realized in the Incarnation. The eleventh of the *Works of Piety* dealing with the Mystery of the Incarnation neatly summarizes the relation of the primary emanation of the Persons of the Trinity as the production "from God within God" (*ex Deo in Deo*), the production of creatures as "from nothing within nothing" (*ex nihilo in nihilo*) and the Incarnation that is the mean between these extremes (*ex nihilo in Deo*): "God takes this created nature [i.e., Christ's human nature] from nothing and not from himself, but he produces it and places it in himself, in his being and in one of his subsistences [i.e., Persons]."[110]

In a late letter (Jan. 1, 1628) to the Carmelite nuns in Paris, Bérulle says, "This Word in God wishes to go out of himself to work. And we ought to heed this and to adore it in every way. And we ought to pay attention and adore the fact that again at another time he went out from himself in another work to effect our salvation." The Eternal Word created the world and "the times and ages" in order to be known and adored: "We adore him in the first moment of creation; we adore him in the work he did in that first moment. We adore him even more willingly because that work of the creation will be concluded [*se terminerer*] in a day of his own when the Word was made flesh and the Creator was made a creature."[111] Speaking of the "days" of creation should not lead us to think of it as a past event. In harmony with

Meister Eckhart and others, Bérulle holds that creation is an ongoing action (*creatio continua*): "Let us adore God always creating, always referring the world to himself, and ruling this world and creating it by a continuous creation, so that the created being is always emanating from God and has no subsistence other than that of a continuous and perpetual emanation."[112] In an Elevation in *Grandeurs* II, Bérulle praises the beauty of the order of nature but reserves higher praise for the order of grace, the emanation that reveals "the admirable and perpetual state of Jesus," because it is based directly on "the noble and primary emanation of the Son in the Godhead."[113]

Bérulle was not much concerned with detailed analysis of the various components and powers of human nature in the manner of many medieval and early modern mystics (e.g., the Spanish Carmelites). His interest is in human activity—annihilating, adhering, adoring, serving, and the like. The cardinal might be described as a Humanist in the sense that he emphasizes both the grandeur and the nothingness of humanity, but it is a resolutely Christological Humanism. A revelatory text is found in *Grandeurs* XI: "The light and power of nature knows no greater miracle than that of humanity. God, creating the world, finished with humanity's production as the final and supreme of his works in the order of nature." Nevertheless, God is the author of both nature and grace, so the miracle of the God-man is far more elevated, because "God himself is enclosed and contained in the circle and circumference of this miracle."[114] Bérulle goes on to note how correct the ancients were to praise "the grandeurs and perfections of humanity," because humans unite in an admirable way the two natures found in creation, the spiritual and the corporeal. The spiritual element is "an image of God and of his sovereignty and work on earth," while the corporeal is "an abbreviation of the universe in its structure and composition." Thus, humanity is the "small world" (*petit monde/microcosm*), which bears both "an abbreviation" (*abrégé*) of God in its spirit and an abbreviation of the whole world in its body, admirably united in the subsistence and the unity of the one same person."[115] In discussing "The Creation of Man" in *Works of Piety* 10, Bérulle notes how both reason and the light of grace provide us with knowledge of the nature of humanity and its composition into two parts: body and soul. Both parts of human nature are necessary, even though Bérulle sometimes stresses the differences between the two, as in *Works of Piety* 168: "He is a miracle on one part and on the other is a nothing. Celestial on one part, and terrestrial on the other. Spiritual on one part, and corporeal on the other."[116]

Bérulle does not dwell much on the traditional theological foundation for Christian anthropology, Genesis 1:26-27, the account of man being made in the image and likeness of God, although it does come up from time to time. In discussing the two emanations of humans from God—that in creation and that in the re-creation of the Incarnation—he says, "In the first God makes us to his image; in the second he makes himself to our image and likeness."[117] Thus, to be made in God's image for Bérulle is not so much a static reality as the gift of the ability to grow into greater likeness to God through the Incarnate Christ—humanity as a capacity for Christ (*capax Christi*) is the essence of Bérulle's theological anthropology.[118] Bérulle's perspective, however, is not so much speculative as salvation-historical.

In his early *Brief Discourse on Interior Abnegation*, based on Achille Gagliardi, Bérulle provided the bare bones of a traditional view of the powers of human nature. Chapter III speaks of renouncing the consolations given to the soul's sensible powers, as well as the spiritual consolations given to the intellect and will. When the inferior and superior powers are stilled and put to rest, at times the soul may receive "divine infusions" in the "supreme and most intimate part of the spirit which some call the *apex mentis*."[119] This brief mention of the standard topic of the soul's deepest/most sublime part, however, rarely appears in Bérulle's mature works, although there are references to the *centre de ame* in the *Life of Jesus*,[120] and the *Elevation to the Most Holy Trinity* speaks of our union with Jesus as "penetrating even to the depths of the human being [*fonds de l'être humain*]."[121] The cardinal's concentration on the saving activity of the God-man did not involve much speculation on the structure of the human soul.

The Incarnation and Christology

Although there have been many forms of Christocentric mysticism in Christian history, Bérulle's stands out for a number of reasons. Auguste Molien's survey of Bérulle provides one overview of the role of the Incarnation, when he speaks of the Incarnate Word as *term*, or goal, of adoration, as well as the *means* of adoration and the *example* of adoration.[122] Perhaps more fundamental is the patristic distinction that Bérulle himself evokes in *Works of Piety* 15 between the *substance* and the *economy* of the mystery:

> The mystery of the Incarnation embraces two principal things, consisting of the state (*état*) and life of Jesus in this new being, which

is to know the substance and the economy of the mystery, the two points often mentioned and distinguished when the ancient Fathers speak of Jesus. The substance of the mystery is explained in a word: God and man. A short word, but one which comprehends created being and uncreated being, and the ineffable but very close and very intimate bond of these two beings, so different and distant. The economy speaks of the dispensation and use of this new life of the God-man in all his states, functions, actions, and mysteries.[123]

The Substance of the Incarnation

Bérulle's Christology is fundamentally Chalcedonian, despite his detractors' accusations of Monophysite, or even Nestorian, tendencies in his thinking. Although his intentions were certainly orthodox, some imprecise or exaggerated expressions found in the *Grandeurs* and earlier works provided material for his opponents that led to later clarifications.[124] *Grandeurs* XI on the birth of the Word in time insists, following the tradition of the Fathers, that in the Incarnation the divine nature becomes incarnate and human nature deified so that all Jesus's actions are "humanly divine and divinely human."[125] "The two natures," he says, "are composed without mixture and confusion, and perfectly conjoined as if they were mixed and properly consistent in their natural properties as if they were separate." This is not a unity in two natures, or in two persons, "but a unity of one person in a diversity of natures perfectly and divinely united together."[126] Thus, Christ is "truly and perfectly God-Man and Man-God."[127]

Bérulle dwells less on Christ's human activity than modern theologians generally do, but "the state [*état*] of the humanity of Christ" is central to his Christology. The state of the humanity of Christ does not exist in a human person, but only in the person, or *subsistence* (as Bérulle likes to say), of the Divine Word. Nevertheless, Bérulle's devotion to the humanity of Christ sometimes makes it sound as though it is a separate thing in itself.[128] It would have been more accurate for Bérulle to have emphasized devotion to Jesus in *both* his human and divine natures. Bérulle sometimes expresses his teaching on the God-man in unusual ways, as when he speaks of the Incarnation as constituting "a second Trinity." Just as in the divine nature there are three persons (subsistences) in one essence, so too in the God-man there are three essences (soul, body, and divinity) in one subsistence.[129] The Hypostatic Union belongs to Jesus alone. Nevertheless, through the Vow of Servitude to Jesus we can come to have some share in the union of Christ's human nature with the Second Person of the Trinity.[130]

With regard to the substance of the Incarnation, we can begin by asking about the motive for the Incarnation—*Cur Deus Homo?* In what may be an early opuscule (OP 5 in OC 3:29–30), Bérulle seems to favor a "Scotist view" of Christ's eternal predestination, though he also notes the "Thomist view," which sees the Incarnation primarily as a remedy for Adam's sin. A number of texts adopt a cosmic Christology, the view that the Incarnation was always intended for the perfection of the universe and human nature. Thus, Bérulle speaks of "the memory of the Incarnation for which it seems that the world was created" (OP 3 in OC 3:24; see also OP 5, 13, 15), or he says, "The greatest of God's works is resolved through the accomplishment in the fullness of time of the work of the Incarnation" (OP 14 in OC 3:62). *Works of Piety* 122 also speaks of the Incarnation as the greatest work ever done in heaven or on earth and lays out a number of reasons for the God-man that favor a Scotist approach.[131] On the basis of texts such as *Works of Piety* 99, however, Michel Dupuy has argued that Bérulle eventually abandoned his Scotist orientation for a more Thomist one.[132] It may well be that Bérulle, like Thomas himself over his career, wavered between the two approaches.[133]

If the substance of the Incarnation is the union of the divine and the human natures in the Person of the Word, the mode of the union and the effect it is meant to have on humans stress *anéantissement*, that key to Bérulle's thought.[134] Concerning Bérulle's Christological *néantisme*, it is misleading to think of *anéantissement* in primarily ontological terms as some kind of total destruction of being.[135] It is more in line with Bérulle to think of annihilation in relational terms. The Word annihilates himself in taking on human nature by entering into a new kind of relation to the Father—from one perspective he still is defined by his mutual relation to his Father, but now, from a new perspective, he has voluntarily emptied himself of his divinity in the act of *exinanition* in obedience to the Father's will. Christ's human nature has no human person (the human person is annihilated), because the nature subsists in the Second Person of the Trinity. In *Grandeurs* IX.iii, Bérulle says that "in the holy and divine union the Word entering into this humanity does not destroy it, or annihilate it, or convert it into the divine essence, but through the same power and the same love which he was abased and joined to this humanity he conserves it now in its created nature . . . and makes it able to receive his grandeurs and his divinity."[136] On the human side, when we are annihilated we do not lose our created being (*ens/être*), but we annihilate "the conduct of our nature" to allow the Incarnate Word to take over all our actions.[137] We surrender our *subsistence*, or way of acting, in order to subsist in the Person of the God-man through what Edward Howells calls a "logic of mutual dispossession."[138] Bérulle puts this clearly in *Works of Piety* 227:

> Just as in the mystery of the Incarnation there is a sort of annihilation of the human nature which is deprived of its proper subsistence or human person in order to be established in the divine Person of the Word, so too in the grace that flows from that adorable Incarnation as a sort of living source, there is a sort of annihilation in ourselves and establishment in Jesus. An annihilation of power and subsistence . . . , but our subsistence is not taken away in the same way [as Christ's]. It is annihilated as far as usage and in morality, and in its authority, and not in its existence.[139]

Bérulle's terminology regarding the emptying process resists easy classification.[140] *Anéantissement* seems to be the general word for both divine and human self-naughting. But *abaissement*, not as strong in its suggestive value, also seems to be used interchangeably for both God and man. *Exinanition* is a term generally used for the Word's emptying out of his divine status as reflected in its scriptural base in Philippians 2:7, but it can also be employed of human self-annihilation. *Abnégation* is a more traditional ascetic word most often applied to the human practice of stripping away aspects of the sinful self, but is also used alongside *anéantissement*.[141] All these words appear in a host of places across Bérulle's writings.[142] In the absence of any complete word study, it is difficult to be precise about the parameters and nuances of each term; nor is it possible to give an even remotely complete review of all the texts in which they appear.

In several places Bérulle enumerates different kinds of *néant*—two, three, or four—but there does not seem to be any overarching model.[143] In the *Works of Piety* 234, for example, Bérulle speaks about God *finding us* in a nothingness that seems to combine both the nothingness of created being and the nothingness of sin, as well as God *meeting us* in the *néant de la grace*.[144] But other texts use triple or quadruple formulae. It may be helpful to try to sketch the cardinal's various ways of speaking about nothing and annihilation into a pattern that goes beyond any particular passage, but that seems reflected in many of his discussions.

There seem to be at least five types of *néant*. The first form is the primordial *néant*, that is, the absolute nothingness implied in *creatio ex nihilo*. This is the root of the second type, creaturely *néant*. Since all things come from nothing and have no real being of their own, and since we are totally dependent on God through *creatio continua*,

Bérulle often waxes eloquent about creaturely nothingness, nowhere more rhetorically than in *Works of Piety* 209, "The Vocation of Christians to Sanctity":

> We are a nothing which tends toward nothing, which searches for nothing, which is occupied with nothing, which is content with nothing, which fills itself with nothing, and which finally ruins and destroys itself through a nothing [i.e., sin] in the place where we ought to be a nothing according to the truth that belongs to us by nature. But we are a nothing in the hand of God, a nothing chosen by God, a nothing consecrated to God, a nothing filled with God, and finally a nothing possessed by God and possessing God; and that belongs to us by grace.[145]

Thus, although we are marked throughout by nothingness, this fact also expresses our capacity for God. It is a matter of relation, as we are told in *Works of Piety* 192, "Oblation to the Holy Trinity": "You are my substance and I am nothing more than a simple relation to You. My goodness is to be from You and to be a pure capacity for You, filled with You."[146] The nothingness of created being is the ontological (as distinct from the soteriological) basis for the vow of servitude that was such an important part of Bérulle's theology and spiritual practice. Such texts also reveal an important aspect of Bérulle's thinking that might be called the law of opposites: only by the recognition of our own nothingness and the annihilation of our created mode of thinking and acting can we fulfill our destiny, that is, to be filled with God and exalted in him.[147] This is the fundamental logic of the Incarnation: the Word emptied himself in order to be exalted by his Father. Bérulle speaks of it as a happy joining of nature and grace—"Just as God in his goodness joins his grandeur to our littleness, so we ought without cease join the abasement in us with elevation in God, in order to conform ourselves to God and to ourselves" (OP 209).

The third form of *néant* is the nothingness of sin, a far worse negation than that of the creature taken in itself. This negation, stemming from Adam's Fall, puts human nature not just in a position of a nothingness dependent on God, but a nothingness that opposes God. This nothingness is given a detailed study in *Works of Piety* 235, which shows that Bérulle's view of fallen humanity is more Augustinian and pessimistic than that of Francis de Sales.[148] It is summarized in a passage from the Preamble to the *Life of Jesus* emphasizing the dire effects of sin and the certainty of damnation had not God through "a new and rare Providence" come to our rescue, "because the nothing and privation of grace to which sin reduced us is much more injurious and deplorable than the pure and simple nothingness of being where we were before creation."[149]

These first three forms of *néant* are reversed by the two final forms, which we might call kenotic *néant*, in the sense that they empty in order to fill. The first of these, the engine for the whole dynamism of *exitus* and *reditus*, is the *anéantissement* of the Incarnation. Throughout his writings, especially in the *Grandeurs*, Bérulle emphasizes the overwhelming love that led the Word to annihilate himself so that humans could be rescued from the nothingness of sin. One representative passage can be found in *Grandeurs* II.i:

> Although Son of God for all eternity, You willed to become Son of Man, and in the fullness of time, despite the grandeurs of your eternal birth, you abased yourself to take a temporal birth, and you annihilated yourself in uniting yourself through love to a human nature in the Virgin's womb! Annihilating love and annihilation of love, which I revere and adore as giving existence and subsistence to a human nature in the grandeur of a divine Person and as having its origin in the excess of infinite uncreated love![150]

As mentioned above, Bérulle seems to have made the breakthrough to emphasizing the Word's "self-annihilation" in the Incarnation as the foundation and model for our own saving self-annihilation during the Verdun Retreat of 1602.[151]

The Word's annihilation has two major components: first, the *exinanitio* by which the Son empties himself of his divine status in taking on a created nature; and, second, the *abaissement* (although other terms are also used) by which Jesus Christ, the God-man, leads a human life of birth, infant weakness, toil, and the suffering that leads to the final annihilation of the cross.[152] In the *Collation for July 1614* Bérulle says that the *communicatio idiomatum* of the God-man allows us to use such phrases as "God is dead," and "God has emptied himself," because "in Christ Jesus there was a double *exinanition*, one of the human person when it does not subsist in the human nature by its proper personality, the other, the *exinanition* of its Divinity when it does not appear in its majesty, but 'in the form of a slave' (Phil. 2:7)."[153] Paradoxically, but in full conformity with the law of the cross, the Word's abasement in taking on human nature is also the source of his new grandeur (that favorite Bérullian term). Emptying out is always in view of a greater filling up. The cardinal invites the reader "to recognize God in man and the grandeur in the abasement through the light of faith and the spirit of truth. God is always God and always great, God in humanity is grand in abasement."[154] The greatest wonder concerning this act of supreme love is that God voluntarily not only unites with the nothingness of human nature in itself, but also joins himself to the worse nothingness of sin, being made "in the likeness of sinful flesh" (Rom. 8:3).[155]

The final form of kenotic *anéantissement* is our imitation of Christ's model, which comes about partly through our own efforts, but more largely through the work of grace. In *Works of Piety* 188, Bérulle speaks of three kinds of fidelity necessary on our way to God. The first two involve our cooperation. The first is choosing God's will above all others: "This is one of the greatest annihilations of the human will in using its liberty, that it no longer has the choice, or the liberty, or even the thought in anything that concerns it so much." The second is a "unity of application that begins the perfect adherence of the spirit with the God who leads us to 'oneness of spirit with him' (1 Cor. 6:17)." But there is more. Fidelity finally "requires that the soul uses all its powers to lose itself and to be annihilated in God according to the way he controls it, until God, after having applied his divine power on the soul, annihilates it himself through its inner and secret operations, which work a kind annihilation on the soul itself, rather different from that which the soul can exercise through its own power over itself."[156] God is the final agent in the fullest sort of annihilation.

This annihilation results in a new kind of "being," one that Bérulle saw Paul proclaiming when he said, "I live now, not I, but Christ lives in me" (Gal. 2:20). In *Works of Piety* 249, he says, "We ought to desire not so much to be as not to be at all, or to be in relation to God and his Only Son, to be naught but a relation to him, [with] all our being in front of the being that is annihilated by grace: 'I live now not I.' . . ."[157] So, we have no new ontological reality, but a new relation—a distinctive moral, spiritual, and mystical bond with God. This is also shown in the distinction that Bérulle makes in the *Works of Piety* between two senses of the "I" (*moi*). In *Works of Piety* 232, in dependence on Catherine of Genoa, he says, "The term 'I' can be understood either *naturally* in signifying the natural subsistence that belongs to each person," and which undergoes no change or annihilation, "or *spiritually* through an addition which sin and separation from God has made in us by way of a property found in our natural being as an accident in its subject and as a quality joined to us by pride, by presumption, and by self-grasping." He continues, "It is this being and this spiritual 'I' that must be lost and annihilated in its being, not so much by us, but by God alone."[158]

To better understand the annihilation of the false "spiritual I" we can turn once again to the *Collation of July 1614*, which describes two kinds of mortification and annihilation. First, there is the general and well-known mortification of the exterior and interior senses and three higher powers of the soul. "But we recognize," Bérulle continues, "another possible mortification or rather annihilation, namely, that of the essence of the soul itself, in which resides a correspondence to the grace by which the soul recognizes that it *totally refers itself to God* [my italics]. When it refers itself in this way and when it receives that grace, there is a kind of *exinanitio* of the soul itself, so that it says: 'My substance is a nothing before You' (Ps. 38:6)."[159] Despite the strong language of annihilation of the soul's essence, it is clear that what has changed is the soul's *awareness* of its total dependence on God. This form of emptying of the self is the living heart of Bérulle's mysticism, to which he often devotes fervent prayers. "'What do you want me to do, Lord Jesus?' (Acts 9:5). I wish all that you wish, O my God! I do not wish to be attached to anything, or to be distant from anything. I wish to be attached to You, O my Savior Jesus, and dependent on You. I wish to be far from myself and to be annihilated in myself so that I am not, so that I only live and work in You and through You."[160] This is the annihilation that truly sanctifies human nature. God first sanctified human nature in Adam, a sanctification lost through sin. The second sanctification found in the God-man is achieved through an "annihilation in nature" by which "a much more noble being is substituted for the one given in creation." This is "a sanctity according to flesh and spirit, a sanctity that will be established forever in his nature, like that which was established in the humanity of Jesus at the moment of the Incarnation."[161]

Bérulle's teaching about God becoming man as the substance of the Incarnation has some unusual implications. I will touch on only two of these here: the Incarnation as a new creation; and the Incarnation as the center of history (*plenitudo temporis*). In one place in the *Grandeurs*, Bérulle distinguishes four different general orders (*états*) of the world: the order of nature; the order of grace; the order of glory; and then, rather unexpectedly, the order of the Hypostatic Union of the Incarnation, which he considers the highest of all, because it alone involves the divine nature directly.[162] He says, "God in creation makes the order of nature, and, at the same time, establishes the order of grace on earth and that of glory in heaven—three different and admirable orders in which humanity has a share. But now there is a new order in the world, now a new state (*état*) in the universe; now a state incomparably higher than the order of glory as the heaven is above the earth, and as glory is higher than the order of grace, and as grace is elevated above the order of nature, and as nature is above nothingness."[163] This new order has the effect of reversing the traditional hierarchical relation of heaven and earth. In the three prior orders, heaven was always superior to earth; paradoxically, now earth, the home of the God-man, is superior to heaven. As he puts it, "This new order follows a change and novelty in the operation of Divine Providence, because it is no longer the heaven that rules the earth, but the earth that rules the heaven, and the First Mover is no longer in the heavens but in the earth, because God is incarnated on earth." This is a kind of reverse Copernicanism: theologically, Jesus is the sun around which every other celestial object revolves, but he is also the "sun-as-earth," because he takes on flesh on our planet.[164] Such a perspective is a radical subversion of the traditional medieval hierarchical view of the universe, not unlike what Nicholas Cusanus had advanced a century and a half previously, albeit from a different perspective. The "newness" of the Incarnation encouraged the cardinal to explore many images to express this "new thing under heaven," such as the identification of Jesus as the "New Ark of the Covenant,"[165] or seeing him as the resurrected phoenix, the image of mystical revival.[166]

Perhaps the greatest novelty of the Incarnation, however, is the fact that, after the Incarnation, we not only have a God to be adored, but we also have gained an "Adoring God." The Incarnate Word is the only person capable of giving God the worship that is his due, something that we can share in when we annihilate ourselves as he did in offering himself to the Father. *Grandeurs* II addresses Christ: "You are the chosen servant, who alone serves God as he should be served, that is, with an infinite service, and alone adores him with an infinite adoration, as he is infinitely worthy to be served and adored." From all eternity God was infinitely adorable, but neither angels nor humans could give him infinite adoration. "Now, O Jesus, you are this adorer, this man, this servant, infinite in power and in dignity to fully satisfy this need and to render this divine homage."[167] *Adoration*, one of the essential elements in Bérulle's mysticism, is thus grounded in Christology. Although we are called to adore God by our creaturely status, we can only adore him adequately through joining ourselves to the God-man. We direct adoration *to* Christ as God, but we adore *with* the God-man who has taken on our nature and elevated it to a new status.

The Incarnation reverses cosmic laws, but it also fulfills Providence's plan for sacred history, something laid out in detail in the first part of the *Life of Jesus*. Bérulle's highly Neoplatonic outlook might seem to conflict with any serious interest in history, but the *Life of Jesus* shows this is not the case. Bérulle's concern for sacred history unfolds in two registers.[168] The first is the universal history of humanity in which all the ages from creation through the time of the Old Testament are seen as preparation and foretelling of the Incarnation as the fullness of time in which redemption is effected through the cross and Resurrection. According to Bérulle, the four thousand years before Christ, the time of nature and then of the law, "tended only to Him [i.e., Christ], spoke only of Him, prefigured only Him, impressed only His name, qualities, and works on our senses and spirit . . . ; it was just as important to imprint Jesus on the world, as that we should have Jesus imprinted on our hearts."[169] For Bérulle, both the Jews and the gentiles (more specifically Rome) prepared the way for Christ: the Jewish people by announcing his coming into the world; the Romans by the establishment of universal peace that was fitting to receive the Prince of Peace.[170] For Bérulle, however, the second register of sacred time is more important for daily life. This is the cycle of the liturgical year from Advent through to All Saints by which believers meditate on and come to share in the mysteries and the saving *états* of Jesus. This aspect is present throughout Bérulle's works but is especially evident in the *Collations*, the sermons, prayers, and observations that Bérulle sent to his fellow Oratorians over the course of several liturgical years. The cardinal's mystical spirituality is eminently liturgical.[171]

The Economy of the Incarnation

The second major aspect of Bérulle's Christology, the economy of the Incarnation, emphasizes its dynamic character. If *néant* is the operative word for grasping the substance of the Incarnation, then *état* is the key for understanding the economy. *État/status* is richer than most understandings we give to the English "state." It has, to be sure, political and juridical implications, but it is primarily a theological and spiritual term, which in general signifies a mode of being as the source for specific forms of acting. *État* has a wide range, being used not only of the created realm but also of the Trinity, as when Bérulle breaks out into a passionate Elevation of praise: "O Divinity, O Fecundity, O Unity, O Power, O Unity of Essence, O Unity of Principle, O Love which encloses, comprehends, encloses the infinite and uncreated state [*l'état infini et incréé*] in its nature, in its Persons, and in its emanations!"[172]

The primary use of *état* concerns the God-man. There are many *états* ascribed to Jesus, but the source of all these modes of being is the *état de union hypostatique*, the state of the Hypostatic Union, by which the

Person of the Word unites the natures of God and humanity.[173] *État* thus first and foremost expresses the unitive state that is the substance of the mystery, but it also is used of all the particular *états* of the life of Jesus, that is, the aspects of his inner life that are revealed in his saving acts and that become the models for our sanctifying union with God in Jesus.[174] In *Grandeurs* VIII, Bérulle says, "There are two sorts of exchange and two kinds of communication of God with man in the mystery of the Incarnation. . . . The one is radical and original and contains, in power and seed, the different states of the mystery, the other is spread out and receives all the fruits of the mystery in abundance. The one constitutes the essence of the mystery, the other corresponds to the state and dignity of the mystery. The one is the depth of the mystery, the other its fullness and joy."[175] Although there are many nuances to the use of *état* in Bérulle, it is the ontological and theological aspects that are given the most weight, although interior and psychological aspects are not lacking in late works, such as the *Life of Jesus*.

Henri Bremond, the rediscoverer of Bérulle, was the first modern scholar to emphasize the importance of *état* in the cardinal's thought, noting the solid and more concrete character of a state in contrast to an action. He summarizes Bérulle's teaching: "The Word Incarnate operates much more by His *states* than by His acts, and His states effect, imprint, in us corresponding states—of humility, patience, gentleness—all of which gradually clothe us with the 'dispositions' of the Christ, leading us towards the state of total servitude, which is the supreme aim of Bérullian direction."[176] Since then, almost everyone who has written on Bérulle has taken up the issue of *état*. On the basis of his detailed study of the term across Bérulle's works, Fernando Guillen Preckler summarizes the characteristics of the term as involving the following aspects: an ontological weight; a free gift of God; an element of passivity; a dynamic character; a permanence, extending to heaven; and an exemplarist aspect in the sense that the states of the mystery of the Incarnation imitate and adore the inner states of the Trinity.[177]

As noted above, Bérulle draws an important distinction between adoring God by action and by state: "There are two ways of serving, one by actions alone and the other by state. We ought to choose this constant, solid, permanent way, and to embrace the life which of itself honors God's majesty and is the origin of many holy and virtuous acts in honor of the state of life which was in the Son of God through the holy mystery of the Incarnation and in which he perseveres eternally in heaven."[178] The state that was given to Jesus in the Incarnation "is eminent and elevated over everything that God has ever produced outside

Himself in the order of nature, or grace, and of glory."[179] Hence, in our own case too, the adoration that comes from *état* is higher than one that proceeds from our own acts and thoughts, because, "it is solid, permanent, and independent of the [human] powers and actions, and is livingly imprinted in the depths of created being [*fonds de l'être crée*] and within the condition of its being."[180] All the *états*, or key points, in the career of Jesus are rooted in the state of the Hypostatic Union. This foundational state, however, expresses itself in different ways and with diverse modalities in the great mysteries of the life of the God-man. Bérulle concentrates on four of these: the state of the Nativity and infancy, the state of the desert (i.e., temptation), the state of the Passion, and the state of glory in the Resurrection. To these he also adds the state of Christ in the Eucharist.[181] As the example of the Eucharist shows, these states are not merely historical past acts; they are present realities meant to be personally appropriated by believers.

The state of the Nativity is important for Bérulle because it embraces both eternity and time.[182] Citing Psalm 2:7 ("You are my Son, this day I have begotten You"), Bérulle, as we have seen, distinguishes three births of the Second Person—from the Father in eternity, from the Blessed Virgin in time, and from the tomb in the Resurrection—and uses them as the basis for the last three discourses in the *Grandeurs*.[183] The second part of Discourse XI considers Jesus's birth from Mary as a mystery of both offering and adoration (OC 7:415-57). This birth, the state in which God becomes fully man and man becomes fully God, is "a new and permanent state that renders homage to the paternity of God." Bérulle says that the Son produces "a new state that honors his eternal state and renders homage to his divine birth through his human birth, a birth in which God truly abases himself to be made Son of Man."[184] What is more, not one but two new states of adoration come from this second birth, because the fecundity of the Blessed Virgin establishes both the state of the Hypostatic Union and the state of Mary as the Mother of God (*Grandeurs* XI.iii [OC 7:436-38]). Bérulle's meditations on the Nativity even led him in a few places to talk about the birth of the Word in our own souls, an important theme of late medieval Northern mysticism.[185] Although the Nativity testifies to the Word's abasement in taking on the lowness of human nature, by the law of opposites it also involves five forms of elevations (*celsitudines*) set out in the *Collation for August 1615*.[186]

Bérulle was always fascinated by the state of Jesus's infancy, especially because it shows the humility of the Word in abasing himself to the limited and dependent conditions of the beginning of human life, the paradox of omnipotent power as powerless.[187] In a similar way, he saw Christ's forty days in the desert "as a state of humiliation and banishment worked by the Holy Spirit in which Jesus was exposed to the beasts and also to the Evil Spirit (Mark 1:13)." During this time of humiliation and abasement, Jesus felt the full weight of being in "the likeness of the flesh of sin" (Rom. 8:3). Bérulle says, "The Son of God seeing that people were in the state of sin, which dishonored God, entered into that same state of sin . . . in order to destroy and annihilate that evil state of sin in which we are born by sanctifying and deifying that state of sin in his Person."[188] It is the state of Jesus's Passion, however, that gains the most attention from Bérulle. No fewer than twenty-one of the *Works of Piety* (OP 74–94) take aspects of the Passion for their subject. It is also discussed in a number of texts in the *Collations* and the *Grandeurs*.

The Passion is central: "God wished his Son to come into this world and not another, and that he take a portion of the same flesh that Adam received from the hand of God and soiled through sin, so that he could condemn sin through the flesh of sin and death through death itself."[189] Again, the paradox of life and death is clear both for our admiration and for our imitation. Jesus's life is the greatest life, but it is a life aimed at death: "The first thought [of the Father], the thought of the death of Jesus, is an eternal thought, and a thought we should adore. It is the thought of the eternal Father to deliver his Son to death."[190] In *Works of Piety* 81, Bérulle identifies five different stages in the progress of the Passion, noting that Jesus came into the world to suffer so that his first thought in Mary's womb was of the cross. The agonies that Jesus suffered in his Passion were a summation of a life that was a perpetual agony and combat: "He came on earth for combat; he went to the Garden of Olives for agony; he mounted the cross for the combat of divine life against divine death."[191] Bérulle meditates on the details of the Passion, such as Jesus's three outcries and the "wound of love," which leaves his heart "eternally open, eternally wounded" (OP 93 [OC 3:272–74]); but he does so in order to move his readers to share in this state of loving death:

> Offer our life and our death to Jesus Christ our Savior in exchange for his life and death which he has given and used for us. O, what a humiliation of the Son of God and the divine grandeur unto death, even death on a cross! O, what forgetfulness and annihilation of himself in order to remember us! O, Lord, that I may forget myself so that I can remember You![192]

Bérulle paid attention to many other states of the life of Jesus, such as the Transfiguration and Ascension, but the other state that was most significant for him was that of the Resurrection, the *état de gloire*, to which he devoted seven of the *Works of Piety*.[193] Bérulle was not like the late medieval mystics who so concentrated on the Passion that they seem to have almost forgotten that Jesus also rose from the dead. For Bérulle, the state of the resurrected Lord goes beyond the issue of reparation for sin that was the motivation for the states of the Incarnation and Passion: "But the Resurrection, which only the Lord worked, was because the Son was sufficiently annihilated in order to be glorified." This is why it is described as "the solemnity of solemnities."[194] The day of the Resurrection is one of the three memorable days of the life of Christ, along with the day of the Incarnation and the day of the cross—signifying respectively mortal life, suffering life, and glorious life (OP 98). Just as one of the greatest and most attractive effects of God's power was the union of the deified soul and deified body of Jesus in the Incarnation, equally powerful is the reunion of deified soul and body in the Resurrection (OP 97).

Bérulle distinguishes between the "being of glory" (*l'être de la gloire*) and the "state of glory" (*l'état de la gloire*). The Incarnate Word never loses the being of glory, but he voluntarily surrenders the state of glory when he comes into the world (OP 103). The restoration to the state of glory is a process that begins with Jesus's prayer at the Last Supper, "You Father, now glorify me with the glory I had with You before the world existed" (John 17:5), a passage that Bérulle exegetes at length in a treatise on glory in *Grandeurs* VIII.[195] The Resurrection represents the restoration of the state of glory, but the glory is not fully manifested during the forty days Jesus spent with his disciples before the Ascension.[196] For Bérulle Jesus's rising spiritualizes both the body and the soul and thus confirms the goodness of the whole creation, material and spiritual.[197]

Furthermore, because "[e]very work of Jesus Christ is meant to be the subject not only of adoration, but of imitation, in order to imitate his Resurrection, we ought to die and live, and to die in order to live, to die to everything that belongs to this earth in order to live in Jesus Christ."[198] Even in this life we can begin to be conformed by grace to the qualities of Christ's glory: his love; his subtlety; his impassibility; his immortality; and his brilliance (*claret*), if not in an outward way, at least "through the light of faith, of prayer, and of contemplation." Bérulle cites Paul about being risen with Christ (Col. 3:1–2), and concludes: "In a word, the true mark of the Resurrection is the taste for the things of heaven, disgust with those of earth, the separation from the things of earth and seeking and desiring heavenly things."[199] The cardinal above all emphasizes the joy (*éjouissance*) that we share with the risen Christ.

All the states of Jesus are set forth for our admiration and imitation, and they all aim at the same goal: servitude, the servitude that allows us to participate in the abasement of the Word, but also in his risen state. Bérulle summarizes: "All [of these] are solid foundations that establish the relation and claim we ought to have with the Son of God through the humble state of servitude we vow to Him in honor of his relation to the Father through the admirable state of his divine and eternal Sonship."[200] He characteristically emphasizes how these states of the life of Jesus testify to his humility, abasement, and annihilation in taking on the human condition,[201] but they also lead to glory and endless joy. With Jesus, as with us, the more perfect the servitude, the more perfect the adoration.

At the conclusion of this brief treatment of this central theme in Bérulle's mystical teaching it may be useful to emphasize once again an important implication of the cardinal's use of *état*. As noted above, state is much more an ontological notion than a psychological or interior one. This means that Bérulle shows little interest in analyzing inner states of prayer, rapture, and union, in sharp contrast to many prior and contemporary mystics. Therefore, we come to unite with Christ's interiority, not through mystical gifts and special graces but through the emptying and self-annihilation that allow us to participate in the Savior's state of servitude. Again, annihilation is the key to help us grasp the Christocentric essence of Bérulle's mysticism.[202]

Bérulle's Mariology

Given the character of Bérulle's Christology, it stands to reason that he would also have a high view of the status of Mary as the Mother of the Incarnate Word. The relation between these two aspects of his thought is well put by Fernando Guillen Preckler: "Just as the Bérullian doctrine of Christ has its final reason and center in 'the state of the Hypostatic Union,' so too, Bérullian Mariology is determined by 'the state of divine maternity.'"[203] Bérulle's interest in Mary is evident throughout his career, from the early *Collations*, which have many passages on Mary and the Marian feasts, through the *Works of Piety* (especially OP 134–50) and the *Grandeurs*, particularly XI. Toward the end of his life, his concern with the Virgin seems to have increased, as is shown by the *Elevation to Offer Oneself to the Virgin*, and the *Life of Jesus*, which, except for the Preamble, is really a meditation on the grandeurs of Mary more than an account of Jesus. The reason for this increasing concern with the role of Mary is expressed several times in the *Life of Jesus*: "To speak of Jesus is to speak of Mary"; and "To speak of Mary is to speak of Jesus, and to honor Mary is to honor Jesus."[204] Marian devotion and spirituality took many forms in Tridentine Catholicism, especially because of the Reformers' attacks on Marian piety. Bérulle explicitly notes the necessity to defend Mary and Marian doctrine against Protestant attacks (e.g., OP 134 [OC 3:364–65]).

Beginning with an emphasis on Mary as the Mother of God, of course, was traditional, with its roots in the Council of Ephesus's declaration of Mary as *theotokos* ("God-bearer"). Bérulle gives this his own twist. In *Works of Piety* 1 devoted to the Feast of the Annunciation, Bérulle places the Incarnation in the middle location of the three parts of Mary's life: the time from her Immaculate Conception to the Annunciation; the time from the Annunciation to Jesus's Ascension; and the third from the Ascension to her own Assumption. The Annunciation marks the first day of the life of God on earth, the time when the Holy Virgin begins to share both in the love and the pains of her Son. This is a mystery that remains forever.[205] Mary's *Ecce ancilla Domini* ("Behold the handmaid of the Lord"; Luke 1:38)[206] is the perfect expression of humility and *abaissement* before God, and thus the source of her elevation to the dignity of divine maternity: "This maternity exists in itself and encloses in its state God's greatest production outside Himself."[207] Mary's most excellent *état* is a paradoxical mixture of non-being and being—the non-being of profound *anéantissement* and the being of *élévation* (*Vie de Jésus* XVII [OC 8:258–61]). The Incarnation, as noted above, is the establishment of a new world, and Mary "is the new creature of the new world, and is herself the first creature of the new world. . . . It is at the instant of the words, *Ecce ancilla Domini*, that the Virgin changes her quality and enters into a new state."[208] Mary thus enjoys a unique *état* shared by neither angel nor human. In *Grandeurs* XI, Bérulle says, "O admirable power of the lack of power of the Infant Jesus who, making himself a small infant, makes the greatest effect and the greatest state in the order of nature, grace, and glory, insofar as he forms and establishes the state of the Mother of God . . . , an order distinct and separate from all the orders that exist among angels and humans."[209]

This new state and order of the divine maternity give Mary a special relation to the Trinity. She becomes a collaborator with the Father in giving birth to the Son. In *Works of Piety* 135, Bérulle says, "She is the chief work of the Trinity. In effect the Father has placed in her the image of his paternity, making her Mother of his only Son, just as he has placed in his Son the image of his substance.... Put otherwise, the Father expresses his essence in the Son, and his paternity in the Virgin, making her Mother of the one of whom He is the Father (although differently, nonetheless quite really and perfectly)."[210] Even stronger is the language from *Works of Piety* 139, where Bérulle speaks of the mutual delight and pleasure that exist between the Father and the Incarnate Son and goes on to say that the Virgin shares in it. He states:

> This complaisance of the Father, I say, is operative in Mary, is communicated to Mary, is applied to Mary, is united to Mary, and is reclothed in the feeling of Mary's heart towards her Son in such a way that the Father in heaven and the Mother on earth are one and make one thing, the one in a divine way, the other in sensitivity in the love of Jesus, since there is a union and harmony between the paternity of the Eternal Father and the maternity of the temporal Mother in the case of Jesus.[211]

The Father giving birth and the Son being born of both divine Father and human Mother do not preclude a role for the Holy Spirit. The *Life of Jesus* XX says that in the heaven of heavens the Trinity is taken up with the Virgin in the work of the Incarnation, and that the Holy Spirit, the third in the order of Persons, is the first in the order of operations by sanctifying, preparing, and elevating the body and the soul of Mary in preparation for the birth (citing Luke 1:35). The Father is the Person who unites himself with the Virgin in order to give birth to the Son in "the new generation of the Person who is born and being eternally born from Him."[212]

The fundamental relation that constitutes Mary is her relation to her Son, the Incarnate Word. In *Works of Piety* 140, Bérulle compares this relation to the subsistence of the Persons of the Trinity in their mutual relations: "You too, O Holy Virgin, O person divine and human together (divine in grace, human in nature), only have a subsistence in the being of grace through a relation to Jesus; you only live through his grace, whereas formerly you lived to yourself through nature."[213] The perfect mutuality of the Son and the Mother is a constant theme in Bérulle. Chapters XVIII–XXIX of the *Life of Jesus* are taken up with the total possession (*occupation*) of the Virgin with Jesus and then of Jesus with the Virgin.[214] This includes the question concerning whether Mary, like Jesus, enjoyed the Beatific Vision in this life. Bérulle is cautious here, noting that, if Moses and Paul were given this privilege, it must definitely also have been accorded to Mary, and perhaps to her even if it had not been given to others (*Vie de Jésus* XXIX [OC 8:304-5]). The category that the cardinal prefers, however, is that of "ravishment" (*ravissement*), which can be described as a form of possession so powerful and pleasing that Mary is constantly ravished, or raptured, into Jesus. Because the Incarnate Word is always present and supremely attractive, "[t]he Virgin is established not by way of an accident, but is a state of perpetual ravishment over an object perpetually worthy of ravishment."[215] This ravishment is nothing else but the loving bond between Mother and Son, the attraction of the heart of Mary to the heart of Jesus, and vice versa.[216]

Mary's ravishment in Jesus involves both her state and the way in which she comes to share in Jesus's interior actions toward his Father. Mary shares in all the states of the life of Jesus (e.g., OP 138, 140, 145), but most especially in his suffering on the cross (OP 141-43). The theme of Mary's compassion, both with Christ on the cross and with the suffering members of the Body of Christ, common in the late Middle Ages, also appears in Bérulle. The cardinal is anxious to stress that Mary's compassion is more than just a natural or even graced sense of sharing in the pain of another, but is actually a special divine gift given her by the Father so that her compassion would be equal to the sufferings of Christ on the cross.[217]

Mary's sharing in the particular states of the life of Jesus is rooted in her deeper participation in the Incarnate Word's dialectic of abasement and elevation. Prior to the Annunciation, Mary was abased in the nothingness of her creaturehood. At the angel's word "she was abased in another nothingness, that is, in the nothingness of the Creator who makes himself a creature. . . . The Virgin entered into a humble and profound state where we ought to bear the abasement and annihilation of God made man through the sacred mystery of the Incarnation."[218] The dialectic of attaining the heights through lowering oneself to the depths means that the Virgin's life is characterized by both supreme love and deepest sorrow. In *Works of Piety* 143, Bérulle concludes, "Love and sorrow are the two equal weights of the scale of the Virgin's soul. O what love the Virgin has for Jesus! O what pain the Virgin suffers over Jesus, pain equal to love."[219]

Finally, we should note that Mary also has an important relation to us as members of the Body of Christ. This is expressed in another of the distinctive themes of Bérulle's Mariology, that of the double maternity of Mary. Mary is both Mother of God and Mother of humans, a maternity that was proclaimed by Christ on the cross (John 19:26-27).[220]

Sometimes the cardinal speaks of Jesus's birth in Mary and outside Mary,[221] that is, the interior birth that set up the primary relation of Mother and Son, and the exterior birth in which Mary begins to give Christ to the world. "The maternity of the Virgin towards us," says Bérulle, "gives her sovereignty over us."[222] Mary's universal queenship over all the orders of humans and angels is a theme well known to Bérulle,[223] and it helps explain why the Vow of Servitude to Mary (which predated the Vow to Christ) was so important for Bérulle as a religious reformer. It was through our taking on the servant state of Mary that we first begin to express our total nothingness and our need for divine grace, and thus there is an intimate bond and no tension between the Vow of Servitude to Mary and the Vow of Servitude to Jesus.[224] The subjection of all the hierarchies to Mary as queen, however, is not the only bond of humans to the Virgin. "Beyond what we call the general dependence [on Mary], there is another special and much more sublime and perfect dependence of certain select souls probably from all orders [i.e., hierarchies] whom the Son of God wished to depend on his Mother in a most special way. These souls we say belong to the chorus spoken of above [i.e., the chorus of Mary]."[225] This special chorus, or order, is what Bérulle elsewhere calls the *comitatus Mariae*, "Mary's band," the hierarchy of those chosen by God to share in Mary's unique position as the Mother of God in a special hidden way. This *ordo* is not identified with any institutional group, although Bérulle encouraged his Oratorian and Carmelite followers to express their desire to join it by signing up for the Vows of Servitude. It was a spiritual or, perhaps better, mystical elite.

The Practice of the Annihilated Life

Although he wrote no systematic works, Bérulle's maturing insights sprang from a coherent theological vision and its mystical implications. When one tries to organize an account of the whole Bérullian program of spirituality and mysticism, however, an overall structure proves difficult to construct. In this last section I will try to lay out some of the more important themes and practices of Bérullian mysticism. The five I will concentrate on are: (1) Adhering to Jesus through Love; (2) Adoration and Apostolic Action; (3) Union and Deification; (4) A Mystical Model: Mary Magdalene; and (5) The Eucharist and Priesthood.

1. Adhering to Jesus through Love
The imitation of Christ is one of the constant themes in the story of Christian mysticism. In the case of Bérulle, imitation takes a distinctive

turn, that of adhering to Jesus in all his states (*états*) and acts, adhesion, as we have seen, being one of the central themes in Bérullian vocabulary. Adhering to Jesus is not something we can do on our own power; it is a supernatural act that needs divine grace. The cardinal does not develop a formal theology of grace but mentions it often. *Works of Piety* 218, "On Grace," is a good summary. Grace is a "participation in God himself and his sanctity." "He communicates Himself through grace and makes us gods by grace, as He is God by nature." Bérulle says that "[g]race is our foundation and heritage," so it behooves us to know our fundamental obligations concerning it: "Humility in receiving it; application to God who gives it to us, and fidelity in using it."[226] The grace that comes to us as members of Christ's Body is both the habitual grace that makes us alive in God after the death of sin, as well as the actual grace that Bérulle describes as prevenient, arousing, aiding, and subsequent.[227] Grace expresses our bond with Christ (e.g., OP 245),[228] and it is infused in us by the Holy Spirit. Bérulle, like a number of mystics and in contrast to Thomas Aquinas, follows the view of Peter Lombard that grace in us is the very Person of the Holy Spirit and not just a created effect—"The Holy Spirit comes into the soul and is not just infused by God, but is God Himself ('Through the Spirit who is given to us'; Rom. 5:5), who communicated Himself to the soul as spirit" in order to make us children of God (Rom. 8:14).[229] In his *Collations*, Bérulle has several passages explaining how we are meant to cooperate with the Holy Spirit within us in our attitudes and actions.[230]

Adhering to Jesus Christ in all his states and actions is a frequent theme in Bérulle's writings, one often treated by his commentators.[231] Adherence is also imitation of Jesus, as *Works of Piety* 35 makes clear: "We ought to adhere to Jesus, and in this adherence to his divine Person who is in continual operation in the production of the Holy Spirit proceeding from Him. And in imitation of Him we ought to be always occupied with eternal and spiritual matters and to work continually towards God."[232] "To adhere to the Son," he says in *Works of Piety* 4, "is to adhere to life, life divine, life eternal, life the source of life, life originating and origin, originating in the Father and origin in the Holy Spirit."[233] Adhering to Jesus in this life is the only way to fulfill the purpose of our creation. As a passage in the *Collations* puts it. "It is enough that the soul adhere to God whatever may be the way that God uses it. It ought not adhere to the means it uses, but only to God himself, whether he be [what seems] best, or, as it may appear to us, harmful. We ought to use these means to that end to which they were ordained by God, namely, that we adhere to Him."[234] Adhering to Jesus in all his states and actions implies a holy exchange in which we offer our life and death to Jesus, who has already given his life and death for us (OP 90). It is the way in which we come to subsist in Christ. "It is not enough," says Bérulle, "for a person to be subordinated, but he ought to be disappropriated and annihilated, and appropriated by Jesus, subsisting in Jesus, given being in Jesus, living in Jesus, acting in Jesus, bearing fruit in Jesus: 'I am the vine and you are the branches' (John 15:5)." Thus, we declare to Jesus, "I establish myself in You as the foundation of my being which has being and subsistence only in You."[235]

We say that we adhere to Jesus, whereas it is really more accurate to say that he is adhering to us through the power of God's love alive in us by grace. Bérulle has a good deal to say about the different forms of love. He insists that God is love, a claim made by many philosophers and theologians, of course, but Bérulle spells this out in his own way. In a passage in *Grandeurs* VIII, meditating on the mystery of the Incarnation, the cardinal says that the God-man reveals that all the divine attributes are transformed into love, the love that conquers both God and man. "Because God is love (1 John 4:8), and is nothing but love, it is in this work where his power, his goodness, his greatness, and his majesty are converted and transformed into love. This mystery is love and nothing but love." This love joins God and man; the grandeur of God and the lowliness of humans are made one in transforming love. "God is man, but it is not his nature, but rather his love that does this."[236] The Incarnation rests on the reciprocity of love between God and human, a mystery known only through faith. Discourse IX of the *Grandeurs* makes this clear:

> Since the happiness of humans has its root and origin in the love of humans for God, that love in turn has its origin in the love that God has towards humans and in the excess of that love of God giving his Son and his love to the world. It is that love that so astonished the Son of God in the sacred text when he says with admiration, "God so loved the world" (John 3:16). In truth it is a point most worthy of astonishment that love—and so great a love—for the world is in the Divinity. It is a secret that the philosophers never penetrated.[237]

Bérulle talks about the love that Jesus has for the world in many texts and different ways, but one set of categories he uses seems to be his own creation. *Grandeurs* XII speaks of how the love Jesus showed in his lifetime was both uniting and separating. "The property of love in itself is to unite, and the property of divine love is to raise up to heaven; on the contrary, the property of the love of Jesus is to separate and to draw Jesus down to earth." The love by which Jesus separated himself from his Father in the annihilation of the Incarnation is for our benefit, as Bérulle shows in the *Elevation* that follows. Jesus's separating love is what allows us to separate ourselves from sin. In high rhetorical fashion Bérulle asks, "Let this love, O Jesus, that is in You, be in us. Let this love that triumphs in You, triumph in us. . . . May this love that divides and separates in You, divide and separate in us, and separate us from sin."[238] The paradox of a love that both unites and separates is expanded upon in an analysis of the three kinds of love that Jesus employs in the work of redemption: separating love, crucifying love, and ravishing love (*amour séparant, amour crucifiant, amour ravissant*).[239] Again, given the reciprocity of love, we are meant to share in each of these modes of love following the model of the God-man. After his Resurrection, Jesus absented himself from entering into the full joy of heaven for forty days, and he explicitly informed the apostles that he needed to separate his physical form from them so that their spiritual love might increase (John 14:28-29). Separating love thus is a blessing in disguise. Addressing the priests of the Oratory on the Feast of the Ascension in 1612, Bérulle told them, "Beyond the acts of love in the Ascension noted above, this other comes to mind: Jesus would not have departed in such a way that he did not leave us a way of joining with him in this state in order that we might satisfy the obligation of always remaining joined with him in the closest way."[240] Separation is a deeper opportunity for loving union.

Crucifying love is more painful than separating love. This is the kenotic love that led Jesus to empty himself on the cross for our salvation—"My God, my God, why have you forsaken me?" (although Bérulle, unlike Francis de Sales, does not concern himself explicitly with Matt. 27:46). We are called upon to adore "the first and eternal thought of God, which is the thought of God's death" (OP 75). And again, "He only came into the world to suffer. His first thought in his Mother's womb, his first offering was to the cross, and before he came into the world, he was totally consecrated to the cross."[241] It is interesting to note, however, that Bérulle seems to use the phrase *amour crucifiant* mostly in relation to our participation in the love that placed the Savior on the cross, as in *Grandeurs* VIII, when he says, "Just as there is a crucifying love, and even a crucifying love in God, why should it be no less powerful among humans and crucify us in Jesus and with Jesus? Even more, just as what is an abasement and disgrace to be crucified and crucified for sinners in the case of Jesus was really his glory and greatness, so too, it is happiness to be crucified for Jesus and with

Jesus, and to be able to say with the Apostle, 'I am attached to the cross with Christ' (Gal. 2:19)."[242] Finally, there is the ravishing love, which represents the overpowering attraction that the glorified Jesus has for those who love him. We have already noted the mutual ravishing love that the Virgin Mary experienced with her Son. Such ravishing love will also be seen in the archetypal lover of the Incarnate Word, Mary Magdalene, who will be treated below.[243]

These three special forms of love are not the only modalities for discussing love used by Bérulle. *Works of Piety* 122 (OC 3:334–36) lays out a general account of the role of Jesus Christ and our loving relation to Him. "For inciting love of Jesus Christ" we start by noting the two great works of divine power: "the creation and glorification of the angels"; and "the sanctification of humans" through a work greater than any done in the heavens, namely, the Incarnation. Six points are noteworthy in considering the Incarnation. The first is that the Incarnate Son is alone worthy to "serve, love, and adore" God as he should be loved; the second is that in Jesus humans are called to an alliance with God "our brother" higher than anything accorded to the angels. The third point centers on the new mode of love this involves: "Note in the third place that humans have been called to a state and a degree of love most grand and eminent. Because of this mystery God has established a greater design of love, of grace, and of glory than he did in creation, because the Incarnation is the greater work and its end is greater."[244] The fourth point is that Jesus's Passion is the model for our suffering in imitation of him, while the fifth point concerns how God's exinanition repairs the harm done by sin. Finally, and sixth, Bérulle emphasizes that the state of love Christians are called to is not only the highest, but is also "a new state of love that God established because of the mystery, namely, the love of Jesus." The nature and the greatness of the new state of Christian love fuel the rhetorical power of the frequent *Elevations* found in the *Grandeurs*,[245] and especially in the 1627 "Elevation to Our Lord Jesus Christ on the Conduct of his Spirit and His Grace towards Saint Magdalene."[246]

(2) Adoration and Apostolic Action
The relation between contemplation and action is another of the major themes in the history of Christian mysticism. Bérulle does speak of contemplation and also references the figures of Mary and Martha from Luke 10, the traditional representatives of the contemplative and active lives. Nevertheless, in a sense Bérulle recasts the issue of contem-

plation and action in his own terms, specifically in what he has to say about adoration and apostolic action.

Adoration, as noted at the beginning of this chapter, is one of the key terms in the Bérullian vocabulary and a major theme in all his works, as shown by Michel Dupuy.[247] That Jesus Christ, the God-man, is the only perfect Adorer of the Father is central to the message of the *Grandeurs*.[248] Insofar as we adhere to Jesus in love we come to share in his state of perfect adoration and thus perform worthy acts of adoration in our daily lives. The state of adoration is, therefore, the source of all our acts of adoration. In *Works of Piety* 22, Bérulle lists the dispositions believers should have with regard to the mystery of the Incarnation. These are *humility* with regard to the greatness of the mystery and our own unworthiness, *simplicity* (not vain curiosity) regarding our inability to grasp the mystery. Third comes *adoration*, which means looking to the Incarnation only in homage and not attempting to understand it. The fourth and fifth dispositions are *admiration* for the dignity of the mystery, and the *affection* that gives us delight in God. Bérulle concludes, "The desire of the soul in contemplation of the mystery should be a desire of homage and belonging and joining with the Holy Trinity, Jesus, Mary, and Saint Gabriel."[249] In this short text, Bérulle brings together a number of terms often used in connection with adoration, such as contemplation, admiration, love/affection, and homage/honor. Although there is no single-model mystical itinerary in his writings, several triple formulations using such terms have been noted as helpful for understanding Bérulle's sense of spiritual progress. For example, in the Introduction to *Grandeurs* II, Bérulle says how when we contemplate Jesus as "the Sun of Justice who gives his light to all who come into the world, we are as it were surprised by astonishment and smitten by love and admiration." Dupuy sees in this "a true initiation in Bérullian mysticism," consisting of contemplation, astonishment, love, and adoration.[250] In Discourse V, speaking of how the Father imprints his being and life on the Son and the Son in turn imprints his condition of Servanthood on us, Bérulle notes "the chain of love and honor that binds us to the Father and the Son and allows us to imitate and adore the reciprocal love and honor that is between them."[251] This suggests a progression of honor, love, and imitation/adoration.

Adoration is that for which humans and angels were created, the full expression of the first commandment of loving God above all things. Nonetheless, while we remain in this life, we are also bound by the second commandment, love of neighbor, so that we are obliged to action, that is, to work for the salvation of others. In Bérulle's case, working for the salvation for others takes on a particular apostolic coloring, due to his efforts as a church reformer, especially in founding and guiding the new Oratorian Order. In a Conference given to the Oratorians on January 1, 1613, Bérulle discussed the conditions for effective apostolic action and raised the question, "What is needed so that the actions referred to our neighbor be useful both to him and to us?" There are three, he says: humility of spirit; reverence for the image of God found in the neighbor; and zeal for the salvation of his soul, which must be very great. If we have these dispositions toward Jesus's human actions, which are also divine because of the Hypostatic Union, "we should not reject asking for the sanctification and deification of at least our own more perfect works that are ordained for the salvation of souls, such as the administration of the sacraments and sermons."[252] Bérulle's thoughts about apostolic action are most often directed to his priests of the Oratory. Priests are called on to recognize that when the good of the neighbor demands it what he calls *devotio sensibilis*, that is, the inner feeling of delight sent by God, needs to be interrupted. *Devotio rationabilis*, which consists in self-denial and love of God, can be possessed in every action, but *devotio sensibilis*, "even though it may be from God, does not always have to be retained by us, but sometimes is lost in the external actions taken up for the usefulness of the neighbor and the glory of God."[253]

Pierre de Bérulle does not develop a detailed doctrine of contemplation, although he does discuss it. *Works of Piety* 38 provides an entry into his thinking on the matter by showing how our call to contemplation is rooted in the life of the Trinity. The Father contemplates the unity of his essence and produces the Son to whom he gives two gifts: the divine essence and the indwelling of his own Person ("The Father is in me," John 14:10). The Son in turn contemplates, loves, and imitates the gift he has received and wishes to give it to a created essence, the humanity that comes from the Virgin. Christians therefore have an essential call to contemplation, because the Father has given them his Son and Word, the flower and fruit of his own contemplation. "There are two kinds of vocations," says Bérulle, "the one by inspiration, the other by state. I say that Christians are called to contemplation not only by inspiration, but by the state and condition of their manner of life and the grace they received in baptism, the sort of grace that elevates them and binds them to God through Jesus Christ his Son, who is his Word, his thought, his contemplation." Thus, by becoming one with Christ in baptism we are called to contemplation by state and essence in this life, and our final goal is the perfect contemplation of God and Jesus Christ in heaven (citing John 17:3).[254] Hence, it is not surprising that Bérulle often speaks about contemplating the grandeurs of God (e.g., OP 7, 12, 22, 26, 129, 349), and that he sometimes uses the term in conjunction with other key words like elevation and abstraction (e.g., OP 64), or prayer (OP 103). But what is the nature of contemplation? It does not seem that Bérulle was much interested in providing a definition of contemplation and its various kinds. There are, however, a few passages in the *Collationes* where Bérulle speaks about a form of direct, or intuitive, knowing of God that may be taken to be a form of contemplation that is higher than but prepared for by ordinary discursive mental and affective acts. For example, in the *Collation for January 1612*, he says, "This simple thought brings it about that the intellectual soul does not wander here and there; it is not lazy, but sufficiently and supremely occupied. This mode of thinking depends on the soul's prior dispositions, by which it is well disposed to be borne into its object by the least impulse of grace."[255] Thus, it appears that at least in the *Collations* Bérulle recognized a form of direct contemplation superior to ordinary cognition, but such discussions are not a major feature in his later writings.

With regard to the relation of contemplation and action, Bérulle's teaching is standard, as expressed succinctly in *Works of Piety* 248: "We love God in contemplation, we honor him in the active life" (OC 4:194). In several places in the *Collationes* Bérulle tells his Oratorian brethren that their calling is to both contemplation and action, not unlike the standard mystical doctrine beginning with Origen and conveyed by Augustine, Gregory, Bernard of Clairvaix, and many others.[256] Bérulle hands on these traditional categories, which need to be evaluated in terms of how they fit with his own thoughts about the nature of *adoration* and its relation to the work of the Oratory.[257]

(3) Union and Deification
Union and deification are two more of the central themes of the Western mystical tradition. Once again, they appear in Bérulle, but in distinctive ways. Our union with the Triune God for Bérulle is not a category separable from the doctrine of the Trinity and the God-man. There is no separate "theology of union" in Bérulle, but our relation to Jesus, the God-man, through annihilation, adherence, servitude, and adoration, is being made one with God through Jesus Christ. Although it goes beyond any particular text in Bérulle's corpus, Edward Howells's analysis of Bérulle's view of union in terms of a relationality that

does full justice to both difference and union shows how the notion of union is inseparable from Bérulle's doctrine of the Trinity and his Christology. In Howells's formulation, "[h]e [Bérulle] finds unity and difference complementary rather than opposed. Human and divine cannot in the end oppose one another but require each other for their distinction."[258] Howells also underlines the truly daring aspect of Bérulle's view of union, namely, the union we attain is not ontologically different from Christ's union, but relationally different. Christ's position remains central, however, in that we attain this union only through the human relationality of the God-man.

This concept of union for Bérulle, as has been noted, is an objective category, one whose experiential aspects were not of great interest to the cardinal. Such an understanding of union is, of its very nature, a deification, a being made "God" by grace and participation, by relation, not by nature. Bérulle makes this clear, for example, in *Grandeurs* VII.i when he says, "We are made gods by participation alone, and not by subsistence as in the Incarnation, and not by essence as in the Trinity, that is to say, it finds it goal [*se termine*] in rendering us temples of the Divinity communicating within the divine Persons and living images of that supreme, divine, and uncreated Being."[259] It is no surprise, then, that Bérulle is among the most insistent voices in Western Christian mysticism on the importance of deification.

No single text in Bérulle will incorporate all the theological implications of his teaching on union, but a survey of a few key passages will help lay out some of its many aspects. Union language is frequent in the *Collations*.[260] Addressing the Oratorians on the Feast of Corpus Christi in 1612, Bérulle emphasizes our union with the adoring Christ: "Let us acknowledge that we are the Temple of God and that Jesus Christ works everything in it that he works in heaven. Here he adores the Father, he prays, he loves. In the same way he also adores, prays, and loves in our soul. Let us love God in union with his love; let us adore in union with his adoration." Later in the same text he talks about having the same purity of heart, love, and intention with which Christ instituted the Eucharist. "The presence of Jesus Christ," he says, "which enkindles us to this purity, love, and union is not in the imagination, but is shown forth in the spirit through living faith."[261] A later meditation on the Ascension in 1615 notes that we are united with Christ not only in his divinity but also in his humanity, so that there is no moment of our lives where we do not have benefit from his life. Jesus lived a double form of life as God and man, something which we cannot experience: "We do not know it, but through his cross we can nonetheless be united to it."²⁶² Union with Christ is central, although we are also united to the Holy Spirit, the Spirit of Christ, who becomes the inner principle of our actions (*Collation for July 1614* in OC 2:208-9).

A number of the *Works of Piety* also discuss union. OP 35, for example, is a succinct summary of much of Bérulle's thought, under the title "Jesus Is the Way in Many Manners." Bérulle begins, "We should adhere to Jesus, and in this adherence, to his divine Person who works continually in the production of the Holy Spirit proceeding from him." Thus, he is the model for all our actions. We should never work alone, "but jointly with God who is our Father, although in dependence on Him, [and] in so strict a bond with him that we seem to be only one same principle with Him and one same spirit, 'The one who adheres to God is one spirit with Him' (1 Cor. 6:17). Jesus Christ in his final days asked his Father that we might be one with Him and his Father, 'That they may be one' (John 17:21)."²⁶³ Therefore, we ought to aim for this unity, as much in our being as in our way of acting. This adherence to Jesus in his humanity comes about through our joining our abasement with the perpetual abasement of Jesus. Thus, our life should be totally possessed by the life of Jesus, since "our life is nothing but a capacity to receive and admire his life." Bérulle goes on to describe six different forms of life in Jesus for our adoration and imitation.²⁶⁴

An *Elevation* in *Grandeurs* II.i also cites John 17:20-23 in praising the connection between our unity and the divine unity the Son enjoys with the Father: "O sacred expression of the Eternal Word! O efficacious prayer of the Only Son of God! O adorable words of unity of the Son with the Father! O desirable prayer of union of the Son with us and of us with Him! O unity! I unite myself then with You in honor of the ineffable union which you have with the Father and the Holy Spirit."²⁶⁵ It is scarcely necessary to collect a mass of union texts from the Bérullian corpus to make the point of its centrality and objective character. One final passage from the *Elevation to the Most Holy Trinity* underlines the fact that our union with God is already permanently established through Christ's Hypostatic Union. What is required on our part is acknowledgment and praise of what is already there. Speaking of the unbreakable bond of God and man in Christ, Bérulle says, "I also want to have an indissoluble bond with you, O Jesus my Savior; You can give me the grace to dispose myself on my part [so that] I adore You in the union that You have wanted to have with us, a union so strong that nothing can dissolve it, a union so intimate that it could not be more intrinsic and immediate, because it penetrates to the depth of human existence [*au fonds de l'être humain*]."²⁶⁶

Such a union of its very nature must be deifying, and deification meets the reader often in Bérulle's pages. As Jean Dagens put it, "The central idea of the spirituality of Bérulle is that through the Incarnation all the actions, all the human states that were corrupted and defiled by the First Man have been deified in the Person of Jesus."[267] Of course, deification comes to us only because the humanity assumed by the Word has been deified in the Hypostatic Union, but the fact that we share this human nature means that the deification of Jesus and our deification can never be separated. The cardinal takes our deification in a strong sense, because we not only receive divinization from God but, due to our union with him, can actually communicate with the divinity, as does Jesus. As he puts it in *Grandeurs* VI, citing John 10:38 ("I in the Father and the Father in me"), "We enter into an excellent communication with the divinity at the present, and, in this inferior world, we are united by certain degrees and levels, in a substantial way with God."[268] The text goes on to cite John 17:22–23. Bérulle's references to our deification are numerous,[269] sometimes making use of traditional images and metaphors, as when he says in *Works of Piety* 163: "We arise from God in creation. We return into God through the glory and in this return we are abyssed and transformed like a drop of water in an ocean of liquid, wine, or something else."[270]

Bérulle had little interest in special mystical gifts and their relation to the reality of Christocentric union and deification. Miklos Vetö noted that the cardinal writes little about mystical experience, because he views things from the divine perspective, not from that of the psychology of the subject.[271] To be sure, Bérulle approves of good mystical consolations, such as Teresa of Avila's wound of love, already so popular in early modern Catholicism.[272] He also has some treatments of "false absorptions," the kinds of self-induced states that Teresa, John of the Cross, and other early modern mystics warned against. Bérulle strongly criticizes those who at Christmastime remain "astonished" and absorbed in a "suspension of mind" before the baby Jesus, not recognizing that there is so much more to God as "infinite object," and that such a suspension "might impede the free act of the will for producing many acts of adoration, love, and self-emptying."[273]

(4) Mary Magdalene: The Model Mystic
The image of Mary Magdalene, sinner and saint, contemplative and apostolic preacher, and, above all, the supreme exemplar (the Virgin always excepted) of ravishing love of Jesus obsessed the religious sensibility of early modern Europe, not least that of Pierre de Bérulle.

The Magdalene was popular all over Catholic Europe, but especially in France due to the legend of her missionary activity in Gaul.

In the *Collations*, Mary Magdalene is frequently held up to the Oratorians as a model. Bérulle says that the Oratorians ought to be particularly devoted to the Magdalene because "the opinion seems quite true" that her conversion was the greatest work of either nature or grace that Jesus Christ worked while he was on earth (*Collation for July 1613* in OC 2:115-16). Speaking of the Magdalene's encounter with the risen Jesus in the garden (John 20:11-18), when she did not at first recognize him, Bérulle says, "The unknown presence of the Son of God did not exercise the effects of love, desire, and the other virtues any less in her soul than the visible presence by which her Lord made himself known." The message is that the grace of Christ in us that we do not feel is often more powerful than the sensible consolations of grace: "Although we do not see God, we are seen by him."[274] In a long meditation given for the Feast of the Magdalene (July 22, 1614), Bérulle places Mary Magdalene in the highest of the hierarchical orders, that is, "the chorus of Jesus which has the greatest part in the love of Jesus." "Reason," he says, "certainly suggests this and the Son of God himself hints at it when he says, 'She has loved much' (Luke 7:47). He loved her much and was much loved by her. It is even probable that she was loved more than many of the apostles; surely, no one denies that He showed her more signs of friendship."[275] In an even longer meditation for the Magdalene's feast in 1615, Bérulle makes use of his teaching about the reversal brought about by the Incarnation so that greater works are now done on earth than in heaven to argue (though he admits it is not a teaching *de fide*) that the love Mary Magdalene showed to Jesus when she washed his feet with her tears (Luke 7:36-50) was superior to the seraphic love of the highest angels. Because "Jesus Christ worked within her a greater work of love than he ever worked in heaven," Bérulle lays out a series of devotions to the Magdalene to be practiced on the eight days of the octave of her feast.[276] Three of the *Works of Piety* are also dedicated to Mary Magdalene.[277]

Bérulle's strong devotion to Mary Magdalene continued on into his later works, reaching a culmination in the twenty *Elevations on Saint Magdalene* addressed to Queen Henrietta Marie, wife of Charles I of England. These cover the whole life of the saint, finding material for praise and imitation, both in the events recounted in scripture and in the legend of Mary Magdalene's thirty years of penance and prayer known from hagiography.[278] This striking work provides a good sense of the high rhetorical style of the late Bérulle. The various Magdalenian themes found in the *Collations* are deepened, supplemented, and integrated into a paean to the overwhelming love of God that Bérulle sees as the essence of the Magdalene's special status among all the saints.

Bérulle opens with the theme of the Magdalene as miracle: "During your time on earth, O Jesus, my Lord, . . . you performed many miracles. . . . However, the rarest choice of your love, the worthiest object of your favor, the masterpiece of your grace, is the Magdalene and you performed the greatest of your miracles for her."[279] Just as the resurrection of her brother Lazarus from the dead was the greatest of Jesus's external miracles, Mary's conversion was the greatest of the higher internal miracles. Once again, the key text is Luke 7:47, where Jesus says that much has been forgiven Mary because "she loved much." That is why she attained an instant perfection at her conversion and why she was made the first member of the new seraphic order of love that begins on earth, not in heaven (*Elevation* I.5). Here, another major theme emerges, that of the feet of Jesus. Mary was converted by kneeling at the feet of Jesus; she stays at the cross also at Jesus's feet; and at the Resurrection Bérulle imagines her at Jesus's feet in the garden. This is a sign of her recognition that it is only by taking on the humbled and abased state of the God-man, by lowering ourselves with him, that we can be elevated to true love: "In her abasement at your feet, she experiences such exalted and powerful prayer that in very little time she makes remarkable progress in the sacred school of your love [*en l'école sacrée de votre amour*]." Bérulle prays that the whole of his life might be equal to one of those moments of love enjoyed by the Magdalene.[280] *Elevation* II concerns how the life of the Son of God on earth restores love to the world, while *Elevation* III returns to the life of the Magdalene, specifically the banquet at the house of the Pharisee recounted in Luke 7. *Elevation* IV is an Ignatian-style meditation on how the Magdalene prepared perfumes for Jesus's anointment after death, and *Elevation* V is a long treatment of the Magdalene at the foot of the cross. *Elevations* VI–VIII deal with the Magdalene at the Resurrection, where another important theme emerges, that of Mary Magdalene as *apostola*. In Jesus's first birth, the first person to see him was the Blessed Virgin; at his birth in the Resurrection the first person was the Magdalene: "The first name you pronounced was her name, the name Mary, the name dedicated to her, in her, to love and patience. The first commission you gave . . . was to her, making her an apostle, but an apostle of life, glory, and love, and an apostle to your apostles."[281]

Elevations IX through XX deal with Mary Magdalene's life after the

Ascension, specifically her thirty years in the desert filled with penitential practices, but even more with intense love of Jesus. Bérulle waxes eloquent over and over in praise of the "desert of love," the school where the Magdalene learns all the mysteries of love of God. *Elevations* XIV and XV show how Mary Magdalene shares in the three forms of love of Jesus mentioned above: separating love, crucifying love, and ravishing love: "I see there a separating love, for Jesus is in heaven, and the Magdalene is on earth. I see there a crucifying love, for Jesus unites himself to her, but as crucified. Moreover he unites himself to her as crucifying. . . . I see there as well a third sort of love, an incomparable love. . . . It is a love that is enraptured at the sight of Jesus, who is no longer crucified but glorified."[282] A series of *Elevations* on the different reasons for giving honor to the Magdalene (XVI–XIX) is brought to conclusion by a prayer to Mary Magdalene in which Queen Henrietta is encouraged to abandon the things of the world, and, like the Magdalene, devote herself to love of God: "That I may separate myself from all things and from myself above all, in order to be totally for Him, imitating your seclusions, your withdrawals [*abstractions*], your divine elevations. That I may be ready to hear the voice of Jesus and his inspirations."[283]

(5) Eucharist and Priesthood

This treatment of the mystical annihilated life in Bérulle will conclude with a few reflections on two things that were of great importance to him and where he had an impact on later Catholic thought: the related issues of the significance of the Eucharist and the priestly hierarchy in whose care the sacrament has been given. For Bérulle there were two essential ways in which the God-man now in heaven is still sacramentally present and accessible in the world: the Mass and the priesthood.

According to Bérulle, "The greatest and most divine action of Jesus Christ on earth thus far seems to be the consecration of the Holy Sacrament of the altar, establishing himself on earth through this 'until the end of the world' (Matt. 28:20), and bestowing through its presence grace and glory to the souls who receive it, and disposing them in soul and body through himself for [final] glory."[284] In Bérulle's view, the reception of Christ in the Eucharist was the central practice of Christian life, the place where the believer not only comes into the direct presence of Jesus, but where the union that is the purpose of salvation is most effectively attained. The description of the five forms of life of Jesus in OP 35 was noted above. At the conclusion of this short work Bérulle says, "To these five forms of life we speak about and which we ought to share in through many other ways we should add some others: his life residing on the altar in the Eucharist, about which he seems to have spoken when he said, 'I will be with you all days until the end of time' (Matt 28:30)," as well as his residence in holy souls. In the Mass, Christ is always offering himself as a sacrifice and giving us to eat as a sacrament.[285] The significance of the Eucharist is perhaps most evident in the passage in *Grandeurs* VII.i–ii where Bérulle discusses the unity of the three greatest Christian mysteries: Trinity, Incarnation, and Eucharist. God's "primitive and eternal communication" is the "cause and exemplar of his temporal communication" in the Incarnation. "The Holy Eucharist," Bérulle goes on to say, "is like an imitation of the mystery of the Incarnation and an application and extension of it to each Christian and faithful soul. . . . In these three mysteries we have the same subject to contemplate and adore."[286] These three states of Jesus are different, but each is worthy of honor, love, and special consideration. In the third mystery, that is the Eucharist, "we adore also the unity of his glorified body accompanied by an admirable fecundity of grace and spirit, because the deified body communicates the spirit, the love, and the grace of Jesus Christ to those who receive it." Adoring and participating in all three mysteries allow us to unite the weak and perishable things of this world "to the supreme unity of the Divinity and to stretch out to the unity of grace and the mystical life [*de la vie mystique*] in which God imprints and communicates to the spirit who is prepared, purified, and lifted up, his holy unity so that it can become one spirit with God . . . , 'Who adheres to God becomes one spirit with Him' (1 Cor. 6:17)."[287]

A number of the *Works of Piety* also treat the Eucharist, especially OP 37, 117, and 119–21. In OP 37, Bérulle shows the role of the Eucharist in divinization. There are, he says, two admirable capacities in Jesus: how he is rendered capable of the fullness of divinity, and how he is "a capacity for souls which he contains in himself, in his authority and power." As part of this second capacity, "Jesus Christ instituted the sacrament of his Body to bind our souls and draw them into the plenitude of the divinity that lives in him according to the admirable and adorable capacity he has to contain them and to give them life and subsistence in him."[288] This is one of the "three chains" spoken of by the Fathers: the chain of consubstantiality that binds the Son to the Father; the chain that binds our nature to God in the unity of the Uncreated Son; and the chain of "the deified humanity and the Man-God to each of us through the efficacy and the singular power of the sacrament of his Body." Bérulle concludes, "To adhere to Jesus is to adhere to life."[289]

Works of Piety 117 is a lengthy and beautiful meditation on "excellences" of the Most Holy Sacrament, while Nos. 119–21 feature exhortations to adore the Holy Sacrament.[290]

To speak of the dignity and role of the Eucharist for Bérulle immediately calls to mind the priesthood into whose hands Jesus placed the consecration and administration of the saving sacrament.[291] *Works of Piety* 280 on "The Different States of Jesus in the Eucharist and the Power of the Priest over Jesus in this Mystery" makes this clear: "The state of Jesus in the Eucharist is principally ours not only because it was instituted for us and our use, but because it was established for us in dependence on the power and operation of priests."[292] Following the Epistle to the Hebrews (Heb. 9:11–28), Bérulle held that Jesus Christ is the one and only priest, the perfect mediator between God and humanity,[293] but he chooses to share this office and function with other human beings (OP 58 in OC 3:197). This gives the priest a unique relation to Christ, as Bérulle explains in OP 290, "On the Perfection of the Priesthood": "Just as the Son is the Image of the Father in the Trinity, and the Father is the prototype and origin of the Son, so too the Son has wished that just as He is the Father's image on earth, there would be priests who would be his image."[294]

Bérulle stresses the dignity of the office of priesthood as the conjoint instrument of the humanity of Jesus working for the salvation of humanity.[295] Priests therefore have an ontological bond with the God-man, as is evident in *Works of Piety* 309 on "The Renewal of the State of the Priesthood." The highest order in the Church is not of the saints, or of the angels, but is "the order of the Son of God himself," to which all priests belong. "This state of priesthood," he goes on to say, "requires two things itself. The first is a very great perfection and similar sanctity, because it is a holy and sacred state in its institution; it is a divine office in its use and ministry. . . . Second, it requires a particular bond with Jesus Christ our Savior to whom we are joined through this ministry in a special manner and through a power so lofty that it does not belong even to the angels in the state of glory." Bérulle says that priests should be "like hosts immolated to his service, just as he deigned to be the immolated Host for us to God his Father, and we should put ourselves wholly into his hands as organs and instruments of his grace, just as he in his humanity is the instrument personally joined to divinity."[296]

Bérulle's understanding of the office and function of the priesthood is essentially hierarchical, deeply influenced by the Dionysian treatises on hierarchy.[297] Like the angels, the priestly order is arranged under its leader to perform the sanctifying actions of purging, illuminating, and perfecting for those who are subject to them. As we have seen in speaking of Mary and Mary Magdalene, Bérulle's conception of hierarchy distinguished a variety of orders/hierarchies and the action and adoration befitting them. All angels and humans are called upon to adore the Son of God in his assumed human nature, but there are many orders of humans to whom special offices are given, of whom the priests are the highest. Beyond these, however, certain very special people, such as the Magdalene, can be chosen by Jesus for an internal sharing in his life and love of a higher kind.[298]

At a time when the state of the priesthood, especially of the diocesan priesthood, was so low and often criticized, Bérulle boldly proclaimed the need for a holy priesthood, even a mystical priesthood. As Paul Cochois says, "[T]he state of passivity or mystical union is by right the normal universe of the priest, because only that state corresponds to the manner in which the Sovereign-Priest takes possession of himself through priestly consecration."[299] In that sense, the ecclesiastical hierarchy and the mystical hierarchy were meant to coincide, just as they do in the angelic hierarchies that are their model. For Bérulle, "The whole of the grace of the Church is given to the priesthood. It is not communicated save by the priest." Therefore, "[j]ust as the great Saint Denys, wanting to give a name to God, called him 'being of beings, superessence' (DN 5.4 and 2), so it is necessary to say that priests are not just angels, but are super-angels [*suranges*]."[300]

For Bérulle, the priesthood was absolutely necessary for the Church: "The Church can and has existed without Religious Orders, but not without priests. And the renewal of the priesthood especially in these times was destined by God and awaited by the world."[301] That is why Bérulle saw the goal of the Oratorians not so much as the establishment of new order, but as part of the broad call for the renewal of the priesthood issued by the Council of Trent (OP 311 in OC 4:602-3). He felt that this was a special aspect of the divine grace at work in the world, as can be seen from his hymn of praise to God the Father for the renewal of the religious orders taking place in his time, especially for the repristination of the priesthood: "'The Father of lights, source of every good' (Jas. 1:7), wished to bestow the same grace and favor on the state of priesthood and pour out his Spirit, his light, and his guidance on many souls for renewing in that order the state of perfection which belonged to it according to its ancient ministry and its first institution."[302] To that end, although he did not write a formal rule for his new society, he structured a form of life conducive to intense contemplative prayer, as well as an active apostolate. Bérulle also left the Oratorians a precious gift, the heritage of his mystical teaching, especially as found in the *Collations* and the *Works of Piety*.

Conclusion

Bérulle is not well known outside France. His life and some of his teaching still arouse controversy. His constant repetitions and often too-fervent style do not make for easy reading. Nevertheless, the French cardinal was an original mystical thinker whose theology sought to integrate the great mysteries of the faith—Trinity, Incarnation, and Eucharist—as much as any of the major figures in the history of Christian mysticism. Time-bound, as are all mystics, Bérulle still manages to set out a powerful position on how to live in the presence of God that serves to inspire as well as challenge. Above all, Bérulle reminds us of the need to annihilate ourselves so that we can live with Jesus: "The life of a person is to abase himself and to be annihilated in himself, to refer himself to God, to unite himself to Jesus, to live and to work in Jesus. God is the goal of goals; Jesus is the medium of mediums, and the medium that contains and encloses the goal."[303]

Appendix: In the Wake of Bérulle

The debate over the term "the French School" was touched upon in chapter 1. Although the characterization still has its defenders, there are so many ambiguities to its use that I have not adopted it for this volume.[304] It may be preferable, as some have done, to speak of a "Bérullian synthesis, or current" (L. Cognet), a "Bérullian School" (J. Le Brun), or "Bérullianism" (Y. Krumenacker). There were many figures, both inside and outside the Oratory, who were deeply influenced by Bérulle's thinking. This group includes religious leaders like Vincent de Paul (ca. 1580-1660), a good friend of Bérulle, the founder of two major religious orders, and the missionary of France.[305] Vincent de Paul's writings, however, are not mystical in the sense that I am using the term. There were other individuals, both men and women, whose lives and writings present mystical teaching imbued to a greater or lesser degree with a deep Bérullian strain. There are a considerable number of these, but the constraints of this volume will allow only brief introductions to four authors. I have chosen to treat them under the admittedly vague rubric of "the wake of Bérulle" to avoid discussions of "school," "influence," "Bérullianism," and the like.

Madeleine de St. Joseph (1578–1637)

Despite some recent work, the story of the role of women in seventeenth-century mysticism still remains to be told.[306] Bérulle, like Francis de Sales, worked closely with several women in a form of spiritual friendship that had an impact on his life and thinking. Foremost among these was Madeleine de St. Joseph, an aristocratic woman he recruited for the first Carmel in Paris and who remained so close to him that Louis Cognet did not hesitate to call her "his inspirer and counselor."[307] Bérulle met the young woman in 1603 and convinced her to join the Carmelite house that was soon to open in Paris. She was a member of the group of women that Barbe Acarie trained as postulants for this first French Carmel, which she entered in 1604. Madeleine founded the second Paris Carmel in 1607, as well as houses in Tours and Lyon. She remained close to Bérulle, especially during her second time as Prioress of the original Paris house between 1624 and 1635. She died on April 30, 1637. Madeleine left a number of letters, as well as a *Life of Sister Catherine of Jesus* (*Le vie de Soeur Catherine de Jésus*), first published in 1628. Sister Catherine (1579–1623) was a member of the Paris Carmel with a reputation for mystical gifts.[308] Only some sections of Catherine's own "little papers" survive. Madeleine used these, as well as her own conversations with the sister, to write an exemplary *vita* of the mystic, which shows a number of resonances with Bérullian thought, such as the emphasis on self-annihilation to allow Christ to take full possession of the soul.[309]

Madeleine's praise for Bérulle is unstinting (she even sided with him against many of the other Carmelite nuns in the controversy over the vows of servitude). Like that of Bérulle, her mysticism can be described as both theocentric and Christocentric. Interior adherence to Jesus and his states as the "door to God" (John 10:9) is absolutely necessary. In Letter 139 she says, "To enter then and leave through this door who is Jesus Christ is a manner of speaking that means to accomplish freely everything that God asks of us, entering into the divinity and going out into the humanity of Jesus Christ." Such going in and going out is to unite contemplation and action—"We enter with Mary and go out with Martha."[310] Like Bérulle and Marie de l'Incarnation (Barbe Acarie), Madeleine therefore criticized any attempt to leave Jesus behind in some kind of imageless contemplation. In Letter 39 she says, "One of the greatest sorrows I bear is to see that the evil spirit has been able to detach so many good souls from the blessed person of our Lord Jesus Christ on the pretext of attaining more sublime realities and thus leading them along the paths of illusion. O my God, what is more sublime than Jesus Christ?" She notes that both "our blessed Father [Bérulle] and our blessed Sister Marie de l'Incarnation" had warned against this dangerous tendency.[311]

A good idea of the Bérullian basis of Madeleine's mystical teaching can be found in Letter 144, written to a Carmelite Prioress.[312] The unnamed Prioress had asked her about the relation of adoration and thanksgiving, and Madeleine responds by arguing for the superiority of adoration, because the act of thanksgiving is included in the act of adoration. "Adoration," she says, "is what God looked for from the beginning in his creatures, . . . because adoration is a duty and a respect that the lesser owes the greater, the subject owes the sovereign Lord. Through it the creature experiences its nothingness in order to offer homage to its Creator." Since men and angels failed in this duty due to sin, God "decided upon the mystery of the Incarnation, where a God would adore God . . . in the state of lamb and victim for God, which is a state of adoration, for it is through sacrifice that adoration is offered." The letter goes on to enumerate three forms of oblation Jesus made of himself: first, at his entry into the world (Heb. 9:10); second, all during his life, but especially on the cross; and third, in the Blessed Sacrament.

The second part of the letter dwells on the necessary relation between love and adoration, an issue on which Madeleine may have had some influence on Bérulle (at least the late Bérulle). She insists, "What is most important to understand is that not only is adoration imperfect without love, but that it does not even deserve to be called adoration, nor is it welcomed by God as such, if love is not its soul and life." Actually, love and adoration "is one and the same duty to which we give two different names because of the different effects it produces." She closes the letter by emphasizing how we are meant to imitate Jesus in his offering of himself as a "perpetual victim." This is most perfectly realized "through holy communion, so that becoming one with him, we can, through this union, offer him to his Father and offer ourselves as well as a holy and acceptable sacrifice in the eyes of his majesty."

Charles de Condren (1588-1641)
Charles de Condren, the second General of the Oratory, was also born into a family of the high nobility.[313] At the age of twelve Charles experienced a mystical illumination, as described in the *Life of Father de Condren* (*La Vie du Père de Condren*) published by his good friend and fellow Oratorian Denis Amelote (1600-1679) in 1643. Amelote

recounts, "[W]hen studying one day . . . he was suddenly aware of his mind being encompassed with a wonderful light, in the radiance of which the Divine Majesty appeared to him so immense and so infinite that it seemed to him that this One Pure Being should alone subsist and that all the universe should be destroyed for his Glory." The illumination also involved the important motif of the "offering up himself and all things in Jesus the Victim." There is also an emphasis on nothingness. "For, being in the abyss of his nothingness before the Divine Holiness and desiring ardently to be sacrificed for his Glory, he was suddenly filled with a particular joy in seeing that the Son of God was ever the Victim of the Father. . . . He recognized that the sacrifice of Jesus Christ was the fulfilling of the zeal of all who themselves desired their immolation, but who were incapable worthily of honoring God by their sacrifice."[314] The vision surely occurred, but the account seems to have been colored by language and motifs later developed by Bérulle.

Destined for a military career, Condren was eventually allowed by his father to study for the priesthood and was ordained in 1614. After making a retreat under Bérulle, he entered the Oratory in 1617. Bérulle was deeply impressed with Condren and groomed him for taking over his position, which Condren did in November of 1629, although much against his will. Condren's natural bent was for a life of prayer and seclusion, but his affable charm, wide learning, deep holiness, and skill as a spiritual director led to his being given a number of public tasks, such as being named confessor to the difficult Gaston d'Orleans, Louis XIII's younger brother. His reticence meant that Condren deliberately wrote very little. Nonetheless, the *Life* by Amelote, as well as some letters and a treatise on the priesthood put together after his death, allow a picture of a mystical teaching that was primarily oral.[315] One of the fullest accounts of Condren's place in French mysticism is still to be found in Henri Bremond's *History*.[316]

Condren's mystical thinking, much like that of Bérulle, emphasizes annihilation and adoration, but with his own accents. He agrees with Bérulle in rooting the nothingness of the creature in creation itself, a nothingness later deepened by the Fall; but for Condren there is a terrible abyss between God and creation that is not ameliorated by a Bérullian doctrine of exemplarism or by the notion of humanity as a capacity for God, something that gives his teaching a strong pessimistic flavor. Condren's view of adoration also differs from Bérulle's in seeing adoration as fundamentally sacrifice conceived of as the annihilation and destruction of the self. Henri Bremond summarized the difference: "Bérulle's theocentrism spontaneously directs itself towards lyrical adoration, that of Condren towards the sacrifice of adoration."[317] For Condren, according to Louis Cognet, "the essence of sacrifice is to be a homage of nothingness to Being through annihilation."[318] Amelote's *Life* makes this act of annihilating sacrifice the heart of Condren's spiritual life: "We need only let it be known that his greatest grace, the one which especially marked the path by which God led his most pure soul, was the grace of sacrifice, love of the sanctity and purity of God, desire for his own annihilation so as to glorify the divine perfections."[319] Of course, the nothingness of fallen humanity cannot on its own offer the sacrifice that bridges the awful gap between the absolute divine Being and worthlessness of the creature, so that the Incarnation becomes almost a metaphysical necessity in order to make the perfect sacrifice possible. Salvation comes to us when the Holy Spirit enters us to allow us to adhere to the states of Jesus, but most especially to the victim-state of the Redeemer. As Condren put it in a letter to a new priest, "We must annihilate ourselves in this action [of offering sacrifice] and be pure members of Jesus Christ, offering what he offers and doing what he does as if we were no longer ourselves."[320] Not surprisingly, the dignity of the priesthood and the importance of the sacrifice of the Mass play a major role in Condren's thought.

John Eudes (1601-1680)
Born in Normandy in 1601, John Eudes entered the Oratory in 1623 and was ordained in 1625.[321] His spiritual formation and early years were decisively shaped by Pierre de Bérulle and Charles de Condren. In 1632, he became head of the Oratory at Caen and in 1634 began preaching the many missions he conducted down to 1676. Eudes wrote a good deal,[322] his most notable work being the *Life and Kingdom of Jesus in Christian Souls* (*La Vie et Royaume de Jésus dans les âmes chrétiens*), first published in 1637, which went through twenty editions in the seventeenth century. The book is a practical handbook of Christian living and the pious practices that foster it, directed to all Christians in the manner of Francis de Sales's *Introduction to the Devout Life*.[323] In 1641, Eudes was asked to investigate the peasant seer Marie des Vallées (1590-1656), a controversial figure who had a reputation for mystical gifts but who also had been obsessed with and sometimes possessed by devils. Eudes, however, accepted her as a genuine mystic and was greatly influenced by her until her death. He was criticized for this relationship, both in his own time and in the modern era, even by those, like Henri Bremond, who bend over backward to try to see Marie as a real mystic.[324]

The year 1643 was a turning point for Eudes. He felt a strong call to begin founding seminaries according to the decrees of Trent. When the current General of the Oratory, François Burgoing (1585–1662), resisted this, Eudes left the order and established a seminary at Caen, as well as a new order, the Society of Jesus and Mary (Eudists), to staff seminaries and preach missions, the two major foci of his apostolate. This led to considerable opposition, not only from the Oratorians but also from the Jansenists whom he regularly attacked. The other major impact of John Eudes in seventeenth-century French piety was his pioneering efforts to spread devotion to the Sacred Heart of Jesus and the heart of Mary. Building on aspects of Bérulle's devotion to Jesus and Mary, Eudes came to see the heart of Jesus as the central expression of the interior loving relation of the Son of God to the Father, and to insist on the unity between the heart of Jesus and that of his mother.

John Eudes used the concrete image of the "heart" in much the same way Bérulle employed *état* (state) as a focus for Christological and Marian devotion. As early as 1646 he introduced a Feast of the Heart of Mary, and in 1672 he pioneered the Feast of the Sacred Heart before the better-known efforts of the Visitandine nun Margaret-Mary Alacoque (1647–1690). According to Paul Milcent, "To all his disciples, John Eudes pointed out the way of a religion of love whose axis was the personal relation of the believer with Jesus Christ. Little by little, all his spiritual thought crystallized around the sign of the heart."[325] Hence, his last major work, published posthumously in 1681, was a treatise entitled *The Most Admirable Heart of the Most Sacred Mother of God* (*La coeur admirable de la très sacrée Mère de Dieu ou la devotion au très saint Coeur de Marie*).[326] As William M. Thompson put it, "His [Eudes] great work on Mary's heart is really a prolonged meditation on how the Marian mystery is grounded in the heart of Father, Son and Holy Spirit."[327]

At the outset of the *Most Admirable Heart* treatise, John provides eight biblical meanings of the term "heart," showing its centrality to his affective mysticism. Heart can refer to (1) the bodily heart; (2) the memory; (3) meditation; (4) free will; (5) the highest point of the soul, that is, "the seat of contemplation, which consists in a most simple gaze and an utterly simple view of God"; (6) the whole interior person; (7) "the divine Spirit, the heart of the Father and the Son"; and (8) the Son of God as the heart of the Father. Heart is therefore a capacious term that embraces all the physical, mental, and even divine relationships in God and between God and humans. Eudes goes on to show how we are to adore God in three hearts that are nonetheless one, just as we adore the Man-God in three unified hearts and honor the

Blessed Virgin in her three-yet-one hearts. The details of the analysis need not detain us, but the upshot is a doctrine of the hearts of Jesus and Mary that involves not only liturgical celebration but also a mystical assimilation and divinization. The *Most Admirable Heart of the Most Sacred Mother* ends with a book on our adoration of the three hearts of Jesus (bodily, spiritual, and divine), in which Jesus tells the adorer: "My Father loves me with an eternal, boundless and infinite love and I love you also with an eternal, boundless and infinite love. My Father makes me what I am, that is, God like him and only Son of God; and I make you, through grace and participation, what I am by nature and essence, that is, gods and children of God."[328]

John Eudes was also concerned with our union with Christ, but not so much with the individual's "mystical" union with Christ, as the general union with the Redeemer in the Mystical Body preached by Paul (e.g., Eph. 5:30). The basic message of the *Life and Kingdom of Jesus in Our Souls* is that because we are one with Jesus we are called to complete the work he began by annihilating ourselves, practicing perfect detachment, and imitating the virtues and acts of adoration he offered to the Father.[329] John Eudes is perhaps not a major mystic, but both the *Life and Kingdom of Jesus Christ* and the *Most Admirable Heart of the Mother of God* contain mystical themes that show the ongoing influence of Bérulle's thought on French mysticism in the seventeenth century.

Jean-Jacques Olier (1608-1657)
Olier is the most interesting of the mystics who wrote in the wake of Bérulle.[330] He is reminiscent of John Eudes in his founding of a new order for seminary work (the Sulpicians) and is similar to his contemporary, J.-J. Surin, as an example of the interconnection between mental health and mystical states. Olier's bout with what today would be called mental illness from 1639 to 1641 was much shorter than that of the Jesuit but seems to have been no less severe. The extent to which this breakdown can also be conceived of as a form of a "dark night" experience is controversial.

Olier was born in Paris and ordained in 1633. His life illustrates the close connections of so many of the French mystics. As an adolescent he met Francis de Sales; Vincent de Paul was his first spiritual director, and from 1635 he was directed by Charles de Condren. True to the Bérullian tradition, Olier took a series of vows of servitude: to Mary in 1633; extended to a vow to Jesus in 1642; and finally a "vow to victimhood" (*voeu de l'hostie*), that is, to Christ's sacrifice in 1644. Throughout his life Olier was a model for combining apostolic mission and contemplative piety. In 1639, a profound illness fell on him that took away his ability to move in body and in soul. He says, "That which God's goodness brought about in my body he also caused in my soul. For he took away the strength from the natural faculties, leaving me languishing in foolishness, stupidities, and imbecilities which only those who have experienced them can understand."[331] Olier also became convinced of his total sinfulness. Fortunately, the cloud lifted on the Octave of Corpus Christi, June 6, 1641.[332] Olier then plunged back into apostolic activity, especially missionizing and founding seminaries, the most important of which was the 1642 Paris foundation at the parish of Saint-Sulpice of which he was the pastor. In 1645, Olier created the Company of the Priests of Saint Sulpice, a group of secular priests who took interior devotion and seminary education as their main apostolate. Between 1649 and 1657 Olier and his associates founded another seven seminaries. In June of 1652 he gave up his position as pastor of Saint-Sulpice due to illness. Paralyzed in 1653, Olier eventually died in Paris on April 2, 1657.

Olier wrote extensively in the last fifteen years of his life. After the death of Condren, his new confessor, Dom Bataille, convinced him to begin writing a spiritual journal. From March 1642 until February 1652, he wrote these *Memoirs* (*Mémoires*), eight volumes of still-unpublished material, containing numerous accounts of the interior revelations given him by God. Revelations he received in 1644 were the source of two books: *The Divine Life* (*La vie divine*) and *The Creation of the World* (*De la création du monde*). In early 1645 he wrote a treatise entitled *The Angels: Divine Fragrances and Sweet Odors* (*Des Anges: Fragrances divines et odeurs suaves*). Olier also left many letters of spiritual direction.[333] Between 1654 and 1656 he composed the most important of his mystical works, *The Crystal Soul: The Divine Attributes in Us* (*L'âme cristal: Les attributes divins en nous*).[334] Olier intended to publish these works before his death, but this did not happen. In the increasingly antimystical atmosphere of the second half of the seventeenth century, Louis Tronson (1622–1700), the third General of the Sulpicians, decided it would not be wise to try to make them public, so they remained unknown until recent years. What was published of Olier's oeuvre (anonymously due to his self-annihilation) were some of his more moral and ascetical writings, which proved to be popular. These include *The Christian Day* (*La journée chrétienne*) of 1655, a series of prayers and meditations designed to sanctify the events of daily life. Also popular was the *Christian Catechism for the Interior Life* (*Catéchism chrétien pour la vie interieure*) of 1656, a more didactic presentation of spirituality centered on attaining union with Christ by mortification and prayer.[335] Shortly after his death, another popular work appeared, the *Introduction to the Life and Virtues of the Christian* (*Introduction à la vie et aux vertus chrétiennes*).[336]

Olier's status as a mystic is not easy to evaluate. Since the late seventeenth century, he has been known through a number of spiritual treatises, such as *The Christian Day* and the *Christian Catechism*, which primarily concern ascetical practices, virtues, and prayer. In recent years the daring mystical treatises that he did not publish in his lifetime have changed our view of his mysticism. These works, which feature bold language about annihilation and a union of indistinction with God, reveal Olier to have been an important voice with links to the traditions of Northern European mystics like Tauler, Ruusbroec, Harphius, and the author of the *Evangelical Pearl*. Thus, Olier takes a place in what the French call the *néantiste* tradition of which Bérulle was a leading figure. Recognizing one's own nothingness in the face of God, becoming "an object of oblivion" (*l'object de l'oubli*), is to serve as "a nothingness capable of God," and therefore to emerge as a "vanished" subject of deifying union.[337]

Like John of the Cross, Olier was suspicious of spiritual consolations and insisted on the way of naked faith. First-person accounts in the *Memoirs* speak about attaining a union of faith with God in prayer and receiving what the Augustinian tradition would have called intellectual visions. For example, on October 10, 1644, he says that when "[h]e was intimately one with God in prayer through a union of faith, I found myself as if in an immense sea which is the great essence of God . . . and [that] made it possible for me to participate in the divine attributes and perfections." He goes on: "I found myself all-powerful in him and I saw through experience what our Savior had only uncovered for me through simple sight and understanding some months when I was writing *The Divine Life*." After citing a key text about union (1 Cor. 6:17), he continues: "Then I saw that this divine union was the source of the magnificent and immense assurance of God. It is in this union that one can do everything, that one can do and see everything. It is in this union that one passes through perils without danger."[338]

Like many seventeenth-century figures, Olier does not cite many mystical authorities explicitly in his writings, although he mentions standard sources, such as the two Catherines (of Siena and Genoa), Gerson, Teresa of Avila, and Francis de Sales. He had read Achille Gagliardi's *Brief Compendium*, and John of the Cross's *Ascent of Mount Carmel*.[339] He testifies to the importance of the Dionysian corpus, but his use of Denys does not so much concern mystical union and negative theology as the role of the Dionysian view of hierarchy on his ecclesiology and theology of the dignity and function of the priesthood.[340]

We can gain a picture of Olier's general teaching from his *Introduction to the Life and Virtues of the Christian*, a primarily moral work that includes a number of mystical themes. The book is divided into fifteen chapters and seems to have been put together by Olier's disciples from a number of earlier writings on the virtues.[341] The recently edited second part deals with "Exterior Conformity with the Mysteries," that is, how the Christian can attain conformity with the mystery of Christ crucified, the mystery of Christ's death, and the mystery of the Resurrection. Participation in the mysteries of Jesus, exteriorly and interiorly, is crucial for Olier.[342] Chapter 1 of the first part introduces the theme of the "religion of Jesus Christ," by which Olier means the love and respect Jesus shows to the Father. As Louis Cognet put it, "Where Bérulle speaks of adoration and Condren of sacrifice, Olier speaks of religion, which includes adoration and sacrifice."[343] Jesus puts his Spirit into believers to "dilate his holy religion so that he and all Christians might become one religious [body] of God."[344] This dilation takes place through annihilation and sacrifice performed in imitation of Christ: "In his sacrifice our Lord claimed to annihilate everything and to sacrifice all things in himself because he had brought everything together in his person. Therefore, it is right that we condemn and sacrifice all things."[345] Christ communicates to us *son état d'hostie*, that is, his state as Host and victim, once on the cross and now on the altar, so that we may be consumed into perfect union with him and his Father (citing John 17:22–23). The second and third chapters of the work deal with the two ways of being conformed to Christ, exteriorly and interiorly, and the two ways the Holy Spirit works in us: as the Spirit of God in giving us the positive virtues, such as fortitude, and then as the Spirit of Jesus Christ in giving us the virtues of humiliation and abasement, such as love of the cross, humility, and poverty. The practice of the latter virtues is the main theme of the treatise, because "the best disposition by which we can be prepared to allow the Spirit to possess us and to be grounded by him in these virtues is interior annihilation [*anéantissement intérieur*]."[346]

This introduction sets the stage for the treatment of the virtues in the remainder of the treatise. Perhaps the most important of these are humility (chap. V) and poverty (chap. XI), because they are both strong expressions of the themes of human nothingness and need for annihilation. In that sense these are not so much moral as ontological virtues, not unlike Meister Eckhart's view of poverty of spirit. Chapter V, which makes use of Achille Gagliardi's *Brief Compendium*, declares that humility is the foundation for all the virtues, because it is the recognition of our nothingness, which makes us vile and abject. Olier analyzes humility in terms of three components. The first is to learn to love our own "vileness, littleness, and baseness," so that we can submit our will and understanding to God in true, interior humility. The second is to love being seen "as vile, abject, nothingness, and sin" by others; the third is to not only want to be known in this way but also to be treated as such. Although some passages in this chapter sound almost like a form of spiritual masochism,[347] the goal is to have God take over completely and thereby gain freedom of spirit: "Thus one is in authentic annihilation and we have nothing but God living and reigning in us. This is why God loves humble souls so much and why he establishes his throne and his domain in them in such an absolute fashion. For there exists in the annihilated person a total freedom to do what he pleases."[348]

Poverty, which is detachment from things in imitation of Christ, is rooted in human nature. God created the human heart empty of any object, so that it could be filled with him alone. By sinning, humans have filled their hearts with all sorts of evil things, so Jesus Christ came into the world to purify the heart. "Thus it follows," says Olier, "that he has established, as the major foundation of our salvation, holy poverty, which tends by its nature to empty the human heart of everything that could fill it, other than God."[349] Exterior poverty is important, but interior poverty, which is yielding to God the use even of the gifts he gives us, is higher. A long consideration of the motives for poverty emphasizes that "Christians be satisfied with him alone and that they come to him as he gives himself to them, in perfect nakedness, having nothing but faith, which helps them to embrace and possess him."[350] A similar emphasis occurs at the end of chapter XV. Olier, here similar to John of the Cross, says that it is not essential that we feel the Holy Spirit in us, or that we "taste experientially the sentiments and dispositions of Jesus Christ." Rather, like Jesus in his dryness and bitterness on the cross, "[w]e must unite ourselves with a pure spirit of sacrifice and faith, that is, with an intangible and obscure yet certain knowledge that God is in us through his holy and divine Spirit."[351]

These themes also appear in *The Divine Life* and *The Crystal Soul*, which Olier seems to have intended to be published together, with the first work serving as a prologue to the second. In these treatises, however, annihilation, naked faith, and union are enriched by being set forth within an ambitious mystical program. *The Crystal Soul* introduces a new master symbol, that of the soul as a transparent crystal in which Christ sits displaying all the divine attributes/perfections: "He intends to give himself to us and to dwell in us as in a throne of crystal by means of which he appears in all his attributes and is visible to us in the eyes of creatures."[352] Consideration of the divine attributes or names naturally calls to mind the Dionysian *Divine Names*.[353] Olier certainly knew this text and models his work on it to some extent, but what he does is different. Rather than concentrating his attention on the names in themselves, he treats his sixteen names/attributes first in God and then at greater length in how they are revealed in us.[354] In a sense, Olier prefers the subjective stance of investigating God's attributes insofar as we see them in the perfected soul. He insists that in God all the attributes are one and the same due to God's *suressential l'Être* and *suréminante vie* (terms frequent in the Sulpician),[355] but in the created realm we are forced to give them different names to bring out the richness of the divine nature. What is remarkable, however, is that God shares these attributes with the soul in a way that established a deep union between the Creator and the creature in which distinction seems to disappear. The main message of the *Crystal Soul* is that God deigns to share all his attributes with the soul, and even more, to give us these attributes in the same way as they are found in the divine nature.[356]

How do we arrive at this sharing in the divine perfections? The answer is annihilation (*anéantissement*) down to the very "depth of the soul" (*fond de l'âme*), the deepest aspect of the human, which has its source in the "divine depth from which it was drawn."[357] In the "Method for Making a Prayer about God and the Divine Attributes" at the start of the treatise, Olier says, "What is needed for communion with God is only a soul that is naked and an enemy of itself, a soul annihilated in its depth [*anéantie en son fond*], which sighs to God to be filled with him" (*Méthode pour faire l'oraison*; ed., 92). In the chapter devoted to "The Conformity of the Will in God," Olier states, "Just as the blessed [in heaven] are totally and in such a way penetrated by him so that they seem to be one thing with him, so too the depth of our soul ought to be penetrated, possessed, and transformed totally in him. This perfect conformity on earth is only found wholly in us with regard to our depth and what is independent of our flesh."[358] Such a position is close to that of many Northern European mystics, beginning with Eckhart, some of whom Olier probably read; but it is clear from his *Memoirs* that this was not a copying from former mystics but was a reflection on his own prayer life.

Annihilation is the leitmotif of the *Crystal Soul*. The theme is obvious from the prefatory "Method for Making a Prayer," where the Sulpician says, "It is highly necessary to aspire to that divine union, highly to desire that union, annihilating one's being and all that is one's own before God, in order to be totally filled and penetrated by him" (*Méthode*; ed., 69). Later in the same section we find the same message: "The only thing to prescribe to such souls is a general state of annihilation [*l'état général d'anéantissement*] of everything that is its own and a great inner emptiness [*vacuité intérieur*] in order to become full of God and to be filled up with his operations" (*Méthode*; ed., 78). Over and over in the chapters that follow Olier stresses the need for annihilation. For example, discussing the means by which we come to share in the attribute of God's perfection in chapter IV, he says, "The preparation for perfection in the ways and the virtue of Jesus Christ is annihilation. In the way in which the soul, empty of itself, is annihilated of its own desires and acts of will, annihilated of its operations, and finally in how its entire self exists in a perpetual and total renouncement of self, it is thereby prepared for perfection."[359]

Annihilation has many equivalents, such as *abandon, abnégation, délaissement* (not unlike Eckhart's "releasement"), *nudité de l'âme,* and *perte* (loss).[360] These terms represent a "word-field" of closely related ways of expressing the total giving up of the created and fallen self to return to the divine origin where the soul is indistinctly one with God. The Sulpician's view of this emptying, stripping, and annihilating is more than just a metaphor for ascetical effort. It is a form of "strong" annihilation, in the sense not of the absolute destruction of what God has created but, as we have seen in the case of Bérulle, of a total negating of our human way of acting and all of what belongs to us (the *propre*), so that God and his divine activity take over the empty place where our ordinary self once lived and worked. In a passage in the *Memoirs*, Olier says this extends even to the depth of the soul: "My depth was in God and was entirely of God [*mon fond était en Dieu et tout de Dieu*], and was able to find nothing in me but God." The sensing soul (*l'âme sensible*) may still be caught in the clouds and feelings of everyday life, but "the depth, which is lost in God, I have found through experience is infinitely distant from me and is lost in the depth of an inexhaustible abyss which cannot be sought out."[361]

The soul is passive in this "decreation" process.[362] Olier says, "When the soul is lifted up to this state of passivity and divine operation, it is passive in the operation, even though it may be acting."³⁶³ (At a later date Madame Guyon will also speak of the soul's "active passivity.") If the soul's task is to annihilate itself and remain passive, from God's side there is action, that is, the strong communication of love and the other attributes that Olier once describes using the Latin term *illapsum*, that is, "a falling, or rushing in" to fill the depth of the soul and its powers.³⁶⁴ This can happen only if the soul remains in "naked faith," as we have already seen.³⁶⁵ Olier often uses strong language about the way the soul in this state must die to itself in all its operations: "It is necessary to be like a dead person who can no longer move by himself and can only receive movement from elsewhere and life from another principle."³⁶⁶ Olier develops the *mors mystica* theme in a detail rarely found. Nevertheless, the whole negating process, so richly set forth in the *Crystal Soul*, is designed for the positive filling of the empty space by the plenitude of the divine attributes through union with God in Christ, a union that Olier describes as deification.³⁶⁷

Jean-Jacques Olier's teaching on union is very much of a "strong" variety.³⁶⁸ Many of his texts are so daring that had they been published in the increasingly antimystical atmosphere of the second half of the seventeenth century they might well have brought investigation and even condemnation. He seems to ignore the kinds of cautions and qualifications that some mystics, such as Tauler, made to their expressions of deep and indistinct union. Thus, he uses the phrase that we become "one same thing" (*une même chose*) with God, without qualification.³⁶⁹ He speaks of our union with God as a "union without confusion" that is like the union of the three Persons in the Trinity.³⁷⁰ In chapter I on the "Existence of God," he says, "He will fill us entirely with himself without mixture or distinction [*sans mélanges ou distinction*; ed., 99]." We become one with God and his attributes in such a unity that he can say: "We will not be more than one sole God: one eternal, one immense, one infinite, in the fullness of majesty, beauty, and splendor. Briefly, all will not be more than one sole God, because 'God will be all in all' (1 Cor. 15:28). He will absorb us, he will consume us, he will abyss us and will annihilate us totally in himself. We will no longer be 'gods,' but one God."³⁷¹ Similar expressions of deep union are found in *The Divine Life*, sometimes using the traditional image of the log and fire: "Then having entered into God and been penetrated intimately in him, we will be one thing (*une même chose*) with him and consequently like him. The wood is totally like fire when it is penetrated by it; the fire absorbs it in itself, it transforms it, it consumes it, and makes it to be one thing with itself."³⁷²

What will remain in the place where "we" once existed will be God at work in and through the annihilated soul, especially in universal love:

> The soul will love God in the neighbor by way of the principle of God himself, who, by dwelling in it, will make it participate in the love which he brings from himself everywhere he dwells. From there comes the immense and infinite love of the saints towards their neighbor. From there comes their ardor and their immense excess, which comes from God loving himself in everything and bringing it about that souls love themselves also in the other person, but through him and in him.[373]

Jean-Jacques Olier's newly published writings are a major addition to the mystical corpus of seventeenth-century France.

Notes

1. The actual source for the phrase is not known, but most modern scholars accept its authenticity; see Jean Dagens, *Bérulle et les origines de la restauration catholique (1575–1611)* (Bruges: Desclée de Brouwer, 1952), 291.

2. Bremond, *History*, vol. 3, part 1, chap. 1, "Pierre de Bérulle" (1–16), and chap. 2, "The Doctrine of Pierre de Bérulle and the French School" (17–132). Bérulle's theocentrism is discussed on 17–35. Bremond also discusses Bérulle in *Histoire*, 3:105–23 (original ed., vol. 7).

3. Balthasar, *The Glory of the Lord: A Theological Aesthetics*, vol. 5, *The Realm of Metaphysics in the Modern Age*, 119–40; quotation from 120.

4. To be sure, many mystics can be said to express a "theocentric Christocentrism" in one way or another, but the phrase is particularly apt for Bérulle because of the explicit and systematic way he integrates these two essential features of the Trinity and the Incarnate Word. The phrase appears in Pierre de Bérulle, *Oeuvres complètes*, 12 vols. (Paris: Oratoire de France/Éditions du Cerf, 1996), 7:269 n. 1 (see n. 13 below).

5. William M. Thompson, "The Christic Universe of Pierre de Bérulle and the French School," *American Benedictine Review* 29 (1978): 320–47, here 336.

6. On this triad, see Miklos Vetö, "La Christo-logique de Bérulle," in *Pierre de Bérulle: Opuscules de piété* (Grenoble: Jérôme Millon, 1997), 7–136, here 117–23.

7. *Exinanition* is based on Philippians 2:5–7, which invites the reader to follow the model of Jesus Christ, who "emptied himself taking the form of a servant" (*semetipsam exinanivit* [Gr. *ekenōsen*] *formam servi accipiens*).

8. Vincent Carraud, "De l'état de néant à l'état anéanti: Le système du néant de Bérulle," *Cahiers de Philosophie de l'Université de Caen* 43 (2007): 211–47; quotation from 245. Bérulle fits within a broad tradition of *néantiste* mysticism. For an introduction, see Alain Gouhier, "Néant," DS 11:64–80, which treats Bérulle on 73–75.

9. Bremond, *History*, 3:107–19; quotation from 108. See also the brief treatment in Cognet, *La spiritualité moderne*, 351–52.

10. See especially Erik Varden, *Redeeming Freedom: The Principle of Servitude in Bérulle*, Studia Anselmiana 152 (Rome: Pontificio Ateneo S. Anselmo, 2011).

11. *Grandeurs* II.iv (*Oeuvres complètes*, 7:123–24; see n. 13 below). I use the translation of Lowell M. Glendon in William M. Thompson, ed., *Bérulle and the French School: Selected Writings*, Classics of Western Spirituality (New York: Paulist Press, 1989), 126.

12. Varden, *Redeeming Freedom*, 209: "The *Élévation*, part meditation, part petition, part spontaneous adoration, stands for the irruption of poetry into theology. It is of its nature an expression of the inexpressible."

13. Pierre de Bérulle, *Oeuvres complètes*, *Oeuvres complètes*, under the general editorship of Michel Dupuy, 12 vols. (Paris: Oratoire de Jésus/Éditions du Cerf, 1995–2005). The volumes are (1) *Collationes* (French translation); (2) *Collationes* (Latin original); (3) *Oeuvres de piété (1–165)*; (4) *Oeuvres de piété (166–385)*; (5) *Notes et entretiens, ordonnances des visites canoniques*; (6) *Court traités*; (7) *Discours de l'état et des grandeurs de Jésus*, vol. 1, *12 Discours* (cited as *Grandeurs*); (8) *Discours de l'état et des grandeurs de Jésus*, vol. 2, *Narré, Vie de Jésus, Élévations*; (9)–(12) *Correspondance*. This edition will be cited as OC with volume and page number. Translations are my own, unless otherwise noted. I will generally not give the French original, unless the vocabulary is important for understanding the point at issue.

14. Besides the volume of Dagens mentioned in n. 1 (which was to have been the first of two), see Auguste Molien, "Bérulle (Cardinal Pierre de)," DS 1:1539–81; Cognet, *La spiritualité moderne*, chap. 9, "Bérulle et sa synthèse spirituelle" (310–59); Paul Cochois, *Bérulle et l'École française* (Bourges: Éditions du Seuil, 1963); and Jean Orcibal, *Le Cardinal de Bérulle: Évolution d'une spiritualité* (Paris: Éditions du Cerf, 1965). There are also a number of books by Michel Dupuy: *Bérulle: Une spiritualité de l'adoration* (Tournai: Desclée, 1964); *Pierre de Bérulle* (Paris: Bloud & Gay, 1964); and *Le Christ de Bérulle* (Paris: Desclée, 2001). Bérulle is also treated in Kołakowski, *Chrétiens sans Église*, 349–435.

15. E.g., Jakob Bachmann, *La notion du temps dans la pensée de Pierre de Bérulle* (Winterthur: P. G. Keller, 1964); Fernando Guillén Preckler, *"État" chez le cardinal de Bérulle: Théologie et spiritualité des "états" bérulliens*, Analecta Gregoriana 197 (Rome: Gregorian University Press, 1974); Anne Ferrari, *Figures de la contemplation: La "rhétorique divine" de Pierre de Bérulle* (Paris: Éditions du Cerf, 1997); and Richard Cadoux, *Bérulle et la question de l'homme: Servitude et liberté* (Paris: Éditions du Cerf, 2005).

16. To the best of my knowledge, the only writings of Bérulle in English are the selections translated by Glendon in Thompson, *Bérulle and the French School*, 107–85. A few of these texts are reprinted in Deville, *French School of Spirituality*, 49–55. Thompson's "Introduction," in *Bérulle and the French School*, 3–106, is the best overview in English of the cardinal and his followers.

17. The best monograph is Varden, *Redeeming Freedom*, cited above. A recent book is Clare McGrath-Merkle, *Bérulle's Spiritual Theology of the Priesthood: A Study in Speculative Mysticism and Applied Metaphysics* (New York: Peter Lang, 2018). English articles will be cited in what follows.

18. A detailed study of Bérulle's rhetoric, arguing for the tight bond between his style and spiritual teaching, is Ferrari, *Figures de la contemplation*.

19. *Grandeurs* obviously calls to mind the Latin *magnalia Dei*, which appears twenty times in the Old Testament Vulgate, but only once in the New Testament (Acts 2:11). The term does not seem to feature in earlier mystical literature but does appear in Teresa of Avila (*Life* 20.9) and is frequent in John of the Cross (*grandeza*); for example, citing only the *Spiritual Canticle*, we find it in 5.1; 7.9; 8.4; 11.10; 13.2; 14/15.2, 3, 27; 24.2, 6; 30.1; 37.8.

20. Dagens studies the major sources of Bérulle and summarizes: "Saint Bonaventure, le capuchin Harphius et le capuchin Canfield sont en effet les grandes sources de la spiritualité bérullien. Mais le source première est saint Augustin, source lui-même de saint Bonaventure" (*Bérulle et les origines*, 45–48). For more on Bérulle as an Augustinian, see Dagens, 36–37, 250, and 267. In the *Grandeurs*, Bérulle sometimes quotes long passages from Augustine; e.g., I.ii; IV.iii; V.iii; and X.iv.

21. Jean Orcibal stressed the influence of Northern mysticism; see his *Le Cardinal de Bérulle*, especially chap. 2. Arguing for a strong influence from the *Evangelical Pearl* is Huijben, "Aux sources de la spiritualité française du XVIIe siècle," *Supplement à La Vie Spirituelle* 26 (1931): [85]-[111], and 27 (1931): [94]-[122].

22. Letter 529 to Père Bertin in Jean Dagens, ed., *Correspondance du Cardinal Pierre de Bèrulle*, 3 vols. (Paris: Desclée de Brouwer; Louvain: Bureux de la Revue, 1939), 3:21.

23. Dagens, *Bérulle et les origines*, book 1, chaps. 3–9 (28–48).

24. See chapter 7 below (414–29).

25. For the *Bref Discours* see the reprint of the 1644 edition found in *Oeuvres complètes de Cardinal de Bérulle: Reproduction de l'Édition Princeps (1644)*, 3 vols. (Montsoult: Maison d'Institution de l'Oratoire, 1960), vol. 2. For an account of the context and content of the work, see Dagens, *Bérulle et les origines*, book 2, chap. 3 (135–49).

26. The "Retreat Notes" were first published by Germain Habert in his *La Vie du Cardinal de Bérulle* (Paris, 1646), and are found in *Oeuvres de piété*, 265 (hereafter OP, in OC 4:238–64). It is possible that Habert edited the original text, but the substance seems authentic.

27. Bérulle's letters sometimes speak about the mystical illuminations (*lumières*) he received, which often gave him confidence in making his decisions (see Varden, *Redeeming Freedom*, 107–9), but he does not refer to these in his other writings.

28. OP 265, Article V (OC 4:245).

29. OP 265, Article XII (OC 4:259–61). Bérulle also speaks of a "suspension of spirit" (*suspender mon esprit*) that lasted three hours.

30. The *Oeuvres de piété* (OP) are available in OC 3–4 in an excellent edition that provides useful information on the occasion, purpose, and date of these pieces, insofar as they can be determined. There is a modern version of some selections from the 1644 edition in Pierre de Bérulle, *Opuscules de piété* (Grenoble: Jérôme Millon, 1997), with a valuable introductory essay by Miklos Vetö on "La Christo-logique de Bérulle" (7–136).

31. See Stéphane-Marie Morgain, *Pierre de Bérulle et les Carmélites de France* (Paris: Éditions du Cerf, 1995).

32. Most of the French accounts of Bérulle go to great lengths to absolve him of blame for the controversies that followed in the story of the French Carmelites.

33. For an account of Bérulle's struggles to found the Oratorians and his plans for the order, see Varden, *Redeeming Freedom*, chap. 5, "Church Reform" (129–59).

34. For an edition, see OC 1 (French translation) and 2 (Latin original).

35. The best English account is Varden, *Redeeming Freedom*, 109–22, whose book is devoted to the theology behind the vows. There is a shorter French survey in Cochois, *Bérulle et l'École française*, 30–41.

36. Théodore Koehler, "Servitude (Saint Esclavage)," DS 14:730–45, who treats Bérulle on 738–41.

37. Bérulle, like most seventeenth-century mystics, was an avid reader of Dionysius. The notion of hierarchy derived from the CH and EH is obvious in his writings (see, e.g., *Grandeurs* XI.xi [OC 7:418]). In *Grandeurs* IV.i he speaks of "the great author, who is called the Areopagite," citing DN 4.15 (OC 7:163). In practice, however, beyond the importance of thinking hierarchically, Bérulle cites a relatively restricted range of texts from the Dionysian corpus, especially the DN (*Grandeurs* III.v uses DN 1.1 and 1.3; *Grandeurs* V.i uses DN 4.3; *Grandeurs* V.ii uses DN 2.7; *Grandeurs* V.iii uses DN 4.3; and *Grandeurs* VI.1 uses DN 2.7). On Bérulle's Dionysianism, see Paul Cochois, "Bérulle et le Pseudo-Denys," *Revue d'histoire des religions* 159 (1961): 173–204; and "Bérulle, hiérarque dionysien," *Revue d'ascétique et de mystique* 37 (1961): 314–53; 38 (1962): 354–75.

38. Varden describes a tripartite model of servitude in Bérulle (*Redeeming Freedom*, 37–44). The first element deals with the origin of servitude in the *néant* of our created nature. The second servitude is that of sin inherited from Adam. The final servitude is that of grace, a servitude that demands our cooperation and recognition of our absolute dependence on God.

39. The translation is from Deville, *French School of Spirituality*, 55–57. Some earlier forms of the vow of servitude may appear in texts in the OP, e.g., 199 (OC 4:77); see also 194 and 195 (OC 4:69–71).

40. According to Varden, "the *Grandeurs de Jésus* is most appropriately read not as a systematic tract, but as an exploratory meditation on the incarnation and as an expression of Bérulle's most intimate aspirations, as a believer called to union with Jesus and as a priest charged to direct the people of God towards the beatific fulfillment of their Christian lives" (*Redeeming Freedom*, 74).

41. On the controversy regarding Bérulle's alleged Monophysitism, see Rémi Lescot, "Introduction historique et théologique," in OC 7:XL–LV.

42. See, e.g., *Grandeurs* II.i (OC 7:95–96), and the discussions in II.ii–iii, V.iii, and VI.iii (OC 7:99–130, 217, 246–47).

43. The *Discours de l'état et des grandeurs de Jésus*, dedicated to Louis XIII, first appeared in February 1623, with six *Discourses*. In the 1625 edition, four more *Discourses* were added, and the posthumous 1644 edition of Bérulle's works split *Discourse* X into three parts, thus making twelve. The titles will give a sense of the whole: (I) The Excellence and Singularity of the Sacred Mystery of the Incarnation; (II) Discourse in the Form of an Elevation on the Mystery of the Incarnation; (III–IV) On the Unity of God in the Mystery; (V–VI) On the Communication of God in the Mystery; (VII–VIII) On the Communication of God in the Mystery; (IX) On Love and the Communication of God in the Mystery; (X) The First Birth of Jesus [from the Father in eternity]; (XI) The Second Birth of Jesus [from Mary in time]; and (XII) The Third Birth of Jesus [from death in the Resurrection]. The *Grandeurs* have been edited by Michel Join-Lambert and Rémi Lescot in OC

7, with an important "Introduction historique et théologique" by Lescot (XIII–LXXI).

44. These developments are most noticeable in the 1623 *Account (Narré)* that Bérulle wrote regarding the controversy. The text is available in OC 8:9–57. On the connection of the vows to baptism, see *Narré* XXIV (OC 8:38–42).

45. See *Narré* XXV–XXVI, XXVIII (OC 8:43–47, 49–50).

46. Varden (*Redeeming Freedom*, 155–59) summarizes four aspects of Bérulle's view of servitude, each present to a greater or lesser degree in the vows themselves: (1) appropriation of origins, that is, recognition of our absolute dependence on God; (2) union with God in adoration; (3) kenotic self-annihilation after the model of Jesus; and (4) submission to divinely instituted authority.

47. The theological nature of Bérulle's involvement in politics has come in for renewed study; see Stéphane-Marie Morgain, *La théologie politique de Pierre de Bérulle (1598–1629)*, Collection "La France au fil des siècles" (Paris: Publisud, 2001), and in English Varden, *Redeeming Freedom*, especially, chap. 6, "Statesmanship" (160–95).

48. The *Mémorial de quelques points servant à la direction des Supérieurs* is found in OC 8:373–406.

49. For an edition, along with the dedicatory letter and an appendix, see OC 8:411–91. Some parts of the Mary Magdalene elevations are translated by Glendon, *Bérulle and the French School*, 172–82.

50. The *Vie de Jésus* was conceived of as the second part of *Discourses on the States and Grandeurs of Jesus* and is edited in OC 8:183–315. A few passages are translated by Glendon in *Bérulle and the French School*, 159–71.

51. These three elevations, probably written in 1625, are "Elevation to Jesus and His Principal States and Mysteries"; "Elevation to the Very Holy Trinity on the Mystery of the Incarnation"; and the "Elevation to the Holy Virgin." They can be found in OC 8:317–48.

52. Thompson puts the relation between the *Grandeurs* and the later works as follows: "While the *Grandeurs* concentrates on man's *universal* participation in Christ, his [Bérulle's] later reflections turn upon the *unique* ways in which this participation is accomplished" ("Christic Universe of Pierre de Bérulle," 340).

53. Molien, "Bérulle," DS 1:1579.

54. On the role of devotion in Bérulle's thought, see Edward Howells, "From Late Medieval to Early Modern: Assessing the Mystical Theology of Pierre de Bérulle," in *Mysticism in the French Tradition: Eruptions from France*, ed. Louise Nelstrop and Bradley B. Onishi, Contemporary Theological Explorations in Christian Mysticism (Burlington, VT: Ashgate, 2015), 169–83.

55. Cochois, *Bérulle et l'École française*, 44 (my trans.).

56. A note to the reader. In this chapter I have generally refrained from trying to judge Bérulle's theological views, although they certainly invite critical reflection. My purpose is primarily to present a clear exposition of what he argues.

57. On the "science of the saints," see Dagens, *Bérulle et les origines*, book 4, chap. 1 (249–69). Similarly, both Bremond and Balthasar spoke of "The Metaphysics of the Saints."

58. On Bérulle's knowledge of both philosophy and Christian classics, see Dagens, *Bérulle et les origines*, book 1, chaps. 2–3 (16–37).

59. Dagens, *Bérulle et les origines*, book 1, chap. 5, "Le Renaissance et l'Ésprit Chrétien" (49–68).

60. Bremond, *History*, 3:20.

61. *Grandeurs* II.i (OC 7:84–85; trans. Glendon, 116–17). Bérulle often compares Jesus with the Sun; see, e.g., *Grandeurs* II, introduction (7:82–83); VIII, introduction (7:289–97); and IX.11 (7:357); as well as *Vie de Jésus* II, XVIII, XXVI, XXVIII (OC 8:218–19, 263, 287, 299); *Discours de la Visitation* (OC 8:351, 355); and *Élévations sur Sainte Madeleine* XIII (OC 8:470).

62. For another treatment of the science of the saints, see *Mémorial* XI–XIII (OC 8:382–86).

63. *Élévations sur Sainte Madeleine* IX, X, XV (OC 8:456, 460, 462, 473–74).

64. See the discussion and texts in Dagens, *Bérulle et les origines*, 252–57.

65. *Collatio Juillet 1614* (OC 2:228).

66. *Collatio Ottobre 1614* (OC 2:245).

67. *Grandeurs* IX.i (OC 8:346–47; trans. Glendon, 148–49 adapted). On the superiority of love over knowledge in Bérulle, see Varden, *Redeeming Freedom*, 48–49.

68. OP 12 (OC 3:57): "Le théologie mystique tend à nous tirer, à nous unir, à nous abîmer en Dieu.... Son unité nous reçoit et nous unit en lui. Et sa plenitude nous perd, nous anéantit et nous abîme dans l'océan immense de ses perfections, comme nous voyons que la mer perd et abîme une gotte d'eau." Another text, OP 246 (OC 4:190) says there is no distinction between mystical theology and practical theology. OP 273, originally in Latin (OC 4:279 and 579), says that the way to God is a "kind of theology, but mystical," because the theology taught there has "a different end and a different spirit" from school theology. On these texts, see Dagens, *Bérulle et les origines*, 370–71.

69. As noted by Carraud, "De l'état de néant à l'état anéanti," 221–23.

70. E.g., *Vie de Jésus* XVII (OC 8:258).

71. On the development of seventeenth-century philosophical views of God, see Jean-Luc Marion, "The Idea of God," in *The Cambridge History of Seventeenth-Century Philosophy*, ed. Daniel Garber and Michael Ayers (Cambridge: Cambridge University Press, 1998), 1:265–304, who notes how mystics like Canfield, Francis de Sales, and Bérulle challenge the philosophical trend toward divine univocity with their insistence on God's transcendence and infinity (270–73). On God as infinite in Bérulle, see, e.g., *Grandeurs* VI.vi and VII.ii (OC 7:238 and 257), among many texts.

72. *Vie*, Préambule (OC 8:201–2). For another text on God as both transcendent and immanent, see *Grandeurs* VI.vi (OC 7:233–37).

73. For a clear expression of Trinitarian theocentrism, see *Grandeurs* II.i (OC 7:86–90).

74. According to Etienne Gilson, *Grandeurs* III–IV constitute the most impressive early modern treatment of God's unity; see Gilson, *La liberté chez Descartes et la théologie* (Paris: F. Alcan, 1913), 170. Texts on the divine unity as the source of the "orders of unity," an important theme in Bérulle, are found, for example, in OP 26 (OC 3:90–91), and *Grandeurs* I.iii, and III.v (OC 7:77–80, 154–60).

75. On God as *Être supreme*, see, e.g., OP 167.10–12 (OC 4:7–8).

76. E.g., OP 8, 12, 20, 25, 38, 126, 127, 190, 192 (OC 3:45–47, 57–59, 77–79, 89–90, 128–29, 344–45, 346–48; 4:59–62, 64–66).

77. The distinction is found in a number of texts; see, e.g., *Grandeurs* IV.iii (OC 7:190-94).

78. *Grandeurs* VI.i (OC 7:225-26; trans., Glendon, 138). He goes on to note the importance of all triads: "Cette trinité de mystères . . . est un nombre sacrè, qui, en la économie de notre foi, rend un honneur et un homage supreme à la Trinité des personnes divines que ses mystères regardent et honorent d'une façon singulière."

79. *Grandeurs* VII.i (OC 7:260).

80. For some other texts on exemplarism in the *Grandeurs*, see XI.i, XII.ii, and iii (OC 7:408-9, 417, 423); see Julian-Eymard d'Angers, "L'exemplarisme bérullien," *Revue des sciences religieuses* 31 (1957): 122-32.

81. See Varden, *Redeeming Freedom*, 60-69.

82. *Grandeurs* III.iv-v (OC 7:152-62). See Cognet, *La spiritualité moderne*, 331-32.

83. *Grandeurs* XI.ii (OC 7:435-36).

84. *Grandeurs* VI.i (OC 7:228). Although it was unusual to speak of the Son as a "Father," Bérulle often uses this expression to indicate Christ's headship in creation on the basis of Isaiah 9:5: "Et vocabitur nomen eius Admirabilis consiliarius, Deus fortis, *Pater futuri saeculi*, Princeps pacis."

85. *Grandeurs* VI.i (OC 7:229; trans. Glendon, 139).

86. *Grandeurs* VII.i (OC 7:257, 260).

87. *Grandeurs* VI.i (OC 7:229): ". . . dès ce bas monde, nous sommes unis, par certain degrees et echelons, substantiellement avec Dieu."

88. *Grandeurs* VI.i (OC 7:230).

89. Vetö, "La Christo-logique de Bérulle," 132-36.

90. *Grandeurs* V.iii (OC 7:203). See Vetö, "La Christo-logique de Bérulle," 129-30.

91. *Grandeurs* IV.iii (OC 7:194-95). The image of the intelligible sphere, originally found in the *Liber XXIV Philosophorum*, is also used in *Grandeurs* VI.i and VII.i (7:235, 257).

92. *Grandeurs* VI.i (OC 7:227). The *diété fontale* reference to Dionysius is in DN 2.7, which reads in Eriugena's version: "Iterum quia quidem est fontalis deitas Pater, Filius autem et Spiritus Dei germinati, et veluti flores et superessentiali lumina" (PL 122:1123C). Bérulle also refers to DN 2.7 in *Grandeurs* V.i and V.ii (OC 7:201, 208-9).

93. *Grandeurs* X.i (OC 7:375-77).

94. *Grandeurs* V.i (OC 7:204).

95. OP 32 (OC 3:111): "Or cette ineffable production de Dieu produisant son Verbe dedans soi-même est la première de toutes les productions divines soit en son essence soit hors de son essence et est aussi le principe et le modèle de toutes."

96. Edward Howells, "Relationality and Difference in the Mysticism of Pierre de Bérulle," *Harvard Theological Review* 102 (2009): 225-43 (quotation from 241, but see the whole discussion on 240-42); also Preckler, *"État" chez le cardinal Bérulle*, 63.

97. A summary text on the Trinity is his *Élévation à la très Sainte Trinité sur le mystère de l'Incarnation* (OC 8:327-36).

98. See, e.g., *Grandeurs* X.iv (OC 7:396-97).

99. *Grandeurs* IV.i (OC 7:163). The reference to Dionysius is to DN 4.15.

100. *Grandeurs* IV.i (OC 7:165–68), using the translation of Glendon, *Bérulle and the French School*, 131–34. Glendon does not translate the moving Elevation to the Holy Spirit found at the end of the passage (7:169).

101. On relation in Bérulle, see Cochois, *Bérulle et l'École français*, 70–72; Vetö, "La Christo-logique de Bérulle," 85–92; and Howells, "Relationality and Difference."

102. *Grandeurs* X.iii (OC 7:384–85).

103. Howells, "Relationality and Difference," 226–27.

104. OP 192 (OC 4:66). There are many similar texts; e.g., OP 248.1 and 249 (OC 4:193–94, 198–99); and *Grandeurs* V.iii (OC 7:215).

105. *Grandeurs* VI.ii (OC 7:238–39).

106. E.g., *Grandeurs* II.i (OC 7:94). Vetö gives a good account of the difference between the created and the graced relationalities ("La Cristo-logique de Bérulle," 86–89, 91), but I think he is misleading in referring to the natural relation as "negative" and the graced relation as "positive." Both are positive, but in different ways.

107. *Grandeurs* V.iii (OC 7:215). On the perfect and absolute relation, see Howells, "Relationality and Difference," 229–30, and 233.

108. See R. Bellemare, *La sens de la creature dans le doctrine de Bérulle* (Ottowa: Desclée de Brouwer, 1959).

109. *Vie de Jésus*, Préambule (OC 8:201–15). The account of creation and fall is in Preamble 6–12 (8:203–6).

110. OP 11 (OC 3:52–53). In line with earlier tradition, Bérulle used *subsistence* and *personne* interchangeably. See OP 208 (OC 4:94): "Selon l'ordre substantiel de la créature, la première chose, c'est la subsistence ou personne à laquelle l'être et la nature appartiennent."

111. OP 53 (OC 3:175).

112. OP 214 (OC 4:116). For other texts on *creatio continua*, see OP 166 and 175.7 (OC 4:3 and 25).

113. *Grandeurs* II.i (OC 7:92–94). This passage is translated by Glendon, *Bérulle and the French School*, 118–20.

114. *Grandeurs* XI.ii (OC 7:423).

115. *Grandeurs* XI.ii (OC 7:424). The notion of humanity as the microcosm appears a number of other times in the *Grandeurs*; e.g., I.iii (7:77), and VIII.iv (7:329).

116. OP 168 (OC 4:10).

117. OP 176 (OC 4:30). Bérulle refers to Genesis 1:26–27 in a number of other places; e.g., *Grandeurs* IV.iii (OC 7:186); VI.i (7:228); and XI.ii (7:425).

118. On this point, see Philip McCosker, "The Christology of Pierre de Bérulle," *Downside Review* 124 (2006): 111–34, especially 123–25.

119. *Bref discours de l'abnegation interieure* III (ed., 656).

120. E.g., *Vie de Jésus* XV (OC 8:252).

121. *Élévation à la très Sainte Trinité* 16 (OC 8:333–34).

122. Molien, "Bérulle," DS 1:1553–57.

123. OP 15 (OC 3:64–65). The critical edition references Athanasius, *Adversus Arianos* 2.45, as one of the patristic texts Bérulle may have had in mind. On the importance of the distinction of substance and economy, see Cochois, *Bérulle et l'École française*, 83–105; and Dagens, *Bérulle et les origines*, 291. The substance

and economy distinction is found also in OP 17 and 18. In OP 19, Bérulle distinguishes the substance, manner, and goal of the Incarnation.

124. On the debates over some of Bérulle's formulations, see Varden, *Redeeming Freedom*, 56-60.

125. The expression is frequent in Bérulle; e.g., *Grandeurs* VI.iii and XI.iii (OC 7:245-46 and 425). This language was found in the Vow of Servitude and was attacked by some.

126. *Grandeurs* XI.iii (OC 7:427-28).

127. *Grandeurs* V.iii (OC 7:219); see also XI.i and XI.iii (OC 7:413, 423-24).

128. See, for example, the way in which Bérulle addresses the humanity of Christ as an object in *Grandeurs* II.i (OC 7:89-90, 94-96).

129. *Grandeurs* III.v (OC 7:154-56).

130. This is laid out in Preckler, *"État" chez le Cardinal de Bérulle*, chap. 4, "L'État de l'Incarnation" (65-99), who summarizes: "La subsistence ontologique de l'humanité du Christ dans le Verbe est rapprochée de la subsistence mystique du chrétien dans le Christ, et toujours à l'aide de ce terme favori" (94).

131. OP 122 (OC 3:324-36). See also OP 204, 279 (OC 4:83-85, 296-98).

132. OP 99 (OC 3:282-83): "Bien plus, meme l'Incarnation suppose le péché et cet anéantissement supreme du Verbe divin dans l'Incarnation suppose Dieu le Père anéanti par le pécheur et dans le pécher par le péché."

133. In his early *Scriptum super Sententias*, Thomas had held either view as legitimate, though by the time of the STh IIIa, q. 1, a. 3 he supported only the motive of remedy for sin. On Bérulle's wavering views, see Cognet, *La spiritualité moderne*, 343-44. Dagens argues that Bérulle's view of the motif of the Incarnation is close to that of Bonaventure as mediated through Harphius (*Bérulle et les origines*, 292-94).

134. Much has been written on Bérulle's teaching on annihilation. See Cognet, *La spiritualité moderne*, 347-59; Dupuy, *Bérulle: Une spiritualité de l'adoration*, chap. 4, "L'Adoration par Anéantissement" (71-96); David Thayer, *"Néants capable de Dieu: Anéantissement*, Freedom and Individuation in the Anthropology of the French School," *Bulletin de Saint-Sulpice*. L'École Française Aujourd'hui. *The French School Today* 22 (1996): 94-107, and "*Kenosis* and *Anéantissement*: The Abnegations of Christ as the Key to Christian Identity—Some Lessons from the French School," *Bulletin de Saint-Sulpice*. Christology. Actualité—Enseignment. *Teaching Christology* 27 (2001): 192-207; and especially Carraud, "De l'état de néant à l'état anéanti" (see n. 8).

135. Dupuy counsels against too strong an ontological reading of *anéantissement* in No. 5 of the "Notes Complémentaires" in OC 3:441.

136. *Grandeurs* IX.iii (OC 7:360).

137. Dagens, *Bérulle et les origines*, 185-87.

138. Howells, "Relationality and Difference," 233-34, 238, 242. See also Bellemare, *Le sens de la creature*, 61-63; and Vetö, "La Christo-logique de Bérulle," 109-10.

139. OP 227 (OC 4:141-42). Vetö notes that there is full annihilation of subsistence in Christ, because there is no human person, but only a participatory annihilation of subsistence in us, in that our human person is not lost, but gives up its own exercise to Christ ("La Christo-logique de Bérulle," 38).

140. Thayer distinguishes three modes of annihilation in the French School:

the *anéantissement* of creation; the *anéantissement* by which Christ frees us from sin; and the *anéantissement* of salvation that forms the crown and completion of the first two ("*Néants capables de Dieu*," 103, 106). Concerning this last he says, "This nothingness before and in divine grace overcomes the incapacitating nothingness of sin and perfects the nothingness of creation by recreating it in plenitude." Useful as these distinctions are, Thayer does not sufficiently highlight how redemptive annihilation is a sharing in the Word's own self-annihilation.

141. For example, while *abnégation* is used exclusively in OP 225 (OC 4:134–37), OP 226 (OC 4:138–39) employs *abaisser* and *anéantir* along with *abnégation*. OP 227 (OC 4:140–42) is entitled "De l'abnégation," but actually uses *anéantissement* throughout. OP 231 (OC 4:148–49), once again titled "De l'abnégation," uses *abaissement, anéantissement, abnégation, exinanition*.

142. Bérulle even employs the term *nudité* synonymously; see OP 185, "De la nudité interieur" (OC 4:48–49). To get some sense of the prevalence of *anéantissement* and related language in Bérulle, I calculate that at least sixty-two of the 373 texts of the OP have important teaching on *anéantissement*.

143. In the *Collatio Juillet 1614* (OC 2:212) Bérulle even speaks of a mysterious annihilation that will take place in heaven, about which we can say nothing now.

144. See Carraud, "De l'état de néant à l'état anéanti," 242–45, dealing with OP 234 (OC 4:155–56).

145. OP 209 (OC 4:98). The text was first written as a letter to the Oratorians, but its form in the OP seems to give it a universal application. For other texts on the nothingness of creatures, see, e.g., OP 166 and 168 (OC 4:3 and 10), as well as *Collationes* (OC 2:192, 248–49, 277).

146. OP 192 (OC 4:68).

147. On the importance of the law of opposites (annihilation/exaltation; weak/strong; etc.) in Bérulle, see Vetö, "La Christo-logique de Bérulle," 40–42.

148. OP 235 (OC 4:157–60).

149. *Vie de Jésus*, Préambule (OC 8:205).

150. *Grandeurs* II.i (OC 7:87–88). For other appearances, see IV.iii (7:188); VII.ii and concl. (7:265, 286); IX.iii (7:355, 360); XI.ii (7:434); and XII.ii (7:469).

151. OP 265, Article V (OC 4:245).

152. On the abasement of Word in the Nativity, see, e.g., OP 41 (OC 3:134–35), while the abasement/annihilation of the Passion is discussed in many texts, e.g., OP 7, 84, 90, 122 (OC 3:43, 253–56, 267–68, 336). There is a series of texts on aspects of the Passion in OP 74–96 (OC 4:235–76).

153. *Collatio Juillet 1614* (OC 2:211). For more on the double *abaissement/anéantissement* of the Word, see, e.g., *Grandeurs* II.iii (OC 7:120–24).

154. *Grandeurs* XI.1 (OC 7:401); see also XII.iii (OC 7:475).

155. *Grandeurs* IX.ii (OC 7:352). For more on the Word abasing himself in sinful flesh, see OP 114, "On Abnegation" (OC 3:316–17).

156. OP 188 (OC 4:53–54). The distinction between two kinds of annihilation—what we can do and what God does—appears as early as the *Bref discours*; see Cognet, *La spiritualité moderne*, 355.

157. OP 249 (OC 4:198). Galatians 2:20 is cited six times in the OP, as well as in *Collationes Décembre 1612* (OC 2:84), *Grandeurs* II.iii (OC 7:119), and *Élévation sur Sainte Madeleine* X (OP 8:459).

158. OP 232 (OC 4:151; my italics). On this distinction, see Carraud, "De l'état de néant à l'état anéanti," 243.
159. *Collatio Juillet 1614* (OC 2:212-13).
160. OP 83 (OC 3:253). For similar prayers for annihilating elevation, see OP 197 (OC 4:73-75); *Élévation à Jésus-Christ* 15 (OC 8:323-24), and *Élévation à la Très Sainte Trinité* 3 (OC 8:328-29).
161. OP 240 (OC 4:171). On the superiority of the "annihilation in God" to the simple annihilation of human existence, see also OP 237 (OC 4:164).
162. *Grandeurs* IV.iii (OC 7:182 ff.).
163. *Grandeurs* IV.iii (OC 7:183). On Jesus as the principle of the new creation, see also OP 211 (OC 4:108-10).
164. Another way of expressing the cosmic role of Christ is found in *Grandeurs* XI.ii (OC 7:361-64), where Bérulle speaks of Christ as the "new world" that unites the visible, intelligible, and archetypal worlds.
165. On Jesus as the New Ark of the Covenant, see, e.g., *Grandeurs* II.iii, VII.iii, XII.i (OC 7:115, 280-81, 461-62).
166. E.g., OP 74, 85 (OC 3:238, 258); *Grandeurs* XII.i (OC 7:462-63).
167. *Grandeurs* II.iii (OC 7:123). See also *Grandeurs* I.i, III.iv, XI.ii (OC 7:68, 152-53, 415-22).
168. The historical dimension of Bérulle's thought is treated by Dagens, *Bérulle et les origines*, book 4, chap. 5 (322-34).
169. *Vie de Jésus*, Préambule (OC 8:208).
170. *Vie de Jésus*, Préambule (OC 8:212-15).
171. On Bérulle and the liturgy, see Cochois, *Bérulle et l'École française*, 167.
172. *Grandeurs* X.iv (OC 7:396).
173. On the newness of the *état de union hypostatique*, see, e.g., *Grandeurs* II.i, II.ii, V.iii (OC 7:88, 102, 217). For a summary, see Preckler, *"État" chez le Cardinal de Bérulle*, 254-58.
174. In discussing the *mysteria vitae Christi* (*mysteria = status*), Bérulle says, ". . . quod maxime fiet si non tam exteriores eius actiones quam interiores in illis patrandis recenseamus" (*Collationes Janvier 1612* in OC 2:14).
175. *Grandeurs* VIII.iii (OP 7:321).
176. Bremond, *History*, 3:54-62 and 124-32 (quotation from 125). On the relation of states and servitude, see also Varden, *Redeeming Freedom*, 69-73.
177. Preckler, *"État" chez le Cardinal de Bérulle*, 252-53.
178. *Grandeurs* V.iii (OC 7:216-17).
179. *Grandeurs* VIII.iv (OC 7:329).
180. *Grandeurs* XI.vi (OC 7:420).
181. For a summary of these states and notes to the many texts where they are treated, see Preckler, *"État" chez le Cardinal Bérulle*, chap. 7, "La diversité des états" (179-212). Preckler also considers the states of Mary Magdalene (213-20), and includes a chap. 8, "Les 'états' de Marie" (221-49).
182. Bérulle devotes fourteen of the OP to the birth of Jesus (OP 39-52 in OC 3:130-72).
183. See the "Introduction aux trois derniers discours" (OC 7:371-73).
184. *Grandeurs* XI.i (OC 7:421).
185. E.g., *Collationes Décembre 1611* (OC 2:11) and *Collationes Décembre 1613* (OC 2:157).

186. *Collationes 1615* (OC 2:288–91).
187. See, e.g., OP 51, "Discours de l'abaissement du Fils de Dieu non seulement à notre nature humaine, mais aussi à l'humble état de l'enfance" (OC 3:160–66).
188. OP 66 (OC 3:221–23).
189. OP 74 (OC 3:237).
190. OP 75 (OC 3:240). At the end of the *Élévations sur Sainte Madeleine* there are reflections on the paradox of *mort vivante et vie mourante* of the God-man (OC 8:458–64).
191. OP 84 (OC 3:256). See also OP 87 (OC 3:260–62) on Jesus's life as a "perpetual sacrifice."
192. OP 90 (OC 3:268). See also OP 91.
193. OP 97–103 (OC 3:278–99). See the treatment in Preckler, *"État" chez le Cardinal de Bérulle*, 197–206.
194. OP 99 (OC 3:283).
195. *Grandeurs* VIII.ii (OP 7:309–19). See also VIII.iv (OC 7:329–34).
196. OP 103 (OC 3:294–96). See also *Grandeurs* XII.i (OC 7:464–67).
197. OP 101 (OC 3:287–89).
198. OP 103 (OC 3:292).
199. OP 103 (OC 3:292–93). For more on the effect the Resurrection ought to have on us, see OP 100 and 101 (OC 3:286, 288).
200. *Grandeurs* V.iii (OC 7:217).
201. To give just two examples, see *Grandeurs* VIII.iii (OC 7:323–24), and OP 115 (OC 3:317–19).
202. Helpful here is the summary on the states in Howells, "Relationality and Difference," 238–42.
203. Preckler, *"État" chez le Cardinal de Bérulle*, 248. See the whole of chap. 8, "Les 'États' de Marie" (221–49).
204. *Vie de Jésus* VI, XV (8:224, 253). See also OP 140 (OC 3:384): ". . . parlant de vos [Mary's] grandeurs, nous parlons des grandeurs de Jésus."
205. OP 1 (OC 3:13–15).
206. Bérulle considers Mary's *ecce ancilla Domini* and *fiat* in several places; e.g., *Grandeurs* XI.ii (OC 7:439–42); and *Vie de Jésus* XV (OC 8:250–56).
207. OP 137 (OC 3:369). An interesting theme that cannot be pursued here is Bérulle's treatment of the "combat" of virginity and maternity in Mary; see OP 149 (OC 3:403–4), and *Vie de Jésus* XII (OC 8:243).
208. *Vie de Jésus* XVII (OC 8:259).
209. *Grandeurs* XI.i (OC 7:441–42). On the new order constituted by Mary, see especially *Élévation à très Sainte Vierge* 6 (OC 8:339–40).
210. OP 135 (OC 3:365).
211. OP 139 (OC 3:382). See also *Grandeurs* XI.iii (OC 7:457–78).
212. *Vie de Jésus* XX (OC 8:269–71).
213. OP 140 (OC 3:384).
214. *Vie de Jésus* XXVIII–XXIX (OC 8:297–309). See also *Collationes April 1615* (OC 2:282).
215. *Vie de Jésus* XXVIII (OC 8:303).
216. OP 139 (OC 3:377–82). In OP 148 (OC 3:401) the heart of Mary is described as Christ's throne.

217. *Collationes Septembre 1615* (OC 2:286-87). For more on Mary's compassion, see OP 142, and especially 143 (OC 3:387-88, 389-93).
218. *Vie de Jésus* XII.16 (OC 8:241); see also XV.19 (8:255).
219. OP 143 (OC 3:303).
220. OP 138 (OC 3:371-72); see also OP 143 (3:389-92).
221. OP 27 (OC 3:91-92), and OP 39 (3:130-31).
222. OP 143 (OC 3:392).
223. On Mary's Queenship, see, e.g., *Collationes Décembre 1613* (OC 2:158-59).
224. On the relation of the two vows, see *Collationes Septembre 1614* (OC 2:234-38).
225. *Collationes Décembre 1613* (OC 2:159). For more on the *comitatus Mariae*, see *Collationes Septembre 1613* (OC 2:132-33), and OP 147 (OC 3:399).
226. OP 218 (OC 4:121-22).
227. OP 247 (OC 4:191-92). For more on the kinds of grace, see OP 301 (4:360-61).
228. The substantial grace that is the essence of the Incarnation is an important theme in the *Grandeurs*.
229. OP 187 (OC 4:51-52). See also OP 163 (OC 3:432-35), and *Collationes Juin 1612* (OC 2:41).
230. E.g., *Collationes Novembre et Décembre 1612* (OC 2:80-85), and *Collationes Mai 1614* (2:194-95).
231. See, e.g., Bremond, *History*, 3:107-19; and Cognet, *La spiritualité moderne*, 351-54.
232. OP 35 (OC 3:119).
233. OP 4 (OC 3:27).
234. *Collationes Décembre 1613* (OC 2:158).
235. OP 244 (OC 4:181-82). See also OP 91 (OC 3:268) on the exchange between Christ and ourselves.
236. *Grandeurs* VIII.iii (OC 7:326-27).
237. *Grandeurs* IX.i (OC 7:349).
238. *Grandeurs* XII.i (OC 7:466-67).
239. For a summary of the three, see Cochois, *Bérulle et l'École française*, 120-23.
240. *Collationes Mai 1612* (OC 2:40).
241. OP 81 (OC 3:249).
242. *Grandeurs* VIII.iii (OC 7:325-26).
243. On *amour ravissement*, see especially *Vie de Jésus* XXVII-XXIX (OC 8:299-303, 307-8).
244. OP 122 (OC 3:335).
245. These elevations are too long to be excerpted here. Some typical examples are *Grandeurs* VIII.iii (OC 7:324-28); IX.i (7:351-52), and XII.i (7:466-67).
246. The *Élévation sur Sainte Madeleine* is found in OC 8:41-83. See especially the *Élévation à sainte Madeleine sur l'excès de son amour divin vers Jésus* (8:473-75), available in English in *Bérulle and the French School*, 180-82.
247. Dupuy, *Bérulle: Une spiritualité de l'adoration*.
248. See the entry "Adoration (adorateur parfait)" in the "Index Thématique" in OC 7:495.
249. OP 22 (OC 3:82-83).

250. *Grandeurs* II, Introduction (OC 7:82), with the accompanying n. 3 of Dupuy.
251. *Grandeurs* V.iii (OC 7:217).
252. *Collationes Janvier 1613* (OC 2:88-89).
253. *Collationes Juillet 1613* (OC 2:115-16).
254. OP 38 (OC 3:128-29). For some other texts about God's self-contemplation, see, e.g., OP 118, 172, and 346.
255. *Collationes Janvier 1612* (OC 2:13). Compare with *Collationes Septembre 1612*, which speak of a *simplex intuitus infinitae bonitatis et praesentiae DEI* (OC 2:64-65), and the discussion of the *simplex consideratio* in *Collationes Janvier 1615* (OC 2:271-72).
256. For some texts on the relation of action and contemplation, see *Collatio Mai 1612* (OC 2:31), and OP 301, 329 (OC 4:360, 445).
257. Adoration and contemplation involve a doctrine of prayer, and Bérulle, to be sure, does discuss prayer, both mental and oral, as well as the way to meditate, in a number of places; see, e.g., *Collationes* (OC 2:93-94, 127-30, 199-201). Bérulle's teaching on prayer deserves a more detailed treatment than can be given here.
258. Howells, "Relationality and Difference," 243. The four points Howells makes on 242-43 summarize the argument of this important article.
259. *Grandeurs* VII.i (OC 7:263).
260. Some important texts are found in OC 15, 33, 40, 45, 47, 84, 94, 208-9, and 300.
261. *Collationes Juin 1612* (OC 2:45).
262. *Collationes 1615* (OC 2:300).
263. OP 35 (OC 3:119). It is interesting to see Bérulle using both 1 Cor. 6:17 and John 17:21, key scriptural union texts, together. 1 Corinthians 6:17 also appears in OP 118 (OC 3:327) and 188 (OC 3:453). Along with these three opuscules, see OP 41 (3:134-35), with a rare use of spousal language, as well as OP 244 (4:181-82), and OP 301 (4:360).
264. The five lives are (1) the divine and uncreated life, (2) the incarnate life, (3) the life of the Viator, (4) the suffering and crucified life, and (5) the glorified life. At the end Bérulle adds the eucharistic life.
265. *Grandeurs* II.i (OC 7:98). For a text on union employing 1 Cor. 6:17, see *Grandeurs* VII.ii (7:269-70). According to the "Index Scripturaire" in OC 7:483-92, John 17:18-23 is cited eight times in the *Grandeurs*, while 1 Cor. 6:17 appears only once.
266. *Élévation à la Très Sainte Trinité* 16 (OC 8:333-34).
267. Dagens, *Bérulle et les origines*, 302.
268. *Grandeurs* VI.i (OC 7:229-30). See Howells, "Relationality and Difference," 242.
269. For a sampling, see *Collationes* (OC 2:36, 71, 89, 290); OP 18, 41, 172 (OC 3:72, 134-35; 4:19); *Grandeurs* IX.i and X.iii (OC 7:350, 388); *Élévation à la Très Sainte Trinité* 4 (OC 8:329); and *Vie de Jésus* XXV (OC 8:282-83).
270. OP 163 (OC 3:434). The image of the drop of water in the ocean of liquid goes back to Bernard of Clairvaux, *De diligendo Deo* 10.28 (*Sancti Bernardi Opera* 3:143).
271. Vetö, "La Christo-logique de Bérulle," 133.

272. See the discussion of *mentis excessus* and *consolationes sensibiles* in *Collationes Janvier-Févier 1614* (OC 2:166-67), which is followed by a treatment of diabolical temptations affecting body and soul.
273. *Collationes Décembre 1614* (OC 2:262-63).
274. *Collationes Avril-Mai 1615* (OC 2:107).
275. The whole of the meditation is found in *Collationes Juillet 1614* (OC 2:218-22; quotation from 221).
276. *Collationes 1615* (OC 2:292-99; quotation from 295). See also the briefer treatment of the Octave of Mary Magdalene in OC 2:283.
277. OP 151-53 (OC 3:406-9). Here a longer opuscule (OP 154 [OC 3:410-16]) is devoted to St. Martha and the active life.
278. The *Élévations sur Sainte Madeleine* are in OC 8:411-83. There is a selection of passages translated by Glendon in *Bérulle and the French School*, 172-82.
279. *Élévation* I.1 (OC 8:414; trans. Glendon, 172).
280. *Élévation* I.5 (OC 8:418; trans. Glendon, 175).
281. *Élévation* VII.20 (OC 8:453-54; trans. Glendon, 178-79).
282. *Élévation* XV.29 (OC 8:474; trans. Glendon, 180-81).
283. *Élévation* XX.35 (OC 8:482).
284. OP 279 (OC 4:296).
285. OP 35 (OC 3:122).
286. *Grandeurs* VII.i (OC 7:260).
287. *Grandeurs* VII.i-ii (OC 7:264, 269-70). The Eucharist features in a number of other places in the *Grandeurs*; see, e.g., OC 7:21, 146-48, 173-76, 201, 226, and 359.
288. OP 37 (OC 3:125).
289. OP 37 (3:125-26, 127).
290. OP 117 (OC 3:320-25), and OP 119-21 (3:327-33).
291. A good short treatment of the theology of the priesthood in Bérulle is Cochois, *Bérulle et l'École française*, "Les pretres de Jésus" (124-33). At greater length, see McGrath-Merkle, *Bérulle's Spiritual Theology of the Priesthood*, especially chaps. 11-13 (209-56). OP 279-293 (OC 4:296-327) all deal with the priesthood. See also OP 306, 309, 323, 329, 339, and 356.
292. OP 280 (OC 4:299).
293. OP 282 (OC 4:302); see also *Grandeurs* III.iii (OC 7:144).
294. OP 290 (OC 4:323).
295. On the special dignity of the priesthood, see the lecture notes to a wide range of authorities in OP 287 (OC 4:309-14). Bérulle's view of the priest as the conjoint instrument of the Word made flesh was criticized by Jacques Maritain, who shows how such a theology confuses the function and the state of the priest and involves serious theological problems. Maritain defends Aquinas's view that only Christ's human nature is a conjoint instrument of the Word (IIIa, q. 62, a. 5); see Maritain, "Apropos of the French School," *Revue Thomiste* 71 (1971): 463-79; reprinted in *Untrammeled Approaches* 1 (1991): 424-41, especially 429-30, and 434-36.
296. OP 309bis (OC 4:387-88). In OP 280 (OC 4:300) he says, ". . . nous sommes ses instruments et coadjuteurs, mais nous agissons et parlons en sa personne et comme si c'était lui-même." See also *Grandeurs* VIII.Conc. (OC 7:337-38).

297. See Cochois, "Bérulle et le pseudo-Denys"; and "Bérulle, hiérarque dionysien."
298. *Collatio Juillet 1614* (OC 2:219-20).
299. Cochois, *Bérulle et l'École française*, 130.
300. OP 290 (OC 4:322-23).
301. OP 320 (OC 4:618). On the difference between the forms of religious life in the orders and the higher priestly charism given by the infusion of the Holy Spirit, see OP 284 (OC 4:304-7).
302. OP 309 (OC 4:385).
303. OP 244 (OC 4:181-82).
304. The most detailed treatment is Krumenacker, *L'école française de spiritualité*. Raymond Deville, *French School of Spirituality*, is a useful survey and collection of texts. The best account in English of Bérulle and his followers (Madeleine de St. Joseph, Jean-Jacques Olier, John Eudes, and some notes on Charles de Condren) is Thompson, "Introduction," *Bérulle and the French School*, 3-101.
305. Ryan and Rybolt, eds., *Vincent de Paul and Louise de Marillac*.
306. For short surveys, see Agnes Cunningham, "Women in the French School: Some No Longer Hidden Faces," *L'École française aujourd'hui. The French School Today. Bulletin de Saint-Sulpice* 22 (1996): 119-37; and Mary Christine Morkovsky, "Women and the French School of Spirituality," in *Surrender to Christ for Mission: French Spiritual Traditions*, ed. Philip Sheldrake (Collegeville. MN: Liturgical Press, 2018), 109-26.
307. Cognet, *La spiritualité moderne*, 362-67; quotation from 362. Magdalene is also treated in Bremond, *History*, 2:238-44; Pierre Seroeut, "Madeleine de Saint-Joseph," DS 10:57-60; and Cunningham, "Women in the French School," 124-27. Thompson's *Bérulle and the French School*, 22-26, discusses her contributions and contains a selection from her letters (191-214).
308. Madeleine's letters were edited by Pierre Serouet, Madeleine de Saint-Joseph, *Lettres spirituelles* (Paris: Desclée de Brouwer, 1965). The *Life* was edited by Jean-Baptiste Ériau, *Une mystique du XVII siècle: Soeur Catherine de Jésus* (Paris: Desclée, 1929).
309. Bremond's account of Madeleine's *Life of Sister Catherine* in *History*, 2:244-53, contains important excerpts from the work.
310. Letter 139 is available in Thompson, *Bérulle and the French School*, 197-98.
311. Letter 39 (Thompson, *Bérulle and the French School*, 191-92). For other references to the danger of bypassing Christ, see 197, 210, and 212.
312. Letter 144 can be found in Thompson, *Bérulle and the French School*, 200-203. For a summary, see Thompson, "Introduction," 43.
313. In English there is an old life by A. Woodgate, *Charles de Condren* (London: Browne & Nolan, n.d.); also in English, in Deville, *French School of Spirituality*, 58-75. Along with the long section in Bremond (see below), there are a number of French treatments: Auguste Molien, "Condren (Charles de)," DS 3:1373-88; Cognet, *La spiritualité moderne*, 382-89; Krumenacker, *L'école française de spiritualité*, 263-68; and C. Pouillard, *Le Père de Condren: Le mystique de l'Oratoire* (Paris: FAC, 1994), which I have not seen.
314. Taken from the translation in Bremond, *History*, 3:294-95. Bremond analyzes this vision on 297-300. Despite the importance of this initiating vision, which

summarizes much of Condren's later teaching, the Oratorian was not noted for visions or ecstasies; indeed, he often criticized them (Bremond, *History*, 3:352-53).

315. Condren's 169 letters are in P. Auvray and A. Jouffrey, eds., *Lettres du Père de Condren* (Paris: Éditions du Cerf, 1943). The treatise *L'idée du sacerdoce et du sacrifice de Jésus-Christ* (1677) was put together and doubtless much edited by several hands after his death. There is a translation by A. J. Montieth, *Charles de Condren, The Eternal Sacrifice* (London: Thomas Baker, 1906; Classic Reprint Series, 2017).

316. Bremond's treatment of Condren occupies the first three chapters of part 2 of vol. 3 of the *History* (243-358). Bremond goes so far as to call Condren "the loftiest religious genius of modern times" (308)!

317. Bremond, *History*, 3:298.

318. Cognet, *La spiritualité moderne*, 387.

319. Amelote, *Vie du Père Condren* 1:43, as cited in Deville, *French School of Spirituality*, 70.

320. Cited in Deville, *French School of Spirituality*, 73.

321. Paul Milcent, "Jean Eudes (saint)," DS 8:488-501; Bremond, *History*, 3:497-572; Cognet, *La spiritualité moderne*, 406-10; Deville, *French School of Spirituality*, 105-35; Krumenacker, *L'école française de spiritualité*, 291-301, 454-62; and Thompson, "Introduction," *Bérulle and the French School*, 19-22, and passim.

322. The standard edition is Joseph Dauphin and Charles Lebrun, eds., *Oeuvres complètes du Vénérable Jean Eudes*, 12 vols. (Vannes: P. Lethielleux, 1905-11).

323. *La Vie et Royaume* is found in vol. 1 of the *Oeuvres complètes*. There are several English versions of the *Life and Kingdom of Jesus Christ*, as well as of some of John Eudes's other works; see the list in Thompson, *Bérulle and the French School*, 342-43. There are also excerpts from the work on 293-321 of *Bérulle and the French School*.

324. Bremond, *History*, vol. 3, part 3, chap. 2, "Père Eudes and Marie des Vallées" (497-535). Bremond is critical of Eudes's acceptance of Marie's claim of obedience to a divine voice that told her to abstain from receiving communion for thirty years as a way of showing her utter obedience to God.

325. Milcent, "Jean Eudes (saint)," DS 8:489.

326. *Le Coeur admirable* has twelve books in three volumes and takes up vols. 6-8 of the *Oeuvres complètes*. There are some excerpts in *Bérulle and the French School*, 326-33.

327. Thompson, "Introduction," *Bérulle and the French School*, 35; see also 53-54, 65, and 86.

328. Thompson, *Bérulle and the French School*, 331-32.

329. At the outset of the *Life and Kingdom of Jesus*, Eudes lays out four foundations for Christian life and holiness: faith, hatred of sin, detachment, and prayer. His notion of detachment involves detachment from the world, detachment from oneself, and (shades of Meister Eckhart) even detachment from God (Thompson, *Bérulle and the French School*, 304-12).

330. Olier is treated in all the accounts of the French School already cited. For an overview, see Irénée Noye and Michel Dupuy, "Olier (Jean-Jacques)," DS 11:737-51. The recent historical study of Bernard Pitaud, *Jean-Jacques Olier (1608-1657)* (Brussels: Lessius, 2017) is now the benchmark for all accounts of Olier's life and times, but see also Michel Dupuy, *Se laisser à l'esprit: L'itineraire spirituel de Jean-Jacques Olier* (Paris: Éditions du Cerf, 1982). There is a bibliography in

Thompson, *Bérulle and the French School*, 339–42. Bremond devoted two chapters to Olier (*History*, 3:359–434) but suppressed a third chapter on "Les singularités de M. Olier," which dealt mostly with the relations between Olier and the controversial mystical woman and prophetess Marie Rousseau (ca. 1596–1680). This chapter is now available in the new French edition, *Histoire*, 1:1353–81.

331. Cited in Thompson, "Introduction," *Bérulle and the French School*, 17.

332. The best account of this period in Olier's life is chap. 6, "Le Crise Spirituelle (1639–1641)," in Pitaud, *Jean-Jacques Olier*, 154–74.

333. É. Levesque, ed., *Lettres de M. Olier*, 2 vols. (Paris: J. de Gigord, 1935).

334. These mystical works have recently been edited by Mariel Mazzocco: *L'âme cristal: Des attributes divins en nous* (Paris: Éditions du Seuil, 2008); *De la création du monde à la vie divine* (Paris: Éditions du Seuil, 2009); and *Des anges: Fragrances divins et odeurs suaves* (Paris: Éditions du Seuil, 2011). In addition, Mazzocco has edited Olier's treatise on the difference between demonic and divine possession, *Tentations diaboliques et possession divine* (Paris: Honoré Champion, 2012). This work includes Mazzocco's synthesis of Olier's mysticism, "Les 'petits mots' d'un aventurier mystique" (135–264).

335. François Amiot, ed., *Catéchisme chrétien pour la vie intérieur et journée chrétienne* (Paris: Le Rameau, 1954). There is a translation of the last pages of the *Journée* in Thompson, *Bérulle and the French School*, 277–87. See also Thompson, "Olier's 'La Journée Chrétienne' as a Guide for Today's Theology," *Bulletin de Saint-Sulpice. Jean-Jacques Olier (1608–1657)* 14 (1988): 113–27.

336. The new edition of this work includes a previously unedited part; Mariel Mazzocco, ed., *Introduction à la vie et aux vertus chrétiennes* (Paris: Honoré Champion, 2016). This is one of the few works of Olier available in English, albeit in an abbreviated form and from an earlier edition; see Thompson, *Bérulle and the French School*, 217–76.

337. On the *néantiste* character of Olier's mysticism, see Mazzocco, "Introduction," *Introduction à la vie et aux vertus chrétiennes*, 20–23. Useful for the analysis of the Sulpician's mystical language is Mazzocco's "Vocabulaire mystique de Jean-Jacques Olier" in her edition of *Tentations diaboliques*, 265–80.

338. This text from the *Mémoires* is cited by Mazzocco in the "Introduction," *La création du monde*, 31–32.

339. On Olier's sources, on which more work is needed, see Mariel Mazzocco, "Les sources mystiques de Jean-Jacques Olier," *Bulletin de Saint-Sulpice. Jean-Jacques Olier (1608–2008). Hier et Aujourd'hui* 34 (2008): 103–16.

340. Gilles Chaillot, "Jean-Jacques Olier: Lecture de Denys L'Aréopagite," *Bulletin de Saint-Sulpice. Jean-Jacques Olier (1608–1657)* 14 (1988): 48–88.

341. The chapters are (1) The Religion of Jesus Christ; (2) The First Way to Conform to Jesus; (3) The Second Way to Conform to Jesus; (4) General Practice of the Virtues; (5) Humility; (6) Pride; (7) Penance; (8) Mortification; (9) Patience; (10) Gentleness; (11) Poverty; (12) Chastity; (13) Obedience; (14) Charity towards our Neighbor; and (15) Accomplishing Works in the Principle of the Christian Life.

342. Olier uses the term *mystère* much as Bérulle used *état*. On Olier's Christology, see Noye and Dupuy, "Olier (Jean-Jacques)," DS 11:141–42; and Michel Dupuy, "Intérieur de Jésus," DS 7:1872–77.

343. Cognet, *La spiritualité moderne*, 404.

344. *Introduction à la vie*, chap. I (ed., 29; trans., 218).

345. *Introduction à la vie*, chap. I (ed., 31; trans., 219).

346. *Introduction à la vie*, chap. IV (ed., 41; trans., 228).

347. The strong Augustinian pessimism of Olier is evident in this section. The Pauline opposition of flesh and spirit is a constant theme in the Sulpician.

348. *Introduction à le vie*, chap. V (ed., 62; trans., 242). In the edition, this text comes at the end of the first section of five; the latter four sections of this, the longest chapter in the work (28 pp.), do not appear in the translation in Thompson, *Bérulle and the French School*.

349. *Introduction à la vie*, chap. XI (ed., 139; trans., 249).

350. *Introduction à la vie*, chap. XI (ed., 150; trans., 261).

351. *Introduction à la vie*, chap. XV (ed., 181; trans., 275).

352. *L'âme cristal*, preface, 59. Mazzocco's note calls attention to how close this is to Teresa's view of the soul as a diamond or crystal in chap. 1 of the *Interior Castle*. The soul as a crystal, however, also appears in a number of other mystics, such as Ruusbroec, the *Evangelical Pearl*, and the contemporary Spanish Carmelite Cecilia del Nacimiento. The image of the crystal is used throughout the *L'âme cristal*, though with slightly different nuances (ed., 71, 77, 219, 240, 270, and 278). It also appears in *La vie divine* (ed., 164–65, 213). For a survey of the use of diamonds, crystals, and other gems as mystical symbols, see Mariel Mazzocco, *Le joyau de l'âme: Diamants et autre gemmes mystiques* (Paris: Albin Michel, 2019).

353. Olier even refers to the DN 2 at one place in the text (*L'âme cristal*, ed., Mazzocco,188).

354. The sixteen attributes treated are Existence (chap. I), Unity (chap. II), Truth (chap. III), Perfection (chap. IV), Infinity (chap. V), Simplicity (chap. VI), Sanctity (chap. VII), Grandeur (chap. VIII), Immensity (chap. IX), eternity (chap. X), Knowledge, (chap. XI), Love (chap. XII), Conformity to the Will of God (chap. XIII), Goodness (chap. XIV), Justice (chap. XV), Strength (chap. XVI).

355. The terms *suressential* and *sureminent* became controversial in the sixteenth and seventeenth centuries, although Olier does not hesitate to use them (e.g., ed., 99, 120, 184, 187, 195, 197–99, 206, 295, 316, 321). They also are used in *La vie divine* (ed., 171, 203, 204). On Olier's use, see Mazzocco, "'Suressential': Aux sources de la langage mystique," 624.

356. This is the constant message of the *Crystal Soul*; for some representative passages, see ed., 65–67, 94–98, 119–23, 147–51, 278–79.

357. *L'âme cristal*, preface (ed., 61): "Elle est renouvelée par la presence de Dieu même au baptême, qui, la régénérant de nouveau, la rend participante du même fond divin d'ou elle avait été tirée"; see also 65, 80, 239, 256, etc.

358. *L'âme cristal*, chap. XIII (ed., 247).

359. *L'âme cristal*, chap. IV (ed., 128). For other texts on annihilation, see, e.g., 83–85, 122, 147–48, 150–51, 164, 236, 253, 289, 292–93, etc.

360. For the meaning of these and other terms in Olier's vocabulary, see Mazzocco, "Vocabulaire mystique de Jean-Joseph Olier." On *délaissement*, see *L'âme cristal*, 162, 290, 304, 326, etc.

361. *Mémoires* for August 30, 1646, as cited in Mazzocco, "Perdersi per Ritrovarsi," 85. See Mazzocco's whole discussion of Olier and other mystics on losing the self (i.e., annihilation) on 86–96.

362. Mazzocco applies Simone Weil's term *décréation* to Olier's view in the "Introduction," *Introduction à la vie et aux vertus chrétiennes*, 23.

363. *L'âme cristal*, Méthode (ed., 93). See also 277.

364. *L'âme cristal*, chap. XIV (ed., 269).

365. E.g., *L'âme cristal*, "Méthode" (ed., 79-80)

366. *L'âme cristal*, chap. VII (ed., 182). See the whole section "Moyens pour entrer en cette sainteté" (175-85).

367. Deification language is scattered through *L'âme cristal*, e.g., 131-32, 159, 270, 272.

368. Olier's view of our union with Christ is strongly eucharistic, but that cannot be taken up here. See *L'âme cristal* (ed., 103, 131-32, 200-201, 210-13); and *La vie divine* (ed., 205-8, 212).

369. For *une même chose* expressions, see, e.g., 233, 237, 245, 319, and on 329 in relation to the union of the Word and the Father.

370. *L'âme cristal*, chap. IX (ed., 212-13). See also the text on 69, where the unity of the Trinity is a model for God's unity in us.

371. *L'âme cristal*, preface (ed., 63). For other strong passages, see, e.g., 68-69, 74-77, 99-100, 188, 232-33, 245-46.

372. *La vie divine*, chap. IV (ed., 186). See also 187, 189-90, 194-95, and 210-13. One passage even uses the term *identité*: "Qui demeure en la charité, il est en Dieu et Dieu est en lui, tant le mélange, l'unité et l'identité est grande et parfait" (195).

373. *L'âme cristal*, chap. XII (ed., 230). The whole of this short chapter, "De l'Amour de Dieu" (229-41), is among the most striking in the treatise.

CHAPTER 5

Other French Mystics of Le Grand Siècle

As mentioned in chapter 1, there is an embarrassment of riches in French mysticism of the seventeenth century, what the French like to call *le Grand Siècle*. This is due not only to the turn to mysticism in France after the Wars of Religion but also to the growing number of mystical texts printed. Even Henri Bremond's eleven-volume *Histoire* did not exhaust this mass of material, although the work stands as a monument that will probably never be equaled. More modestly, the account given here has highlighted the two figures I judge to be the most significant of the era (Francis de Sales and Pierre de Bérulle), as well as some of their followers. Along with a look at some of the mystics who initiated the great era of French mysticism (chapter 2), this final chapter on French mysticism will concentrate on rounding out a partial picture by investigating six mystics who contributed much to the revival of mysticism in the seventeenth century. Most of these, not surprisingly, belong to religious orders: Louis Lallemant and Jean-Joseph Surin were Jesuits; Jean de Saint-Samson and Lawrence of the Resurrection were Carmelites; and Marie de l'Incarnation (Marie Guyart) was an Ursuline. In addition, I append a brief treatment of the mysticism of Jansenist Blaise Pascal, perhaps the most important lay mystic of the time.

Jesuit Mystics

In one sense, the Jesuit Order started in France, because it was while he was a student at Paris from 1527 to 1535 that Ignatius of Loyola gathered his first six disciples, who vowed to go to Jerusalem and work for the "good of souls." After the papal approval of the "Company of Jesus" in 1540, Ignatius's followers soon spread to France and took up their apostolic work and educational ministries. In France, as in other places, the Jesuits also played important political roles as preachers, advisers, and confessors to kings and nobility. The Jesuits were natural allies of the intransigent Catholics of the Holy League during the Wars of Religion. In 1594, an attempt made on the life of Henry IV by a former student of the Jesuits, Jean Châtel, led Henry to exile the order from the kingdom from 1595 to 1603. The Jesuits remained suspect to many, although this did not prevent some of them, such as Henry's confessor, Pierre Coton (1564–1626), from exercising positions of power. Coton, a noted spiritual author and friend of Barbe Acarie, Francis de Sales, and Bérulle, was also one of the voices calling out for a renewed commitment to prayer and interior spirituality in the Jesuit Order.[1]

Joseph de Guibert, the historian of Jesuit spirituality, has justly spoken of "the enormous mass of spiritual writings of the French Jesuits of the seventeenth century."[2] Not all of these writers were mystics. The mystical element was controversial among the seventeenth-century Jesuits, as it had been among the sixteenth-century Spanish followers of Ignatius.[3] Some Jesuit authorities expressed coolness, even hostility, to an emphasis on mystical prayer that they thought might detract from the Jesuit charism of commitment to apostolic action. A good expression of this suspicion is found in the popular handbook written by Alonso Rodriguez (1538–1610), *The Practice of Perfection and the Christian Virtues*, published in Spanish in 1609 and soon translated into many languages. Rodriguez treats meditation in detail but discourages his readers from all kinds of infused contemplation. Around 1576, Balthasar Alvarez (1533–1588), the Jesuit confessor and friend of Teresa of Avila, got in trouble with the Jesuit authorities in the province of Castile for his teaching on the "prayer of silence" and was deleted to the Jesuit General Everard Mercurian (General 1573–81), who in 1575 had already banned the Jesuits from reading a number of mystical authors. The outcome of the Alvarez affair remains murky, but it expresses the antimystical side of Jesuit spirituality. Alvarez's teaching became known in France mostly through the translations of the works of his prolific student Luis de la Puente (Du Pont). Mercurian's successor, Claudio Aquaviva (General 1581–1615), issued a general letter to the order in 1590 that approved the use of contemplative prayer, while still emphasizing apostolic service. Nonetheless, both the French Jesuit mystics considered here, Louis Lallemant and Jean-Joseph Surin, experienced criticism of their mystical teaching.

Louis Lallemant

Lallemant was born in 1587, entered the Jesuits in 1605, and had a fairly uneventful life as a teacher and administrator. In 1622, he became rector and master of novices at the Jesuit house at Rouen, where in 1628-31 he was the instructor for the Tertians, the Jesuits making the special third year of noviceship. Here he guided a number of later Jesuit mystical writers, such as Jean-Joseph Surin and Jean Rigoleuc (1595-1658). In ill health, Lallemant went on to the Jesuit house at Bourges, where he died in 1635. Lallemant published nothing during his lifetime. It was not until 1694 that Pierre Champion edited and published the *Spiritual Doctrine* (*Doctrine spirituelle*), based on materials collected by Rigoleuc and Surin about their teacher. For years there was discussion about how much of the *Doctrine* is actually from Lallemant and what came from Rigoleuc and others, but the recent edition by Dominique Salin establishes that the book contains basically what Lallemant himself wrote down during his lifetime.[4] The Jesuit may have hesitated about publishing his defense of mystical prayer because it had become controversial. Lallemant's instructions to the Tertians were denounced to Rome by some of his fellow Jesuits, precipitating a letter from the General Muzio Vitelleschi (General 1615-45) to the Jesuit Provincial, which noted, "It is said at Rouen that the Instructor [Lallemant] is completely mystical [*totus mysticus*] and that he wants to steer the whole world to the extraordinary in devotion. I am astonished, because he was proposed as especially apt for this instruction. These extraordinary modes are foreign to the role of the Instructor, who, above all, ought to have the spirit of our vocation and to hold himself to the standard manner of the Company."[5] This was not Vitelleschi's first or last criticism of what he considered dangerous mystical tendencies among the French Jesuits.[6] Nevertheless, the General did not remove Lallemant from his post.

Some aspects of the *Spiritual Doctrine* reveal the dangers that Vitelleschi and others found in the Jesuit's contribution to mysticism. Lallemant's stress on the necessity for the inner illumination of the Holy Spirit, as well as his emphasis on contemplative prayer, was bound to annoy antimystical Jesuits. Furthermore, other mystical themes found in the work, among them annihilation and the role of freedom of spirit, while widespread, were often subject to suspicion. By and large, however, *Spiritual Doctrine* is a clear, at times rather "scholastic," presentation of the stages of the inner life aimed at attaining union with God.[7] As the work comes down to us, the content is Lallemant's, written down at various times during his stay at Rouen (1622–31), but its structure was put together by his disciples. While admitting that Lallemant does not equal the greatest mystical teachers, Bremond praised him saying, "As a grammar of mysticism, as a manual of initiation to the contemplative life, nothing can be preferred to him."[8]

The work is organized according to seven "principles," beginning with "The View of the End," and proceeding to "The Idea of Perfection," "The Main Ways to Perfection," "Purity of Heart," "Docility to the Leading of the Holy Spirit," "Recollection and the Interior Life," "Union with Our Lord," and closing with "The Order and Degrees of the Spiritual Life." Each of these principles is in turn divided into sections, chapters, and articles, not unlike medieval *summae*. These seven headings should not be considered as discrete theses, but rather as charting a journey, "one that begins with the experience of human emptiness and terminates with union with God in Christ—and all under the direction of the Holy Spirit."[9] Bremond identified four main themes in Lallemant's teaching: (1) the "second conversion" to a deeper spiritual life, which, for Jesuits is the Tertian year; (2) the criticism of any active apostolate that is not grounded in a deep interior life; (3) the importance of guarding the heart, as a special form of Ignatian discernment; and (4) the need for submitting to the guidance of the Holy Spirit. These headings are helpful, but there is much more in the *Spiritual Doctrine*, which is basically a treatise on perfection, conceived of as total spiritual accomplishment. None of the mystical themes was original (Lallemant demonstrates considerable knowledge of many mystics),[10] but the synthesis was new and reflects his intention to try to return the Jesuits to a more interior and mystical mode of spirituality.

The short first principle begins by asserting that God alone can make us happy and saying that the emptying of self in perfect submission is necessary to attain felicity in union with God—"The heart is a void that can be filled only by God."[11] Principle II on the "Idea of Perfection" is divided into two sections: the first of three chapters on perfection in general, and the second with six chapters on the perfection particular to the Jesuit Order. Perfection in general consists in seeking God in all things, especially through the sacraments, faith, and the virtues of the Christian life. Jesuit perfection takes as its model Ignatius, the ideal representative of the contemplative in action (prin. II, sect. II, chap. 1, art. 3). It is here that Lallemant takes up the theme of two conversions, the first by which saints and religious "give themselves up to the service of God; the other by which they devote themselves entirely to perfection" (prin. II, sect. II, chap. 6, art. 2). In the case of the Jesuits, this latter is the period of the tertianship, when the Jesuit should commit himself to three necessary things. The first is total love of our Lord with Ignatius as his deputy; the second is sincere contempt of self. To attain these, says Lallemant, it is necessary to seek out "the heart of Christ and to enter there often to consider the annihilated Word and the very sacred humanity annihilated in the Passion."[12] The third thing is *l'esprit de recollection*. Regarding this item, Lallemant stakes out his position regarding the necessity for recollection and contemplation in the life of the Jesuit: "If some should say that there is danger lest a habit of recollection should interfere with the active duties of zeal to which our vocation obliges us, I reply that the very reverse is the case, and that it is certain that a man of prayer will do more in one year than another will in his whole life."[13] Thus, the goal of Lallemant's teaching, as it is for all Jesuits, is effective apostolic action, but he says that apostolic action without contemplative grounding will be ineffective, even dangerous.[14] At the end of his treatment on the perfection to which Jesuits are called, Lallemant cautions spiritual directors to avoid two opposed dangers: either giving credence to directees who imagine that "the least sensible sweetness" means they are already experiencing the graces of the great saints, or the opposite of keeping minds too low by never mentioning contemplation, heavenly visitations, or extraordinary favors. "In deciding cases of conscience," he concludes, "more dependence must be placed on the lights of the Holy Spirit, which constitutes the science of the saints, than on human reasoning."[15]

The third principle deals with purity of heart, which has been rightly described as a core issue of the book. The six chapters here are straightforward, treating the nature and properties of purity of heart, its four degrees, the things from which we must cleanse the heart, how to preserve purity of heart, and how to guard the heart. According to Dominique Salin, the short treatise on guarding the heart "is a veritable précis of Ignatian mysticism, constituting without doubt Lallemant's most original contribution to the Jesuit tradition."[16] The fourth principle on "Docility to the Leading of the Holy Spirit" is also part of the core message. This long section (125 pages in the edition) provides the essence of what Dominique Salin has called Lallemant's "mysticism of the docility to the Spirit."[17] Two key themes are intertwined here and throughout the *Doctrine*, namely, the importance of the inner light provided by the Holy Spirit and the need for discernment of spirits (a good Ignatian theme) to determine how best to follow the Spirit's promptings. For Lallemant, the inner guidance of the Holy Spirit is the essence of spiritual progress. We must follow God's will insofar as we see it in hopes that God will gradually manifest his inner will of good pleasure to us more fully (prin. IV, chap. 1, art. 2). What is especially needed is discernment of spirits: "Let us watch with care the different movements of our soul. By such attention we shall come gradually to perceive what is of God and what is not. That which proceeds from God in a soul which is subjected to grace is generally peaceable and calm. What comes from the devil is violent and brings with it trouble and anxiety."[18] The Jesuit recognized that this emphasis on the inner light of the Holy Spirit could be controversial, so in article 3 of chapter 1 he responds to four objections. First, he says that the inner illumination he speaks of is not that of the Calvinists, who subject the church to the inner light in his view. Second, this teaching does not destroy religious obedience to superiors, because the articles of faith and vowed obedience always trump interior inspiration, which may, however, be proved right in the end. Third, inner illumination does not remove the need for deliberation and counsel in our actions. Finally, to those who reply that they have never experienced such illumination, Lallemant says that they need to make greater efforts to empty themselves before such gifts can be given them (prin. IV, chap. 1, art. 3). He concludes, "The two elements of the spiritual life are the cleansing of the heart and the direction of the Holy Spirit. These are the two poles of all spirituality."[19]

The emphasis on the Holy Spirit leads Lallemant to a discussion of the seven gifts of the Spirit as essential to progress in the life of perfection. This was not a new theme, since mystics and theologians such as Gregory the Great, Thomas Aquinas, and Jan van Ruusbroec had all dwelt on the seven gifts. The Jesuit's teaching relies much on Thomas, but the discussion allows him to develop some distinctive aspects of his own spiritual teaching. For example, in treating the highest gift of wisdom he not only discusses it in Thomistic fashion as a form of connatural knowing of God (citing STh IIaIIae, q. 45, art. 2), but he also uses the supremacy of wisdom among the spiritual gifts to underline the fact that raptures and ecstasies are not the highest graces.[20] In treating the gift of understanding, he sets out a brief treatise on how to interpret scripture (prin. IV, chap. 4, art. 2), while the gift of knowledge allows him to emphasize that both action and contemplation are necessary for the soul's progress (art. 3).

Principle V is a brief consideration of the interior life defined as the thoughts and affections comprising the operations of God in the soul and our cooperation with these (prin. V, chap. 1, art. 1). The interior life must be joined to external action (prin. V, chap. 3, art. 2), and it is a life in which the will must be cultivated more than the understanding (chap. 4, art. 1). Chapter 4, art. 2, says that God leads souls by two ways: "Some he guides by interior lights, consolations, and sentiments of devotion; and this way is the most dangerous.... Others are led by reason and faith, assisted by the ordinary aids of actual grace.... And this road is the safest and leads most directly to perfection, because therein we walk more in spiritual poverty and humility."[21]

Principle VI dealing with "Union with Our Lord" is also long and expresses the Christological aspect of the instructor's mysticism. Lallemant often speaks of union with God as the goal of the spiritual life; in this principle and in the last he discusses what union actually is. Principle VI is divided into three sections. The first deals with knowledge of our Lord and is basically a treatise on the Incarnation. A Bérullian influence is detectable in the treatment of the three forms of annihilation of the Incarnate Word (prin. VI, sect. I, chap. 2, art. 2), in the discussion of the four states (*états*) of the life of Christ (sect. I, chap. 3), and in the attention given to the dignity and glory of the Blessed Virgin in the Incarnation (sect. I, chap. 4). In section II, the Salin edition restores an important part of the treatment of the love of our Lord. This is chapter 1bis devoted to "The Exercise of Love towards Jesus Christ." The chapter distinguishes three kinds of love toward Christ, that is, "the operations of Jesus Christ himself in the well-disposed soul."[22] These are *affective love, effective love,* and *passive love.*[23] *Amour affectif* entails four different kinds of affections: a desire for the good and glory of Jesus; the complaisance the lovers of the Word have for his goods and glory; the sorrow they feel over their sins; and finally, their confidence in the Savior and their abandonment into his hands.[24] *Amour effectif* consists in becoming like Jesus by three practices: general mortification of sensuality; attaining the liberty of spirit (*liberté d'esprit*) that reaches to "a holy indifference where everything is equal"; and total surrender to Jesus so that souls act as his instruments, "recognizing that it is no longer they that act, but that another spirit works in them and through them concerning things that are far distant from [their] abyss of nothingness and the misery in which they are plunged."[25] Finally, *amour passif* consists in four operations of wounding and suffering that the Savior inflicts on the loving soul, categories that Lallemant appears to have adapted from Richard of Saint-Victor's *Four Degrees of Violent Charity*.

The second chapter of section II of principle VI deals with the reasons we should love Jesus in the sacrament of the altar. Article 4 treats four kinds of "admirable union we have with Our Lord in the Holy Sacrament." The first is the local presence of the sacred humanity; the second is the moral union of the mutual love that binds us to him in communion. The third is of a higher order, namely, "the extraordinary effects which the Holy Sacrament produces in the soul and body," especially in those saints who testify that they have touched the sacred flesh and tasted the precious blood. "The fourth," says the Jesuit, "is a union, not indeed substantial or essential, but accidental, the most perfect that can possibly be in this kind [of union]. By it we are united immediately to the Body and Blood of Jesus Christ, and by means of his Body and Blood to his Soul and his Divinity." Lallemant's expressions of this union are unusual, even radical: "His Body becomes blended with our body, his Blood with our blood; whence there results in us an accidental change which makes us like our Lord."[26] Section III of the long principle VI deals with the imitation of Christ in nine chapters, including a rare reference to "the mystical generation of Jesus Christ in souls" (prin. VI, sect. III, chap. 4).

The seventh and last principle deals with "The Order and Degrees of the Spiritual Life" and is actually a treatise on prayer, especially contemplative prayer. As reconstituted by Salin, principle VII contains two treatises on prayer, probably dating from different periods. As found in the standard editions, the first treatise starts with a brief consideration of prayer in general (chap. 1), meditation (chap. 2), and the affective prayer of the advanced (chap. 3). The bulk of this treatise is a long treatment of contemplation in the ancient sense of the whole of the contemplative life (chap. 4 with nine articles). Salin introduces a second treatise (chap. 3bis), which bears the title "An Introduction Touching on Mental Prayer and the Three States of the Spiritual Life." Part I of this deals with the meditation of beginners (two arts.); part II, with the affective prayer of the advanced (two arts.); part III has eight articles treating the prayer of silence and the practice of the presence of God for elevated souls.[27] Let us first analyze this second treatise and then say a bit about the treatment of contemplation in the first treatise.

In chapter 3bis, Lallemant introduces prayer as "a gift of God that depends much more on grace than on our own effort and work; the Holy Spirit is its author and master" (art. 1). Three articles are devoted to the various forms of the meditation of beginners, while two articles are given to the prayer of affection of the advanced, which Lallemant says does not need to form distinct activities as meditation does but can rest in "contemplation by simple regard towards Jesus Christ, his perfections and virtues" (prin. VII, chap. 3bis, II, art. 1). The third stage is the prayer of silence, which is "a simple and respectful gaze at God, a loving attention to God's presence, and a sweet repose of the soul in God."[28] This simple gaze is not any particular act of knowledge but is a "confused and universal notion of Sovereign Being," which represents God better than all distinct ideas.[29] Lallemant says that it takes place in "the depth of the soul [*le fond de l'âme*], where God resides as in a secret sanctuary," a place that is closed to most people through their own fault. Perhaps somewhat nervous about introducing this speculative mystical theme, Lallemant cites a long list of mystical authors who have spoken of it.[30] The remainder of the discussion deals with practical issues concerning the prayer of silence, such as the different states of souls in the prayer (art. 2); dryness and desolation in the prayer (art. 4); how to discern true from false forms of the prayer of silence (art. 3); how to know if you are called to the prayer of silence (art. 6), and the like. We are reminded that Louis Lallemant was writing as an instructor of novices.

The second treatise on prayer found in the long chapter 4 on contemplation takes Teresa of Avila as a major resource, she being cited seven times. Lallemant begins by identifying two kinds of contemplation: ordinary and extraordinary. "Ordinary contemplation is a supernatural habit, by which God raises the powers of the soul to sublime knowledge and illuminations, lofty sentiments, and spiritual tastes." Extraordinary contemplation "consists in raptures, ecstasies, visions, and other extraordinary effects." "In this prayer," he continues, "we place ourselves before God. We remain thus without making distinct or repeated acts, occupied either with a simple regard toward God with respect and love, or some pious feelings that God gives, which last an hour, two hours, one day, two days. . . . The presence of God becomes almost continual with some very pure souls."[31] The gift of the sense of the presence of God is the first step in contemplation (art. 2), and Lallemant argues that it is necessary for the apostolic life (art. 4). Article 5 seems to start all over again, defining contemplation as "a perception of God, or of divine things, simple, free, penetrating, certain, proceeding from love, and tending to love," and then explaining each of these characteristics.[32] Article 6 speaks of the various effects of contemplation: elevation, suspension, admiration, ravishment, and ecstasy, using the authority of a number of ecstatics and mystical authors.

The final three articles on contemplation consist of a kind of grab bag listing the diverse degrees of contemplation set down by various mystical writers, beginning with the affective model taken from Richard of St. Victor's *Four Degrees of Violent Charity* (art. 7). This rather disorganized collection of materials allows Lallemant to introduce several terms that do not feature in his usual expositions, such as *mort mystique* and *deification* (art. 7, ed., 380). Article 8 sets out a different fourfold model of the essence of contemplation: (1) the knowledge and love of God given by devotion; (2) the divine darkness taken from Dionysius's *De mystica theologia* 1; (3) a state "When God elevates the soul to an extraordinary way of acting with regard to supernatural objects," that is, the realm of raptures and ecstasies; and finally (4) "when the soul no longer acts through the imagination, the medium through which raptures and ecstasies are caused, but is wonderfully enlightened by God by means of mental species or intellectual illuminations."[33]

At the end of the *Spiritual Doctrine*, chapter 9 gives Lallemant's judgment on the differing degrees of contemplation, favoring an intellectualist, Augustinian model of three ways of knowing God: through sense, through imagination, and through direct intellectual apprehension. He seeks, not totally successfully, to link this pattern to the four kinds of contemplation given in chapter 8. At the conclusion, the Jesuit sets out four modes of the soul's union with God conforming to the four kinds of contemplation. The first and best is "an habitual union by which the principal powers of the soul remain continually united to God at all times, even amidst the disturbance of exterior actions and the most urgent affairs." (This is what Teresa of Avila would have called the mystical marriage, although the Jesuit does not cite her here.) "The second kind of union . . . is when the will is united to God, but not all the other powers," although the imagination does not disturb the soul. "The third is when the will is united to God, but not in such a way that it is not sometimes distracted and harassed."[34] There should be a fourth kind of union to conform to the four kinds of contemplation, but Lallemant names only three. This puzzle, as well as the heterogenous nature of this last part of the *Doctrine* and the fact that principle VII contains two accounts of prayer, all remind us that the work is a compilation rather than a finished treatise. Nevertheless, Louis Lallemant's *Spiritual Doctrine* is one of the most important monuments of Jesuit mysticism.

Jean-Joseph Surin

Surin is a figure who puzzles, troubles, and amazes—one whom Stanislas Breton spoke of as "a mystic of excess."[35] Surin was rediscovered in the twentieth century, largely through the work of Henri Bremond and then Michel de Certeau.[36] Surin wrote much, and much has recently been written about him. What follows is only a sketch based on a few of his writings. Despite these limitations, it is important to say something about how this enigmatic figure fits into the story of seventeenth-century French mysticism.[37]

If Louis Lallemant's life was placid, Surin's was anything but.[38] Born in Bordeaux in 1600, he entered the Jesuits in 1616 and was ordained in 1626. He completed his tertianship in Rouen under Lallemant's supervision during 1629–30. Surin was one of the generation of young Jesuits from Aquitaine whose devotion to mysticism was deleted to Rome and raised the ire of the General Vitelleschi for following a spirit that was "alien to the Order." The young priest's interest in mystical matters and his quest for experiential certitude are revealed in a famous letter. In 1630, while on his way from Rouen to Paris, for three days he shared a coach with a young illiterate of eighteen or nineteen who was remarkably enlightened about the spiritual life. "He spoke to me," says Surin, "almost the entire morning on the various states of the most perfect union with God, the communication of the three divine Persons with the soul, of the incomprehensible familiarity of God with pure souls, [and] of the secrets God had allowed him to know concerning his attributes." Surin, who seems to have been in a spiritual crisis, told the young man of his own inner difficulties. The Jesuit found the incident life-changing. "In short, he told me such a number of good thoughts that I am not capable of writing them down. I am sure that those three days have been worth many years of my life." Surin's long letter, which taps into a tradition about illiterate laymen teaching divine secrets to learned priests that goes back to fourteenth-century stories about John Tauler, became quite popular and circulated in several forms and many languages, as Michel de Certeau has shown.[39]

Surin worked for a few years as a missionary in Protestant regions. Despite his poor health, the Jesuit authorities sent him and another Jesuit to Loudun in December of 1634 to assist in the exorcism of the community of Ursuline nuns who claimed to have been subject to a diabolical possession since 1632. This event was the most noted of the public spectacles of exorcism that the French church and state used to prove the superiority of Catholicism over its Reformed foes.[40] Surin's program of prayer and exorcism was directed to the abbess Jeanne des Anges (1605–1665), who was filled with demons. By October of 1636 he had freed her from most of the devils that possessed her, but at a price. According to his later autobiographical accounts of the events, the *Triomphe de l'amour divin sur les puissances de l'Enfer* and the *Science expérimentale des choses de l'autre vie*,[41] in order to free the nun Surin opened himself up to the power of the devil, who soon possessed him:

> He implored God with tears to give him that girl [Mother Jeanne] so that he might make her into a perfect religious, and was moved to pray for that with such ardor that one day he could not keep from offering himself to the Divine Majesty to be burdened with the evil of that poor girl and to participate in all her temptations and sufferings, to the point of asking to be possessed by the devil, provided He agreed to give him the freedom to enter into her and devote himself to her soul.[42]

Surin suffered greatly from attacks by demons during Lent of 1635, to the extent of feeling that there were "two souls" within him: "I feel the state of damnation and know it, and feel as if pierced with arrows of despair in this foreign soil that seems to be mine." Later he says, "I can feel the devil coming and going in me as in his house."[43] In 1636, Surin left Loudun, exhausted and mentally and spiritually troubled. On February 7, 1637, Jeanne des Anges claimed to have received a vision of her angel and St. Joseph, who anointed her with a healing balm and inscribed holy names on her hand. Nonetheless, in October of that year Surin was commanded to return to Loudun to help drive out Behemoth, the last devil who possessed her. After her "miraculous" cure, from April to September of 1638 Jeanne undertook a triumphal tour through France to show off her tokens of divine intervention and receive the plaudits of the king, Cardinal Richelieu, and the powers of church and state. The result for Surin was not so triumphant. What followed was a descent into madness ("melancholy" in the seventeenth century), a certainty of his own damnation, and many years of infirmary imprisonment and terrible mental suffering. Surin's trials are described in detail in the *Science expérimentale*, including the "terrible vision of Jesus Christ" as he appears to the souls in hell.[44] During much of this time Surin was in a catatonic state; at other times he tried to commit suicide. No wonder the story has attracted so much attention and diverse judgments.

The Jesuit gradually began to get better beginning around 1650. Although not yet able to write, by 1654 he started to dictate his mystical works, such as the *Catéchisme spirituel*. By 1655, he was able to write and even to preach. He sent numerous letters to a wide circle of friends and admirers (594 survive).⁴⁵ Surin's definitive release from his troubles came on June 9, 1656. Oppressed once again by a conviction that he was damned, he fell on his bed and made an act of total submission to God's will even if it meant his damnation. This act of *resignatio ad infernum* (Rom. 9:5) was followed by a flood of divine peace in his soul.⁴⁶ Surin continued to write at a great pace, including the *Dialogues spirituels* and the *Contrats spirituels*. He composed and published mystical poetry, such as the *Cantiques spirituels*.⁴⁷ Along with the two accounts of the exorcism and his personal trials, Surin worked on his (*Spiritual Guide*) *Guide spirituel pour la perfection* in 1660–61, the work that he considered his best.⁴⁸ In 1665, he published *Questions importantes à la vie spirituelle: Sur l'amour de Dieu*, which contains a response to the Jesuit critics of mysticism, like Vitelleschi.⁴⁹ When he died in April of 1665, Surin left a mass of material, some published, much unpublished.⁵⁰

The account here will be based primarily on the *Spiritual Guide*. Given the fact that Surin said that this work was his best and most penetrating, this limited approach will at least give a general idea of Surin's mysticism. Different authors have characterized Surin's teaching in diverse ways. Henri Bremond spoke of both Lallemant and Surin as representing "mystical moralism" (*le moralisme mystique*), that is, "the fusion realized by these masters between the most mortifying asceticism and the highest mysticism, between Saint Ignatius and the Pseudo-Dionysius."⁵¹ Michel de Certeau, on the other hand, spoke of the "incisive lucidity, . . . an understanding that comes from experience," found in Surin's thinking, and thus characterized him as trying "to present an experimental science of the spiritual life" by tracing "its logical structure in the successive phenomena which the soul experiences and which mark the development of a human life created by God."⁵² For Certeau, Surin's mystical thought was not so much a theological system as a practical program that begins with the determination to surrender totally to God, moves through a continual struggle against the self guided by the practice of discernment, to strive toward pure love of God. The mystical gifts that characterize this process revolve around two themes also found in Lallemant: the inner testimony of the Holy Spirit, and a "universal and confused [i.e., nondistinct] notion of God," that is, "a perception of union with God that is the foundation of the spiritual life."⁵³

Elements of both these approaches can be seen in the *Spiritual Guide*, although the purpose of the work is to provide a handbook for the reader to recognize his or her situation on the road to perfection. Something like Francis de Sales's *Introduction to the Devout Life*, the *Spiritual Guide* includes counsels about both the ascetical and the mystical aspects of the journey, but it emphasizes the mystical goal and seeks to defend it against its critics. The book is divided into seven parts: part I on Perfection in General; part II on Matters relating to Perfection in Particular; part III on the Virtues; part IV on the Aids to Perfection and Supernatural Acts; part V on the Regulation of Natural Actions; part VI on Perfection and Extraordinary Matters; and part VII on Mystical Matters. In parts II, IV, and especially VI and VII, the polemical aspect of Surin's treatise comes to the fore. In 1657, the Ancient-Observance Carmelite friar Jean Chéron (1596–1673), a professor at the University of Bordeaux, had published an *Examen de la théologie mystique*. Chéron admitted the possibility of mystical graces but argued against almost all the contemporary proponents of mysticism, including such respected figures as Teresa of Avila and John of the Cross.[54] Surin set out to answer him.

Perfection for Surin, as for Lallemant, was not moral perfection as such but the perfection by which the person attains the goal intended by God: "Perfection taken in its whole understanding is the best state [*état*] that a person can have in this life as taught by Jesus Christ and gained through his merits." It is true happiness, because it fulfills the three principal instincts leading to contentment: greatness, delight, and the possession of the best things. This opening paragraph of chapter I of part I introduces one of the characteristic features of the *Spiritual Guide*, that is, the way in which each section of each part is divided into threes. This tripartition was perhaps a mnemonic device, but it gives an often artificial flavor to the book. Thus, chapter II talks about three false ideas of perfection, and chapter III discusses the important first stage of perfection in terms of its three qualities: its universality (i.e., it surrenders everything to God); its sincerity; and its resolution to surpass all the difficulties that lie ahead.[55] The same pattern continues for the rest of part I.[56] It is clear from part I that Surin intended the book to be a practical guide for a general audience.

Part II of the *Spiritual Guide*, dealing with particular issues regarding perfection, is more directly concerned with mystical themes, such as recollection (chap. I), renovation of the spirit (chap. VII), the true interior (chap. VIII), and the presence of God (chap. IX). True recollection comprises the effort to gather and unify the soul's scattered powers within, followed by directing full attention to God, and the proper use of the heart, which means that the spiritual soul should be concerned with the things of God and not those of the world. There are two sorts of recollection: the one is the result of our own efforts (Surin does not use the term "acquired"), and the other is "that which comes from the infusion of grace and the operation of the Holy Spirit."[57] After two chapters devoted to the religious life, Surin returns to topics of importance to all Christians, such as prudence, the role of natural activity in relation to grace, and renewing the spirit when it has grown lax. Chapter VIII, on the true interior, has important mystical content. Surin specifies three things proper to the interior person. The first is a lack of concern for all exterior things; the second is concentration of one's actions on three interior practices—attention to the presence of God, discernment regarding one's interior actions, and ruling our actions to the end that "the person does not properly act but that God acts in him."[58] This surrender to divine activity is the third thing proper to the interior person. One who has attained this state reaches a condition of joy and repose in which God dwells in him as in his temple. The comparison of the soul to God's temple or palace, says Surin, is the common teaching of "the mystical doctors" (*docteurs mystiques*), such as Gerson, Augustine, and Teresa of Avila.

At this point, Surin launches his first attack on (the unnamed) Fr. Chéron, condemning those (like the Carmelite) who deny such teaching because they "examine supernatural matters more from their natural judgment than from the light of the saints."[59] The Jesuit takes this objection further in part II.IX with a discussion of how the soul should strive to make God present. There are three degrees of this presence. The first is to call God to mind by the use of faith according to which we know that God is everywhere. The second is to remember that God dwells in us as in his temple (1 Cor. 3:17). Again, Surin appeals to "those mystics" (e.g., Benet of Canfield and Francis de Sales) who have spoken about the "keep" (*donjon*) of the castle of the soul: "This is a spiritual keep, that is, an internal faculty of the soul where God communicates himself to the soul notwithstanding the attacks which she receives from the impressions in other parts of the soul."[60] After citing further authorities, Surin again divides his material, speaking of three degrees of this form of God's presence in the soul. The first was already referred to above, "the soul tastes the Being of God in its depth [*en son fond*], in general and non-distinctly [*confusément*], without any distinct knowledge." The second is when the soul senses it is united to Christ by grace and in the Eucharist. The third is Trinitarian: "It is to feel the three divine Persons residing in the soul and to be conversing with them." "All this," says the Jesuit, "has been treated by different mystical authors," among whom he names Teresa. Surin closes by noting that God's omnipresence can be known by both reason and faith, but that he is talking about something that goes beyond these initial levels through the gift of grace. In one of the most beautiful passages in the work, the Jesuit praises this new and more profound sense of God's presence in all things as a recognition that "everything is surrounded by God as in an ocean of love and goodness."[61]

The third part of the *Spiritual Guide* is a treatment of the virtues. From the perspective of mysticism, the most important chapters are those on charity (chap. III) and on abandonment into God's hands (chap. VI). As the love of God, charity has three forms. Active love (*amour aggissant*) is the love the soul has toward God in order to execute all that pertains to God's glory, while suffering love (*amour patissant*) is the love that gives itself over to sufferings, both external and internal, for God's sake. To illustrate the highest forms of this love, Surin cites both Teresa and John of the Cross. Finally, there is the "joyous love" (*amour jouissant*), that is, the joy of possessing God in this life that has been described by saints like Bernard, Gerson, and Teresa as a mystical marriage. Surin goes on to specify three aspects of this marital love: the divine kiss (Song 1:1); the divine embrace; and divine union, that is, the joining of bride and bridegroom, as taught by the *docteurs mystiques* (1 Cor. 6:17 and John 17:23 are cited). This is all standard mystical teaching in which Surin advances little that is new, leaving in doubt, at least with regard to this book, the claim of Certeau that a new experiential science of mysticism is coming to birth in the Jesuit.

The most interesting aspect of part IV of the *Spiritual Guide* is what it has to say about mystical literature. Again, there is a kind of fusion of the old and the new. Surin begins part IV by talking about the three kinds of prayer and those that practice them (chap. I), and he goes on to investigate the examination of conscience (chap. II) and questions about confession (chaps. IV–V). More space is given to communion and the frequency of its reception (chaps. VI–VIII), given the fact that Jansenist strictures against frequent reception of the sacrament were growing. The long chapter III, dealing with sacred reading, gives us a sense of Surin's concern to make sure that good mystical literature is not neglected either by religious or laity.[62] The chapter contains an annotated bibliography listing about fifty spiritual writers, patristic, medieval, and modern, including such figures as Blosius, Alvarez de Paz, Teresa, John of the Cross, Francis de Sales, Thomas de Jesús, Juan de Jesús-Maria, and Balthasar Alvarez. In discussing those he calls "the mystics," Surin begins with respected names such as Dionysius, Bonaventure, Denis the Carthusian, Gerson, and Blosius, but he also mentions four "profound authors" (Tauler, Ruusbroec, Harphius, and

Suso), who treated the same materials but "the reading of whom is dangerous for some because of the terms and the perspective they use to explain supernatural things." (These are the same mystics whom Everard Mercurian had forbidden Jesuits to read in 1575.) Surin says these authors have been misunderstood by the scholastic theologians who do not grasp the meaning of mysticism, but have been defended by the "theologians who are not only scholastic but also mystics," such as Bellarmine, Suarez, and Lessius.[63] Surin admits that the language used by these mystics is extraordinary but says that it must be so, because the matters they treat of are "so high and sublime."

Part V of the *Spiritual Guide* deals with the regulation of natural human elements, such as food, clothing, social relations, illness, reading, friendship, and even marriage, showing how all these aspects of life can help the reader on the path toward perfection. Part VI returns to the consideration of mysticism, specifically regarding what Surin calls "extraordinary matters." He begins with right intention (chap. I), religious simplicity (chap. II), and holy freedom (chap. III), which he defines as "the power to do what others do not dare to do without fear and with God's spirit." An example is the kind of austerity practiced by Francis of Assisi. After treating of the folly of the saints (chap. IV), Surin returns to sacred reading in another long chapter on mystical authors.[64]

Once again, the Jesuit displays his wide knowledge of mystical literature, as well as his opposition to Chéron and other antimystics. According to Surin, this chapter will not deal with all those who have written about spiritual things in general, but only "those who have spoken of the secret operations of grace," of whom he names about thirty, including many recent Spanish mystics and contemporary figures. Again he takes the opportunity to attack those who blame these authors and say that they talk fantasy. At this juncture, Surin lays out a detailed case against Chéron, rebutting a number of the arguments the Carmelite advanced against the mystics. The first is that "mystical science" rests on a poor foundation, because it appeals to experience, and the experiences of the mystics are often different. Surin answers that it is not so much a question of opposed experiences as experience being expressed in different ways. The second point concerns the language of the mystics who use extravagant allegories that obscure spiritual matters, such as Teresa's description of the soul as an interior castle. Surin shows that many respected mystics have employed such language over the centuries, and even more surprising terms. A third objection is that the mystics use extraordinary terms to express common and vulgar things. Surin's response is that mystics, such as "Saint Denys," are talking not about common things but about "the secret ways of God," and thus they must use sublime words to explain such high matters. (VI.V; ed., 250–51). To the question how learned theologians like Chéron can have so little grasp of the language of the mystics, Surin answers, "Science does not suffice. It is not enough to have read Aristotle, the medical experts, and even to possess theology, but it is necessary to have the proper dispositions for the internal things of God and the supernatural operations of his Spirit." Docility and humility are also needed, "because mystical science is totally different from Scholasticism, so that to know the one is not for that reason to know the other" (VI.V; ed., 252). He uses Teresa of Avila as an example. Her *Life* tells of how some learned men at first thought she was subject to diabolical illusions, but truly holy and wise theologians like Peter of Alcántara and Francis Borgia realized that her inner experiences came from God.

Towards the end of the chapter, Surin takes up the issue of whether mystical prayer and special experiences are proper for Jesuits. To those who say that St. Ignatius was suspicious of mysticism, Surin answers that there is no evidence for this, although the founder was suspicious of those given to lengthy prayers who did not practice mortification. Although Fr. Mercurian banned the reading of certain mystics who were "strongly abstract" (*fort abstraits*), Fr. Aquaviva encouraged reading the mystics. Surin continues, "Saint Ignatius was frequently raptured and lifted above the ground in his prayers, as was Francis Xavier" (VI.V; ed., 258). Surin closes with a discussion of the many famous theologians (Bonaventure, Gerson, Lessius, etc.) who encouraged the reading of the mystics.

The following three chapters take up a key issue in medieval and early modern mysticism: the discernment of spirits. The Jesuit begins with a chapter on extraordinary graces, which also takes on Fr. Chéron for his attack on such gifts of the Holy Spirit. Surin says there are two kinds of people who are suspicious of gifts that go beyond ordinary grace, such as visions, elevations, locutions, and the like. The first group, among whom he numbers Chéron, says that such experiences are always dangerous. But, says Surin, the scriptures and history demonstrate that there have been many saints who have received such graces, although he allows that some people have been led astray by them.[65] There is, however, a second group who distance themselves from extraordinary graces who are less blameworthy. These are those who say that people who have received such gifts ought to turn away from them out of prudence and humility. There are three kinds of people in this group. The first are those who do not care about such gifts, recognizing that spiritual progress consists in attaining virtue and not in enjoying "God's caresses." The second group refuses them out of humility, and the third has extreme indifference to them. Surin places John of the Cross in the last camp, arguing that the Carmelite's advice about rejecting special experiences (e.g., *Ascent of Mount Carmel* 2.11) means that we should adopt an attitude of "abnegation and disengagement" toward them.

Chapter VII discusses spiritual illusions and the reasons why some fall into these, while chapter VIII is devoted to the three "[h]idden deceptions which frequently come upon those who travel on the road to perfection." Given that the goal of the spiritual life is union with God, the most dangerous of these deceptions is when the devil deceives the will into thinking that a person can maintain some attachment to creatures and not give everything to God. No, argues Surin, "I say even more, that there is little difference with regard to divine union between someone who is attached to some small creature and someone who has great attachments." It makes no difference whether a bird is bound to a snare by a thread or a rope—it still cannot fly. The difference is not between small attachments and large attachments but between any attachment and the detachment needed to attain union with God.

In part VII of Surin's *Spiritual Guide* Teresa of Avila emerges as a main authority. Here the Jesuit devotes eight chapters to "mystical matters" (*choses mystiques*). The first three deal with mystical prayer; then two chapters concern ecstasy and rapture. Given Surin's own sufferings, it comes as no surprise that chapters VI and VII deal with mystical dereliction—the "Purgatory of the Soul" and the "Hell of the Soul." These partly autobiographical chapters form a classic account of this aspect of mysticism. Finally, chapter VIII treats the last stage of the path to perfection, spiritual marriage.

The three stages of mystical prayer begin with the prayer of quiet and silence, which is "a repose which the soul takes in thinking of God without working much by its own effort."[66] Surin analyzes four different terms for this kind of prayer (prayer of the presence of God, recollection, quietude, and silence) and proceeds to treat it in terms of two questions. The first is whether the soul can remain still without any operations. The Jesuit says that the doctors and mystics seem to differ on this, but his answer is that during this prayer the soul enjoys both great knowledge and great affectivity, but only through God's action, not its own. To the question as to who is apt for this prayer, Surin answers, following Suarez, that not all people have the capacity for this prayer. The second stage of mystical prayer is called the prayer of transport and of familiar conversation with God (Surin cites Teresa's *Life*, chap. 17). The third degree is the prayer of union, which is "that in which the soul uses all its faculties . . . so that it can with all its power receive and embrace God who is present to it."[67] To the question about the difference between this stage of prayer and the first, Surin responds by distinguishing between the first prayer, where "the soul can be united in its depth [*en son fond*], but still empty in the imagination," and the third stage, where every power is occupied by God in a full and absolute way and the effects are much greater.

Concerning ecstasy, Surin once more returns to answering the objections of Fr. Chéron that ecstasy is against God's intention, because God wishes human beings to gain merit in this life. But, counters Surin, God approves of sleep in which no merits are gained. More important is the treatment of rapture (*ravissement*) in chapter V. Rapture is defined as an attraction from the summit of the soul moving the inferior powers to be attentive to some lofty good. There are three kinds of rapture: (a) purely natural; (b) diabolical; and (c) divine, which is when "[o]f his goodness God wishes to communicate to the soul in this way and draw it to himself on high and make the operations of the lower powers cease until the soul receives what it is He wants to give her."[68] During this state the soul can be held by God without receiving any distinct act of knowledge, but with divine delight in its depth, or the soul can be given some form of divine knowledge, as we see in the case of the prophets and apostles. Rapture is the highest actual grace, according to Surin, although as a transient experience it is inferior to the spiritual marriage, which is a habitual state.

The purgatory of the soul and the even more terrible hell, things that the Jesuit had experienced for years, are part of God's preparation for perfect union. Surin's analysis of mystical purgatory, based on his own life and the witness of mystics like Angela of Foligno and Teresa, is once again divided into three. The three kinds of suffering that the soul undergoes are, first, the sense of being damned; second, a frightful censure of its whole life; and, third, various "great and difficult torments." These torments include the sense of hanging or suspension (like Angela of Foligno), suffocation (like Teresa), and of being crushed (Surin does not name anyone here, but such an experience came to the Flemish mystic, Jan van Leeuwen). Mystical hell increases all these sufferings "to excess and their extremity." Surin cites Teresa again, John of the Cross in the *Dark Night*, as well as a number of other mystics, as witnesses to this most terrible aspect of the road to perfection. He also mentions how God may permit souls who suffer such trials to seem as if they are insane, as in his own case. To the charge that such suffering comes from "melancholy," or mental illness, he responds that this is certainly possible, but we must distinguish three kinds of sufferers: those whose trials come only from nature; those who receive them from grace to help test the soul; and those cases where both nature and grace are at work (VII.VII, ed., 308–12).

The final chapter of the *Spiritual Guide* takes up spiritual marriage, using the writings of Teresa, John of the Cross, and Tomás de Jesús, thus showing how important the Carmelite mystics were for the Jesuit. Surin says that this state, which consists in familiarity, conversation, and friendship with God, usually comes after much practice of virtues and suffering, especially the terrible purgatory he has just spoken about. There are three main benefits of this state. The first is "a plunging of the soul into divine essence, which is a union in its depth (i.e., the origin of all its operations), in its center, and in its most intimate being with God." The effects of this union are a perpetual light in the soul, along with a perpetual taste for God, and a perpetual inclination to do good.[69] The second benefit is frequent communication with Jesus Christ and the three Persons of the Trinity. The principal communication is when the Word unites itself to the soul and imprints its divine Being through a substantial touching, which is an "intimate furnace that instructs the soul not only through faith but through the experience of what God is" (VII.VIII, ed., 316). The third benefit comprises all the treasures and riches of this blessed condition, including "the caresses, above all the furnace enkindled in the depth of the soul whose flame touches the heart" (ed., 317). Surin dwells on the delights of this flame of love, which drives the soul onward, so that "[i]t fulfills what is written [in scripture], that 'the way of the just proceeds like the day to noon' (Isa. 58:10), and, because God is infinite and without measure, it does not find a stopping point in this same love" (ed., 318). On this note of mystical epektasis, that is, infinite loving stretching out into God, Jean-Joseph Surin ends his handbook.

Carmelite Mysticism

The introductory chapter has already mentioned the presence of both Teresa's reformed Carmelites in France and the homegrown Carmelite reform of Touraine. A number of the Discalced Carmelite nuns would qualify as mystics, as revealed in the *vitae* written about them,[70] but my attention here will be on one male mystic from the Touraine reform, Jean de Saint-Samson, and one from the Teresian reform, Brother Lawrence of the Resurrection.

Jean de Saint-Samson

In 1600, there were about a hundred male Carmels in France divided into eight provinces. In most of these, however, religious practice had sadly decayed. As early as 1582, some friars at the Carmel at Rennes had tried to introduce ancient liturgical practices but had been rebuffed by their fellow friars. Over the next decades, the movement toward reform grew slowly both at Rennes and at the Carmelite *studium generale* at the Place Maupert in Paris. Under the leadership of Philippe Thibault (1572–1638), a friar who was also associated with the Barbe Acarie circle and Pierre de Bérulle, the reform gradually gained ground. The renewal of vows taken by the community at Rennes on April 21, 1608, is seen as the establishment of the Touraine reform, which stressed mental prayer, silence, and poverty, as well as a renewed liturgical life. This reform soon spread throughout France and abroad among the Ancient Observance Carmelites.[71]

If Thibault provided the leadership, the spiritual heart of the reform came from the blind lay brother Jean de Saint-Samson. Born Jean du Moulin at Sens in 1571 into a well-to-do family, he was blinded at the age of three by smallpox. Orphaned at ten, he lived with his maternal uncle between 1581 and 1597, where he acquired some education, but especially skill playing a number of musical instruments. In 1597, he went to Paris to live with an older brother. After the death of his brother in 1601, he was reduced to poverty but eventually found employment as an organist at various churches, including the Carmelite church at the Place Maubert. Jean had been devoted to prayer and contemplation from his youth. From about 1604 to 1606 he participated in spiritual reading groups led by the friars, which must have been where he acquired much of his knowledge of mystical literature. Against custom, he was accepted as a Carmelite lay brother at the house at Dol-de-Bretagne in 1606, where he remained until 1612. He transferred to the Carmel of Rennes in 1612, which was now the center of the reform movement. Philippe Thibault was at first suspicious of Jean, but the humble and devout lay brother won him over, and Philip appointed him to work on the formation of the young friars.

As spiritual director and master of the novices who would soon carry the reform throughout France, Jean had a strong impact on the spread of the Touraine reform. From about 1615 he also began dictating at a furious pace, both in prose and poetry. Upon his death on September 14, 1636, he left a mass of material of some four thousand pages. In his last years, Jean acquired disciples. Fr. Joseph de Jésus collected his writings, and a selection (of a thousand pages) was published by Fr. Donatien de Saint-Nicholas as *Oeuvres spirituelles et mystiques* in 1558-59. The antimystical reaction in France, especially around the Quietist controversy, relegated Jean to obscurity for centuries, a position from which he has only recently begun to emerge. A Carmelite project to publish all his writings in ten volumes is under way.[72] English translations are sparse, as are English studies of his thought.[73]

Despite his blindness, Jean de Saint-Samson appears to have had considerable knowledge of mystical literature, which he would have gained from discussion and having books read to him. He knew standard patristic and medieval authors and was familiar with a number of Northern European mystics, such as Ruusbroec, Thomas à Kempis, Hendrik Herp, the *Evangelical Pearl*, and the Pseudo-Tauler *Institutiones*. One work that influenced him was the *Mantelet of the Spouse* by the Flemish Franciscan Frans Vervoort (d. 1555). Jean also appreciated the writings of Catherine of Genoa; among the Spanish mystical authors, he used Luis de Granada and Teresa.[74] Jean de Saint-Samson's mysticism, however, was very much a personal development, not a learned phenomenon.

Like John of the Cross, Jean de Saint-Samson communicated his mystical message in both prose and poetry. We know that he often sang these poems, whose metric systems were based on those of the great French poet Pierre de Ronsard (d. 1585). Only five of Jean's poems were published, leaving 127 others in manuscript.[75] Jean's prose style is not easy. Given that his works were dictated and that he did not revise, the treatises tend to be badly organized and digressive. Since he often dealt with deep mystical issues, Jean himself admitted that some of what he has to say may be obscure to those who have not experienced such things. Given the size of his *oeuvre*, as well as the fact that only a part of it has been edited, what follows will be only an initial attempt at a sketch based on two of his treatises, *The Goad* (*L'éguillon*), an introduction to his spirituality,[76] and the *Epithalamium*, whose full title, *The Marriage Song of the Divine and Incarnate Bridegroom and the Divine Bride in Conjugal Union with Her Spouse*, suggests its content.

The Goad, written for his friend Bishop Antoine Revol, provides an overall sense of the Carmelite's spiritual program, which centers on "the life and spirit of love in love itself " (*vie et esprit d'amour en l'amour mesme*). The eight chapters set out the practices, both internal and external, for advancing in the spiritual life to union with God. Citing Bernard on the Song of Songs (*Sermo super Cantica* 83.4), Jean notes that love offers "a double goad to help you ever more vigorously on your course to its goal" (*Au Lecteur*, ed., 32). The journey is a familiar one, beginning with chapter 1 on knowing oneself, God, and his love, which stresses the need to remove all mortal and venial sins from one's life. Toward the end of the chapter, Jean emphasizes something found throughout the treatise: the contrast between two styles of life— the "scientists" who study only nature and conduct their lives on this basis, and those who live by the spirit (chap. 1, ed., 42–43). Chapter 2 deals with the contrast between the infinity of God and the nothingness of the self, a familiar theme in French seventeenth-century mysticism. Jean concentrates on gaining the proper attitude, not on giving advice about specific practices, noting that we should be satisfied with whatever state God sets us in. Love is the real goad of spiritual progress, so chapter 3 treats love as the mistress of all the virtues (an Augustinian theme). Jean's digressive exposition here touches on one significant mystical theme, namely, how to evaluate states of ecstasy. The Carmelite admits that these are beyond most people, but he also cautions against too much importance being given to ecstatic states, because they often indicate an immature spiritual development more dependent on one's own efforts than on a passive and powerful gift of God.[77] Chapter 4 continues the love theme by discussing how to perform good works for the love of God alone.

The second part of *The Goad* moves into more mystical matters. Chapter 5 discusses how to persevere in the exercise of the love of God, noting, "It is in ordinary situations, as I have always said, that the Beloved plays his amorous game within his Spouse, and he truly demonstrates his fidelity when she suffers languor and desolation."[78] Chapter 6 on "The Mystical Life" constitutes a brief consideration of aspects of mystical teaching, not a formally organized treatise. For Jean, the mystical life is the work of the Holy Spirit pouring its wisdom into the soul. Again, he contrasts the mystical way of ecstatic contemplation with the academic research that takes pleasure only in intellectual curiosity. The mystical way is designed to arouse the affections, because love is the goad of all the virtues needed to attain higher states of consciousness of God. These higher states comprise the simple gaze of contemplation, as well as the true ecstasy of those "aspiring" to God.

The theme of aspiration, already mentioned in several earlier chapters, emerges in chapter 7 as a major theme of this and other works of the blind Carmelite. What he has been describing, according to Jean, is nothing other than "mystical science" (*la science mystique*), that is, a state beyond description. He says, "Not a few saints have said marvelous things about it, and yet all their words are nothing compared with the reality. Here one is clothed with God and all his attributes as with a garment. Here one experiences the fullness of divine generations. Here without cease God comes totally anew, and in return the soul goes to God with all her desire. The whole creature is immersed completely in the eternal sea, where it is suspended in a state higher than its own."[79] In this chapter Jean frequently cites the agreement between his teaching and those he calls "the genuine mystics."

With chapter 7, "The Art of Aspiring," we reach the heart of the work. Short ejaculatory prayers of love to God had been a part of Christian mysticism for centuries. In the later Middle Ages, they had been emphasized by the author of the *Cloud of Unknowing*, whom Jean would not have known, as well as Hendrik Herp, whom he certainly knew.[80] As Hein Blommestijn has shown, aspiration as a prayer practice in which God inspires the human to a prayer of union that makes the two into one is central to Jean de Saint-Samson.[81] Jean begins this chapter by claiming that the practice of aspiring is the purest and simplest form of the mystical way. Aspiring is not just affectionate conversation, but "is an expression of love: a love so purely and radically expressed that it transcends all loves that are comprehensible to the senses, the reason, or intellect. By the impetuosity and force of the Spirit of God, it arrives at union with God, not by chance but by a sudden transformation of the spirit in God."[82] Hence, aspiring is not so much a human activity as it is the action of the Holy Spirit in the aspirer.[83] Aspiring, however, usually begins with the "affective and relaxed prayer of meditation" in which a person considers and imagines the divine works he desires to know, the way a dog chases a hare. But when the dog captures the hare it is not allowed to eat it, but hands it over to the owner. So too, what is discovered by mental effort is handed over to the will so that it can be ignited and nourished. Sensitive souls will be quite fit for this exercise, about which the mystics have written much (Luis de Granada is cited). Jean also discusses the simple loving gaze of contemplation, which he seems to be distinguishing from aspiring.

Jean de Saint-Samson suggests that both the sensitive souls for whom aspiring is easy and the less sensitive souls for whom it is difficult eventually will have their wills drawn into "the amorous bosom of love," where they become love itself "insofar as it is possible for any creature in this life."[84] What must be avoided, he cautions, is too much exertion of either head or heart, which could block the Spirit's action. When the exercise is received by the soul, he goes on, "it can easily, powerfully, and sublimely create the union beyond union (if I may say so) of the loving creature in God, its blessed Lover."[85] Thus, loving aspiration is both the means and the end to union. It is God at work in us. "Just as we live, move, and exist in Him (Acts 17:28), it is in Him that we must flow back with the most active and unflagging current."[86] Having laid out what he says is "the excellence of the true mystics in their own mystical way," the Carmelite closes this chapter with a model of the exercise of aspiration. This is a rather lengthy prayer, not unlike one of Bérulle's Elevations, mingling conversation with God (questions and answers), reflections on God's gifts, and acts of thanksgiving, praise, and resolution to love God more effectively.

The final chapter of *The Goad* deals with the life of renunciation. "Renunciation," according to Jean, "is the complete abandonment of the whole self to God, with no reservations regarding length of time or nature of action."[87] Such genuine abandonment can be practiced in every life situation. Again, the Carmelite emphasizes that only God has the power to raise a person to this level of knowing and loving, as the "greatest mystics" and he himself have always taught. Later on, he distinguishes between individual acts of mortification and renunciation, which "concerns prolonged situations that we find most difficult and aggravating." By undergoing these with "our amorous desire and our amorous suffering" we can eventually arrive at a state of resignation.[88] The remaining pages of chapter 8 contain a rather disconnected series of reflections on the dangers of the active life, the mistake of confusing God's gifts for holiness itself, and the nature of what he calls "mystical holiness" and the "mystical life." Those who have arrived at this state are "the true friends of God [who] remain hidden to their fellow humans, and their unique vocation, demanded by the life of true renunciation, is to remain as unrecognized as possible."[89]

Perhaps the most remarkable of Jean de Saint-Samson's works is the *Epithalamium*, an ecstatic prose-poem of over nine hundred lines, praising the mystical marriage between the human bride and the divine Bridegroom.[90] Like most of the blind brother's works, it is hard to date; but we can presume it is a mature work. Jean taps into the long tradition of epithalamia, or wedding songs, going back to the Song of Songs.[91] Like John of the Cross's "Cantico espiritual," it is a rewriting of the Song, whose images appear about two dozen times. There are several peculiarities about Jean's use of the Song. The most striking is that he makes almost no appeal to the most often-used image of the Song, the kiss (Song 1:1).[92] The Carmelite speaks of the bed (*lict*) of the two lovers (Song 1:15; 3:1; see ll. 323, 600, 603) and once refers to their bridal chamber (Song 3:4; l. 484), but his favored image is the embrace shared by the bride and Bridegroom.[93] Perhaps no other epithalamium equals Jean's in the excessive character of its love language and its daring presentation of the deep union between God and human. Excessive love had been an important theme in Christian mysticism since the twelfth century, especially among female mystics. Yet few if any mystical works give so much emphasis to "the excessive," both in its language and its teaching, as Jean's *Epithalamium*. As an experiment in creating a new language of ecstatic experience, this prose-poem is reminiscent of Richard Rolle's *Melos amoris* in removing all barriers to the rushing force of what Jean called "excessively excessive love" (*l'amour excessivement excessif*, l. 858).[94]

We know that Jean de Saint-Samson dictated his works, and it is possible that at least some of the *Epithalamium* was dictated while the brother was in ecstasy. At times, the author (let alone the reader) seems to get lost, but the narrative always rushes ahead. As Ivan Scicluna puts it, "When his thought reaches untranslatable peak experiences, he ends up creating unusual, reduplicated adverbial expressions to express absolute superlatives."[95] As might be expected, Jean delights in paradox and oxymoron, and frequently appeals to the ineffability of what he is trying to say,[96] even inventing the phrase "ineffably ineffable" (*ineffablement ineffable*) to drive the point home.[97] The positivity of the Carmelite's language of excessive love is moderated not only by these appeals to ineffability, but also by at least one passage of an apophatic nature. In section 15, the bride dwells on the problem of trying to put the "ineffably ineffable vision and rest" she has enjoyed with the Bridegroom into words, asking, "What value is there in expressing things that are through things that are not, as much as expressing things that are not through those that are?" She continues, "Where is the truth in all this," that is, in the object that has enraptured her and which she feels flowing within her, "if not in you who are beyond being and the eminence of being, in the eminence of non-being, and in being and beyond being through the power of supereminent negation?"[98]

This passage points to another characteristic of Jean's style, the use of the language of *suressential* and its cognates, which he probably learned from Hendrik Herp and his disciples.[99] Thus, the Carmelite uses *sureminente negation* (l. 286), *surpassion* (l. 678), *suressential embrass-*

mens (ll. 814–15), *sureminente et suressentiel amour* (l. 819), *sureminente force* (ll. 871–72), and *existence suressentielle* (ll. 830–31). Jean sometimes even reduplicates superessential formulae, speaking of *suressentielle sureminence* (e.g., ll. 782–83, 803, 808–9). The language of supereminence and superessential is another aspect of the delight the Carmelite takes in paradox and passing beyond. An example is found in the concluding lines of the address of the bride in the first part, where she says:

> Oh! I fail totally! Oh! I cannot take any more. I die and expire of love and comfort in your superessential breast, whose exquisite and delightful beauty powerfully ravishes me [in] the life of love and comfort, in love and beyond love, in repose and fruition and beyond repose and fruition, in simplicity beyond ineffably ineffable simplicity, in the ineffable beyond the ineffable.[100]

Before taking a look at the teaching of the *Epithalamium*, it will be helpful to get a sense of the work's structure. After a "Prologue" (ll. 5–39) setting out the main theme of love, the *Epithalamium* divides into two unequal parts. The first (sections 2–35, ll. 40–649) is the impassioned address of the bride either rejoicing with the Bridegroom in their "common delight" (*commune jouissance et repos*),[101] or else begging him to come to visit her and return her to their shared love-union. The *ludus amoris*, the game of love that alternates between the presence and the absence of the Bridegroom is an important theme (e.g., sections 30 and 31). Although the bride is addressing the beloved Other, Jean's notion of a union of identity means that it is really the Bridegroom who is speaking in his total oneness with the vanishing bride. He gives her to speak of love and to be moved to union (e.g., section 13, ll. 241–57). In the second part (sections 36–50, ll. 650–910), the speaker is the Bridegroom. Here the language is still suffused with excessive love, but the tone is more instructional, as the God-man attempts to put indistinct union into fallible human words. One way in which Jean highlights the inexpressibility of mystical consciousness is when both God and the soul appeal to the "secret" that they alone share (e.g., ll. 406–8, 837–40).

One does not look to the *Epithalamium*, which describes itself as a *science experimentale* (l. 797), for explicit doctrinal teaching, but there is obviously a view of the divine nature and its relation to humanity undergirding the passionate effusions of the work. The picture of God that emerges shows the Carmelite's affinity with the dynamic view of God found in Northern mystics like Ruusbroec, Hendrik Herp, and the *Evangelical Pearl*. God is the supremely simple One, and Jean uses the expressions *simple unique* (e.g., ll. 705, 708) and *tres simple unique* (ll. 717-18). Thus, in section 39 he says that, by the "ineffably ineffable embraces" of the lovers, "through an outpouring of the simple total into the *simple unique*, . . . infinitely beyond the understanding, the comprehension, and beyond being in the being of being, through the same *simple unique*, . . . that [love] seizes its mutual and life-giving object" (ll. 703-13). Section 40 also speaks of the cycle of love as taking place "in the impetuous power of *simple unique*" (ll. 728, 733).[102] But the "simple unique" is also the God who is Trinity. In describing the mystical marriage in section 14, the bride begs her companions to sing a new song of praise (see Ps. 98:1) for "the profound and total consummation of the divine marriage," which takes place "in his own divine unity, where the three Persons of the Trinity reside for the completion of their active and joyous happiness, taking sufficient and total delight and [having] mutual and interconnected contemplation of one to another and of one in the other."[103] Jean does not mention the Trinity often, but it is present by implication in his language of "flow" (*flus*, etc.), which he shares with the Northern mystics.

Flus is the dynamic divine energy that begins in the Godhead, overflows into creation, and is the source of the "return," the *reditus* by which God brings back into himself the human person and all things. The language of flow exists on three levels: (1) within the Trinity itself; (2) in the overflow from God into creation; and (3) between the lovers as they flow back into the supernal source. In section 10, Jean describes the two "likenesses" of the Bridegroom, the Word of God. Before his love for the bride was made manifest in the Incarnation, the Word possessed only his own likeness which he received "from the total and eternal flow from the Principle of your eternal production in its infinite fecundity, through which you are similar to the Source itself, distinct from itself in itself" (ll. 201-4). The second likeness of the Word is the humanity he takes on "so as to render me totally similar to yourself in myself, made yourself of yourself, in yourself and for yourself" (ll. 207-9). Flow not only refers to the production in the Trinity but also to God's creation of the universe (section 8, ll. 158-63). The bride also uses the term to describe the mutual flowing into each other of the two lovers, praising "our very simple flow of divine delights, which is, in the uniqueness of us both and for us both, our same rest, without distinction or difference of what we are" (section 34, ll. 622-25). These uses are all taken from the bride's speeches, but the language of flow is actually more frequent in the Bridegroom's address to the bride, where the term describes not only the mutual flowing of the lovers, but the way in which the divine energy flows back into itself (*reditio completa in seipsam*). This language is especially prevalent in sections 38–40. In section 38, for example, the Bridegroom tells the bride: "You have flowed out [*flueé*] of yourself into me, into the eternal expanse and enjoyment of your Bridegroom." This flow is part of the great cycle of flowing, because the Bridegroom praises the unity of the bride's fruitfulness that has allowed her "to return to the total enjoyment of what is simple, fruitful and unique in the infinite power of the love of the *simple unique*, equally flowing from every fecund distinct thing as from its simple, originary, and present Principle."[104]

Jean's *Epithalamium* does not set out a theological anthropology, such as a description of the powers of the soul, although in several places he does say that union with God takes place in the "supreme center of the soul" (e.g., ll. 100–102, 833). In speaking of the soul's relation to God and its indistinct union with the Bridegroom, however, Jean makes remarkable claims about the soul's infinity. Just as the Word's "revenge" for humankind's sin was to take on flesh in order to be able to marry the bride (sections 9–10), so too the bride takes her vengeance in return by "plunging myself unceasingly in the power and strength of my infinite love for you, in you, from depth to depth, until by dint of acting and suffering in love I become totally reduced and consumed in your love."[105] As this text and others show,[106] Jean de Saint-Samson here picks up the theme of the double infinity, or the double bottomless abyss of God and the matching depth of the soul, as the "place" of deep union, a teaching that stretches back as far as Hadewijch and was found in mystics such as John Tauler and the author of the *Evangelical Pearl*. The double infinity motif is also implied in the way that Jean dwells on the matching beauty of the bride and the Bridegroom, particularly a passage in section 16, where he says, "Who is it then who will be astonished to see me beautiful in your outstanding beauty, O my Bridegroom? No, one will not be astonished to behold me publically declare myself totally beautiful (Song 4:7). If I ever do this, [it will be because] coveting my beauty as you do, you perfect it to its utmost fulfillment of and in your infinity, for your complete satisfaction."[107] This passage is reminiscent of a text in John of the Cross about the mutual beauty of the lovers (*Spiritual Canticle*, stanza 36), although the French mystic seems to go beyond the Spanish friar in his conviction of the soul's infinity.

Jean's *Epithalamium* is fundamentally about union—the whole text is nothing but an ecstatic hymn to marital union. Scarcely a line is without a reference to the joining of the bride and the groom. Still, it may be helpful to point to some aspects of union highlighted by the Carmelite. This unity, which he refers to in a typically excessive formula as "unity uniquely unique" (*unite uniquement unique*), is *experientially* an erotic mutual and total satisfaction (*jouissance*);[108] *theologically* it is a melding of natures as a form of deification so that humans can be spoken of as divine; *concretely* it is a devouring of each nature by the other; *eschatologically* it is a mystical death of the human person to be fully realized in heaven; *sacramentally* it is a eucharistic union, and, *finally*, a "union without distinction and difference." A number of these notes, especially that of indistinct union, were controversial, but the Carmelite did not hesitate to use them. Let us look at just a few texts that may help us to understand the vision behind his rhetoric.

The total mutuality of the union between the bride and the Bridegroom is a leitmotif of the *Epithalamium*. This is rooted in the mad, excessive love that each lover has for the other. God's infinite desire to be one with humans is matched by the infinite longing for God that he places in the soul. In fact, it might be more accurate to say that this desire *is* the soul. In section 5, for example, the bride praises "the power of our impetuous and conjugal love, which enraptures us everywhere equally with gladness in our common enjoyment and repose and which makes us hold one another, one for the other, ever more tightly in the power of our unique embraces."[109] The bride embraces the Bridegroom in both his divinity and his humanity: "Why are you astonished if in the activity of my impetuous love I embrace you entirely naked [*je vous embrasse tout nud*], entirely divine in your divinity, and entirely divine in your humanity, . . . one sole and divine person [*suppost*] in your divinity and your humanity" (section 7, ll. 151–55). The theme of deification appears throughout the *Epithalamium*. In section 33, for example, the bride speaks of the truth of the excesses of love with its "simple embraces" that bring her to "where I am divine-human and human-divine [*ou je suis divine humaine et humaine divine*] in the total all-comprehending and incomprehensible fullness, which not even your Bride in her capacity as such understands" (ll. 594–97). Other passages boldly speak of "our divinity" (*nostre divinité*, ll. 829, 847).[110]

The *Epithalamium* says nothing about the church, nor should it be expected to. It does, however, devote two sections to the Eucharist. In section 17, the Carmelite says, "I have infinite hunger and thirst to possess you personally and totally under the mantle of your loving sacrament, instituted in the force of the excess of your own love for me."[111] (Jean appears to have often had his ecstatic experiences in relation to receiving the Eucharist.) The reference to infinite hunger and thirst here touches on another aspect of how Jean treats of union, namely, his use of the language of the bride and the Bridegroom devouring each other in their mutual embraces (*personnellement et totalement engloutir*).[112] The excessive devouring force of the embraces of the two lovers can only end in death, the *mors mystica* that many mystics have referred to. Toward the end of her speech, the bride cries out, "Ah, my Love and my Bridegroom, if you hold me and grasp me more powerfully, you will doubtless make me die of gladness and love. It is true that I desire such a death so much that I already feel it infinitely sweet and delightful."[113] In section 48, the Bridegroom tells the bride that when she died in him of the "power of my excessively excessive love" she did not even plead with the angels "to surround you with flowers and sustain you with apples" (Song 2:5) in order to remain alive so that she could love him in a way "suitable and satisfactory to the insatiable famished longing of your loving desire" (ll. 857–65). Nonetheless, the soul continues to long for real death, because, as the Bridegroom tells her, union will only reach its perfect state in the eschatological joy of heaven (see sections 42–45).

Jean de Saint-Samson does not shy away from speaking of union as "without distinction or difference," the kind of language about a unity of indistinction often considered dangerous in mystics from Meister Eckhart on.[114] Like Eckhart, he sometimes even says this union involves a transformation that restores the soul to its original state of existence in the divine essence, its virtual being. One of the boldest uses of this language comes at the beginning of the Bridegroom's speech to the bride:

> . . . through this same action of the divine game [of love] [*action du jeu divine*] equally active in us both, I fill you and delight you through me and in me, and through all that I am, in whom you are totally transformed beyond all degrees of transforming love, since you have attained your original essence which I am [*ton essence originaire que je suis*], in which you will live and dwell like myself, without distinction or difference from myself, who am your rest, your total happiness, and your total paradise.[115]

Jean de Saint-Samson is a daring mystic who deserves to be better known.

Lawrence of the Resurrection

Lawrence of the Resurrection's life (1614–1691) extends beyond the chronological boundaries set for this volume, especially due to his posthumous involvement in the Quietist controversy, but he will be included here as a witness to how Discalced Carmelite mysticism moved into seventeenth-century France. Although formed within the tradition of Teresa, John of the Cross, and the Spanish Carmelite mystics of the early seventeenth century, Lawrence is a special voice—not quite the *idiota illiteratus* of Surin's young layman in the carriage, but a pious and unassuming cook and sandal maker of a community of reformed Carmelite friars in Paris. There is considerable irony in the story of this attractive figure and his subsequent audience. Due to the fact that François Fénelon cited him in support of his views in the *Maxims of the Saints*, as well because several early editions of Lawrence's works were produced by Protestant sympathizers of the Quietists, Brother Lawrence suffered an eclipse in French Catholicism. At the same time, he was being translated and widely read among German Pietists, English Methodists, Quakers, and many American Protestants.[116] Catholic students of mysticism finally woke up to the importance of Lawrence in the twentieth century, and it seems fair to say that he is now one of the most widely read and ecumenical mystical authors of the great century of French mysticism.[117]

The Discalced friars came to France in 1606 with a foundation in Avignon. By 1611 they had opened a house in Paris in the Rue Vaugirard. Born in Lorraine as Nicholas Herman, the young man experienced a mystical enlightenment at the age of eighteen but served for some years as a soldier in the Thirty Years' War.[118] Wounded in 1635, he entered the Paris Carmel in 1640 and was professed in 1642 with the name Lawrence of the Resurrection. His first ten years among the Carmelites was a period of intense inner trials, including a sense of damnation, such as we have seen in the case of Surin. In an autobiographical letter written to his spiritual director probably in 1683, he testifies that there were times "I thought I was willingly damning myself, that there was no salvation for me."[119] According to his biographer, "The fear of self-deception began to take strong hold of his heart, and his state appeared so uncertain that he no longer knew what would become of him. This consequently caused him such terrible torments that he could only convey them by comparing them to those of hell."[120] Convinced that he was damned, Brother Lawrence, again like Surin, made an act of perfect submission to God: "Without thinking of what would become of him, and without concerning himself with his sufferings (as troubled souls would do) he consoled himself by saying, 'Come what may, at least I will do everything for the love of God for the rest of my life.'"[121] Having come through the fire of mystical dereliction,

Brother Lawrence arrived at a state of inner peace, balance, and mystical insight.

A simple man without advanced education, Lawrence had, by the late 1650s and early 1660s, begun to acquire a reputation among those interested in the spiritual life. At this point, a learned Parisian cleric, Joseph de Beaufort (1635–1711), steps into the picture. Beaufort interviewed Lawrence several times in 1666–67 and eventually wound up gathering and editing his sparse writings, as well as composing two biographical accounts. Brother Lawrence was in ill health for many years, yet his fame as a holy person and spiritual guide grew and he received a number of important visitors, including Fénelon. He died at the age of seventy-seven on February 12, 1691. What we know of Brother Lawrence is largely due to Joseph de Beaufort, but there is little reason to think that it is a perversion of the Carmelite's simple, yet deep, message about the practice of the presence of God.

In his *Eulogy*, Fr. Beaufort tells us, "He [Lawrence] maintained that the practice of the presence of God was the shortest, easiest way to arrive at Christian perfection, the form and life of virtue, and the great protection from sin. He insisted that this practice required only courage, good will, and the truth of deeds rather than words" (*Eulogy* 32; trans., 13). As Lawrence himself put it in his *Spiritual Maxims*, "The holiest, most ordinary, and most necessary practice of the spiritual life is that of the presence of God. It is to take delight in and become accustomed to divine company, speaking humbly and conversing lovingly with Him all the time, at every moment" (*Maxims* 2.6; trans., 36). Chapters 5 and 6 of the *Maxims* form the heart of Lawrence's teaching. "The [practice of the] presence of God is an application of our mind to God, or a remembrance of God present, that can be brought about by the imagination or the understanding" (*Maxims* 5.20; trans., 39). Testifying to the fact that he has been practicing this "general and loving awareness of God" (*regard general et amoureux en Dieu*) for forty years, Lawrence says that the practice is a habit formed by constant acts of fixing the mind on God. While the exercise may be somewhat difficult in the beginning, it soon becomes easy. Lawrence recommends making use of short aspirations, such as "My God, I am completely yours"; or, "God of love, I love you with all my heart" (*Maxims* 6.30; trans., 41). Eventually, the practitioner can hope to reach the state of interior recollection that Beaufort describes as follows: "He [Lawrence] says that as soon as he is free from his occupations, and often even when he is most taken up with them, the recesses of his mind or the innermost depths of his soul are raised with no effort on his part and remain suspended [*demeure comme suspendue*] and fixed in God, above all things, as in its center and resting place."[122] The two main means to acquire the practice of the presence are "great purity of life" and "great fidelity to the practice." "We must take special care," he says, "that this inner awareness [*regard intérieur*], no matter how brief it may be, precedes our activities, that it accompanies them from time to time, and that we complete all of them in the same way. Since much time and effort are required to acquire this practice, we must not get discouraged when we fail, for the habit is only formed with effort, yet once it is formed we will find contentment in everything" (*Maxims* 6.27-29; trans, 41). The major benefits of the practice are an increase in faith, hope, and love that are open to all; God alone can grant the special grace given to a few in which the practice "becomes one continuous state, because the soul constantly practices this exercise in the presence of God" (*Maxims* 7.36; trans., 43).

Brother Lawrence's simple, yet profound, mystical teaching rests on a solid basis that has a distinct "Sanjuanist" flavor that he would have absorbed during his half-century in the Paris Carmel. Like John of the Cross, Lawrence emphasizes the three theological virtues, but especially faith. Over and over again, he insists on the importance of faith. As a passage in the *Ways of Brother Lawrence* puts it, "Faith was the only light he used, not only to know God in the beginning, but from that point on; he wanted only to be instructed and led by faith in all God's ways."[123] Without adopting the detailed anthropology of John of the Cross, or Teresa, and not setting forth any distinct mystical itinerary, Lawrence joins with his predecessors in insisting that the supreme contact with God takes place in the "depth and center of the soul."[124] Also like John of the Cross, he is suspicious of consolations from God, especially ecstasies and visions. What is essential is not spiritual pleasure but total surrender to God and the indifference to created things that accompanies this. Some of Lawrence's expressions of holy indifference indicate why Fénelon and after him Quietist sympathizers like Pierre Poiret liked to cite him. Fr. Beaufort reports, "He said that he thought neither of death, nor of his sins, nor of paradise, nor of hell, but only of doing little things for the love of God, since he was not capable of doing great things."[125] Also, according to Beaufort, "He admired nothing, nothing surprised him, and he feared nothing."[126]

For Lawrence of the Resurrection the goal of the practice of the presence of God is union, and chapter 4 of the *Spiritual Maxims* is devoted to union, which Lawrence divides into three kinds: habitual, virtual, and actual. Habitual union is union by grace; virtual union takes place in the course of actions in which we remain united to God (presumably in activities like mental prayer), while the most perfect form, actual union, is described as a divine intervention, a powerful stirring of the soul that is "more intense than fire and more luminous than the sun." Yet, paradoxically, it is also deeply apophatic: "It is, rather, an 'I don't know what,' of the soul, gentle, peaceful, spiritual, respectful, humble, loving, and very simple, that upholds us and incites us to love God, to adore him, and even embrace him with unspeakable tenderness that experience alone can enable us to understand."[127] This divine action takes place in the will, not the intellect, because the will can in some respect comprehend God by love. Lawrence says that "tastes and sentiments of the will are in the soul as in their object [*terme*], and its operation, which is properly love, terminates in God as in its end [*se termine à Dieu comme à son fin*]."[128]

The practical simplicity and depth of Brother Lawrence's message are evident in his handful of letters. His ecumenical popularity today can be at least partly explained by the fact that his practice of the presence of God is a good expression of what some modern theologians have called "everyday mysticism," that is, the conviction that God can be sought and found in every place and at every time. As Lawrence once put it, "It is a big mistake to think that the period of mental prayer should be different from any other. We must be just as closely united to God in our activities as we are during our times of prayer" (*Conversations* 4.46; trans., 98). Or again, and more concretely, it is illustrated in something Brother Lawrence once told Fr. Beaufort: "I flip my little omelette in the frying pan for the love of God, and when it's done, if I have nothing to do, I prostrate myself on the floor and adore my God who gave me the grace to do it, after which I get up happier than a king. When I can do nothing else, it is enough for me to pick up a straw from the ground for the love of God."[129]

Ursuline Mysticism and Marie de l'Incarnation

As noted in chapter 1, the spread of the Ursuline Order in France was one of the great success stories of French Catholicism after the Wars of Religion. No order appears to have set up more houses in the kingdom during the seventeenth century. The history of the Ursulines is also important for evaluating the contribution of women to what Bremond called the *invasion mystique* that swept over France in the first half of the seventeenth century. Women mystics in the Reformed Carmelites,

Reformed Benedictines, the new order of Visitandines, and others proliferated. Bremond's *Histoire* treated many of these women, but their sheer numbers show why there is still no general account of the women of this period. Bremond was also a pioneer in emphasizing the importance of the Ursuline mystic Marie de l'Incarnation, or Marie Martin, née Guyart (1599–1672), whom he dubbed the Teresa of New France.[130]

Next to Jeanne Guyon (1638–1717), the controversial Quietist whose story will be taken up in the next volume, Marie de l'Incarnation is the best known of the seventeenth-century French female mystics. Her extensive writings are available in modern editions;[131] English translations exist for many of her works,[132] and there is an extensive secondary literature, both in French and in English.[133] Marie's mysticism is presented primarily in two semi-autobiographical *Relations*, one of 1633 and the other of 1654, accounts of her spiritual life ordered (she says) by her confessors, and in the later case also requested by her son, Claude Martin (1619–1699), a Benedictine monk.[134] There is, however, more to her mystical oeuvre, notably 278 surviving letters (out of thousands), as well as some minor prose pieces. Both of the *Relations* and the *Letters* present the course of Marie's life story, suggesting that a good way to treat this important mystic is to begin biographically.[135]

Born in 1599 into a family of moderate means at Tours, Marie was married at seventeen to Claude Martin and was left a widow at nineteen with a young son also named Claude, who had been born in 1619.[136] From her infancy, Marie had been drawn to a life of piety, and she records having received a vision of Christ at the age of seven.[137] Her intense piety increased after the death of her husband. The young widow experienced a life-transforming conversion through a vision she received on March 24, 1620, the Feast of the Annunciation. While she was on her way to work, she suddenly had a powerful inner experience:

> Suddenly I was brought stock-still, both inwardly and outwardly. Even my thoughts were abruptly brushed aside. Then, in an instant, my inner eyes were opened and all the faults, sins, and imperfections that I had committed since my birth were shown to me in most vivid detail.... At the same moment I saw myself immersed in the blood of the Son of God, shed because of the sins which had been shown to me; and furthermore, realizing that it was for my salvation that this Precious Blood had been shed, I think I would have died in terror had God's goodness not sustained me.[138]

This experience of the redemptive power of the blood of Christ is reminiscent of Catherine of Siena, although Marie here emphasizes the personal and not the universal character of the redeeming blood. Marie often referred back to this decisive moment of her conversion to a higher mystical life.[139] During the next eleven years, however, Marie, along with her young son Claude, lived in her brother-in-law's house and assisted him in his business.

Despite Marie's difficulties and distractions, the years from 1620 to 1631 were the foundation of an extraordinary mystical career. Both the surviving fragments of the *Relation of 1633* and the later *Relation of 1654* witness to the events of this period, and Guy Oury has stressed the importance of her ten earliest letters written to her first confessor, the Feuillant Cistercian, Raymond of Saint-Bernard, as providing direct and unfiltered evidence for her mystical life at this early time.[140] In these letters, Marie describes periods of ecstatic union with the Incarnate Word as the Spouse of the soul; she also tells of visions granting insight into the three Persons of the Trinity and even of attaining union with them. These advanced mystical gifts did not preclude periods of desolation and suffering from the absence of the divine Lover. In the *Relation of 1633*, she also talks about reading mystical classics, such as Dionysius and Teresa of Avila, to help her understand what she was undergoing.[141] The stress for Marie, however, is always on her own experiences, not spiritual reading. A few texts will give us a sense of the richness of the early stages of her mystical journey.

Marie's first letter to Raymond of Saint-Bernard, probably written in 1626, opens with an Elevation to the divine majesty: "O breadth, O length, O depth, O height (Eph. 3:18), infinite, immense, incomprehensible, ineffable, adorable! You exist, O my great God, and all that is does not exist save insofar as it subsists in you and through you. O eternity, beauty, goodness, purity, cleanness, love, my center, my beginning, my end, my beatitude, my everything!"[142] She continues on an apophatic note, saying that wherever she finds herself, "I am not able to see myself save as absorbed and abyssed in that incomprehensible Being, nor regard creatures except in the same way." God is in all things and all things in God as "a great and vast ocean" that totally envelops her. Marie's Letter II (1626?) speaks of a vision of the Trinity, which appears to be the first of the three visions of the Trinity enumerated in the *Relation of 1654* (the three were given in 1625, 1627, and 1631). Some of the language the young widow uses is reminiscent of other French mystics, such as Pierre de Bérulle. Fragment 32, for example, describes special illuminations concerning the divine attributes. Here she launches into another rhetorical elevation praising God's attributes and then says, "After this great taste my spirit was occupied in each of the divine perfections, where it consummated itself in acts of adoration, admiration, annihilation and abandonment towards that great All"[143]

Marie enjoyed a special relation to the second Person, the Incarnate Word. The *Relation of 1633* describes a uniting of her heart with that of Jesus, a mystical experience similar to those recounted by other women (Fragment 27; ed., 1:191). She was also given an interior illumination "about the mystery of the Incarnation and the union of the Word with the sacred humanity of Jesus Christ" (Fragment 29; ed., 1:193). A crucial experience was that of Pentecost 1627, as recounted in the *Relation of 1633* and later in the "Eighth State of Prayer" in the *Relation of 1654*.[144] "At that moment," she says, "this adorable Person seized my soul and, embracing it with indescribable love, united it to himself, taking it as his spouse." She explains, "When I say he embraced it, this was not in the manner of human embraces. There is nothing sensual which approximates this divine action, but I must express myself in these earthly terms since we are composed of matter. It was through his divine touches and by being enfolded in his love that I in turn loved him in a union so complete that I was no longer aware of myself, having become one with him." Subsequently, Marie claims that "[t]he soul is kept continually in this loving ecstasy, no longer living in itself, but in him who keeps it wholly absorbed in his love." She says that afterward she read about such love union in the Song of Songs, although the depth of what she has experienced went far beyond human words.[145]

The *Relation of 1633* describes a number of other mystical experiences that took place in the period prior to 1631. For example, Marie underwent feelings of intense interior desolation, despite remaining convinced that she was still married to the divine Spouse (Fragment 31; 1:197-200). She also talks about how her union with Jesus was most strongly felt at the time of receiving communion, which she did almost daily (Fragments 13, 38-39, and 48; 1:170, 214-16, 227-28). Fragments 44-46 (1:224-26) feature a reflection on the *mors mystica*, or loving death of the soul in the embrace of the Divine Lover. Marie also testifies to having received the "wound of love" like Teresa of Avila. Fragment 50 speaks of how her heart suffered new inflammations and felt like it was broken in pieces in a form of martyrdom: "I felt these blows in my heart as if someone pierced me. This was not an imagination, but I really suffered this, which caused me extreme pain, but it was also very pleasing and one would want to have it repeated without cease" (1:230-31).

The Ursulines had established a convent at Tours in 1622, and after much deliberation Marie decided to enter that house on January 25,

1631. In large part Marie's choice of the Ursulines over the stricter life of the reformed female Cistercians (Feuillantines) was based in her commitment to a life where contemplation could co-exist with apostolic action.[146] Her decision to embrace religious life was controversial, since it involved abandoning her eleven-year-old son, Claude.[147] Such "abandonment" of a child had a long history in Christian hagiography about giving up all things, including family, for the single-minded pursuit of the kingdom of God (see Matt. 10:37). This was similar to what Jane de Chantal had done when she left her children to help Francis de Sales found the Visitandines, although Marie went further, breaking with seventeenth-century convention by not leaving Claude any patrimony. Such acts, hard to comprehend today, have recently come in for renewed study, if not to condone them, at least to try to make them more understandable to modern readers whose expectations and experiences of family and mother–child relationships are so different.[148]

Marie flourished in the religious life, though not without gnawing doubts about having left her only child behind. In 1633, her Jesuit confessor, George de la Haye, ordered her to write down the story of her mystical gifts, the *Relation of 1633*. Marie's visions and ecstasies continued during the early years of her religious life. One of the most striking accounts is that of an annihilating union with the Trinity found in Fragment 67 of the 1633 *Relation*, an event that presumably dates to around 1631–32.[149] Marie says that the experience began in her cell on the Feast of the Guardian Angels. Her spirit was powerfully drawn to Christ, the Master of the angels, who united her to himself but also gave her a sense that a more powerful gift was to come. Her agitation over this lasted for several hours until she had to go to the chapel for prayers. Here, in front of the Blessed Sacrament, she felt a great tenderness that completely changed her as her senses began to fail. "Instantly," she says, "my understanding was illumined with a vision of the Most Holy Trinity which revived my knowledge of its grandeurs. Then by a profound love, this whole Divine Majesty united itself to my soul, giving itself to me with an outpouring I would never know how to explain." All three Persons absorbed her in such a way that she simultaneously saw herself in all three, "Or, to put it better, I saw myself in both their Unity and their Trinity simultaneously." She saw herself as a "pure nothing abyssed in the All" (*pur néant abîmé dans le Tout*).[150] This constituted a joy similar to that of the Blessed in heaven, and she goes on to say, "I understood once again that it was here I found real annihilation of my soul in God by a true union of love." In this "profound union" Marie sensed herself totally taken over by the Trinity: "My actions never came from myself but were produced in me by him in whom I was totally lost. He gave himself completely to me and I let him take everything to himself."

By 1635 Marie was beginning to instruct the other nuns, as can be seen in her *Expositions on the Song of Songs*.[151] As the result of a dream vision, however, she became convinced that God wanted her to go to New France (Canada) to help convert the native peoples to the Christian religion. In this revelation, the apostolic aspect of her mysticism was given a new direction. As with Teresa of Avila, for Marie it was not enough to be an ecstatic contemplative; she felt the call to be a contemplative in action.[152] Against strong odds, but with the financial support of powerful patrons, Marie and a group of nuns were able to leave for Canada in 1639. Marie-Florine Bruneau speaks of Marie's "triple vocation of mystic, missionary, and historiographer of the New World."[153]

Founded in 1609, the French colony in cold Quebec grew slowly and is said to have had only about two to three hundred inhabitants when Marie and the first group of Ursulines arrived after a difficult voyage. Marie may have hoped to take up a more active missionary role, but the local ecclesiastical officials insisted on full cloister. Nonetheless by setting up schools for the native Amerindian girls, Marie and the other Ursulines did have a remarkable apostolate in Canada over more than thirty years. She and her community "acculturated" (to use a modern term) to some degree, at least within the limits set by seventeenth-century society and religion. Their cloister school sought to convert, instruct, and "civilize" the indigenous women. As a part of this process, Marie learned several of the Indian languages and taught and wrote catechetical materials in them. All the while, however, she was engaged in an intense, often difficult, inner spiritual journey. Since 1641, her son Claude, who had entered the Benedictine Order, had been writing her about their conflicted history and her own spiritual path.[154] After numerous solicitations, and with the approval of her Jesuit confessor, Jerome Lalemant, she finally sent him her spiritual autobiography, the *Relation of 1654*. Marie insisted that this text was for Claude's eyes alone, an injunction he observed until after her death in 1672. Then Claude, now an important scholar in the Reformed Benedictine community of Saint-Maur in Paris, moved into high gear to edit (extensively) and publish his mother's writings, as well as a *Life of the Venerable Marie of the Incarnation*, all of which appeared in 1677. The irony of this is that the young Claude, whose abandonment is portrayed so movingly in the correspondence between him and "his most cruel mother," became the shaper of her story and subsequent fame. Perhaps this is what she had hoped for all along.[155]

The mystical journey laid out in the *Relation of 1654* is striking and sometimes puzzling.[156] It does not conform to traditional mystical itineraries, especially the threefold pattern of purification, illumination, and union, but rather follows a life story that mingles states of ecstatic union with periods of inner trial and experiences of desolation. Although the text has been described as "mystagogical" in the sense that it was designed in part to inspire Claude to a life of mystical prayer, it is scarcely meant as a model for others in the manner of Teresa's *Interior Castle*. It is Marie's story, not a paradigm of the mystical life in general. The thirteen sections into which Marie divides the book are chronological. Although she calls them "states of prayer" (*états d'oraison*), they do not provide formal teaching about modes of prayer (e.g., meditation, contemplation, prayer of quiet, etc.), but rather reveal the story of Marie's relations to God. The *Relation* is too rich to try to present all the mystical experiences the Ursuline recounts, but a sketch of the thirteen stages with comments on a few of the more noteworthy incidents will give a sense of this remarkable mystical text.

The "First State of Prayer" (I in vol. 2:160–73; trans., 41–48) tells the story of Marie's life up to the time of the death of her husband in 1620. The "Second State of Prayer" (II in vol. 2:181–203; trans., 49–55), dealing with the period 1620–22, begins with the life-altering vision of the blood of Jesus. Even at this initial stage, Marie testifies that she was given "an intimate bond [*liaison*] with Our Lord Jesus Christ in all his sacred mysteries from his birth to his death" (2:190; trans., 53). Under the guidance of the Feuillant fathers, she tried to use Ignatian methods of meditation but found that they gave her headaches, although she says she was assisted by reading Francis de Sales's *Introduction to the Devout Life* (2:192; trans., 55). Marie also took a vow of chastity at this time. The "Third State of Prayer" (III in vol. 2:200–203; trans., 56–57) is a relatively brief account of some of her early mystical experiences that apparently also took place in 1622. The "Fourth State of Prayer" (IV in vol. 2:205–32; trans., 58–64), which treats the period from 1622 to 1624/25, is a rich account of a variety of mystical gifts. Marie says that she experienced a continuing inner colloquy with the God-man in her understanding and will. She emphasizes the purity of heart and total abandonment to divine providence necessary to be immersed in the "great ocean" that is God (a favored image). She also describes a "state of prayer which withdraws the support coming from the sacred humanity of Our Lord" (2:208; trans., 59), which she says is a gift that enabled her soul to advance by working lovingly for her neighbor in patient humility. In this state, Marie came to see the need for a spiritual director, and her Feuillant confessor apparently encouraged her in the extreme mortifications she undertook during these years. Here we also find emphasis on the Bérullian teaching on the nothingness of the soul, as well as a strong erotic fixation and attaining the "kiss of the mouth" (Song 1:1). Marie testifies that her love for the Divine Bridegroom gave her both inner peace and intense suffering—"In another respect divine love keeps it [the soul] in agony, an agony which it feels keenly but cannot express" (2:216; trans., 64).

In the "Fifth State of Prayer" (V in vol. 2:218-32; trans., 65-73), treating 1625, Marie speaks about her call to the religious life, where she was convinced she would be able to enjoy the perfect practice of the poverty, chastity, and obedience that she had already adopted in private vows. At this time, however, Marie also began to experience the first of the many series of inner trials that afflicted her throughout her life. She was tempted to give up her severe penances; she worried about the future of her son whom she loved very much, and she experienced inner doubts, fears, and restlessness. Nonetheless, she abandoned herself to God, knowing that the trials were sent to purify her soul. The alternation of suffering and consolation is evident in the fact that it was during this same period that Marie experienced the exchange of hearts with Jesus referred to above.[157]

The "Sixth State of Prayer" (VI in vol. 2:233-46; trans., 74-80) features the first of the three visions of the Trinity recounted in the *Relation*. This theological showing of the Trinity and the highest choir of angels took place in May 1625. Marie speaks of the generation and spiration of the interchange of the three Persons, and says, ". . . in a flash I understood the unity, the distinctions, and the operations both within the divine Persons and those which culminate outside them" (2:234; trans., 74). Such theological language leads one to think that this vision was likely to have been retouched by Claude before he published it. This vision took place in "a very clear light," and Marie takes the opportunity to describe the three kinds of light that come from God: pure light; light and love intermingled; and pure love. She analyzes these gifts with frequent references to the Song of Songs,[158] noting that they are part of the preparation for the spiritual marriage. As she continues to describe the "intimate caresses" that lead up to spiritual marriage in the second part of State VI, Marie not only uses passages from the Song but also makes an appeal to the ineffability of the soul's experience (one of many such appeals). She says that she never heard or read anything to equal what she has experienced, perhaps because the spiritual authors preferred not to speak of them out of reverence, or perhaps because they feared to scandalize people (2:242; trans., 78). Finally, after the Trinitarian illumination Marie says she spent almost a year in ecstatic enlightenments concerning the divine attributes, which inner experiences did not, however, prevent her from performing her customary works of charity. Again, the union of contemplation and action is vital.

During the period from 1627 to 1631, Marie underwent the "Seventh State of Prayer" (VII in vol. 2:251–75; trans., 81–95). This state opens with the second vision of the Trinity received in May 1627, one that was directed more toward pouring love into the will than understanding into the intellect. The account closes with Marie's entry into the Ursuline monastery in Tours. We have already looked at this second vision and the accompanying marriage to the Word above, so here I note only some of the special graces that went along with the spiritual marriage. The soul now has no further desires, says Marie, because it possesses the Divine Lover, having passed away in a gentle and sweet death (VII.23). Although she continues to burn inwardly in the fire of divine love, Marie describes how she is outwardly active in instructing, consoling, and nursing the many workers in her brother-in-law's business. Marie's inner bridal song to her Lover, nevertheless, often made it difficult for her to concentrate on outer activities. The loving touch and embrace of the Bridegroom also involves suffering and fiery purification (VII.25). Eventually, the sweetness of her union with the Word produced a state of serenity in both the higher and lower parts of her nature (VII.27).

Marie de l'Incarnation, mystic and novice, rapidly adapted to the Ursuline life, as we see in the account of the "Eighth State of Prayer" (VIII in vol. 2:279–99; trans., 96–107). This period lasted from 1631 down to her full profession on January 25, 1633. After her entrance as a novice, Marie continued to enjoy inner loving union with the Incarnate Word, although she sensed that another great grace was soon to be given her. This was the third of her visions of the Trinity. This half-hour transport in which the Father, Son, and Holy Spirit came to completely possess her soul is described in language fairly close to the account given in the *Relation of 1633* discussed above.[159] Marie says that singing in choir "took me so completely out of myself that as I went about the monastery I was in a constant state of ecstasy. It was the same while I was at work" (VIII.34; trans., 102). All was not well, however, because Marie also tells of how she was assailed by diabolical temptations. The devil even appeared to her and tried to take over her body in the way the malign spirit was thought to have done to the contemporary Ursulines of Loudun (VIII.35). Meanwhile her Feuillant confessor, Fr. Raymond, had left Tours, so Marie took the Jesuit George de la Haye as her confessor, an able and sympathetic director who calmed her fears, and, despite her reluctance, ordered her to begin writing down her mystical experiences in the *Relation of 1633*.

The "Ninth State of Prayer" (IX in vol. 2:302–19; trans., 108–18), detailing events from 1633 to 1635, is important for the information it provides about Marie's entry into an apostolic mode of life. She had already been given the gift of uniting contemplation and action, but now the active aspect of her vocation was to take a distinctive apostolic turn. Once again, this new stage happened by means of a visionary experience, in this case a dream vision of Christmas, 1633. In it Marie saw the Blessed Virgin with the infant Jesus atop a little church in "a great, vast country, full of mountains and valleys and thick fogs," which she was to later recognize as Canada, her special place for exercising her apostolic calling (IX.37). The Blessed Virgin kissed Marie twice, but the mystery of the vision was hidden from her until she realized that the kiss of the Virgin was a sign that, although she could not travel through the world to win souls, she could do what she could by instructing the young sisters within the novitiate (IX.38). This was a foretaste of what she would do in Canada for over thirty years. The Virgin's kisses were the sign of entering into a new state: "At the age of thirty-four, or thirty-five, I entered into that state which, as it were, had been shown me and of which I had remained in expectation. This is an outpouring of apostolic spirit, . . . which took possession of my soul so that it could no longer live except in him and by him" (2:309–10; trans., 112). Marie's imagination (like that of the later Thérèse de Lisieux) wandered wide over the globe, imagining how she might spread knowledge of the gospel, but the real call came to her in a subsequent vision that made it clear that the "great, vast country" she had seen was Canada, the New France that the French were seeking to exploit for both financial and religious reasons. "The country of Canada," she says, "was my home and my country" (IX.41). The Ninth State of Prayer, then, has nothing to do with new ways of praying but is an expression of Marie's increasing apostolic commitment. The brief account of the "Tenth State of Prayer" (X in vol. 2:323–33; trans., 119–24) forms a kind of coda to this, describing the time between about 1635 and 1639 when Marie wrestled over how to fulfill her apostolic calling to go to Canada.

The final three "States of Prayer" recount the long period in Marie's life between her setting sail for Canada in 1639 and late 1654, when she sent her spiritual journal off to her son Claude. Mother Marie de l'Incarnation had almost another twenty years to live, and her later teaching is available to us in the more than 120 letters that survive from the period 1654–1671, but we will not take these up here. The "Eleventh State of Prayer" (XI in vol. 2:339–59; trans., 119–35) is mostly autobiographical, recounting the events of 1638–39 leading up to her departure for Canada. Marie's raptures and inner loving conversations with Jesus continued, although she had to deal with doubts and external objections concerning the Canadian venture. Nonetheless, God sent her a three-day rapture in which she saw everything that was later to happen in New France (XI.46). Finally, all difficulties were overcome and Marie and several other nuns, along with Madame de la Peltrie, who had financed the expedition, set sail on May 4, 1639. After a difficult and dangerous three-month voyage, they reached Quebec on August 1 (XI.47).

The long accounts of the Twelfth and Thirteenth States of Prayer (roughly 1639–42 and 1643–53) are not easy to follow, especially because they veer back and forth between descriptions of ongoing union with her Divine Spouse in the "center of the soul" and accounts of intense inner sufferings, diabolical temptations, and descriptions of mystical dereliction.[160] Thus, the negative side of the mystical path for Marie de l'Incarnation was not a stage along the way to permanent higher enjoyment but was a constant aspect of her life of loving union and apostolic service. What emerges clearly in these last parts of the *Relation of 1654* is the need for accepting the condition of absolute victimhood in relation to God, whatever consolations might be given or withdrawn.

The "Twelfth State of Prayer" (XII in vol. 2:367–412; trans., 136–55) provides information about the early days of the new Ursuline house in Quebec with its five sisters, but is largely given over to the account of Marie's "dark night" experiences that began in 1639 and lasted intermittently until 1647. Marie says that she soon lost the inner peace she had enjoyed during the voyage, and because the powers of her soul had been annihilated at their center by God, she felt plunged into darkness. "While in this state," she goes on, "I entered into another yet more painful. I saw myself, it seemed to me, despoiled of all the gifts and graces God had given me, as well as of all my talents, both interior and exterior." This feeling of self-contempt grew strong to the extent that she saw herself as far from God, even at the mouth of hell:

> I saw myself as though plunged into hell, full of sadness and bitterness arising from a temptation to despair which was born in the darkness I did not understand. I would have been lost if God had not sustained me by a secret strength. Sometimes I was suddenly brought to a halt and it seemed to me that I actually saw myself on the brink of hell with flames pouring forth from the mouth of the abyss to engulf me. I felt impelled to let go and hurl myself down to displease God whom this impulse led me to hate.[161]

Marie says she also had a desire to throw herself into hell to satisfy God's justice regarding her sinfulness, although a simple act of faith drew her back from the precipice. Poised between defiance of God and willingness to be damned for God if that should be his will, Marie says that her inner suffering was like being in Purgatory, but a Purgatory where she never lost sight of the Word Incarnate, who was purifying all her powers, although not affecting the "center of the soul," which was always his pure dwelling place. The temptation to throw herself into hell over contempt for God caused her to feel that she was condemned for all eternity, a situation attested to by John of the Cross and a number of other mystics (XII.52).[162]

The "revolt of the passions," as Marie terms it, lasted three years and was accompanied by intense feelings of aversion toward the people around her. She saw all this as a painful but necessary part of the purging of the last remnants of sinfulness from her life: "The critical and jealous spirit of pure love is inexorable and makes itself obeyed without compromise, for it forces the soul to recognize and experience that the spirit of love is the enemy of both compromise and relapse" (XII.54; trans., 148). In this paradoxical condition, the Incarnate Word continued to dwell in the center of the soul in "an intimate habitual and continuous union" (*une union intime, habituelle et continuelle*) while the imperfections in the powers were being purged until the soul could abandon everything in a "total annihilation" (*entier anéantissement*) (XII.55).

The "Thirteenth State of Prayer" (XIII in vol. 2:418–66; trans., 156–78) covers the period from 1647 to ca. 1653. It opens by noting that, through the assistance of the Blessed Virgin, the nun was finally freed from "the revolt of my passions and my temptations to aversion" on August 15, 1647. The Ursuline was now free to enjoy the peace and insights from her habitual union with Incarnate Word (XIII.61). At the end of 1650, the monastery burned to the ground, an unfortunate event which Marie accepted "in loving conformity to the holy will of God" (XIII.62). The thirteenth state recounts the decision to rebuild the monastery, which was not completed until 1653. During the rebuilding process Marie was sustained by a new experience of inner union with the Blessed Virgin (XIII.64). True poverty of spirit and a sense of victimhood had been important to Marie since the time of her conversion. Now, toward the end of her account, she launches into a more theological and didactic mode in "a little discourse to explain the despoilment of the soul, the state of victim, and true and substantial spiritual poverty" (XIII.65).

This "little discourse" of chapter 66 forms a recapitulation and culmination of Marie's inner journey based on a theological analysis of her inner states rather than the kind of description of experiences found in the previous states of prayer.[163] She says that God created the free rational soul with a destiny to reach toward its highest good. God aids it in this search, providing "streams of light and fire" that allow the soul to attain holy raptures (Song 1:4 and 8:4 are cited). But the soul is enjoying *its* pleasure in these states and therefore lacks the absolute interior purity that God as the jealous Lover demands—hence, the process of painful purgation of the soul that Marie had experienced throughout her life, especially since she arrived in Canada. First, the sensitive and lower parts must undergo excruciating privations. It is at this point that the distinction between the lower and higher parts of the soul can be discerned, she says, but this is only the first step in the state of victimhood. The higher part of the soul (memory, understanding, and will) is still enjoying light and love, but "the Spirit of God, who wants everything for himself," now suspends the intellect and renders it incapable of its ordinary acts. The will, however, still enjoys intimacy with her Divine Spouse. It too must be conquered by the Divine Spirit, the source of all purity. The Spirit suspends the will, just as he had suspended the memory and intellect. "Behold, then, the victim," says Marie, "in that state in which the Spirit of God, loving infinitely the purity of souls espoused to the Son of God, reduces them in order to bring them to that condition where he wishes to take his pleasure in them" (2:458; trans., 173). The Spirit's action is profoundly painful, especially because the soul cannot delight in religious things. The will is dead, although the soul in its unity and center remains embraced by the Word and shares with him "a sweet and loving breath which never ends [*un respir doux et moureux qui ne finit point*], the exchange of spirit to Spirit and from spirit into Spirit" (2:459; trans., 174). Even this breath, however, is imperfect and must go. "He consumes this," says Marie, "and here at last is the sacrifice of the victim, and here, finally, that true pure, and essential purity of spirit."[164] This is the culminating mystical state of the Ursuline, finally attained in the 1650s, although the process had been ongoing since her conversion in 1620.[165] It is a form of imitation of Christ, especially Christ sacrificed on the cross for the salvation of humanity.[166] Victimhood was to remain her ideal for the remainder of her life. In one of the last letters Marie wrote to her son Claude in October, 1671, she says, "I do not want anything more for you or for me than the perpetual state of being a victim."[167]

Marie de l'Incarnation is the first major transatlantic mystic. Her apostolic mysticism was formed and nurtured in France, but her particular path to loving union with her Divine Bridegroom was brought to fruition in the "new place" of Canada to which she journeyed, both geographically and spiritually.

Appendix
Jansenism and Mysticism: The Case of Blaise Pascal

Seventeenth-century France had a profound effect on modern Catholicism not only due to the many religious orders founded at the time, as well as the mystics we have reviewed, but also because it saw the origins of two great theological controversies that have troubled Catholicism almost down to the present. One of these was directly mystical, the Quietist debate over the relation of active religious practice and passive states of pure love. The history and implications of Quietism are too large to be taken up in this volume but will be the starting place for volume 7 of *The Presence of God*. The other movement, one given the perhaps inadequate name of Jansenism, was primarily a theological dispute over grace and free choice and its implications for Christian living, although, because of the latter aspect, it included important spiritual dimensions.[168] To some extent Jansenism was a continuation of the debates over the heritage of Augustine that had marked Western Christianity since the fifth century and that had flared up significantly in the sixteenth century in Catholic and Protestant polemics.

The public starting point of the Jansenist controversy was the posthumous publication in 1640 of the vast tome *Augustinus* of the little-known Low Countries bishop Cornelius Jansen (1585–1638). The strict predestinarian views of the late Augustine, revived by Jansen and his followers, roiled the rest of the seventeenth century and continued on into the eighteenth century. The pessimism and moral rigorism of Jansenism, or the Jansenist spirit, continued to affect aspects of modern Catholicism far beyond 1800. Jansenism was primarily a theological and moral movement, not a mystical one, but it did attract Blaise Pascal (1623–1662), one of the premier figures in French religious and intellectual history, and certainly a mystic, at least in his last years.[169]

Jansen's intention was to mount an attack on what he thought of as laxist views regarding the relation of the necessity of efficacious grace and the role of human freedom in Counter-Reformation theology, especially that of the Jesuits (e.g., Luis de Molina). His return to Augustinian predestinarianism and pessimism also had a strong moral component, featuring a rigorist view of spiritual practice and ecclesiastical discipline and a restricted view of access to the Eucharist as a sacrament too holy for frequent reception. On the theoretical side, the Jansenists attacked the system of probabilism, the view that in questions of moral conduct it is lawful to follow any solidly probable opinion, even though the opposing view may be more probable. Probabilism too was often associated with the Jesuits.[170]

In writing the *Augustinus*, Jansen was aided by his friend, Jean Duvergier de Hauranne, abbé de Saint-Cyran (1581–1643), a noted scholar. Saint-Cyran was friendly with many of the key religious figures of the day, such as Vincent de Paul, Pierre de Bérulle, and Jean-Jacques Olier. He too sought a strict Augustinian reform of theology and morals. Saint-Cyran was close to the important aristocratic Arnauld family whom he won over to the Jansenist cause. In 1635, he became the spiritual director of the female Cistercian abbey of Port-Royal in Paris, which was led first by Angélique Arnauld and then by her sister, Agnès Arnauld. These two women and their niece and later abbess, Angélique de Saint-Jean, were important female leaders of the Jansenist party, as well as religious thinkers in their own right. Antoine Arnauld (1612–1694), the young brother of Angélique and Agnès, was ordained in 1641 and immediately retired to Port-Royal, where he began extensive writings in favor of the Jansenist position. After the death of Saint-Cyran, he emerged as the theological leader of the group, especially through his widely popular *Frequent Communion* (*De la fréquente communion*) of 1643 (he was against it), and *Apologies for Jansenius* (*Apologies de M. Jansénius*) of 1644. Both Saint-Cyran and Arnauld attracted the ire of the Jesuits and the theologians of the Sorbonne, but they had many supporters among the serious-minded clergy, religious, and aristocracy. The key moment in the history of early Jansenism came in 1653, when Pope Innocent X condemned five propositions taken from Jansen's *Augustinus*. The Jansenist defense of their position in the following dispute involved a distinction between fact (*fait*) and law (*droit*), namely, that the pope was correct in law to condemn these five positions as heretical, but in fact they were not actually found in the *Jansenius*. The denouement of this complex quarrel cannot delay us here.

Blaise Pascal was recognized as a genius from his earliest years. His first major contributions were made in mathematics and physics, including the invention of a calculating machine. While living in Rouen in 1646, he came in contact with the Jansenist Deschamps brothers and became sympathetic with the movement. Back in Paris, he read widely in Augustine, the works of Saint-Cyran and Arnauld, and especially the Bible. His sister Jacqueline entered Port-Royal in 1652, and he made long visits there. Previously a rather mediocre practitioner of his faith, Pascal grew more and more serious, but his religious life was intellectually and personally unsatisfying, and in September 1654 he wrote his sister complaining about his spiritual state as being one of "quiet desperation." God intervened on the night of November 23, 1654, in the form of a grace whose brief narrative is among the most famous texts of mystical conversion in Christian history. Pascal immediately wrote down an account of the event, which he says lasted about two hours. He then sewed this paper, the *Memorial*, into his coat, where it was discovered after his death. Although the original is lost, we can be confident of the authenticity of what has been handed down.[171]

Pascal was not a trained theologian, but he did know the Bible exceedingly well. The *Memorial* is a tissue of biblical citations, combined with his own brief exclamations, petitions, and comments on what had taken place. The most obvious biblical resonance comes at the beginning: "FIRE. God of Abraham, God of Isaac, God of Jacob, not of the philosophers and scholars." This cannot but recall the theophany of Exodus 3:2–6, God's appearance to Moses in the burning bush, where He announces himself to the frightened Moses with the same formula. Pascal then sets down brief words to hint at what he felt: "Certainty, certainty, heartfelt [*sentiment*], joy, peace." Pascal, like Moses but unlike the carnal Jews, had encountered "The God of Jesus Christ," as testified to both by the New Testament ("My God and your God"; John 20:17) and by the Old ("Thy God shall be my God"; Ruth 1:16). The impact of the encounter is then drawn out with further brief axioms: "The world forgotten and everything but God. He can only be found by the ways taught in the Gospels. Greatness of the human soul. 'O righteous Father, the world had not known thee, but I have known thee' (John 17:25)." The first part concludes with another expression of rapture: "Joy, joy, joy, tears of joy."

The second part of the *Memorial* emphasizes Pascal's reflection on his sinful past and conversion to a new life. "I have cut myself off from him," he says, followed by a scriptural text relating to abandonment of God (Jer. 11:13). Then comes a tortured question, "My God wilt thou forsake me?" (Matt. 27:46), and a prayer, "Let me not be cut off from him forever!" The only way not to be cut off is by adhering to Christ. Here Pascal quotes John 17:3: "And this is life eternal, that they might know thee, the only true God, and Jesus Christ whom thou has sent." The rest of the second part is a repetition of the confession of sin, a fervent petition, and a resolution for the future: "I have cut myself off from him, shunned him, denied him, crucified him. Let me never be cut off from him! He can only be kept by the ways taught in the Gospel. Sweet and total renunciation." Finally, there are three additional lines, not found in all copies of the text, but seemingly authentic. These comprise a maxim of surrender ("Total submission to Jesus Christ and my director"), a reflection on the reward for this ("Everlasting joy in return for one's day's effort on earth"), and a final promise taken from the Bible ("I will not forget thy word"; Ps. 119:16).

Among the many remarkable things about the *Memorial* is that Pascal does not attempt to describe the actual experience beyond the powerful invocation of *FEU* at the start, thus implicitly emphasizing the ineffable nature of the revelation. What he describes are the effects of the experience on his inner state, his confession of sin, his resolutions for the future, as well as the repeated plea "not to be cut off." The text is thus a summary of Pascal's whole life: past sin, present enlightenment, and future resolution. Pascal thought of the experience as a divine sign that he was numbered among the elect; it gave him the foundation for the last eight years of his life, during which he devoted himself to prayer, acts of severe asceticism, and the desire to spread the deeply Augustinian message that we can do no good on our own, but only through the grace of Jesus Christ.[172]

Although Pascal denied being a full-fledged member of the Jansenist faction on several occasions, after the November 1654 experience he became more closely associated with Port-Royal and its adherents. This involved him in his most polemical, satiric, and popular writing, *The Provincial Letters (Les Provinciales)*, which began to appear in January of 1656 (there were eighteen in all). Arnauld was in danger of condemnation by the doctors of the Sorbonne and appealed to Pascal to help in his defense. Hence, *The Provincial Letters*, which, perhaps unfairly but nonetheless brilliantly, set forth the major theological issues about grace and freedom and related matters in an accessible and entertaining style that delighted the public. The main target was the Jesuits, who were skewered with such skill that all their attempts to answer the charges did little to limit the damage. *The Provincials*, however, do not represent what Pascal really wanted to do, which was to construct a convincing rational defense of rigorous (i.e., real) Christianity, a systematic work he intended to call *Apologie de la Religion Chrétienne*.

Pascal's health, never strong, had begun to fade, so that by the time that he undertook serious work on his apology, his memory had weakened and he began to write down his thoughts ca. 1656–58 on pieces of paper that he was only partially able to organize before his death. These dossiers, plus a mass of uncollected materials, were put together posthumously by his disciples and titled *Pensées*, first published in 1670. The *Pensées*, universally recognized as Pascal's most enduring work, is disorganized and unfinished, and perhaps for that reason immensely attractive in the way in which it invites the reader to think along with and even complete Pascal's brilliant, if at times obscure, insights and observations.[173]

The *Pensées* is an apologetic work, not a mystical one, although it touches on important mystical themes. This collection of thoughts is based on the grace given Pascal in the mystical experience of 1654 and what had guided his life of severe asceticism and contemplative piety in his declining years. It was, in a sense, a witness to a mystical life, rather than being an attempt to set it in words. Nonetheless, the *Pensées* give us insight into the mind and heart of a profound thinker and a remarkable mystic. Pascal's final years were difficult. His health continued to decline. The *Provincial Letters* were condemned and burned in 1660. There was much agonizing by Pascal and other Jansenists at Port-Royal about whether to sign the various "Formularies" drawn up by the French clergy to ensure obedience to the papal condemnation of Jansenius. Ill and worn out, Pascal died on August 19, 1662, just over thirty-nine years of age.

A full treatment of the *Pensées* would demand attention to its philosophical, theological, apologetic, and biblical dimensions. That cannot be done here. I will briefly touch on some major themes and concentrate on those sections that are particularly relevant for his mysticism. One of the best entries into Pascal's thought is section XI of part 1 entitled "At Port-Royal" (No. 149). Pascal starts with an evocation of a fundamental theme: "Man's greatness and wretchedness are so evident that the true religion must necessarily teach us that there is in man some great principle of greatness and some great principle of wretchedness. It must also account for such amazing contradictions."[174] So, the true religion must show that there is a God whom we are bound to love and who is our sole bliss. It must also acknowledge our darkness and unrighteousness due to sin. Finally, "It must account for the way in which we thus go against God and our own true good. It must teach us the cure for our helplessness and the means of obtaining this cure" (ibid.). The philosophers and other religions are not up to this task, but "the Wisdom of God" speaks and gives an account of creation, Fall, and man's present wretchedness. The wisdom of the philosophers cannot relieve man of the pride and concupiscence that block his way to God. Recognition of our vileness leads us to be aware that we know as little of our own selves and our capacities as we do of God's nature, so it is only the humility that admits that "since we do not know of ourselves what we are, we can learn it only from God" (trans., 79) that will help us. Another text written at Port-Royal sums up the dialectic of wretchedness and greatness thus: "It is certain that as man's insight increases so he finds both wretchedness and greatness within himself. In a word man knows he is wretched. Thus he is wretched because he is so, but he is truly great because he knows it."[175]

In No. 149, Wisdom turns to salvation history, saying, "I mean to show you clearly, by convincing proofs, marks of divinity within me which will convince you of what I am, and establish my authority by miracles and proofs that you cannot reject, so that you will then believe the things I teach" (trans., 79). Here the apologetic nature of the *Pensées* is clearly to the fore. The first of the teachings that Wisdom summarizes is that of God's predestinating will to redeem humanity. Some seek the way of salvation, but other men "have shown themselves so unworthy that it is right for God to refuse some, for their hardness of hearts, what he grants to others by a mercy they have not earned" (ibid.). That is why Wisdom incarnate in Jesus Christ comes in a hidden fashion so as to be recognized only by those who sincerely sought him. Wisdom concludes, "There is enough light for those who desire only to see, and enough darkness for those of contrary disposition" (trans., 80). It is no accident that this apt summary of the Jansenist position was written at Port-Royal itself.

The text from Port-Royal raises the question of the role that fallen reason and human knowing play in the process of redemption. Helpful in this connection is Pascal's teaching about the three incommensurable orders found in human nature. No. 45 says that both of the principles of truth (reason and the senses) deceive us. This is because they are part of three basic orders that are the foundation of three different types of persons. No. 931 clarifies: "There are three orders: flesh, mind and will. The carnal are rich men and kings. Their interest is in the body. Inquirers and scholars: their interest is in the mind. The wise: their interest is in what is right."[176] The reason that pertains to the world of inquirers and scholars is real but limited. Its use is indispensable throughout the *Pensées*, but Pascal uses reason to show the limits of reason in the search for real truth and ultimate happiness. Section XIII on "Submission and the Use of Reason" contains striking formulations on the use and limits of reason. No. 173, for example, says, "If we submit everything to reason our religion will be left with nothing mysterious or supernatural. If we offend the principles of reason our religion will be absurd and ridiculous." Or Nos. 182 and 183, which state, "There is nothing so consistent with reason as this denial of reason;" and "Two excesses: to exclude reason, to admit nothing but reason."[177]

Above and beyond reason is the realm of wisdom, the heart, and charity. The heart too is a source of truth. "We know the truth," says Pascal in *Pensée* 110, "not only through our reason but also through our heart. It is through the latter that we know first principles, and reason, which has nothing to do with it, tries in vain to refute them."[178] The knowledge that comes from the heart and instinct is what reason has to base all its argument on: "Principles are felt, propositions proved, and both with certainty though by different means" (ibid.). Pascal expresses the wish that we could know everything by instinct and feeling, but nature determines that most of what we know comes from reasoning, only a bit through the heart. This reaches into the core of Pascal's apologetics: "That is why those to whom God has given religious faith by moving their hearts are very fortunate, and feel quite legitimately convinced, but to those who do not have it we can only give such faith through reasoning [this is apologetics], until God gives it by moving their heart, without which faith is only human and useless for salvation."[179] The most famous expression of this truth comes later in the *Pensées* when Pascal says, "The heart has its reasons of which reason knows nothing: we know this in countless ways." Therefore, "[i]t is the heart which perceives God and not the reason. That is what faith is: God perceived by the heart, not by reason."[180] Yet, even the perception of God by the heart has limits in this life.

The God who predestines some to be saved and others to be damned is a hidden God (Isa. 45:15, "Truly you are a hidden God"; see No. 242). As the famous text on "The Wager" shows (Nos. 418–26), Pascal does not try to prove God's existence, but rather to show that it is a more rational *choice* to bank on the supposition that God exists rather than the opposite. The proof of God's existence comes from man's goodness and even his evil: "So it is not only the zeal of those who seek him that proves God's existence, but also the blindness of those who do not seek him."[181] Pascal's deep suspicion of fallen human nature and even of the physical universe makes it evident that the only real and secure way to know God is through faith (i.e., heart-knowledge) in Jesus Christ. Nonetheless, meditation on the coincidence of opposites revealed both in the physical universe and in man as the microcosm reveals something of God and of the terror of the fallen human situation, thus opening us to the redeemer and his saving message. The wonderful text on the "Disproportion of Man" (Nos. 199–201) is a good illustration of this.[182] Contemplation of the vastness of the universe shows that it is "the greatest perceptible mark of God's omnipotence that our imagination should lose itself in that thought" (trans., 89). Contemplation of man, an equally astounding prodigy, "a new abyss," reveals the existential knowledge of man as poised between the dual abysses of infinity and nothingness, a recognition involving both wonder and terror. Pascal explores how the most valiant efforts of the human mind run up against ineluctable limitations, not only in knowing the universe but also in knowing ourselves: "Man is to himself the greatest prodigy in nature, for he cannot conceive what his body is, and still less what his mind is, and least of all how a body can be joined to a mind. This is his supreme difficulty, and yet it is also his very being" (No. 199; trans., 94). Hence, the famous conclusion: "Man is only a reed, . . . but he is a thinking reed. . . . Thus, all our dignity consists in thought. . . . Let us then strive to think well; that is the basic principle of morality" (No. 200; trans., 95). But thinking well is not enough, because "[t]he eternal silence of these infinite spaces fills me with dread" (No. 201; ibid.). The solution to the dread of the human condition and even human thinking cannot come from the self. No. 202 concludes, "Be comforted; it is not from yourself that you must expect it, but on the contrary you must expect it by expecting nothing from yourself."

Jesus Christ, "the long-expected One," brings the message of salvation and the grace that redeems those who are open to God. *Pensée* No. 189 begins: "We know God only through Jesus Christ. Without this mediator all communication with God is broken off. . . . All those who have claimed to know God and prove his existence without Jesus Christ have only futile proofs to offer."[183] Hence, "Without scripture, without original sin, without the necessary Mediator, who was promised and came, it is impossible to prove absolutely that God exists, or to teach sound doctrine and sound morality" (ibid.). But it is not by the miracle of the Christian religion, or even by the wisdom of its teaching that we are saved. "None of this can change us and make us capable of knowing and loving God, except the virtue contained in the folly of the Cross."[184]

The importance of the folly of the cross for Pascal is evident in the meditation on "The Mystery of the Cross" that comes toward the end of the *Pensées*.[185] This has long been seen as the most mystical part of the work, and it reveals the depth of Pascal's devotion to the suffering Christ. Pascal fixes his attention on Christ's Passion, not in the manner of those late medieval meditations that presented the Savior's external bloody sufferings, but through a consideration of the Lord's inner condition and even his human relation to his disciples. The focus of Pascal's attention is not on the crucifixion itself, but on the Agony in the Garden of Gethsemane. "Jesus," Pascal begins, "suffers in his Passion the torments inflicted upon him by men, but in his agony he suffers the torments which he inflicts on himself." God the Father brings this on his Son: "This punishment is inflicted by no human hand, but an almighty hand, and only he that is almighty can bear it" (trans., 312). Jesus seeks comfort from the three disciples he brought into the Garden, but they are asleep and indifferent to him. Suffering this anguish in "the horror of the night," for the first and only time Jesus complains, "My soul is exceedingly sorrowful, even unto death" (Matt. 26:38). Like some medieval mystics (e.g., Mechthild of Magdeburg), Pascal universalizes this suffering: "Jesus will be in agony until the end of the world. There must be no sleeping during that time" (trans., 313). Jesus, afraid of death and uncertain of the will of the Father, prays until he is sure of the proper course of action, going forth then to meet his death. Jesus brought about the salvation of the disciples while they slept and has done this for each of the righteous while they slept in the nothingness before they were born and in the sleep of sin of their lives. Pascal emphasizes the message we are to take from this event: "Jesus tears himself away from his disciples in order to enter into his agony: we must tear ourselves away from those nearest and dearest to us in order to imitate him" (trans., 314). The meditation next turns to a theme that we have seen in Francis de Sales and others, that is, the need for obedience to necessity and events, the masters that God himself sends us (that is, God's will of benevolence).

The second part of the "The Mystery of the Cross" is a conversation between Jesus in his agony and Pascal as representing the devout soul. Jesus opens with a dozen statements expressing both messages of encouragement (e.g., "You would not seek me if you had not found me") and questions for testing (e.g., "Do you want it always to cost me the blood of my humanity while you do not even shed a tear?"). Then the text turns into a dialogue, when Jesus says, "If you knew your sins, you would lose heart." Pascal responds, "In that case I shall lose heart, Lord, for I believe in their wickedness on the strength of your assurance." No, Jesus says, the whole purpose of this conversation is to show you that I want to heal you, and that "[a]s you expiate them [your sins] you will come to know them, and you will be told: 'Behold thy sins are forgiven thee.'" The conclusion is a poignant summary of Pascal's life of surrender since the experience of the *Memorial*: "Lord, I give you all" (*Seigneur je vous donne tout*). The final part of "The Mystery of Jesus" starts with three more admonitions by Jesus and continues with Pascal's further considerations of the meaning of the sufferings of the Lord. According to Pascal, Pilate is the exemplar of the "falsely righteous," who have not made a total conversion and therefore continue to do both good deeds and bad.[186] When I recognize that "Jesus was made sin for me," he says, "I know that I must add my wounds to his, and join myself to him and he will save me in saving himself" (trans., 315). Finally, no further sins must be added, especially those of our judging what is good and what is evil. In a passage that might have been written by Francis de Sales or Lawrence of the Resurrection, Pascal concludes, "Do small things as if they were great, because of the majesty of Christ, who does them in us and leads our life, and great things as if they were small and easy, because of his almighty power" (trans., 316). "The Mystery of Jesus" summarizes Pascal's meditations on the mystical experience given him in 1654, a message that he felt called upon to communicate to others even within the context of a book of what was essentially apologetic reasoning.

It is in and through our union with Jesus Christ, especially as members of his Body, the church, that union with God the Father becomes possible. Pascal's sense of our oneness in Christ, especially in the poor and the outcast, is moving, especially in going beyond the Christian community to embrace all humanity. *Pensées* No. 946 is an example: "Consider Jesus in every person and in ourselves. Jesus Christ as father in his father, as brother in his brothers, Jesus Christ as poor in the poor, Jesus Christ as rich in the rich, Jesus Christ as priest and doctor in priests, Jesus Christ as sovereign in princes, etc." Jesus took on our unhappy condition, "so that he could be in every person and a model for every condition of man."[187] This is even more strongly put in No. 931, which says, "I love all men as my brothers, because they are all redeemed. I love poverty because he loved it. I love wealth because he affords me the means of helping the needy. I keep faith with everyone. . . . I try to be just, genuine, sincere and loyal to all men, and I feel a special affection for those whom God has most intimately joined to me." These, says Pascal, are now his "feelings," and, "[a]ll the days of my life I bless my Redeemer, who implanted them in me and who made a man full of weakness, wretchedness, concupiscence, pride, and ambition into one free from these evils."[188] (These texts about God's universal love seem to conflict with Pascal's Jansenist view of a strict divide between the saved and the damned, but that issue cannot be taken up here.) Other passages concentrate on the love that binds the members of Christ's mystical Body into one. Thus, No. 372 says that not only do the members have life in the Body, but that "in loving the body it [the member] loves itself, because it has no being except in the body, through the body, and for the body. 'But he who is joined to the Lord is one spirit'" (1 Cor. 6:17). Hence, "we love ourselves because we are members of Christ. We love Christ because he is the body of which we are members. All are one. One is in the other like the three Persons"—a rare mention of the Trinity in the *Pensées*.[189]

These passages about our unity in Christ cast light on Pascal's appeals to the language of uniting with God and coming to share in and participate in God through deification. Pascal was not interested in presenting a detailed discussion of union with God and its various types; his point was rather to emphasize that becoming one with God was the goal of the Christian life, a truth that had been directly revealed to him when the divine fire descended in 1654. Thus, at the conclusion of the important *Pensées* 131 he says, "[I]t is clearly evident that man through grace is made like unto God and shares his divinity, and without grace he is treated like the beasts of the field."[190] In one place Pascal says, "It is incredible that God should unite himself to us" (No. 149; see also No. 231), yet this is part of the paradox of faith. "Christianity is strange," he says; "it bids man to recognize he is vile, and even abominable, and it bids him to want to be like God." And yet, "[h]ow little pride the Christian feels in believing himself to be united to God!," because he knows this is God's doing alone.[191] The Christian religion "teaches the righteous, whom it exalts even to the participation in divinity itself" that they still bear the source of corruption within themselves and thus are prone to error, misery, death, and sin. Therefore, "it makes those whom it justifies tremble and consoles those whom it condemns" with the hope of salvation.[192] The reason for the gift of deifying union is well summarized in No. 239: "Man is not worthy of God but he is not incapable of being made worthy. It is unworthy of God to unite himself to wretched man, but it is not unworthy of God to raise him out of his wretchedness."[193]

The *Pensées* are the extension of the mystical experience recounted in the *Memorial*. They are an act of *confessio* to God and before his fellow believers. In *Pensée* No. 418, Pascal says, "If my words please you and seem cogent, you must know that they come from a man who went down upon his knees before and after to pray to this infinite and indivisible Being, to whom he submits his own, that he might bring your being also to submit to him for your own good and for his glory: and that strength might thus be reconciled with lowliness."[194]

Notes

1. See the account of Coton's 1606 memorandum regarding Jesuit renewal in Certeau, chap. 8, "The 'Little Saints' of Aquitaine," in *Mystic Fable: Volume One*, 245–48.

2. Joseph de Guibert, *La spiritualité de la Compagnie de Jésus: Esquisse historique*, Bibliotheca Instituti Historici S.I. 4 (Rome: Institutum Historicum S.I, 1953), 341. Bremond devoted the whole of volume 5 of his *Histoire* to Jesuit authors of the seventeenth century.

3. For a brief account of the Spanish Jesuit mystics and the opposition they encountered, see McGinn, *Spain*, 386–91.

4. Louis Lallemant, *Doctrine spirituelle*, Nouvelle edition augmentée, établie et présentée par Dominique Salin (Paris: Desclée de Brouwer, 2011), especially the "Introduction" (7–46). There is now a translation: Louis Lallemant, *The Spiritual Doctrine* (Chestnut Hill, MA: Institute of Jesuit Sources, 2016). I will make use of the older and less complete text, *The Spiritual Teaching of Father Louis Lallemant of the Society of Jesus, Preceded by an Account of His Life by Father Champion, S.J.*, ed. Alan G. McDougall (London: Burns Oates & Washbourne, 1928). I will make my own versions of the new texts found in the Salin edition.

5. Translated from the text given by Salin in his "Introduction," 10–11.

6. See Certeau, *Mystic Fable: Volume One*, 251–70.

7. For a brief treatment, see Buckley, "Seventeenth-Century French Spirituality: Three Figures," 28–68, here 53–63. Most of the literature is in French. Along with Salin's excellent "Introduction," see Bremond, *Histoire*, 2:447–86 (new edition); de Guibert, *La spiritualité*, 345–51; Cognet, *La spiritualité moderne*, 424–40; and Georges Bottereau, "Lallemant (Louis), jésuite, 1588-1635," DS 9:125-35. Another English study is Tibor Bartók, "Louis Lallemant and his *Doctrine spirituelle*: Myths and Facts," in *A Companion to Jesuit Mysticism*, ed. Robert A. Maryks, Brill's Companions to the Christian Tradition 78 (Leiden: Brill, 2017), 112–38. Bartók sees Lallemant's *Doctrine* as a mystical expression of Claudio Aquaviva's call for interior renewal in the Jesuit life.

8. Bremond, *Histoire*, 2:485.

9. Buckley, "Three Figures," 56.

10. Lallemant's sources include patristic figures, like Clement of Alexandria, Athanasius, Gregory of Nyssa, Augustine, Dionysius, Gregory the Great, and Isidore of Seville. Among the medievals, he cites Bernard of Clairvaux, Richard of St. Victor, Thomas Aquinas, Francis of Assisi, Bonaventure, Catherine of Siena, Vincent Ferrar, and Catherine of Genoa. He also uses recent authors, such as Lawrence Giustiniani, Francis Suarez, Balthasar Alvarez, Francis de Sales, and especially Ignatius of Loyola, Francis Xavier, and Teresa of Avila. John of the Cross appears only once.

11. *Doctrine*, prin. I, chap. 2, art. 3 (ed., 56; trans., 31).

12. *Doctrine*, prin. II, sect. II, chap. 6, art. 2 (ed., 101). Lallemant was not a Bérullian, but one cannot exclude the influence of Bérulle in passages like this and other references to the self-annihilation of the Word (prin. VI, sect. I, chap. 2, art. 1 [ed., 254-55]; prin. VI, sect. III, chap. 6 [ed., 315-17]; and prin. VII, chap. 3bis, part 3, art. 3 [ed., 356]), as well as to our own self-annihilation (e.g., prin. IV, chap. 4, art. 7 [ed., 207]; and prin. VII, chap. 3bis, part 3, art. 6 [ed., 361]).

13. *Doctrine*, prin. II, sect. II, chap. 6, art. 2 (ed., 101; trans., 69).

14. On apostolic action as the underlying theme of the *Doctrine*, see Buckley, "Three Figures," 60-62.

15. *Doctrine*, prin. II, sect. II, chap. 6, art. 5.2 and 3 (ed., 109-10; trans., 78). Lallemant mentions *la science des saints* in several other places.

16. Salin, "Introduction," 20.

17. Ibid., 40.

18. *Doctrine*, prin. IV, chap. 1, art. 1 (ed., 154-55; trans., 109).

19. *Doctrine*, prin. IV, chap. 2, art. 1 (ed., 158; trans., 132).

20. *Doctrine*, prin. IV, chap. 4, art. 1 (ed., 176-77; trans., 130-31). Lallemant says that raptures and ecstasies indicate that the soul has not yet attained perfection in prin. VII, art. 1, art. 6, and art. 8 (ed., 365-66, 374-77, and 382-85).

21. *Doctrine*, prin. V, chap. 4, art. 2 (ed., 246; trans., 197-98).

22. *Doctrine*, prin. VI, sect. II, chap. 1bis (ed., 279-89). This chapter is not found in the old English translation.

23. The distinction between *amour affectif* and *amour effectif* is found in Francis de Sales, *Treatise on the Love of God*, Book VI.1, and is based on Bernard of Clairvaux, *Sermo super Cantica Canticorum* 50 (*Sancti Bernardi Opera* 2:80-81).

24. *Doctrine*, prin. VI, sect. II, chap. 1bis (ed., 280-84). The first two affections mirror Francis de Sales's *amour de bienveillance* and *amour de complaisance* (*Treatise on the Love of God* I.13, etc.).

25. *Doctrine*, prin. VI, sect. II, chap. 1bis (ed., 284-87). This is one of the few places in the text where Lallemant insists on the nothingness of the soul taken in itself: "Car d'un côté se voyant dans le néant, étant convaincues qu-elles ne sont que pur néant" (286-87).

26. *Doctrine*, prin. VI, sect. II, chap. 2, art. 4 (ed., 296-97; trans., 232-33).

27. *Doctrine*, prin. VII, chap. 3bis (ed., 332-64).

28. *Doctrine*, prin. VII, chap. 3bis, III, art. 1 (ed., 348). This definition is based on Francis de Sales, *Treatise on the Love of God* VI.3.

29. Salin ("Introduction," 349 n. 1) notes that this is close to John of the Cross's idea of contemplation as consisting in *essa noticia general y confusa* (*Ascent of Mount Carmel* 2.14).

30. *Doctrine*, prin. VII, chap. 3bis, III, art 1 (ed., 350-52). These include

Augustine, Francis de Sales, and Jesuits such as Suarez, Alvarez de Paz, Louis Dupont, Balthasar Alvarez, and Maximilian Sandaeus. Lallemant uses the expression *fond de l'âme* in only a few other places (e.g., ed., 393). *Doctrine*, prin. II, sect. I, chap. 1 speaks of the *centre de l'âme* (ed., 65).

31. *Doctrine*, prin. VII, chap. 4, art 1 (ed., 365–66; my trans.).

32. *Doctrine*, prin. VII, chap. 4, art. 5 (ed., 372–74; trans., 263–64). According to Salin (ed., 372 n. 11), the definition and characteristics are taken from Alvarez de Paz, *De inquisitione pacis*, liber V, II, chap. 1.

33. *Doctrine*, prin. VII, chap, 4, art. 8 (ed., 382–85; trans., 273–75). Here Lallemant conforms more to the late Teresa of the *Interior Castle* in relegating raptures and ecstasies to the penultimate stage.

34. *Doctrine*, prin. VII, chap. 4, art. 9 (ed., 387–89; trans., 278–80).

35. Stanislas Breton, *Deux mystiques de l'excès: J.-J. Surin et Maître Eckhart*, Cogitatio fidei 135 (Paris: Éditions du Cerf, 1985).

36. Several of Certeau's writings about Surin are available in English, notably the sections in *The Mystic Fable: Volume One*, 179–87, and chap. 7, "The Enlightened Illiterate" (206–40). Surin also makes partial appearances in *The Mystic Fable: Volume Two*. Surin's role in the exorcism at Loudun is treated in Certeau's *The Possession at Loudun* (Chicago: University of Chicago Press, 1996), chap. 13, "The Time of Spirituality: Father Surin" (199–212). In addition, there is a short introduction by Certeau, "Jean-Joseph Surin," in *Spirituality through the Centuries: Ascetics and Mystics of the Western Church*, ed. James Walsh (New York: P. J. Kenedy & Sons, 1964), 293–342, as well as chap. 7, "Surin's Melancholy," in Certeau, *Heterologies: Discourse on the Other*, Theory and History of Literature 17 (Minneapolis: University of Minnesota Press, 1986), 101–15.

37. The literature about Surin reflects the ambivalence of his story. Bremond devotes three chapters to him in *Histoire* (2:538–642). Guibert discusses him with some caution (*La spiritualité de la Compagnie de Jésus*, 352–55). Cognet, *La spiritualité moderne*, does not mention him at all. Surin is important for those who stress the disruptive nature of seventeenth-century mysticism; see, e.g., Kołakowski, *Chrétiens sans église*, chap. 7 (436–91); and Houdard, *Les invasions mystiques*, chap. 7 (275–99). See also Moshe Sluhovsky, "Mysticism as an Existential Crisis: Jean-Joseph Surin," in Maryks, *Companion to Jesuit Mysticism*, 139–65.

38. For an introduction, see Michel Dupuy, "Surin (Jean-Joseph), jésuite, 1600–1665," DS 14:1311–25.

39. M. de Certeau, "The Enlightened Illiterate," in *The Mystic Fable: Volume One*, whose translation (207–10) I cite here. See also Rob Faesen, "A French Mystic's Perspective on the Crisis of Mysticism: Jean-Joseph Surin (1600-1665)," in *Mysticism in the French Tradition: Eruptions from France*, ed. Louise Nelstrop and Bradley B. Onishi (Burlington, VT: Ashgate, 2012), 149–67.

40. For a discussion, see Carlos Eire, *Reformations: The Early Modern World, 1450–1650* (New Haven: Yale University Press, 2016), 655–59.

41. Jean-Joseph Surin, *Triomphe de l'amour divin sur les puissances de l'Enfer en la possession de la Mère supérieure des Ursulines de Loudun, exorcisée par le Père Jean-Joseph Surin, de la Compagnie de Jésus; et, Science expérimentale des choses de l'autre vie*, Collection Atopia (Grenoble: Jérôme Millon, 1990).

42. Surin, *Triomphe de l'amour divin*, chap. 2 (ed., 27). Translation of Certeau, *Possession at Loudun*, 202.

43. Cited from Surin's correspondence by Certeau, *Possession at Loudun*, 208.
44. *Science expérimentale*, seconde partie, chap. IX (ed., 206-7).
45. Surin's correspondence was edited by Michel de Certeau, *Jean-Joseph Surin, Correspondance* (Paris: Desclée de Brouwer, 1966). About 450 of the letters date from the last decade of his life. See also Patrick Goujon, *Prendre part à l'intransmissible. La communication spirituel à travers la correspondance de Jean-Joseph Surin* (Grenoble: Jérôme Millon, 2008).
46. *Science expérimentale*, seconde partie, chap. XV (ed., 241-42). See the discussions in Certeau, "Jean-Joseph Surin," 294-95; and Faesen, "French Mystic's Perspective," 136-38.
47. There are two modern editions of Surin's poetry: Étienne Catta, ed., *Poésies spirituelles suivies des Contrats spirituels*, Études de théologie et d'histoire de la spiritualité 15 (Paris: Vrin, 1957); and Benedetta Papàsogli, ed., *Cantiques spirituels de l'amour divin*, Biblioteca della Rivista di storia e letteratura religiosa: Testi e documenti 16 (Florence: Leo S. Olschki, 1996).
48. Jean-Joseph Surin, *Guide spirituel pour la perfection*, ed. Michel de Certeau (Paris: Desclée de Brouwer, 1963).
49. Jean-Joseph Surin, *Questions importantes à la vie spirituelle: Sur l'amour de Dieu*, ed. Aloys Potter and Louis Mariès (Paris: Téqui, 1930). See the discussion in Faesen, "French Mystic's Perspective," 158-62.
50. The task of sorting out the history of Surin's writings and publications was begun, but alas not completed, by Michel de Certeau, "Les oeuvres de Surin," *Revue d'ascétique et de mystique* 40 (1964): 443-76; 41 (1965): 55-78.
51. Bremond, "Surin e le moralisme mystique," in *Histoire*, 2:606-42; quotation from 640.
52. Certeau, "Jean-Joseph Surin," 293-94.
53. Ibid., 302-6, and the texts cited there. Like Lallemant, Surin took this language over from John of the Cross (e.g., *Ascent of Mount Carmel* 2.14.6 and 12; *Living Flame of Love* 3.34). On the relation of John of the Cross and Surin, see Michel de Certeau, "Jean-Joseph Surin, interprète de Saint Jean de la Croix," *Revue d'ascétique et de mystique* 46 (1970): 45-70 (69-70 on the *notion universelle et confuse*).
54. On the importance of the polemical context and Chéron, see Certeau, "Introduction," in *Guide spirituel*, 39-50. See also Johannes Brenninger, "Chéron (Jean)," DS 2:821-22.
55. *Guide spirituel* I.III (ed., 74-75). On the importance of the "premier pas," see Certeau, "Introduction," 28-31.
56. Chapter IV gives three difficulties that hinder folk in the first stage. Chapter V provides three reasons why people do not make progress, while chapter VI discusses three hidden obstacles. Chapter VII treats three faults that people commit on the path of perfection; chapter VIII treats three aspects of true virtue, while part I concludes with chapter IX's discussion of the three things that comprise true service of God.
57. *Guide spirituel* II.I (ed., 101-3).
58. *Guide spirituel* II.VIII (ed., 130-31).
59. *Guide spirituel* II.VIII (ed. 132-34). This is the first of ten attacks Surin launches against Chéron and his sympathziers. The points he makes are almost always the same: (1) the critics try to judge supernatural matters with the rational

intellect; (2) they do not recognize the special character of mystical discourse; and (3) they reject the teaching of great saints and masters approved by the church.

60. *Guide spirituel* II.IX (ed., 136).
61. *Guide spirituel* II.IX (ed., 137-39).
62. *Guide spirituel* IV.III (ed., 175-83).
63. Ibid. (ed., 178-79).
64. *Guide spirituel* VI.V (ed., 244-60).
65. *Guide spirituel* VI.VI (ed., 261-63). Certeau's note on 263 indicates that Surin may be referring to his contemporary Jean Labadie (1610-1674), a Jesuit who left the order in 1639 to become a Calvinist and later a sectarian.
66. *Guide spirituel* VII.I (ed., 283).
67. *Guide spirituel* VII.III (ed., 287).
68. *Guide spirituel* VII.V (ed., 293).
69. *Guide spirituel* VII.VIII (ed., 314-15).
70. For a brief sketch of some of the Carmelite female mystics, see Cognet, *La spiritualité moderne*, 361-68.
71. See Janssen, *Les origines de la réform des Carmes*, who treats Jean de Saint-Samson on 233-54.
72. The critical edition under the general editorship of Hein Blommestijn includes: *Oeuvres Complètes*, vol. 1, *L'éguillon, les flames, les fleches, et le miroir de l'amour de Dieu propres pour enamourer l'âme de Dieu en Dieu mesme* (Rome: Institutum Carmelitanum, 1992); vol. 2, *Méditations et Soliloquies 1* (Rome: Institutum Carmelitanum, 1993); vol. 3, *Méditations et Soliloquies 2* (Rome: Edizioni Carmelitane, 2000). Volumes still to appear include vol. 4, *Traités Mystiques 1*; vol. 5, *Traités Mystiques 2*; vol. 6, *Commentaire sur la Règle des Carmes*; vol. 7, *Traités de direction spirituelle 1*; vol. 8, *Traités de direction spirituelle 2*; vol. 9, *Cantiques spirituels*; and vol. 10, *Lettres* (to appear in 2019). (I thank H. Blommestijn for this information.)
73. The only published English versions are in *Prayer, Aspiration and Contemplation from the Writings of John of St. Samson, O. Carm., Mystic and Charismatic*, ed. and trans. Venard Poslusney (New York: Alba House, 1975). The volume is not very useful, however, because the selections are arranged thematically, with no indication of their actual source. There is a brief introduction and a text in Steven Payne, *The Carmelite Tradition*, Spirituality in History (Collegeville, MN: Liturgical Press, 2011), 78-85.
74. On John's sources, see Suzanne-P. Michel, "Jean de Saint-Samson, mystique carme, 1571-1636," DS 8:703-10; and Blommestijn, "Introduction générale," in *Oeuvres Complètes*, 1:13-15.
75. One of Jean's longest poems, "Cantique Spirituel Saint Sepulchre de Iesus-Christ," has been edited, translated, and studied by Robert Stefanotti, *"The Holy Sepulchre Canticle" of John of St. Samson (1571-1636): A Synecdochical Study of His Spiritual Imagery, Language and Style* (Rome: Gregorian University Dissertation, 1991).
76. The *Equillon* is in *Oeuvres Complètes*, 1:29-135. With the kind permission of Hein Blommestijn, general editor, I will make use of the unpublished English version of Maurice Cummings, originally intended for the edition but unfortunately not published with it.
77. *L'éguillon*, chap. 3 (ed., 63-64; trans., Cummings [279-80]).
78. *L'éguillon*, chap. 5 (ed., 81-82; trans., Cummings [300-301]).

79. *L'éguillon*, chap. 6 (ed., 90; trans., Cummings [311]).
80. McGinn, *Varieties*, 132-33.
81. Hein Blommestijn, "Aspiring as a Mystagogical Journey of Prayer," in *Seeking the Seeker: Explorations in the Discipline of Spirituality; A Festschrift for Kees Waaijman on the Occasion of His 65th Birthday*, ed. Hein Blommestijn et al.(Leuven: Peeters, 2008), 549-61.
82. *L'éguillon*, chap. 7 (ed., 98; trans., Cummings [319]).
83. According to Blommestijn, "During the mystical process aspiring is transformed from a consciously practiced and orally or mentally expressed prayer into a very simple and essential aspiring. . . . I am becoming a passive participant and spectator, while God is acting in me in the first person" ("Aspiring as a Mystagogical Journey of Prayer," 557).
84. *L'éguillon*, chap. 7 (ed.,101-2; trans., Cummings, [323]).
85. *L'éguillon*, chap. 7 (ed., 102; trans., Cummings [324]).
86. *L'éguillon*, chap. 7 (ed., 103-4; trans., Cummings [325]).
87. *L'éguillon*, chap. 8 (ed., 111; trans., Cummings [333]).
88. *L'éguillon*, chap. 8 (ed., 115; trans., Cummings [338]).
89. *L'éguillon*, chap. 8 (ed., 118; trans., Cummings, [348]).
90. The *Epithalamium* is in *Oeuvres Complètes*, 2:335-60, but I will make use of the reprint of this edition in Elisabeth Hense and Edeltraud Klueting, *Die dunkle Stille: Das Epithalamium von Jean de Saint-Samson als spirituelles Dokumentationstheater* (St. Ottilien: EOS Verlag, 2012), 60-113, which conveniently numbers the lines of the text (911 in all). In English, see Ivan Scicluna, "*L'Epithalme* of Jean de Saint-Samson (1571-1636)," *Studies in Spirituality* 18 (2008): 289-311. With the kind permission of Hein Blommestijn, editor of the *Oeuvres*, I have also been able to consult Scicluna's English version, which divides the text into fifty sections. I will cite according to section and line (l. and ll.), mostly adapting Scicluna's rendering.
91. For an introduction, see Suzanne-P. Michel, "Épithalme," DS 4:907-9. In the 1620s, a contemporary of John's, Claude Hopil (d. 1630), composed two epithalamia based on the Song of Songs. See Claude Hopil, *Meditations sur le Cantique des cantiques et Les douces extases de l'âme spirituelle*, ed. Guillaume Peyroche d'Arnaud (Geneva: Droz, 2000).
92. The one exception appears to be section 28 (ll. 480-81), which speaks of *mutuelles ambrassades des esgalles*.
93. Jean does not actually quote Song of Songs 2:6 ("Laeva eius sub capite meo et dextera illius amplexabitur me"), but it is hard not to think that he has this image in mind in his numerous references to the embraces (see, e.g., ll. 112, 119, 125, 152, 169, 446, 498, 522, 590, 602, 614, 621, 655-56, 667-68, 699-704, 720, 814-15, and 821-22).
94. Elsewhere he speaks of *l'amour infinement excessif de nostre Espoux* (ll. 237-38; see also ll. 752-55). For other passages on *amour excessif*, see, e.g., ll. 301-12, 454, 463, 773, 839-40, and 865. *Exces/excessif* characterizes many other nouns: *excessif secret* (l. 419); *exces de parolles* (l. 543); *douleur excessive* (ll. 578-79); *profonds excéz* (l. 857); *admiration excessive* (l. 884); and *excés de ma beauté* (l. 900). A passage in section 33 (ll. 585-87) speaks of "the force of our present enjoyment [*jouissance*], excessive far beyond the excess of comprehension and expression."
95. Scicluna, "*L'Épithalme* of Jean de Saint-Samson," 297.

96. Key texts on ineffability include ll. 17-22, 50-78, 116-32, 270-86, 352-57, and 540-45.

97. *Ineffablement ineffable* appears in ll. 171, 274-75, 531, 647-48, 703-4, and 888-89.

98. *Epithalamium* 15 (ll. 277-86): "Et que sert il d-exprimer les choses qui sont, par les choses qui non sont pas, tout autant que d'exprimer celles qui ne sont pas, par celles qui sont? . . . Car dittes moi, . . . , ou est la verité de tout cecy . . . , sinon en vous qui estes au dela de l'estre et l'eminence de l'estre, et en l'eminence du non estre, en l'estre et au dela de l'estre par force de sureminente negation?"

99. See Mazzocco, "'Suressentiel,'" who mentions Jean de Saint Samson on 618.

100. *Epithalamium* 35 (ll. 643-49; trans. Scicluna adapted). Sometimes, says Jean, language fails and the love encounter must end in silence (e.g., ll. 87-94, 540-45, and 565).

101. *Commune jouissance* (sometimes *ineffable jouissance*), along with *embrassemens*, are Jean's favorite terms for the love union enjoyed by the bride and groom.

102. Both sections 39 and 40 (ll. 697-745) in which the Bridegroom addresses the bride are examples of how difficult it often is to follow the train of Jean's thought.

103. *Epithalamium* 14 (ll. 261-69; trans. Scicluna adapted).

104. Section 38 (ll. 685-97; trans. Scicluna adapted). In section 39, similar language is found in ll. 715-18, while section 40 is filled with flowing (ll. 726, 736-37, 743-45). *Flux* also appears in later sections (e.g., ll. 755, 760, 869).

105. *Epithalamium*, section 11 (ll. 219-23; trans. Scicluna). See also the references to the soul as infinite (l. 493), and to the *l'infini excéz de moy mesme* (l. 610).

106. For example, section 4 (ll. 83-94) and section 20 (ll. 345-50).

107. *Epithalamium*, section 16 (ll. 294-300; trans. Scicluna adapted). See also section 23 (ll. 391-95) and section 26 (ll. 441-50).

108. Jean de Saint-Samson's *Epithalamium* talks constantly about the mutual love and embraces to the bride and groom, but except for the sections where there is heavy use of the images of the Song of Songs (e.g., sections 28 and 33), there is little sexually erotic flavor to the work.

109. *Epithalamium*, section 5 (ll. 110-12). For some other passages on mutuality, see, e.g., section 9 (ll. 172-97), section 18 (ll. 322-33), section 25 (ll. 437-40), section 29 (ll. 490-501), section 30 (ll. 518-35), section 31 (ll. 556-65), section 37 (ll. 664-78), etc.

110. For some other texts on deification, see section 5 (ll. 103-6), section 8 (ll. 159-62), section 12 (ll. 239-40), section 41 (ll. 746-50), section 43 (ll. 781-84), and section 44 (ll. 800-805).

111. *Epithalamium*, section 17 (ll. 309-12). See also section 25 (ll. 420-40).

112. For references to mutual devouring, e.g., ll. 345-49, 460-65, 544-51, 712-15, and 724.

113. *Epithalamium*, section 34 (ll. 626-29). For some other references to the *mors mystica*, see ll. 619-21 and 650-53.

114. For references to *union sans distinction ni différence*, see, e.g., ll. 330-33, 460-63, 551, and 621-25.

115. *Epithalamium*, section 36 (ll. 656-63; trans. Scicluna adapted).

116. To cite just one example, the American Quaker mystic Thomas R. Kelly

(1893-1941) praises Brother Lawrence, along with Augustine and the *Imitation of Christ*, as speaking "the language of souls that live at the Center" (*A Testament of Devotion* [New York: Harper One, 1992], 55).

117. The critical edition and introduction to the works by and about Brother Lawrence is Conrad De Meester, *Écrits et entretiens sur la pratique de la presence de Dieu*, Epiphanie (Paris: Éditions du Cerf, 1996). There is an English translation by Salvatore Sciurba, *Writings and Conversations on the Practice of the Presence of God* (Washington, DC: ICS Publications, 1994). I will cite this version. Brother Lawrence's sparse writings include seven chapters of *Spiritual Maxims* (trans., 35-43) and sixteen *Letters* (trans., 49-84). In addition, his biographer, Joseph de Beaufort, records four *Conversations* he had with Lawrence (trans., 89-99). Beaufort's two biographical sketches are the *Eulogy* (trans., 5-24) and the *Ways of Brother Lawrence* (trans., 113-24). The brief treatise called *The Practice of the Presence of God* (trans., 105-8) is Beaufort's anthology of some passages from the *Spiritual Maxims* and *Letters*.

118. In the *First Conversation*, Brother Lawrence recalls his conversion at eighteen: "One day in winter while he was looking at a tree stripped of its leaves, and he realized that in a little while its leaves would reappear, followed by its flowers and fruit, he received a profound insight into God's providence that has never been erased from his soul. This insight completely freed him from the world, and gave him such a love for God that he could not say it had increased during the more than forty years that had passed" (trans., 89).

119. *Letter* 2 (trans., 53).

120. *Eulogy* 22 (trans., 10).

121. *Ways of Brother Lawrence* 13 (trans., 117). *Letter* 2 puts it this way: "When I accepted the fact that I might spend my life suffering from these thoughts and anxieties—which in no way diminished the trust I had in God and served only to increase my faith—I found myself changed all at once" (trans., 53).

122. *Maxims* 5.22 (trans., 40). This "suspension" should not be thought of as an ecstasy, because Lawrence shows himself rather negative toward ecstatic states, which he judged evidence of a kind of spiritual gluttony (*Conversations* 2.10; trans., 91).

123. *Ways of Brother Lawrence* 5 (trans., 114). Many other texts emphasize the centrality of faith; see, e.g., trans., 16-19, 78, 81, 83, 90, 95, 119, and 121.

124. References to the *fond et centre de l'âme* are frequent. Along with the passage already cited, see trans., 50, 53, 54, 59, etc.

125. *Conversations* 2.29 (trans., 94).

126. *Ways of Brother Lawrence* 20 (trans., 118).

127. *Maxims* 4.15-18 (trans., 38-39). The phrase *mais c'est un je ne sais quoi* is taken from John of the Cross; see *Spiritual Canticle*, strophe 7 (*un no sé qué que quedan balbuciendo*). The adjectives describing the experience are based on John's *Living Flame of Love* 3.38 and 43.

128. *Maxims* 4.19 (trans., 39).

129. *Ways of Brother Lawrence* 10 (trans., 116); see also *Ways* 14 (trans., 118).

130. Bremond devoted three chapters to Marie de l'Incarnation in *Histoire*, 2:709-850.

131. The prose works were edited by Albert Jamet, *Écrits spirituels et historiques*, 4 vols. (Paris: Desclée de Brouwer, 1929-39). This edition will be cited by volume

and page. Marie's 278 surviving letters were edited by Guy-Marie Oury, *Marie de l'Incarnation (1599–1672): Correspendance* (Solesmes: Abbaye Saint-Pierre, 1971).

132. The most accessible English versions are by Irene Mahoney, *Marie of the Incarnation: Selected Writings*, Sources of American Spirituality (New York: Paulist Press, 1989). Mahoney translates the whole of the *Relation of 1654*, as well as selections from some other works. I will use her versions, unless otherwise noted.

133. For a summary, see Guy-Marie Oury, "Marie de l'Incarnation," DS 10:487–507. In English, see Anya Mali, *Mystic in the New World: Marie de l'Incarnation (1599–1672)*, Studies in the History of Christian Thought 72 (Leiden: Brill, 1996); and Marie-Florine Bruneau, *Women Mystics Confront the Modern World: Marie de l'Incarnation (1599–1672) and Madame Guyon (1648–1717)*, SUNY Series in Western Esoteric Traditions (Albany: State University of New York Press, 1998). For an analysis of the relation of Marie and her son, see Mary Dunn, *The Cruelest of All Mothers: Marie de l'Incarnation, Motherhood, and Christian Tradition* (New York: Fordham University Press, 2016). French literature is large. An important biography is Guy Oury, *Marie de l'Incarnation*, 2 vols. (Solesmes: Abbaye Saint-Pierre, 1973); see also Thérèse Nadeau-Lacour, *Marie Guyart de l'Incarnation: Une femme mystique au coeur de l'histoire* (Paris: Artège, 2015), and the essays in Raymond Brodeur, ed., *Femme, mystique et missionnaire: Marie Guyart de l'Incarnation* (Quebec: Les Presses de l'Université de Laval, 2001).

134. Both *Relations* have "Supplements." The *Relation of 1633*, written at the request of her Jesuit confessor, George de la Haye, is found in *Écrits* 1:149–309, with the 1636 Supplement in 1:310–39. The *Relation of 1654* is found in *Écrits* 2:151–476, with the 1655 Supplement in 2:481–98.

135. An insightful account of Marie's life is Natalie Zemon Davis, "Marie de l'Incarnation: New Worlds," in her *Women on the Margins: Three Seventeenth-Century Lives* (Cambridge, MA: Harvard University Press, 1995), 63–139.

136. What we know about the first part of Marie's life is mostly through the "First State of Prayer," from the *Relation of 1654* (ed., 2:160–73; trans. Mahoney, 41–48).

137. *Relation of 1654*, "First State of Prayer" (ed. 2:160–61; trans., 41–42). Such early visions of Christ, of course, were typical of women mystics, as we see in the cases of Mechthild of Magdeburg and Catherine of Siena.

138. *Relation of 1654*, "Second State of Prayer" (ed., 2:181–82; trans., 49). On the "Vision of the Blood," see Nadeau-Lacour, *Marie Guyart de l'Incarnation*, chap. 5 (pp. 69–85).

139. On the importance of this conversion experience, see Mali, *Mystic in the New World*, xvii–xviii, and chap. 2 (32–55).

140. Guy-Marie Oury distinguishes two kinds of writing in Marie's oeuvre: first, texts written close to the experiences described, and, second, later reflections on her life and mystical experiences, as we find in the *Relations* ("Mystique de l'immanence et mystique nuptiale," in Brodeur, *Femme, mystique et missionnaire*, 157–67). The ten early letters (1626–35) can be found in Oury, *Correspondance*, 1–22, and are discussed in his "Mystique de l'immanence et mystique nuptiale," 163–67.

141. The *Relation of 1633* does not survive as a complete text, but Jamet was able to reconstruct large parts of it (seventy-two fragments) from its use by Claude Martin in *La vie de la Vénérable Mère Marie de l'Incarnation*. Fragments 1–52 (1:149–

236) are especially important for Marie's mystical itinerary. Fragment 6 (ed., 156) mentions reading Dionysius, while Frag. 8 (ed., 160) speaks of Teresa.

142. Letter I in *Correspondance* (ed. Oury, 1; my trans.).

143. *Relation of 1633*, Fragment 32 (1:201; my trans.): "Mais après ce grand attrait, mon esprit fut occupé en chacune des perfections divines, où il se consommait en actes d'adoration, d'admiration, d'anéantissement et d'abandon à l'endroit de ce grand Tout." The language of annihilation and abandon is found in several other fragments; see, e.g., Frags. 24, 32, 40, 53, 60, 67, 71 (1:187, 202, 218, 254, 255, 272, 299, 305). *Abnégation/anéantissement* is also found in Marie's letters; e.g., Letter LXXXI (ed. Oury, 228).

144. The Pentecost experience involved both the second vision of the Trinity and the marriage with the Incarnate Word; see *Relation of 1633*, Fragments 34–35 (1:204–11), and the *Relation of 1654*, "Seventh State of Prayer," 22–23 (2:251–57; trans., 81–84). On these visions, see Nadeau-Lacour, *Marie Guyart de l'Incarnation*, chap. 8 (119–34).

145. *Relation of 1654*, "Seventh State of Prayer," XXV (2:260–61; trans., 86–87).

146. On Marie's attraction to the Ursulines because of their commitment to apostolic service, see *Relation of 1633*, Fragment 56 (1:261–62; trans., 183).

147. For her account of the difficulty she had in leaving her son, see the *Relation of 1633*, Fragments 60–61 (1:270–77; trans., 186–87).

148. See Dunn, *Cruelest of All Mothers*. Dunn has also published a translation and study of forty-one of the eighty-one letters Marie wrote to her son in *From Mother to Son: The Selected Letters of Marie de l'Incarnation to Claude Martin* (Oxford: Oxford University Press, 2014). For more on the relation of Marie and her son, see also Bruneau, *Women Mystics Confront the Modern World*, chap. 3.

149. *Relation of 1633*, Fragment 67 (1:298–300; trans., 192–93).

150. Although she is a *pur néant*, Marie also says that she is "entirely apt for him who is my All" (*toute proper pour lui qui est mon Tout*). The similarity of this to Bérulle's teaching on the soul as a nothing capable of receiving God (see chap. 4, 208) is striking. There is no direct evidence that Marie read Bérulle or his followers, but a number of features in her mysticism can be seen as parallel developments to the Bérullian approach.

151. The *Entretien spirituel sur l'Épouse des Cantiques* is in *Écrits* 1:387–404. For a discussion, see Mali, *Mystic in the New World*, 138–45. In the *Relation of 1633*, Fragment 68 (1:304–5) Marie claims to have been given the gift of understanding the meaning of the Bible by God himself (see also *Relation of 1654*, XIII.60 [224–28]).

152. Others have noted the importance of the combination of contemplation and action for Marie; see, e.g., Mali, *Mystic in the New World*, 99–101; and Dunn, "Introduction," in *From Mother to Son*, 24–25, 31.

153. Bruneau, *Women Mystics*, 78–79.

154. There are many examples of epistolary exchanges between mystics and their confessors/advisors, but the letters between Maria and her son Claude, especially with regard to her inner life, are a new phenomenon.

155. On the ways in which Claude reworked his mother's writings, see Davis, "Marie de l'Incarnation: New Worlds," 128–34.

156. For an interpretation of the *Relation of 1654*, see Mali, *Mystic in the New World*, chap. 3 (56–89). I will cite the text from *Écrits*, vol. 2, by "State of Prayer" (e.g., II), chapter (e.g., 3), and page number.

157. The account in *Relation of 1654*, IV.16 (2:228-29; trans., 71) is almost identical to that in *Relation of 1633*, Fragment 27 (1:191). See also "Supplement" V (2:485).

158. The Song of Songs plays a notable part in the *Relation of 1654*, being referenced twenty-five times. These citations cluster in States VI (six quotations) and XIII (five quotations).

159. *Relation of 1654*, VIII.33 (2:285-87; trans., 99-100). See *Relation of 1633*, Fragment 67 (1:298-30; trans., 192-93).

160. Bruneau observes that the time in Canada saw a reduction in accounts of ecstasy and visions, although the visions do not totally cease (*Women Mystics*, 43-44).

161. These passages are from XII.51 (2:376-78; trans., 141).

162. This description of the temptation to despair is followed by a chapter (XII.53) that is essentially a long first-person confession of her sinful life to God.

163. XIII.66 (2:452-61; trans., 171-75). On this text, see Nadeau-Lacour, *Marie Guyart de l'Incarnation*, 259-63; and especially Anya Mali, "L'état de victime et le 'petit discourse' mystique," in Brodeur, *Femme, mystique et missionnaire*, 211-20.

164. XIII.66 (2:460; trans., 174). The last part of this chapter also insists on the need for external crosses.

165. XIII.66 is not actually the final chapter of the *Relation*. The last two chapters (XIII.67-68) are a kind of appendix in which Marie ties the state of victimhood back to her experiences of union with the three Persons of the Trinity.

166. On the theme of victimhood, see Giuseppe Manzoni, "Victimale (Spiritualité)," DS 16:531-45, who surprisingly does not mention Marie.

167. *Correspondance*, Letter CCLXXVI (ed. Oury, 938): ". . . parce que je ne veux rien ny pour vous ny pour moy, qu'un perpetual état de victime."

168. For a short consideration of the spiritual dimensions of the two movements, see Dupré, "Jansenism and Quietism," 121-42. Dupré emphasizes that the Jansenists and Quietists began as movements of theological and spiritual reform. The spiritual and mystical dimensions of the Jansenist authors were studied by Bremond, *Histoire*, 2:25-409, "L'École de Port-Royal: La Conquête mystique."

169. It is not possible to give even a short list of the books devoted to Pascal. There is a chapter on "La Prière de Pascal," in Bremond, *History*, 2:231-96. Two accounts by major twentieth-century thinkers are Hans Urs von Balthasar, *The Glory of the Lord: A Theological Aesthetics*, vol. 3, *Studies in Theological Style: Lay Styles* (San Francisco: Ignatius Press, 1986), "Pascal" (172-238); and Leszek Kołakowski, *God Owes Us Nothing* (Chicago: University of Chicago Press, 1995), part 2, "Pascal's Sad Religion" (113-97). For Pascal as mystic, see F. T. H. Fletcher, *Pascal and the Mystical Tradition* (Oxford: Basil Blackwell, 1954).

170. The literature on Jansenism is large. For an introduction, see Louis Cognet, chaps. 2 and 3 of part 1, "The Leadership Position of France," in *The Church in the Age of Absolutism and Enlightenment*, ed. Wolfgang Müller et al., History of the Church 6 (New York: Crossroad, 1981), 24-57.

171. The text of the *Mémorial* was included as No. 913 of Pascal's *Pensées* (on which see below). The edition used here is Pascal, *Oeuvres complètes*, edited by Louis Lafuma (Paris: Éditions du Seuil, 1963), where the *Mémorial* is on 618. The translation is A. J. Krailsheimer, *Pensées* (Baltimore, MD: Penguin Books, 1966), 309-10.

172. There are many analyses of the *Mémorial*; see especially Bremond, "Le 'signe' de feu," in *Histoire*, 2:254–74; and chap. 3, "The *Mémorial*," in Fletcher, *Pascal and the Mystical Tradition*, 29–42.

173. The *Pensées* have been edited in many forms and with different numeration. Krailsheimer uses the Lafuma edition and numbering. Section 1 consists of twenty-eight parts under headings classified by Pascal himself (*Pensées* Nos. 1–382). Section 2 contains thirty-one parts with titles by the early editors (*Pensées* Nos. 383–829). Section 3 has three parts relating to miracles (Nos. 830–912), and section 4 contains fragments gathered under the headings of A (The *Memorial*, No. 913), B (some Fragments and *The Mystery of Jesus*; Nos. 914–74), and C (Fragments on Self-Love; Nos. 975–93).

174. *Pensées* No. 149 (ed., 520; trans., 76). The misery and grandeur of the human condition is a constant theme; see, e.g., Nos. 24, 68, 114, 117, 121–22, 127, 198, etc.

175. No. 122 (ed., 514; trans., 61).

176. No. 933 (ed., 624; trans., 322). See Fletcher, *Pascal and the Mystical Tradition*, chap. 5, "The Three Orders," 50–60.

177. Nos. 173, 182, 183 (ed., 523; trans., 83–85). For further reflections on the limits of reason, see Nos. 45, 76, 188, and 418.

178. No. 110 (ed., 513; trans., 58).

179. No. 110 (ed. 513; trans., 58). For more on the nature and necessity of faith, see, e.g., Nos. 131, 226, and 423–24.

180. Nos. 423–24 (ed., 532; trans., 154).

181. No. 163 (ed., 522; trans., 82). In another text Pascal says that it is actually original sin that reveals human nature to us. *Pensées* No. 131 (ed., 515; trans., 65): "It is, however, an astounding thing that the mystery furthest removed from our ken, that of the transmission of sin, should be something without which we can have no knowledge of ourselves."

182. No. 199 (ed., 525–28; trans., 88–95).

183. No. 189 (ed., 524; trans., 85–86).

184. No. 291 (ed., 539; trans., 121).

185. No. 919 (ed., 619–21; trans., 312–16).

186. In No. 378 (ed., 546; trans., 137) Pascal speaks of total conversion as involving "self-annihilation before the Universal Being."

187. No. 946 (ed., 624–25; trans., 324).

188. No. 931 (ed., 623; trans., 321).

189. No. 372 (ed., 346; trans., 136).

190. No. 131 (ed., 516; trans., 66).

191. These two passages are Nos. 351 and 358 (ed., 544; trans., 133–34).

192. No. 208 (ed., 529; trans., 97).

193. No. 239 (ed., 531; trans., 102–3).

194. No. 418 (ed., 551; trans., 153).

PART II

Mysticism in Other Catholic Areas

Chapter 6

English Recusant Mysticism

The Recusant Situation

The religious history of sixteenth-century England is a story of dramatic actions and bewildering shifts of power.[1] Henry VIII broke with the papacy and declared himself head of the English church in the Act of Supremacy of 1534, but Henry was far from a Reformer in theology, liturgy, or customs, although there were many supporters of Protestantism among his advisors. Under his sickly son Edward VI (ruled 1547–53) England turned in a strongly Protestant direction of the Genevan, not the Lutheran model, but the succession of his half-sister, Mary Tudor ("Bloody Mary"), reversed all this. For five years Mary strove to re-Catholicize the realm through a heavy-handed campaign of persecution of the Protestant heretics (about three hundred were executed). She was succeeded by her half-sister, Elizabeth, in 1558, who was to reign until 1603.

Under Elizabeth, England became definitively Protestant, though of a distinctly English version that stressed the *via media*, that is, a middle road between rituals and offices inherited from medieval Catholicism and the newer Protestant polity, theology, and liturgy of Geneva. In 1559, three acts of legislation marked a clean break with Rome: a new Act of Supremacy that reaffirmed the monarch as the "only Supreme Governor" of the church; the Act of Uniformity, which required all churches to follow the vernacular Book of Common Prayer first issued in 1552 under Edward; and the Elizabethan Injunctions, which spelled out directives for doing away with "popish rituals" and the like. This Elizabethan Settlement left English Catholics in difficult straits: Were they to give in and abandon their religion? Were they to attempt resistance? Were they to try to alter the queen's mind? Were they to dissemble their views? Even, were they to flee the realm? Things got even worse in 1570, when Pius V unwisely excommunicated Elizabeth and released Catholics from allegiance to her. Several local revolts against Elizabeth failed, and Philip II's blunder of trying to invade England to restore Catholicism with the "Invincible Armada" of 1588 led the vast majority of the population to consider Catholicism the enemy both politically and religiously.

The liturgical question was especially pressing. Catholics no longer had their own churches and liturgies, but many refused to attend the state church services and thus became guilty of the crime of *recusancy* (Latin: *recusare*). Recusants became the name for those Catholics who resisted the Elizabethan Settlement, both at home and abroad, since a number of loyal Catholics, especially of the gentry and clergy, began to leave England for the Low Countries and France, and even for Spain, Portugal, and Rome.[2] The recusants set up printing presses to produce apologetic and religious works in English to smuggle back to nourish their brethren at home, including the so-called Douai-Rheims translation of the Vulgate (NT in 1582; OT in 1609–10). They also established colleges, both for the education of the Catholic gentry and especially for the training of priests willing to risk their lives by returning to England to minister clandestinely to the faithful. Within the colleges there were tensions between the Jesuits, who took over the administration and teaching of many of the institutions, and the secular priests. Both groups, however, sent missionary priests back to England to suffer martyrdom (it has been calculated that about 160 Catholics, both priests and laity, were executed under Elizabeth). The recusants soon began to establish religious houses of various orders: Jesuits, Benedictines, Franciscans, Dominicans, Carmelites, Carthusians, including twenty-two convents for women.[3] The English Benedictines were especially active, founding no fewer than five male houses and eight convents for nuns.[4] Originally three groups of English Benedictines competed for the English mission, but eventually the three united to form the English Benedictine Congregation, recognized by Paul V in 1616. Their first General Chapter was held at St. Gregory's monastery in Douai in July of 1621. Most of the Benedictine houses for women were under the control of the local bishop, but the Benedictine priests, Rudesind Barlow, the President of the English Congregation, and Benedict Jones, Superior of the London District, were instrumental in setting up the convent of Our Lady of Consolation at Cambrai in 1623, a house that was subject to the English Congregation. While the spirituality present in the recusant colleges and religious houses was often influenced by the Ignatian model fostered by the Jesuits, there were also present elements of the spiritual teachings of Francis de Sales, largely taken from his 1608 *Introduction to the Devout Life*. It was the merit of the Benedictine houses, especially of Douai and Cambrai, to introduce a third strain into English recusant spirituality, a teaching given the name "Bakerism" after its originator, Fr. Augustine Baker.[5]

Augustine Baker (1575-1641), Bakerism, and *Sancta Sophia*

A poem appearing in *Sancta Sophia*, a posthumous edited digest based on Augustine Baker's writings, hails him with the words: "As in Sable lines laid o're a silver ground / The face of that mysterious Man is found, / Whose secret life and publish'd Writtings prove, / To pray is not to talke, or thinke, but love. . . ." "That mysterious Man" is appropriate for Baker.[6] Baker remains in many ways a mystery. Was he an important mystical thinker, or only a second-rate compiler of mystical texts? Is there coherence to his teaching, or is it a mishmash of the views of others with internal inconsistencies? Is it fair to measure him against the great mystical thinkers of the previous generation, especially Teresa of Avila and John of the Cross, whom he knew and cites as authorities for his views?

The learned Baker brings together a number of major strands of Western mysticism—first, the monastic tradition that Cuthbert Butler called "Western mysticism"; second, the great age of English mysticism in the fourteenth century;[7] and, third, contemporary Continental mysticism of the early modern period. Baker's attempt to return to the early monastic tradition can be seen, for example, in his stress on contemplative prayer over Ignatian meditation, his emphasis on the Holy Spirit as the only true spiritual director, and his opposition to contemporary (again read Ignatian) forms of examination of conscience.[8] Among the fourteenth-century English mystics, Baker knew Walter Hilton and the anonymous *Cloud of Unknowing* well, and also had some acquaintance with Richard Rolle and Julian of Norwich.[9] Baker sought to combine these two mystical traditions with aspects of the Northern European mysticism of the later Middle Ages represented by authors such as "Thaulerus" (mostly pseudo-Tauler), Hendrik Herp (Harphius), as well as more modern figures, such as Blosius

(Louis de Blois), and two contemporary Capuchins: Benet of Canfield and Constantin de Barbanson.[10] He also knew the writings of Teresa, John of the Cross, and other Spanish mystics. The names of some forty mystical authorities appear in *Sancta Sophia*, and these (and others) are cited in his authentic texts. Despite the frequent use of so many mystical authors, however, Baker was not just a compiler—his mysticism has its own distinctive style.

An Eccentric Monastic Life

David Baker was born in Abergavenny in Wales on December 9, 1575, the last son of a "Church papist," that is, someone who conformed to the Church of England but remained Catholic at heart.[11] At the age of twelve he went to school at Christ's Hospital in London, where he remained before matriculating at Broadgates Hall in Oxford in 1590. He was there for two years but did not take a degree, returning to Abergavenny for several years where he began the study of law, a vocation he pursued at the Inns of Court. Upon the death of his elder brother, Richard, in 1598, his father recalled him to Abergavenny. At this stage, young Baker lived a totally secular life, but this changed in 1600 when a miraculous escape from drowning led to his conversion and to much reading of controversialist texts about the true religion, a course that led him to convert to Catholicism in 1603.

David Baker decided to become a Benedictine and joined the Reformed Benedictine house of Santa Giustina in Padua on May 27, 1605, taking the name Augustine after the monk-missionary who helped convert England. This was his first conversion, as entry into religion was often called. The Ignatian meditative prayer style followed at Santa Giustina did not suit him, however, and his health (never strong) soon gave way, so he returned to England in 1607, where his legal expertise assisted in guaranteeing the legal continuity of the new English Benedictines with the ancient English Congregation.[12] In 1608, Baker took up a life devoted to contemplative prayer and study (his second conversion), while staying at the houses of devout Catholic laity. The later spiritual autobiography in the *Secretum* says he soon attained a high stage of contemplation, what he afterward called "passive contemplation." As he later described it, using the third person:

> And now as touching his passive contemplation itself he can say little in description of it, partly because it being a pure spiritual work it is not explicable in words, and partly for that now it is out of his and my

memory, being so many years since it was acted. But as far as memory now serveth I say that it was a speaking of God to the soul. . . . Yet was it not a seeing of God. Note that our author of the *Cloud* saith how that a person, while he is in this life, shall still have the cloud of unknowing between him and God.

Baker insists that neither active nor passive contemplation can grant a vision of the essence of God in this life. He then gives important particulars about this early event: "The said contemplation fell to our scholar in the forenoon, about eleven of the clock. . . . He had—according to his wont—spent the forepart of that morning in his mental prayer that had been somewhat long and continued." Several times "the spirit of prayer came upon him. . . . And the last time was a little before the said eleven of the clock, whereupon he was raised to the said contemplation." Baker says that such experiences need a long preparation of prayer, until the one praying can go no further, and "God becometh the sole worker, as He is in all such passive contemplations." He even records the duration: "The same contemplation of our scholar lasted not, as I think, above the space of half a quarter of an hour, or at most but for one quarter of an hour. And it was with alienation from senses; I mean, in a rapture."[13]

The gift of ecstatic passive contemplation did not recur, however, and Baker soon fell into a state of tepidity and desolation (ca. 1610–19), during which he gave up mental prayer. Not even his ordination to the priesthood in 1613 helped him overcome his spiritual malaise. He later bewails the fact that he had no good director who could have apprised him of the fact that times of desolation often follow upon periods of ecstatic prayer. It was probably in 1619 or 1620 that a reading of the *Speculum humanae perfectionis* of the Carthusian Johannes Landspergius, as well other works, convinced him to return to a strict regimen of mental prayer (his third conversion). An autobiographical passage in one of his treatises on contemplation (*Book G*) says:

> I also knew a man who, findinge or conceivinge that he could not meditate, & having a good will, he tooke in hand the plaine exercise of acts that is taught & sett downe by Blosius in the *Institution* (Cap. 10) & he therein continued . . . very constantly, & at length (after some time) came to an exercise of aspirations wherin he continued but a very short space, beinnge called & taken out of them in a passive contemplation.[14]

Baker never afterward gave up his contemplative practice.

For a few years Fr. Baker stayed in England, but in 1624 the situation for Catholic priests had become more dangerous, so he crossed over to the English Benedictine house of St. Gregory in Douai in Belgium. He remained there for only a few days, however, because his friend, Fr. Leander Jones, prior of Douai, appointed him as an unofficial spiritual director (not confessor) to the new community of English Benedictine nuns established at Cambrai. The nine years that Baker functioned in this capacity were central to his life and teaching.

The account of his prayer life between about 1620 and 1630 that Baker gives in the autobiographical part of his *Secretum* is detailed. His descriptions of his prayer and its pyschosomatic effects are often curious. For one thing, Baker insists that during this long period he did not regain a state of "passive contemplation" in which only God is at work—in other words, his prayer was different from the early experience of union cited above. Second, Baker was fixated on his feelings of "God's working within him" in both physical and mental ways. These "workings" are never quite defined; perhaps Baker did not know how to, which is why he could only describe them. He insists that the "workings" primarily come from the will, but he describes them in corporeal ways. There are two major accounts in the autobiographical part of the *Secretum*. The first seems to come in the period between 1620 and 1624 before he came to Cambrai. After a year and a half of the prayer of forced acts of the will (i.e., active contemplation), the divine "workings" in the will were sent forth into his body. He says, "And at first they came into the extreme parts of it, as into the hands and feet, and afterwards into the arms and legs; and in these places the working seemed to be and there continued for the space of about a year, by little and little drawing to the middle part of the body, . . . till at last it seemed to be whole about the breast." The exercise in the breast lasted about a year, but was succeeded by something even stranger: "Therehence by little and little the working went upwards and came into the neck . . . and thence went higher into the head, and it seemed to him that it brake forth in his eyes, so that he thought if any man had well regarded his eyes, he must note some alteration in them." Here Baker refers to the *Cloud's* teaching about how some would-be mystics who proceed by imagination alone and look like men that are out of their wits, but he insists that his "working up into the head" was not of this sort. His long explanation of the experience, laced with references to his mystical sources (the *Cloud*, Tauler, Harphius), however, does little to really explain the nature of the "working" that lasted for two or three years.[15]

A second account seems to come from 1629, as he describes "His Present State" while at Cambrai. According to this description, it was mid-Lent in 1627 when "there happened and fell suddenly in and upon his head such an alteration that he greatly wondered at it, nor could he tell what to make of it. He doubted that he should have died upon it; and yet, when he considered the case, he imagined that it was an extreme cold that he had taken." But it was not a cold, and Baker admits that he cannot tell whether its cause was natural or supernatural. The effects described, however, were spiritual. First, a shortening of his prayer regimen. Whereas he previously devoted most of the day to prayer, he now turned his energies more to writing and translating. "The second effect of the said ascent into the head," he says, "was that he found himself in greater light and facility for penning of some spiritual things than he had before."[16] The psychological aspects of these and other of Baker's accounts of his strange experiences raise questions that cannot be pursued here.[17]

Although Baker's style of spiritual direction and his emphasis on the importance of contemplative prayer for enclosed nuns were unusual at the time when many religious houses had been won over to an emphasis on Ignatian meditation, he soon gained support among many of the sisters, especially Dame Gertrude More, whose father's resources supported the foundation, and her friend Dame Catherine Gascoigne. The nuns not only asked Fr. Baker for books about contemplation but also begged him to put down his own teaching in writing. Baker responded with alacrity and incredible energy, and between 1627 and 1632 composed forty or more writings (many quite long). None of these works was written for publication; rather, they were for the spiritual instruction of the nuns. Baker's prolix and repetitive style (his serpentine prose, as it has been called) makes them often difficult reading. But the treatises were treasured by Benedictine nuns and monks over the centuries, so that many survived the ravages of the French Revolution when the Benedictine houses were disbanded.

Augustine Baker's type of direction and advice about prayer were not welcome to all. Fr. Francis Hull, the newly appointed confessor for the Cambrai nuns, soon took issue with him, accusing Baker of a number of theological errors, such as Illuminism, the heresy of the recently condemned Spanish *Alumbrados*. (Baker's stress on the priority of divine "calls," or "inspirations" was easily misunderstood.) The clash between the two Benedictines seems to have been as much personal as doctrinal. Hull was a rigid confessor and a supporter of the necessity of meditation for all, as well as probably being jealous of Baker's influence over the nuns. The upshot was that both Baker and Hull were asked to write statements (*Protestationes*) of their positions for the Benedictine General Chapter that met at Douai in August of 1633. The appointed commission approved Baker's teaching, both in the "Protestation" and in his writings, but enough of a scandal had emerged that both men were removed from Cambrai, Baker going back to St. Gregory in Douai, and Hull being sent to St. Edmund's in Paris. Baker spent the next five years at Douai, although he did not live in community, but as a kind of residential hermit. He continued his prodigious writing, though in a different vein, since his audience now was male monks and theological students. Many were attracted to his teaching and spiritual direction ("Bakerism," as it came to be called).

The final chapter in Augustine Baker's life also involved controversy. The major theologian of St. Gregory's was Fr. Rudisind Barlow (1585–1656), who at first had been favorable to Baker. In 1638, however, they fell out, although it is hard to know whether personal conflicts or differences of view were more important. In any case, Baker wrote an *Introduction to a Treatise on the English Mission*, which painted a negative portrait of an unnamed monk, who could not be other than Fr. Rudisind. In light of the dissension in the community that followed, the President of the English Congregation agreed that Baker should be sent back to England, despite his age and frailty. For the last three years of his life Augustine Baker lived quietly in London or with country friends, often in danger of arrest, imprisonment, and execution. His contemplative life grew even stronger, and he described himself to his disciple Leander Prichard as being *totus in passionibus*, which he explained as not due to physical suffering, but as being once again given the grace of passive contemplation.[18] Augustine Baker died on August 9, 1641.

Baker's Writings

Modern lists of Baker's writings exist, so there is no need to try to record all the titles of his more than sixty works here.[19] The Benedictine translated all or part of many spiritual works, either as stand-alone texts, or by way of long insertions into his own collections.[20] The distinction between original writings and translations almost vanishes in Baker, who was certainly a "bookish" mystic. Although English Benedictines continued to read some of Baker's works over the centuries, his wider reputation rests on a book that is really not his. After Baker's death some of the Benedictines seem to have begun making summaries of his teaching. In 1653, the English Benedictine Congregation commissioned Fr. Serenus Cressy (1605–1674) to prepare a summation of "Bakerism," based on Baker's surviving manuscripts. Cressy's efforts were published in 1657 as *Sancta Sophia*, a reduction to about two hundred thousand words of Baker's more than a million words of repetitive prose.[21] Most previous Baker scholarship has presumed that *Sancta Sophia* represented a fair synthesis of Baker's many writings from the 1620s and 1630s, but this supposition has recently been questioned. John Barrett, for example, summarizes a critical view of Cressy's procedure by arguing, "The process whereby Cressy created the digest of Baker's texts involved a large scale re-interpretation of the material he worked upon, both at a structural level, and at the level of paragraph and even sentence structure."[22] So, until we have more detailed textual studies of the relation between the many authentic writings and *Sancta Sophia*, it is important to remember, as one investigator puts it, that in reading the *Sancta Sophia*, "We don't read Baker: we read Cressy."[23] Three factors fuel this hermeneutic of suspicion: first, Baker did not write with publication in mind; second, he never intended to write a synthesis of his teaching; and, third, the arrangement and structure of *Sancta Sophia*, often praised, are Cressy's work, not Baker's.[24] Hence, in what follows I do not speak of Baker as the author of *Sancta Sophia*, which is Cressy's summary of what he understood to be "Bakerism." Nonetheless, *Sancta Sophia* is an important and influential part of the early modern mystical tradition and deserves attention.

Cressy's edition went on being used. In the nineteenth century, Norbert Sweeney (1821–1883), prior of Downside abbey, produced an improved version of the Cressy text (1876). This has been often reprinted and is still the most-cited version.[25] In the early twentieth century, the English Benedictine Justin McCann (1882–1959) took on the task of reading, editing, and writing about Baker. He claimed to be the only person for almost three hundred years who had read *all* of Baker, and he cautioned that the world was probably not ready for modern editions of the wordy Welshman. This judgment did not deter J. P. H. Clark from beginning to edit all Baker's works. For more than three decades Clark has been issuing editions of many of Baker's unpublished writings under the auspices of the Salzburg-based Analecta Cartusiana.[26] Detailed studies of these works have already begun to provide us with better ways to discriminate between Baker and "Bakerism."[27]

Two texts, however, that will be used in the following account need some introduction. In 1629–30, Baker wrote a hybrid text he called the *Secretum sive Mysticum* (the title probably based on Isaiah 24:16: *Secretum meum est mihi*).[28] This melange includes: (1) an autobiographical account of the Benedictine's mystical experiences;[29] (2) an edition and commentary on the *Cloud of Unknowing*;[30] and (3) materials relating to Baker's spiritual teaching given to the nuns of Cambrai, including a number of long translations of mystical sources (e.g., Blosius, Barbanson, etc.). Messy and complicated as it is, the *Secretum* brings us closer to the real Baker than *Sancta Sophia*. The second text to note is the life that Baker wrote of his deceased penitent, Gertrude More (1606–33). This work attracted the attention of Benedict Weld-Blundell (1857–1931), who produced two volumes under the title *The Inner Life and Writings of Dame Gertrude More* (London: R. & T. Washbourne, 1910–11). The first volume contains a highly edited version of Baker's *The Life and Death of Dame Gertrude More*, while the second volume has Gertrude's three writings edited by Baker: the *Confessiones Amantis*, fifty-three prayers and acts of thanksgiving; various "Fragments"; and *The Apology of Dame Gertrude*, a defense of the style of contemplative prayer she learned from Baker. The many deficiencies of the Weld-Blundell text led to the preparation of a new version of the *Life* by Ben Wekking in 2002.[31]

Augustine Baker, both the "real" Baker of the authentic treatises and the "reworked" Baker of *Sancta Sophia*, is a fascinating but problematic figure. One of the most influential studies on Baker is by David Knowles in his 1961 *The English Mystical Tradition*. Knowles had a deep appreciation of Baker as a spiritual guide and teacher, noting that *Sancta Sophia* "is the only original work in English that gives magisterial guidance over a great part of the spiritual life."[32] But Knowles did not agree with Baker's teaching about the highest forms of mystical union (at least as they are found in *Sancta Sophia*), and he was quite put off by Baker's account of his own mystical experiences. With the possible exception of the "passive contemplative" experiences of the early part of Baker's life, Knowles judged that "[w]hatever he may have experienced it was not mystical union with God."[33] Knowles's criteria for authentic mystical union, however, are based on Teresa of Avila and John of the Cross, and, to a lesser extent, the *Cloud of Unknowing*. Not everyone agrees, especially today, with taking the great Spanish mystics as the benchmark for evaluating all mystics. In a review of Knowles's book Thomas Merton complained that Knowles wrote out of "a kind of scholarly compulsion to deny and reject, as if the most important task of the student of mysticism were to uncover false mystics."[34] In an essay about Baker's mysticism, E. I. Watkin, while admitting inconsistencies and problems in the English Benedictine, judged that *Sancta Sophia* is "safe, sober, solid, simple and sublime," and is "the ripe fruit of the English mystical tradition confirmed, clarified, and enriched by the more scientific mystical theology of the Counter-Reformation."[35] Again, this judgment applies primarily to *Sancta Sophia*.[36]

The Teaching of "Sancta Sophia"

This treatment will be divided into two parts. The first will consider what *Sancta Sophia* has to say about the preparatory stages, or foundations, of the "internal life," that is, the interior life in general, as characterized by spiritual direction and reading, docility to inspirations, solitude, and mortification. The second part will consider prayer, the core of the mystical life, and its three degrees: meditation; the prayer of immediate forced acts of the will; and what the text speaks of as "mystical contemplation." I cannot engage in a comparison of Cressy's digest with Baker's thought as found in the treatises, but I will bring in material from the *Secretum* and other texts where appropriate.

A. Foundations

Sancta Sophia is a massive and repetitive book, but it does have a structure. David Knowles characterizes it as "a carefully arranged series of instructions for one engaged upon the religious life, and especially the monastic contemplative life."[37] The work is divided into three "Treatises." The first bears the title "Of the Internal Life in General" and has three sections and twenty-five chapters.[38] The Second Treatise concerns the "First Instrument of Perfection, viz., Mortification" and has two sections: "Mortification in General" (eight chapters), and "Certain Special Mortifications of the Passions" (fifteen chapters). The Third Treatise is "Of Prayer" and has four sections. Section 1 deals with "Prayer in General and Its Divisions" (seven chapters), while section 2 is on the "First Degree of Internal Prayer," that is, meditation (five chapters). Section 3 concerns the second degree of internal prayer, "Exercises of Immediate Forced Acts of the Will" (seven chapters). Finally, section 4 deals with contemplation, mystical prayer in the true sense, as well as the desolation that often follows it (six chapters). There is a long appendix comprising six collections of model short prayers, or "Devout Exercises of Immediate Acts and Affections of the Will."[39]

Augustine Baker never studied theology and at times expressions of suspicion toward Scholastic theology are found in his authentic writings, as well as in *Sancta Sophia*. Cressy's digest does not engage in speculation, either on the nature of God or on anthropology. Nevertheless, it presupposes a view of human nature as composed of a union of body and soul, two parts that were meant to be fully in harmony but that since Adam's Fall have been in conflict. The powers of sensation constitute the lower part of the human composite, while the superior part consists of the powers of memory, intellect, and will. *Sancta Sophia* is voluntaristic and affective—the intellect is important but cannot lead to contemplative prayer, which is reserved to the affective power.[40] In the long run, however, the highest form of contemplation is rooted in something that goes beyond both intellect and will, what the text variously calls "the summity, or top, of the spirit" (based on the Latin *apex spiritus*), or the "center of the spirit," or the "depth of the spirit."[41] This is a teaching found in many mystics, but *Sancta Sophia* does not engage in speculation on it. More distinctive of the text's understanding of humanity is its notion of "propensities" (or "propensions"), that is, natural and habitual inclinations of thought and feeling manifested in human behavior. These propensities fall into the two broad categories of attractions either to the active or to the contemplative way of living, but they differ markedly in individuals. Supernatural grace builds on these propensities, as God works in us through our inclinations. Their existence, individual characteristics, and how to use them formed a crucial part of Baker's practice as a spiritual director.[42]

In cultivating the contemplative life, *Sancta Sophia* distinguishes three different areas of concern: external aids, the more important interior aids, and practices necessary for making advance in the life of prayer leading to contemplation. The external aids are two: the spiritual director and the use of spiritual reading. (Baker was a skilled spiritual director, as can be seen in his *Life and Death of Dame Gertrude More*.) Nonetheless, the goal of spiritual direction, according to *Sancta Sophia*, was gradually to efface the role of the director by teaching the penitent/advisee about how to open herself up to the action of the true and only interior teacher, the Holy Spirit. The text advises the instructor "not to teach his own way, nor indeed any determinable way of prayer, etc., but to instruct his disciples how they may themselves find out the way proper for them . . . ; in a word, that he is only God's usher, and must lead souls in God's way and not his own."[43] *Sancta Sophia* has sane advice for dealing with the interior distractions that often affect scrupulous souls—what it calls "riddance" and "patience." Riddance is giving the soul some "ease and latitude" with regard to external acts that are not obligatory, while patience is needed for dealing with aridities and desolations.[44] One of the crucial themes for understanding spiritual direction is that of the "liberty of spirit" that must be allowed to souls striving for contemplation.[45] The second external aid is reading spiritual books, a list of which is provided in section 2, chapter 3 (ed., 87). Spiritual reading is second only to prayer itself, but *Sancta Sophia* says that God can bring even unlettered souls to the heights of contemplation.[46]

Much greater importance is to be given to the interior aids, especially the "calls and inspirations," which are indispensable to spiritual progress. According to David Knowles, Baker's (i.e., *Sancta Sophia*'s) teaching here is valuable and original.[47] According to *Sancta Sophia*, "the spirit of corrupt nature" and "the Divine Spirit" are constantly at war in fallen humans, and contemplative souls must train themselves to be attentive and obedient to "the divine inspirations [that] are necessary forasmuch as concerns the proper and essential actions of Christian virtue, which receive all their meritoriousness from the said inspirations."[48] The divine inspirations spoken of are not extraordinary events, such as visions, locutions, and the like, about which the text advises caution;[49] they are the inner motions and illuminations by which the Holy Spirit communicates promptings about either a course of action to be followed, or, more often, things to be omitted or avoided.[50] They are a kind of actual grace, though presumably a higher species than the actual graces necessary for every saving act.[51]

Sancta Sophia 1.2.9 distinguishes inspirations from calls. Inspirations are only internal, whereas "the term of divine calls imports both an external ordination of God, and also his internal operation in our souls suitable to the external call" (ed., 128). The commands of religious superiors, and indeed all the duties attendant on our state of life as Christians, are external calls. The internal inspirations God gives us in their regard are intended "not only simply to direct and incline us to perform all Christian, regular, and other duties with readiness and cheerfulness, but to do them with perfection and purity of intention, in and for God only, as if he had immediately and visibly imposed them on us" (ed., 128–29). Purity of intention, that is, doing things only for God's sake, is one of the key elements in *Sancta Sophia*. Purity of intention is nothing else but docility to the inspirations of the Holy Spirit.[52] Thus, it is not so much the value of the act, or even of its goal, but the degree of purity of intention with which it is done that is central. James Gaffney summarizes his position: "It is Baker's teaching that supernatural merit necessarily depends on an actual or virtual purity of intention, which depends in turn on correspondence with divine inspiration, whereby the agency of man is made instrumental to the initiative of God."[53]

The more the contemplative leads a pure and inner life, the more he or she will be aware of these promptings. But there are three impediments that hinder attentiveness to inner inspirations. The first is distracting images, which the contemplative can remove through living an "abstractive life," that is, one separated from the world. The second is "unruly passions," which are curbed by a life of mortification, while the third is the lack of "that indifference and liberty of spirit which is necessary to all that will seriously follow the divine guidance in all the ways that they are then led by it."[54] Presumably the habit of recollection and the practice of patience are of major assistance in acquiring this indifference and freedom of spirit. The struggle to overcome the three impediments and arrive at a life of inner attentiveness to the divine inspirations is well expressed by one of the frequent motifs of the book—the contrast between the distracting multiplicity of ordinary active life and the simplicity of the contemplative life. Adam's life in paradise was characterized by unity and simplicity, but the Fall introduced him "to miserable multiplicity, and from peace to endless war."[55] "Inner-livers," then, are striving to regain as far as possible the Adamic state, an ancient monastic theme.

Sixteenth- and seventeenth-century mystics were haunted by the specter of Illuminism, the notion that a divine inner light was the essence of true religion and that external religious practices were secondary, perhaps even dispensable. This is what the Spanish *Alumbrados* were accused of (rightly or wrongly), and the teaching can certainly be found among some of the Radical Reformers and with the English Quakers, who were soon to come on the scene. It is no accident that Fr. Baker was subject to similar accusations. Baker certainly held that the exterior rules and structures of the religious life were designed to facilitate attention to the inner promptings of the Holy Spirit, and not vice versa. Despite a number of strong statements about how inner illuminations outweigh all exterior things, especially in some of his other writings, *Sancta Sophia* works hard to absolve Baker of real Illuminism, although some of his disciples may have veered in an Illuminist direction.[56] *Sancta Sophia* 1.2.9 deals with objections against Baker's teaching on inspirations and argues both that external calls overrule internal ones, and especially that the authority of religious superiors ought to overrule inspirations, even in things not of obligation (ed.,

129-31). Baker's 1633 explanation of his views, the "Protestation of Father Anonimus and his Scollers: or a Declaration of his doctrine and practise in the matter of the Divine Call," was approved by the General Chapter of the Benedictine Congregation.[57] The issue, however, did not go away. The conflict between inspirations and the claims to obedience of external authority was a key issue in the history of mysticism, and the debate about whether Baker had stepped over the line in some of his statements about the primacy of inner inspiration continued.[58] In his preface to *Sancta Sophia*, Cressy mounts an extended defense of Baker's view of the necessity of divine inspirations, despite the fact that "the fanatic sectaries which now swarm in England more than ever, will be ready to take advantage from hence to justify their frenzies and disorders; all of which they impute with all confidence to divine inspirations, illuminations, and impulses."[59] The edition also reprinted "A Memorial" written by Baker's friend Fr. Leander de S. Martino, defending Baker's teaching. This ends with a brief summary of the doctrine of divine calls that has Fr. Baker's own written approval.[60]

A question that surfaces during the discussion of calls and inspirations concerns the extent of the call to the contemplative life. Are all people called to contemplation? Baker was a Benedictine much influenced by the *Cloud of Unknowing* with its clear preference for the contemplative life. There is an obvious preference for the contemplative life over the active in *Sancta Sophia* (e.g., 1.1.1-3), something that may seem retrograde in light of how mystics like Ignatius of Loyola and Teresa of Avila argued that being a "contemplative in action" (*contemplativus in actione*) was the highest stage of the mystical life. When one searches *Sancta Sophia* carefully, however, one can discover qualifications about the preference for the pure contemplative life. First of all, the text insists that contemplation is open to all believers,[61] and, second, it instructs contemplative religious who are called to active duties and obligations about how to maintain their inner union with God, in other words, to become contemplatives in action, as far as possible.[62]

Section 3 of treatise 1 forms an investigation of "The School of Contemplation," which teaches the necessary practices and modes of life that aid in progress to contemplation. Solitude is an essential practice, but it is something that, while more easily practiced in the religious life, cannot be denied to those who live in the world (1.3.1). Hence, the work includes a chapter on how secular persons may learn to adapt the counsels it gives primarily to religious to their own situations (1.3.2; ed., 140-45). What follows are eight chapters of advice to those in the religious state, who formed the primary audience for the work.

Treatise 2 concerns mortification, one of the two practices necessary for the contemplative life, prayer being the other. Although inferior to prayer, mortification is equally necessary for the soul's progress. The presentation is clear and sober, dealing with "Mortification in General" and "Mortifications of the Passions." These chapters contain much useful ascetical advice. In terms of the preparation for mysticism, the most important aspect of this section is the distinction between necessary and voluntary mortifications (2.1.5; ed., 218–25). Briefly put, *Sancta Sophia* counsels that the soul's willing submission to the necessary mortifications involved in all human life is an essential part of the preparation and growth of mystical prayer, while voluntary mortifications, where a person chooses to inflict some special ascetic practice on the self (often in imitation of the saints) is unwise, even dangerous, unless a divine inspiration to do so has been made explicitly clear. The major general forms of mortification of life for contemplatives are four: (1) abstraction of life, (2) solitude, (3) silence, and (4) peace, or tranquility of mind. These are discussed in section 1, chapters 6–8.

Section 2 of treatise 2 deals with the mortification of the passions, that is, the affections. The four basic passions (love, anger, fear, and sorrow) are discussed in considerable detail in fifteen chapters. The discussion of love, the root of all the passions, is especially important (2.2.2–5; ed., 241–65).[63] Love is defined as "an internal complacence and inclination to an object from the goodness or beauty believed to be in it" (2.2.2; ed., 243) and is differentiated into two inseparable forms: the love of desire for our own pleasure, and the love of friendship, where we seek not our own good but the good of the other. "Charity," says the text, "is . . . a love of friendship to God, and for his sake only to men or ourselves" (2.2.2; ed., 245). Charity, as the director of all our actions, is nothing else than "the Purity of intention, by which we do refer all that we do or suffer to the love and glory of God" (2.2.4; ed., 249). There is also a long discussion of the relation of love of God and love of neighbor, that is, the ordering of love (2.2.5; ed., 255–65). Along with love, the most important virtue treated is humility in chapter 13 (ed., 309–20). *Sancta Sophia*, in line with many contemporary mystics, such as Benet of Canfield and Constantin de Barbanson, stresses the absolute nothingness of the soul as the root of the virtue of humility. There is a great difference, though, between general intellectual knowledge of our nothingness and "the feeling or perception of it." This feeling comes in two versions. The first is when the soul is so raised above the body that it loses "all care and solicitude about it." The second is more powerful and properly mystical. It takes place when, after periods of desolation, the soul "begins to have a more perfect feeling of her not-being, consisting in an abstraction from the soul herself and all her faculties and operations, all of which are so lost and annihilated in God, that in her exercises of most pure prayer she cannot perceive distinctly any working either in the understanding or will, not being able to give an account of what she does when she prays."[64]

B. *Sancta Sophia*'s Teaching on Prayer and Mystical Contemplation

The treatment of the three degrees of prayer in treatise 3 of *Sancta Sophia* constitutes the heart of its teaching about the union with God possible in this life.[65] In one place the text even speaks of this as "mystical union."[66] *Sancta Sophia* does not, of course, use the word "mysticism" but employs the qualifier "mystic/mystical" often and in many contexts. The most frequent is "mystic authors," who can also be called "mystical doctors," or just "mystics." But we also find "mystical contemplation," "mystic matters," "mystic affairs," "mystic exercises," and "mystical theology" (surprisingly just once).[67]

Of particular interest is a passage in the *Secretum* where Baker says, "Some mystic authors have laid certain terms or names upon such contemplations [his active and passive contemplations] as they themselves had experienced; the which names I shall here set down, without any explication of them, though I think it not amiss to make you acquainted with such of those names and terms as I have met with in books." This list that follows includes "*Unio Mystica*, A Mystick Union," for which he does provide an explanation: "Here I mean a passive union; for the active union is another kind of union; the which active union is sometimes in it or in its effect also called transformation. And both active and passive union is sometimes called a deification." He continues with other key terms: "In these unions are sometimes understood annihilations, the mystick death of the soul, the mystick liquefaction or melting of the soul, mystick fervor and languishing."[68]

Right from the start *Sancta Sophia* insisted that the "infinite variety of paths and fashions" for seeking God all tended "to the same general end, which is the union of our spirits with God by perfect love."[69] This union, to be sure, is just a pale shadow of the final union to be realized in heaven, "the inconceivably happy union" with God in mind, will, and affections "which consists in a returning to the divine principle from whom he flowed."[70] Union language is frequent throughout *Sancta Sophia*,[71] and this language always goes together with that of prayer and contemplation. According to the outset of treatise 3, the whole "internal contemplative life" involves two duties, mortification and prayer. Having treated the former in treatise 2, "[w]e are now henceforward to treat of the other most noble and divine instrument of perfection, which is prayer," by which we attain the reward of all our efforts, "union with God, in which alone consists our happiness and perfection."[72]

The definitions of prayer given in chapter 1 of treatise 3 are traditional. Prayer is "an offering and giving to God whatsoever he may justly require from us." Or, prayer is "an elevation of the mind to God," that is, "an affectuous actuation of an intellective soul towards God, expressing, or at least implying, an entire dependence on him as the author and fountain of all good." It is also "a desire and intention to aspire to an union of spirit with him" (ed., 341–42). "Since in prayer alone the soul is united to God . . . , by consequence, it is of all other actions and duties the most indispensably necessary" (ibid.).[73] External, that is, vocal, prayer is not prayer at all, *unless* it is accompanied by inner intention, in which case it can become an instrument to bring a soul to contemplation.[74] The book's main concern, however, is with internal or mental prayer, specifically affective prayer. This can be: (1) imperfect and acquired, or (2) perfect and that which is called properly infused prayer. Perfect infused prayer is the "prayer of contemplation," which *Sancta Sophia* says is the prayer taught by many mystical authorities, as well as Teresa and John of the Cross.[75]

The second section of treatise 3 is devoted to meditation, the first degree of internal prayer. This section begins by noting the conformity between these three stages of prayer and the traditional three ways of purgation, illumination, and union.[76] Meditation is discursive and primarily uses the understanding and the imagination to consider its objects, which include "the infinite joys of heaven, the sublime mysteries of faith, the blessed humanity of our Lord, the glorious attributes of divinity, etc." (chap. 1; ed., 399). It is the first stage of the ascent of interior prayer—necessary, especially for beginners but soon to be surpassed by the "inner-livers."[77] *Sancta Sophia* does not undervalue meditation, but it obviously thinks that most contemplative religious, especially religious women, who have a greater natural propensity for contemplation than men,[78] should soon pass to the higher stages of internal prayer. At the end of section 2, chapter 5 takes up the controverted question of whether meditation on Christ's Passion may be left behind in the move to higher prayer. Contrary to the positions of Benet of Canfield and Teresa, who argued that consideration of Christ's

Passion can never be abandoned, *Sancta Sophia* argues that "a due liberty of spirit should [not] be abridged for any pretext whatsoever. The ground of which liberty is this, that a soul is to make the experience and proof of her own spiritual profit to be the rule and measure of all her spiritual exercises." Souls may find themselves unable to meditate on the details of Christ's Passion as they once could, but they can exemplify the Passion both in their internal prayer by showing similar acts of love, humility, and patience as Christ did on the cross, and by practicing these virtues in their outward lives. Truly perfect souls will have the imagination so perfectly in union with the superior soul that "a view of the humanity of our Lord will drive the soul more deeply into the Divinity."[79] In the felicitous formulation of Edmund Power, "the Passion is indeed important, but in the higher reaches of prayer, it is to be experienced and lived rather than meditated upon by means of the understanding."[80] The treatment of meditation ends with a discussion of the signs indicating when the move from discursive meditation to the higher stages of prayer is called for.

The discussion of meditation on the Passion raises the issue of how christological the teaching of *Sancta Sophia* may be said to be. The treatise is not systematically christological in the way that the works of someone like Pierre de Bérulle are. In one place, however, *Sancta Sophia* talks about the "Nothingness" of the Incarnate Word in a manner that seems close to Bérulle, but this is, admittedly, an outlier.[81] In reading through *Sancta Sophia*, one is not struck by a plethora of references to the life of Christ or inner devotion to Jesus, although these appear from time to time, especially in relation to the Passion.[82] An anomaly, however, is created by a look at the "Exercises" of Acts and Aspirations that Cressy added to the volume. Many of these are affective expressions of personal love for Jesus of a typically Baroque form. While the text of *Sancta Sophia* is abstract, these prayers are of a strongly affective Jesus devotion.

The second degree of internal prayer is called "Exercises of Immediate Forced Acts of the Will" and marks the entry "into the ways of contemplation." These are explained: "For the exercises of the will are the sublimest that any soul can practice, and all the difference that hereafter follows is only either in regard of the greater or lesser promptitude, or in regard to the degrees of purity wherewith the soul produces such acts."[83] Thus, the life of prayer is a continuum more than a series of discrete stages, a fact that is evident in the subsequent admission that, at the beginning of the exercise of forced acts of the will, there is always some degree of meditation and the use of images.

Only gradually will the soul learn to reject all distinct images and rely on "that obscure notion which faith informs us of God's totality and incomprehensibility; and this only is truth, whereas all distinct images are but the imperfect shadow of truth."[84] *Sancta Sophia*, then, has an anti-intellectual view of prayer, though this relates primarily to the discursive and conceptualizing function of the intellect.

The important first chapter of section 3 sets out the broad lines of two forms of contemplative prayer. The first, which is under discussion here, is the exercise of forced acts or affections of the will, that is, acts and affections that are not based on intellectual discourse but that come immediately from a person's disposition. They are "forced," because at the beginning they do not flow naturally but require voluntary effort. They differ from the "exercise of aspirations" pertaining to the highest form of contemplation, not so much in substance but by reason of "the facility wherewith they [i.e., the latter] are produced without force, foresight, or election, purely flowing from the impulse of the Divine Spirit . . . , the constant exercise of which is proper and perfect contemplation."[85] In other words, forced acts are primarily acquired and elicited by human effort, though always under the influence of grace, while aspirations are infused by God and produced without effort. *Sancta Sophia* also distinguishes between the "acts" and the "affections" of the will. Acts (e.g., humiliation, resignation) are made in the superior will without the concurrence of sense nature, while the lower affections (e.g., love, joy, hope, desire) are immersed in sensation. The affections are useful, but souls must strive to rise above sense love into the superior spiritual will whose operations alone can perfect them.

In order to illustrate the point *Sancta Sophia* concludes with "a collection of several patterns of exercises by acts of the will and holy affections," as well as some perfect aspirations, designed to aid in the practice of contemplative prayer. These are of many kinds to fit the variety of souls and their stage in the contemplative path—some pertaining more to the purgative way (remorse, fear, contrition) and some more to the illuminative and unitive ways (adoration, resignation, love).[86] The rest of section 3 of treatise 3 concerns acts of resignation to the Divine Will (chap. 3), how to pray in times of distraction (chap. 4), praying in sickness (chap. 5), and the use of discretion, not only in mortifications but also in the stages of prayer (chap. 6).

Contemplative prayer in the truest sense of the word is the subject of section 4 of treatise 3, although it had been discussed in a number of earlier places in *Sancta Sophia*.[87] The text's view of contemplation, especially its division between active and passive contemplation, has elicited much discussion. *Sancta Sophia* begins with the "accepted general notion of the word contemplation, but since this generally involves "mental seeing and quiet regarding of an object," it will not do for the text's anti-intellectual view of contemplation. So, *Sancta Sophia* provides a second meaning to the word, one that has nothing to do with the commonly accepted view: "There is a mystic contemplation which is, indeed, truly and properly such, by which a soul without discoursings and curious speculations, without any perceptible use of the internal senses or sensible images, by a pure, simple, and reposeful operation of the mind, in the obscurity of faith, simply regards God as infinite and incomprehensible verity, and with the whole bent of the will rests in him as (her) infinite, universal, and incomprehensible good."[88] This definition highlights an essential issue of the text's understanding of contemplation, namely, the priority of the will. But what role does intellect have? This is a problem for the rest of the chapter.

Angels contemplate God perfectly without sensible forms. "Our perfection," according to *Sancta Sophia*, "will consist in approaching as near as may be to such an angelical contemplation of God without sensible forms, and as he is indeed proposed by faith, that is, not properly represented, but obscure notions imprinted in our minds concerning him." So, there is nothing to perceive or imagine "but an inexhaustible ocean of universal being and good, infinitely exceeding our comprehension; which . . . we love with the whole possible extension of our wills, embracing God beyond the proportion of our knowing him."[89] Citations are made to Tauler, Harphius, and others about the need for annihilating external and internal senses and drawing the powers of the intellectual soul up into "that unity which alone is capable of perfect union with God." *Sancta Sophia* says it will not try to determine if such expressions "will abide the strict examination of philosophy." While it allows that even the "pure operations" of the soul have some connection with the "internal senses and sensible images" according to the Scholastics, nevertheless, the text claims that the operations in the pure degree of prayer are so subtle, pure, and immaterial, that the soul "cannot perceive at all that she works by images." The key is that these "pure intellectual operations" are not in the intellect at all. We read, "On the contrary, they are exercised in a manner wholly by the will, for in the proper aspirations the soul hath no other use of the understanding but only antecedently to propose an object, which is no other but only a general obscure confused notion of God, as faith darkly teaches, and this rather virtually than directly and expressly, the main business being to elevate the will and unite it to God so presented."[90] *Sancta Sophia* thus seems to assume that the intellect has no function other than to make images and create concepts, a position that eliminates, or at least severely restricts, any role for knowing, even intuitive and connatural knowing, in mystical union. The *intellectual* soul no longer needs the intellect!

The tradition of placing the acme of mystical contemplation in loving union beyond intellect (often called "Affective Dionysianism") goes back at least to the thirteenth century with Thomas Gallus and Bonaventure.[91] Both of these mystics, and their successors in the later Middle Ages, however, recognized a role for higher dimensions of intellect, one that had an important, though not final, place in leading to mystical union at the height of the spirit (*apex spiritus*). Restricting the intellect to the level of discourse and image seems to leave *Sancta Sophia*, and perhaps also Baker himself, in a more consistently anti-intellectual position than most of the mystics in the tradition of Affective Dionysianism.

What is essential to chapter 1, however, is not so much the rather problematic attempts of *Sancta Sophia* to deal with the relation of intellect and will in the ascent to "perfect mystical union or contemplation," but the distinction of mystic contemplation or union into two kinds: (1) active and ordinary, that is, "an habitual state of perfect souls by which they are enabled . . . to unite themselves actively and actually to God by efficacious, fervent, amorous, and constant, yet withal silent and quiet, elevations of the spirit"; and (2) "passive and extraordinary; the which is not a state but an actual grace and favor from God, by which he is pleased at certain times, . . . to communicate a glimpse of his majesty to the spirits of his servants."[92] Active contemplation is habitual and constant, acquired by the soul's efforts as empowered by grace, while passive contemplation is transitory, infused, and totally dependent on God.[93] As the account of the two forms of contemplation proceeds in chapters 1 to 4, however, things become more murky. The intentions of *Sancta Sophia* are, as ever, practical. It does not try to sort out "these great variety of ascents and descents," but turns to the prayer proper to the state of active contemplation in chapter 2.

The prayers characteristic of active contemplation are "purely spiritual operations of the will." These aspirations, or elevations, are "certain short and lively affections of the soul, by which she expresses a thirsty longing after God, such as these: 'My God when shall I love thee alone?' 'When shall I be united to thee?'"[94] These expressions can also be used in meditation and in the prayer of immediate forced acts, but they take on a different modality in the state of active contemplation, because (1) they tend directly to God; (2) they involve no images of God, but only the confused notion dependent on "obscure general faith"; (3) they have no preceding discourse; (4) they come without deliberation from the Holy Spirit; (5) they do not last long in imperfect contemplatives; and (6) they are more efficacious than the "immediate acts" of the second stage of prayer as proceeding from "a more habitually perfect ground."[95] In line with the teaching of the twentieth-century English Benedictine John Main, Laurence Freeman suggests that these aspirations are not that different from the practice of the prayer of the mantra advocated by Main and close to the monologistic prayer formulae found in Cassian and the *Cloud* author, both well known to Baker.[96] The criteria for the prayer of aspirations given in the text are detailed and practical, as is the note that the soul that comes to the state in which she makes constant aspirations is able to do so in the midst of the activity of external business, because the understanding is not involved in them and is therefore capable of attending to other things. This long chapter closes with a discussion of five benefits the soul accrues in "this sublime exercise" (ed., 517–19), the third of which is its effect on the understanding. "Now the soul," says *Sancta Sophia*, "loses all remembrance of itself and of all created things, and all that she retains of God is a remembrance that he cannot be seen or comprehended"—that is, "the cloud of unknowing."

The next two chapters treat the several sorts of passive unions. One may well wonder, if active union is identified with "the highest possible mystical contemplation," what is the status of these passive acts of union. The answer seems to lie in the distinction between the ordinary form of union taught by such mystical authorities as the *Cloud*,[97] and the extraordinary forms given by divine gift to only the few (e.g., Teresa). *Sancta Sophia* insists that "perfect union is only in this of Aspirations," but admits there are infinite degrees: "How much soever it increases, it will never exceed that obscure light which faith affords, which is the most perfect light that we can have in this life. . . . [I]n perfect contemplation this light of faith is the only light." As in John of the Cross, *Sancta Sophia* emphasizes the absolute necessity of the darkness of faith in attaining mystical union.[98]

There are still problems about the categories of active and passive contemplation. David Knowles judged that Baker exhibited "real confusion in the degrees of the spiritual life and the principles of mystical theology," to the extent that "Fr. Baker failed to arrive at an adequate definition of contemplation." The reason for this was twofold, according to Knowles. The first was that Baker failed to realize that no effort or emotion of the will (e.g., aspirations) can be "a proximate means of union with God," but only the virtues of faith in the intellect and hope and charity in the will. The second, taken from John of the Cross, was the failure to emphasize the need for passive purgation of the intellect and will. Thus, Baker's unfortunate distinction between active and passive contemplation, which muddles the dictum that "contemplation is to receive."[99] Baker's distinction is certainly not that of John of the Cross, but is it radically confused? E. I. Watkin sought to show that whatever confusions Baker's distinctions may have, they are not quite so radical as Knowles imagines. He argues, "Baker's active contemplation is the mystical contemplation usually called passive"; that is, it is fundamentally infused and effected by the operation of the Holy Spirit in the darkness of faith, and thus can be identified with the highest form of passive contemplation as taught by Teresa and John of the Cross, if not in all regards.[100] Watkin's argument seems closer to the intentions of *Sancta Sophia*, although the debates are by now antiquated.

Chapters 3 and 4 of section 4 of *Sancta Sophia* give an extended discussion of passive contemplative union, the level where God alone is at work and the soul is totally passive. In passive union, "God reveals himself to the soul by a supernatural species impressed in her, in which he is the only agent, and she is the patient."[101] The text divides the supernatural graces given in passive contemplative union into two forms: those given to the sensible part of the soul, and what are called "intellectual gifts"—although one may well ask, How can there be gifts given to an intellect that has already been left behind? In sensible unions, the least perfect are those given to the outward senses (e.g., apparitions, physical manifestations), while the higher are those communicated to the inner sense, such as raptures, ecstasies, and internal visions. The latter do have a role in mysticism, so *Sancta Sophia* provides twelve rules for discerning true gifts from false (3.4.3; ed., 522–25). Chapter 4 treats the perfect passive unions that are purely intellectual. Here the divine mystery is presented immediately to the understanding without images or discourse. These begin inwardly through the agency of what are called "divine inactions," or inward workings (*inwerken*, an originally Flemish term). "Herein," says the text, "God is not seen as he is, yet he is clearly seen that he is and that he is incomprehensible." These divine passive unions are "far more strait and immediate than any of the former; a union exercised more by the will than the understanding, although the effect thereof be to refund great light into the understanding." So, both will *and* understanding seem to be involved, contrary to what was claimed earlier. This light, however, is *in caligine*, that is, in the darkness of faith, "in which God is more perfectly seen, because there is nothing seen that is not God." Properly speaking, it is above both intellect and will "in that supreme portion of the spirit which is visible to God alone, and in which he alone can inhabit."[102] Chapter 4 closes with a description of the three main benefits that passive union brings to the whole soul, intellect, will, and imagination and senses (3.4.4; ed. 533–36).

Chapter 5 concerns the desolation that usually follows union and how the devout soul should deal with this, because of the many benefits it can bring when properly understood.[103] Based on Baker's reminiscences of such "most terrible unexpected desolation," Cressy presents a consoling message of how to deal with such trials so that the soul will not be tempted to succumb to this condition but will recognize that "out of this darkness God produces light and strength from this infirmity." Beyond what can be sensed in the faculties, the soul still remains "in constant union and adhesion to God" in the center of the spirit. If she practices tranquility of mind and exercises resignation, she will attain many rewards, including "a new light to penetrate into the mystery of our Lord's desertion in the garden and on the cross, and from this light a most inflamed love for him." The experience produces transcendence of God's gifts, profound humility, and a state of full confidence in God in the midst of present suffering, as well as of any possible future affliction. "For what has a soul left to fear that can with a peaceable mind support, yea, and make her benefit the absence of God himself."

In a concluding chapter (3.4.6), *Sancta Sophia* summarizes "the end of all these exercises of mortification and prayer." The end is love: "All these favors, therefore, and all these sufferings do end in this: namely, the accomplishment of this love in our souls, so that all our perfection consists in a state of love and in our entire conformity with the divine will."[104] Love has many states and degrees, but it is "divinely beautiful in all." So it is clear that it is love, not prayer as the means to attain love, that is the real goal.

This state of perfection seems to be higher than passive contemplation (another of the anomalies in Baker's account). Passive contemplations were temporary divine favors, but, following Barbanson, Baker now says that "this new union is not only now a gift and operation of God that is of short continuance, nor only simple actual infusions, . . . but the very foundation, state, and disposition of the soul is changed, reversed, and reformed by divine grace, which being a participation of the Divine Being, and, consequently, making us partakers of the divine nature, confers on us a stable and permanent state in regard to our interior."[105] This habitation of God in the souls of the perfect who contemplate him in the "absolute obscurity of faith," according to *Sancta Sophia*, is called by "some mystic writers" . . . "the union of Nothing with Nothing," that is, the union of the divested soul that now "being nowhere corporally or sensible, is everywhere spiritually and immediately united to God, this infinite Nothing."[106] The state of union is thus a state of perfect No-thingness. Who the mystic writers are that Baker has in mind here is not clear. The *Cloud* author may be included, but *Sancta Sophia* goes on to cite Canfield. More tellingly, the last authority cited is a rare reference to Dionysius: "[I]n this perfect state the soul's desire is to be nowhere, and she seeks nothing that either sense or spirit can fix upon. Such souls can taste and comprehend what St. Denis meant in his Instruction to Timothy: 'But thou, O Timothy, relinquish the sense and sensible operations, . . . and according to thy utmost possibility raise thyself in ignorance and renouncing of all knowledge, to a union with God above all substance . . . and knowledge.'"[107] It is difficult to know if this perfect union of the two "Nothings," divine and human, is a stage beyond active and passive union/contemplation, or their higher synthesis.

The *Sancta Sophia* is an impressive handbook of the contemplative life from its origins to end. Although directed to religious, it is not without relevance to those who do not lead an enclosed life. Aspects of its teaching have been controversial from the start, and it is difficult to say whether its teaching, as well as that of Baker's that forms its foundation, is fully coherent. He might well not have cared, since Baker was not a man of theory but a spiritual guide, a bit of a controversialist, and an avid reader of mystical literature who cited at length, but rarely paused to see if his authorities were in agreement. That said, *Sancta Sophia*, his almost-treatise, is among the most important English mystical texts.

Baker's Disciples among the Benedictine Monks and Nuns

We have already noted Fr. Baker's younger Benedictine disciples, especially Fr. Leander Prichard and Fr. Peter Salvin, both of whom wrote lives of Baker. Prichard's *Life and Writings of the Venerable Father,*

F. Augustine Baker was written about 1643,[108] while Salvin's *Life* was penned for the nuns of Cambrai in 1646. Salvin's text contains a good short summary of Baker's teaching on mortification and prayer.[109] A third *Life* was written by Serenus Cressy.[110]

Born Hugh Paulinus Cressy, the Yorkshireman was an Oxford graduate and fellow of Merton College. Ordained in the Established Church in 1629, he served in several important ecclesiastical positions. During the turmoil of the English Civil War he went abroad, where his doubts about Anglicanism led him to convert to Rome in 1646. He wrote a much-discussed defense of his conversion, the *Exomologesis* in 1647, before becoming a Benedictine at St. Gregory's in Douai in 1649.[111] Although Cressy never met Baker, he was deeply influenced by his mystical teaching, as shown not only by his efforts in producing *Sancta Sophia* (1653–57), but also by his publishing of two English mystics favored by Baker, Walter Hilton's *Scale of Perfection* in 1659 and Julian of Norwich's *Revelations* in 1670 (the first printing of the noted mystic). Cressy's preface to *Sancta Sophia* shows how well he had synthesized Baker's thought and modified some of its exaggerations. After the Restoration, Cressy returned to England, where he engaged in a controversy with the Anglican divine Bishop Edward Stillingfleet (1635–1699), who attacked Baker, Julian of Norwich, and other mystics as "Fanaticks" in his *A Discourse concerning the Idolatry practised in the Church of Rome* (1672). Cressy responded with a treatise *Fanaticism fanatically imputed to the Catholick Church by Dr. Stillingfleet* (1672) and an *Epistle Apologetical* in 1674.[112] Cressy noted that to attack the mystics is also to attack St. Paul, and he was not impressed with Stillingfleet's wide learning, saying, "He may by such a way of writing beget in the minds of the vulgar sort of readers a high opinion of the vastness of his unnecessary reading and his well-furnished library."[113]

Baker's greatest seventeenth-century influence, however, was on the Benedictine nuns for whom he served as spiritual advisor. Recent decades have seen a great increase in our knowledge of the English Recusant nuns. According to Laurence Lux-Sterritt, "Thanks to ... recent studies across a range of disciplines we know more than ever before about English religious women in exile."[114] These studies have mined the cache of primary sources that exists for the twenty-two houses of Recusant nuns, telling us much about many aspects of their lives, including their spirituality and mysticism.[115] There were two lines of the convents of Benedictine nuns. The first line was begun with the convent of the Glorious Assumption of Our Lady founded by Lady Mary Percy (1570–1642) at Brussels in 1598. Percy's interest in mysticism is evident from her role in putting out an English translation of *An Abridgement of Christian Perfection*.[116] The spirituality of the Brussels community was primarily Jesuit, although this led to debates and divisions among the nuns. The situation grew so grave that in 1624 a group of the more strongly Jesuit-leaning nuns left to found a new house at Ghent. This community became noted for the many mystical gifts (visions, raptures, etc.) recorded about some of its members.[117] Ghent was the mother house of three daughters: Boulogne in 1652; Dunkirk in 1662; and Ypres in 1665. The line of Cambrai, which we have seen was founded in 1623 under strictly Benedictine auspices, was not so prolific. Its only foundation was at Paris in 1651, although this house came under the authority of the archbishop of Paris in 1657.

"Ghent stands out as a supporter of the idiosyncratic use of the supernatural which was typical of the Jesuit missionaries in England. . . . The Cambrai (and Paris) papers offered an array of mystical writings, but were shy on the topic of sensate experience."[118] This, of course, is due to the Bakerite heritage, which these two convents did so much to preserve. A number of nuns left spiritual writings, poems, and personal notes, such as Margaret Gascoigne (1608-1637), Clementia Cary (1615-1674), and Barbara Constable (1617-1684). Here I will concentrate on the two nuns who were closest to Fr. Baker and did the most to defend his teaching: Catherine Gascoigne (1600-1676) and Gertrude More (1606-1633).

Catherine Gascoigne was a member of an aristocratic family from Yorkshire, many of whose members entered religious life.[119] She joined the original group of Cambrai nuns at Douai and was thus a founding member. She was Fr. Baker's earliest and most faithful adherent and served as prioress of the Cambrai convent for much of her life (1629-41 and 1645-73). In 1655, Fr. Claude White, the President of the Benedictine Congregation, demanded the surrender of all the Baker manuscripts in the possession of the convent to purge them of "poisonous doctrine." Catherine and the community bravely resisted and Fr. White fortunately died later that year.[120] Catherine wrote an early defense of Baker ("Father Anonymous") and his method of prayer that was submitted to the 1633 General Chapter of the Benedictines that acquitted him of error. Surviving in a 1743 manuscript, it is a short document but a good summary of some of the basic points of Baker's teaching.[121]

Gertrude More (born Helen), Catherine's friend, had a larger impact. A great-great-granddaughter of the martyred Chancellor Thomas More, she was raised by her pious father, Cresacre More. Although her father had funded the Cambrai venture, the lively and rather difficult Helen at first did not really have a vocation to the cloistered life, taking it on only because a favorite priest recommended it. In her early years in the convent, as Baker sets out in his *Life and Death of Dame Gertrude More*, she was personally unhappy, a trial to those around her, and close to leaving the religious life. At first she rejected Baker's nondirective spiritual direction, but her friend Catherine advised her to continue, and soon Baker's advice began to affect her deeply. She was converted to the life of interior prayer and rapidly advanced to high mystical states. Her tragic early death from the plague in 1633 was certainly a blow to the community. Baker took on the task of writing *The Life and Death of Dame Gertrude More*, and he also edited her *Spiritual Exercises*, which were not published until 1658.[122]

Baker's *The Life and Death of Dame Gertrude More* was written during his time at Douai (ca. 1633–36). The original is lost and none of the eight surviving manuscripts has the whole text. The structure of the book is basically chronological with a Prelude and Four Stages, or Stations.[123] Much of the text is didactic rather than biographical—a vindication of Baker's teaching and a description of his method of spiritual direction. The book is not a conventional hagiography, since Baker is open about Gertrude's character faults, especially in her early years in the convent. The basic motifs of teaching are all present in *The Life and Death*: propension, abstraction, introversion, the role of the director, divine inspirations and calls,[124] purity of intention, the conflict between multiplicity and simplicity, mortification, the different kinds of prayer,[125] contemplation, and union with God (sometimes spoken of as "adhering").[126] In short, we might think of *The Life and Death* as a kind of exemplary account of what came to be called "Bakerism."

According to Baker, Gertrude's nature, by which "she seemed to have four, or five, repugnant or contrarie qualities or conditions," did, however, give her a natural propensity for introversion, but she did not know how to activate it. Her early years in the convent were miserable, both for her and for others. She could get nothing out of Jesuit-style meditation. Through Baker's guidance she came to realize the basic rule of the spiritual life, surrender to the action of the Holy Spirit. He says, "And none but the divin spirit was able to guide or reforme her, or to bring her to the immediate waie for reformation. . . . And indeed such Reformation could not be wrought, but by having her brought into a Simplicitie in Soule; that is an immediate disposition to Union with God." Gertrude perceived that the only way for her was that of obedience to the "divin Call," so that she took as her motto: "*Regarde your Call,/that's all in all.*"[127] Having surrendered to her divine call, the young nun made rapid progress in contemplative prayer. In a section on "Prayer and Mortification," Baker says that "finding and treading the right waie of the spirit, that is a Secret and Mystick waie, is not discovered but by a divin internall light gotten by the meane of Praier, and pursued with the use of answerable mortification." Both mortification and prayer are necessary, but prayer is higher, because it is "the Union of the soule with God in her three powers."[128]

Baker has extended discussions of Gertrude's manner of life, especially her conduct with regard to both obligatory and indifferent matters (stage 2.16–17). He also emphasizes that she did not use the Ignatian style of examination of conscience employed by the active religious orders, but rather followed the advice of St. Benedict about the internal watchfulness proper to the contemplative life (stage 2.18). While Gertrude's usual mode of prayer was the fourth and highest of Baker's divisions, the "prayer of sensible affection," her health often made it difficult for her to produce such affections, so she would be content with what Baker calls "the prayer of aridity." Her patience at such times had its reward, he says, because God gives enlightenment of the intellective soul and strengthening of the will even in times of aridity.[129] Baker spends a good deal of time treating Gertrude's trials, as well as describing her mortifications under three categories of doing, abstaining, and suffering.[130]

Stage 3 of *The Life and Death of Dame Gertrude More* is both polemical and instructive, dealing as it does with the conflict over contemplative prayer that Baker, Gertrude, and the other Cambrai nuns waged against the objections raised by Fr. Francis Hull, the convent's official confessor. Although the arguments are at times tedious,[131] this section allows Baker to deepen his teaching on prayer and obedience, especially in the section, "Why Gertrude and Her Associates Should Not Relinquish their Form of Prayer."[132] Following on a long treatment of "propensities" of mystics, that is, their "natural tendencies to seek after God" (stage 3.28; ed., 185–214), Baker provides two important chapters on Gertrude's manner of prayer and union with God (stage 3.31–32; ed., 229–58). The propension for introversion that urges Gertrude to seek God in her interior moves her toward two things: "The one is to seeke a Simplicitie in her owne soule, which is by denudation of it from all created images, the which Simplicitie onlie makes her capable of an Immediate Union with the Divin Simplicitie. Secondlie it urgeth her to seeke after the Simplicitie of the pure Divinitie abstracted from all bodies and images of bodies."[133] This stripping of images extends even to the noblest image of all, that of the humanity of the Savior, which in some cases, like Gertrude's, cannot always be used as a step to the Divine Simplicity. This is why Christ in John 16:7 told the apostles that it was necessary for him to depart from them.

Since God alone is infinite, "Divinitie is the infinite and bottomlesse Center and resting place for a mans soule, to whome all other things are but narrow and improper. . . . The same Divinitie also is the proper vast Element, wherein the soule of man should finde life and infinite life. But furth out of the said Element of hers she is like unto a great whale that were to come into a narrow brooke, that runneth into the sea, in which brooke the whale hath no sufficient scope to swimme and fullie to plunge itself."[134] This kind of union in the center takes place through sensible affections in the intellective soul, not sensate devotions in the sensible nature; but Gertrude, like John of the Cross, also found that in habitual contemplation spiritual delight could descend into the sensible nature (*sensualitie*), so that "sensualitie and spirit [would] both join in their exercise in their severall maners, but yet the Superior soule still retaining the supereminence . . . , and so nothing obscured by sensualitie, but rather by it more elevated into height of spirit, and concurring to the actions of it."[135] Baker closes this important account with further analysis of love as the only power able to effect such union. He summarizes, "And this case to which she was come is that that is called Contemplation, the which is a prompt, easie, and cleere immediate conversation and treatie [treating] of the Intellective soule with the Divinitie, though apprehended onlie according to the notion of faith."[136] It should be pointed out that as high as this form of active contemplative union is, it is still what Baker calls "ordinary contemplation" in which human effort is at work under divine grace. It is therefore to be distinguished from the more sublime supernatural "Passive Contemplation, wherein God doth discover [show] him self in a more cleer maner then is onlie the light of faith . . . and that by certein speciall created speciesses."[137]

Stage 4 is a brief account of Gertrude More's exemplary death. She contracted smallpox about July 29 of 1633 and saw Fr. Baker the last time on July 31, as he departed for the Douai Chapter. Her death was difficult; her patience and resignation admirable. Having made her confession, she placed all her confidence in God and said that she did not want to see Fr. Baker or other male spiritual advisors. When Catherine Gascoigne asked her about Baker, she responded, "God rewarde him . . . for what he hath donne to my soul: and God rewarde him for all he hath donne to this house, that he should bring a soule to such a passe that comming to die she hath nothing to trouble her, but to relie wholie uppon God."[138]

Gertrude More left a number of spiritual writings that were collected and organized by Baker. These include the *Apology* she wrote in defense of Baker's teaching about prayer and obedience, which was sent to the General Chapter of 1633.[139] This is an explanation of Baker's view of obedience and its relation to divine calls, which hews closely to her master's expositions.[140] She testifies that at the beginning of her life in the community her "heart had grown hard as a stone" so that "nothing could have been able to mollify it but by being put into a course of prayer, by which the soul tendeth towards God and learneth of him the lesson of truly humbling herself."[141] This is what Baker taught her. She contrasts Baker's way with the way of meditation taught by the Jesuits, and, indeed, the treatise shows quite a negative attitude toward the Society of Jesus.[142] Her other major opponent is bad spiritual direction, the kind, like that of Francis Hull, which does not recognize the individual needs of each penitent, but insists on rigid external obedience.[143] More's basic point is not to question the need for external obedience; indeed, obedience to superiors and confessors is to be listed among the divine calls given to the soul. Nonetheless, she feels that the teaching of the Jesuits and others slights the far more important internal obedience that is needed for progress in contemplation. True obedience is patient and full inner subjection to God. "This is the obedience that Fr. Baker so much commends," she says, "and wishes souls to make right use of in their obedience to Superiors."[144] Full obedience to the interior call of God is the pathway to contemplative union, and More closes her *Apology* on a mystical note. "Let us rest in him alone," she says, "and not in anything that is or can be created. Let us not seek the gift, but the Giver. Let us seek no other comfort but to be able (without all comfort) to be true to him." The soul must will to serve God without any reservation, "till such time as we may be swallowed up in the bottomless ocean of all love, and praise God in himself, in whom, and by whom only, we can praise him as we ought."[145]

Dame Gertrude's mystical writings come in both prose and verse, and a number of examples of both were cited in *The Life and Death*.[146] Some of the poems seem fairly accomplished; others rather pedestrian.[147] The major prose collection is what Baker called the *Confessiones Amantis; or, The Confessions of a Loving Soul*. These are fifty-three soliloquies, some short, some longer, reminiscent of acts of *confessio* found in Augustine's *Confessions*.[148] These were composed for different liturgical feasts and include acts of thanksgiving, confessions of sin, praise of

God's benefits, and many petitions. The prayers are often repetitious, featuring major themes of the teaching Baker had given to the nuns. These include liberty of spirit, of which Gertrude says, "For I find that where I seek myself there I am caught, as it were, in a snare, and where I forsake myself there I become more and more capable of that true liberty of spirit which carrieth the soul above herself and all created things that she may more perfectly be united to Thee."[149] Obviously, union with God is also a major feature, as it was for the *Sancta Sophia*. In one place Gertrude prays for full union thus: "We sigh and make our moan to Thee while it is daily said to our soul, 'Where is thy God?' (Ps. 41:4). Yes, even as I say so, speaking to Thee, where Thou, my Lord art; and when shall I without all mean [intermediary] be united to Thee, that my love may be entirely bestowed on Thee, and nothing but Thyself live and reign in me."[150] The way of the cross as an *imitatio Christi* is also mentioned in a number of places.[151] Thanksgiving for Fr. Baker's teaching occurs several times (e.g., *Conf.* XXIV, XXIX, XXXI, XXXIV, and XXXVII), and there are discussions of the role of obedience and the relation of superiors and subjects (e.g., *Conf.* XLIII and XLIX).

The overarching theme of the *Confessiones Amantis*, however, is love, both yearning love for God and active love of neighbor. This is evident, for example, in *Confessio* XXVIII, which deals with love of God and love of neighbor, using Psalm 118:38 to beg God for the purity of love that will enable her to "sigh and pant without ceasing after Thee," but also proclaiming, "Oh, how sincere, then, are our affections, when we love our neighbor only in and for Thee!"[152] Among the most striking of the presentations of love of God is that in *Confessio* XVIII, which makes use of the Song of Songs and the game of love between the soul and Christ. Gertrude begins by contrasting God's presence, which always rejoices her heart, with God hiding his beautiful face, when her soul "becomes exceedingly obscured and troubled—yes, even overwhelmed in darkness and misery." She is as "one sick with love for her absent Beloved." While others continue to talk about the Beloved, she can only write about him, hoping that he shall soon return to see "how she is languishing with love" (Song 2:5). "She sleeps, but her heart wakes" (Song 5:2), because nothing can satisfy her unquiet heart but the presence of the Beloved. Wounded with the pure love of God, she is sometimes admitted to "unspeakable joys and delights," "yet out of Thy care for her Thou suddenly turnest away Thy face," until she learns to love the Beloved only for himself. The lesson is given: "If she bears this with a resigned mind, making Thy will her law above all the desires of her heart, and sitting solitary like a turtledove (Song 2:12), Thou wilt in good time assuredly return."[153] The last of the *Confessions* written shortly before her death is an impassioned prayer for her coming reward in which she asks her Lord and God: "Speak peace to my soul, that I may be capable of hearing Thy voice, more sweet than all things whatsoever. Speak to my heart, but speak so as I may hear Thee."[154] Gertrude More's *Confessions* are typical of much seventeenth-century piety. Her writings may not be major mystical literature, but they testify to the importance of Fr. Baker as a teacher and guide of souls committed to the mystical path to loving union.

IV. A Recusant Mystical Poet: Richard Crashaw

In *Mysticism in the Reformation* (volume 6, part 1 of *The Presence of God*), I presented a brief account of the mystical poets of the seventeenth-century Anglican *via media*, figures like John Donne, George Herbert, Thomas Traherne, and others. Different in temperament and Catholic in confession was Richard Crashaw (1612/13–1649).[155] His poetry, which has often been described as the epitome of the Baroque, has been variously interpreted.[156] Its sometimes overexuberant aspects have been criticized by many, but it is hard to deny that some poems of this converted Puritan achieve a level of ecstatic celebration of union with God rarely found in literature. Crashaw has also been criticized for his feminine sensibility with its attendant gender malleability, something that has come in for renewed attention in recent decades, and often for a more positive evaluation.[157] Judgments on Crashaw's place in the English literary canon are too varied to try to survey here. I look at him as an example of an English poet who deliberately strove for a mystical effect. The nineteenth-century critic Edmund Gosse claimed him as "the one great Catholic mystic in the English language of the seventeenth century."[158] On a rather more shrill note, the mid-twentieth-century English Catholic critic E. I. Watkin concluded his essay on Crashaw with the peroration: "What is religion? Ask Crashaw. What is mysticism? Ask Crashaw. What is love—the love which is religion and mysticism's crown? Ask Crashaw."[159] Ronald A. Knox was more succinct: "Crashaw's poetry was all religion, and Crashaw's religion was all poetry."[160] Even more recent critics cannot escape discussing Crashaw as the English mystical poet par excellence. In the words of his recent editor, Richard Rambuss, "Crashaw was a seriously sensationalist writer. His poetry amounts to the most sustained endeavor among English poets to render—and by rendering stimulate—ecstasy."[161]

Crashaw once again raises an issue often discussed in the volumes of *The Presence of God*: What is the relation of poetry to mysticism? The English poet may not provide a theoretical answer, but he does function as a fine example of the poet mystic.

We have little knowledge of Crashaw's inner life, but the witness of his poetry makes it clear that mystical Catholicism, especially that of Teresa of Avila, was central for him. His life was short, but not without major developments. Richard was born in 1612/1613, the son of a noted Puritan anti-Popish divine, William Crashaw. Much of Richard's life centered on Cambridge, where he matriculated in 1631. Educated at Pembroke and Peterhouse, he became part of the Laudian, High Church wing of Anglicanism, which favored elaborate liturgies and devotions. He had to flee Cambridge under threat from the Puritan Parliamentarians in 1643. By 1644 he had left the country for Leiden and converted to Catholicism; by 1645 he was in Paris, where he received support from Henrietta Maria (Charles I's wife) and her circle of court ladies. Now a Catholic cleric, he went on to Rome (1646–49), where he served in various ecclesiastical positions in the entourage of Cardinal Pallotta until he was made a canon of the Holy House of the Virgin Mary of Loretto in April 1649, a premier shrine of Tridentine Catholic devotion. He died soon afterward on August 21, 1649.

Our knowledge of Crashaw's character depends to a large degree on prefaces to his poetry. The anonymous "Preface to the Reader" of the 1646 edition of *Steps to the Temple*, possibly written by his friend Joseph Beaumont, praises the author as "our divine poet" whose poems can lift the reader "some yards above the ground" and "tune thy soul . . . into a heavenly pitch; and thus refined and borne up upon the wings of meditation. In these Poems thou mayest freely talk of God, and others of that other state." After rounding on secular love poets, the preface continues: "Reader, we style his Sacred Poems, *Steps to the Temple*, and aptly, for in the temple of God, under his wing, he led his life in St. Mary's Church, near St. Peter's College [both in Cambridge], . . . where, like a primitive saint, he offered more prayers in the night, than others usually offer in the day; there, he penned these poems, *Steps* for happy souls to climb heaven by." The author also includes fulsome praise of Crashaw's academic learning.[162] The posthumous collection *Carmen Deo Nostro* (1652) was edited by his friend the English convert Thomas Carre (born Miles Pinkney), a priest at the court-in-exile of Henrietta Maria. (Carre was responsible for the first English translation of Francis de Sales's *Treatise on the Love of God*.) In a witty prefatory poem, "Crashawe, The Anagram. He was Car," Carre also praises

Crashaw's personal piety: "Nor fears he [i.e., Carr] check praising that happy one / Who was beloved by all; dispraised by none. / To wit, being pleased with all things, he pleased all. / Nor would he give, nor take offense; befall / What might. . . ."[163] The picture of Crashaw as prayerful and pious, as well as beloved and inoffensive, is complemented by his devotion to celibacy. As he put it in an epigram "On Marriage": "I would be married, but I'd have no wife, / I would be married to a single life."[164]

The history of the publication of Crashaw's poems is complicated. Most were written "while the author was still with the Protestants," but he revised many before publication. The first edition, as noted above, was the 1646 *Steps to the Temple*, consciously presenting itself as a kind of prologue to George Herbert's *The Temple* published in 1633. It contained fourteen sacred poems and fifty epigrams, mostly based on his Latin versions, as well as thirty-three secular lyrics under the title *The Delights of the Muses*, the most famous being "Music's Duel," a poem based on the long tradition of a contest between a nightingale and a lutenist. (The musical character of Crashaw's poetry has often been noted.) These poems were reprinted, often with additions and alterations, in 1648 under the title *The Delights of the Muses*, along with some new pieces. The *Carmen Deo Nostro* of 1652 contains the final forms of thirty-seven sacred poems. This collection has a more or less liturgical sequence as befitting the title based on Psalm 40: "The Lord put a new song into my mouth, a song to our God (*Carmen Deo Nostro*)." I shall concentrate on these final poems, with some attention to the earlier versions. There has been some debate in recent years about whether to consider Crashaw an Anglican or a Catholic poet. This seems misplaced. For a number of years he was content to be a member of the most pro-Catholic wing of the Established Church, but when the Civil War showed him that this was not a possible option, he embraced the Catholicism to which he had always tended, whether or not we wish to consider him, as T. S. Eliot once put it, a "natural born convert."[165] Certainly, no one, even among the Catholic poets of Italy, Spain, and Germany, encapsulates Baroque mystical poetry as well as does Richard Crashaw. This seems to be a generally accepted judgment, despite the ongoing disagreement about what exactly constitutes the "Baroque."[166]

Almost all who have written on Crashaw have noted his stress on emotion and affectivity, despite the considerable poetic intelligence that went into the construction of his poems. Again to cite T. S. Eliot, "Donne might be called a voluptuary of thought; Crashaw could be called a voluptuary of religious emotion."[167] Crashaw's insistent appeal to religious affectivity is evident throughout his poems, even when they are also examples of metaphysical wit. As Anthony Low put it, "[A]ffective or sensible devotion, which has been overlooked by most critics writing on seventeenth-century poetry, is probably the neglected key to a sympathetic entry into his work."[168] This affectivity fits in well with many of the spiritual and mystical currents of seventeenth-century Catholicism. When we read Crashaw, it is not hard to think of his older contemporary, Augustine Baker (whom he would not have known), advising his nuns to abandon rational meditation and surrender themselves to the prayer of affective aspirations. There is, to be sure, not just an affective but also a flamboyant character to Crashaw's verse, which is exactly why so many critics have seen it as the epitome of the Baroque style.

Crashaw's poetry has often been seen as more than just flamboyant, but as strange, weird, grotesque, bizarre, in bad taste. Its intense physicality, even eroticism, especially in relation to spiritual events and states, has troubled a number of critics. Notwithstanding the sensuous images that Crashaw employs, however, there is a lack of sensuality in his poetry, because his images function as masks or markers for the spiritual world where all the action really takes place.[169] In the words of R. V. Young, "Crashaw's purpose is to take advantage of the rapturous and pleasurable associations of sensuous, erotic language, but to subvert its usual, especially physical references."[170] The poet's fascination with blood and tears, with wounds and swoons, with smells and tastes, as well as the disconcerting way in which male and female roles are sometimes reversed, has led some to characterize him as an "idiosyncratic extreme in the adoption of Continental modes of sensibility."[171] This may be true from the perspective of one aristocratic strand of English poetry, but Crashaw is both an English poet and a representative of the international Baroque. From the viewpoint of European Baroque piety, as well as from the long-range perspective of the development of Catholic devotion from the twelfth century on, many aspects of Crashaw's images and conceits seem less strange, although he often takes traditional themes in new and surprising directions. There are many medieval examples in prose, verse, and image of drinking Mary's milk and sucking Christ's blood. This is not to defend everything Crashaw ever wrote, or to assert that all the poems are on the same level. The fact that the poet himself continued to edit and work on his poems (not always for the better) is evidence that he was often dissatisfied with the result. Crashaw's reputation has waxed and waned over the centuries, but he has rarely been neglected.

Richard Crashaw brought to his poetry not only an unusual religious sensibility and great versifying skills but also the impressive knowledge of a Cambridge scholar. His command of classical languages was superb. He had good French and taught himself Italian and Spanish. From the poetry alone it is difficult to know just how widely read he was in the traditions of mystical literature, but it is safe to say his knowledge was extensive. He was deeply influenced by sixteenth- and seventeenth-century Catholic mysticism. This is especially evident with regard to Teresa of Avila, who for Crashaw as for most of his contemporaries, was the exemplar of ecstatic love for Jesus.[172] Crashaw's three poems dedicated to Teresa are the finest poetic tribute to the mystic of Avila. Also evident is the influence of Francis de Sales. "The Author's Motto" that prefaces the 1646 *Steps to the Temple*—"Live Jesus, live, and let it be, / My life to die, for love of thee"—is taken from de Sales's *Treatise on Divine Love*, first published in 1616.[173] Francis's influence on Crashaw can be seen in a number of details of the poems,[174] but, as Marc F. Bertonasco has shown, it extends more widely. An optimism about the triumph of God's love, a stress on the ability of the fallen will to be turned back to God, and an avoidance of predestinarian and "hell-fire" motifs all speak to a kind of Salesian atmosphere to Crashaw's religion.[175] How far Crashaw may have been familiar with some other contemporary French mystics, such as Pierre de Bérulle, has yet to be fully investigated, although Gary Kuchar has argued for a Bérullian input to Crashaw's Christocentric apophaticism.[176]

The quasi-liturgical structure of the *Carmen Deo Nostro* reflects a central aspect of Crashaw's poetry—his desire to unite affective mysticism with the liturgy of the church year.[177] Many of the poems in the collection are performative liturgical hymns, acts of praise for the God who goes beyond all naming, but not all hymning. The book, like the liturgical year, has both its "Temporal Cycle" of major feasts and a "Sanctoral Cycle" honoring saints. The Temporal Cycle begins with the feasts of the Christmas season, and moves on through the Passion, Corpus Christi, and Marian feasts, especially the Assumption.[178] Crashaw celebrates these festivals with original hymns, as well as with his adopted translations of six of the church's liturgical hymns. These inventive versions can be seen as "descants," that is, ornamented variations on the original "plainsong" melody of the hymns.[179] The Sanctoral Cycle is abbreviated to the three famous hymns to Teresa of Avila and two in honor of Mary Magdalene. There are, of course, a number of other poems in the collection, but the liturgical core is hard to miss. There is no space here to comment on all these poems, but an analysis of some will, I hope, provide an entry into the special character of Crashaw's poetic mysticism.

After some preliminary pieces, Crashaw begins *Carmen Deo Nostro* with four poems for the Christmas season that form a unit, since the underlying issue of the dark that becomes light and the light that becomes dark introduced in the first poem is magnificently taken up in the last.[180] The first entry is "To the Name above Every Name, the Name of Jesus, a Hymn." Although the Feast of the Holy Name of Jesus is actually celebrated between New Year's Day and Epiphany, it is fitting that this long and accomplished poem begins the series. It is a hymn to the mystery of the Incarnation revealed in the saving and ineffable name of "Jesus," a name that Crashaw actually never voices in the poem, because, as Richard Rambuss puts it, "Crashaw's poem is in effect an endeavor in lyricizing the ineffable."[181] Anthony D. Cousins summarizes: "The *Hymn* to the Holy Name . . . offers a comprehensive and Christ-centered analysis of sacred love, one whose ideas are basic . . . to the thinking on sacred love throughout his poems."[182] Louis Martz has seen the poem as the ideal expression in Crashaw's oeuvre of the carefully constructed meditative poems of the sixteenth and seventeenth centuries.[183]

Devotion to the name of Jesus went back for centuries, and Crashaw may well have known Bernard of Clairvaux's sermons on the name of Jesus and the Pseudo-Bernadine "Jesu dulcis memoria" that serves as the Vesper hymn for the Feast of the Holy Name.[184] The poem's seven sections begin with an Introduction: "I sing the Name which none can say / But touched with an interior ray: / The Name of our new peace; our good; / Our bliss: and supernatural blood: / The Name of all our lives and loves. / Hearken and help, ye holy doves!"[185] Before the actual hymn begins, Crashaw prefaces three long sections: (1) an address to the soul to go out to summon all nature to "this great morning's mighty business" (lines 13–45); (2) the actual invitation to all the powers of nature and art to join together into "the long and deathless song" (lines 46–87); and (3) another self-address to the "heart" to encourage it to mingle its love-notes with the music of the heavens (lines 88–114). The hymn itself commences with a plea to the Name to come from heaven and reveal itself on earth (lines 115–50): "Come, lovely Name! Appear from forth the bright / Regions of peaceful light / Look from thine own illustrious home, / Fair King of Names, and come." All nature waits for the coming of the Name, including humans: "Come, lovely Name; life of our hope! / Lo we hold our hearts wide ope." The coming of the Name is synonymous with the coming of the day that will illuminate what is later called "our dark world" (line 161).

The sixth section (lines 151–96) is a celebration of the appearance of the Name, beginning with a stately measure: "Lo, where aloft it comes! It comes, among / The conduct of adoring spirits, that throng / Like diligent bees, and swarm about it." The major emphasis of this section is a synesthesia of sight, taste, and smell. The Name is the "birth of our bright joys," but is also addressed: "O dissipate thy spicy pow'rs / (Cloud of condensed sweets) and break upon us / In balmy show'rs; / O fill our senses, and take from us / All force of so profane a fallacy / To think aught sweet but that which smells of thee." And later: "Sweet Name, in the each syllable / A thousand blessed Arabias dwell; / A thousand hills of frankincense; / Mountains of myrrh, and beds of spices, / And ten thousand paradises / The soul that tastes thee takes from thence." The soul is invited to make this multitude of sweet-smelling comforts and mercies its own: "Happy is he who has the art / To awake, / And to take them / Home, and lodge them in his heart." In the conclusion or epilogue (lines 197–239) the note of personal appropriation of the riches of the Name becomes more emphatic. Martyrdom and wounding (favorite Crashavian themes) come to the fore, as the soul is invited to imitate the martyrs of old, who wore the Name "in the center of their inmost souls." The torturers of the martyrs did nothing more than to allow them to demonstrate by their wounds "That impatient fire / The heart that hides thee barely covers." Invoking "the wit of love," that is, the ingenuity and organizing power of burning love for the Name, Crashaw says, "Each wound of theirs was thy new morning; / And reenthroned thee in thy rosy nest, / With blush of thine own blood thy day adorning, / It was the wit of love o'erflowed the bounds / Of wrath, and made thee way through all those wounds. / Welcome dear, all-adorèd Name! / For sure there is no knee / That knows not thee" (see Phil. 2:9–11).

The following poem, "In the Nativity of Our Lord God, a Hymn Sung as by the Shepherds," is shorter and simpler, but no less accomplished.[186] It is in the form of a mini-drama, featuring the give and take of a Chorus of Shepherds and two figures familiar from Virgil's *Eclogues*, Tityrus and Thyrsis. Sometimes the figures sing in single voices, sometimes together; at other times the full Chorus repeats what has been sung. In this poem the interplay of night and day, dark and light, become stronger, as Jesus, the true Sun, makes the midnight of his birth more bright than day: "Come we shepherds whose blessed sight / Hath met love's noon in nature's night; / Come lift we up our loftier song / And wake the Sun that lies too long" (lines 1-4). Along with the reversal of night and day, a major theme is the ability of the Incarnate Word to transform the physical world, and, by extension, the world of the human heart.

The Chorus invites Tityrus and Thyrsis to testify to the miracle of night becoming day through the appearance of the "noble infant," which they do individually and then together. The drama then shifts to the problem of what the "poor world" could have to offer to "this starry stranger." Thyrsis's answer is that the babe is the Lord of heaven and earth and will decide what is worthy of him: "Proud world, said I, cease your contest / And let the mighty babe alone. / The phoenix build's the phoenix' nest. / Love's architecture is his own, / The babe whose birth embraves this morn, / Made his own bed ere he was born" (lines 44-49), an image that seems to be a reference to the bosom of the Virgin to be mentioned shortly. Where will the babe rest his head? Not in the falling snow, which is pure white but too cold, and not in the "rosy fleece" of the seraphim, warm but perhaps not pure enough. Tityrus gives the answer: "No, no, your King's not yet to seek / Where to repose his royal head. / See, see how soon his new-bloomed cheek / Twixt's mother's breast is gone to bed. / Sweet choice, said we! No way but so / Not to lie cold, but sleep in snow" (lines 65-70). Mary's bosom, though part of the created world, is purer and warmer than all else in earth and heaven. The full Chorus brings the whole paradoxical tableau together as it hymns: "Welcome, all wonders in one sight! / Eternity shut in a span. / Summer in winter. Day in night. / Heaven in earth, and God in man. / Great little one! whose all-embracing birth / Lifts earth to heaven, stoops heav'n to earth" (lines 79-84). But that is not the end. Two further "Welcome" stanzas follow. The first carries forward the praise of the Virgin, specifically of the breasts that nourish the babe, while the second concerns the fittingness of the simple shepherds as the worshipers of the "dread Lamb." They promise to return in the spring with fitting offerings to further the purifying process by which they will become a holocaust to God: "Each of us his lamb will bring, / Each his pair of silver doves; / Till burnt at last in fire of thy fair eyes, / Ourselves become our own best sacrifice" (lines 105-8). The hymn ends on this note of mystical transformation.

The brief poem on "New Year's Day" in the *Carmen Deo Nostro* is a slightly revised version of "A Hymn for the Circumcision Day of Our Lord" in *Steps to the Temple*. It has a brief reference to the circumcision as the first shedding of Jesus's blood, prophetic of the cross,[187] but is more concerned with Jesus as the true light of the world overcoming even the brightness of the sun. This theme is further developed in the next hymn, one of Crashaw's richest, "In the Glorious Epiphany of Our Lord God. A Hymn Sung as by the Three Kings."[188] Austin Warren finds this poem the most "metaphysical in style and intent" in Crashaw's oeuvre, due to its careful structure following through the contrast between natural and supernatural light, but the poem is also deeply Dionysian, an exercise in the dizzying permutations of day and night as a symbolization of the interplay of cataphatic, apophatic, and hyperphatic (beyond both positive and negative) theologies found in the writings of Pseudo-Dionysius. Along with Henry Vaughan's "The Night," it is a premier expression of Dionysianism in English poetry.[189] For a fuller appreciation of the subtlety and profundity of "In the Glorious Epiphany," I recommend Gary Kuchar's article; here I lift up only a few dimensions.

The opening lines of the hymn shared by the three kings of the Feast of Epiphany and the chorus announce a major motif—the difficulty of discerning true dark and true light. The dialogue commences: "1st King: Bright babe! Whose awful beauties make / the morn incur a sweet mistake: / 2nd King: For whom th'officious [eager to please] heav'ns devise / To disinherit the sun's rise, / 3rd King: Delicately to displace / The day, and plant it fairer in thy face" (lines 1–6). The babe is invited to look up to see the East represented by the Magi come "to seek herself in thy sweet eyes." The strangeness of the journey of the Magi through a dark that is too light is deepened in what follows: "1: We, who strangely went astray, / Lost in a bright / Meridian night, / 2: A darkness made of too much day, / 3: Beckoned from far / By thy fair star, / Lo at last have found our way" (lines 15–21). They have found their way to the babe in whom all opposites coincide, where the universe is embraced in the divine mystery, and where all time becomes one. Then the general voice cuts in: "Chorus: To thee, thou day of night! Thou East of West! / Lo we at last have found the way. / To thee, the world's great universal East. / The general and indifferent day. / 1: All-circling point. All cent'ring sphere. / The world's one round, eternal year. / 2: Whose full and all-unwrinkled face / Nor sinks nor swells with time or place; / 3: But everywhere and every while / Is one consistent solid smile" (lines 22–32).[190]

Having set up the Neoplatonic, indeed Dionysian, dialectic governing the interplay of dark and light in the path to God, the following sections of the poem spell this out further in both speculative and historical terms. The speculative part begins with a series of split, ambiguous, pronominal references also found in other mystics—Who is speaking to whom about what? As the Kings put it, "1: To thee, to thee / From him we flee / 2: From him, from whom by a more illustrious lie, / The blindness of the world did call the eye; / 3: To him, with these mortal clouds hast made / Thyself our sun, though thine own shade" (lines 43–47). The long historical exploration about the rejecting of the worship of the false sun found in pagan religion witnessed to by the Magi's conversion to the true Sun of Christ (lines 48–132) is a bravura example of Crashaw's metaphysical wit, but the essential light–dark, day–night dialectic remains strong and is even heightened toward the end of the hymn. This is first shown by way of the Passion, when the eclipse during Jesus's three hours on the cross announces the sun's penance for daring to usurp the glory of the true Son/Sun: "That forfeiture of noon to night shall pay / All the idolatrous thefts done by this night of day; / And the Great Penitent press his own pale lips / With an elaborate love-eclipse / to which the low world's laws / Shall lend no cause" (lines 149–54). The sun's eclipse at the crucifixion teaches all creation no longer to mistakenly think of God in positive fashion (e.g., God is beautiful), but negatively—their new wisdom is to enjoy his "blot" (the eclipse as the image of negative theology) as a reference to "a large black letter" that better spells the divine unknown beauties. At this point, Crashaw openly reveals the Dionysian background behind what has been building from the beginning. The lines are dense but pregnant with meaning: "By the oblique ambush of this close night / Couched in that conscious shade / The right-eyed Areopagite / Shall with a vigorous guess invade / And catch the quick reflex, and sharply see / On this dark ground / To descant thee" (lines 189–95). More than a few paragraphs of explanation would be needed to unpack the meaning of this summary of mystical apophaticism. All that can be noted here is how Crashaw cannot let Dionysius go at this stage, praising him as "that reverend child of light, / By being scholar first of that new night, / Come forth great master of the mystic day; / And teach obscure mankind a more close way / By the frugal negative light / Of a most wide and well-abusèd night / To read more intelligible thine original ray" (lines 205–11). It is astonishing that in the literature devoted to the heritage of Dionysius this, perhaps the finest evocation of Dionysian thought in poetry, finds so little echo.

 Few, if any, of Crashaw's other poems come close to the fusion of theological insight and metaphysical wit found in the Nativity poems, but many illustrate the Crashaw of the usual criticism—the over-the-top Baroque sensualist of supercharged images. Some of the Passion poems are relatively restrained, such as his composition "The Office of the Holy Cross" and his version of the Vesper hymn for Passiontide of Venantius Fortunatus, the "Vexilla Regis."[191] Three relatively short lyrics dwell more on the bloody figure of Christ on the cross. These are typified in "Upon the Body of Our Blessed Lord, Naked and Bloody": "They'have left thee naked, Lord, O that they had! / This garment too I would they had denied. / Thee with thyself they have too richly clad; / Opening the purple wardrobe in thy side. / O never could there be garment too good / For thee to wear, but this, of thine own blood."[192] Crashaw's poems on the Passion revel in the gaze on the naked wounded body of the Redeemer, as well as invitations to drink of the blood of Jesus from the wounds that are also mouths to which we can press our lips to be satisfied. These images may seem strange today, but read against contemporary Continental Passion piety, both in prose and verse, Crashaw is scarcely anomalous.

Among the most accomplished of Crashaw's Passion poems is his very free rendition of the "Stabat Mater dolorosa," traditionally ascribed to the Franciscan mystic Iacopone da Todi and used for the Feast of the Seven Sorrows of the Blessed Virgin (Friday of Passion Week, and also September 15). As Austin Warren puts it, "This is the most successful of Crashaw's paraphrases, for, though he has appropriated the substance of da Todi's poem, he has completely reshaped it, translated it into his own sensibility as well as into English, and made of his own version an independent work of art."[193] This transmutation was made possible because the motifs of the original Latin version (tears, blood, wounds, spears, nails, inflammation, inebriation, compassion, and the like) were so close to Crashaw's own Passion piety. Above all, Crashaw heightens the role of the poet in the drama of the suffering of Son and Mother, making him the third person (indeed, the younger brother) in the family tragedy: "Come wounds! Come darts! / Nail'd hands! And pierced hearts! / Come your whole selves, sorrow's great son and mother! / Nor grudge a younger brother / Of griefes his portion, who (had all their due) / One single wound should not have left for you."[194]

Crashaw's contributions to the Feast of Corpus Christi were also translation-adaptations of liturgical hymns, the "Adoro Te Devote" used in the thanksgiving after Mass, and the "Lauda Sion Salvatorem," the sequence for the Mass. Both of these are ascribed to Thomas Aquinas. Crashaw's rendering of the "Adoro Te Devote" as "The Hymn of Saint Thomas in Adoration of the Blessed Sacrament," is quite a free version, while the "Lauda Sion Salvatorem, the Hymn for the Blessed Sacrament" sticks close to the original. The English poet's rendition of the "Dies Irae. The Hymn of the Church, in Meditation of the Day of Judgment" (first written as a sequence for Advent; later used in the Requiem Mass) is also quite free and more personalized than the Latin original. The last of Crashaw's liturgical adaptations is the Marian hymn "O Gloriosa Domina" for the Feast of Mary's Assumption (August 15).[195]

With regard to what I am calling the Sanctoral Cycle of the *Carmen Deo Nostro* we can start with the two hymns to Mary Magdalene, the converted sinner whose feast is celebrated on July 22, one of the most popular saints, not only in the Middle Ages but also in the early modern period, as can be seen, for example, in the case of Pierre de Bérulle (see chapter 4, 232-35). In art, as well as in prose and poetry, the Magdalene meets us everywhere. Crashaw's poems on the Magdalene are among his best known, the short poem "The Tear," and the longer "Saint Mary Magdalene, or The Weeper."[196] This poem, which Mario Praz called a "necklace of conceits" and a "rosary of epigrams," is a good example of the loose-structured, "pile-on" character of this form of much Baroque poetry. A number of its images have been criticized as in poor taste, although many did not originate with Crashaw. If one is looking for structure and continuity of argument, "The Weeper" is likely to disappoint. It is a succession of witty, often paradoxical, conceits designed to praise the beauty of the Magdalene's repentance and to present her as the most devoted of all lovers of Jesus, flowing with tears and drowned in a sea of liquid images.

Crashaw's "A Hymn to the Name and Honor of the Admirable Saint Teresa, Foundress of the Reformation of the Discalced Carmelites, Both Men and Women," first appeared in the 1646 *Steps to the Temple* but was probably written earlier. Robert T. Petersson calls it "his most accomplished, most fully developed work."[197] According to Austin Warren, "In the 'Hymne,' one of Crashaw's four or five best pieces, he unites the two themes intensely dear to him—martyrdom and mysticism."[198] Crashaw appears to have read Teresa's *Life* in the original Spanish, although there were English versions. Interestingly, during the years he was in Rome (1646-49), G. L. Bernini was at work on his famous "Saint Teresa in Ecstasy" in the Cornaro Chapel of S. Maria della Vittoria, although Crashaw would not have seen it. The hymn falls into three parts, with the first two based on incidents recounted in the *Life*, while the third part projects the reader into the saint's apotheosis (her feast day is October 15). The three parts demonstrate the saint's ascent to glory, beginning on earth in childhood, moving to the heaven on earth of the ecstasy of the mature Teresa, and ending with the full reward of heaven.

The overarching theme of the poem is love, as announced with the sonorous "o" sounds of the opening lines: "Love, thou art absolute sole lord / Of life and death." But Crashaw will present not love in general but love as mystical marriage and inner martyrdom. In setting forth his case the poet does not begin by appealing to "Those thy old soldiers, great and tall, / Ripe men of martyrdom," but rather to the "milky soul of a soft child," that is, the six-year-old Teresa, who tells us in the *Life*, chapter 1, of her attempt to go off to the Moors to suffer martyrdom. Along with the theme of love, part 1 (lines 1-64) introduces other key words, such as blood, heart, fire, and death, that will recur throughout the poem. This part explores the paradoxes of the child Teresa desiring what she does not really know, but still functioning as an exemplar of the martyrdom of love: "She never undertook to know / What death with love should have to do, ... Yet though she cannot tell you why, / She can love and she can die" (lines 19-24). The ancient theme of the *mors mystica*, strong in many of Teresa's works, is a constant in Crashaw's Teresa poems. This is why the saint's true home is only where she can become a martyr of love: "Since 'tis not to be had at home / She'll travel for a martyrdom. / No home for her confesses she / But where she may a martyr be" (lines 44-47). The home for Teresa's martyrdom, however, will be not the land of the Moors, but the convent of the Bride of Christ.

The second part of the poem (lines 65-128) starts with the turn to the mystical life: "Sweet, not so fast! Lo thy fair spouse, / Whom thou seek'st with so swift vows, / Calls thee back, and bids thee come, / T'embrace a milder martyrdom" (lines 65-68). (This is the first of four appearances of the word "spouse.") This part is based on Teresa's account of her transverberation in chapter 29 of the *Life*, the subject of so many artistic portrayals, not least the famous Bernini statue. In her new location, Teresa hears the words: "Thou art love's victim; and must die / A death more mystical and high" (lines 74-75). The meditative descant that follows on the transverberation account (lines 79-119) is one of the longest presentations of ecstasy in poetry. First, there is a description of the wounding dart of love: "His is the dart must make the death / Whose stroke shall taste thy hallowed breath; / A dart thrice dipped in that rich flame / Which writes thy spouse's radiant name / Upon the roof of heav'n" (lines 79-83). This is followed by a description of "love's soldiers," the seraphim who bear the dart (lines 91-96). The result is the sweet pain of the *mors mystica*, the death that gives life: "O how oft shalt thou complain / Of the sweet and subtle pain. / Of intolerable joys; / Of a death, in which who dies / Loves his death, and dies again. / And would forever so be slain" (lines 98-102).

Teresa is wounded not just once but continuously, so that the wounds weep healing balsam until they can come together to melt her soul into a single lump of incense in order to exhale her to heaven, where she will be welcomed by Mary the Queen of Heaven as figured in Apocalypse 12 (lines 106–28). The third part of the poem (lines 129–82) is a hymn to the glorified Teresa. Crashaw is too wise to try to describe heaven in detail; rather, he pictures the greeting the saint receives from the whole heavenly court, especially her Divine Spouse. All her good works will be there waiting for her, so that "all in one [shall] / Weave a constellation / Of crowns, with which the King thy spouse / Shall build up thy triumphant brows" (lines 141–44). Teresa will also see the effects that her book (taught by Jesus) is having in the world, as well as "thousands of crowned souls," both Carmelites and non-Carmelites, who, inspired by her words and example, are following the Lamb to heaven. "And so / Thou with the Lamb, thy Lord, shalt go; / And whereso'ere he sets his white / Steps, walk with him those ways of light / Which who in death would live to see, / Must learn in life to die like thee" (lines 178–82). For Crashaw, as for so many in the seventeenth century and after, Teresa is the very model of the mystical life.

Crashaw's second poem on Teresa is "An Apology for the Foregoing Hymn as Having Been Writ When the Author Was Yet among the Protestants."[199] It is both a defense for turning Teresa's Spanish into English ("O 'tis not Spanish, but 'tis heaven she speaks!"), as well as a disquisition on two kinds of ecstatic inebriation: the bestial form that turns humans to animals; and the ecstatic form that makes human into angels.[200] Following Song of Songs 2:4 and Isaiah 63:3, the poet asks to be able to follow Teresa into the mystical inebriation of the love of Christ: "Let the King / Me ever into his cellars bring / Where flows such wine as we can have of none / But him who trod the winepress all alone, . . . wine / That can exalt weak earth; and so refine / Our dust, that at one draught, mortality / May drink itself up, and forget to die" (lines 37–46).

The last of Crashaw's trilogy to Teresa is "The Flaming Heart," a poem that begins with an extended conceit on the piercing of Teresa's heart. Crashaw had seen a picture of a small seraph plunging his spear into the passive, swooning figure of Teresa, but felt that such an image got it all wrong. Teresa and her love for God should be the active figure; the angel is mere bystander.[201] In a typical metaphysical conceit Crashaw writes, "You must transpose the picture quite, / And spell it wrong to read it right; / Read him for her, and her for him, / And call the saint the seraphim" (lines 9–12). For some sixty-eight lines the poem pursues rather tiresome versions of the conceit, ending with "His be the bravery of all those bright things, / The glowing cheeks, the glistering wings; / The rosy hand, the radiant dart; / Leave her alone the flaming heart" (lines 65–68). The conclusion is more effective, an impassioned hymn to Teresa's wounded heart and a plea for the poet's conversion to divine love and loss of self (lines 69–92). The wounded heart is love's best weapon, because it can pierce others with the example of its love: "Live here, great heart; and love and die and kill; / And bleed and wound; and yield and conquer still. / Let this immortal life where'er it comes / Walk in a crowd of loves and martyrdoms. / Let mystic deaths wait on't; and wise souls be / The love-slain witnesses of this life of thee" (lines 79-84).

This is where the poem ended in its 1648 form—a rather objective presentation of the power of Teresa's flaming heart. But Crashaw added a third part that appears in the 1652 printing (lines 85–108), what Louis L. Martz called "the richest fiery shower of Baroque imagery to be found anywhere in Crashaw's poetry,"[202] a shower that turns subjective, because it contains the poet's personal prayer to the saint: "O sweet incendiary! Show here thy art, / Upon this carcass of a hard, cold, heart; / Let all thy scattered shafts of light, that play / Among the leaves of thy large books of day, / Combined against this breast at once break in / And take away from me my self and sin" (lines 85–90). This plea for mystical transformation is followed by a coda (lines 93–108), reprising the message of praise for the saint and the plea for personal conversion. These lines, a kind of ecstatic litany, have been widely admired and I give them here in full: "O thou undaunted daughter of desires! / By all thy dow'r of lights and fires; / By all the eagle in thee. All the dove; / By all thy lives and deaths of love; / By all thy large draughts of intellectual day, / And by thy thirst of love more large than they; / By all thy brim-filled bowls of fierce desire; / By thy last morning's draught of liquid fire; / By the full kingdom of the final kiss / That seized thy parting soul, and sealed thee his; / By all the heav'ns thou hast in him / (Fair sister of the seraphim!) / By all of him we have in thee; / Leve nothing of myself in me. / Let me so read thy life, that I / Unto all life of mine may die." *Mors mystica* indeed.

There is one other poem of Crashaw's, less well known, that is important for his claims as a mystical poet. "Prayer; an Ode Which Was Prefixed to a Little Prayerbook Given to a Young Gentlewoman" is not generally considered one of Crashaw's most successful poems, but it is interesting for its adaptation of erotic love language from secular poetry in the service of mysticism, although the marriage does not seem totally successful.[203] The poet attaches the poem to a copy of "a little volume, but great book! / A nest of newborn sweets" (lines 1-2), that is, a copy of the *Book of Common Prayer*. Concerning this book says Crashaw, "It is love's great artillery / Which here contracts itself, and comes to lie / Close couched in your white bosom: and from thence / As from a snowy fortress of defense, / Against the ghostly foes to take your part, / And fortify the hold of your chaste heart" (lines 15-20).

Using this book of prayer will prepare the heart for the coming of "The spouse of virgins and the Virgin's son" (line 45). But the poet goes on to warn the recipient that if she is not ready for the Bridegroom, but leaves her "chaste abode / To gad abroad / Among the gay mates of the god of flies [i.e., Beelzebub], . . . Doubtless some other heart / Will get the start / Meanwhile, and stepping in before / Will take possession of that sacred store / Of hidden sweets and holy joys" (lines 49-64). The poem goes on to describe these sweets and joys with a series of mystical images, such as inner locutions, as well as "Amorous languishments; luminous trances; / Sights which are not seen with eyes; / Spiritual and soul-piercing glances" (lines 70-72). Yet more, "Delicious deaths; soft exhalations / Of soul; dear and divine annihilations; / . . . And many a mystic thing" (lines 77-83). Toward the end of the poem, the poet repeats the message: remain at home and wait, or the Divine Lover will go elsewhere, visiting the "Selected dove / Whoe'er she be" that is prepared for him. This happy soul is described as taking an active erotic role in the conjunction. She will "Seize her sweet prey / All fresh and fragrant as he rises / Dropping with balmy shower / A delicious dew of spices" (lines 107-10; see Song 5:5). What is more, "She shall have power / To rifle and deflower / The rich and roseal spring of those rare sweets / Which with a swelling bosom there she meets" (lines 115-17). In that way "she shall discover / What joy, what bliss, / How many heav'ns at once it is / To have her God become her lover" (lines 122-24). This is strongly erotic stuff, but R. V. Young and others contend that God here is merely substituted for a human lover and that the images of love's delight have not really been transformed in the service of sacred love.

Crashaw's poems do not really open a door to his own inner experience, save to witness to his desire that God come and warm his cold heart by the fire of divine love. The little we know about the external aspects of his life indicates that this very private person was looked upon as a rare ascetic, a man of great prayer, and of a mild and winning disposition. Whether or not Crashaw experienced special mystical gifts himself is not decisive for the issue of his status as a mystical poet. Both his person and his poetry make such status difficult to deny, as suggested by the verse accolade of his friend Abraham Cowley's "On the Death of Mr. Crashaw," which apostrophizes, *"Poet* and *Saint!* To thee alone are giv'n / The two most sacred *Names* of *Earth* and *Heav'n.*"[204]

Notes

1. Eire, *Reformations,* chap. 13, "England, Wales, Ireland, and Scotland, 1521-1603" (318-65).

2. For a general account, see John Bossy, *The English Catholic Community 1570-1850* (New York: Oxford University Press, 1976). On the Recusants, see J. C. H. Aveling, *The Handle and the Axe: The Catholic Recusants in England from Reformation to Emancipation* (London: Blond & Briggs, 1976).

3. See Peter Guilday, *The English Catholic Refugees on the Continent 1558-1795,* vol. 1, *The English Colleges and Convents in the Catholic Low Countries, 1558-1795* (London and New York: Longman, Green, 1914); he treats the Benedictines in chap. 7 (215-83). The English nuns abroad have recently been given massive treatment in Caroline Bowden, ed., *English Convents in Exile, 1600-1800,* 6 vols. (London: Pickering & Chatto, 2012).

4. David Lunn, *The English Benedictines, 1540-1688: From Reformation to Revolution* (New York: Barnes & Noble, 1980).

5. On Baker's place in the three strands of Recusant spirituality, see Aidan Bellinger, "Baker's Recusant & Benedictine Context," in *That Mysterious Man: Essays on Augustine Baker OSB, 1575-1641,* ed. Michael Woodward (Abergavenny: Three Peaks Press, 2001), 42-56. For an overview, see Liam Peter Temple, "English Benedictine Mysticism, 1605-1650," in *Mysticism in Early Modern England* (Woodbridge: Boydell Press, 2019), 19-44.

6. For recent literature, see the essays in Woodward, *That Mysterious Man*; and Scott, *Dom Augustine Baker (1575-1641).* (I thank Prof. Peter Tyler for making this work available to me.) The few monographic studies of Baker include Anthony Low, *Augustine Baker* (New York: Twayne, 1970); and James Gaffney, *Augustine Baker's Inner Light: A Study in English Recusant Spirituality* (Scranton, PA: University of Scranton, 1989). An important unpublished work is John Douglas Barrett, *"Such a World of Books": Spiritual Reading in the Cambrai Treatises of Fr. Augustine Baker OSB* (Ph.D. dissertation, Heythrop College [University of London], 2011). I thank Prof. Edward Howells for sending me a copy of this dissertation.

7. Placid Spearritt, "The Survival of Medieval Spirituality among the Exiled English Black Monks," in Woodward, *That Mysterious Man,* 19-41; and David Lunn, "Father Augustine Baker (1575-1641) and the English Mystical Tradition," *Journal of Ecclesiastical History* 26 (1975): 267-77.

8. Thomas Merton, "Self-Knowledge in Gertrude More and Augustine Baker," in Merton, *Mystics and Zen Masters* (New York: Dell, 1961), 154-77.

9. On Baker's "mystical canon" and its relation to the medieval English mystics, see Elisabeth Dutton and Victoria Van Hyning, "Augustine Baker and the Mystical Canon," in Scott, *Dom Augustine Baker,* 85-110.

10. For an appreciation of Baker's sources, see John P. H. Clark, "Augustine Baker, O.S.B.: Towards a Re-Assessment," *Studies in Spirituality* 14 (2004): 209-24.

11. Baker himself left some autobiographical writings that can be found in *Memorials of Father Augustine Baker and Other Documents Relating to the English Benedictines*, ed. Justin McCann and Hugh Connolly, Publications of the Catholic Record Society 33 (London: Privately printed for the Society by J. Whitehead & Son, Leeds, 1933), 3–52. In addition, there are three lives. The first is by his relative and *socius* Fr. Leander Prichard and can be found in McCann and Connolly, *Memorials of Father Augustine Baker*, 53–154. A second life is by another Benedictine friend, Fr. Peter Salvin; the third is by Fr. Serenus Cressy. These last two lives are in *The Life of Father Augustine Baker, O.S.B. (1575–1641) by Fr. Peter Salvin and Fr. Serenus Cressy*, ed. Justin McCann (London: Burns, Oates & Washbourne, 1933).

12. On November 21, 1607, the ninety-year-old Dom Sigebert Buckley of Westminster, who had spent many decades in jail for refusing to recognize the English church, affiliated two English monks of the Cassinese Congregation with Westminster Abbey, thus establishing the continuity of English Benedictinism.

13. The account is found in the *Secretum*, edited and introduced by John Clark, Analecta Cartusiana 119.7 (Salzburg: Institut für Anglistik und Amerikanistik, 1997), 57–59. I cite from the modernized version found in Justin McCann, *The Confessions of the Venerable Father Augustine Baker* (London: Burns, Oates & Washbourne, 1922), 59–61.

14. *Directions for Contemplation: Book G*, ed. John Clark, Analecta Cartusiana 119.13 (Salzburg: Institut für Anglistik und Amerikanistik, 2000), 29. See the discussion in J. T. Rhodes, "Blosius and Baker," in Scott, *Dom Augustine Baker*, 133–52, here 139–41.

15. I use the translation of McCann in *Confessions of Father Baker*, 94–100 (quotations from 94–96). The original texts can be found in Clark, *Secretum*, 34–35.

16. McCann, *Confessions of Father Baker*, 115–16; the original is in Clark, *Secretum*, 249–50.

17. There is a treatment by Richard Lawes, "Can Modern Psychology help us understand Baker's *Secretum Sive Mysticum?*," in Woodward, *That Mysterious Man*, 211–33.

18. *Life and Writings of the Venerable Father, F. Augustin Baker*, No. 280, in McCann and Connolly, *Memorials of Father Augustine Baker*, 152.

19. Justin McCann listed sixty-eight works in his "Register of Fr. Baker's Writings," appendix 2 in *Life of Fr. Augustine Baker*, 160–201. See also Michael Woodward, "Bakerdata: An Annotated Bibliography of Published Texts and Secondary Sources," in idem, *That Mysterious Man*, 260–72.

20. Among the whole and partial translations (not a full list) are Luis de la Puente's *Life of Balthasar Alvarez*; Constantin de Barbanson's *Secret Paths of Divine Love*; a number of works of Louis de Blois; Achille Gagliardi's *Breve Compendio*; Pseudo-Tauler's *Institutiones divinae*; parts of Harphius's *Theologia mystica*; parts of Benet of Canfield's *Rule of Perfection*; parts of Walter Hilton's *Scale of Perfection*; and, of course, his edition of and commentary on the anonymous *Cloud of Unknowing* and *Book of Privy Counselling*.

21. Anselm Cramer, "Baker's Editors: Cressy to McCann," in Woodward, *That Mysterious Man*, 245–59.

22. Barrett, *"Such a World of Books,"* chap. 1 (29–80; quotation from 45).

23. Cramer, "Baker's Editors," 246.

24. Lunn summarizes, "Whereas the MSS give us the language of the living

teacher, as he sat in the parlour at Cambrai, prejudiced, emphatic, repetitive, this is lost in Cressy's version. Instead, we have a masterpiece of mystical theology" (*English Benedictines*, 213).

25. I will use the 1948 reprint, under the title *Holy Wisdom* (London: Burns, Oates & Washbourne). This includes the hundred pages of "Certain Patterns of Devout Exercises or Immediate Acts and Affections of the Will" (563–662), left out of many editions but central to understanding the second and third stages of prayer presented in the book.

26. Over thirty volumes have appeared as parts of the Analecta Cartusiana vol. 119, published by the Institut für Anglistik und Amerikanistik of the Universität Salzburg. Among the most important of these are Baker's *Directions for Contemplation* given the identifying letters *D, F, C, H,* and *G*. On the dating of these and other works, see John P. H. Clark, "Towards a Chronology of Father Augustine Baker's Writings," in Scott, *Dom Augustine Baker*, 111–32.

27. Again, see Barrett, "*Such a World of Books,*" whose chaps. 2–5 provide such a study concerning the view of spiritual reading found in the authentic writings and that in *Sancta Sophia*.

28. The edition is Fr. Augustine Baker, *Secretum*, edited and introduced by John Clark. For an account of the text, see John Clark, "Augustine Baker's *Secretum*: Sources and Affinities," in Woodward, *That Mysterious Man*, 123–35.

29. These autobiographical texts were excerpted and modernized by McCann in *Confessions of Venerable Father Augustine Baker*, 41–150.

30. A modernized version of the commentary appears in *The Cloud of Unknowing and Other Treatises by an English Mystic of the Fourteenth Century with a Commentary on the Cloud by Father Augustine Baker, O.S.B.*, ed. Justin McCann (London: Burns, Oates & Washbourne, 1947), 150–214.

31. On the problems of the Weld-Blundell text, see Ben Wekking, "Baker's Biography of Dame Gertrude More," in Woodward, *That Mysterious Man*, 155–73. The new edition is Ben Wekking, *Augustine Baker O.S.B., The Life and Death of Dame Gertrude More Edited from All the Known Manuscripts*, Analecta Cartusiana 119.19 (Salzburg: Institut für Anglistik und Amerikanistik, Universität Salzburg, 2002).

32. David Knowles, *The English Mystical Tradition* (London: Burns, Oates & Washbourne, 1961), chap. 9, "Father Augustine Baker" (151–87; quotation from 153).

33. Ibid., 167. On Knowles's denial that Baker has an adequate definition of contemplation, see 163–65, 171–72, and 183–85.

34. Merton, *Mystics and Zen Masters*, 147.

35. E. I. Watkin, *Poets and Mystics* (London and New York: Sheed & Ward, 1953), chap. 9, "Dom Augustine Baker" (188–237; quotation from 235).

36. For another evaluation of Baker as mystic, see Low, *Augustine Baker*, chap. 3 (53–74).

37. Knowles, *English Mystical Tradition*, 176.

38. The three sections deal with "The Contemplative Life in General" (six chapters), "Holy Inspirations" (nine chapters), and "Solitude and Religious Profession" (ten chapters).

39. Given the articulated structure of *Sancta Sophia*, I will cite by treatise, section, and chapter, as in 1.1.4 (i.e., treatise 1, section 1, chapter 4).

40. Low, *Augustine Baker*, chap. 4, "Reason and Will" (75–95).

41. For uses of these terms in *Sancta Sophia*, see 41-42, 151-52, 216, 334, 345, 397, 492, 510, and 540-41. The terms also occur in the *Secretum* (e.g., 27, 31, 192, 198, 215, and 228).

42. See *Sancta Sophia* 1.1.2 (ed., 34-38); and the discussion in Gaffney, *Augustine Baker's Inner Light*, 29-31.

43. *Sancta Sophia* 1.2.2, "Of an External Director" (ed., 73-86; quotation from 85).

44. *Sancta Sophia* 1.2.2 (ed., 83-84). Later, in 2.2.8-11 (ed., 278-304), there is a long discussion of three forms of scrupulosity.

45. "Freedom of spirit," of course, is not license, or following one's own desires; it is freedom to obey the promptings of the Holy Spirit. The need for *libertas spiritus* (2 Cor. 3:17) is a constant throughout *Sancta Sophia* (see, e.g., ed., 80, 100, 102, 136, 178, 223, 228, 252, 253, 383, 412-13, 418, 420, 421, 423, 426, 461, 470, etc.).

46. The relation between *Sancta Sophia* and the "Cambrai Treatises" on spiritual reading has been examined by Barrett in *"Such a World of Books."*

47. Knowles, *English Mystical Tradition*, chap. 10, "Epilogue," 192: "[T]he two most valuable single elements in his [Baker's] scheme, the prayer of acts of the will and the teaching on inspirations, are largely his own contribution and owe nothing directly to the medieval mystics."

48. *Sancta Sophia* 1.2.4 (ed., 92). The inspirations are often discussed (see, e.g., 1.1.1-3; 1.2.1-9; 2.2.14; and 3.4.3). The most detailed study is Gaffney, *Augustine Baker's Inner Light*, 31-41, on *Sancta Sophia*. In chap. 3, "Baker's Teaching on Inspiration in Other Works" (57-123), Gaffney provides a detailed discussion of the full range of Baker's teaching; see also Low, *Augustine Baker*, chap. 5, "Inspiration" (96-117).

49. On the cool attitude to special mystical experiences, see *Sancta Sophia* 1.2.1 (ed., 72), as well as 3.1.5 (ed., 369-70), and 3.4.3 (ed., 529).

50. Inspirations are the direct work of the Holy Spirit (e.g., 1.2.6); but, unlike the contemporary Jesuit mystic Louis Lallemant, who also defends the necessity for divine illuminations, *Sancta Sophia* does not develop this teaching in light of the traditional seven gifts of the Holy Spirit.

51. *Sancta Sophia* 1.2.6 (ed., 104-12).

52. Jean Lécuyer, "Docilité au Saint-Esprit," DS 3:1471-97, which mentions Baker, albeit briefly.

53. Gaffney, *Augustine Baker's Inner Light*, 91; see also 139-41.

54. The three impediments are treated in *Santa Sophia* 1.2.5 (ed., 98-104; quotation from 100).

55. *Sancta Sophia* 1.1.1 (ed., 31).

56. Cressy clearly "cleaned up" or omitted some aspects of Baker's teaching on illuminations in creating the *Sancta Sophia*. Gaffney (*Augustine Baker's Inner Light*, 94-98) notes some passages from the *Inner Life of Dame Gertrude More* that seem to conflict with what we read in *Sancta Sophia*.

57. The text of the "Protestation" is available in Baker's *Life and Death of Dame Gertrude More* (Wekking ed., 347-50).

58. Even after his exhaustive treatment of the issue of inspiration vs. authority in Baker, Gaffney makes the conclusion: "Indications like these seem to indicate that Baker never did, in fact, bring his doctrine of inspiration wholly to terms with the claims of obedience" (146).

59. *Sancta Sophia*, "Preface" (ed., 11-19; quotation from 14). Cressy's preface is discussed by Gaffney, *Augustine Baker's Inner Light*, 117-23.

60. *Sancta Sophia*, "A Memorial" (ed., 554-62), is discussed by Gaffney, *Augustine Baker's Inner Light*, 112-14. Even today, the adequacy of Baker's insistence on the inner light provokes discussion; see Gaffney, chap. 4, "Review and Critique of Baker's Doctrine," 125-50; and Lawes, "Can Modern Psychology Help Us Understand?," 217-19.

61. See *Sancta Sophia* 1.3.1 (ed., 136), and 3.4.2 (ed., 514-15).

62. See the discussion in *Sancta Sophia* 3.3.4 (ed., 457-65), and 3.4.2 (ed., 514-15).

63. On love in Baker, see Gordon Mursell, "'On Being Loved': The Assurance of Divine Love in the Works of Augustine Baker," in Scott, *Dom Augustine Baker*, 65-83.

64. *Sancta Sophia* 2.2.13 (ed., 319).

65. This section seems to have been influenced by the discussion of prayer in part II of Constantin de Barbanson's *Secret Paths of Divine Love*; see Edmund Power, "The Spirituality of *Sancta Sophia*," in Scott, *Dom Augustine Baker*, 14.

66. It is significant that, in speaking about the soul "attaining to perfect and mystic union" (3.3.2; ed., 444), *Sancta Sophia* says it is following Blosius, who as we saw above (chap. 2, 39, 42), introduced this language in the sixteenth century.

67. On the use of the language of "mystic" in Baker, see Dutton and Van Hyning, "Augustine Baker and the Mystical Canon," 94-95, 98-99.

68. *Secretum* (ed. Clark, 260-61). The list of terms bears interesting comparison with Maximilian Sandaeus's work (see chap. 8, 474-79), which was published only a few years later.

69. *Sancta Sophia* 1.1.2 (ed., 35).

70. *Sancta Sophia* 1.1.1 (ed., 29).

71. Union is one of the most frequent terms in the book, occurring close to a hundred times (among the most important appearances are 40-44, 129, 150, 196-98, 254, 259, 286-97, 318-19, 342, 396, 401, 497, 506-7, 519-31, and 545-46). Union language is also common in the *Secretum* (important uses include 84-85, 119, 186, 189-91, 196, 247, and 254).

72. *Sancta Sophia* 3.1.1 (ed., 341).

73. Prayer is certainly necessary, but, as Gaffney points out (*Augustine Baker's Inner Light*, 134-35), Christian teaching has always seen love of God and love of neighbor as the most essential and necessary practice. Cressy's introduction implicity corrects Baker on this, and *Sancta Sophia* later has texts that equate prayer and love.

74. *Sancta Sophia* 3.1.2 (ed., 347-48) discusses three degrees of attention to external prayer, especially the Divine Office, the third of which is identified with habitual union. Thus, vocal payer can accompany all three forms of internal prayer (see 3.2.1; ed., 402-3).

75. *Sancta Sophia* 3.1.2 (ed., 349-51).

76. *Sancta Sophia* 3.2.1 (ed., 395-97).

77. Chapter 1 of section 2 contains a helpful thumbnail sketch of the three stages of prayer (ed., 398-402).

78. Baker, like a number of mystics, believed that women had a greater affinity

for mystical prayer than men, as can be seen in the Cambrai Treatises, as well as *Sancta Sophia* 1.1.3 (ed., 40); and 1.3.1 (ed., 136-37).

79. *Sancta Sophia*, 3.2.5 (ed., 423-24).
80. Power, "Spirituality of *Sancta Sophia*," 1-18; quotation from 16.
81. *Sancta Sophia* 2.2.12 (ed., 313).
82. See, e.g., *Sancta Sophia* 3.3.2, 3.4.6 (ed., 442, 540).
83. *Sancta Sophia* 3.3.1 (ed., 431).
84. Ibid. (ed., 435).
85. Ibid. (ed., 432).
86. *Sancta Sophia* 3.3.2 (ed., 437-39). The "Patterns of Devout Exercises" at the end of *Sancta Sophia* take up a hundred pages. Some are christological (ed., 567-88); some deal with contrition (ed., 592-606). Other groups seem designed for the higher stages of contemplation, e.g., Four Exercises of Pure Love of God (ed., 607-11); Holy Exercises of Acts of the Will (ed., 623-29); and Holy Exercises of Resignation (ed., 630-49).
87. For earlier discussions of properly contemplative prayer, see *Sancta Sophia*, 38-42, 111-12, 238-40, 317-19, 400-402, and 433-34.
88. *Sancta Sophia* 3.4.1 (ed., 502-4).
89. Ibid. (ed., 505).
90. Ibid. (ed., 506-7).
91. For an account of this aspect of the background to Baker, see Peter Tyler, "Mystical Writing as *Theologia Mystica*," in Scott, *Dom Augustine Baker*, 51-63.
92. *Sancta Sophia* 3.4.1 (ed., 505). In the *Secretum*, Baker also often mentioned active and passive contemplation; see, e.g., 14-15, 21, 57-59, 66-67, 252-53, and especially 26-66.
93. Active contemplation is also infused. E. I. Watkin provides the following definition: "Active contemplation . . . may be described as a deliberate attention and adherence to God as he is known by faith without image or concept, a union which, when this contemplation is developed and infused, is evidently produced by the action of God" (*Poets and Mystics*, 222).
94. *Sancta Sophia* 3.4.2 (ed. 509-10).
95. Ibid. (ed., 512-13).
96. Laurence Freeman, "Baker and the Contemplative Ideal," in Woodward, *That Mysterious Man*, 191-201, especially 199-200. *Sancta Sophia* 3.1.4 (ed., 364) appeals to Cassian's view of monologistic prayer.
97. In the *Secretum* (e.g., 7-9) Baker explicitly says that the *Cloud*, Benet of Canfield, and Barbanson all teach the doctrine of active contemplation.
98. *Sancta Sophia* 3.4.3 (ed., 520). There are many texts on the darkness of faith throughout the book, particularly in treatise 3 (e.g., 36, 39, 400, 403, 434-35, 492, 503, 505, 507-8, 511, 533, 545, etc.).
99. Knowles, *English Mystical Tradition*, 183-85.
100. Watkin, *Poets and Mystics*, 205-25; quotation from 214. After an extensive discussion, Watkin summarizes his view of Baker's teaching on the forms of contemplation under five points (224-25).
101. *Sancta Sophia* 3.4.3 (ed., 520).
102. *Sancta Sophia* 3.4.4 (ed., 532-33). The text says that the mystics call the supreme portion by many names ("summit of the mind, the fund and center of

the spirit, the essence of the soul, the virginal portion, etc."), but there is really no name proper to it.

103. *Sancta Sophia* 3.4.5 (ed., 536–41). In the *Secretum*, Baker speaks of four states or conditions of souls: active and passive contemplation, and desolation and temptation (see 265–66). These states of desolation were mentioned in earlier places in the text (e.g., 285, 448–49, 464). Part 2 of the *Secretum* contains a rich treatment of the "State of Privation and Desolation" that cannot be taken up here (198–270).

104. *Sancta Sophia* 3.4.6 (ed., 541–42).

105. *Sancta Sophia* 3.4.6 (ed., 544). The language of deification found here is infrequent, but present elsewhere in the work (e.g., 42, 251, 255, 306, 518).

106. On the union of Nothing with nothing in Baker, see Christopher Armstrong, "Augustine Baker and the Union of Nothing with Nothing," in Woodward, *That Mysterious Man*, 136–54. On God and the soul as both *nihil*, see also *Secretum*, 23–24, 52–53, and 264–65. The original (and more striking) location of this passage appears to be a fragment of 1633 titled "Of That Mystick Saying, 'Nothing and Nothing Make Nothing," which was edited by Justin McCann in his article "Father Baker's Tercentenary," *Downside Review* 79 (1941): 355–71, here 369–71.

107. Ibid. (ed., 546). The quotation is from MT 1.

108. Prichard's *Life and Writings* is edited in McCann and Connolly, *Memorials of Father Baker*, 53–154.

109. *Life of Father Augustine Baker*, chap. 1.6–15, in McCann, *Life of Father Augustine Baker, O.S.B.*, 8–13.

110. Cressy's *Life of the Venerable Father Augustine Baker* was written as a preface to the edition of *Sancta Sophia* but proved to be too long. A modernized version can be found in McCann, *Life of Father Augustine Baker*, 51–153.

111. On Cressy, see Lunn, *English Benedictines*, 131–33; and Dom Hilary Steuert, "A Study in Recusant Prose: Dom Serenus Cressy, 1605–74," *Downside Review* 66 (1947/48): 165–78, 287–301.

112. For an account of the controversy, see T. A. Birrell, "English Catholic Mystics in Non-Catholic Circles I," *Downside Review* 94 (1976), 60–81, here 78–81.

113. Cited in ibid., 80.

114. Laurence Lux-Sterritt, *English Benedictine Nuns in Exile in the Seventeenth Century: Living Spirituality* (Manchester: Manchester University Press, 2017), 8. Lux-Sterritt discusses mysticism in chaps. 6 and 7. The range of this new research on the Recusant nuns is evident in the six volumes of Bowden, *English Convents in Exile, 1600–1800*.

115. Volume 2 of *English Convents in Exile, 1600–1800*, edited by Laurence Lux-Sterritt, is devoted to *Spirituality*.

116. On this text, see chap. 7 (417). On the translation, published in St. Omer in 1612, see Lux-Sterritt, *English Benedictine Nuns*, 119. Mary Percy is discussed in Lunn, *English Benedictines*, 198–201.

117. On the propensity of the Ghent nuns to talk about their visions, ecstasies, and miracles, see Lux-Sterritt, *English Benedictine Nuns*, 200–211, 237–38, 251. A good example of a visionary and ecstatic was Lucy Knatchbull (1584–1629), professed at Brussels in 1611, who was a founding member of Ghent in 1624 and abbess from 1624 to 1629. For some of her visions and ecstasies, see Lux-Sterritt, *English Benedictine Nuns*, 200–202.

118. Lux-Sterritt, *English Benedictine Nuns*, 251.

119. On Catherine Gascoigne, see chap. 1 in *In a Great Tradition: Tribute to Dame Laurentia McLachlan, Abbess of Stanbrook by the Benedictines of Stanbrook* (New York: Harper & Brothers, 1956), 3–29.

120. The story is told in ibid., 23–27.

121. The text is available in Lux-Sterritt, *English Convents in Exile*, 2:463–66.

122. *The Spiritual Exercises of the Most Vertuous and Religious D. Gertrude More . . . Confessiones Amantis: A Lovers Confessions* (Paris: Lewis de la Fosse, 1658). There is a recent facsimile reprint in *Gertrude More*, ed. Arthur F. Marotti, *The Early Modern Englishwoman: A Facsimile Library of Essential Works. Series II, Printed Writings, 1641–1700*: Part 4, Volume 3 (Burlington: Ashgate, 2009).

123. I will cite from the edition of Ben Wekking, *The Life and Death of Dame Gertrude More*. The sections are as follows: (1) Prelude (Gertrude's early life, 1606–23); (2) Stage 1, her difficult first years as a nun (1624–25); (3) Stage 2, where she finds her true spiritual way (1626–31); (4) Stage 3, featuring more treatment of her contemplation and the debate over Baker and Gertrude's method of prayer (1631–33); and (5) Stage 4, treating her last illness and death in August 1633. On the structure of the work, see Wekking, "Introduction," xxiv–xxvii.

124. The teaching on inspirations and calls, the focus of the dispute between Fr. Baker and Fr. Hull, is featured in stage 3.33–37 (ed., 258–304).

125. There is a treatise on the "Four Kinds of Prayer" in stage 2.11-14 (ed., 61–79).

126. Wekking has a discussion of many of these themes ("Introduction," xxvii–xliv).

127. *Life and Death*, stage 1.6 (ed., 25–26).

128. *Life and Death*, stage 2.15 (ed., 82–83).

129. *Life and Death*, stage 2.20 (ed., 118–19).

130. *Life and Death*, stage 2.21-24 (ed., 121–51). Baker also discusses Gertrude's sufferings in stage 3.30 (ed., 221–29).

131. The polemical attacks on Hull are mostly found in stage 3.34 and 36 (ed., 265–70, 279–91).

132. *Life and Death*, stage 3.26 (ed., 155–80).

133. *Life and Death*, stage 3.31 (ed., 229–30).

134. Ibid. (ed., 231). Baker goes on to include a poem by Gertrude on the theme of union with God the center through the power of love (ed., 232).

135. Ibid. (ed., 234). For more on how the love in the superior part of the soul overflows into lower sensible love so that the two work in harmony, see 3.32 (ed., 247).

136. Ibid. (ed., 237).

137. *Life and Death*, stage 3.32 (ed., 251).

138. *Life and Death*, stage 4.38 (ed., 316–17).

139. I will cite the *Apology* from the modernized version edited by Dom Benedict Weld-Blundell, *The Inner Life and the Writings of Dame Gertrude More*, vol. 2 (London: R. & T. Washbourne, 1911), 209–90. In the facsimile reprint of the 1658 original edition, the *Apology* appears first with a separate pagination from the other writings (see Marotti, *Spiritual Excercises*, 7–112).

140. There is a study of the *Apology* in Gaffney, *Augustine Baker's Inner Light*, 102–12. On More's understanding of prayer and obedience, see also Arthur F.

Marotti, "Saintly Idiocy and Contemplative Empowerment: The Example of Dame Gertrude More," in *Mysticism and Reform, 1400–1750*, ed. Sara S. Poor and Nigel Smith, ReFormations: Medieval and Early Modern (Notre Dame, IN: University of Notre Dame Press, 2015), 151–76.

141. *Apology* 4 (ed., 214).

142. Although she admits that the Jesuits have the perfection of the active life, her remarks are in general negative; see *Apology*, 227, 250–54, and 258–59.

143. Hull's name is never mentioned, but it is obvious he is the target of comments in *Apology*, 217–18, 244–47, and 281.

144. *Apology* 11–12 (ed., 219–20); see also 224–26, 261–63, and 282–83.

145. *Apology* 69 (ed., 288–89).

146. Not much has been written on Gertrude More as a mystic, but see Marion Norman, "Dame Gertrude More and the English Mystical Tradition," *Recusant History* 15 (1979): 192–211.

147. Among the better poems are those collected and studied by Dorothy L. Latz, "The Mystical Poetry of Dame Gertrude More," *Mystics Quarterly* 16 (1990): 66–82.

148. I cite from the modernized version of the *Confessiones Amantis* in Weld-Blundell, *Inner Life and the Writings*, 3–142. In the facsimile of the 1658 edition, the *Confessiones* appear first with their own pagination (Marotti, *Spiritual Exercises*, 1–237). In addition, there are a number of "Fragments" (Weld-Blundell, 145–206). Augustine is singled out for praise in the *Confessiones*, both in Gertrude's poetry (*Conf.* I; ed., 11) and in her prose (*Conf.* X; ed., 45–46).

149. *Conf.* XXXVI (ed., 104; for more on liberty of spirit, see 4, 15, 20, 38, 52, 63).

150. *Conf.* XII (ed., 54–55; for more on union, see 15, 19, 25, 33, 43–44, 50, 62, 76, 91, 104, etc.).

151. On the way of the cross, see *Conf.* IX, XI, XIX, and XXVII (ed., 43, 51, 65, 79).

152. *Conf.* XXVIII (ed., 83–85).

153. *Conf.* XVIII (ed., 63–64). Another fine text on love is *Conf.* XXV (ed., 75–78).

154. *Conf.* LIII (ed., 141).

155. Helpful introductions to Crashaw include Douglas Bush, *English Literature in the Earlier Seventeenth Century, 1600–1660* (Oxford: Clarendon, 1962), 146–50; Anthony Low, "Richard Crashaw," in *The Cambridge Companion to English Poetry: Donne to Marvell*, ed. Thomas N. Corns (Cambridge: Cambridge University Press, 1993), 242–55; and Richard Rambuss, "Richard Crashaw: A Reintroduction," in *The English Poems of Richard Crashaw*, ed. Richard Rambuss (Minneapolis: University of Minnesota Press, 2013), xvii–lxxxiv. On Crashaw as a spiritual and mystical figure, see Ronald Arbuthnott Knox, *Literary Distractions* (London and New York: Sheed & Ward, 1958), chap. 4, "Richard Crashaw" (59–77).

156. The Baroque character of Crashaw's poetry has elicited a large literature. Classic accounts are Austin Warren, *Richard Crashaw: A Study in Baroque Sensibility* (Ann Arbor: University of Michigan Press, 1939); Mario Praz, "The Flaming Heart: Richard Crashaw and the Baroque," in Praz, *The Flaming Heart* (Garden City, NY: Doubleday Anchor, 1958), 204–63; Louis L. Martz, "Richard Crashaw: Love's Architecture," in Martz, *The Wit of Love* (Notre Dame, IN: University of Notre

Dame Press, 1969), 111–48; and Robert T. Petersson, *The Art of Ecstasy: Teresa, Bernini, and Crashaw* (New York: Athenaeum, 1970).

157. On Crashaw's "femininity," see the discussions in Low, "Richard Crashaw," 245–48, 252, as well as Rambuss, "Richard Crashaw: A Reintroduction," lx–lxxi, and the literature cited there.

158. Cited in Rambuss, "Richard Crashaw: A Reintroduction," lxiii.

159. E. I. Watkin, "Richard Crashaw," in *Poets and Mystics*, 136–63; quotation from 162.

160. Knox, *Literary Distractions*, 60.

161. Rambuss, "Richard Crashaw: A Reintroduction," xxii.

162. "The Preface to the Reader" to *Steps to the Temple (1646)*, cited from Rambuss, *English Poems of Richard Crashaw*, 5–6. All citations will be from this edition.

163. Rambuss, *English Poems*, 151.

164. Ibid., 124.

165. T. S. Eliot, "Richard Crashaw," in *The Varieties of Metaphysical Poetry by T. S. Eliot*, ed. Ronald Schuchard (San Diego: Harcourt Brace & Compnay, 1993), 161–84; quotation from 163.

166. For a recent attempt to characterize the main features of the Baroque, see Peter Davidson, *The Universal Baroque* (Manchester: Manchester University Press, 2007), "Introduction" (124).

167. Eliot, "Richard Crashaw," 168.

168. Low, "Richard Crashaw," 245. See also Low, *Love's Architecture: Devotional Modes in Seventeenth-Century English Poetry* (New York: New York University Press, 1978).

169. Helpful in this connection is Marc F. Bertonasco, *Crashaw and the Baroque* ([Tuscaloosa]: University of Alabama Press, 1971), 88–90. See also Petersson, *Art of Ecstasy*, 124–26.

170. R. V. Young, *Richard Crashaw and the Spanish Golden Age*, Yale Studies in English 191 (New Haven: Yale University Press, 1978), 88.

171. Janel Mueller, "Women among the Metaphysicals: A Case, Mostly, of Being Donne for," *Modern Philology* 87 (1989): 142–58; quotation from 144.

172. The most complete study of Crashaw's relation to Spain and Spanish mysticim is Young, *Richard Crashaw and the Spanish Golden Age*, especially chap. 4, "The Wound of Love and the Dark Night of the Soul; Crashaw and Mysticism" (79–112).

173. For the motto, see Rambuss, *English Poems*, 8. The source is Francis's *Treatise on Divine Love*, book 12, chap. 13. Crashaw's friend Fr. Thomas Carre produced the first English version in 1630, but Crashaw might have read it first in French.

174. See A. F. Allison, "Crashaw and St. François de Sales," *Review of English Studies* 24 (1948): 295–302.

175. Bertonasco, *Crashaw and the Baroque*, chap. 2, "The Influence of St. Francis de Sales," 45–93, especially 59, 74–79, and 85–90.

176. Gary Kuchar, "A Greek in the Temple: Pseudo-Dionysius and Negative Theology in Rchard Crashaw's 'Hymn in the Glorious Epiphany,'" *Studies in Philology* 108 (2011): 267–75, especially 268, 271, 275, 279–80, 283–86, and 295.

177. On the liturgical context of Crashaw's poetry, see Eugene R. Cunnar, "Opening the Religious Lyric: Crashaw's Ritual, Liminal, and Visual Wounds,"

in *New Perspectives on the Seventeenth-Century English Religious Lyric*, ed. John R. Roberts (Columbia: University of Missouri, 1994), 237–67, especially 239–40.

178. It is something of an anomaly that the *Carmen Deo Nostro* does not include a hymn for Easter, although the Divine Epigrams in *Steps to the Temple* has a three-stanza poem on "Easter Day" (*English Poems*, 29).

179. The six hymns are "Vexilla Regis," "Stabat Mater," "Adoro Te Devote," "Lauda Sion," "Dies Irae," and "O Gloriosa Domina." On the character of these versions as "descants," see Warren, *Richard Crashaw*, 151–58.

180. On the unity of the four poems, see A. R. Cirillo, "Crashaw's 'Epiphany Hymn': The Dawn of Christian Time," *Studies in Philology* 67 (1972): 67–88, especially 68–73.

181. Rambuss, *English Poems*, 381.

182. Anthony D. Cousins, *The Catholic Religious Poets from Southwell to Crashaw: A Critical History* (Westminster MD: Christian Classics, 1991), 134.

183. Louis L. Martz, *The Poetry of Meditation: A Study of English Religious Literature of the Seventeenth Century* (New Haven: Yale University Press, 1954), 337–52.

184. Bernard's devotion to the name of Jesus is evident in his *Sermones super Cantica* 15 (*Sancti Bernardi Opera* 1:82–88), as well as in *Sermo 1 in Vigilia Nativitatis* and *Sermo 1 in Circumcisione*. The "Jesu dulcis memoria" is a late twelfth-century Cistercian composition. On devotion to the name of Jesus, see Irénée Noye, "Jésus (Nom de)," DS 8:1109–26 (which does not mention Crashaw!).

185. The 239-line hymn will be cited from Rambuss, *English Poems*, 157–64.

186. The Nativity Hymn of 108 lines is in Rambuss, *English Poems*, 165–69. The earlier and rather different version from *Steps to the Temple* is in ibid., 37–40. On the poem, see Martz, *Wit of Love*, 142–47; Young, *Richard Crashaw and the Spanish Golden Age*, 93–99; and Kerby Neill, "Structure and Symbol in Crashaw's *Hymn in the Nativity*," *Publications of the Modern Langage Association of America* 63 (1948): 101–13.

187. The *Steps to the Temple* has a poem "Our Lord in his Circumcision to his Father" (Rambuss, *English Poems*, 27) whose subject is the blood of the circumcision as the "firstfruits of my growing death," and the "knife [as] the spear's praeludium." This poem is not reprinted in the later collection.

188. "In the Glorious Epiphany of Our Lord," in Rambuss, *English Poems*, 172–79, was first published in the 1648 version of *Steps to the Temple*. There are many treatments; see Warren, *Richard Crashaw*, 147–51; Young, *Richard Crashaw and the Spanish Golden Age*, 99–112; Cirillo, "Crashaw's 'Epiphany Hymn,'" 67–88; and especially Kuchar, "Greek in the Temple," 261–98.

189. On "The Night," see McGinn, *Reformation*, 249–51.

190. Many things about these remarkable lines are worthy of study. Here I note only "All-circling point. All cent'ring sphere," which is Crashaw's rendering of the famous definition of God originally found in the *Liber XXIV Philosophorum* as the *Sphaera intelligibilis cuius centrum est ubique, cuius circumferentia est nusquam*. It is interesting to note that the major study of this central theological motif, Dietrich Mahnke, *Unendliche Sphäre und Allmittelpunkt* (Halle: Niemeyer, 1937), does not reference Crashaw.

191. For these poems, see Rambuss, *English Poems*, 181–95.

192. The three Passion poems are in Rambuss, *English Poems*, 204–7. These poems originally appeared in *Steps to the Temple*, 26, 28, and 29–31. There is

also an unpublished poem, "In cicatrices Domini Jesu" (Rambuss, *English Poems*, 276).

193. Warren, *Richard Crashaw*, 157. Warren's brief treatment (156-58) is a good summary.

194. The full title is "Sancta Maria Dolorum, or The Mother of Sorrows. A Descant upon the Devout Plainsong of *Stabat Mater Dolorosa*" (Rambuss, *English Poems*, 200-203; quotation from 202-3).

195. These hymns can be found in Rambuss, *English Poems*, 208-19.

196. "The Tear" of forty-eight lines is found only in *Steps to the Temple* (Rambuss, *English Poems*, 14-15). There is a short appreciative comment by T. S. Eliot (*Varieties of Metaphysical Poetry*, 171-74), although he thought the poem referred to the Virgin Mary and not Mary Magdalene. The early version of "The Weeper" from *Steps to the Temple* had 140 lines in twenty-three stanzas. Crashaw reworked the poem extensively for the *Carmen Deo Nostro* (Rambuss, *English Poems*, 223-29) to reach thirty-one stanzas and 186 lines. Many critics have written on the poem, e.g., Praz, *Flaming Heart*, 222-31; Bertonasco, *Crashaw and the Baroque*, chap. 3 (94-117), who sees it as a meditation in the style of Francis de Sales; and Patricia Badir, *The Maudlin Impression: English Literary Images of Mary Magdalene, 1550-1700* (Notre Dame, IN: University of Notre Dame Press, 2009), 169-80.

197. Petersson, *Art of Ecstasy*, 127. See the whole of Petersson's insightful analyis of the poem (127-56). There are many treaments; among them Warren, *Richard Crashaw*, 139-46; Young, *Richard Crashaw and the Spanish Golden Age*, 70-73, 80-90, 114-20; and Cousins, *Catholic Religious Poets*, 159-67. The poem appears in all three books of Crashaw's verse. Petersson prefers and reprints the 1648 version (107-12), because it incorporates Crashaw's revisions to the first edition and does not have the typographical errors that appeared in the 1652 version.

198. Warren, *Richard Crashaw*, 146.

199. Rambuss, *English Poems*, 236-37.

200. It has been noted that the contrasting forms of inebriation were also discussed by Francis de Sales, *Treatise on the Love of God*, book I, chap. 10; and book VI, chap. 6.

201. For the poem, see Rambuss, *English Poems*, 238-41. Martz (*Wit of Love*, 122-31) tentatively identifies the picture with a scene of the transverberation painted by the Antwerp artist Gerhard Seghers.

202. Martz, *Wit of Love*, 130.

203. The first version of "Prayer, an Ode" appeared in the 1646 *Steps to the Temple*, and the second revised form in *Carmen Deo Nostro* (Rambuss, *English Poems*, 58-61, 243-46). The first version is addressed to a Mrs. M. R., who has not been identified. For discussions of the poem, see Young, *Richard Crashaw and the Spanish Golden Age*, 30-34; and Martz, *Wit of Love*, 137-40.

204. Quoted in Warren, *Richard Crashaw*, 60-61.

CHAPTER 7

Mysticism in Italy (1500–1675)

Introduction

The history of Italy during the period 1500–1575 has important differences from Spain, France, and Germany.[1] Like Germany, Italy was a "multi-state polity," but its relation to the Holy Roman Empire was different, since it was only in the time of Charles V that Italy was to some extent under the emperor (1530–55). There were small intellectual groups in Italy (often called "Evangelical," sometimes *Spirituali*) who sympathized with some aspects of the criticism the Reformers directed against abuses in the church, but aside from a few notable converts to the Reformation who had to flee the peninsula, Italy did not have a Protestant problem and did not experience the religious wars of Germany and France. Unlike the unified state-church of Spain, Italy was split into a number of contending political entities. There were five major states—the Kingdom of Naples, the Papal States, the Duchy of Florence, the Republic of Venice, and the Duchy of Milan (with many minor powers). Having the papacy as both a contender in its involved politics and as the universal head of the true church introduced obvious complications into Italian history, especially when papal political objectives conflicted with its universal claims.

Italy's problem was not only regional conflicts between the major entities on the peninsula but also the fact that from 1494 to 1530 it was the "cockpit of Europe," where great powers, especially the Hapsburg Empire (and later Hapsburg Spain) and the kingdom of France, vied for a control of Italy that would give them a preponderance in Europe. Italy was ravaged with wars—but dynastic, not religious, wars. The damage inflicted by these wars reached a culmination in 1527 with the sack of Rome by rebellious troops of the Catholic emperor Charles V, an event of seemingly apocalyptic dimensions to contemporaries. Nonetheless, history went on, and during the period from 1530 until ca. 1560, while Charles was the nominal ruler of Italy, internecine conflict receded during a period of stabilization. With the defeat of the last French incursion into Italy and the Peace of Cateau-Cambrésis in 1557, a fifty-year period of peace and consolidation ensued. By the end of the sixteenth century, Italy was probably the most densely populated and richest area in Europe.[2]

From the perspective of religion, there was a similar dynamic: a period of conflict and debate, followed by a time of consolidation. Criticism of aspects of medieval religious life and the papacy was strong at the beginning of the sixteenth century. These were exacerbated by the outbreak of the Reformation (1518) and the failure of popes such as the Medici Leo X and Clement VII to mount an effective response. Nonetheless, reform was not just a "top-down" operation. What has come to be called "Catholic Reform," that is, the proliferation of more limited attempts at personal and institutional reform "from below," were strong, especially in Italy in the first half of the sixteenth century.[3] Furthermore, while it is easy to criticize the political failures of many late fifteenth- and early sixteenth-century popes, the great achievement of the Renaissance papacy was its encouragement of the glory of High Renaissance art, whose greatest practitioners, such as Michelangelo (1475-1564), produced works of art not only of surpassing aesthetic merit but also of real theological and spiritual significance.[4]

Catholic Reform was evident in the growth of confraternities, in the reform of religious orders that had grown ossified, and in the foundation of new orders and religious congregations. In 1497, a circle of laity and clergy in Genoa centered on Catherine of Genoa (Caterina Fieschi Adorno) founded the Oratory of Divine Love to deepen their commitment to prayer and apostolic action. The movement spread to other places in Italy and in 1524 gave birth to the Theatines, an order of Clerks Regular, or priests engaged in pastoral work but living under vows and according to a rule of life. Another such congregation of priests was the Roman Oratory, whose spiritual leader was the Florentine Filippo Neri (1515-1595), active in Rome from the 1550s, although the group did not receive papal approval until 1575. The reform of the ancient

Camaldolese Order of monks was organized by a group of Venetian aristocrats under the leadership of Paolo (Tommaso) Giustiniani (1476–1528). The Franciscan hermit Matteo da Bascio (1495–1552) and his followers established a new and more rigorous branch of the Franciscans, the Capuchins, in 1528. Girolamo Seripando (1492–1563) reformed the Augustinian Order by writing new constitutions and making sure they were adopted throughout the order. The most successful of the new apostolic orders was the Jesuits, founded by the Basque Ignatius of Loyola but centered in Italy. Ignatius and his early followers arrived in Rome in 1537 and won papal approval in 1540. The list could go on, but it is obvious that these new foundations and renewals of older orders were vital to religious life in Italy during this period.

With regard to the papacy, under Paul III (1534–50) the wheels of reform slowly began to move.[5] Paul established a Commission of Cardinals who issued a *Consilium de emendenda ecclesia* in 1537 and eventually called for an ecumenical council that began its deliberations at Trent in northern Italy, a territory in imperial lands, in 1545. The council met over three disconnected sessions (1545–47, 1551–52, and 1562–63) with a fluid number of participants, surviving a number of attempts by both popes (especially Paul IV) and political powers to kill it off. The history of the Council of Trent, and its achievements and failures, has recently been well laid out by John O'Malley.[6] Trent set down important doctrinal norms in opposition to Protestant teaching and instituted many general reform decrees for laity, priests, religious orders, and bishops, though saying nothing about the reform of the papacy and the curia. Although far from perfect, Trent marked an important turning point for the church in Italy, since most of the attending bishops were Italian and sought to implement the reforms when they returned to their dioceses. The popes after Trent (Pius IV, Pius V, Gregory XIII, Sixtus V), were generally reformers, although some still practiced nepotism and other abuses. They furthered the process known as "Tridentinism," that is, the confessionalization by which the newly confident Roman Catholicism of the period after 1565 through the actions of popes, bishops, priests, and religious, as well as Catholic rulers and laity, established a coherent "Catholic identity," though often in a rather rigid way.[7]

It is hard to provide a general picture of the political and cultural situation in Italy in the seventeenth century. There were a number of crises in the first three decades of the century that challenged the optimistic last half of the preceding century. Severe economic depression kicked in about 1610, exacerbated by attacks of the plague in the early

1630s. In 1606, Paul V put Venice under brief Interdict, an event that in the long run undermined the authority of the papacy in relation to sovereign states. Wars broke out across the Italian peninsula and France was able to intrude into Italian politics once more. A number of scholars have pointed to a gradual hardening of the Tridentine view of papally led Catholicism in the first half of the seventeenth century. Concern for the teaching of correct doctrine shifted away from arguing against the heretical Protestants (a lost cause) to theological disputes within the Catholic world, as the popes and the Holy Office stepped in to determine truth or preclude debate. Examples include the controversy over grace and freedom that pitted the Jesuits against the Dominicans (the *de auxiliis* debates of 1598–1607); the condemnation of Galileo in 1633; and the decree against the *Augustinus* of Cornelius Jansenius in 1642. The greatest crisis of the era was the outbreak of the Thirty Years' War in 1618. This terrible conflict did not affect Italy to the extent it did northern Europe, but it sucked the papacy into a struggle that killed millions, changed little, and showed that Catholic states, like France, would pursue their own national interests, whatever the papacy might desire. The triumph of national politics over more universal Catholic concerns only increased in the second half of the seventeenth century when the French ruler, Louis XIV, sought to reduce the pope to a kind of chaplain for French hegemony.

The more positive side of this impressionistic sketch is to point to the cultural glory of Rome, as well as other Italian states, in the seventeenth century—the age of the Baroque triumph still so evident in the Eternal City. Urban VIII (1623–44) may have been something of a failure as a political and theological figure, but he was a magnificent patron of the arts, especially through sponsoring the work of G. L. Bernini (1598–1680), the greatest artistic figure of the time. Bernini's genius in depicting ecstatic mystical states in sculpture, best known through his Cornaro Chapel portrayal of Saint Teresa but evident in many other works,[8] shows that in Italy Baroque culture was an integral aspect of the triumph of the Counter-Reformation view of the church and the establishment of the Catholic Tridentinism, which in various transmutations was to last for three hundred years.

Sixteenth- and seventeenth-century Italy also shared in many of the spiritual currents and devotional practices of both the Catholic Reform era and post-Tridentine Catholicism noted above in the case of France (see chapter 1), as many surveys of Italian spirituality have shown.[9] While not as richly studied as French spirituality of the early modern period, the seventy years since Giuseppe de Luca published the first number of the *Archivio italiano per la storia della pietà* has seen significant research on the topic.[10] The "great spirituals" (*grandi spirituali*) of the sixteenth century should not be seen just from the perspective of the reaction of Catholicism to the Protestant threat, but as the flowering of developments rooted in the spirituality of the late Middle Ages,[11] while the mystics of the seventeenth century have their own spiritual physiognomy and are not just a preparation for the Quietist controversy.[12]

Along with the new and renewed religious orders and congregations mentioned above, there are many other important currents to Italian religious life of this era, only a few of which can be noted here. Of great importance was the more effective teaching of doctrine, especially through the production and use of catechisms. There was a significant renewal of sacramental life, especially the more frequent use of the sacrament of penance. The Council of Trent called for a renewal of the priestly life and mandated the creation of seminaries to foster a better educated and more devout clergy. Carlo Borromeo (1538–1584) encouraged reform of the priesthood and became the model for the kind of reforming pastoral bishop fostered by the council. There was a strong ascetic flavor in much of the spirituality of the late sixteenth and seventeenth centuries, as well as a desire to disseminate sound spiritual teaching to the laity. These tendencies and others coalesce around the important theme of "spiritual combat," which produced one of the masterworks of the period, *Il combattimento spirituale* of the Theatine Lorenzo Scupoli (1530–1610).

The widely read *Spiritual Combat* is not a mystical text but an ascetical manual about the Christian life as warfare against the enemies of salvation: the world, the flesh and its passions, and the devil.[13] Scupoli was born in Otranto, but little is known about him before his entry into the Theatines in Naples in 1569, where he was influenced by Gaetano da Thiene, the founder of the order, and Andrea Avellino, later canonized. He served in several Theatine houses, especially in Milan during the reforming times of Carlo Borromeo. For reasons unknown, in 1585 Scupoli was condemned and imprisoned for three years by the Theatine General Chapter and spent the rest of his life under a cloud. He was not rehabilitated until a few months before his death in 1610. The first edition of the *Spiritual Combat*, published anonymously in 1589, had only thirty-three chapters and was apparently written for a nun, since the audience is addressed in the feminine. Scupoli, however, continued to add material in later years, including thirty-three chapters of "Additions to *The Spiritual Combat*." The definitive edition published shortly after his death at the end of 1610 had sixty-six chapters, as well as the "Additions," and even named him as the author.

The sixty-six chapters have six basic parts: (1) distrust of self (chaps. 1-2); (2) confidence in God (chaps. 3-6); (3) the central section on overcoming faults (chaps. 7-26), achieving victory over Satan (chaps. 27-32), and attaining virtues (chaps 33-43); (4) prayer and meditation (chaps. 44-52); (5) the reception of communion (chaps. 53-56); and finally (6) various pieces of advice, especially on dying (chaps. 57-66). The *Spiritual Combat* is not particularly well organized, but its solid and practical advice about the spiritual life made it into a remarkable best-seller across denominations, a book still read today. Six hundred editions are said to have been published over the past four hundred years. Almost all the spiritual and mystical teachers of the seventeenth century read and praised it. Francis de Sales, who discovered it during his time studying law at Padua, always kept a copy on his person so that he could read in it when time allowed.

There were a number of other spiritual classics produced at the end of the sixteenth and the beginning of the seventeenth century that tell us much about Italian post-Tridentine piety. A good example is *The Mind's Ascent to God by the Ladder of Created Things* (*Ascensus mentis in Deum per Scalas Rerum Creaturarum*) of the Jesuit cardinal Roberto Bellarmino in 1612. Bellarmine (1542-1621), saint and Doctor of the Church, was one of the great minds of the era.[14] He was best known as a controversialist, and his three volumes of *Disputations about the Controversies of the Christian Faith against the Heretics of the Age* (1586-93) were the first systematic refutation of Protestant theology. Bellarmine was a respected teacher at both the University of Louvain and the Jesuit Collegio Romano. The last decade of his life, however, was devoted to biblical and spiritual writing. The greatest fruit of this was *The Mind's Ascent to God*, of which Bellarmine says in his dedication: "I do not read my other books unless I am forced to; this one I have already read gladly three or four times, and I have resolved to reread it frequently in the future."[15]

Despite its title, and the fact that Bellarmine praises Bonaventure's *Mind's Journey into God* in his introduction, the book is not really mystical. Rather, it is a typical Renaissance panegyric designed to lift the mind to admiration and love of God through the consideration of created things. Bonaventure had constructed his ascent in *The Mind's Journey* around six stages. The first two considered God "in and through" creatures, while the second two turned inward to find God "in and through" the rational mind, and the last two transcended the mind and all creation to attain mystical contact with God and the crucified Christ. Bellarmine, however, is interested only in the first two levels of ascent, that is, the physical universe and the human being as the *imago Dei*. At the end of his introduction, Bellarmine makes it clear that he is writing for the average believer, not mystics who have been given special graces. "For us mortal men," he says, "it seems that no ladder of ascent to God can be open except through the works of God. Those who by a singular gift of God are admitted to paradise by a different road and hear mysteries of God which it is not lawful to utter (2 Cor. 12:4) are better said not to have ascended, but to have been carried up."[16] So, this is not a book for the raptured or those seeking special contact with God. Bellarmine's decidedly "a-mystical" treatment fits in well with that camp in the Jesuit Order that remained suspicious of mystics and mystical writing. The cardinal pursues his theme with ingenuity and power through fifteen steps; the rhetoric is rich, the content largely doctrinal.[17] The treatise was written in Latin, but Bellarmine obviously meant it for a wide audience, as was indeed the case. In the years that followed there were some sixty editions in fifteen languages.

Collaboration and Controversy:
Isabella Berinzaga and Achille Gagliardi

Since the thirteenth century there have been many examples of fruitful collaboration between female mystics and their male friends, advisors, and confessors, who may or may not have been mystics themselves. In this volume we have already studied the well-known case of Francis de Sales and Jane de Chantal. In Italy at the end of the sixteenth century we have the example of "the Milanese lady," Isabella Berinzaga (1551-1621), and her confessor and scribe, the Jesuit theologian Achille Gagliardi (1538-1607). This collaboration produced a mystical classic widely read in the seventeenth century, *The Brief Compendium of Christian Perfection* (*Breve compendio di perfezione cristiana*), but it also led to the silencing of both figures by Clement VIII in March of 1601.

Based on the research of Mario Gioia, we now have a good sense of the unfolding of the at times gripping story of how this book came to existence.[18] Gagliardi was born in Padua in 1538, entered the Jesuits in 1559, and was educated at the Collegio Romano.[19] He received his doctorate in 1568 and began a distinguished teaching career in Rome, Turin, and Padua, before being sent to the Jesuit church of San Fedele in Milan at the request of Carlo Borromeo in 1580. Isabella Berinzaga (Lomazzi) had attended Mass there since 1568 and had taken spiritual direction from the Jesuits. Berinzaga was born into a noble family in 1551, and as a young girl had already received high mystical graces.[20] Like many female mystics, she also suffered from a number of illnesses, as well as mysterious sufferings caused by her sharing in Christ's Passion. In 1579, the Jesuit general, Everard Mercurian, sent Fr. Sebastiano Morales to Milan to investigate Isabella's mystical claims, which the latter so strongly vindicated that she was given the unusual title *figliola della Compagnia e sotto l'obedientia de i padri* ("little daughter of the Company under the obedience of the fathers").

Gagliardi appears to have had little to do with Isabella for his first several years in Milan as he fulfilled apostolic tasks for Carlo Borromeo, but this changed in 1584 when he assumed the office of her spiritual director. From May 1 until about September 15 of that year he gave her the *Spiritual Exercises* and recorded her prayer experiences. Gagliardi was astonished by her mystical insights. Isabella became for him, as a number of medieval mystical women had for their confessors and advisors, not only a messenger from God but also a living source of grace. Writing to the Jesuit general Claudio Aquaviva about Isabella in 1593, he says, "There are many worthier than I who have received cures [from her]. I only profess before God that I have had such experiences within me and outside me many times, that I have seen real spiritual miracles for the good and incredible changes in souls, and so great a strength of spirit and revival of [spiritual] practice that I am obliged to hold that the powerful hand of the Almighty is hidden within [her]."[21] It is clear that the Jesuit theologian and the young Milanese woman had entered into a deep spiritual friendship, as Achille seems to hint at in a text from the second part of the *Brief Compendium* when he speaks of "two deiform souls having between them the greatest sympathy and the most powerful mutual love, along with the greatest self-denial [*spropriatione*]; for the greater glory of God they do not care a bit if they are far from each other, and they do not get disturbed over whatever happens, however serious it be."[22] Apparently in late 1584 and into 1585 Gagliardi worked up Isabella's own records (these do not survive),[23] as well as his notes of their conversations, into an experiential mystical account, *Through the Way of Annihilation (Per via di annichilazione)*, thus emphasizing one of the central themes of the Milanese woman's mysticism. According to Mario Gioia, Isabella can correctly be termed the "author" and Gagliardi the "redactor" of this text,[24] which, although it survives in four manuscripts, did not see publication until 1994.

During 1585, Achille Gagliardi decided to recast the material from Isabella's personal account into a theological treatise on the mystical life, what became the *Brief Compendium*. Gagliardi's considerable knowledge of theology and mystical sources is evident in the treatise, as is its Ignatian substructure. The Jesuit never mentions sources in the work, but, given the importance of the theme of annihilation both in *Through the Way of Annihilation* and the *Brief Compendium*, it is obvious that Gagliardi was well acquainted with late medieval Northern mystics, such as Ruusbroec, Suso, Herp, and especially the pseudo-Tauler, *Institutiones spirituales*, all of which were available in Latin translation.[25] During the course of the next fifteen years, the treatise was subject to several investigations and some rewriting but was generally approved and welcomed by its readers. Why it became controversial was due to its connection with disputes within the Jesuit Order about how far the Jesuit way of life should be open to interior, or contemplative, prayer.

Ignatius himself was a mystic and contemplative, but also the founder of an order committed to apostolic activity. What for the saint may have been easy to reconcile, has not always been so for his followers, so the history of the Jesuit Order ("our Company") has featured a series of controversies over the proper role of contemplation in Jesuit life. Teresa of Avila's Jesuit confessor Balthasar Alvarez and his interchanges with General Everard Mercurian in the 1570s are a case in point.[26] In 1575, Mercurian also forbade the reading of certain mystical authors without special permission.[27] Similar tensions over mysticism were found in France in the 1630s, as noted above.[28] Gagliardi's problems with Claudio Aquaviva (general 1581–1615), Mercurian's successor, form another chapter in this story. What seems to have exacerbated this conflict is that the order was dealing not just with the writings of Jesuits themselves, but with mysticism of a female "little daughter of the Company," whose message, as filtered through Gagliardi, was influential on those Jesuits who wished to reform the order and turn it in a more contemplative direction (*reformatores/riformatori*).

The full story cannot be told here, but we need to note that in the 1580s and 1590s a group of Jesuits referred to as *riformatori* had emerged, people who condemned the spiritual ossification in the order and sought to renew it by greater emphasis on the interior life. Berinzaga's mysticism, as conveyed through Gagliardi's *Brief Compendium*, became a rallying point for the group.[29] Opposing views soon emerged, attacking the Milanese mystic and questioning the frequent contact that Gagliardi had with her. Fearing a schism in the order, or an appeal to the papacy to intervene, Aquaviva heeded these voices and gradually restricted Gagliardi's access to the mystic. In late 1594, he was compelled to leave Milan. The denouement came in 1600–1601, when Gagliardi was called to Rome for an investigation as to whether his writings should be given a positive or negative *censura* by the order. The decision was unfavorable, so Gagliardi could not publish, and he and Isabella were restricted to "eternal silence." This judgment was given before Clement VIII, but in an "extrajudicial hearing" (not a case before the Inquisition). The main theological witness was Roberto Bellarmino, Gagliardi's onetime classmate. Bellarmine's opposition to mysticism comes through in the records of the events. In a letter written to Aquaviva on March 10, 1601, summarizing the hearing, Bellarmine says, "He [the pope] recognized (as happened by the grace of God) that the matters written in these books are new and dangerous, so that this whole business was ended by imposing perpetual silence on him [Gagliardi] to calm him down." Regarding Isabella Berinzaga, Bellarmine goes on to say that "she should abandon similar dangerous imaginations or illusions, and walk by way of the safe road of Christian perfection."[30] Gagliardi had defended himself but submitted to papal judgment and went back to Brescia and then on to Modena, where he had only a few years to live. Isabella Berinzaga lived on for two more decades out of the public eye, although her funeral attracted many who hailed her as a saint.

The protagonists were reduced to silence, but their book was not. The *Brief Compendium* enjoyed a remarkable history. Jesuits who studied in Italy brought manuscripts to France at the end of the century, where it saw publication in three forms (all the early printings were anonymous). An anonymous translator brought out an abbreviated form, the *Abrégé de la perfection chrétienne* at Paris in 1596, which was reprinted at Arras in 1599. The young Pierre de Bérulle produced another version, also called *Abrégé* in 1597 (a second edition appeared in 1598). In 1620, the Jesuit Etienne Binet published a complete version in Paris under the true title, *Bref discours de la perfection chrétienne*. One of the early French versions was the basis for the English translation of 1612 published at St. Omer by Dame Mary Percy, prioress of the English Benedictine convent at Brussels. The first Italian version appeared at Brescia in 1611, with a second at Verona in 1612. It was not until 1614 that the Naples edition named Gagliardi as the author. After 1620, ten Italian versions and ten French versions appeared down to 1700. There were four Spanish versions (some ascribed the text to Teresa of Avila or John of the Cross!), as well as four Latin, eight German, and two Flemish. The fact that some of the teaching in the *Brief Discourse* seemed close to that found in Miguel de Molinos's *Spiritual Guide* of 1675, and that the book was also edited by the Protestant Pietist Pierre Poiret in 1697, led to its being placed on the *Index of Forbidden Books* in 1703 (it was removed in 1899). Although reprinted ten times in the eighteenth century, the *Brief Compendium* fell out of sight in the nineteenth century, only to be rediscovered in the 1930s.[31]

Through the Way of Annihilation, the experiential source of the *Brief Compendium*, was unknown until recent decades but deserves notice as one of the foremost witnesses to the theme of mystical annihilation so prevalent in early modern mysticism. It is also one of the most interesting personal accounts of mystical graces in the period. The structure of the work is traditional—the division of the spiritual life into the purgative, the illuminative, and the unitive ways. Within these sections there are numerous short chapters that reflect the meditations that Fr. Achille gave Isabella during her taking the *Exercises*. The form of these meditations, however, is unusual, in that they are expressions of the immediate relation between the two real protagonists of the text: God and Isabella.[32] The content is also new. Isabella's account of the purgative way, for example, is not about the traditional purgation of vices as the first stage of the spiritual life, but rather tells the story of how purgative annihilation brought her to the heights of mystical union with God. She sets this in widest perspective, that is, a discussion (chaps. 1-3 [17-27]) of how purgation is always necessary as an essential activity of created being, both in this life and the next. All creatures, humans on pilgrimage, the blessed in heaven, the angels, the Blessed Virgin, and even the humanity of Jesus, need purgation. This is because the essence of purgation is annihilation—recognizing the nothingness of all created things in relation to God's majesty. As she puts it, "The blessed, according to the level of each before God, are purged, annihilating themselves before the Divine Majesty, recognizing and thanking him for the gift [*talento*] they have received."[33] Thus, purification, annihilation, and humility are the marks of all created reality, even the human nature of Jesus—a position prescient of what will be later developed by Bérulle. The major portion of the Way of Purgation (chaps. 4-11 [28-60] deals with Isabella's life of purgation through interior and exterior trials. This leads to the summary of chapter 12 [61-70, pp. 137-43] where the mystic lays out the kinds of annihilation and the various lights, or illuminations, they provide the soul. The chapter is entitled: "On annihilation acquired through these and other means; its grades, and the new progress she [Isabella] desires to make."

There are three kinds of annihilation and seven lights, according to Isabella. The first annihilation is "when God gives light and the feeling of one's own lowness in the time of prayer, in a way that penetrates much into her." This is imperfect, because outside of prayer the soul still resents humiliation. The second form is "when [a person] enters into this nothingness within an intimate heart and feels an effective desire to be known and considered as vile and from nothing." This produces greater fervor in the service of God. "The third is when the creature truly ought to know and consider itself as nothing, and feels great joy in this, because from it is born greater glory to God. From this annihilation is born a greater illumination of the knowledge of God, indeed so great that it makes the soul to come to unite itself to God on a high level."[34] The soul divests itself (*una spoliatione*) to such a degree that there is no medium whatsoever between it and God and it wills whatever God wills. Isabella then discusses the six means by which the three grades of annihilations are obtained (two for each level), before closing off with an account with the seven lights that the three annihilations grant to the soul. The three lights of the third annihilation are supernatural lights of the highest kind, ones that bring the soul to participation in the divine essence, an excess of knowledge of God's immensity, and full knowledge of the properties and attributes of God. Although they are "indescribable" (*indicibile*), Isabella does describe them, primarily in terms of love and with the beautiful example of God and the soul as two lutes sounding in harmony. The chapter ends with a rhetorical love-dialogue between the soul and God. Soul says, "What have you seen in me, Lord, that you have given me such great graces?" The Lord responds, "I have placed myself in you, and have seen me in you, drawing you on by love." Then the soul: "Oh, the light that you have shone in this my darkness, what I call darkness, since these things are very little, this [is] my darkness! The abyss of this my nothingness exclaims to you, my most beloved Lord, you are Nothing through excess, you who cannot be comprehended, containing all things above all things."[35] Isabella concludes, "This is what happened to this soul in the purgative life." Thus, Isabella Berinzaga joins many other early modern mystics in emphasizing the paradox of annihilation—it is only by totally giving up the self that the soul attains the fullness of union with God.

The longest part of *Through the Way of Annihilation* is that dealing with the illuminative way (ed., 144–228). These fifty-five chapters are divided into three sections corresponding to three kinds of virtues. Ten chapters deal with the virtues toward the self, beginning with an important treatment of humility. Then chaps. 11–22 treat of virtues toward the neighbor. The large third section (chaps. 23-55) deals with virtues toward God, but this is somewhat misleading. After chapters on faith, hope, fear, and hatred of sin (charity is left to part 3), Isabella turns to prayer (chap. 27 [123]) for the remainder of the illuminative way. After several general chapters on prayer, the work takes up meditation, particularly the Jesuit style of meditation on the mysteries of Christ's life to which a long succession of chapters is devoted (chaps. 35-46). The final chapters 47-55 concern various issues relating to prayer, with the two final chapters devoted to contemplation. Just a few remarks can made about the third part of this long section.

Faith was a fundamental virtue for the mystics, especially in the era of the disputes between Catholics and Reformers. It is not surprising to see Isabella draw it into her program by distinguishing two kinds of faith: "The one is that light with which a person believes the Most Holy Trinity and the other articles, and this is common to all Catholics and is necessary for salvation. The second is that light with which God through the way of annihilation draws the soul to union with himself, and this is proper to the great friends of God."[36] As is typical with all the chapters on the virtues, the second part of the chapter testifies to how Isabella has demonstrated this virtue throughout her life, including the faith of annihilation by which a light of faith "drew her to union with the divine essence, to the extent that she seemed to become one thing with God [*una medesima cosa con Dio*] by participation, according to how it is written, 'I have said, you are gods'" (Ps. 81:6).[37] Isabella's teaching on prayer, beginning with chapter 27, distinguishes no fewer than seven kinds.[38] She spends the most time with acquired meditation-contemplation (chaps. 32-53), but the second section ends with two chapters on infused contemplation that introduce the reader to the third part of the treatise.

For Isabella, meditation is active, discursive, and given to many; contemplation is passive and given to few. She defines it as follows: "Contemplation supposes that the soul be passive in the path of meditation and that it be well deprived of every thought and desire [*affetto*] that does not belong to heaven, and that, placed in its nothingness, it is raised up above itself by means of the love of God to come to the divine gaze, where it is fixed in God, thinking of nothing but his attributes, if that is granted to it. It is not able to ask for anything at all, nor make any other act of love or reverence, if it be not wished by the Lord."[39] The passivity of this lengthy definition contains some of the elements that were later to feature in the Quietist controversy. Colloquy (the sixth form of prayer) in its perfect form is a conversation with God as "with one friend to another." It is an expression of contemplation, as is exclamation (the seventh form of prayer), which is a crying out to God "from the vehemence of love or sorrow." In her usual mode of explanation, Isabella goes on to analyze eight levels or steps of contemplation. The illuminative way closes with a second, rather different, and "more important" (*maggiore*) division of eight progressive levels of contemplation, written by Isabella herself and given to Gagliardi for inclusion in the work.[40] This description of the forms of mystical contemplation makes use of standard terminology but contains passages of great originality.

The third part of *Through the Way of Annihilation* is brief but weighty, tying together the main themes of love, annihilation, and union with God. Despite the lofty nature of the eight forms of contemplation just described, the five kinds of union set out in this part are much higher. Charity/love is the key: "The Lord has shown that charity is a joining with God and a total conformity with his divine will. Its excellence is what Saint John describes when he says, 'God is charity, and he who remains in charity remains in God and God in him' (1 Jn. 4:16)."[41] The Lord says that "union is nothing else but the joining [*congiuntione*] of the soul with God." Its excellencies are twofold—"a high and singular participation in God," and a fruition and delight in God that leads to deeper union by way of inflamed love. In accordance with the fundamental theme of the treatise, "The one way to arrive at this union is the way of annihilation, and the greater the light that derives from this, the more powerful will be the union."[42] Isabella went on to tell Fr. Gagliardi about five different forms of union she had received.

The first was given her in 1572, after practicing annihilation for many years. As she went to pray "with a great rebellion," God rewarded her for her efforts by granting her "a stupendous illumination" regarding all her sins, so that she felt a sorrow that might have killed her. Along with this came an illumination concerning the love of God in creating all things and a corresponding sense of the nothingness of creation. This was a new form of annihilation greater than what she had previously experienced [164; ed., 230-31]. The account that follows is central:

> Through the means of this annihilation and self-knowledge, she drew very near to the love of God, as she said, and was drawn to the divine presence, that is, to the place where God is in heaven and above all created things. There she saw with her intellect a light in the manner of a ray descend from God into her soul, which light

caused in her another great light that through the reflection of the first light returned to God, as a mirror reflects the light of the sun and redoubles it. These lights caused not only the presence of God, but also that the soul was in God himself.[43]

After the illumination, God infused into her the gift of a participation in his goodness and a high and direct knowledge of himself and his attributes. The gift of the illumination of the intellect was accompanied by a corresponding gift to the will—"a love and fruition and enjoyment of God without any of the changes involved in languor, enflaming, liquefaction, or other similar accidents or tastes." This shows that Isabella believed that union was superior to the types of gifts found in contemplation alone. The "vehemence" of these gifts to intellect and will "made it seem that she was transformed in God and made one same thing with him [una cosa medesima con lui], not with regard to being, because created being cannot be changed into the Uncreated, nor the Uncreated into the creature, but only by way of the operation and force of love." (Isabella's careful formulation is fully orthodox.) This union was ecstatic and prolonged. She told Gagliardi that it lasted six hours the first time and more or less on succeeding occasions. She also explained that it was neither the light of faith, nor the light of glory enjoyed in heaven, but midway between these as a "participated glory" (una gloria participata).[44]

The other four forms of union are not given as detailed a consideration. Like other mystics, Isabella Berinzaga did not consider her experiences of ecstatic union as a purely personal grace. This is shown in the second form of union she describes. Frequently asked for counsel and spiritual advice by others, she says that God would give her a familiarity and union with him without rapture and in it reveal to her things that would be helpful to her petitioners ([165], ed., 233–34). The third form of union began at Easter of 1584. Once again, annihilation is central: "Before the union there was an annihilation much different from the former kind, because it derived immediately from God, making a comparison between his greatness and her lowness. . . . Nonetheless, it was more profound and stronger than all the others, a feeling within herself as if she were divested of existence and reduced to nothing. . . . In the other annihilations she thought she was nothing in herself, because everything was from God, but in this one the thought was so powerful that in truth she seemed to become nothing [le pare in verità diventar niente]." Immediately after this annihilation, the Lord came to her in a different way. Instead of taking her up into heaven, he came down into her and joined himself with her. She continues, "And therefore, the knowledge and love given in this union was much greater and more efficacious than the other; it transformed her and united her with him in a double way."[45] A fourth form of union happened on Palm Sunday in the same year. This is described as a much greater knowledge of the divine attributes than what had been given earlier; it also provided knowledge of the glory of the saints and martyrs in heaven. It was nonecstatic: "In this union the soul is not drawn outside itself, but rests fully in the senses, in such a way that reasoning or treating with other people, or with whatever noise it hears, it is not disturbed and hindered by it" ([167]; ed., 236–37).

The final form of union is Christ-centered, an expression of the Passion-piety of Isabella as subject to trials within and without that she saw as sharing in Christ's sufferings on the cross. She tells us, "On June 21, 1584, being in a struggle with great pains, as mentioned above,[46] the Lord gave her a feeling and a conformity with his sufferings, and the more, "so great a union with the members in which Christ suffered that it seemed that her head was that of the Lord who suffered in her, and she had the hands of the Lord in hers, and so also with the other members." She goes on: "And this was through the Lord's love for her, causing union and conformity of reciprocal pains and love." This might be called a union of compassion, especially because the Lord revealed to her that she could offer her pains for other people ([168]; ed., 237–39). This brief review hopefully shows why Isabella Berinzaga's *Per via di annichilazione*, a recent discovery, deserves to be more widely known, not only as a remarkable personal account of the road to mystical union but also as one of the major witnesses to the early modern fascination with the theme of annihilation.

Achille Gagliardi's decision to recast the content of Isabella's narrative into a shorter treatise on mystical annihilation of an almost geometrical form produced a document that had considerable impact for over a century.[47] The original form of the work, which Gagliardi seems to have first intended for his fellow Jesuits,[48] consisted of a short introduction followed by discussions of three "States of Annihilation," with the first state being subdivided into six stages.[49] A few later editions, as well as Gioia's recent critical text, add to this first part a longer second part, the *Appendice*, which contains an explanation of the *Breve compendio* (called *Secondo compendio di perfezione*) and a number of other comments and "Spiritual Exercises." This Appendix was not well known in the seventeenth century, but is helpful for elucidating the meaning of the often terse text.[50]

The introduction to the *Brief Compendium* starts with the notion of perfection, a central theme in many early modern mystical treatises, and, more specifically, the need to have "a resolute and effective desire" to attain perfection (*BC* [1–2]; ed., 179–80).[51] Gagliardi then discusses the two principles of the practice of perfection: "The first is a very low estimation of all creatures, but above all of the self, with respect to God. . . . The second is a very high estimation of God, not by way of penetrating concepts of theology and similar things, . . . because these are not necessary, but by way of prompt and great submission of the will and the whole person to the Divine Majesty."[52] The ontological foundation of this voluntaristic spiritual program is laid out in more detail in the *Second Compendium*. Implied in the principle of the low estimation of the self are three terms central to the text: "*Annihilation* is a very low concept and estimation of the self with a prompt resolve of the will to put this into practice. *Disappropriation, or divestment* (*spropriatione*) is an abnegation and total despoiling of ourselves and of all that might impede the greater perfection and glory of God. *Indifference* is a disposition of soul that renders it docile and at ease with divine withdrawal (*sottrattione*), and any other movement or ordination of God in his ineffable providence."[53]

The "low estimation of creation" expressed in the triad of annihilation–disappropriation–indifference constitutes the first level for the spiral ascent of the soul to participation in God's loftiness. This negative triad works together with the positive triad of "the high estimation of God" expressed as conformity–unanimity–deiformity. Gagliardi says, "The practice of working in this way with the use of the two principles leads the soul to the union and transformation with God that is called deification, not yet mystical by way of rapture and elevation of mind and the powerful longings [*affetti vehementi*] that derive from it." The Jesuit downplays mental ecstasy, "[b]ecause this [kind of mental deification] is subject to many illusions and is very tiring with danger of weakness of body and ruin of mind." What he prefers is "a solid deification, real and general by way of the will fully conformed and made stable, transformed into the divine will through perfect love." All believers are capable of such deification based on sanctifying grace, whereas the "many other gifts of light and divine longings" are not of the essence of deification but are "gratuitous gifts of grace" (*gratiae gratis datae*) that God gives to people according to his good pleasure. The *Second Compendium* explains deification in terms of the second triad of terms expressing the path to perfection: "*Conformity* [*La conformità*] consists in consenting to, accepting, and following everything that God wishes and ordains for us, however repugnant or hard it is. *Uniformity* [*La uniformità*], beyond conforming itself to the divine will in the same desire, joins to this a conformity to the divine will in itself through an act of regard and immediate love of it, something that removes all repugnance. *Deiformity* [*La deiformità*] joins to this a total transformation of our will into the divine will, taking it totally as our own will, as if we were deprived of our own."[54] Gagliardi's view of deifying union is therefore not ecstatically intellectual but is primarily affective, based on faith, hope, and charity, and therefore open to all.

The first state of perfection deals with the six stages or rungs of the ascent toward annihilation understood as a humble and loving union with God without any mediation (*BC* [7-37]; ed., 186-226).[55] The text proceeds in a linear, almost mathematical, fashion with divisions and subdivisions too numerous to be detailed here. The first state begins by laying out four modes of knowing and estimating the self as nothing, and then gives four forms of putting this knowledge into practice ([7]; ed., 186-90). The first grade ([8-12]; ed., 191-94) is that of disappropriation, withdrawal, and conformity by both desire (*affetto*) and practice (*opera*) with regard to things indifferent to salvation. Withdrawal here means practicing indifference when God takes things away from us, as when he gives us sickness rather than health. This leads to conformity of the will to God through perfect love, and even transformation— "This is the ecstasy of will not intellect; it is much higher than that [of intellect] and deifies the soul much more."

The second grade of the same triad ([13-15]; ed., 195-97) deals with disappropriation, withdrawal, and conformity regarding "holy and spiritual things," not in themselves but "insofar as under the appearance of holiness there can be mixed in and hidden self-love and [our own] interest."[56] What the Jesuit has in mind here is the "spiritual gluttony" (*gola spirituale*) that sates on interior delights and consolations and blocks the soul's advance to true deiformity, which is better achieved through "spiritual crosses." The third grade of the triad of disappropriation, withdrawal, and conformity ([16-21]; ed., 198-201) deals with one of the roadblocks in the ascent. Having passed through the first two levels, the soul often receives "lights, desires, and affects of solid virtue, . . . which are pure principles and means of solid virtue and have their home in the higher part of the person." Nonetheless, a person may embrace these lights "with hidden self-delight" and hence slide back to the level of nature and "fall into the vanity of pride and vain persuasion of great virtue, from which arise many deceptions and illusions." Similar advice had been given by many mystical teachers.

The account of the fourth grade ([22–29]; ed., 201–10) deals with an even more subtle problem, specifically what to do when "desires for solid virtue" and contemplative rest are impeded by human situations, such as when contemplation has to yield to apostolic action. This often leads to "suffering, anxiety, and worry," which are really expressions of our own self-interest, that is, they proceed from "self-love, and although without sin, are impediments between God and the soul." In order to destroy this barrier, Gagliardi recommends a complicated itinerary of six practices (ed., 203–6). Above all, the soul needs to "acquire a sure trust and filial security that the God who has given the desire [for increase in virtue], will also give the perfection when he wishes." If the soul can "leave God for God," that is, give everything over into his hands, "there will follow the highest transformation and deification, to which also usually follow gifts and unusual illuminations worthy of such and so great a love of God."[57] Gagliardi applies this teaching regarding releasement to three specific kinds of desire: the desire for heaven, the desire for annihilation itself, and the desire to suffer. All are good, but if they are desired in the wrong way, out of our own self-interest and thus cause anxiety rather than cheerfulness, they are to be shunned. The Jesuit holds up Christ as the perfect model of true self-surrender and cheerfulness.

The last two stages of the process of disappropriation—withdrawal and conformity—concern temptations, first in the lower part of human nature, and second in the higher powers. The fifth level (*BC* [30–34]; ed., 211–16) concerns how God permits the advanced soul to suffer "grave temptations, similar to and greater than those it was accustomed to suffer at the beginning of its conversion." The soul is in real danger of backsliding at this point, so Gagliardi gives four pieces of encouragement for holding fast in this mysterious situation where God is trying the soul. Above all, the soul must "continue to abase itself in its nothingness," knowing that merit is gained through resisting temptation. Once again, Christ is proposed as the model, the Christ in the Garden of Olives, who suffered in his lower nature but said, "Not my will, but Yours be done" (Luke 22:42). This is to share in his crucified love. The sixth level (*BC* [35–37]; ed., 216–26) moves on to temptations affecting the higher parts of the soul and seems to be a kind of "dark night" that features "darkness, blindness, tedium, difficulty, rebellion and great cowardice, confusion and great oppression, with the appearance that it will not be possible to return to [our] first good intentions." This, says Gagliardi, is "a great danger" in which the soul can fall into "many disorders."

Achille Gagliardi provides five insights for understanding such temptations, and then five practices for dealing with them. The first insight is to remember that these trials come from God in order to purify the soul. The second is the important distinction between a "direct act" (*atto diretto*) and a "reflex act" (*atto riflesso*). The direct act is the actual willing of the object (e.g., an act of obedience); the second is the judgment and satisfaction we take in such an act. God is still working with us in the direct act, but in temptations of this sort he removes the reflex act and we are left in misery. He does this, third, to remove subtle motives of self-interest that may still hinder deeper union with him. In the fourth place, God's withdrawal allows pure love to operate more effectively in our good actions, and, fifth, this grants a "high and living imitation of Christ, our Lord," in his suffering in the Garden. "In summary," says the Jesuit, "this state is a supreme test that God gives to his elect, a living imitation of Christ, a martyrdom more noble than mere external martyrdom, founded in the deepest humility, and much more secure than any other, and of greater merit" ([37]; ed., 224). The sixth stage closes with five practices for dealing with such temptations. Essentially, the soul needs to redouble its efforts at annihilation and disappropriation until it reaches a condition of being totally subject to divine action, that is, *pati divina*.[58] This is not only to be a sacrifice to God, but to become a real holocaust.

The second and third states of the original *Brief Compendium* are quite short.[59] The second state (*BC* [38-44]; ed., 226-34) confronts the problem of the will itself *insofar as it is still our will*. The problem was not new. Its first explicit appearance comes in Marguerite Porete's *Mirror of Simple Annihilated Souls* at the end of the thirteenth century.[60] Granted that the annihilated person now has a pure direct will totally disappropriated of self-interest, isn't there still something *of us* in it? In dependence on Isabella Berinzaga's teaching,[61] Gagliardi affirms that it is possible for God "to take away little by little the power to do such acts" (*sottrare a poco a poco il poter fare tali atti*), removing the one after the other, until he has taken away all of them, except the power to conform oneself to the divine will" ([39], ed., 227). Such a soul, in the midst of temptations and trials, does not perform any good acts but "stands as it were in [a state of] being acted upon and in [its] being" (*star così con patire et esser*). "There does not remain any other operative force in relation to act, but only to undergo everything for the love of God and to be itself content with this" ([39-40]; ed., 227-28). Gagliardi calls this a "passive quiet" (*quiete passiva*), like a lamb before its shearer. This withdrawal of all activity from the soul brings about a situation in which "the soul cannot perform any action, no matter how high and holy it is, but only stands voluntarily undergoing [*patendo*] what God permits to it" ([41-42]; ed., 229). The soul is meant to respond to this withdrawal of the ability to act with a renewed act of annihilation, recognizing its nothingness and lowness, as well as freely divesting itself of activity and the acts of virtue. Even worse interior trials and sufferings may follow, but the soul is to act like a very patient little lamb and suffer everything. Paradoxically, the result is "a purely passive conformity to the divine will, incomparably greater than the former, and an inexplicable deification and a purely passive act, which is no longer oblation" and the like, "but much more, like a giving oneself to be God's prey" ([43]; ed., 230-31). State 2 closes with three implications of the loss of active will. The first is that external acts, now as coming from God, are more effective than before. The second is that God does not remove his good gifts and habits but only our ability to act. The third is that the now passive soul can rest in two states of ecstasy. The first is in relation to the intellect, when the soul "is drawn into its depth or womb, which these mystics call the *apex animae*." With the ability to operate removed, the soul has the greatest readiness for God acting within it to produce "far more sublime acts of thanksgiving, of love, and union with him. . . . This is what these mystics call *pati divina*." Although Gagliardi admits intellectual ecstasy, he remains suspicious of it, preferring the ecstasy of the will as "a practical and most virtuous ecstasy," in which the Lord lifts it up and "works in it fully what pleases him, and this is a *pati divina* in a much higher mode" ([44]; ed., 233-34).

The third state of the *Brief Compendium* is even shorter ([45-51]); ed., 236-41), dealing with "the ultimate state and the most sublime of all," that is, "when the Lord withdraws himself and takes away not only the activity [of the soul], but also the passivity, letting the will rest naked in all and through all." The soul should not resist or oppose itself to this, "but let itself be a non-self-will [*si fa non propria volontà*], divested of all self-movement" (47], ed., 238). At this stage there is no proper will left, since it has given over its rights to another. Whatever acts the soul does are not its own; it does not will them, even with a will conformable to the divine will. "The divine Will wills them to be done, and therefore they are done as immediately willed by the divine Will" ([48]; ed., 239). Gagliardi cites the well-known text of Galatians 2:20 ("I live now not I, but Christ lives in me") and again points to Christ's renunciation of his own will in the Garden of Gethsemane (Luke 22:42). The final paragraph summarizes the message:

Here the annihilation, disappropriation , and withdrawal shine out in the highest way. It is not conformity, but much more, because with such a renunciation the will is bound, absorbed and abyssed in God, where it loses all its own property. It rests in God's property, most highly deified through perfect identity in relation to the divine property. And [it has] this with the practical and real mode already described. *The End. Praise God.*[62]

A comparison of *Through the Way of Annihilation* and the *Brief Compendium* is difficult to avoid here. Both texts have the same co-authors, though in different combination. Rarely in the story of Christian mysticism have two works been so closely related, but there are also differences. The *Brief Compendium* has the advantages of concision and clarity, but at the expense of the moving personal tone found in *Through the Way of Annihilation*. Influential as it was, the *Compendium* appears dry and formalized in comparison to the message expressed more creatively, passionately, and personally in *Through the Way of Annihilation*. This "scholasticization" seems to be what Gagliardi intended for his Jesuit audience, but it may not be what modern readers of the mystics find most meaningful. In any case, the *Brief Compendium* and *Through the Way of Annihilation* deserve greater recognition as among the classics of Christian mysticism.

A Selection of Women Mystics

Late medieval and early modern female mystics of Italy were notable for their paranormal mystical gifts, especially ecstasy, although ecstasy and levitation cannot be restricted to women, as shown by the example of Joseph of Cupertino (1603–1663). Ecstasy is one of the oldest themes in Christian mysticism; the literature on it is extensive, especially with regard to women.[63] A number of studies have been devoted to ecstasy in early modern Italy.[64] With regard to ecstasy, mystics have insisted on the difference between the essential reality of mystical contact with God—the loving union with the God present within—and external paranormal gifts and graces given to some. In popular piety, however, the sense of admiration and awe for these extra gifts has often overwhelmed the historical record.[65]

There was a significant group of mystical women in sixteenth- and seventeenth-century Italy.[66] Almost all were ecstatics; many also left written records, most often letters, but sometimes other forms of writing.[67] Scholarship on the mystical women of early modern Italy has pointed to some differences between these mystics and their medieval predecessors. For example, Claudio Leonardi noted that, in the wake of the Tridentine insistence on full enclosure for women religious, it was more difficult for female mystics to exercise a prophetic role or to be involved in civic affairs the way some medievals, such as Catherine of Siena, could.[68] The early modern female mystics, like many of the late medieval women, were centered on sharing in the sufferings of Christ on the cross. Their sometimes disturbing acts of penance, as well as the physical and spiritual trials they endured, were part of an inherited cultural-spiritual paradigm in which women came to be seen as emblematically connected with the suffering body of Christ. Nevertheless, as E. Ann Matter has suggested, the sixteenth- and seventeenth-century female *imitatio Christi* "became a more conformist and less expressive manner of self-interpretation," especially when "carefully regulated by the patriarchy of posttridentine Catholicism."[69] Another possible shift concerns the "discernment of spirits" (*discretio spirituum*), which was an important weapon in the church's armory for determining the difference between true and false visionaries and ecstatics. The creation of handbooks and judicial investigations for "discerning spirits" began in the fourteenth century and continued for many centuries.[70] Such handbooks continued to be produced in early modern Italy, as we can see in Federico Borromeo (1564–1631), cousin of Carlo Borromeo and also a reforming archbishop of Milan, who published a treatise *On Ecstatic and Deluded Women* (*De ecstaticis mulieribus et illusis*] in 1616.[71] Traditionally, three sources of "spirits" were identified (God, the self, and the devil), and rules were laid down for determining which of the three was the more likely source in particular cases. In the medieval period many women were accused of being mislead by the devil; but, given the seventeenth-century obsession with the growing power of the devil,[72] it may well be that the seventeenth century saw a greater link between ecstasy and diabolical activity.[73] In the context of early modern Italy, the investigation of mystics and the ferreting out of heretical error and diabolical deception were further regularized by the creation of the Roman Inquisition by Paul III in 1542, although the power and reach of the Inquisition did not come into its own until the pontificate of Paul IV (1555–59).[74]

It is not possible to treat all the Italian mystical women of this period, but a brief look at a few may illustrate some general patterns. Most of these women's repute was limited to Italy; a few, like Maria Maddalena de'Pazzi, became more widely known. We will look at a Dominican, a Franciscan, and a Carmelite, since the role of religious women was dominant at this time.

St. Caterina de'Ricci, O.P. (1522–1590)

Caterina Ricci, born of an aristocratic Florentine family in 1522, became a Dominican at the age of thirteen at the convent of San Vincenzo in Prato, a house under the influence of the spiritual reform associated with Savonarola (d. 1498).[75] Caterina was not an ideal candidate for profession as a nun, because she seemed to be slow, incompetent, even mentally challenged. The biographical materials put this down to her almost constant ecstasies. She was professed in 1536, however, and soon became physically and mentally seriously ill. On May 22, 1540, she was miraculously cured on the anniversary of the death of Savonarola. Catherine's ecstasies increased, particularly her reliving the events of Christ's Passion every Friday. Her fame grew, both inside and outside the convent. In 1552, she was elected prioress and in the following year her ecstasies mysteriously ceased. She continued as prioress for many years, dying in 1590. During this latter part of her life, Caterina emerged as a reformer and builder, a major sponsor of many charitable works, and an extensive letter writer (over a thousand are known), someone in contact with many of the major figures of the day (Pius V, Philip Neri, Carlo Borromeo, Maria Maddalena de'Pazzi, and others). The letters often contain general spiritual advice, but do not speak about her mystical gifts. She was influenced by Catherine of Siena, but her letters, unlike those of the Sienese mystic, do not have a prophetic or a doctrinal emphasis. Putting together Catherine the early ecstatic and Catherine the capable prioress is not easy.[76]

Some first-person accounts of Catherine's ecstasies come down to us, probably written down by her fellow nuns and later corrected by her. Devotion to Christ in his Passion is prominent in many of these, as are the themes of annihilation and marriage to the Savior. Her erotic relation to Jesus can be seen in the account of an ecstasy of May 10, 1542, where she says, "O my Jesus, why do you show me so much love! Oh, how ingrateful I am! However bad I have been to you, you always do something better for me. My Jesus, Oh!, you have kissed me. For mercy's sake, do not kiss me. You are mistaken; you should go to others, not come to me."[77] Caterina often complains about the severity of the pains she suffers during her weekly sharing the Lord's Passion. On August 27, 1542, she breaks out into a fervent prayer: "Oh! My Spouse, make me die with you, so that although I suffer on Friday and Saturday, you will restore me later on Sunday. You know that I suffer voluntarily for your love, but in a way that I have not willed. I am asking you to remain dead in my heart on Saturday." Caterina in a sense turns the tables on Jesus "by telling him about her Passion and cross."[78]

Caterina's letters often deal with the business of the convent and her charitable works, but they also give spiritual advice to her family, to other Dominicans, to rulers and prelates, and especially to her many disciples to whom she often writes in a tender, sometimes even a teasing, way. Humility and obedience are frequent themes, but the main message is the need to practice the love of God and neighbor, which she characterizes as pleasant, prudent, and above all strong.[79] Some letters lay down a basic spiritual program,[80] while others stress how the Feast of Christmas is a time for spiritual renewal. Writing to her disciple Filippo Salviati in 1560, Caterina even refers to the mystical theme of the birth of the Son in the heart. She says, "Although his coming was only once, nevertheless every year holy Church brings us back to this mystery, because human frailty is great. . . . So this wonderful call and astounding news by which our loving Mother announces to us the coming of our Savior. . . . For he comes now no longer to be born into this universe, but rather into the tiny world of the human heart."[81] Toward the end of her life Caterina wrote to the nuns of San Vincenzo about the importance of Christmas: "You have all celebrated the Nativity of Jesus Christ the Son of God, and I am certain that all of you—not equally, but each according to her capacity—have been reborn with him through a holy desire to lead a new life, leaving the old one completely behind for whoever wants it. You will have made up your minds to follow wholeheartedly the dear Bridegroom of your souls, imitating him through the whole of your life, following his example, and looking at yourselves as reflected in his life, which always shines before the mind's eye like the very brightest of mirrors."[82] Caterina's letters may not be mystical texts in themselves, but they make use of mystical themes.

Maria Domitilla Galluzzi, O.F.M. Cap. (1595–1671)

Born Servetta Galluzzi in Acqui in Piedmont in 1595, from her early years she exhibited a strong desire to suffer along with Christ, the fundamental characteristic of her life and writings. In 1616, she entered the Capuchin convent in Pavia, taking the name Domitilla. Here she immediately began to have ecstatic visions connected with the Blessed Sacrament and especially with Christ on the cross. We know a good deal about Sister Domitilla, since the nuns of the convent collected her writings and materials relating to her life in view of a canonization process, which, alas, never got off the ground, for reasons that will become clear below. These writings begin with a commentary on the *Rule of Saint Clare* (*Lume sopra la prima Regola di S. Chiara*), based on a vision of 1619. From 1618 on, Domitilla had been receiving mystical visions of the Passion, especially during Lent and Holy Week. These were particularly strong in 1622, so her confessors commanded her scribe, Sister Beatrice Avite, to begin to write them down as Domitilla described them. The result was the 1624 *Passion of My Savior* (*La Passione del Mio Signore*), her most popular work (ten manuscripts survive). A large part of the twenty-six chapters of the work is a kind of running commentary on the Passion narrative in John. Paolo Fontana, the editor of the text, describes it as "a nexus of mystical experience, biblical commentary, and liturgy."[83] The other major work was the *Vita*, a mixed work containing the *Passion* and more accounts of her visions written at the command of her confessors in the mid-1620s.[84] There was also a series of meditations on the spiritual exercise known as the "Forty Hours" (*Quarant'hore di meditatione mentale*), and eighty or more letters in her *Epistolario*. None of her writings was published in her lifetime.

Domitilla's mystical writings date from the 1620s; her ecstatic experiences seem to have ceased around 1630. The visions, however, brought her fame, both within and outside the convent over the following decades, as her letters testify. No doctrinal objections seem to have accompanied their diffusion until the 1650s, when she became embroiled with the Inquisition.[85] Her trial and eventual silencing were connected to the complicated case of the Pelagini, a devout group associated with the Oratory of St. Pelagia established at the Valcamonica in Piedmont in 1641. The Pelagini, who had supporters in Milan, taught mental prayer practices and ran into opposition from the local clergy, who claimed they disvalued all forms of vocal prayer. The group seems to have been affected by millenarian ideas about the reform of the church as well. The movement was eventually condemned by the Inquisition in 1658. During the 1650s they had come under the influence of the strange figure of Giuseppe Francesco Borri (1627–1695), doctor, alchemist, and prophet, who was convinced of his call to be the millenarian reformer of the church. Borri visited Domitilla in March of 1658, soliciting her help. It is difficult to know just how strongly she supported him (she later denied it), but the association led to the nun's being called before the Inquisition in 1659 and eventually being sentenced to perpetual silence and a kind of house arrest in the convent until her death in 1671. The Inquisition also investigated her writings in 1660, eventually handing them on to the noted Cistercian mystic and theologian Giovanni Cardinal Bona (1609–1674). His determination, mostly on the basis of the *Vita*, was as follows: "I do not sense in these writings the usual efficacy of the word of God that might move the reader's soul to piety. Here there is no sense of devotion, but much arrogance. . . . She shows herself greatly addicted to her own judgment. For this reason and for many others I omit here for brevity's sake, I determine that these writings ought not be permitted to be published."[86] It is difficult to know if Galluzzi's silencing was a case of guilt by association, or something more serious. In any case, her history once again witnesses to the growing suspicions of mysticism in the late seventeenth century.

There will be no attempt here to give a full picture of the mystical teaching of the controversial ecstatic Maria Domitilla Galluzzi.[87] Nonetheless, a look at some visionary narratives from her three major works, the *Lume* (i.e., *Commentary on the Rule of St. Clare*), the *Vita*, and the *Passione*, may provide some sense of her mysticism. Domitilla's account of the 1619 vision that produced the *Lume* is revealing of the purpose of this work, her most scholarly treatise.[88] She tells us:

> One night after Matins, fifteen days before the Most Blessed Nativity, in the third year of my profession, at the age of twenty-three, I found myself in front of the Most Blessed Sacrament in the act of leaving the choir to go to the dormitory with the other mothers and sisters, more than ever lost in the abyss of my nothingness [*più che mai inabissata nel mio niente*]. I found myself overshadowed by a great light in which I ardently enjoyed God . . . , and in his Majesty I understood the way in which the Holy Rule was observed in the time of Holy Mother Clare. . . . Out of obedience I agreed to write down as much as I could, a small part of that light, since I do not have words to express it fully.[89]

This is an intellectual vision, befitting the theological nature of the *Commentary* as a gloss on Clare's *Rule*. The vision of light "overshadowing" the nun (see the account of the Incarnation in Luke 1:35) provides a divine warrant for the unusual fact of a woman writing a commentary on a rule written by a woman for women.

More characteristic of Sr. Domitilla's usual highly pictorial and somatic visions are the experiences recounted in the *Vita*, as well as the initial showings of the *Passione*. Many female mystics, not least Catherine of Siena, had found in the blood of Christ a central symbol for their teaching, a versatile instrument for unpacking the many dimensions of meaning in the process of salvation leading to union with God. Domitilla is not so much interested in the various meanings of blood as in the experience of being physically immersed in Christ's blood. As Paolo Fontana puts it, Domitilla experiences the Passion as "a true blood bath" (*un vero bagno di sangue*).[90] Domitilla is not just a witness to Christ's bloody Passion, but, like a number of female mystics before her, an active participant. At times she feels herself nailed to the cross with Christ. She sweats blood and displays the marks of the Passion on her body before the eyes of the other nuns. Her blood-soaked garments become relics that help spread her fame. Blood, however, is not defiling or upsetting but lovely and attractive. Again as with other mystics, blood for her often transforms itself into sweet-smelling roses.[91]

Much of this powerful Passion mysticism is expressed in the vision of 1622 that Domitilla recounts at the beginning of the *Passione* and repeats in part elsewhere. She tells of how she had retired to her cell one night and had the following either dream-vision or experience in the eyes of the mind. She saw a famous "servant of God" (Teresa of Avila?) who was disciplining herself for love of God and she felt great sorrow that she herself did so little penance. Then, "I saw come before me a most beautiful and lovable Crucified Christ who, with his rays of infinite love, set me on fire with the great flames of his divine love." She made the sign of the cross to assure her that the vision is really of Christ (the devil would not be able to abide the holy sign). Christ does not flee but comes down to her "with such great sweetness and clearness of his divine goodness that he united his most blessed head to my unworthy one, his most holy face to mine, and his holy feet to mine, and thus, all united to me so very tightly, he took me with him onto the cross, so that I seemed to be crucified with him, and that all the stains of his most holy body stained my unworthy one. And feeling such pain from him, I felt myself totally aflame with the most sweet love of this most sweet Lord. . . . Thus in the air for a great piece, I was made to feel, enjoy, and suffer his pains from head to foot, as if the most holy wounds of all his most holy body were imprinted on me, but in particular those of his most holy hands, feet, and side."[92] While this vision has clear reminiscences of Francis's stigmata, it also has distinctive characteristics of Domitilla, such as the attention to the stains of blood. Maria Domitilla Galluzzi's mysticism strove to internalize Christ's sufferings, but in such a way that they could once again become externally visible in the body of the ecstatic. Having won her position as bride of Christ through sharing in his sufferings, Domitilla is given the ultimate reward. In one text Christ tells her: "O my spouse, for my part tell your confessor that through you has come the hour when my Father will be adored in spirit (John 4:23) . . . and that you enjoy me without any shadow in seeing. . . . This is the most secure level, far from any deception, and no greater thing can be given to any soul loved by me. . . . For nothing greater is given to the citizens of heaven than the grade I give to my beloved spouse."[93]

St. Maria Maddalena de'Pazzi, O. Carm. (1566–1607)

The most important female mystic of sixteenth-century Italy was Maria Maddalena de'Pazzi, a Carmelite nun of Santa Maria degli Angeli in Florence. Although Maria's house was Carmelite, it was untouched by the Spanish Teresian reform; its dominant piety was under Jesuit and Dominican influence.[94] Maria Maddalena was an original, a mystic with a new form of conveying God's presence/absence in her life. Her mysticism not only shares the Passion-centered character of the other Italian ecstatics but is also an original contribution to the issue of attempting to express the inexpressible Word of God, and thus has important implications for investigating the nature of mystical discourse. It is no surprise, therefore, that a number of studies have been devoted to the Carmelite mystic, both in Italian and in English.[95]

Maria Maddalena's writings were edited (uncritically) in seven volumes between 1960 and 1966.[96] These works are not really her "writings." They are transcriptions of her ecstatic statements taken down and edited by a team of nun amanuenses from her convent. Such a procedure was not entirely new in the story of mysticism, but the mechanics of how some of the sisters formed a group for recording and checking what they heard from the ecstatic is unusual. Their editorial comments are frequent, and these nuns doubtless had much to do with shaping the corpus of writings ascribed to the saint. She herself was ambivalent about these writings, since there is record that when she discovered some of the manuscripts and realized they were about her she threw them into the fire.

The development of Maria's "writings" is best reviewed through her biography. Born Caterina of the noble family de'Pazzi in Florence in 1566, she received her first ecstasy at the age of twelve. She entered the Carmelite convent of Santa Maria degli Angeli in 1582 and was professed in 1583. After a mysterious illness early in 1584, she received a succession of fifty ecstasies during the forty days between May 27 and July 4, 1584. Dutifully recorded by her amanuenses with the approval of the mother superior and her confessor, these became *The Forty Days*

(*I quaranta giorni*).⁹⁷ A second series of raptures and messages began at Christmas 1584 and continued until June 4, 1585, and were taken down under the title *The Discourses* (*I colloqui*).⁹⁸ These conversations, some short, but others of considerable length, are the heart of the mystic's message. During this period Maria is also recorded as having received a number of the standard mystical gifts known from the lives of female ecstatics, such as an exchange of hearts with the Blessed Virgin (March 5, 1584; *Discourse* 20), the reception of an invisible stigmata (April 15, 1585; *Discourse* 33), and an exchange of hearts with Jesus on May 17–18, 1585 (*Discourse* 48). Eight more days and nights of visions and revelations were recorded between June 8 and June 15 of that year.⁹⁹ On June 16, 1585, Maria Maddalena entered into a period of severe trials characterized by diabolical attacks that lasted until June 10, 1590. These conversations and encounters with the devil were recorded in two books of *Probations* (*Probatione*).¹⁰⁰ Mixed in with the dated sequences of ecstatic pronouncements were some other revelations, especially about the necessity for moral reform in the church, letters written in ecstasy to a number of people, as well as some meditations and other writings.¹⁰¹ This large corpus is available in English (at 1,585 pages).¹⁰² Maria's ecstasies did not prevent her from taking on several positions of authority within the convent. Like the two ecstatics already noted in this section, Maria's raptures eventually ceased. She received no raptures during her final illness from 1604 to her death in May 25, 1607.¹⁰³ Parts of Maria's writings were included in the *Vita* that her last confessor, Vincenzo Puccini, published in Florence in 1611. This work, translated into Latin and other languages, fostered her reputation, so Maria was beatified in 1626 and canonized in 1669.

Like most female ecstatics, Maria Maddalena rarely mentions sources. One book that we know she read and used was the Italian meditation manual of the Spanish Jesuit Gaspar Loarte.¹⁰⁴ Several other collections of meditations were available to her in the convent library. Augustine's *Confessions* and Catherine of Siena's *Letters* were important for her, as was Tauler, probably mostly through the popular Pseudo-Tauler, *Institutiones divinae*. Another contemporary resource was the Italian version of Louis of Granada's *Introduction to the Symbol of the Faith*. It is possible that she may have had access to Achille Gagliardi's *Brief Compendium*, which was circulating in manuscript form among the Jesuits by the late 1580s.¹⁰⁵ Maria's mysticism, however, is expressed not in learned treatises but in long ecstatic utterances in which we overhear, if only in part, the mystic's inner conversations with God (and often the devil too).

The characteristics of Maria's special mystical discourse, a type of narrative theology, needs to be investigated first. As the studies of Giovanni Pozzi, Armando Maggi, and others have shown,[106] Maria Maddalena de'Pazzi is an important witness for exploring the limits of language for expressing mystical contact with God. The accounts of her ecstasies read as quasi-stenographic, though this may well be in part a sophisticated literary device. Despite their basic narrative form, Maria's revelations are not easy reading—they confuse; they are filled with ellipses and silences; they mix together Italian and Latin sentences in ways that impede the comprehension of many individual sentences, although the overall direction is usually clear. The "real" author is God speaking in Maria, sometimes in ways that are relatively clear; at other times obscurely both in the words and the ellipses that dot the text and leave the reader trying to imagine what might have been said on the other side. As Armando Maggi puts it, "She neither speaks to the Word, nor does she speak with the Word; *she attempts to speak the Word*."[107] Speaking the Word in human discourse, however, is impossible; it testifies to an absence more than a presence. This is why the texts of her later revelations are filled with gaps indicating her silences. This oscillation between positive verbal utterance and negative verbal annihilation is among the most novel of her verbal strategies. In a sense we are invited to the impossible task of (re)constructing the original oral event of the discourse that is the foundation of the fragmentary text that is its surviving imperfect witness.[108] The *Discourses* ask us to engage in a non-ending (at least in this life) mystical praxis.

To help understand this strange language, it is useful to begin from the foundation of Maria's mysticism: the nature of God as communication (*comunicatione*). In *Discourse* 45, the Divine Spouse tests the beloved through "a test of annihilation," because he had annihilated himself in becoming man (a theme later taken up by Bérulle). Maria, like so many seventeenth-century mystics, has a powerful sense of the need for annihilation understood as the recognition of our created nothingness.[109] The test of annihilation given here involves nine qualities of the Bridegroom; significantly, the last of these is communication. Maria says:

> Then comes communication which is God's being. Oh communication! And what do you communicate, Word? To whom do you communicate? Why do you communicate? Oh, you communicate in order to make death into life, darkness into light, prison into freedom, a servant into a lord, a slave into a son. And what do you communicate? You communicate yourself. . . . And what is the goal of your com-

munication? So that communication can be communicated, and, as you said, you communicate yourself so much that everything that the Father has disclosed to you (citing John 15:15) you disclosed to us."[110]

The divine nature, therefore, is communication itself, as we also see in a text from *Discourse* 48, which addresses the Word: "Oh Word, what led you down to earth? Love. What leads us up to heaven? Blood. What led you to us other than your being which is pure communication" (Maggi, 263)? The same *Discourse* speaks of the contemplation of the Father and the Soul of the Word according to a series of contemplations (*risquardi*), among them the "contemplation of communication" (*risquardo di communicatione*).[111] Furthermore, the three forms of the "clarification of the Word" (Jn. 17:5)—the Word's self-contemplation before the creation of the world, the contemplation of the three Persons in the Trinity, and the contemplation the "humanate Word" received in the Father's bosom—are all described in terms of mutual communication of the Persons in the Trinity and their desire to communicate in creating.[112] God's nature as communication demands our communicative response. Maria's letter to Caterina de'Ricci of August 10, 1586, says: "I say that God is communicative; we ought also to be communicative in communicating the illumination that God has communicated to us, especially that by which we are able to aid his creature to return to him."[113]

God is communication; indeed, *pure communication.* An important text in the long *Discourse* 48 features a conversation in which the Father teaches the soul about the divine nature as purity. The soul asks to know what God's purity is and the Father responds, "My purity is such an intrinsic thing that neither you nor others, . . . will ever be able to understand it fully. . . . This purity is in fact my own being."[114] God's intrinsic and immense purity was shared with creatures in their preexistent state through the "milk" of their original participation in God, but was lost in original sin. The Father continues, "When this innocence was lost, in order to recuperate that purity there was no remedy but to bathe and drown in that second source of blood coming from the humanate Word."[115] Milk and blood are the two essential fluids that express the communication between God and humans.[116] In order to regain God's purity, it is necessary to strip away all created things. Mirroring something like Meister Eckhart's notion of true poverty of spirit, the Father later tells the soul, "Of daughter and spouse *Unigeniti Verbi mei*, . . . one needs to dwell in nothing, because one acquires this purity by being nothing, by understanding nothing, by knowing nothing, by dwelling in nothing, and by wishing nothing, nothing, nothing."[117] Communication and purity, therefore, are two sides of the same coin of divinity—God's communication is absolutely pure, and the divine loving purity desires to communicate itself to the preexistent soul and restores fallen humans to their original state of purity through the Blood of the "Humanate Word."[118]

All three divine persons are mutually communicative in the mystery of the Trinity,[119] but the focus of most of the mystic's discussion of divine communication is the Word made flesh. A central biblical text for the Carmelite is the Johannine passage, *Verbum caro factum est* ("The Word was made flesh," John 1:14), a text she returns to frequently.[120] The very beginning of the *Discourses* states, "On Tuesday, January 1, 1584, the Feast of the Holy Name of Jesus, we gathered, in the name of Jesus, with the beloved soul [Maria].... We started by asking her what the Lord had wanted to communicate to her on Christmas night [and she] started with the words of St. John: *Et Verbum caro factum est* and also *In principio erat Verbum et Verbum erat apud Deum*."[121] It is no surprise that the Word (*Verbo*) occurs in all of Maria's *Discourses*, because it is the central name for understanding our relation to God, the ultimate communicator. A passage from *Discourse* 38 says, "... your idea, your might, your goodness, everything is a language *in Verbo Domini. In Verbo Domini* I had hoped, rested, and abandoned my soul.... The Word, proceeding from the Word, communicates us the Word and unites us to him. She meant that the Word of God, which is pronounced by the mouth of the humanate Jesus, communicates to us and unites to its source, Jesus himself, while he utters it and we listen to it."[122] The union achieved through hearing the Word, and the deification it grants, are among the major themes of Maria's mystical teaching, but, given the nature of her revelations, they are not given independent treatments but are woven throughout the course of the narratives.[123] The Word is meant to speak, to utter; we are meant to hear and listen, but the issue with which Maria (and other mystics) wrestle is the necessary paradox when the infinite Word meets our fallible, imperfect, finite hearing, as well as all our attempts to (re)utter what was said. This paradox is the basis of the unusual form of Maria's *Discourses* and other revelations.

Maria's problem was not new—it is a version of the age-old issue, "How to speak of the ineffable." Her solution was novel: to inscribe the paradoxes, limitations, and failures of communicating with God into the structure of the text itself. Hence, the strangeness of the *Discourses* and related texts. God addresses the mystic, often through a passage from the text of the liturgy in Latin, inviting her response. This introduces another unusual aspect of the *Discourses*: their mixture of Latin and Italian, something which has not yet been sufficiently studied.[124] Maria knew Augustine's *Confessions* and had doubtless noted that a third of this text consists in biblical citations. She too cites the Vulgate Bible often and also quotes liturgical Latin texts. Thus, she is using God's own words to address him. More surprisingly, she makes up numerous quasi-biblical passages of her own. Did Maria know Latin? A passage in *Dialogue* 33 says that "it was a wonder to hear her, especially inasmuch as she said everything in Latin, which ordinarily she does not understand. Nor does she know how to speak a Latin of the psalms which are said every day. And on this evening it seemed that she knew grammar like a doctor."[125] The miraculous gift of using languages one does not understand is a hagiographical topos used about many women mystics, but we are still left with the problem of how to understand Maria's frequent use of Latin, without which her texts would be incomprehensible. In the *Confessions*, God never speaks to Augustine directly; scripture is his voice. In the *Dialogues*, Maria cites the Bible and creates biblically sounding texts, presumably as given her by God, probably because the loftiness of the communication demands the use of the formal sacral language.

The experience behind the *Discourses* and Maria's other writings was essentially oral, and this obviously cannot be recaptured today. What we have is the fixation of her overheard and broken conversations in a series of *Dialogues* taken down by others. The peculiar genre of these texts was the creation of her scribes during the two-year course of what seems to have been an almost daily flood of revelations. The revelations of the *Forty Days* and of the first twenty-nine of the *Dialogues* are relatively straightforward narratives in which the scribes attempt to take down what Maria tells them after the event and edit the material into a comprehensible format. With *Dialogue* 25 on the Feast of the Annunciation (March 25, 1585), things change.[126] This discourse highlights the role taken by St. Augustine, whom she calls her "big papa" (*il suo babbone*), and who writes on her heart the key words, *Et Verbum caro factum est*, in letters of gold for the divinity and letters of blood for the humanity. (The biblical text is repeated four more times in the *Dialogue*.) The first part of the revelation is in the narrative form of the earlier showings, where Maria tells the nuns what has been revealed to her, but this switches in the middle of the *Dialogue* as the compilers say, "Because she did not know how to tell us anything beyond what has been written, we shall therefore write these words here in the way in which we had them from her mouth. And we shall leave a space from one phrase to the other, so that we can see when she was silent, and when she began anew, and what she said quickly."[127] The new mode of presentation is obvious in her first remarks after going into a new rapture: "How well that Word takes his place [*silence*]. Such great lowliness equal to you [*silence*]. In the bosom of the Father is his greatness, and he was made little and the little womb has become great. How shall the exalted valleys not become low before you who are inscrutable in your greatness and incomprehensible in your littleness?" [*silence*].[128] The ensuing conversations with the Blessed Virgin and with Augustine feature the same alterations of speech and silence.

In the later *Dialogues*, narrative content is never abandoned but is increasingly enriched and qualified by a series of performative techniques that alert us to the fact that it is not only *what* Maria said but *how* she said it that is significant (although we cannot really recover this). The words themselves and who is speaking them are obviously important—her interlocutors include the Father, the *Verbo*, the Blessed Virgin, various saints, also devils, her fellow nuns, and at times she seems to be talking to herself. How the words are said is also significant, because the text sometimes notes the tone of her voice and a kind of ventriloquism in which she uses a grave voice when the Father or Son is speaking, and a mild one when she speaks on her own. As Armando Maggi points out, the silences in the *Dialogues* are not simple. There are several kinds of silence: the silence of unheard words from the *Verbo*; silences indicating a pause in her meditations; and silences coming from a sense of despair in trying to articulate what she has heard.[129] These last are often linked with another textual feature, the frequent use of exclamations of several different kinds. Even the many repetitions of these texts need to be carefully considered. A number of the ecstasies, particularly those in which Maria relives Christ's Passion, are actually one-woman mini-dramas in which the mystic uses different locations within the monastery to act out the events of Jesus's last days and employs dramatic actions and even stage props such as a crucifix.

The complex of strategies found in the *Dialogues* is rooted in Maria's fixation on the Second Person of the Trinity as *Verbo*. The *Verbo* is the perfect expression of the hidden Father, but this infinite Word is not expressible in finite terms. What the *Verbo* can say to us and, even more, what we can comprehend of this *Verbo* are always imperfect and fragmentary. Maria's revelations are a collection of such fragments, both in form and in content. Without ever engaging in a formal discussion of the relation of positive and negative discourse about God, the Carmelite's ecstatic outbursts, which conceal more than they reveal, are in essence a series of exercises on the paradox of the necessity and the impossibility of speaking about God. The fact that this large corpus of God-language was created without direct appeal to the theological categories of the relation of the cataphatic and the apophatic may be taken as a sign that such matters are inherent in mystical discourse, whatever the theological background.

Maria Maddalena's peculiar form of mystical discourse is found throughout her writings, to greater or lesser degrees. I will try to give a few examples of how she uses this discourse with regard to several of the major aspects of her teachings. The first concerns the saving Passion. Like so many Italian mystics of the time, Christ's sufferings in his Passion dominated Maria's religious sensibility. Both the *Forty Days* and the *Dialogues* contain raptures extended over the end of Holy Week in which the Carmelite relived the events that Christ suffered in the last three days of his life. The visionary shares Christ's sufferings, converses with him (often in words we do not hear), and not only imitates Christ but *becomes Christ* in his sufferings. This occurs on an invisible internal level but is manifested in an external acting-out of the details of the events, a public theater in which Maria moves from place to place in the convent to indicate new scenes in the drama and engages in extravagant actions—changing her countenance, screaming out, throwing herself on the ground, speaking in the name of other participants, and so on. From the time of Margaret of Cortona in the mid-thirteenth century, female mystics had acted out the Passion in public, or quasi-public, settings. Maria's use of this form of activity makes the convent into a *theatrum sororum*, a theater for devout nuns in which they can meditate on the meaning of the Passion. With Maria Maddalena de'Pazzi we not only have the most detailed of "Passion Plays," but also a kind of script of the inner motivations and sentiments of some of the major actors.

There are five Passion accounts in Maria's "writings," all fairly lengthy, so we cannot comment on them all. The first is found in Revelation 20 of the *Forty Days* and occurred on June 14–15, 1584 (Thursday night and Friday, but not in Holy Week).[130] Here Love draws her to follow Christ's Passion, despite her illness. In a state of ecstasy she describes for her nurse and the other sisters the details of the Passion hour by hour. She not only sees Jesus's sufferings but engages in conversation with the disciples, Judas, and Pilate. The revelation is highly visual; Maria sees all the events as she stares at a crucifix in her hand, which acts as a mirror in which she beholds the events "exactly when they really took place." The reporters give a detailed account of the words, gestures, and physical state of Maria over the long hours from "the first hour thirty minutes of Thursday night until the eighteenth hour of Friday."

The second reliving of the Passion, found in *Dialogue* 36, took place on Good Friday, April 20, 1585.[131] The nun scribes tell us at the beginning that they are writing down what they saw with their own eyes and heard with their own ears during the mystic's ecstasy, rather than what she told them later. The first scene (nonscriptural) is when Jesus goes to his mother and tells her about his imminent Passion. Here Maria makes a Latin comment: "Thus God so loved the world so that he gave his only Begotten Son [*silence*], and he loved Mary and did not make everything known to her."[132] "This blessed soul [Maria]," the scribes continue, "spoke sometimes with Jesus and sometimes with the Virgin and sometimes with herself. And between one speech and the next, she kept silent for a while as she usually does" (Maggi, 98). A mixture of discourse with Jesus and meditation on the prerogatives of Mary as Mother of God and the sufferings she endured during the Passion follows.[133] Then the mystic rushed upstairs to the highest room in the convent, which for her became the upper room of the Last Supper account (John 13–17). Once again, this section of the Passion Play features a meditation, this time primarily on Jesus's washing of the feet of the apostles, the *mandatum*, and his giving them communion (Maggi, 103–8). Then the mystic moves on to the convent dormitory, which is the scene of Christ's agony in the garden (Maggi, 108–10). There follow accounts of the capture of Jesus, his interview at the house of the chief priest Annas, as well as the house of Caiaphas, and Pilate's palace (Maggi, 110–14). Not only the many changes of location, but the mystic's different actions and gestures are faithfully recorded. Maria's words are few in comparison with her sufferings: "During this time of the Passion... she spoke very little and so low because she had difficulty in articulating the words, given the intense suffering she felt inside and the great pain she showed externally. Indeed, she could hardly cry, but once in a while she gave those deep screams of hers."[134] The scene of Christ's scourging at the pillar demands a new location, where she also reenacts Pilate showing Jesus to the people (Maggi, 116–19). Here the mystic's prayer to the Father encapsulates the message of redemption: Kneeling down on the landing of the stairs, she prayed to the Father, saying, "Father, do not regard the thoughts of these impious people [the Jews], but regard the salvation of the human race [*silence*]. Father, accept the anguish and the suffering of your Word for the comfort and consolation of your elect" [*silence*].[135]

The final scenes of the way of the cross have Maria Maddalena walking through the convent for more than an hour in imitation of Christ carrying his cross; she ends by imitating Christ on the cross as she stretches out on the floor of the oratory, allowing her hands and feet to be fastened down (Maggi, 119-21). As she repeats Christ's seven last words, she gradually seems to die. With the text of John 19:30 ("And inclining his head he gave up the spirit"), Maria slowly relaxes and awakens and in a weakened state is put to bed. The scribes, who note that they were not able to write everything down, later interviewed her: "We asked her if, when she went to these places, she followed Jesus and saw him. She said that yes, she saw him and suffered with him to the point that sometimes she felt as if she were Jesus himself [*tal modo che gli pareva alcuna volta esser lo stesso Jesu*], as we could infer by the way she recounted this to us."[136] This lengthy account provides a good picture of Maria Maddalena de'Pazzi's Passion piety.

There are two more reenactments of the Passion in the mystic's corpus. *Dialogue* 44 of May 7, 1585, is unusual by beginning with some pages devoted to reviewing the events in Christ's life prior to the Passion (infancy, baptism, miracles), before presenting Jesus's sufferings with a particular emphasis on how the Holy Spirit leads Jesus on in all these events.[137] The inspiration of the Holy Spirit is the motivating force in everything in the Redeemer's life.[138] This revelation also features Maria's struggles with the devils, later prevalent in the text of her *Probations*. The second book of the *Probations* contains a final reenactment of the Passion, which took place on March 26, 1592.[139] This is elaborated in sixteen scenes often involving conversations. The first scene features Christ and his mother, and the second contains dialogues between the Lord and the apostles. The later fourteen scenes follow the standard itinerary of the Passion.[140] These four accounts of the Passion are completed by another revelation, that found in *Dialogue* 48, the longest of the mystic's ecstatic accounts, which tells the post-Passion story, that is, how Maria participated in Jesus's forty hours in the tomb from late Good Friday to early Easter morn. This showing was given to her on May 17, 1585.[141] This reliving of Jesus's death and memorial deepens the mystic's theology of redemption in significant ways but is too long to survey here.

Two shorter *Dialogues* can help fill in some of the other significant aspects of the mysticism of Maria Maddalena de'Pazzi. The first is *Dialogue* 39 on the marriage of the Word and Maria's soul; the second is the last of the dialogues, *Dialogue* 50 on the Ascension.[142] Mystical marriage to the Word (and less frequently to the Father and the entire

Trinity) is an ancient theme, often expressed through the language of the Song of Songs.[143] Maria Maddalena's form of this mystical event in *Dialogue* 39 has many distinctive features.

On April 28, 1585, a young girl took the veil and was received into the convent of Santa Maria degli Angeli. Witnessing this, Maria went into an ecstasy that follows a three-part structure: (1) a phase where the soul sees its sins and suffers for them; (2) the Word's forgiveness of these sins and marriage to the soul; and (3) the soul's new understanding from the marriage and her act of thanksgiving and praise for this wonderful gift.[144] During this first ecstasy Maria sees two angels writing down in books the words that the young novice says during the ceremony and the good deeds that she has done in her life, thus mirroring what the other nuns will write down about what Maria says in ecstasy. Late the evening of the same day, Maria enters into a second ecstasy, which is recorded by her amanuenses. The first part of what she sees centers on sin, both the sins of the world and her own sins (ed., 3:13–17; trans. Maggi, 125–27). Maria's sufferings at the sight of these sins and her recognition of the ingratitude of humans in sinning against the Savior who died for them lead to a series of three outbursts of fragmented discourse in Italian and Latin expressing her distress. For example: "Oh Word, let me die a living death, so that I can carry out your project. 'All have turned aside; all alike have been made useless. There is no one who does good, not a single one' [Ps. 52:4] [*silence*]. Oh, let blindness see, whose seeing gives it pain, whose pain gives it glory; this glory is its beatitude, and its eternity is incomprehensible, inscrutable, and can be understood only by you, for you, and in you [*silence*], but no novelty is a novelty to me! [*silence*].[145] This tortured sequence seeks to express both the bodily and the inner pain of the mystic's confrontation with sin. Such a shattering of the self leaves her open to diabolic attack, as she tells her scribes after she comes out of the ecstasy. The suffering, though, had a purpose. The scribes comment, "We think that the Lord let her experience this to purge her because that night he wanted to give her the great present of his wedding ring in order to marry her as he had done to Saint Catherine of Siena. Indeed, that night was the eve of that anniversary when Jesus, Catherine's Spouse, had taken her to heavenly marriage rites."[146]

This leads into the second act in the drama, the marriage of the Word and Maria, which begins with the nun exclaiming: "'Oh immense generosity' [*O liberalità immensa*]. [*silence*]. When she began to see the gift that Jesus wanted to give, she began to rejoice greatly and said [these are the explanatory comments of the scribes]: 'No one will be crowned who has not fought valiantly' (1 Tim. 2:5). [*silence*]. 'O Word, you too! [*silence*]. She wished to say that he had also married Saint Catherine [another comment]. [*silence*]. 'Oh Word, [*silence*] Oh, your holy hands are so adorned and full of wedding rings for your spouses."[147] Maria Maddalena asks Christ to allow both St. Catherine and St. Augustine to come to the wedding, which she wants kept secret, that is, that the ring should not be visible. Now as a true spouse, Maria has a request to make: that all the other spouses (i.e., the other nuns) should realize this, their true vocation. She then asks Jesus to inscribe three verses on her wedding ring, statements central to the mystical message that St. Augustine had already written in her heart: *Verbum caro factum est*, for the Incarnation; *Sanguis unionis* for Holy Monday; and for tonight, *Puritas coniunsit Verbum ad Maria, et Sponsum ad sponsam* [Purity joined the Word to Mary, and the Bridegroom to the bride].[148] The nun-scribes say that Maria remained in ecstatic joy throughout the night with "her face so beautifully rose-colored that it looked like milk and blood" (the two sacred liquids). Maggi notes that this part of the revelation mixes both present and future tenses. This seems to indicate that the marriage to Jesus is both a present event and one to be completed in the eschatological future in heaven.

The third part of the account of Maria's marriage to Jesus is a description of the ring ceremony, an account of the knowledge that she gains from this, and her reaction to and praise of the gift she has been given (ed., 3:19–27; trans. Maggi, 129–34). Despite her unworthiness, she offers herself to the Trinity in the blood shed by Jesus her Spouse. With Saints Catherine and Augustine holding her hand, Maria receives the ring from Jesus. After quietly enjoying the gift, she wonders how she, like Catherine of Siena, will be able to preserve the wedding ring. Her answer: "I will use it as a very bright mirror, in which, by constantly contemplating it [*continuo sguardando*], I will see how in this wedding the generosity, goodness, and gentleness of my Word have united with the Holy Trinity, to whom he has married my soul" (ed., 3:20–21; trans. Maggi, 130). So, Maria's marriage is not just to the Word but also to the Holy Trinity (something not unknown in earlier mystical traditions). Maria's contemplation of what she sees in the mirror of the ring is expressed in a series of twelve future actions of seeing (*vedro*) that summarize key mysteries of Christian belief.[149] First, "I will see the Word in myself, and myself in him. And he will be crucified in myself, and I will be crucified in him," citing Galatians 2:20, a favorite text for expressing union. Second, "In that ring I will see the Word my Spouse stay in his Father's bosom in a motionless motion [*immobile moto*] that can never cease because of his vehement desire to redeem the creatures."[150] In "this mirror" she goes on to see the Word resting in Mary's womb, the wondrous deeds and the virtues of the Word made flesh, and the infinite love for us he shows in the sacrament of the Eucharist. "I will also see the blood he has shed to bathe us, in which we can continuously wash our souls of our constant faults" (ed., 3:22; trans. Maggi, 131). She also sees "the love with which the Word has prepared his glory for us," as well as the different kinds of holy souls that receive places in parts of his Body and are united to him. This leads Maria to make "a continuous letting go of myself in my Word" (*una continua relassatione di me stesso in esso mio Verbo*), so that the Word himself actually performs all her works (ed., 3:23-24). This "letting go," not unlike the actions of detachment (*abgescheidenheit*) and releasement (*gelassenheit*) of the Northern mystics,[151] allows Maria to see how the Word draws souls to himself by various paths that are all manifestations of the one road of love.[152] She sees further mysteries: the purity that united Mary to the Word; Catherine's loving-kindness and Augustine's sanctity; and all the good works that she is to perform. After another long pause Maria three times repeats one of her favorite Psalm texts: *Eructavit cor meum verbum bonum* ("My heart belched forth a good word," Ps. 44:2),[153] which she explains as "I [belched forth] the espousal of the Word to my soul" [*silence*]. Not my heart, but your [the Word's] side; no *verbum*, but the bond of a ring, of union, of love, of preciousness." There follows a passage of fragmented sentences in Latin and Italian giving praise to God.[154] A final evocation of the necessity of "releasement" (*rilassatione*) leads to Maria's thanking the Word for the gift of marriage by offering him all the drops of blood he spilled for her. In summary, Maria's teaching about mystical marriage does not concern itself with the erotic details of the love encounter between God and human but concentrates on the union forged by the redeeming blood of the "humanate Word" and insight into the divine mysteries that comes with it.[155]

Christian mystics have insisted on the difference between any experience of God that can be enjoyed in this life, however exalted, and what is reserved for the life to come. In a sense, Maria Maddalena's final dialogue deals with this issue, because in this revelation Jesus ascended into heaven is the model for the coming final reward. Many of Maria's late revelations are difficult to understand, not least the Ascension *Dialogue*. What follows is a brief introduction to a text that in places is scarcely comprehensible, because Maria's ecstatic outpourings often do not seem to have much logical connection. Nevertheless, there is a kind of broad structure to *Dialogue* 50, with the first part consisting of a two-scene rapture that occurred, apparently intermittently, during the evening and night of the Feast of the Ascension (ed., 3:382-403; trans. Maggi, 268-81), while the second part is a revelation about Maria being awarded divine purity (ed., 3:403-10; trans. Maggi, 281-86).

At the beginning of the first scene of the opening revelation, the mystic responds to the call of the Eternal Father, who girds her for battle against her demonic foes. She asks the Father to explain John 17:2, Christ's prayer, "Glorify me, Father, with the glory I had with you before the world existed." The answer to this request deals more with what the status of the soul, now united with her divine Spouse, must ask for herself: "She must ask for the being she had before the world was [*silence*], but what did I have before the world was? Since I was and was not? [*silence*] What was my being before I was? A non-being and great being, much greater than now, because it was the idea of your mind."[156] Maria Maddalena, like many mystics before her, appeals to the theme of the soul's preexistence in the Word, which is non-being from our present perspective, but truly "great being" in its oneness with God. In the dense pages that follow (ed., 3:386-90; trans. Maggi, 269-72) Maria tries to shed light on this higher being by identifying three characteristics of the pre-creational self that is one with God: *purity, copiousness,* and *beauty*. These characteristics are lost in created being, which has knowledge of its own being and is therefore distinct from God. Nevertheless, the soul can regain its glory, although in a different way, through participation in the glory of the Word's divinity and humanity: "The soul will see that the Word's Blood has given it such a purity, through which the soul unites with God in such a deep manner that neither a thought, nor a word, nor a desire, nor a deed, nor a glance would be able to separate it from its union and enjoyment of God" (ed., 3:388; trans. Maggi, 270-71).

At this point the second scene of the first revelation commences— Maria's entering into a conversation Jesus is having with the Virgin Mary and the disciples, apparently at the time of the Ascension (ed., 3:390-403; trans. Maggi, 272-81). Exactly what this might contribute to the discussion of the ascended Christ is not clear, but it appears to be connected to "the adornments of the heart" that the risen and ascended Jesus grants to the bride in order that she may know the virtue of his heart more profoundly. These adornments are divided into three classes, and Maria asks for the adornments in the middle of the divine heart, because they can be shared both by those in heaven and those still on earth (the right and the left sides). These are three: the charity that unites the soul to God; the justice that gives each his due; and the love (different from charity) that is the compendium of all virtues. These three adornments with their Trinitarian dimensions are infused into the soul in a ceremony that seems to mimic the soul's marriage to the *Verbum*. What follows this ceremony is a conversation of the Ascended Word with the Blessed Virgin, raising her to the level of a co-redemptrix (ed., 394-96; trans. Maggi, 275-76). Mary's status, however, is tied to her virginity, so the next section is an extended (in places very difficult) gloss on the role of virgins in the church (ed., 3:396-99; trans. Maggi, 276-78).

According to her amanuenses, Maria came out of this rapture about 8:00 A.M. in order to attend Mass and receive communion with the other nuns but then went back in ecstasy around 9:00 to remain in rapture until 5:00 P.M. The record of this brief revelation is more directly related to the feast (ed., 3:399-403; trans. Maggi, 279-81). Christ invites her to ascend with him into the Father's bosom, and she sees Mary's body and soul also go up (the Assumption). At this stage Maria Maddalena complains that she does not want to be alone, so she asks Jesus how many other souls he will take with him to heaven. The answer is given in a series of obscure distinctions of kinds of souls ascending to heaven. In conclusion, the scribes tell us that they saw Maria standing up and gazing to heaven, showing "such a majesty that for us she resembled Jesus when he ascended to heaven." They then record the mystic's hymn to the ascending Lord.

The second part of *Dialogue* 50 is a difficult "rapture about purity" (*ratto della purità*), which Maria received beginning about 11:30 P.M. on Ascension Eve (ed., 3:403-10; trans. Maggi, 281-86). The purification is Trinitarian, because the Father's essence purifies the mind, the Son's essence purifies the will, and the Holy Spirit purifies the memory, while the unity of the Trinity purifies the whole soul, and the humanity of the Word purifies the body. The person who receives this purification, like the Blessed Virgin, "will make it communicating for those who are able to receive it and understand it." The result is an "intellect abyssed, dead, and vivifying, which understands nothing, seeks nothing, and in seeking everything, understanding everything, will lead a dead life; and here will live enlightened, and with a dead light it will enlighten the other thirsting minds, even though they don't know this purity."[157] This paradoxical situation is reminiscent of the totally detached person of late medieval mystical traditions, one whose releasement allows for a full engagement in spreading the message of attaining God to other eager souls. The pages that follow primarily concern Maria's regaining her original divine purity in the divine idea before creation but are too convoluted to be amenable to a short summary (ed., 3:404-9; trans. Maggi, 282-85). The revelation ends with a vision of two columns that inspire Maria Maddalena to continue "to live as dead" (*viver morta*) here in the world. The notion of living as dead resonates with other places in her corpus where Maria talks about the final stage of the soul's realization of its purity as the death that comes from total releasement. In the *Revelation* given on the Sixth Day, for example, she enumerates the kinds of love—passive love, anxious love, satisfying love, and dead love. Concerning the last she says:

> The last love is dead, because it does not desire anything, it does not wish anything, it does not long for or search out anything. By the dead relaxation it has made of itself in God [*per la morta relassatione che ha fatta di sé in Dio*], [the soul] does not desire to know him, nor to understand him, nor to taste him. It wants nothing, knows nothing, and does not want to do anything. . . . [*silence*]. All these kinds of love lead to the Word, but one therefore must dwell only in the last one, I say, in dead love, of which the Word lets his spouse taste a bit. [*silence*].[158]

Maria Maddalena de'Pazzi's mysticism has an unusual theological depth despite its difficult form. The strange features of how her message reaches out to us in writings that are not her own, and that even by the usual standards of mystical discourse often remain opaque, make her a test case for exploring the limits of language in talking about God. The Florentine nun invites theoretical analysis perhaps more than any other early modern mystic.

Early Modern Italian Male Mystics

After the thirteenth century, the tally of male mystics in Italy was reduced. To be sure, there are a number of religious men of the Late Middle Ages whose names appear in the history of mysticism and also writers between 1500 and 1675 who leave us mystical works. Unlike the figures in France and Spain, however, most of the Italian male mystics do not seem to have had much influence outside the context of a particular religious order, or their Italian locality.[159] Many of the Italian saints from this period became well known, such as Filippo Neri, Carlo Borromeo, and Giuseppe Cupertino. Their hagiographers often ascribe mystical graces to them, but their writings do not add to the history of mystical traditions. In concluding this chapter, I will look at two of the

Italian male mystics of the period, one from the sixteenth century, the Camaldolese monk Blessed Paolo Giustiniani, and one from the seventeenth century, the Cistercian monk and later cardinal Giovanni Bona.

Blessed Paolo Giustiniani (1476-1528)

Paolo (born Tommaso) Giustiniani is a prime example of the fusion of Renaissance humanism with ecclesiastical reform and contemplative piety.[160] Born of an aristocratic Venetian family in 1476, Tommaso's conversion from the world was not just a turn to the monastic life but a dedication to its most extreme form, the eremetical ideal of extreme asceticism and separation from the world. After extensive studies, especially of the Stoic philosophers, Tommaso entered the hermitage of Camaldoli in 1510. His attempts to reform Camaldoli failed, so in 1520 he and some followers left that monastery and founded the community of the Hermits of St. Romuald near Ancona, where he died in 1528. He wrote a good deal, both in Latin and in Italian, in many genres, writings not edited until recently.[161] Along with his humanistic education, Giustiniani was widely read in monastic literature and mysticism, from the *Apophthegmata Patrum* and Cassian to the writings of Cistercians like Bernard and William of St.-Thierry. He writes, above all, in praise of the eremetical life of deep contemplation, for which he composed a *Regula* in 1520, updating the original rule of the founder of the Camaldolese, St. Romuald.

The eremitical context of Giustiniani's writings is always evident, but the inner message of the centrality of loving contemplation has wider dimensions for all those desiring to lead a more perfect life, as can be seen in his *Secretum Meum Mihi* (*My Secret Is Mine*), a favorite passage for many mystics taken over from Isaiah 24:16.[162] The treatise was based on a mystical experience that Giustiniani received during the celebration of Mass on August 7, 1524, in which he was illuminated to grasp the necessity of dying to self in order to live only for God. The experience was so overwhelming that he immediately began to write and quickly finished this treatise on the love of God. Perfect love of God, however, is a difficult goal, so much of the work is concerned with analyzing how to overcome the barriers set up by self-love. The work is scholastically schematized into six parts (*Ragionamenti*), each beginning with a biblical quotation.[163]

The First Argument, *Ad nihilum redactus sum et nescivi* ("I am reduced to nothing and have no knowledge," Ps. 72:22) deals with how the sinful soul reduces itself to nothing through love of God. Giustiniani distinguishes four kinds of annihilation (*annientamento*), thus taking his place in the tradition of mystical annihilation. The first two kinds are bad: (1) the soul is reduced to nothing when it does not know it is in sin; and (2) the soul is still nothing when it recognizes its sin and seeks the aid of grace. The second two annihilations are good: (3) the soul is reduced to nothing through the love of God so that it lives in God alone; and (4) the soul is reduced to utter nothingness when it does not love itself or even know itself, or even know God in itself, but only knows God in God. (This final state of annihilation is close to some of the strong forms of annihilation found in mystics like Marguerite Porete and her successors.)[164] At the conclusion of this analysis, Giustiniani inserts a prayer expressing the mystery of God's ineffability: "Give me then, O Lord, I beg you, such a conversion to you, such a union with you, such a conversion that I may have such a taste and enjoyment of you that the intellect cannot grasp and the pen cannot express, that I may be so totally united and drawn into you that I may love you, taste you, enjoy you!"[165]

The Second Argument takes the well-known Pauline text for its title, *Vivo, iam non vivo, sed in me vivit Christus* ("I live now, not I, but Christ lives in me," Gal. 2:20). This investigates the three forms of life of the loving soul, the third of which echoes the fourth form of annihilation: "Thus, the soul lives through love, but it does not live in itself nor in God, nor does God live in it, but only God lives in God. And the soul lives because it is transformed in God, when it loves neither itself in itself, nor itself in God, nor God in itself, but only God in God [*solo Dio in Dio*]."[166] *Solo Dio in Dio* is the central theme of the treatise. The Third Argument is under the title, *Deus caritas est, et qui manet in caritate in Deo manet et Deus in eo, et erit Deus omnia in omnibus* ("God is love, and one who remains in love remains in God and God in him, and God will be all in all," combining 1 John 4:16 and 1 Cor. 15:28). This section (ed., 61–66) treats the three transformations of the soul through love. The long Fourth Argument, entitled *Dilige Dominum Deum tuum ex toto corde tuo* ("Love the Lord your God with your whole heart," Deut. 6:5; Matt. 22:37), introduces the six modes or qualities of love, which end with the quality of love "when the soul loves God in God."[167] The Fifth Argument bears the title *Et proximum tuum sicut te ipsum diliges* ("And love your neighbor like yourself," Matt. 22:39) and seeks to show how pure love of God does not exclude proper love of self and neighbor.[168] Love of God and love of neighbor are never split, but by the very act of directing all our love to God we also love ourselves and our neighbor in the highest way possible. Finally, the Sixth Argument, *Certus sum quia nihil me poterit separare a caritate dei* ("I am sure that nothing can separate me from the love of God," Rom. 8:35), speaks of the unchanging peace of the soul that loves God in God.[169] A passage from near the end of this section illustrates the character of Giustiniani's rhetoric: "O blessed is the soul that arrives at that peace, to which I do not believe it is ever, ever, possible to arrive at in any other way, if not with the love that is not only in God, but that is God alone, and not in itself, but in God. The more that this love is only love of God in God, the more the soul distances itself from any other form of love or tries to insert any other loving affection."[170] While there is a certain flavor of abstraction in Giustiniani's divisions and subdivisions, *My Secret is Mine* testifies to the deep mystical insights of the Camaldolese hermit.

Giovanni Bona (1609–1674)

Giovanni Bona was born at Mondavi in Piedmont in 1609 and entered the Feuillant reform of the Cistercian Order, famous for its asceticism, at Pignerol in 1625.[171] Ordained in 1633, he spent five years as a hermit before becoming a prior and later abbot. Bona was called to Rome to serve as the General of the Cistercian Order from 1651 to 1654, and at the behest of Pope Alexander VII, again from 1657 to 1664. Bona was a consultant to many Roman Congregations, and Clement IX made him a cardinal in 1669. He died in Rome in 1674. Bona was famous for both learning and piety and wrote extensively on liturgical matters. He was also noted for his ascetical and mystical works. His best-known work (seventeen printings in the seventeenth century alone) was his 1658 *Initiation to Heaven containing the Best Part of the Holy Fathers and Ancient Philosophers*, an ascetic manual of thirty-five chapters organized according to the traditional threefold pattern of beginners, proficients, and perfect.[172] This was intended to accompany his main mystical work, the *Short Cut to God by Way of Anagogical Actions and Ejaculatory Prayers* (*Via compendii ad Deum per motus anagogicos et orationes iaculatorias*), which he subtitled as *Liber Isagogicus in Mysticam Theologiam*, that is, an introductory guidebook.[173] Bona was disappointed that this work did not achieve the success of the ascetical treatise (only four seventeenth-century editions). In addition, the Cistercian wrote a treatise on discernment of spirits (*De discretione spirituum in vita spirituali deducendorum*, 1671), as well as a posthumous *Cursus vitae spiritualis* (1674).

The Short Cut to God deserves to be better known, because it is a useful and in some ways original summary of mystical theology written on the eve of the outbreak of the Quietist controversy. Bona was learned (the book is filled with citations helpfully identified at the end), and he intended his small book to be a précis of the history of mystical theology. But he was more than just a compiler; the Cistercian had a distinctive approach (as well as an elegant Latin style). His originality is most evident in his stress on anagogic and ejaculatory prayer, where he fits into a tradition on the role of aspirations/ejaculations in the path to God, one that was strong from the later Middle Ages through the early modern period. Nonetheless, the central role he gives to aspirations is unusual—ejaculatory prayer is the "shortcut" to mystical union.[174] As Sabrina Stroppa has shown, *The Short Cut to God* is also a good example of the seventeenth-century conviction that mysticism has become a special theological "science," contrasted with scholastic "science," by its foundation in experience and its own technical language and procedures. As a handbook of the new science, however, *The Short Cut to God* does not talk about the author's own experience,[175] but presents the *indocta sapientia* ("unlearned wisdom") of mystical theology through a technique of accumulating different sources as a way of approaching, but never actually attaining, the ineffable mystery.[176]

The work falls into two parts. The first ten chapters set out the foundations of *mystica theologia* and introduce the importance of aspirations in general, while chapters 11–20 present examples of the aspirations that are meant to prepare for the higher prayer of contemplation. (The parallel with the aspirations found in *Holy Wisdom* of Augustine Baker published in the same year of 1657 is striking.) The second part closes with a summary chapter *De amore dei*.[177] A brief look at the first part will provide a sense of Bona's *Short Cut to God* as a representative mystical text of the late seventeenth century.

The first chapter introduces what had by now become a common theme: the difference between scholastic and mystical theology: "There are two ways to go to God, as the best authorities assert. The one they call scholastic and common; the other mystical and secret. Both are a 'gift from heaven, coming down from the Father of lights' (Jas. 1:7), but there are many differences between them."[178] A long list of these differences follows—Bona's usual technique of accumulation. The mystical path, however, is double, consisting of the active (cataphatic) and passive (apophatic) way, as taught by Dionysius (MT 1). The passive way is higher: "Thus, freed from all hindrances [this way] promises what is to come, that is, to be anagogically lifted up to the ray of divine darkness and drawn on by God, because then the soul is raptured and absorbed in a divine way, which is the passive way, building upon the prior disposition of the active way."[179]

Chapter 3 addresses the question, "What Is Mystical Theology"? Bona says that it is "the unlearned wisdom [*indocta sapientia*] higher than all human wisdom, by which the mind recognizes [*agnoscit*] its God without discursive reasoning, and takes hold of him, and tastes him without reasoning. Mystical theology is the totally hidden conversation of the mind with God." He goes on: "It is experimental wisdom, the loving of God, divinely infused, by which the mind, purified of every disorder through the supernatural acts of faith, hope, and charity, is intimately joined to God."[180] After treating how mystical theology differs from both scholastic (i.e., rational) theology and symbolic theology, Bona discusses what the Neoplatonic philosophers knew of mystical theology, citing Tauler that their mystical theology was purely natural. Finally, he locates the source of true mystical theology in "the essence of goodness and the cause of all things, the superessential Trinity," and specifies its goal as union with God and deification (cap. III.5; ed., 16–17). Chapter 4 treats the dispositions favoring mystical theology and the impediments hindering it, again with the citation of numerous mystics, both men and women.[181]

Mystical union, by now an accustomed term, is the subject of chapter 5. It is not the local union by which God is present to all things, and is not the union of charity given Christians through sanctifying grace. Rather, "[i]t is the very secret and hidden union, not penetrated by those without the experience and difficult to explain, which takes place in the soul's powers, that is, in the intellect and will. These attain God and are joined to him by their own vital acts. The supreme joy of this life consists in this union, and it is a kind of foretaste of future glory."[182] It is interesting to note here that Bona stresses the soul's powers, not its essence, or the *apex mentis*, or the *fundus animae*, although he does mention these in later chapters.[183] Both powers, according to Bona, are brought into "the vast solitude of divinity," where the Father strips the intellect of all images and elevates it above reason, the Son fills the intellect with divine clarity, and the Holy Spirit enflames the will so that whatever is mortal in us is absorbed into immortal life (cap. V.2; ed., 27). Bona generally does not employ the language of mystical annihilation, but he does so in chapter 5, as he explains the nature of union. He says, for example, "Here the loving soul flows away, dies to itself, and as if reduced to nothing [*velut ad nihilum redacta*], sinks down into the abyss of eternal love." He speaks of union as "the perfect imitation of Christ," and "a marvelous transmutation," and as "the annihilation of the soul before God and a mystical death" (cap. V.2-3; ed., 28-29). Attaining mystical theology, however, is "a very difficult task, an arduous path, and a very high summit inaccessible to human efforts" (cap. V.5; ed., 30-31). How, then, can we have any hope of reaching it? The answer is anagogic prayer. "I say that the short cut to God, to the peak of mystical theology, to intimate union with the Word is anagogical acts and the exercise of aspirations."[184]

Chapters 6, 7, and 8 are devoted to the nature, proofs for, and sources of aspirations. First the definition is given: "Aspirations are certain very brief prayers, whether in the mind alone, or conceived and spoken at the same time by mind and mouth, by which the faithful soul, in any place or time, and frequently invoked, raises its heart and will to God day and night."[185] Aspirations are "anagogical actions," because they lead above; they are also called "ejaculatory prayers" (*orationes iaculatoriae*), because they are like arrows and javelins thrown toward the heart of God; and they are also called "affections" (*affectus*) as expressing the loves and desires of the heart and proposals of the will (cap. VI.2; ed., 36). Bona says they were used by Christ and other biblical figures and were employed by many saints, from the Desert Fathers down to recent saints, like Francis de Sales (cap. VI.3-5; ed., 36-44). Chapter 7 (ed., 45-60) gives advice about how to make aspirations and observes that they are generally most useful for souls in the illuminative way who are on the road to contemplation (VII.5), although chapter 8 notes that there are aspirations for all three stages of the mystical path (beginners, advanced, and perfect; see VIII.5).[186] The states of beginners and proficient belong to the active life, while the perfect attain the contemplative life. This is the love that constitutes Christian perfection, which, Bona says, "is not an affective love, desirous [*affectuosus*], as they say, but is an effective, practical, and obedient love, which completely withdraws the will from its own good, subjects it to God, and makes it conform to God's will both in its deciding and commanding. Indeed, tender and soft affections are lazy and empty, and nothing dries quicker than tears [*lacryma nihil citius arescit*]."[187]

Chapters 9 and 10, which complete the first part of *The Short Cut to God* treat of the nature and kinds of contemplation. As is typical, Bona gives a number of definitions, cites numerous authorities, and provides several divisions of the kinds of contemplation.[188] After discussing the signs for the transition to contemplation (cap. IX.1-2; ed., 71-74), he says that "[c]ontemplation consists in a certain sweet, peaceful, and lovable vision of eternal truth, which, without a variety of discursive acts, is said to behold God, truly gazing and penetrating with immense love and admiration, and such great certitude and clarity, that it is 'face to face,' as Scripture says of Moses."[189] It is more in the will than in the intellect (IX.4; ed., 80–81). Its objects include God and all things related to God; its proximate cause is the Holy Spirit through the mediation of the seven gifts of the Spirit (IX.5, ed., 81–83); and its goal is union with God. It is not a result of human effort but is God's gift alone, although few have attained it due to the time and effort needed and the frequent long trials that usually precede it (cap. X.5-6; ed., 100–104). At this point Giovanni Bona summarizes the first part of his *Isagoge* and concludes with his own hymn, *O fons decori luminis*: "O fountain of beautiful light, / O serene light of the stars, / God, the most pure fire, / the lasting strength of hearts, / Always by voice, by prayer, / By grateful mind, I lay claim to you, / Singing of my salvation, / From the sun's first light until evening."[190]

Conclusion

To say that the sixteenth- and seventeenth-century Italian mystics did not have the impact of the male and female Italian mystics of the thirteenth through fifteenth centuries should not be taken as a slight or dismissal. The women and men treated above, just a selection of a large group, each in her or his way, illustrate the varieties of Catholic response to the challenges of the time. Although the Reformation was not a direct threat to Catholic faith in Italy, it was a constant presence, affecting how believers lived their faith. Writing out of a consciousness of the direct presence of God seems to have become more and more centered on records of ecstatic experience at this time, although these revelatory narratives often contain deep theological teachings. This is especially true of the women mystics of the period. Learned clerics wrote treatises on the new "scientific" view of mystical theology in a variety of ways: sometimes based on their own experience (Paolo Giustiniani); sometimes as a summary of mystical traditions (Giovanni Bona); sometimes in an interaction with the experiential witness of others, especially women (Achille Gagliardi). This era in Italian mysticism has yet to reveal its full contours and inner richness to contemporary study.

Notes

1. For a short account of Italy during much of this period, see Eric Cochrane, *Italy, 1530–1630* (London: Longman, 1988).

2. Ibid., 172.

3. Documents relating to Catholic reform movements before Trent are translated by John C. Olin, *The Catholic Reformation: Savonarola to Ignatius Loyola. Reform in the Church 1495–1540* (New York: Harper & Row, 1969).

4. Using Michelangelo's Sistine Chapel frescoes to argue the point, David Tracy has recently contended that the leading Catholic thinkers of the time "are not the official theologians but rather the great artists" ("The Catholic Imagination: The Example of Michelangelo," in *Heavenly Bodies: Fashion and the Catholic Imagination*, ed. Andrew Bolton (New York: Metropolitan Museum of Art, 2018), 10–16.

5. For a nuanced view of the popes and reform, see William V. Hudon, "The Papacy in the Age of Reform, 1513–1644," in *Early Modern Catholicism: Essays in Honor of John W. O'Malley, S.J.*, ed. Kathleen M. Comerford and Hilmar M. Pabel (Toronto: University of Toronto Press, 2001), 46–66.

6. John W. O'Malley, *Trent: What Happened at the Council* (Cambridge, MA: Belknap Press of Harvard University Press, 2013). See also Cochrane, *Italy, 1530–1630*, 145–53.

7. Giuseppe Alberigo, "From the Council of Trent to Tridentinism," in *From Trent to Vatican II: Historical and Theological Investigations*, ed. Raymond F. Bulman and Frederick J. Parella (Oxford: Oxford University Press, 2006), 19–37, especially on the two models of reception of Trent: pluralist and centralized.

8. See Anthony Blunt, "Gianlorenzo Bernini: Illusionism and Mysticism," *Art History* 1 (1978): 67–89.

9. A useful survey from 1971 is "Italie. IV: Période Moderne (16e-18 siècles)," DS 7:2236–73, especially Mario Scaduto, "A. Le 16e siècle" (2236–52); and Massimo Petrocchi, "B. Le 17e siècle" (2252–58). More recent surveys include Tullo Goffi and Pietro Zovatto, *La spiritualità del Settecento: Crisi di identità e nuovi percorsi*, Storia della spiritualità (Bologna: Edizioni Dehoniane, 1990); Massimo Petrocchi, *Storia della spiritualità italiana* (Turin: Società Editrice Internazionale, 1996); Sabrina Stroppa, *Sic arescit: Letteratura mistica del Seicento italiano*, Biblioteca della Rivista di storia e letteratura religiosa: Studi 8 (Florence: Olschki, 1998); Pietro Zovatto, ed., *Storia della spiritualità italiana* (Rome: Città Nuova, 2002); and Massimo Marcocchi, ed., *Spiritualità e vita religiosa tra Cinquecento e Novecento* (Brescia: Morcelliana, 2005).

10. See the survey of research by Massimo Marcocchi, "Per la storia della spiritualità in Italia tra il Cinquecento e il Seicento," in Marcocchi, *Spiritualità e vita religiosa*, 11–45.

11. For an introduction, see Massimo Petrocchi, chap. 6, "I grandi spirituali del Cinquecento," in Petrocchi, *Storia della spiritualità italiana*, 84–101.

12. Massimo Petrocchi, chap. 11, "Un Seicento spirituale italiano non formalistico," in Petrocchi, *Storia della spiritualità italiana*, 166–83.

13. For a recent translation and account, see Hudon, *Theatine Spirituality: Selected Writings*, 42–65 (Introduction), and 112–236 (Text). *The Spiritual Combat*

does not lack all reference to mystical themes. Chapter 54 on how to receive the sacrament of the Eucharist and chapter 55 devoted to preparation for communion both contain references to loving union with Christ in the Eucharist (Hudon trans., 192–93, and 197).

14. See James Brodrick, *Robert Bellarmine, Saint and Scholar* (Westminster, MD: Newman Press, 1961).

15. I cite from the translation by John Patrick Donnelly and Roland J. Teske, *Robert Bellarmine, Spiritual Writings*, Classics of Western Spirituality (New York: Paulist Press, 1989), 49.

16. Bellarmine, *Mind's Ascent*, "Introduction" (trans., 53).

17. The meditations are: step 1 (man as microcosm); step 2 (world as macrocosm); step 3 (the earth); step 4 (waters and fountains); step 5 (air); step 6 (fire); step 7 (the heavens, sun, moon, and stars); step 8 (the rational soul); step 9 (angels); step 10 (God's essence as compared to bodily greatness); step. 11 (God's power as compared to bodily greatness); step 12 (God's wisdom as compared to bodily greatness); step 13 (practical wisdom); step 14 (God's mercy); and step 15 (God's justice in comparison with bodily greatness).

18. Mario Gioia edited both texts produced by the collaboration of Gagliardi and Berinzaga: *Per via di annichilazione: Un testo di Isabella Cristina Berinzaga redatto da Achille Gagliardi S.I.*, Aloisiana 25 (Rome: Gregorian University Press, 1994); and *Breve compendio di perfezione cristiana: Un testo di Achille Gagliardi S.I. Saggio introduttivo ed edizione critica*, Aloisiana 28 (Rome: Gregorian University Press, 1996). The account given here will depend on the two "Introduzioni" by Gioia (*Per via di annichilazione*, 21–39; and *Breve compendio*, 15–97). There is a fairly large literature, which Gioia uses and often supersedes, so it will not be much cited here. All translations from these two texts are my own. Gioia's editions are not without criticism; see Sabrina Stroppa, "L'annichilazione e la censura: Isabella Berinzaga e Achille Gagliardi," *Rivista di storia et letteratura religiosa* 32 (1996): 617-25.

19. See Ignacio Iparraguirre and André Derville, "Gagliardi (Achille), jésuite, 1537/38–1607," DS 6:54–64.

20. For a biographical sketch, see Gioia, "Introduzione," *Per via di annichilazione*, 28–39.

21. Cited in Gioia, *Breve compendio*, "Introduzione," 54–55.

22. Gioia, *Breve compendio, Appendice* (ed., 338).

23. Nevertheless, some of Isabella's writings are still extant: five brief letters and chapters 4 and 5 of a *Vita* that the Jesuits of S. Fedele ordered her to write. These chapters are available in Gioia, *Per via di annichilazione*, 245–92.

24. Gioia, "Introduzione," *Per via di annichilazione*, 19.

25. On Gagliardi's *Compendio* and his acquaintance with Northern European mystics, see Rob Faesen, "Achille Gagliardi and the Northern Mystics," in *A Companion to Jesuit Mysticism*, ed. Robert A. Maryks (Leiden: Brill, 2017), 82–111.

26. McGinn, *Spain*, 387–90.

27. The mystics put under ban included Ramon Llull, Henry Suso, John Tauler, Jan van Ruusbroec, Hendrik Herp, John Mombaer, Alonso de Madrid, and the female mystics Mechthild of Magdeburg and Gertrude of Helfta.

28. See chapter 5, 274–75.

29. For a review of the conflict, see Gioia, "Intoduzione," *Breve compendio*, 29–45; and Faesen, "Achille Gagliardi and the Northern Mystics," 83–85.

30. Cited in Gioia, "Introduzione," *Breve compendio*, 84. A treatment of the *censura* is found in Stroppa, "L'annichilazione e la censura."

31. In the early 1930s important articles on the *Breve compendio* were written by R. P. Villers, M. J. Dagens, G. de Luca, and Henri Bremond. Bremond gave the first extended treatment in 1933 in his *Histoire*, vol. 11, part 1, chapter 1, "Isabelle Bellinzaga [sic], Achille Gagliardi et la charte de l'amour" (new ed., 4:525-59).

32. Gioia, "Introduzione," *Per via di annichilazione*, 53. Gioia's edition does not number the chapters but gives section numbers, e.g., [35]. I will cite by section and page of the edition.

33. Gioia, *Per via di annichilazione*, [22], ed., 105-6.

34. Gioia, *Per via di annichilazione*, [61], ed., 137.

35. Gioia, *Per via di annichilazione*, [69], ed., 142-43.

36. Gioia, *Per via di annichilazione*, [115], ed., 180.

37. Gioia, *Per via di annichilazione*, [116], ed., 181.

38. The seven kinds of prayer are vocal, ejaculatory, cogitation (discursive considering of God, but without an affective elevation), meditation (discourse with elevation), contemplation (immediate union with God), colloquy, and exclamation (see [123], ed., 187).

39. Gioia, *Per via di annichilazione*, [154], ed., 218.

40. Gioia, *Per via di annichilazione*, [159-60], ed., 222-28. The eight forms of contemplation discussed are: interior fire, unction, ecstasy, speculation, taste, quiet, liquefaction, and the brightness of glory.

41. Gioia, *Per via di annichilazione*, [161], ed., 229.

42. Gioia, *Per via di annichilazione*, [162], ed., 229-30.

43. Gioia, *Per via di annichilazione*, [164], ed., 231.

44. Gioia, *Per via di annichilazione*, [164], ed., 232-33.

45. Gioia, *Per via di annichilazione*, [166]; ed., 234-35.

46. This appears to be a reference to earlier descriptions of suffering with Christ, as in [32], ed., 118.

47. For a survey of the use of the *Breve compendio* in seventeenth-century France, see Papàsogli, *Gli Spirituali Italiani e il "Grand Siècle,"* 22-29.

48. See Gioia, "Introduzione," *Breve compendio*, 100-103.

49. I will use the edition of M. Gioia referred to above. The first part takes up only 63 pages, as compared to 146 pages for *Per via di annichilazione*. There is some debate about whether annihilation is the subject of all three states, or if the *primo stato* is the preparation for the later two states of true annihilation (see Faesen, "Achille Gagliardi and the Northern Mystics," 89).

50. In what follows I will refer to the *Breve compendio* with section number and page (e.g., *BC* [2]; ed., 180). I will cite the *Secondo compendio* in similar form (e.g., *SC* [2*]; ed., 249). The *Appendice* is fairly long (ed., 245-338).

51. There are analyses of the content of the *BC* in Gioia, "Introduzione," 130-50; and Faesen, "Achille Gagliardi and the Northern Mystics," 88-91.

52. *BC* [3]; ed., 181-82. Gioia ("Introduction," 132) notes the similarity of these two principles to Ignatius's "Principle and Foundation" in the *Spiritual Exercises* 23.

53. *SC* [2*]; ed., 249-50. Disappropriation (*spropriatione*) is further explained in *SC* [157*]; ed., 326-27, as a derivation and participation in God, because although God the Father possesses the fullness of all things, "he disappropriates himself

of all that with peace, sureness, and infinite greatness of spirit, and, in effect, communicates it all to the Son and the Holy Spirit." In a similar fashion ([158*]; ed., 329) indifference (*indifferenza*) is "the highest divine perfection," because in exercising his will toward creatures, God freely gives to both good and bad, "not ceasing to love and give gifts" even to the evil.

54. *SC* [4*]; ed., 250. Gioia ("Introduction," 115–24) has an extended treatment of these terms.

55. Gioia ("Introduction," 130–45) has a good summary of the first part.

56. *BC* [13*]; ed., 195. Self-love (*amor proprio*) is the great enemy of annihilation, and Gagliardi devoted a long section to it in the *Appendice* [*SC* 108*–142*], ed., 287–306.

57. *BC* [25], ed., 206. The notion of "leaving God for God," originally found in Meister Eckhart but also present after him in many late-medieval Northern mystics, such as the Pseudo-Tauler, *Institutiones spirituales*, is one of the clearest signs of the influence of these mystics on Gagliardi (Faesen, "Achille Gagliardi and the Northern Mystics," 92).

58. *Pati divina*, "to suffer or to undergo divine things," a term taken over from Dionysius (DN 2.9 [648B]) appears several times; see Gioia, "Introduction," 114–15.

59. There is a translation of the second and third states of the *BC* by John Arblaster and Timothy Page in Faesen, "Achille Gagliardi and the Northern Mystics," 103–8.

60. On Marguerite Porete and the letting go of the created will in the process of annihilation, see McGinn, *Flowering*, 261–65. On the relation of Porete and Gagliardi, see Juan Miguel Marín, "A Beguine's Spectre: Marguerite Porete [d. 1310], Achille Gagliardi [d. 1607], and Their Collaboration across Time," *The Way* 51.3 (2012): 93–110; and Faesen, "Achille Gagliardi and the Northern Mystics," 93–96.

61. Gioia points to texts in the *Per via di annichilazione*, such as [108]; ed., 173.

62. *BC* [51]; ed., 241.

63. Literature on ecstasy includes the multiauthor, "Extase," DS 4:2045–2189; Jean-Noël Vuarnet, *Extases féminines* (Paris: Arthaud, 1980); and U. Occhialini et al., eds., *L'estasi* (Vatican City: Libreria Editrice Vaticana, 2003).

64. The historical account of Massimo Petrocchi (*L'estasi nelle Mistiche Italiane della Riforma Cattolica* [Naples: Libreria Scientifica Editrice, 1958]) mostly treats late medieval Women (Catherine of Bologna, Catherine of Genoa, Camilla Battista da Varanno), but does deal with Maria Maddalena de' Pazzi (69–77). Helpful are the essays and illustrations in Giovanni Morello et al., eds., *Visioni ed Estasi: Capolavori dell'arte europea tra Seicento e Settecento* (Milan: Skira, 2003).

65. The best account of paranormal gifts is still Herbert Thurston, *The Physical Phenomena of Mysticism* (Chicago: Henry Regnery, 1952). Thurston does not devote a separate chapter to ecstasy (there is just too much evidence), but ecstasy often accompanies the other gifts he discusses (e.g., levitation, stigmata, telekinesis, luminous phenomena, bodily elongation, etc.). Thurston describes his approach thus: "As I have more than once previously noted, it is not the aim of this volume to solve problems, but to present facts" (233).

66. A useful anthology of Italian mystical women is Giovanni Pozzi and Claudio Leonardi, eds., *Scrittrici mistiche italiane* (Genoa: Marietti, 1988). Early modern fig-

ures included are Battistina Vernazza (1497-1587), briefly treated in McGinn, *Varieties*, 329; Paola Antonia Negri (1507-1555); Caterina Ricci (1522-1590); Isabella Cristina Berinzaga (1551-1624); Caterina Vannini (1562-1606); Maria Maddalena de'Pazzi (1566-1607); Caterina Paluzzi (1573-1645); Maria Domitilla Galluzzi (1596-1671); and Brigida Morello (1610-1679). Missing from this volume are figures such as Orsola Benincasa (1547-1618), who is treated in Herbert Thurston, *Surprising Mystics* (Chicago: Regnery, 1955), chap. 5 (111-21), as well as the Carmelite mystic Giovanna Maria della Croce (1603-1673), whose *Vita* and eleven volumes of *Rivelazioni* were only recently published. This list is not exhaustive.

67. The literary and theological contributions of Italian women mystics are studied in the essays in Dino S. Cervigni, ed., *Women Mystic Writers*, Annali d'italianistica 13 (Chapel Hill: University of North Carolina Press, 1995), which contains a useful "Bibliographical Essay" by Cristina Mazzoni (401-35). For an overview, see Marlena Modica Vasta, "Mystical Writing," in *Women and Faith: Catholic Religious Life in Italy from Late Antiquity to the Present*, ed. Lucetta Scaraffia and Gabriella Zarri (Cambridge, MA: Harvard University Press, 1999), 205-18.

68. Claudio Leonardi, "La santità delle donne," in Pozzi and Leonardi, *Scrittrici mystiche italiane*, 43-57, here 54-56.

69. E. Ann Matter, "Interior Maps of an Eternal External: The Spiritual Rhetoric of Maria Domitilla Galluzzi d'Acqui," in *Maps of Flesh and Light: The Religious Experience of Medieval Women Mystics*, ed. Ulrike Wiethaus (Syracuse, NY: Syracuse University Press, 1993), 60-73, here 72.

70. See McGinn, *Harvest*, 73-76.

71. On Federico Borromeo and his treatise, see Massimo Lollini, "Scrittura obbediente e mistica tridentina in Veronica Giuliani," in Cervigni, *Women Mystic Writers*, 351-56.

72. For an overview, see Eire, *Reformations*, chap. 23, "The Age of Devils" (618-59); and Moshe Sluhovsky, *Believe Not Every Spirit: Possession, Mysticism, and Discernment in Early Modern Catholicism* (Chicago: University of Chicago Press, 2007).

73. An example of a "failed mystic," who claimed that her deceptions regarding mystical gifts, as well as her lesbian relation to one of the other nuns, were the result of demonic possession is Benedetta Carlini (1590-1661), abbess of the Theatine convent in Pescia. See Judith Brown, *The Life of a Lesbian Nun in Renaissance Italy* (Oxford: Oxford University Press, 1986).

74. John Tedeschi, *The Prosecution of Heresy: Collected Studies on the Inquisition in Early Modern Italy* (Binghamton, NY: Medieval and Renaissance Texts and Studies, 1991).

75. Much of the scholarship devoted to Caterina, as with a number of these female mystics, is difficult to access in the United States. Thus, I have not seen Dionisia Trosa, *Prolegomeni alla spiritualità di S. Caterina di Ricci* (Florence: Olschki, 1975). For introductions, see Raffaele Cai, "Catherine de Ricci (Sainte)," DS 2:326-27; and Mauro Regazzoni, "Il 'Vissuto' Mistico," in Zovatto, *Storia della spiritualità italiana*, 399-423, here 401-3.

76. The materials by and about Caterina Ricci were edited by Domenico Di Agresti in the *Collana Ricciana* published by Olschki in Florence (five volumes of the *Epistolario*, 1973-75; and nine volumes of the *Fonti*, 1963-76). There is a brief English account and a translation of some of her letters in Domenico Di Agresti, ed.; Jennifer Petrei, trans., *St. Catherine de'Ricci, Selected Letters* (Oxford: Dominican Sources, 1985).

77. The Italian text can be found in Pozzi and Leonardi, *Scrittrici mistiche italiane*, 389.
78. Ibid., 391.
79. Di Agresti, *Selected Letters*, "Introduction," xi–xiii.
80. For an example, see the "Letter to a Sister" of November 18, 1549 (Di Agresti, *Selected Letters*, 14–15); and the "Letter to the Nuns of San Domenico, Lucca," of October 1571 (ibid., 39).
81. Di Agresti, *Selected Letters*, 41; see also the "Letter to Salviati" of December 22, 1561 (ibid., 48–49).
82. "To the Sisters of San Vincenzo," late January, 1590 (Di Agresti, *Selected Letters*, 15–16).
83. Paolo Fontana, *Santità femminile e Inquisizione: La "Passione" di Suor Domitilla Galluzzi (1595–1671)*, Fontes Archivi Sancti Officii Romani 3 (Rome: Libreria Editrice Vaticana, 2007), 93–94.
84. The *Vita* has been edited by Olimpia Pelosi, *Vita da lei narrata (1624)*, Studi e testi 6 (Chapel Hill, NC: *Annali d'italianistica*, 2003).
85. For an account of Galluzzi's difficulties with the Inquisition, see Fontana, *Santità femminile e Inquisizione*, 59–88.
86. I translate from the quotation given in Fontana, "Parte I," 77.
87. Along with Fontana, "Parte I: Suor Domitilla Galluzzi dall'esperienza mistica al processo," in Fontana, *Santità femminile e Inquisizione* (7–94), several recent essays are helpful for Galluzzi's mysticism: E. Ann Matter, "The Personal and the Paradigm: The Book of Maria Domitilla Galluzzi," in *The Crannied Wall: Women, Religion, and the Arts in Early Modern Europe*, ed. Craig A. Monson (Ann Arbor: University of Michigan Press, 1992), 87–103; eadem, "Interior Maps of an Eternal External," 60–73; and Olimpia Pelosi, "Tra *eros* e *caritas*: Le 'pene d'amore' di Maria Domitilla Galluzzi," in Cervigni, *Women Mystic Writers*, 307–32.
88. On the *Lume*, see E. Ann Matter, "The Commentary on the Rule of Clare of Assisi by Maria Domitilla Galluzzi," in *Creative Women in Medieval and Early Modern Italy: A Religious and Artistic Renaissance*, ed. E. Ann Matter and John Coakley (Philadelphia: University of Pennsylvania Press, 1994), 201–11.
89. Cited from the translation in Matter, "Commentary," 204.
90. Fontana, *Santità femminile e Inquisizione*, 57.
91. On the relation of blood and roses, see Fontana, *Santità femminile e Inquisizione*, 43–58.
92. The text can be found in Fontana's edition of the *Passione* in *Santità femminile e Inquisizione*, 100–101. I use Matter's translation from "Interior Maps," 64–65.
93. My translation from the text given in Pelosi, "Tra *eros* e *caritas*," 328.
94. On the history of Santa Maria degli Angeli, see Armando Maggi, *Uttering the Word: The Mystical Performances of Maria Maddalena de'Pazzi, a Renaissance Visionary* (Albany: State University of New York Press, 1998), 6–8.
95. Major studies in Italian include Carmelo C. Catena, *Santa Maria Maddalena de'Pazzi carmelitana: Orientamenti spirituali ed ambiente in cui visse* (Rome: Institutum Carmelitanum, 1966); Bruno Secondin, *Santa Maria Maddalena de'Pazzi. Esperienza e dottrina* (Rome: Institutum Carmelitanum, 1974); and Luca M. di Girolamo, *Santa Maria Maddalena de'Pazzi: Esistenza e teologia a confronto*, Vacara Deo 21 (Rome: Edizioni Carmelitane, 2010). The best study in English is Maggi,

Uttering the Word; see also Maggi, "The Voice and the Silences of Maria Maddalena de'Pazzi," in Cervegni, *Women Mystic Writers*, 257–81. Other essays in English include Karen-edis Barzman, "Cultural Production, Religious Devotion, and Subjectivity in Early Modern Italy: The Case Study of Maria Maddalena de'Pazzi," in Cervegni, *Women Mystic Writers*, 283–305; Antonio Riccardi, "The Mystic Humanism of Maria Maddalena de'Pazzi," in Matter and Coakley, *Creative Women in Medieval and Early Modern Italy*, 212–36; and Charlò Camilleri, "To Be Is to Gaze and Be Gazed At: Vision in Maria Maddalena de'Pazzi's Mysticism," *Studies in Spirituality* 19 (2009): 35–46.

96. Bruno Nardini et al., eds., *Tutte le opere di Santa Maria Maddalena de'Pazzi dai manoscritti originali*, 7 vols. (Florence: Nardi, 1960–66). An anthology of texts was later edited by Giovanni Pozzi, *Le parole dell'estasi*, Piccola Biblioteca 163 (Milan: Adelphi, 1984).

97. Nardini, *Tutte le opere*, vol. 1.

98. *I colloqui* are found in *Tutte le opere*, vols. 2–3. There are also fifty of these. Since March 25 marked the New Year in Florence, these discourses were recorded over a period of some five months between late 1584 and early 1585 in the Florentine calendar.

99. These *Revelatione e intelligentie* are found in *Tutte le opere*, vol. 4. Since there were raptures each day and each night there are sixteen in all.

100. The *Probatione* are found in *Tutte le opere*, vols. 5–6.

101. These materials are gathered in *Tutte le opere*, vol. 7. The tally of Maria's letters (only twelve in this edition) needs to be augmented by those in Chiara Vasciaveo, ed., *"Constretta dalle dolce verità, scrivo": L'Epistolario completo* (Florence: Nerbini, 2007).

102. There is a full translation in five volumes by Gabriel N. Pausback, *The Complete Works of Saint Mary Magdalen de'Pazzi, Carmelite and Mystic (1566–1607)* (Aylesford, IL: Carmelite Friars, 1969–75). More accessible, and with a good introduction, is the selection by Armando Maggi, *Maria Maddalena de'Pazzi: Selected Revelations*, Classics of Western Spirituality (New York: Paulist Press, 2000). Maggi includes six of the fifty revelations of *The Forty Days* and five of the fifty *Colloquies*, but he translates many of the longer and more important texts.

103. A helpful analysis of Maria Maddalena's raptures is Ermanno Ancilli, "Marie-Madeleine de Pazzi (sainte), carmélite, 1566–1607," DS 10:576–88, with cols. 578–81 on the nature of her ecstasies. In the *Quaranta giorni* No. 34 Maria has an interesting reflection on the nature of her raptures: "Furthermore, he gave me this abstraction of soul from body so that the soul could better unite itself completely with God; in consequence, since it is then more noble and powerful, the soul causes the body to remain thus immobile and, giving it life, the soul makes the body enjoy, together with itself, at least some little bit of what the soul savors in this union that it has with God" (ed. 1:214; trans. Pausback 1:106).

104. Gaspar Loarte, *Instrutione et avertimenti per meditare la passione di Cristo nostro redentore, con alcune meditationi intorno ad esse* (Rome, 1571). On Loarte, see Manuel Ruiz Jurado, "Loarte (Gaspard), jésuite (1498–1578)," DS 9:949–52; on Maria's use of Loarte, see Maggi, *Uttering the Word*, 95–97.

105. On Maria's possible sources, see di Girolamo, *Santa Maria Maddalena de'Pazzi*, 43–50.

106. Pozzi, "Introduzione," *Le parole dell'estasi*, 15–46; Maggi, *Uttering the*

Word, and especially the summary essay, "The Voice and the Silences of Maria Maddalena de'Pazzi"; and di Girolamo, *Santa Maria Maddalena de'Pazzi,* 121-34.

107. Maggi, *Uttering the Word,* 4.

108. Maggi, "Voice and the Silences," 279: "Maria Maddalena's request to her audience is conveyed through the absence of voice. We must 'complete' this mystical work . . . by perceiving a fundamental absence: that of the visionary's voice. Indeed, our imagination cannot fill this 'gap' in a positive way by imagining her voice. It is actually through her absent voice, however, that the Saint can still speak to us."

109. Maria often talks about the need for annihilating the self through the practice of the utmost humility, which is really the recognition of our nothingness. Nevertheless, annihilation is more than just a moral practice; it is an attempt to acquire the divine No-thingness, or purity, as we can see in God the Father's discourses on the relation of humility and purity in *Dialogue* 48 (ed., 3:344-48; trans. Maggi, 246-48). Here, the soul says, "Oh eternal Father, yes, yes, I understand that if the soul wishes to be able to have it [purity], it must dwell in nothing, but only in you with perfect purity" (trans., 246).

110. *Coll.* 45 (ed., 3:191-92; trans. Maggi, 199). The text and Maggi's translation read *la luce in tenebre* (i.e., changing light into darkness), but this appears to be an error, so I have reversed it in the translation given here ("darkness into light").

111. Maria's teaching on contemplation is expressed through the noun *risquardo* and the verb *risquardare.* For a summary, see Maggi, "Introduction," *Selected Revelations,* 33-37. *Risquardo* implies a mutual gaze—when we gaze at the Word we recognize that he is gazing at us. *Risquardo,* therefore, always implies communication. On the mutuality of the gaze, see Camilleri, "To Be Is to Gaze and Be Gazed At."

112. *Probatione II* (ed., 6:62-67; trans. Maggi, 312-14). Maria says little about creation, but a few passages show her adherence to the traditional view of creation as the *exitus* and *reditus* of all things to their divine source. See, e.g., *Colloquio* 36 (ed., 2:395; trans. Maggi, 107), where we read, ". . . as with every other creature, I came from your idea, everything must go back there [*silence*], we must go back there where we came from."

113. *Renovatione della Chiesa* (ed., 7:108; my trans.).

114. *Coll.* 48 (ed., 3:339; trans. Maggi, 242): "Però che questa purità propriamente è il mio essere." The whole section devoted to the discussion of purity is found in ed., 3:339-48; trans. Maggi, 242-48.

115. Ibid. (ed., 3:341; trans. Maggi, 243). The *Verbo humanato,* Maria's distinctive name for the God-man, is frequent in her corpus.

116. On milk and blood (and water) in Maria's writings, see Maggi, "Introduction," *Selected Revelations,* 26-33.

117. *Coll.* 48 (ed., 3:344-45; trans. Maggi, 246).

118. This is suggested by an earlier section in the conversation of the Father and the soul that treats the "Sentence that brings the communicaton of my divinity" (*Consiglio che apporta comunicatione della Divinità mia*) (ed., 3:331-32; trans. Maggi, 235-36).

119. Maria's theology of the Trinity cannot be taken up here. For a few important texts, see *Quaranta giorni* No. 19 and 47 (trans. Maggi, 73-74, 92); *Colloquio* 44

(Maggi, 161–63); and especially *Probatione* II (Maggi, 311–14), where the Father is compared to a book, the Son to a mirror, and the Holy Spirit to a fountain.

120. According to the indices of volumes 2 and 3 of the edition, John 1:14 is cited fifteen times in the *Colloqui*.

121. *Coll.* 1 (ed. 2:51; trans. Maggi, 16).

122. *Coll.* 38 (ed. 2:435; trans. Maggi, 17).

123. For this reason, I will not give a separate account of Maria's teaching on union and deification here. For some important texts, see *Coll.* 22 (ed. 2:234); *Coll.* 46 (ed. 3:246); *Probatione* II (ed. 6:174); and *Revelatione e intelligentie* (ed., 4:256).

124. See, however, the discussion in Maggi, *Uttering the Word*, 177–78 n. 19.

125. *Coll.* 33 (ed., 2:333; trans. Pausback, 2:229).

126. *Coll.* 25 (ed. 2:264–80; trans. Pausback 2:176–88).

127. *Coll.* 25 (ed., 2:269; trans. Pausback, 180). The comments of the amanuenses on explaining, qualifying, and shaping the *Dialogues* deserve more study than can be given here.

128. *Coll.* 25 (ed. 2:269; my trans.).

129. Maggi, "Voice and the Silences," 275–77.

130. *Quaranta giorni* 20 (ed. 1:156–80; trans. Maggi, 75–91).

131. *Coll.* 36 (ed., 2:381–420; trans. Maggi, 97–123).

132. *Coll.* 36 (ed., 2:382; trans. Maggi, 98): Sic Deus dilexit mundum ut filium suum unigenitum daret. . . . Et dilexit Mariam et non fecit cognita de omnia. The first part of the Latin sentence is scriptural (John 3:16), while the second part is the mystic's creation.

133. *Coll.* 36 (ed., 2:382–87; trans., Maggi, 98–102). As befitting a Carmelite, the Virgin Mary plays a large role in Maria's mystical teaching. For a treatment, see di Girolamo, *Maria Maddalena de'Pazzi*, chap. 4, "Maria, Madre del Signore" (209–64).

134. *Coll.* 36 (ed., 2:409; trans. Maggi, 115–16).

135. *Coll.* 36 (ed., 2:414; trans. Maggi, 119).

136. *Coll.* 36 (ed., 2:420; trans. Maggi, 123).

137. *Coll.* 44 (ed., 3:134–61; trans. Maggi, 166–79).

138. On Maria's teaching about the Holy Spirit, see di Girolamo, *Santa Maria Maddalena*, chap. 3, "Il Ruolo dello Spirito Santo" (159–208).

139. *Riprobatione* II (ed., 6:47–86; trans. Maggi, 301–26).

140. These locations are (3) the room near the Cenacle where Jesus finished his last address, (4) Gethsemane, (5) the betrayal by Judas, (6) the house of Annas, (7) the house of Caiaphas, (8) before Pilate, (9) before Herod, (10) the return to Pilate, (11) Jesus's scourging, (12) the crowning with thorns, (13) the *Ecce Homo*, (14) Pilate's judgment, (15) the way of the cross, and (16) Calvary.

141. *Coll.* 48 (ed., 3:285–370; trans. Maggi, 218–83). This text is given a full analysis in Maggi, chap. 3, "The Wedding, the Funeral, and the Memorial of the Word," in *Uttering the Word*, 93–118. According to Maggi, *Coll.* 48 "is the performance of an act of remembrance," in which "[t]he Word becomes the memory of the Word" (94).

142. *Coll.* 39 (ed., 3:11–27; trans. Maggi, 124–34) is discussed in Maggi, *Uttering the Word*, 80–93. *Coll.* 50 can be found in ed., 3:382–410, and is translated in Maggi, *Selected Revelations*, 266–86.

143. See Pierre Adnès, "Mariage spirituel," DS 10:388-408, who mentions Maria on 394.

144. The three parts are identified by Maggi, who structures his analysis on this basis; see *Uttering the Word*, 80.

145. *Coll.* 39 (ed., 3:14; trans. Maggi, 126 adapted).

146. *Coll.* 39 (ed., 3:16; trans. Maggi, 127).

147. *Coll.* 39 (ed., 3:17; trans. Maggi, 128 adapted).

148. *Coll.* 39 (ed., 3:19; trans. Maggi, 129).

149. At the end of Section 2 of *Coll.* 39, the scribes explain the relation between "seeing" and "uttering" as follows: "As she has explained to us many times, in her raptures she sees and perceives more than one thing at the same time. She utters, however, what the Lord wants her to because by herself she neither knows how to speak nor what to say."

150. *Coll.* 39 (ed., 3:21; trans. Maggi, 130).

151. For Maria's understanding of *relassatione*, see Maggi, "Introduction," *Selected Revelations*, 36-38.

152. *Coll.* 39 (3:24; trans. Maggi, 132-33). Maria identifies five different kinds of love here: *amor secreto, amor forte, amor fervente, amor quieto, amor puro*. On Maria's various enumerations of the kinds of love, see Maggi, "Introduction," *Selected Revelations*, 43-53.

153. Maria uses Psalm 44:2 in a variety of ways. In *Coll.* 12 (ed., 2:152), after she receives the Word, she (or the Word acting in her) "belches him forth." In the *Quaranta giorni* No. 21 (ed., 1:180) she sees the Father "belch forth the Word," that is, all creatures in the Word.

154. *Coll.* 39 (ed., 3:25-26; trans. Maggi, 133-34). After this there is a brief vision of the nuns of the convent under the protective mantle of the Blessed Virgin.

155. Blood, what Maria often refers to as the *sanguis unionis*, is one of the dominant themes in her corpus. A key passage is in *Colloquio* 48, where the Father discourses on the "Sentence of union." He says, "My dear daughter, what kind of a sentence is this? Sentence without sentence. . . . I communicate myself and I communicate the unity which is the idea of my essence, every time you offer me my Word's Blood. Your offer of his Blood is so powerful, that with it you can unite what you want. If you want to unite man with God, you can be sure that with that Blood he will be united" (ed., 3:323; trans. Maggi, 230). For a summary of the different uses of blood in Maria, see Maggi, "Introduction," *Selected Visions*, 26-33.

156. *Coll.* 50 (ed., 3:386; trans. Maggi, 269): "Ma ha a chieder l'esse che haveva inanzi ch'el'secolo fussi. [*silence*] Ma che havevo io inanzi ch'el'secolo fussi? [*silence*] Che non ero e ero? [*silence*] Che era il mio essere inanzi che io fussi? Un non essere e grande essere, molto più che non è hora, perché era nell'iddea della mente tua."

157. *Coll.* 50 (ed., 3:404; trans. Maggi, 282 adapted). For another text on the "dead life," see *Coll.* 46 (ed., 3:199-200).

158. *Revelatione*, Sixth Day (ed., 4:211; my trans.). The theme of "wanting nothing, knowing nothing, and doing nothing" goes back to Marguerite Porete and Meister Eckhart and appears frequently in early modern mystics, as we have seen.

159. A partial list of the Italian male mystics/mystical authors of the time would include Battista Carioni da Crema, OP (ca. 1460-1543); Bl. Paolo (Tommaso) Giustiniani, a Camaldolese (1476-1528); Giovanni da Fano, OFM Cap (d. 1539);

Serafino da Fermo, a Lateran canon (1496-1540); Achille Gagliardi, SJ (1537-1607); Virgilio Cepari, SJ (1564-1621); Sisto de'Cucchi, OFM Cap (1585-1630); Giovanni Cardinal Bona, OCist. (1609-1674); and Bl. Carlo da Sezze, OFM Cap. (1613-1670). Again, this is not a complete list.

160. Giustiniani attracted the interest of the great monastic historian Jean Leclercq, who wrote the best monograph on him, *Un humaniste eremite: Le bienheureux Paul Giustiniani (1476-1528)* (Rome: Edizione Camaldoli, 1951). Leclercq also wrote the entry in the DS: "Giustiniani (Paul), camaldule, 1476-1528," DS 6:414-17, as well as an introduction in English, *Alone with God: A Guide to the Hermit Way of Life, Based on the Teachings of Blessed Paul Giustiniani* (London: Hodder & Stoughton, 1961).

161. *Trattati, lettere e frammenti dai manoscritti dell'Archivio dei Camaldolesi di Monte Corona nell'Eremo di Frascati*, 3 vols. (Rome: Edizioni storia e letteratura, 1967-2012).

162. Although there are more recent editions, I will use the first modern edition, *Secretum Meum Mihi, o dell'amor di Dio: Ragionamenti sei* (Frascati: Sacro Eremo Tuscolano, 1941), with a preface by the Benedictine scholar Anselm Stolz.

163. The edition has a helpful outline of the "Six Arguments" (*Ragionamenti Sei*) that structure the work (ed., 19-23). A Seventh Argument was planned but does not survive. There is a good discussion of the Arguments with numerous translations in Leclercq, *Alone with God*, 162-83.

164. The four annihilations are found in *Secretum Meum Mihi*, I (ed., 45-53).

165. Ibid. (ed., 53). See also the translation of the earlier part of the prayer in Leclercq, *Alone with God*, 171-72.

166. *Secretum Meum Mihi*, II (ed., 54-60). I translate from the summary in ed., 20. See Leclercq, *Alone with God*, 166-68.

167. *Secretum Meum Mihi*, IV (ed., 67-116). See the analysis in Leclercq, *Alone with God*, 169-71.

168. *Secretum Meum Mihi*, V (ed., 117-48); see Leclercq, *Alone with God*, 173-78.

169. *Secretum Meum Mihi*, VI (ed., 149-63); see Leclercq, *Alone with God*, 180-83.

170. *Secretum Meum Mihi*, (ed., 161-62).

171. For an introduction, see J.-M. Canivez, "Bona (Jean)," DS 1:1762-66. The best recent study is Stroppa, *Sic arescit: Letteratura mistica del Seicento italiano*, part 1 (15-76).

172. I will use the edition of the *Manuducatio ad Caelum* found in Ioannis Cardinalis Bona, *Opuscula Ascetica Selecta* (Freiburg-im-Breisgau: Herder, 1911), 3-117. After two introductory chapters, the purgative way is treated in chapters 3-18, concentrating on the seven deadly sins and the passions and powers of the soul. Chapters 19-31 deal with the life of the proficients, especially the use of solitude and the various virtues. The final chapter 35 is a very brief treatment of the state of perfection.

173. D. Ioanne Bona, *Via compendii ad Deum* (Rome: Ang. Bernabò a Verme, 1657). Both the *Manuducatio* and the *Via compendii* were written ca. 1650-53.

174. For an overview, see E. Vansteenberghe, "Aspirations," DS 1:1018-25, who mentions Bona several times.

175. *Via compendii*, "Praefatio ad lectorem" (n.p.): "Tam ultro ipse fateor me rem sublimem, non mea, sed aliena experientia edoctum scripsisse; sicut scriptum

est, *credidi proper quod locutus sum.*" Later Bona insists that the mystical sources he cites are, indeed, founded on *experientia* (cap. V.4, ed., 29–30).

176. Stroppa, *Sic arescit*, chap. II.2, "Una approssimazione all'ineffabile: l'accumulo" (43–52).

177. The aspirations of part 2 include the following: cap. XI with nine decades of "groaning aspirations" for beginners; cap. XII with nine decades of pious apsirations for the proficient; and cap. XIII with ten decades of "loving sighs" for the perfect. Cap. XIV contains acts of praise of different virtues, while cap. XV has a collection of aspirations to Jesus, the Blessed Virgin, and the saints. Cap. XVI has ten decades of aspirations based on the name and attributes of God; cap. XVII features ten decades on the life of Jesus; and cap. XVIII has *motus anagogici* based on the created universe. Finally, cap. XIX has a diary of aspirations for every time and aspect of the day.

178. *Via compendii*, cap. I.3 (ed., 3). Bona returns to the differences between scholastic and mystical theology in several other places; e.g., cap. VI.5 (ed., 44).

179. *Via compendii*, cap. II.1 (ed., 7–8).

180. *Via compendii*, cap. III.1 (ed., 12–13).

181. *Via compendii*, cap. IV (ed., 18–25). Bona here gives the first of his many citations to John of the Cross (ed., 19). Other recent male mystics mentioned include Victor Gelen, Constantin de Barbanson, and Francis Suarez. Among the female mystics cited are the three Catherines (of Siena, of Bologna, and of Genoa), Angela of Foligno, Gertrude the Great, Mechthild of Hackeborn, Brigid of Sweden, Baptista Vernazza, and Teresa of Avila. Maria Maddalena de'Pazzi is later cited (cap. X.6; ed., 103).

182. *Via compendii*, cap. V.1 (ed., 26).

183. Citing John of the Cross, Bona once refers to the *centro animae* (cap. IX.3; ed., 77). He equates the *apex mentis* and the *fundus animae* in cap. X.7 (ed., 106–7): "Mens vel apex spiritus est nudus ac Deiformis animae fundus. Id est simplex animae essentia imagine Dei insignita." *Apex mentis* also occurs in cap. III.2 (ed., 14), while *fundus animae* is found in cap. VII.2 and 6 (ed., 49, 54).

184. *Via compendii*, cap. V.6 (ed., 31).

185. *Via compendii*, cap. VI.2 (ed., 34–35).

186. Cap. VIII.2 (ed., 62–64) lists the three sources for aspirations, namely, the world around us, conscience within us, and the Bible.

187. *Via compendii*, cap. VIII.6 (ed., 69).

188. *Via compendii*, cap. X.2 (ed., 86–90) lists the following kinds of contemplation: *acquisita/infusa*; *pura/mixta*; *positiva/negativa*; and *clara/caliginosa/supereminens*. X.3 (ed., 90–98) treats the divisions of contemplation found in a number of authorities, such as Richard of St. Victor, Bonaventure, Thomas Aquinas, Thomas de Jesús-Maria, and Victor Gelen.

189. *Via compendii*, cap. IX.4 (ed., 78).

190. *Via compendii*, cap. X.8 (ed., 108). Bona was a noted Latin poet.

CHAPTER 8

Mysticism in Catholic Germany and the Low Countries (1525–1675)

Introduction

It is difficult to generalize about Catholicism in German-speaking lands in the sixteenth and seventeenth centuries because of the political fragmentation of the Holy Roman Empire into many kingdoms, principalities, duchies, imperial cities, prince archbishoprics, and the like. This gave German Catholicism a more dispersed and local flavor than seventeenth-century France. Still, loyalty to the Hapsburg dynasty and the system of the "Imperial Church" (*Reichskirche*) in which many high clerics, as well as religious institutions, exercised a power both secular and spiritual, provided a fundamental basis for the century-and-a-half of Catholicism after the rise of Protestantism.[1]

During the period ca. 1525–1555, it looked for a time as though Germany might be totally lost to Catholicism, as about two-thirds of German territories went over to Protestantism. Catholicism began to experience a revival during the troubled 1540s and 1550s, and the Peace of Augsburg of 1555, which formulated the principle that the ruler determined the religion of his territory (*cuius regio eius religio*), guaranteed the political and religious stability necessary for Catholic survival. During this time, the Council of Trent (1546–63) began to lay down the doctrinal and disciplinary reforms that go under the broad name of the Counter-Reformation. Although many of the decisions of Trent were adapted only slowly and in piecemeal fashion in Germany, the council set a benchmark for a renewed and confident Catholicism. From 1555 to the outbreak of the Thirty Years' War in 1618, Catholicism experienced the form of consolidation of identity that is spoken of today as "confessionalization." An important factor in this process was the influence of the Jesuit Order. In 1543, a Dutch student, Peter Kanis (1521-1597), entered the Jesuits. He went to Rome, where Ignatius of Loyola soon recognized his gifts and in 1549 sent him back to German-speaking lands to foster reform and combat Lutheranism. Peter Canisius, as he came to be known, preached throughout Germany, set up schools and universities, and wrote a series of successful catechisms in the 1550s. Canisius and the other Jesuits played an important role in educating the Catholic elite and the clergy.

The Catholic recovery fostered a growing militancy against Protestantism that was cultivated by the Hapsburg dynasty ruling the Holy Roman Empire. The result was the outbreak of the devastating series of religio-dynastic conflicts called the Thirty Years' War, which ravaged Germany between 1618 and 1648. This was the last and probably the worst of the religious wars of early modernity, a conflict whose effects were felt throughout Central Europe.[2] It has been estimated that perhaps a third of the population perished by violence, starvation, or disease. The first decade of the war was generally favorable to the Hapsburg Ferdinand II, who in 1629 issued the Edict of Restitution, which restored to Catholics many ecclesiastical holdings taken over by Protestants. The tide turned in the 1630s with the incursion of the Protestant king of Sweden, Gustavus Adolphus, into the fray. In the last and most destructive period of the war (1635–48), the French monarchy, guided by Cardinal Richelieu and then Cardinal Mazarin, supported the Swedish and German Protestants against Ferdinand II and his son, Ferdinand III. The Treaty of Westphalia, which ended the destruction, pretty much returned the political and religious situation to what it had been in 1624. General disgust with the horrors of religious conflict led to the decline of militancy on both sides during the following century.

From the 1630s on, a cultural shift that greatly affected Catholic Germany was the emergence of the "Baroque Catholicism" that dominated Germany until the mid-eighteenth century. "Baroque" is a term that has been used to describe the art, music, literature, and religion of the time between the Renaissance and the rise of Neoclassicism in the eighteenth century. The term is mostly used to characterize the exuberant, emotional, and sensuous style of art and literature created in sixteenth-century Italy that in the seventeenth century spread to Germany, Eastern Europe, Spain, the Spanish New World, and even to France and England. Baroque resists any easy or generally agreed-upon definition. Since its appearance in art-historical discussions in the late nineteenth century (Heinrich Wölfflin, 1888), it has been discussed and debated by major twentieth-century scholars of art and literature (e.g., Mario Praz, 1925; Benedetto Croce, 1929; Eugenio d'Ors, 1935; Victor Tapié, 1961; Paolo Portoghesi, 1966; Robert Harbison, 2000; Giovanni Careri, 2003; etc.).[3] Though this idea is often associated with Counter-Reformation Catholicism, there were Protestant and Orthodox manifestations of the Baroque in the seventeenth century and beyond.[4] With regard to seventeenth-century Germany, Marc Foster has characterized Baroque Catholicism as "a religious synthesis that incorporated the high culture of Baroque literature and architecture [presumably that from Italy] and the more popular aspects of a highly developed and diverse religious practice.... It was a dynamic synthesis, with a constantly shifting mix of devotional practices, and it was often highly regional and even local in its practice and institutions."[5]

Although not as productive as contemporary France in the writing of mystical literature, Catholic Germany did make its contribution in the early modern era.[6] Both Protestants and Catholics wrote mystical works and poems during this century, but, given the Catholic emphasis of this volume of *The Presence of God*, I shall not give any extended treatment of Protestant mystics.[7]

The Jesuits[8]

The German Jesuits, although crucial to the maintenance and revival of Catholicism in German-speaking lands, did not produce the rich mystical literature that characterized the French followers of Ignatius. In his monumental *La spiritualité de la Compagnie de Jésus*, Joseph de Guibert devotes only ten pages to German Jesuits of this period as compared with twenty-three pages for the French.[9] There were, of course, noted Jesuit spiritual authors who did not write about mysticism, of whom the most famous was the prolific Jerome Drexel (1581–1638), longtime preacher at the Imperial Court in Vienna. Peter Canisius himself showed an interest in mystical literature.[10] As a young student at Cologne he was influenced by Nicholas van Esch, a priest involved with Beguines and an editor of mystical texts.[11] Both men were friendly with the Carthusians of the St. Barbara Priory in Cologne, who were pioneers in translating, editing, and publishing the major works of Northern mysticism that were to play such a large role in France and Spain. Canisius began his writing career by editing the sermons of John Tauler in 1543.[12] His many activities over the next half-century seem to have precluded any further attention to working on mystical texts. Two seventeenth-century Jesuits, however, do deserve attention for their contributions to mysticism.

The first is Maximilian Sandaeus (van der Sandt, 1578–1656), born in Amsterdam, who entered the Jesuits at Rome in 1597 and taught at Würzburg and Mainz before dying at Cologne.[13] Sandaeus was a prolific author who is purported to have said, "I have written as many books as the years I have lived." Aside from his polemical works and many spiritual and theological treatises, he is best known for two works in defense of mysticism. The first is the *Mystical Theology or Divine Contemplation of Religious People Defended from Calumnies* (*Theologia mystica seu contemplatio divina religiosorum a calumniis vindicata*), published in Mainz in 1627. The second, more famous, work was the *Key for Mystical Theology* (*Pro theologia mystica clavis*), put out in Cologne in 1640.[14] The late sixteenth and seventeenth centuries saw the growth of two new types of books that reflected the changes in the understanding of *mysticus* and *theologia mystica*. The first was the production of summaries of spiritual theology usually under the rubric either of "perfection" (*De perfectione . . .*) or of "mystical theology" (*theologia mystica*). The second was vocabularies or *onomastica*, that is, alphabetical summaries and defenses of the expressions of the "mystics" (*mystici*), as they were now called.[15] Sandaeus's two works reflect these tendencies. The Jesuit did not create the new genre of the explanation and defense of the "obscure words and expressions" used by the mystics to "manifest the proper meaning of their discipline." The Carmelite Diego de Jésus had included an appendix defending some of John of the Cross's "mystical expressions and doctrine" in his 1618 edition of the saint's works, and another Carmelite, Nicolás de Jesús-María, produced a longer apology of the language of John and other mystics in 1631.[16] Sandaeus's work, however, was larger and more systematic. As Michel de Certeau has shown, these works speak to a new moment in the history of Western mysticism, one that was both "scientific" in the sense of treating *theologia mystica* as a distinct new discipline, and apologetic in defending mysticism against its critics, an increasingly necessary endeavor as the seventeenth century progressed.[17] We can get a sense of why Sandaeus felt it was necessary to mount this counterattack, as well as the way in which he understood and presented the mystics, by a brief look at the *Key for Mystical Theology*.

The *Clavis* gives us a good insight into the status of the new understanding of *theologia mystica* in the first half of the seventeenth century, with regard both to its use of sources and to its choice of topics. Sandaeus had an extensive knowledge of mystical traditions. Although he uses both the "older" and the "newer" mystics, his favorite authorities are the Northern mystics of the past two centuries, especially Tauler (mostly, however, through the *Institutiones Taulerianae*), Ruusbroec, Harphius, and Blosius, whom he calls "the best Master of the Mystics" (*optimus Mysticorum Magister*; *Clavis*, 374). The older authorities he cites most often are Augustine, Dionysius, Gregory the Great, Bernard, Bonaventure, and Gerson. Sandaeus also uses a number of recent and almost contemporary sources. Constantin de Barbanson is the most often referenced, but Ignatius of Loyola, Teresa of Avila, and John of the Cross also appear.[18] Unusual sources that appear only once or twice (e.g., Origen, the *Theologia Deutsch*, Suso, and Pico della Mirandola) testify to the wide range of his reading.

The structure of the *Clavis* is alphabetical, but also scholastically organized under various divisions, often featuring what Sandaeus calls *disquisitiones*, which are really a form of *quaestio* that divides the material into its component issues. The Preface (*Praeambula*) with five chapters provides a sense of what the Jesuit was trying to accomplish. The first chapter addresses the issue of the occasion and usefulness of the work; the second gives a definition. "Mystical theology, if you look to the etymology," says Sandaeus, "signifies the hidden and covered knowledge of God and divine things, which is possessed by some special people, so that it ought not, or is usually not, manifested to others."[19] In typical fashion, the Jesuit gives several more definitions, before describing the "mystical theologian" as "[a] perfect contemplative, one who having put the passions to sleep, overcome his defects, inheres to God alone, and seeks him in all things and knows how to find him" (chap. 2, ed., 4). In the important third chapter Sandaeus lays out the main principles governing the work, namely, the defense of the special nature of mystical theology as contrasted with other forms of discourse and knowledge. He says, "Mystics have their way of speaking [*suum stylum*], so that whatever care is taken to subvert their formulas of speaking, proper language, and phrasing [i.e., of mystical theology] will not be worse than what happens when any discipline, art, or science, as can be shown from other disciplines, which have their different topics used by alien ways of speaking and writing" (*Clavis*, ed., 4). Sandaeus doubles down by claiming, "The mode [*character*] of the mystics is obscure, knotty [*involutus*], elevated, sublime, abstract, and in a way inflated. Their way of speaking has frequent hyperboles, excesses, improprieties. Their terms make, if not discover, exaggerations [*grandiloquia*], which is why their critics accuse them of grandstanding [*granditas affectata*] (*Clavis*, ed., 4). Like his Spanish predecessors, Sandaeus goes on to defend the peculiarities of mystical discourse, such as its neologisms, its heavy use of metaphors, its employing of dissimilar symbolism in the manner of Dionysius, and its necessary appeals to ineffability. "Mystical words hide more than reveal," according to the Jesuit. This is especially the case with the language of love. "Love has its own logic [*dialectum*]," he says, "in which the mystics often speak. In it, the usual expressions of love are not to be taken in the proper sense, but metaphorically [*per tropum*] according to the desire of the lovers" (*Clavis*, ed., 8–9). The Jesuit also notes that mystical language employs terms not much used in the scholastic theology of his day, but that have an ancient and orthodox provenance, such as *illapsus immediatus in anima* ("[divine] immediate descent into the soul"), *amor mysticus omnis cognitionis expertus* ("mystical love exceeding all knowledge"), and *fundus animae potentiarumque eius distinctione* ("the ground of the soul and its distinction from its powers"). Finally, he defends the appeal of the mystics to experience by noting that in recent time experience has proven that many long-accepted notions turned out not to be true (e.g., that the torrid zone of earth could not support life). Why, then, not believe the experience of the holy persons who have given their lives over to prayer?[20]

Sandaeus's defense of the mystics is revealing, not only because he relies so heavily on mystics like Tauler, Ruusbroec, and Harphius, which some Jesuit generals had forbidden, but also because he defends mystical expressions, such as *inactio* (*inwerken*, i.e., God's descent to take over the soul's operations) and *unio essentialis* (*weselike einung*; essential union), that had recently been attacked.[21] The large number of terms and themes treated provide an excellent road map of the state of "mystical science" in the first half of the seventeenth century. Major topics are treated in considerable detail. The longest section, that devoted to *Amor*, takes up thirty-seven pages and discusses 106 different kinds of love, such as *amor rationalis, amor amicitiae, amor concupiscentiae, amor unitivus, amor super-fervidus, amor purus, amor essentialis, amor ecstaticus,* and *amor super-essentialis*. The section devoted to *Contemplatio* is shorter (three pages), although it defines twenty-five different kinds. *Deificatio* and *deiformitas* occupy twelve pages, with each term being examined in four careful treatments (*disquisitiones*). Sandaeus is insistent on the fact that *deificatio/deiformitas* must be seen as accidental, not essential. As he puts it, "The teaching of the mystics is that deity essentially belongs only to God the Father, the Son, and the Holy Spirit. Personally, it belongs to the man Christ who is the partner of the divine nature by the Hypostatic Union. . . . The faithful and the just are partners [*consortes*] of the divine nature, although accidentally, as all ought to admit, through the gift of sanctifying grace, which is an accident infused by God" (*Clavis*, ed., 178). Many other typical mystical themes and terms are discussed,[22] as well as images and symbols favored by the mystics.[23]

A major treatment, as might be expected, is given to the related terms *unio* and *unitas* (*Clavis*, ed., 365–72). Union is treated in five *disquisitiones*. The first asks about the different kinds of union. In treating the meaning of *unio mystica*, Sandaeus refers the reader back to twenty-two issues taken up in his earlier work on mysticism. The second *disquisitio* addresses the question, "What is mystical uniting [*Quid sit unitio mystica*]?" Uniting is union in process (*in fieri*) and is defined as follows: "Mystical uniting is that action by which the mind of the contemplative is joined to God in a certain hidden manner. Mystical union is the end of this uniting, through which the contemplative mind remains joined to God" (*Clavis*, ed., 366). To the third question, that is, whether union is immediate or not, Sandaeus responds by quoting Harphius's rendering of Ruusbroec's three modes of union (with medium, without medium, and without distinction). He seems to accept even the third union as one arrived at "in essential love, through which, with the essential union it has with God, infinitely exceeds its intellect" (*Clavis*, ed., 368). The fifth *disquisitio* denies that union should be conceived of as a formal uniting with God (i.e., that God becomes the form of the soul) but accepts the controversial terms *unio essentialis* and even *unio sine distinctione*, at least as understood by Ruusbroec. The treatment of *unitas* is briefer with only three *disquisitiones*. The second of these accepts the terms used by Dionysius, Tauler, Ruusbroec, and Harphius of *unitas supereminens, essentialis, deiformis*, but insists on understanding these in an orthodox way: "Super-eminent unity, which is also essential to the soul, is the peak and apex of the mind. In this unity the mystic becomes like God through grace and the virtues."[24]

Sandaeus several times warns against the "false mystics" (*pseudomystici*; e.g., *Clavis*, ed., 11, 182, 295–96), but he does not name names. It is clear, however, that although he was willing to employ words and terms that some in his time thought dangerous, he was careful and precise about the theological understanding of mystical discourse, however special it might be in its own domain. One good example can be found in his treatment of that key seventeenth-century theme *annihilatio* (*Clavis*, ed., 99-103). He begins by distinguishing between philosophical, or scholastic, annihilation and mystical annihilation. "Mystical annihilation," as he defines it, "is according to likeness [*similitudinaria*], improper, moral, and signifies the perfect cessation of preceding qualities and affections in a person. . . . Clearly the being [*esse*] that existed does not cease; this union is not physical, but moral. And thus the person is other than he had been."[25] Therefore, when the mystics write that the contemplative's soul is annihilated in mystical union, "[t]hey are to be understood not according to philosophical or physical annihilation, but of mystical and moral." He then distinguishes between two kinds of mystical annihilation, the intellectual annihilation by which we recognize that we possess nothing of our own that deserves the gift of grace, and affective annihilation by which "a person so desires to be cast down and humiliated that he is held as nothing by everyone" (*Clavis*, ed., 101-2). Under the related term *annullatio* Sandaeus cites with approval Peter Blomeveen's "Introduction" to Harphius's *Theologia mystica* to the effect that "[i]t would be foolish to believe that the Mystical Doctor wanted to assert that the rational soul is annulled or converted into God, because the second is totally impossible and the first is quite absurd. This would be as if in order to be made blessed, it would be necessary to be reduced to nothing, when indeed, someone who does not exist cannot be made blessed" (*Clavis*, ed., 102). This view would seem to rule out all "strong" annihilation language. Nevertheless, the Jesuit goes on to make a distinction that brings him closer to some mystics who insist on annihilation of our own operations: "Annulling and annihilation are to be understood of the unlikeness of our spirit to God, and also regarding our own activity [*propriae actionis*]. Our spirit in some way ceases from this activity when it undergoes 'inaction' [*inactio/inwerken*], that is, the internal operation of the Spirit of God" (ibid.).[26] A position like this would allow for Bérulle's understanding of annihilation, although there is no evidence that the Jesuit had read the French cardinal. Another example of the Jesuit's careful treatment of controversial issues is his entry on *resignatio ad infernum* (the "impossible supposition" of some French mystics). Sandaeus recognizes that many mystics, in dependence on Paul (Rom. 9:3) use such language, but he insists that the mystics do not teach "resignation to eternal damnation" insofar as it involves the lack of grace and hatred of God. What the mystics mean by these expressions is that "they would remain resigned, patiently suffering even the pains of hell for God's glory, if that seemed to be God's desire" (*Clavis*, ed., 315).

Another German Jesuit who made a contribution to mysticism is Friedrich Spee von Langenfeld (1591–1635).[27] Spee was born at Kaiserwerth near Düsseldorf and received a humanist education at the Jesuit College in Cologne. He entered the order in 1610, did his novitiate at Trier and philosophical studies at Würzburg. Ordained in 1623, Spee taught at Paderborn and Cologne. During these early years he wrote numerous *Spiritual Songs* (*Geistliche Lieder*), for which he is best known today, since many of them are still used in the Catholic liturgy. At Cologne in the late 1620s he wrote the *Golden Book of Virtues* (*Güldenes Tugend-Buch*), a popular moral handbook on faith, hope, and charity. Spee was involved in giving spiritual succor to those accused of witchcraft during these years of the height of the Witch Craze in Germany. This experience convinced him that accusations of witchcraft were a hoax, so in 1631 he published (anonymously) a treatise called the *Criminal Warranty, or Procession against Witches* (*Cautio criminalis, seu Processio contra Sagas*) addressed to the civil authorities responsible for the cases against witches. His authorship became known, however, and he was attacked by persecuting bishops and others. To forestall his opponents, the Jesuit provincial sent him to Trier to teach moral theology. It was here that Spee completed his major mystical work, the collection of fifty-two lyrics on the love between God and the soul he called the *Resisting-Nightingale* (*Trutz-Nachtigall, oder geistlich-poetisch Lustwaldlein*), although the work was not published until 1649.[28] Trier was caught in the midst of the Thirty Years' War, and Spee served as a chaplain for sick soldiers. While performing this apostolic work, he caught the plague and died on August 7, 1635.

Well known for his German hymns, widely admired (at least today) for his opposition to the Witch Craze, Spee has also been much studied by scholars of German Baroque literature. According to Wilhelm Emrich, "Friedrich Spee ... had the merit, along with, and even shortly before Martin Opitz, of creating a completely new, formally complete, lyric poetry in the early years of the seventeenth century."[29] Spee has been less often treated as a mystic,[30] and he is virtually unknown in the English-speaking world. Here I can only provide a few introductory remarks.

Spee is universally recognized as a typical Baroque poet, part of a distinctive international literary movement (ca. 1580–1680) found in almost all the countries of Western and Eastern Europe, as well as in Spanish Latin America, as Harold B. Segel has shown.[31] It is not surprising that a good deal of the poetry of the Baroque era was religious and mystical in nature. Friedrich Spee's lyrics are a case in point. The Jesuit's poetry, however, is different from the better-known and more speculative poetry of Johann Scheffler, or Angelus Silesius. (Scheffler, as we shall see below, combined both the speculative and the affective dimensions of mysticism in his work.) Friedrich Spee was resolutely affective. Two themes dominate the *Resisting-Nightingale*: the burning desire of the soul-bride for the Divine Bridegroom; and the impulse to praise God for the beauties of creation (something that helps explains his popularity among the German Romantics).

Friedrich Spee's *Resisting-Nightingale* has three basic groups of poems: (1) Nos. 2-18, lyrics on the love of the human and divine spouses, illustrating *amor concupiscientiae*, or love of desire; (2) Nos. 20-29, poems praising God for creation expressing *amor benevolentiae* (love of delight); and (3) Nos. 30-50, a series of Eclogues, or shepherd songs, with Christ as the loving shepherd. Among the love poems are two unusual examples of the traditional form of the "echo-poem."[32] In the praise poems there is also a doctrinal lyric, "A Very High Praise-Song in which the Mystery of the Hidden and Very Holy Trinity will be Portrayed, both Theologically and Poetically, as Far as Possible." This poem might be compared with John of the Cross's poems on the Trinity, especially Nos. 1-2 of his "Romances."[33]

An example of the poems praising God for creation is No. 25, "Another Praise on the Works of God" ("Anders Lob auss den Wercken Gottes").[34] The nine stanzas are reminiscent of the psalms that praise God through his creation, but the lyric does not call on created things to praise God, as in the Psalms but is directed to humans to render adequate thanks to the Creator by pondering the wonders of his works. Stanza 1 addresses the musical instruments of praise as if they were living beings, while in stanzas 2-6 every distich begins with "Who?" (*Wer*), inviting the reader to meditate on the source of all the beauties of creation: "Who has in silver and in gold / The moon and sun adorned? [*Wer hat in gold- und silber-stück / Die Sonn und Mond gekleidet?*]." The answer to the constant hammering question "Who?," already obvious, is made explicit in the last three stanzas. Stanza 7 proclaims, "It is Our Lord, alone, alone, / Who does these deeds perform; / If but the trumps His word make known, / Peace follows on the storm. / Then hasty run toward His hand / The creatures of his mind [i.e., humans], / Full of His might will every land / Rich birth of marvels find." One may, of course, question whether this is a mystical poem, but it is arguably a form of Christian nature mysticism in which God is experienced in and praised through his creation.

More central to the *Resisting-Nightingale* are the poems of erotic longing of the bride for the Bridegroom. These are influenced by the language and images of the Song of Songs but are also colored by the traditions of pastoral love poetry, beginning with Greek and Latin literature (Anacreon, Virgil, etc.), and moving on to more recent Petrarchan models. Spee's lyrics are all about longing, burning, and desire. Actual union, whether erotically conceived, or as some kind of daring merging with the Beloved, is generally absent. Thus, Bernard Gorceix identifies three dominant structures in Spee's poems: (1) optimistic confidence in God; (2) praise for the good Creator; and (3) the theme of desire that organizes and channels the first two.[35] As in the Song of Songs, the Jesuit poet sets his love scenes within natural settings that provide a context emphasizing the more-than-personal dimension of the love relation with God. The main theme, however, is the powerful Jesus-devotion characteristic of Catholic Baroque literature.

As an illustration, we can look at No. 3, "The Spouse of Jesus Laments Her Heart's Flame" ("Die Gesponss Jesu Klagt Ihren Hertzenbrand"), a poem of seven stanzas.[36] The poet-lover sets the natural stage in stanzas 1–3 by painting a picture of how the flame of love in his heart is constant, no matter what the time of day or season of the year. But what is this flame? Stanza 4 tells us, "The flame of which I think / Is Jesus Christ's sweet name. / And bone and marrow sink / All strangely in its flame. / Of loving born of pain! / Oh pain born lovingly! / Oh in my heart remain / For all eternity!" The translation cannot do justice to the antithetical conciseness of the original.[37] The remaining stanzas repeat the basic message in various tropes. The love the soul has for Jesus is both torment and satisfaction, hunger and feeding, "sweet fire" and "bitter flame," desire and repose. There is no closure here, only patient waiting to escape the world while one experiences the paradoxical wounded fulfillment of a love that cannot be fully satisfied in this life.[38] Such unresolved but dynamic tension between polarities is characteristic of Spee's mystical love lyrics.

Johannes Scheffler (Angelus Silesius)

Life and Works

The one German mystic from this period who is known to more than a few specialists is Johannes Scheffler (1624–1677), who renamed himself Angelus Silesius, the "Silesian Angel." His main work, *Der Cherubinischer Wandersmann* (*The Cherubic Pilgrim*), is among the most original mystical texts of the seventeenth century. The literature on Scheffler is mostly in German;[39] there is a considerable amount in French,[40] though far less in English.[41]

Silesia was a borderland between modern Poland, Germany, and the Czech Republic, a territory of contention between Catholics and Protestants, as well as political struggles between the Hapsburgs and other powers. It was home to many religious and esoteric currents, as can be seen in the case of the noted mystic Jacob Boehme, who died the year that Scheffler was born.[42] Scheffler's family was Polish and Protestant and had to flee persecution to take up residence in Breslau (Polish Wrocław). The young man received an excellent education in the schools of the city and went on to study medicine, first at Strassburg, then at Leiden, and finally at Padua, where he took a degree in 1648. In the openness of Dutch Leiden the young scholar seems to have come into contact with esoteric material, such as the writings of Jacob Boehme, and other mystical, and perhaps even Kabbalistic, literature. Such writings were anathema to the rigid Lutheran dogmatism in which he had been raised, as was the exuberant Counter-Reformation Catholic piety he experienced during his time at Padua. In 1648, Scheffler returned to Silesia to become the physician of Count Sylvius Nimrod of Würtemberg-Oels. During the next few years he became close to Abraham von Franckenberg (1593–1652), the foremost disciple of Boehme, who left Scheffler his extensive library when he died, a collection that included a number of mystical and esoteric texts.[43]

This reading, as well as Scheffler's inner life, began to move him in a strongly mystical direction. In 1652, he was prevented from publishing a book of extracts from the medieval mystics by the Lutheran court preacher, a setback that seems to have helped him decide that the form of Christianity he felt called to was not Protestant orthodoxy, but Roman Catholic mystical spirituality. He converted to Catholicism on June 12, 1653, an event that precipitated a public exchange of vituperative pamphlets between Protestants and Catholics. In 1657, Scheffler published the first five books of *The Cherubic Pilgrim*, although he had begun working on these Alexandrine two-line epigrams as early as 1650, when he was still a Protestant.[44] In the same year he put out *Holy Joy of the Soul, or Spiritual Shepherd Songs* (*Heilige Seelenlust oder Geistliche Hirten-Lieder*), five books of pastoral poems (204 eclogues) about the love between the soul and the shepherd Jesus (*Jesulein*, or "little Jesus").[45]

In 1661, Scheffler was ordained a priest and during the next few years served in various ecclesiastical positions, although he also continued giving medical assistance to his flock.[46] He also began publishing a series of strong attacks against Protestantism, culminating in a collection he called *Ecclesiologia* that came out in 1677, the year of his death.[47] In 1675, he published a series of poems on the "four last things" (death, judgment, hell, and heaven), the *Sense Description of the Four Last Things* (*Sinnliche Beschreibung der vier letzten Dinge*). Also in 1675 he put out the second edition of his main work, *The Cherubic Pilgrim*, adding a sixth book rather different in tone from the first five.[48]

Scheffler's last contribution to mysticism came out in 1677. This was his translation of one of the masterworks of sixteenth-century mysticism, the anonymous Dutch *Great Evangelical Pearl*, which Scheffler translated from the Latin edition of 1545.[49] The brief preface he wrote to this version summarizes his commitment to conveying mystical wisdom to a wide audience. Scheffler praises the *Pearl* as "truly an incomparable treasure." He goes on, "I dare to say it is the one costly pearl among all spiritual books for the sake of which one ought to sell all the other books to buy this one alone." The purpose of this book and all other spiritual works is to cast off the "old man" and put on the "new man, who, following God, is created in holiness and justice and all the godly virtues, so that we may finally gain the state where we are changed totally and fully (like glowing iron in fire) into God, one spirit with him, and ourselves becoming the living book of eternal life in and with Christ Jesus."[50]

Sources, Style, and Perspective

1. Sources

Johann Scheffler was well educated and widely read. What survives of his library indicates the range of his interests, including alchemical works, radical spiritualist mystics (Valentin Weigel), and six works of Jacob Boehme. This list (numbered I–XXXIX now in the Breslau library), as well as mystical authors named in the "Preface" (*Vorrede*) to *The Cherubic Pilgrim*, demonstrates that the Silesian was familiar with a broad range of Catholic mysticism. With regard to medieval authors, he possessed volumes of Bonaventure, Hugh of Balma, Mechthild and Gertrude of Hackeborn, Tauler and Pseudo-Tauler, Ruusbroec, the *Theologia Germanica* (or *Theologia Deutsch*) Bridget of Sweden, and Savonarola. Of sixteenth- and seventeenth-century authors, he had the *Evangelical Pearl*, Blosius, John of the Cross (a Latin version), Victor Gelen, and Sandaeus's *Clavis*, which he extensively annotated.[51] Many of these names are mentioned in the "Preface," along other important mystical authors, such as Augustine, Bernard of Clairvaux, William of St.-Thierry (masquerading as Bernard in the *Golden Letter*), Harphius, Denys the Carthusian, Tomás de Jesús, Nicolás de Jesús-María, and Marina de Escobar, a Spanish mystic whose life was written by Luis de la Puente. Sandaeus is singled out for special praise: "Along with these, especially Maximilian Sandaeus of the Society of Jesus who has beyond measure served the lovers of this divine art with his *Mystical Theology* and *Key*" (ed., 25–26). Sandaeus was a major resource for Scheffler, but there is an important difference between them: whereas the Jesuit summarized mystical authors under alphabetical headings, the Silesian forged something new out of tradition. What his background in Christian mystical literature makes clear is that it is difficult to think of Scheffler as an esoteric or aberrant mystic, although he did make use of themes from Boehme and alchemy from time to time.

What was Scheffler's relation to the Northern European mystical tradition stretching from Meister Eckhart to such sixteenth-century figures as Blosius and the *Pearl* author? Many have noted the sometimes striking similarities between Eckhart and Scheffler but have said that he could have had only indirect connection with the Dominican Meister through Tauler and others, such as Ruusbroec.[52] This is true in the main, but now we know that there is authentic Eckhartian material in the *Institutiones divinae* ascribed to Tauler, a text that Scheffler knew.[53] Many of the more speculative aspects of *The Cherubic Pilgrim* (e.g., the Godhead/God distinction, God as *ein einig ein*, the soul's preexistence in God, the eternity of creation, the birth of the Word in the soul, union of identity, and so on) are the Silesian's reworking of themes that go back to Eckhart, but there are also real differences. Among the most important is the presence of a strong nuptial mysticism that is lacking in Eckhart (though present in Suso). Also significant is the difference in the mode of presentation. As Isabelle Raviolo summarizes, "If Eckhart conceptualizes, Silesius reinvests these theological concepts in order to integrate them into a poetic form (*une poétique*) where the reader is no longer invited to follow a preaching program, but to listen to a mystical chant."[54] Alois M. Haas makes a similar point, although not in terms of a contrast between Eckhart and Scheffler, when he says that the Silesian's intent was "to transpose teaching into life and belief into experience."[55] These observations raise the issue of the poetic style of Scheffler's mysticism.

2. Style

Conveying mystical insight in poetic form had been a part of Christian tradition for centuries. In adopting a poetic mode of presentation, *The Cherubic Pilgrim* was not breaking new ground. Even with regard to the particular poetic form, the Alexandrine distich, or couplet, Scheffler was not a pioneer. He was a friend of the Silesian Protestant humanist, poet, and mystic Daniel Czepko, whose *Six Hundred Single Distichs of the Wise* (*Sexcenta Monadistica Sapientium*) had been published in 1648. A detailed comparison of these two Silesian mystical poets is outside the scope of this presentation, but such an investigation would be revelatory for understanding this poetical moment in the history of Western mysticism.[56] Johannes Scheffler may not have been an innovator in choosing Alexandrines, but the way in which he uses this style, fusing form, expression, and message into a vehicle that at once attracts, incites, and often puzzles the reader in its revealed concealment is often striking. Scheffler's fusion of a distinctive rhetorical form (the epigram expressed in the rigid confines of the Alexandrine) and challenging mystical message (often compared to Eckhart and his followers) was something new—a style that continues to attract many readers and doubtless repels others, who find it perhaps too clever, facile, even artificial. The distichs of *The Cherubic Pilgrim* can be all of these, but they are often much more. It is up to the reader to determine what is moving, what is brilliant, and what is pedestrian. Scheffler's main intent was to arrest his audience with a shock of mystical insight and compel them to new ways of thinking.

The Alexandrine takes its name from the poetic form first used in the Old French *Alexander Romance*—two lines of twelve or thirteen syllables each with a strong caesura and end rhyme. The form lent itself to epigrams, that is, aphorisms of a witty or satirical nature. It was widely used in poetry of the Renaissance, Baroque, and early modern periods. Most of *The Cherubic Pilgrim* is written in these distichs, although there are some four-liners and a few longer poems. The distichs are given titles and usually stand alone, though a key word in one distich may be picked up in the following two-liner, often to be reversed or enriched. There are also groups of distichs that treat the same topic.[57]

Since there is no real order in the distichs, it is obvious that they were intended to be mini-meditations, aphorisms designed to inspire the reader to deeper consideration of the topic in question. Some scholars (e.g., von Balthasar, Haas, and Schmidt) have stressed the meditative aspect and seen a background in Ignatian meditation techniques aimed at spiritual conversion.[58] Some of the couplets are straightforward, but many are puzzles built on antitheses, either of opposition or reversal. As Maria M. Böhm puts it, "In Angelus Silesius we will find all possible combinations of antithetical structures, whether logical or contradictory, strictly formal or poetically free. Antithesis is the core of Angelus Silesius' *Formgebung*, the way he gives form to his thought."[59] An example of antithetical opposition dealing with the same subject can be found in CW 1.45: "Wer nichts begehrt, nichts hat, nichts weiss, nichts liebt, nichts will, / Der hat, der weiss, begehrt und liebt noch immer viel" ("The one who does not desire, nor possess, nor know, nor love, nor will, / Still does possess, does know, does desire and love very much").[60] An example of an antithetical reversal where the subject changes back and forth is CW 2.180: "Ich bin nicht Ich noch Du: du bist wohl Ich in mir! / Drum geb ich dir, mein Gott, allein die Ehrgebühr" ("I am neither I nor You; you are clearly I in me! / Therefore, I give you, my God, alone the honor" [ed., 145; my trans.).

Oxymora and paradoxes abound in Scheffler's distichs. The mini-contemplations of these couplets are at once lyric in form and aphoristic and paradoxical in their rhetoric. Many of the paradoxes seem unrelieved, at least on the level of ordinary logic. As Mariel Mazzocco puts it, "The secret harmony of the *Cherubinischer Wandersmann* pours forth the dissonances and antitheses nourished by the Alexandrines. Nonetheless, this paradoxical character does not imply a resolution of the antitheses, but their overcoming (*dépassement*). Far from reducing the contradictions it expresses, the paradox exalts and exacerbates them."[61] Paradox is strong in religious writing, especially in mystical texts. As Matthew Bagger suggests, "Religion celebrates paradox because it forms the basis for techniques of self-transformation."[62] Scheffler's *Cherubic Pilgrim* is a good example of teaching by paradoxical aphorism, although similar methods had been used before in Christian mysticism. Although he would not have known this literature, Scheffler's couplets are reminiscent of the "centuries," that is, the groups of a hundred short mystical aphorisms that Evagrius Ponticus, the fourth-century monastic teacher, used to convey his message. The desert father's aphorisms were usually brief and often cryptic or paradoxical.[63] They were not meant to be read quickly but to be pondered, just like Scheffler's Alexandrines. The ambiguities of Evagrius's centuries and Scheffler's distichs invite the reader to abandon the surface of the text and plunge into the issues presented in search of deep mystical meaning. Thus, Scheffler's verses often seem incomplete, spurring the reader to try to find the full significance. Bernard Gorceix summarizes this aspect: "The distich appears as an endeavor, always directed to being checked, to search out adequate language to express the living dynamism that leads to mystical union."[64] In his anthology of mystical texts, Harvey J. Egan offers this summary of Scheffler's mystical style: "By blending images, themes, paradoxes, aphorisms, antithetical statements, and dissonance, these couplets dazzle, delight, and unite both the mind and the heart with the object of their longing: the ineffable God."[65]

3. The Angelic Perspective

What I mean by the angelic perspective is suggested by the new name that Johannes Scheffler chose for himself (Angelus Silesius), as well as by the title of the poem, *Der Cherubinischer Wandersmann*. Why the new name, and what does it have to do with the figure of a "Cherubic Pilgrim"? An investigation may cast light on some of the issues about the work that have puzzled readers and initiated considerable debate.

Since the time of the Dionysian writings, especially the CH, the role of the angelic hierarchies had been important in mystical traditions.[66] The mystic's ascent to union with the Ineffable, according to Dionysius, is powered by divine grace acting in and through the nine hierarchies of the angelic host. This general ascensional process was given a more systematic form in the thirteenth-century commentaries on the Dionysian corpus by Thomas Gallus, which emphasized Seraphic love as the height of the mystical path and is therefore often characterized as "Affective Dionysianism." This tradition was influential on many Franciscan mystics, such as Bonaventure, whose *Mind's Journey into God* was familiar to Scheffler. Becoming angelic in form (angelization), especially in the case of the highest hierarchy (Thrones, Cherubim, and Seraphim), was an influential way of presenting the mystical ascent. Hence, for Bonaventure, Francis of Assisi is the *vir seraphicus* par excellence (Scheffler himself calls Francis a Seraph in CW 3.47). Scheffler's new name, *Angelus Silesius*, indicates his taking on a form of angelization that was revelatory of the message he wished to convey.

Scheffler's two major works reflect this angelic self-understanding, with *Der Cherubinischer Wandersmann* (CW) expressing the contemplative knowledge of the Cherubim and *Heilige Seelenlust* (HS) the burning love of the Seraphim. Gorceix insists on the need to study both the "Cherubic face" and the "Seraphic face" of the mysticism of the Silesian Angel.[67] The love of the Seraphim represents the highest angelic order, but both love and knowledge are necessary for the soul seeking union, as Scheffler says in CW 3.196: "Wisdom gazes at God, Love kisses him: / Alas, that I am not full of love and complete wisdom."[68] While Seraphic love of Jesus is most evident in *Holy Joy of the Soul*, the Seraphic side of the Silesian Angel is by no means lacking in *The Cherubic Pilgrim*, as the numerous couplets relating to love in general and to nuptial love of Jesus demonstrate. To cite just a few examples. CW 1.83 proclaims, "What joy must there be when God entrusts himself to his Bride / In his Eternal Son through his Spirit." CW 2.38 says, "You can recognize God as your Lord in any way you want, / I will give him no other name but my Bridegroom." Calling to mind the Song of Songs, CW 3.78 speaks of the "Spiritual Shulamite": "God is my Solomon, I am his Shulamite, / when I love him with all my heart and he summons me to him."[69] Book 5 has a series of couplets on God as Love (5.241–46), and there are many more. The frequency of the themes of love and the nuptial couplets in every book show that it is possible to grasp both sides of Scheffler's angelization program from *The Cherubic Pilgrim*, although perhaps not to the fullest extent.[70]

There is still another dimension to the angelic perspective. In her essay "The Speculative Mysticism in *Der Cherubinischer Wandersmann* of Johannes Angelus Silesius," Louise Gnädinger analyzed the centrality of the angels to the Silesian's mysticism. "And so," she states, "Scheffler's presentation and concept of mystical contemplation and union with God, something that was the result of his reading of medieval and contemporary spiritual writers, but certainly also of his own experience, is especially clear in the angelic theme."[71] Gnädinger also shows that Scheffler not only took on the role of the Cherubim and the Seraphim in his journey to God, but that he sometimes spoke about going *beyond* the angelic realm and addressed his readers from a perspective of absolute oneness with God achieved in and through Christ. Being both angelic and "Super-Angelic" (*Überengelkeit*, CW 2.44) may help solve some of the problems that confront the reader in approaching *The Cherubic Pilgrim*.

In the course of the CW, Scheffler speaks of himself as not only writing from the perspective of the Cherubic contemplative (e.g., CW 2.184) and the Seraphic lover (e.g., CW 2.254, 3.71, 5.211) but also as sharing in the life of all three orders of the highest hierarchy of the angelic world, that is, the Thrones, Cherubim, and Seraphim. For example, CW 3.165 says, "Drei wünsch ich mir zu sein: erleucht wie Cherubim, / Geruhig wie ein Thron, enbrannt wie Seraphim" ("Three things that I would like to be: radiant as the Cherubim, / Tranquil as a Throne, enflamed as the Seraphim").[72] As exalted as these three orders are, there are a number of couplets where the Silesian asserts that human beings can go beyond any angel.

The "Super-Angelic" theme appears early in book 1.3 in a four-line poem: "Away, away, you Seraphim, you cannot give me life! / Away, away, all you Angels and what you all look at! / I do not want you now: I cast myself only / Into the uncreated sea of the naked Godhead."[73] The theme is often repeated. For example, in CW 3.203: "How boldly we are viewed! The highest Seraphim / Are covered before God; naked we may come to him." Again, in CW 4.145: "I, man, am far more noble than all the Seraphim, / I can be what they are; they never what I am."[74] To fallen humanity this realization of our oneness with God above all the angelic orders comes only through Christ: "The world is a pure nothing, the angels are the same: / Thus, I will be God and man in Christ Jesus."[75]

We can conclude that there is a double perspective in *The Cherubic Pilgrim*. On the one hand, Scheffler writes as a pilgrim (*viator*), a person on his way through life empowered by being able to share in the contemplative knowledge of the Cherubim, as well as the intense love of the Seraphim. On the other hand, he also can write from the perspective of a blessed soul in heaven (*comprehensor*), who enjoys oneness with God through the God-man who has taken on our human nature. John Tauler once accused the opponents of Meister Eckhart of not understanding the perspective of his preaching on union with God, saying, "One loving master taught you and told you about these matters, and you did not understand him. He spoke from eternity, and you took it as referring to time."[76] Something similar is claimed by the Silesian, "Time's like eternity, eternity like time, / Unless you do yourself between them draw a line."[77] Even clearer is CW 5.127: "The soul, eternal spirit, is itself above time: / It lives already here an everlasting life."[78] When the Silesian speaks from the perspective of the "Super-Angelic" *comprehensor*, one already enjoying eternal life here below, he is able to make daring claims about union with God that cannot but seem exaggerated, even dangerous, to those who are still on the pilgrim path.

Johann Scheffler's Cherubic Mysticism

As mentioned earlier, there has been much debate about the nature of Scheffler's mysticism. Concentrating on some verses (and often misunderstanding them), some interpreters have seen him as a pantheist,[79] an esotericist, or a kind of perennialist mystic better compared to Eastern rather than Western mystics. Others have doubted the sincerity of his conversion to Catholicism. Yet others have struggled to put together the speculative depth of *The Cherubic Pilgrim* with the effusive Baroque piety of *Holy Joy of the Soul*, and especially with the savage polemicism of his anti-Protestant works.[80] Recent scholarship, however, has tried to see Scheffler as a whole and has emphasized his deep knowledge of and rooting in the Christian mystical tradition, despite the novel aspects of his message and its form of presentation.[81] Debate about the nature of Scheffler's contributions to the mystical tradition will surely continue, but there can be no doubt that he created an impressive form of mysticism, at once speculative in its insights into the relation of God and humanity and emotional in its Jesus devotion. Many have seen this achievement as a synthesis of the traditions of late medieval Northern mysticism and the effusive Jesus piety of early modernity, especially as found in the popular devotions encouraged by the Jesuits. This may be true as a broad description, but it risks depriving Scheffler of his originality.

The kaleidoscopic character of *The Cherubic Pilgrim* precludes a distich-by-distich analysis, which would not be a synthetic interpretation but merely an extended commentary. The attempt at a broad picture given here will suggest the richness of some of the themes that seem necessary to grasp the message that the "Silesian Angel" wished to convey. It will be divided into two main parts: (1) The Mystery of Divine–Human Reciprocity; and (2) Dynamics of the Return to the Source.

1. The Mystery of Divine–Human Reciprocity
More than most mystics, the Silesian insisted on the reciprocal relation of God and the human person. It is true that there are many couplets that stress the difference between the divine nature and created humanity, but that is only one side of the story. On the deeper level, from the perspective of the "Super-Angelic," God needs man as much as man needs God. At the beginning of *The Cherubic Pilgrim* a series of distichs announces this challenging message. The first (CW 1.8) says, "I know that without me God cannot live a minute: / If I were annihilated, he would have to give up his spirit." The Silesian goes on: "That God is so blessed and lives without demand, / He has as much from me, as I have received it from him." CW 1.10 puts the same point in correlative terms: "I am as great as God; he is as small as me; / He cannot be over me, nor I under him." CW 1:11 expresses this interdependence through the image of fire and its illumination: "God is in me the fire

and I in him the light: / Aren't we totally one [*gemein*] in each other?"⁸²
We are reminded of Eckhart's daring statement in German Sermon
52: "If I did not exist, God would also not exist. That God is God,
of that I am a cause; if I did not exist, God too would not be God."⁸³
These couplets are introduced by a four-line poem that speaks about
the need for going beyond God, again evoking an Eckhartian theme,
the desert. CW 1.7 says, "Where is my dwelling place? Where I and
you can never stand. / Where is my final goal, toward which I should
ascend? / It is beyond all place. Where should my quest then be? / I
must go beyond God and into the desert flee."⁸⁴ This set of verses does
not explicitly mention the God/Godhead distinction used by both
Eckhart and Scheffler, but it suggests that the two mystics have much
the same message about the two aspects of the divine nature. "God"
conceived of as Creator is distinct from man as created being, but if we
go beyond that "God" to attain the desert of the "Godhead," then the
Creator God depends on us as much as we do on him. The mystery of
our identity with the Godhead is the foundation of the reciprocity of
God and human in Scheffler's thought. The God/Godhead distinction
seems to be behind the cryptic distich in which Scheffler, again not
unlike Eckhart, announces that we both live and die in God: "Die or
live in God! You must rightly do both, / Because a person must die in
God and God will also live."⁸⁵

The Divine Nature
The fact that the Godhead lies beyond all that can be expressed gives
rise to the many paradoxes in which the Silesian poet delighted. The
inexpressibility of God, the divine nature as both "named by all names"
(*omninominabilis*) and "unnameable" (*innominabilis*) is explicit in couplet CW 5.196: "One can give the highest God every name, / But again
one cannot ascribe any of them to him."⁸⁶ In the interplay of God and
Godhead, the God that can be given all names and the Godhead that is
utterly unnameable, the complexity of the Silesian's message unfolds.
Scheffler often evokes the Godhead, but, as befits his presentation by
antithesis, one has to construct what *Gottheit* means from many couplets. CW 1.249, for example, says "The Godhead makes God the way
that 'Goldness' makes gold" (ed., 87). In CW 2.12–13, two couplets
equate the Godhead with virginity (*Jungfrauschaft*) understood as pure
emptiness (*Lauterkeit*). The first states, "What is virginity? Ask what
the Godhead is! / Still you know pure emptiness, so you know them
both."⁸⁷ In CW 3.168 the Godhead is described as a fountain (*Brunn*):
"The Godhead is a fountain! From it all things come forth / And they

return there, so that it is also a sea [*Meer*]."⁸⁸ This brings together two of the Silesian's favorite aquatic images, long popular with mystics, to symbolize the procession (*exitus*) and return (*reditus*) of all things to the hidden divine source. The invocation of the sea in this couplet, a traditional image for the limitless expanse of divine being, is one that Scheffler applies both to *Gott* and the *Gottheit*.⁸⁹ CW 6.171–74 features a succession of distichs on God as ocean/sea and our sinking into total oneness with God. "The little drop becomes the sea, when it arrives at the sea: / The soul becomes God when it is taken up into God" (6.171; ed. 442; my trans.). CW 6.174, entitled "In the Sea the Many are One," even employs a term created by Eckhart to describe this absolute oneness: "Many grains of wheat are in bread, a sea is many drops of water: / So too our manyness in God becomes a Simple One [*ein einges Ein*]."⁹⁰ This Eckhartian term, probably known through Tauler, is found in a number of other couplets.⁹¹

Other forms of language used to portray the God/Godhead relation also recall Eckhart and other Northern mystics. Among these is the image of blooming. CW 1.81 says, "You are born from God, and so God blooms in you, / And his Godhead is your sap and adornment."⁹² Another Eckhartian image for the Godhead is used, though sparingly, namely, the "abyss" (*abgrunt*): "How deep the Godhead is no creature can grasp: / In its abyss even the soul of Christ must vanish."⁹³ There are, however, limits to Scheffler's use of Eckhartian language. For example, the term *grund* is only rarely used (three times by my count).⁹⁴ Jacob Boehme's neologism *ungrund* is used once: "God is certainly an *Ungrund*, yet to whom he shows his face / Must climb the summit of the eternal mountain."⁹⁵ The Silesian poet made use of images and terminology from the Eckhartian tradition, but not in a slavish way.

The attributes that Johannes Scheffler uses for the divine nature are those of the Christian theological tradition, especially oneness, being, eternity, love, and the like. He does not, however, always use them in expected ways. As the formula *ein einges Ein* indicates, the pure and simple Oneness of the divine nature is central for the Silesian. Book 5 opens with eight distichs on God as One and the way in which all multiplicity flows from and returns to the One. The first sets the theme: "Everything comes forth from the One and must go back into the One, / Where it will never be 'twoed' and exist in multiplicity."⁹⁶ Just as all numbers come from one, so all creatures have their origin in divine Oneness (5.2, 3, and 8). All will eventually be *ein einges Ein*: "All is one in the One, when two returns to One, / It has essentially a Single One become."⁹⁷ The divine unity appears throughout *The Cherubic Pilgrim*.

The Silesian, however, also insists that God is supreme being. For example, "The animal is known through instinct, the human through knowledge; / The angel through contemplation; God through being [*Wesen*]."⁹⁸ This Being, however, is not a concept or idea grounding an "onto-theology": "What is God's Being? Are you asking about my Limitation? / Yet know that it is a 'Beyond-Being' [*Überwesenheit*]." Thus, God's Being, just as his other attributes, is radically above all human conceiving.⁹⁹ This is why in CW 2.55 the Silesian says that God's mode of being is *eigentlich* (belonging to him alone), so that he cannot be said to live and love the way in which we do.¹⁰⁰ Even if God cannot be said to love the way in which humans love, Scheffler follows the Bible and Christian tradition in often speaking of God as love. This can be seen in another group of couplets, this time from CW 5.241–46, where we read: "There is no name that rightly belongs to God: / One can only call him Love (1 John 4:8), because it is so worthy and refined."¹⁰¹ In speaking of God as love, the Silesian uses another image for the divine nature hallowed by tradition: the circle and the point. CW 5.212 says, "The middle point of love is God and also the circumference: / In it love rests and loves everything in it in equal fashion."¹⁰²

These and the other usual attributes that Scheffler uses of God should not mislead us into thinking that his view of the divine nature is merely traditional. As we have seen, all of these positive terms are qualified by the apophatic imperative the Silesian shares with Dionysius, Eckhart, and his followers. *The Cherubic Pilgrim* sometimes seems to echo the expressions of John of the Cross that we must abandon everything created and take a path of negation that seems impossible to human efforts: "*God is Outside the Creature.* Go where you cannot go; see where you cannot see! / Hear where there is no sound; so you will be where God is speaking."¹⁰³ Echoing John of the Cross's "I know not what" in speaking of God, is the following couplet on eternity: "What is Eternity? It is not This or That, / Not Now, not Thing, not Naught; it is 'I know not what.'"¹⁰⁴ Scheffler's negative theology reaches a culmination in the six-line poem in CW 4.21, entitled *The Unknown God*, based on Dionysius's MT 5:

> No one knows what God is. He is not Light, not Spirit,
> Not Delight, not Oneness, not what is called Godhead,
> Not Wisdom, not Understanding, not Love, Will, Goodness,
> Not a Thing, not an Un-thing, not Being, not Mind [*Gemüte*].
> He is what I and you and no creature
> Ever knew before we became what he is.¹⁰⁵

The Silesian poet, like Eriugena, Eckhart, and others, does not shy away from speaking of God as "Nothing" (*nichts*), that is, the transcendent No-thing that lies beyond both light and darkness. In the distich entitled "God is Light and Darkness," he says, "God is pure Lightning and Dark Nothing / Which no creature can see with its own light."[106] Scheffler's God is the Trinitarian God of Christianity, as he makes clear throughout *The Cherubic Pilgrim*. The Silesian speaks of the Trinity often, both in traditional ways and in others that are more unusual. Since the twelfth century, Power, Wisdom, and Goodness had been seen as attributes ascribed to the three Persons. Scheffler uses the triad to characterize the activity of the Trinity: "Almighty Power holds the world, Wisdom governs it, / The Good blesses it; isn't God present here?"[107] Ruusbroec and his followers had spoken of the triune God as uniting both inward rest and loving dynamism. This view may be behind the distich in CW 5.283: "Because God is Trinitarian, he has rest and desire: / Rest comes from the Oneness, Desire from the breast of the Trinity."[108] Also traditional is the way in which the Silesian teaches that all three Persons are involved in the process of our salvation.[109] More unusual Trinitarian imagery also occurs. For example, Scheffler makes use of geometrical imagery, although this was not unknown in earlier tradition. CW 4.62 says, "God-Father is the point, out of him flows God the Son / The line; God the Holy Spirit is both the surface and the crown."[110] Like Jacob Boehme, Scheffler employs alchemical images, as in CW 1.257: "That God is triune, as every plant reveals; / Sulpher, salt, mercury are all in one concealed."[111]

Creation and Human Nature
Creation is in essence the manifestation of God, as the opening couplets of book 4 show. The poet says, "The unmade God in the midst of time, / Becomes that which he never was in all eternity"; and, "The uncreated light becomes a created being, / So that his creature can be completed only through it."[112] To the unwary this might look like pantheism, but to the theological tradition that sees creation as theophany, the fact that all things are God made manifest does not negate the truth that the unknown God is also always infinitely more than the world.[113] To call Silesius a "pantheist" makes little sense, just as accusations of pantheism against mystics like Eriugena, Eckhart, and Nicholas of Cusa are the result of an anachronistic projection of the Enlightenment *Pantheismusstreit* into earlier Christian history.

To the question of why God made the world, the Silesian has a simple answer—We don't know (CW 4.126)! In line with Eckhart and others, Scheffler suggests that creation can be conceived of as God's play: "*God Plays with Creation*. Everything is a game that the Godhead makes for itself: /It has conceived of creatures for its own pleasure."[114] Divine Wisdom (*die Jungfrau*) made the world and also redeems it (CW 3.195), and all creatures seek their rest in returning to God (CW 1.110). Once again, the Silesian reminds of us of Eckhart by insisting that, because there is no time in God, creation must be an eternal act (*creatio aeterna*): "Who will write down the year when God created the world? / It was not other than the first year of his Origin [*Urstands*]."[115] Again like Eckhart, this implies that creation was not just something in the past but is God's continuous act (*creatio continua*; see CW 4.165). The purpose of creation as theophany is to praise God (e.g., CW 1.264 and 4.193), as well as to reveal him, which Scheffler describes using the ancient image of creation as book: "Creation is a book, who reads it wisely, / Will find within the Creator well revealed."[116] Fundamentally, creation was made to show us the way to God (CW 3.102).

Among creatures, human nature takes a special place as both *imago Dei* and even *imago Trinitatis*.[117] Man as *imago Dei* has both a protological and an eschatological aspect. Protologically, CW 5.239 asks, "You put the question, why did God make me according to his image? / I say there was no one who brought him anything else." The following distich expresses the eschatological function: "When is the person brought back again to God fully? / When he is the model according to which God made him."[118] In other words, when the *imago* has been fully realized in us, we have returned to where we were first made. Scheffler's anthropology is not a detailed analysis of the components of human nature, its parts and powers. Rather, he is interested in the fundamental condition of humanity and its relation to God. A foremost issue is humanity's virtual existence in the divine mind—the fact that the true human is its ideal existence in God and not its particular and divided existence here below.

That all things have existed eternally as exemplary ideas in the mind of God was common teaching in the patristic and medieval world, although it had begun to be questioned from the time of William of Ockham in the fourteenth century. Angelus Silesius was still a firm believer: "The rose which here on earth is now perceived by me, / Has blossomed thus in God from all eternity."[119] And again: "In God everything is God; a single little worm, / That is in God as much as a thousand Gods."[120] This is especially true of humanity, the creature that has the capacity to know its ideal status: "Before I was I, I was a God in God: / Therefore, I can be that again, if I only die to myself."[121] There are several implications to be drawn from this teaching. One is that the soul remains a mystery even to itself: "I do not know what I am; I am not what I know: / A thing and not a thing, a little dot and a circle."[122] While there is thus a certain fragility, insecurity, and confusion in the human "I" taken in itself,[123] the true self ("Ich") is properly neither in space nor in time: "You are not in a place, the place is in you! / If you cast it out, Eternity will already be standing here."[124] This true self can be said to create time (CW 1.189), and to see all things as one, that is, the way they exist in the eternal now of God: *"The Equality.* I wonder what to do! To me it's all the same: / Place, no-place, eternity, time, night, day, joy and pain."[125] This transcendental "I" stands firm in God.

Like his French contemporary Jean-Jacques Olier, the Silesian uses the image of the soul as a crystal. The very first couplet of *The Cherubic Pilgrim* proclaims: "Pure as the finest gold, hard as a granite stone, / Wholly as crystal clear your mind [*Gemüte*] must become."[126] The term *Gemüte*, meaning mind, or inner spirit, which had been used by fourteenth-century mystics like John Tauler, is quite frequent in Scheffler. References to the major powers of the soul, such as intellect and will, also occur often enough, but there is no developed psychology of the faculties. The Silesian employs the Eckhartian term the "spark of the soul," but rarely;[127] he does mention Eckhart's view of the soul as both virgin and wife in a few places.[128] Scheffler has little concern for creating a systematic anthropology but is focused on how the soul in its uncreated/created nature responds to God.

The Mutuality of God and Humanity
As mentioned at the beginning of this section, what is remarkable about the Silesian poet is his insistence that, whatever the differences, God needs humanity as much as humanity needs God. The theological root of this claim is in the preexistence of the soul in God, a traditional teaching. Its implications had been explored by Eckhart and others, but perhaps no one pushed the limit-expressions of this teaching more strongly than the Silesian. This may be one of the reasons why those who have investigated him according to the categories of Aristotelian logic, with its either-or stance, have often seen him as a pantheist, or as radically confused. Looked at in terms of his mystical predecessors, however, the Silesian was taking his place in a long tradition. There are many texts on the mutuality of God and human, so only a few will be cited here. Such couplets are especially frequent in book 1. For example, CW 1.97 states, "God cannot make even a little worm without me! / Did I not hold it in being with him, it would have to break

apart at once."[129] The reciprocity pertains not just to creative activity but also to how God and the human interact; that is, the more we give ourselves to God, the more he must enter into us. As CW 1.138 states, "The more you can come out of yourself and be poured out, / The more must God with his Godhead flow into you."[130] One of the most striking of Scheffler's expressions of this comes from book 1.278: "I am God's Other-He [*ander Er*]: he only finds himself in me, / It is what will be like and similar to him in eternity."[131] This bold claim asserts that man is destined to fulfill God—dangerous heresy to some, but a logical conclusion to those who have understood what it means for God to have created humanity as the *imago Dei*.

Passages in the later books of *The Cherubic Pilgrim* repeat the message. For example, CW 2.201 has an Eckhartian ring: "Tell between me and God the only difference? / It is (put in one word) nothing but otherness [*Anderheit*]."[132] In book 3.202 the Silesian uses the theme of the wound of love (Song 4:9): "God cannot be wounded by anything, he has never received any pain: / And yet my soul can totally pierce his heart."[133] Book 5 also has couplets expressing how God and humanity need and complete each other. For example, CW 5.48 says that in order to escape death both God and man must work together: "Two must accomplish it; I cannot without God, / God cannot without me, make me escape death."[134] Mystics like Eckhart and Tauler had insisted that if the human person empties himself out in detachment and humility, God of his overflowing nature must come down to fill him. Silesius says the same: "Man, if your heart is like a valley, God must pour himself into it, / And surely so freely that he must fill it to overflowing."[135] The intimate need God has for us and our need for God grounds what the Silesian poet has to say about the path to mystical union.

2. The Dynamics of the Return
Three major issues will be taken up here. The first is the role of Christ the God-man in the return, including our marriage to Jesus and the birth of the Word in the soul. The second concerns the mystical practices the Silesian inculcates, which may be divided into two major components: the positive aspect, that is, love of God; and the negative aspect, the stripping away of the created self suggested by terms such as detachment, annihilation, poverty, silence, and especially releasement (*Gelassenheit*). Finally, we will consider his teaching on the nature of mystical union and deification. An important issue to keep in mind in considering the poet's presentation of the path to God is that he is not interested in psychological analysis of the inner states of the

mystic, but rather focuses his attention on the objective reality of the process by which we realize the deep union we always possess in the eternal "Now."[136]

The Role of Christ
Angelus Silesius shared the Christological emphasis of so many of the seventeenth-century mystics, although his way of expressing this was different from the French mystics.[137] The Silesian does not engage in theological analysis of the nature of the Incarnation. His Christology is devotional: the soul's love for Jesus as Redeemer is expressed as devotion to the mysteries of Christ's life, especially his birth and Passion, but there is not really a developed doctrine of the "states" of Christ's life, such as we find in Bérulle.[138] This form of Christology culminates in numerous couplets dealing with the marriage between the soul and Jesus. The final component in Scheffler's treatment of Christ is his teaching on the birth of the Word in the soul, something he takes over from the Eckhartian tradition.

Jesus-devotion, relatively rare in books 1 and 2, is frequent in books 3–5. Book 3 opens with thirty-two couplets on the birth of Christ and the events surrounding it, beginning with one on *"The Crib of Jesus.* This wood is costlier than Solomon's throne, / Because in it lay the true Son of God" (3.1; ed. 167). A number of these couplets concern praising Jesus with music: "Chant, all you angels, chant! With hundred thousand tongues / To this most blessed Child is scarcely homage done. / Oh! If only I were without a voice and tongue / I know that I could sing straightway the sweetest song."[139] Many of the distichs express the poet's amazement at the infinite God taking up his dwelling in a little infant. After the Christmas collection there follows a series of couplets (3.34–44) devoted to the cross and the Passion. Book 3 ends with another series of distichs on Christ's birth (3.239–49), and book 4 has a second Passion section (4.46–53). A number of individual couplets, especially on the Passion, appear in books 4 and 5. A good example is 5.82: "Tell me where love is found in her most cherished place? / Where to the Cross she's bound, for her Beloved's sake."[140]

Devotion to the humanity of Christ is meant to lead to his divinity, as Augustine and many others had taught. The Silesian agrees: "If you would like to catch the dew of divinity, / Unwaveringly adhere to its humanity."[141] The key to this adherence is to follow in Christ's footsteps, the *imitatio Christi* theme: *"This is Where You Must Begin.* Man, if you want to stand always with the Lamb of God, / You must here already go in his footsteps."[142] Such an imitation will result in the image of Christ being formed in us, as we are told in 5.264: "Man, when your heart before God is soft and pure as wax, / Then will the Holy Spirit impress the image of Jesus in it."[143] This image, however, is not a merely individual possession. The Silesian poet has a strong sense of the unity of all believers in the Risen Christ: "Multiplicity is God's enemy: this is why he draws us to become so one, / that all people shall be one thing in Christ."[144] Scheffler was thus a strong proponent of the Pauline doctrine of the Body of Christ. Christ's universal role in history is also emphasized: "The first and last man is Christ alone, / Because from him everything comes forth, and in him everything is concluded."[145]

The devotion to Jesus expressed in *The Cherubic Pilgrim* reaches a fulfillment in the marriage between Jesus, the Divine Bridegroom, and the soul-bride. Like many other mystics, Scheffler teaches that the marriage is made to the Incarnate Second Person of the Trinity, but that all three divine Persons are involved. This is set out in a six-line poem in book 3:

> The bride is my soul, the Bridegroom God's Son,
> The Priest is God's Spirit, and the Godhead's throne
> Is the place of the wedding. The wine which makes me drunk
> Is my Bridegroom's blood, the food is especially
> His divinized flesh. The chamber and the hall
> And the marriage bed is the Father's breast in which
>   we have sunk down.[146]

Scheffler turns to the Song of Songs 2:4 to describe the sacred marriage: "*From the Song of Songs.* The King himself leads the bride into the wine-cellar, / That she may choose for herself the very best wine. / So too God will do with you when you are his bride: / He has nothing in himself that he does not entrust to you."[147] Sweet kisses and marital union with the Bridegroom are described in a number of couplets (e.g., CW 3.51, 3.68, 3.235, 5.310). The Silesian poet insists that every soul can aspire to be a bride (CW 4.40), but there are conditions—the soul must bloom like the lily in virginal chastity (5.180, and 5.260). In another couplet he describes the kind of soul that becomes a bride, using an Eckhartian formula: "The soul that knows nothing, wants nothing, and loves nothing but the One, / Must today become the Bride of the eternal Bridegroom."[148]

The Silesian also reminds his readers of the suffering the spiritual marriage entails, especially the pains of love that wound the heart and make it melt like wax (CW 4.170–71). The biblical theme of the wound of love (Song 4:9) decrees that for the bride to be like the Bridegroom, she too must be wounded: "I must be wounded. Why? Because / My eternal Bridegroom, the Savior, was found full of wounds. / What is the importance of this for you? It is not fitting / When the bride and Bridegroom are not like each other."[149] In sum, the bride is the "most cherished child, . . . who rests in God's arms and bosom" (CW 2.10), where she enjoys the great reward of continued and increasing loving familiarity with the Bridegroom (CW 4.138).

Like Henry Suso, Johannes Scheffler has a mysticism that embraces both spiritual marriage with its erotic language and the Eckhartian theme of the birth of the Son in the soul (both appear in about forty couplets). He does not appear to try to show the connection between these two major mystical themes but sets them out side by side in his rhyming couplets. *The Cherubic Pilgrim* features three groups of distichs dealing with the birth of the Son. The first is in book 4.204-7, beginning: "The one whom God has born as his son on earth, / He can never more be separated from God." This essential (*wesentlich*) birth is said to be the whole point of holiness (4.205); those who live in unity and pure peace have the essence of virginity born in them (4.206). The final couplet describes the characteristics of such a son: "The person who remains in God, enamored and released, / He will be especially chosen as son of God."[150] The second group (5.249-52) has several couplets that stress the eternal nature of the birth—what takes place in us is the same as the Son's eternal procession from the Father (5.250-52). The last collection on the divine birth comes in book 6.129-34. Here the fact that God eternally bears me as his son is said to be the highest joy and delight (6.131), because bearing the Son from eternity is "God's single blessedness" (6.132). As the final couplet daringly puts it: "*To Be Born from God is to be Totally Divine.* God gives birth to nothing but God: if he bears you as his son, / You will be God in God, Lord on the Lord's throne."[151] Despite its poetic form, Silesius's doctrine of the birth of the Son in the soul is quite as daring as that of his forebears.

The Silesian poet sees the divine birth as necessary for salvation: "Were Christ to be born a thousand times in Bethlehem, / And not in you, you would remain lost forever."[152] Thus, the birth is described as God's highest blessing (CW 2.252, 4.230, 5.352), and also as a great mystery. As with Eckhart and his followers, to be born a son of God is also to be called upon to bear God with God: "*Out and In. Birthing and Being Born.* If in truth you can be born from God / And again give birth to God, you are able to go both out and in [*gehst du aus und ein*]," that is, receive God in yourself and bring him out to others.[153] This is why a number of couplets point to Mary as the model for the birthing process: "I must be Mary and bear God from out myself, / In order that he may eternally grant me blessedness."[154] The birthing motif is the crown of the Silesian's teaching on the role of Christ in bringing human beings to union.

Practices on the Cherubic Path
Johannes Scheffler's couplets describe attitudes and practices necessary for the pilgrim's journey. The essential positive practice is the love of God. Since God is love, as we have seen above, we must then become love in order to attain him (CW 1.71, 4.80, 5.317). Love is the inner life of all the virtues (CW 2.233, 5.289), and the holy person acts only from love (5.276). The love that draws us to God is actually "God's eternal power, his fire, and the Holy Spirit" (CW 5.296; ed., 367). Loving God, therefore, is inscribed into our mind [*Gemüt*] from creation (CW 2.36). The Silesian even has a version of the Augustinian motto "Love and do what you will" (*Ama et fac quod vis*): "*God Wants Only One Thing From Us.* A single word God speaks to me, to you, and all: / Love! If we do that through him, we must give him pleasure."[155] In dependence on Paul (1 Cor. 13:13), Silesius refers to love as outlasting faith and hope (CW 3.160, 3.230). Love, he says, does not seek any reward save God (CW 2.47, 5.293), and the love of God is always generous, unlike the love of the world (CW 4.87). Probably echoing Bernard of Clairvaux, Scheffler emphasizes that the true way of loving God is to love him without measure: "The person who loves God rightly does so without measure and goal; / God is so sweet and good that one can never love him enough."[156] Pure love is the essence of holiness (5.226).

Scheffler emphasizes the power of love. CW 2.2 says, "Love is a magnet which draws me into God; / And what is yet greater, it draws God into death [i.e., on the Cross]."[157] Eckhart had spoken about God being "compelled" to come down and fill those souls who emptied themselves through perfect detachment. For Silesius, love is the force that can compel God: "If it was not God's wish to raise me above God, / I should compel him thus, by force of sheerest love."[158] There are several groups of couplets on love in book 5 that sum up Scheffler's teaching. The first is in CW 5.199–201. CW 5.199 says that love's true object can only be the Highest Good, while 5.200 speaks of love's transformative power: "Man, you are what you love, and you will be changed into that: / You will be God, if you love God, and earth, if you love earth." Finally, 5.201 expresses the traditional theme of the ordering of love (Song 2:4): "*The Well-Ordered Love.* If you love God who is above you, your neighbor as your own life, / and what else there is below you, you will love rightly and evenly."[159] A little later on, in CW 5.212 (ed., 350; my trans.), the poet uses the point and circle image to describe love's nature: "The middle point of love is God and also its circumference: / You are at rest in him, and you love all in him in an equal fashion."[160]

An important point about love in Christian mysticism is the relation between knowledge of God and love of God. I have already cited CW 3.196, which says that the soul wants to be full of both the wisdom that beholds God and the love that kisses him. CW 6.220 says that love follows on the contemplative beholding (*aufs Schaun*) of eternal things. Despite this reciprocity, love remains supreme. Silesius holds that the ultimately unknowable God can still be loved: "I love one single thing, it is to me unknown; / And since I know it not, I chose it for my own."[161] When he compares love and knowledge, the poet insists that love is higher than knowing and brings us closer to God: "The nearest way to God is through the door of love: / The way of knowledge brings you there only very slowly."[162]

Under the heading of practices of negation we can include such important themes as detachment, poverty of spirit, releasement, silence, and annihilation of self. Most of these were rooted in the traditions of Northern European mysticism of the Late Middle Ages, but they were also important for many early modern mystics. Scheffler's teaching on these negations is summarized in a couplet on "not-seeking": "*One Finds God By Not-Seeking.* God is neither here nor there: someone anxious to find him, / Had best have hand and foot, body and soul, bound"; that is, our efforts to gain God may easily lose him. We have to empty ourselves and let go so that God can act in us.[163] Scheffler's distichs convey much epigrammatic wisdom about these emptying practices.

Detachment (*Abgeschiedenheit*) is a term that Scheffler does not employ often, though he mentions it occasionally, as in CW 2.67: "Because detachment does not make itself the same with anything, / It must be without desire like a virgin."[164] In CW 5.209, the purity of detachment is identified with the highest form of life: "Friend, you will want to know: the very highest life / Is to be detached and to stand surrendered to God."[165] More common than detachment is insistence on absolute poverty, the inner surrender of all will, knowledge, and possessing that Eckhart taught. Under the title "Poverty Is Divine," CW 1.65 says, "God is the poorest thing, he stands totally empty and free: / Therefore, I say well and truly that poverty is divine."[166] One notes here the Eckhartian language of *bloss und frei*, and the Silesian's couplets often employ similar terms, such as "empty" (*leer*), "poor" (*arm*), and "free from" (*ledig*). A number of other distichs deal with poverty, such as CW 2.148, 5.80, 5.344, and 6.167. The Silesian considered poverty important enough to devote a short collection of distichs to it in book 4.210-14. The first of these expresses the core of his message: "The poverty of our spirit consists in inwardness, / By which one denies everything and even himself."[167] Scheffler's poetic fragments make it difficult to construct a developed teaching on the nature of true poverty, but his insistence on its necessity is much in line with his German and Dutch predecessors.

A related negative theme is "annihilation," which we have treated in detail with regard to the French mystics. The Silesian poet talks about annihilating all self-interest and even the self, but not to the extent that we find in French mysticism. A few distichs are clear about the need for "Self-Annihilation": "Nothing elevates you more over yourself as annihilation [*Vernichtigkeit*]: / The person who is the more annihilated has the more divine likeness."[168] A similar message is found in CW 5.332, where we read: "In God annihilated [literally: 'gone beyond'], I shall arrive again, / Where from eternity I have forever been."[169] As a result of this "going-beyond," the soul comes to regain its primordial existence in God.[170]

The traditional mystical terms that Silesius employed most often were *gelassen/Gelassenheit*, the releasement of created things, the self, and even of God (at least the "idol-God" of our own construction). Releasement, he insisted, is necessary to break free of the boundaries of the narrow self and open up to God's action. Thus, Scheffler is one of the last major exponents of mystical releasement preached by Eckhart and his followers.[171] These terms appear about twenty times. A number of these occurrences have an Eckhartian note in teaching that it is necessary to leave even God. For example, CW 2.292: "*The Most Secret Releasement*. Releasement pleases God: but to leave God himself, / Is a releasement that few people understand."[172] Another couplet says much the same: "A holy person's greatest work and task on earth / Is to let go of God and be one with him."[173] Releasement is what makes a person one with God without difference: "A ground-released person is ever free and one: / Can there be any difference between him and God?"[174] Such a person has already attained blessedness (CW 4.39, 5.70), and has his heart written in the book of life (CW 5.106). Releasement is presented in many other distichs.[175]

The Silesian poet also had an important teaching on the role of silence in the mystical path. The requirement for silence in the face of the overwhelming mystery of God has very old roots, both in the

Bible (e.g., "Be still and see that I am God"; Ps. 45:11) and in the post-biblical mystical tradition.[176] Silesius's poetry, as pointed out by Mariel Mazzocco, contains a sophisticated teaching on the interrelation of sonorous images (e.g., creatures as the voices of God: CW 1.264 and 270) and the silence needed for hearing God's voice.[177] CW 1.240 puts it well: "*The Silent Prayer.* God far exceeds all words that we can here express: / In silence he is heard, in silence worshipped best."[178] In the original edition of *The Cherubic Pilgrim*, Scheffler appended to couplet 1.19 a note to Sandaeus's *Mystical Theology* regarding the "prayer of silence": "*The Holy Silence.* How blessed is the man who neither desires nor knows, / Who (understand me rightly) gives neither praise nor glory to God."[179] The root reason for the need to praise God in silence is because God himself is silent: "*One Praises God in Silence.* Do you think, O poor man, that your mouth's cry / Is the correct song of praise for the silent Godhead?"[180] Paradoxically, silence is the highest activity as CW 2.19 says, "It is good to be busy, it is much better to pray; / Still better it is to come before God the Lord dumb and silent."[181] This is because God's speaking within can be heard only when we are silent and still (CW 5.330).

Union and Deification
Many of the couplets already cited address the indistinct union with God that is central to the message of *The Cherubic Pilgrim*. I will close by presenting a few of the most important passages on union and deification. Silesius never uses the term "mystical union," which had been pioneered by French mystics but appears not to have entered into German mysticism in the seventeenth century. Becoming one with God had been expressed in many ways throughout the Christian tradition, and the distinction between the loving union of the divine and human wills (*unitas spiritus*) and union language that presents oneness of indistinction (*unitas indistinctionis*) is only a heuristic tool for surveying complex individual terrains. Silesius has several couplets where he speaks about how love makes us one with God's will: "The highest peace that the soul can enjoy, / Is to know itself to be one as far as possible with God's will."[182] Such a union of wills, however, is not the major thrust of his teaching. As we have seen above in his use of the Eckhartian formula of becoming "a single One" (*ein einges Ein*) with God (e.g., 4.184, 5.321, etc.), as well as in his descriptions of God as the immeasurable sea into which we become absorbed (6.171–74; see also 4.153), Silesius's teaching on union emphasizes a merging of God and human that seems to exclude otherness, at least on the deepest level. To give a

few examples. In CW 4.181 he says, "The blessed soul knows nothing of otherness; / She is one light with God and a splendrous beauty." Couplet 4.10 insists that union removes "otherness" (*Anderheit*): "No man has ever known perfect felicity, / Until his otherness is drowned in unity."[183] We have already noted a number of couplets containing the same message (e.g., 2.201). One couplet says that only by withdrawing from multiplicity can we come to oneness with God: "When a person draws away from multiplicity / And turns himself back to God, he comes to oneness."[184] The presentation of union is more paradoxical in two distichs that come earlier in book 2. CW 2.178 seems to assert the continuing duality of God and the soul: "There are but you and I; and when we two are not, / The heavens will collapse, God will no more be God." The following distich reverses this by claiming that the two are really one and that this identity enhances the importance of heaven: "Ah yes! If I were you and you in me a single one, / So heaven would be heaven a thousand times over."[185] One can suggest that these two couplets reflect diverse perspectives: the first from the outlook of created being; the other from that of indistinct union. Attaining union, according to Silesius at least, can be instantaneous as a matter of a change of attitude: "Man, you can more easily see yourself one with God, / Than to open your eye; if you only want it, it happens!"[186]

The Silesian realized that his teaching on union might seem dangerous or heterodox to some. Hence in the "Foreword for Remembering" (*Erinnerungs-Vorrede*) that he wrote for *The Cherubic Pilgrim*, he not only listed the many theologians and mystics he had used but also defended and explained how to read his paradoxical couplets. Addressing the "God-hungry reader," he reviews his writings and the Cherubic and Seraphic spirit he writes in before noting how "the following rhymes" contain "many strange paradoxes and contrary statements" concerning the little-known "keys for the hidden Godhead, and for union with God and the divine Being, as well as for divine likeness and deification, or becoming God." Because of the terseness of their presentation, he says, "they can easily be given a condemned sense or an evil meaning, and so you should note to remember this beforehand." Scheffler then lays out several authorial principles. The first is "that it was never the author's meaning that the human soul should or could lose its createdness, so that it would be changed through deification in God, or in his uncreated Being, something that cannot happen through all eternity." Even Almighty God cannot do this. Citing Tauler, he says that deification means "that we are God through grace [*dass wir Gott wären aus Gnaden*], by which we, together with him in everlasting love, are able to possess a single blessedness, a single joy, and one single Kingdom." Thus, in heaven we shall *appear* to be God because of our transformation and union with the divine nature, and so we can be called "A Light in the Light, a Word in the Word, a God in God." The second principle is Christological. Because the Father has only one Son, Scheffler says, "We are now sons in Christ, and so we must also be what Christ is, and have the same being that the Son of God has." He again cites Tauler in defense of this Eckhartian teaching.[187]

The indistinct union that the soul has always enjoyed in its eternal being is therefore also deification (*Vergötterung*), one that is eternally present, but that is now being temporally given in a new way in Christ.[188] Like other Western mystics, Silesius was no stranger to the theme of deification. The temporal dimension of deification ties it to the Incarnation, that is, the traditional motif that God became man so that man might become God, which is echoed by Silesius in several places (e.g., CW 1.220, 3.16, and 3.20). His holistic view of deification as union with the God-man is set forth in CW 1.216: "God is my spirit, my blood, my flesh and my limbs: / How shall I then not be totally 'through-goded' (*ganz durchgottet*) with him?"[189] Other couplets bring out further dimensions of the deification theme. In order to become God, we need to "dis-image" (*entbilden*) our created reality, language reminiscent of Eckhart. The word is used in CW 2.54: "Dis-image yourself, my child!, if you want to be like God, / And be in silent rest yourself your own Kingdom of Heaven." This dis-imaging involves the paradox of loving without feeling and knowing without knowing in order to be "more God than man" (CW 2.59).[190] It is a going beyond both loving delight and painful wounding (CW 1.293). The process is described as an "overforming" (*Überformung*; CW 3.114), as "eating and drinking God" (2.120), and as melting into God: "*God Works Like Fire.* Fire melts and unites; if you sink into your Origin, / So must your spirit be melted into one with God."[191] In the final analysis, deification (as Meister Eckhart also taught) is a returning to the status where we were before we were created: "The person who is as if he were nothing, and were never created, / He (O Blessedness) has become purely God."[192]

The Cherubic Pilgrim is one of the major monuments of German mysticism, a Baroque reimagining of many of the themes of the Northern European mysticism that began at the end of the thirteenth century. Johannes Scheffler's contribution rests not only in the way in which he combined early modern forms of Jesus-mysticism with older Germanic speculative insights, but also in the paradoxical epigrammatic verse he employed to convey his message. The Cherubic and Seraphic perspectives, as well as the "Over-Angelic," can be found in this mystical collection. But Silesius wanted to do more than just impress his readers with his cleverness. He wanted to convert them. As the concluding couplet of *The Cherubic Pilgrim* says: "Freund, es ist auch genug! Im Fall du mehr willst lesen, / So geh und werde selbst die Schrift und selbst das Wesen" ("Friend, this is now enough! In case you want to read more, / Then go, and become yourself the writing and the reality"; 6.263; ed. 461).

Mysticism in the Low Countries: Maria Petyt

The conflicts between Protestant and Catholic that marked German-speaking lands between 1525 and 1675 also affected the Low Countries, or Spanish Netherlands (present-day Belgium and Holland were ruled by the Spanish Hapsburgs at the start of the period). The seventeen independent provinces that constituted the Low Countries had passed from the rule of the Dukes of Burgundy to the Hapsburgs under Charles V. From the 1550s French Calvinist influence had begun to grow, first in the ten southern provinces (Flemish and Wallon-speaking) and then into the seven Dutch-speaking provinces in the north. In 1549, Charles V declared the seventeen provinces a single entity under Hapsburg rule. During the reign of his son, Philip II, an Iconoclastic Revolt by Calvinists in 1566 marked the beginning of the "Eighty Years' War," which was not only a religious struggle between Protestants and Catholics but also a war of independence. As Carlos Eire has remarked, "The conflict played a large role in the development of the Dutch Republic, one of Europe's first tolerant societies, and, simultaneously, in the decline and ultimate demise of Spain, one of its most intolerant ones."[193]

Philip II sent the Duke of Alba to put down the revolt and most of the Protestants were driven into the northern provinces. Fighting went on under his successor, the Duke of Parma, until in 1581 the northern provinces, now solidly Protestant, declared independence from Spain, while the southern Catholic provinces stayed under Hapsburg rule. Finally, in 1609 Philip III signed a twelve-year truce that effectively recognized the independence of the northern Dutch Republic. Fighting broke out again in 1619 as part of the Thirty Years' War, and it was not until the Treaty of Westphalia of 1648 that the United Provinces of the north were guaranteed freedom. Warfare commenced again in the second half of the seventeenth century when Louis XIV pursued his dynastic ambitions, first against the Spanish Netherlands, and then against the Dutch Republic. Three wars (1667–68, 1672–78, and 1688–97) led to much death and destruction, but little ultimate gain for Louis.

From the twelfth century on, and especially in the late Middle Ages, the Low Countries made strong contributions to the spiritual life of Europe. In the period ca. 1530–60, the Eastern Netherlands (Gelderland) saw a flourishing mystical movement among beguines and their monastic and clerical advisors, as the production of the *Evangelical Pearl* and the *Arnhem Mystical Sermons* demonstrate. These figures and anonymous writings were treated in *The Varieties of Vernacular Mysticism (1350–1550)*, because in many ways they are a late medieval phenomenon.[194] It has sometimes been thought that the religious wars that afflicted the Low Countries beginning in 1566 marked the end of the productive period of Netherlandish mysticism, but this is not at all the case.[195] Even in the midst of the Eighty Years' War there were mystics, as Jan Pelgrim Pullen (1520–1608) demonstrates.[196] Pullen was a diocesan priest noted for his austere life, his skill as a confessor and spiritual director, and his mystical gifts. He is said to have written as many as seventy mystical treatises, although only twenty-odd have been identified. Many of these are short, but the *Three Books about the Object* (*Drie boecxkens van het Voorwerp*) is quite long. Part of one of his short works, *The Conversation with the Anchoress of Ghent* (*Samenspraak met de cluysenersse tot Gent*), is now available in English.[197] In this text the teaching is that of the anchoress Claesinne van Nieuwlants (ca. 1540–1611), but how much is due to Pullen's editorial intervention is difficult to determine. This discussion about the need for annihilation to draw near to God and attain essential union is revelatory for the period of the late 1580s, when mystics like Benet of Canfield in France and Isabella Berinzaga and Achille Gagliardi in Italy were also creating doctrines of mystical annihilation.[198] Pullen's teachings about annihilation, the "superessential life," union, and divinization are rooted in the tradition beginning with Ruusbroec and carried on by the mystical circles in the Eastern Netherlands in the preceding generation.

In the early seventeenth century, the Low Countries, like France, were the scene of a mystical controversy over the role of Christ in the path to God and the place of human activity in final union.[199] We have already made reference to the attacks on Benet of Canfield (chapter 2, 51–52) in this regard. These objections came largely from Spanish Carmelites active in spreading the Carmelite Reform in the Spanish Netherlands. The key early figure is Jerónimo Gracián (1545–1614), Teresa's friend, who, after being cast out of the Discalced Order, wound up in the Spanish Netherlands in 1607. In 1609, he wrote a treatise called *The Life of the Soul* against those who set perfection in "total annihilation" and, in 1611, issued a work against Canfield, Lawrence of Paris, and the *Theologia Deutsch* under the provocative title, *Ten Lamentations on the Miserable State of the Atheists of Our Time*.[200] More telling of the conflict between the heirs of Teresa and the adherents of the tradition of Northern mysticism were two unpublished treatises of Tomás de Jesús (1564–1627), the most important Discalced mystical author of the generation after Teresa and John of the Cross, who had been sent to Flanders in 1610 to found new Carmelite houses and combat Protestant errors.[201] Despite the fact that Tomás at times used expressions taken from the Northern mystics in his own works (e.g., "supereminent contemplation"), these two works attacked numerous errors in Tauler, Ruusbroec, the *Theologia Deutsch*, Herp, and Canfield. They witness to the considerable misunderstanding between two important mystical traditions, that of Carmelite Spain and that of the late medieval Northern mystics.

Chapter 2 above has shown the importance of the Capuchin mystical authors of the period ca. 1590–1630 in France. The Capuchins were also active in the Low Countries and contributed to the mysticism of the time. Benet of Canfield's *Rule of Perfection* was widely read and translated into Flemish in 1622 and again in 1623. Constantin de Barbanson was born in the Low Countries and translated two Flemish treatises in his *Anatomy of the Soul* as examples of mistaken interpretations of Canfield. John the Evangelist of Bois-le-Duc (1588–1635) entered the order in 1613 and wrote a number of mystical treatises, centering on the importance of annihilation. These include *The Kingdom of God in the Soul* (*Het Ryck Godts inder zielen*) published in 1637, and the Latin work, *The Division of the Soul and Spirit* (*Divisio animae et spiritus*), published in 1652 and translated into Flemish in 1677/78.[202]

The Carmelite Maria Petyt (1623–1677)

In the later seventeenth-century the Low Countries did not lack for mystical authors, of whom the third-order Carmelite Maria Petyt is the most important (she was an almost exact contemporary of Johannes Scheffler).[203] Although little known outside the Low Countries, Maria was a significant mystical voice.[204] She was born into a merchant family and was well educated, spending a year and a half in a convent at St.-Omer to learn French.[205] As an adolescent she wavered between a life of prayer and more worldly concerns but was inspired by reading works like the *Imitation of Christ* and Benet of Canfield's *Rule of Perfection*. In 1642, she entered the convent of the Canonesses of St. Augustine at Ghent but did not remain long due to illness. For a time she lived in a beguinage at Ghent, but soon she and another woman took up an anchoritic life near Ghent. Receiving spiritual direction from Carmelite friars, Maria professed as a Carmelite tertiary around 1645, taking the name Maria of St. Teresa. Like many other women in the seventeenth century, Maria was strongly influenced by Teresa, both as model and as teacher.[206] In 1647, she took the well-known Carmelite Michael of St. Augustine (1622-1684), a proponent of the Touraine Reform among the Flemish Carmelites, as her spiritual director. He remained in this capacity for the rest of her life, although his many duties meant he often had to counsel her through letters.[207] In 1657, Maria's desire for a stricter life led her to move to a hermitage (*De Cluyse*) attached to the Carmelite church in Mechelen, where, along with a small group of other religious women, she remained for the last two decades of her life.[208] Early in this period she experienced four years or more of a kind of Dark Night experience, which probably had much to do with the emphasis on annihilation in her mystical teaching. From about 1658 on, Maria also received many visions, imaginative and intellectual, mystical and prophetic. She died on November 1, 1677.

Friar Michael had Maria write a spiritual autobiography. This document and the many letters they exchanged formed the basis for his four-part, two-volume *Life of the Worthy Mother Maria of St. Teresa* (*Het Leven vande Weerdighe Moeder Maria a Sta Teresia*), the major source for her mystical teaching.[209] The Flemish material, however, is not the only source for Maria Petyt's mysticism. In 2009, Esther van de Vate found some folios in a manuscript in the Carmelite archives in Rome that contained a fragmentary part of a Latin *Vita* of Maria, also composed by Michael of St. Augustine, which shows that her mysticism was tied to a prophetic charism (remember Elijah as founder of the Carmelites).[210] Maria's prophetic persona was politically involved with the Dutch War of Louis XIV (1672-78), a struggle in which the Carmelite's mystical visions and experiences of union led her to take the side of the French king against the Hapsburg rulers of the lower Netherlands. She based this change of her natural allegiance on Louis's opposition to Jansenism and the heretical Calvinists of the Dutch Republic, prophesying that the French king's coming victory (of which God had assured her), would be the beginning of the conversion of Protestants and other heretics to the true faith.[211] This view was naturally controversial and went against the commands of her spiritual director. Michael of St. Augustine did record this mystical material in his Latin *Vita*, but significantly did not publish it in his volumes of her writings. He even adds the disclaimer: "Whether these things come forth from a divine spirit or not, I leave it up to others who are capable of examining and weighing such things. I just refer to those things with the same sincerity in which they were written by her and entrusted to me."[212] Nonetheless, to have accounts of mystical union so closely tied to a partisan political program is unusual. Elisabeth Hense describes it as an example of "prayer . . . seen as a political act." The discovery of Maria Petyt's political involvement provides us with a new dimension on this Flemish mystic, indicating that more work needs to be done to determine the full contours of her thought.[213]

Scholars who have written on the Flemish texts that Friar Michael edited from what Maria communicated to him have presented her mystical teaching in various ways. In his 1939 introduction, the Carmelite scholar and future martyr Titus Brandsma sketched Maria Petyt's career according to a fourfold model: (1) an early stage of severe asceticism, followed by (2) her putting herself under the direction of Friar Michael, which led to (3) the gradual deepening of her mystical life through the exercise of imitating the life and virtues of Jesus as a way of attaining union with God. For Brandsma, the fourth stage was distinctive of the Flemish Carmelite, the attaining of a *Marielijck*, or "Mary-form life," in which she gains a place in Mary's heart to attain full union with Jesus and with the Trinity.[214] According to Brandsma, the "practice of devotion to Mary introduced Maria to the actual Mary-form life, which she describes as a higher degree of perfection than the usual union with God as our greatest good. She sees it as a strengthening of our life with God, because, living with Mary, we can at the same time live in a better and more intimate union with God." In this Mary-form life, all of her actions are performed "in, for, through, and with Mary."[215] Although devotion to Mary is not prevalent in the Latin *Vita*, it is strong in the Flemish writings. The Carmelite insists that her devotion to Mary strengthens rather than detracts from her union with God. "It is in the Divine Being as in a mirror," she says, "that I behold, honor, and love our all-lovable Mother, and that I pray to her. I behold her as making but one with the Divine Mirror, with this ineffable Being."[216]

Titus Brandsma's account does not put much stress on the theme of annihilation, which is central to the analysis of Paul Mommaers. Speaking of Maria's autobiography, he says, "The themes characteristic of seventeenth-century mysticism (annihilation, the role of Christ) are treated in an illuminating way."[217] Mommaers notes that Maria attained the prayer of quiet shortly after beginning her mystical path, but that she then had to endure four years of painful purification during which the experience of mystical annihilation reduced her to nothing. Mommaers cites the following passage from the Flemish *Life*: "I found myself all at once as if devoured in the immeasurable grandeur of God, like a little spark which one can no longer perceive when it is thrown into a great fire." She continues, "The totally pure Nothing, or annihilated soul" goes beyond all creatures, and even itself, moving toward "God who is its center," until, "flying beyond everything, it is lifted into God—the Nothing has disappeared into the divine All."[218] It was on the basis of this annihilating purification, according to Mommaers, that Maria Petyt attained the mystical marriage where she experienced divine touches (*toetsen*). This is the "transformed life" (*overvormde leven*) in which she enjoys moments of "superessential contemplation" (*overwezenlijke schouwing*). This state is essentially Christological, a life lived in imitation of Christ and in union with the annihilated God-man in his suffering and abandonment. Mommaers notes the visionary and mariological aspects of Maria Petyt's teaching but stresses annihilation and union with Christ.

Albert Deblaere's summary of Maria's mysticism is a detailed, philologically rich analysis of the story of her life as told to her confessor, one that also stresses the role that annihilation played in her mystical path.[219] The first stage, according to Deblaere, was the passage from meditation to contemplative prayer under the guidance of Michael of St. Augustine. Here, through the practice of purifying both the sensitive and the higher powers of the soul, Maria attained an introversion to the "ground of the soul" where she became capable of receiving infused grace and practicing the first stage of mystical prayer—intimate prayer.[220] Deblaere describes "intimate prayer," which involves abstraction and the lack of mediation, as the permanent foundation for Maria's contemplative life. In a text from 1671 she says, "I contemplate God in obscurity, in the night, in my ground, with a peaceful quiet or perfect silence of all the soul's powers, with a gaze of the spirit, very simple and intimate. The gaze itself is more passive than active." Such contemplation, according to Deblaere, accords with the teaching on prayer found in Ruusbroec and Herp, but Maria describes it in a more personal and direct fashion.[221]

The consoling gifts of intimate prayer, however, can feed the soul's hidden egoism and lead a person to care more about God's gifts than about God, so Maria Petyt, like many mystics, had to endure a trial of dereliction and affliction for some four or five years in which God withdrew from her and she underwent terrible sufferings, both interior and exterior. She says that her aridity at times brought her to a state of mind in which she was convinced she had lost God's grace forever; at other times she contemplated suicide. Maria's vivid descriptions echo those of other mystics who had experienced such dereliction.[222] Having been reduced to true humility and absolute dependence on God alone, Maria Petyt finally attained the state she calls "essential resignation." She often speaks of this as a state of "annihilation." In one passage she says, "It seemed to me that now my dwelling was established in a deep valley, in the humiliation of being, in the scorn, the distrust, and the annihilation of myself." She recognizes that she is a "Nothing" before the "All" of God, and speaks of being "sweetly occupied in annihilation of herself and of everything created in the unending and infinite being of God." Deblaere says that this "spirituality of annihilation" is one of the salient traits of Maria's mysticism.[223]

On the basis of the recently published Latin *Vita*, which presents evidence of Maria's late mystical states (1672–76), it is possible to add some further observations to these accounts of her mystical gifts, though the fact that her unitive experiences were directed to a political program, rather than to a teaching about how to attain deeper consciousness of God, is troubling. Maria's model, Teresa of Avila, also lived in the midst of a world of contention and conflict, but her writings about the path to union were designed to instruct her readers, especially her sisters, about the life of contemplative prayer, not to advance a particular political agenda.

The *Vita* is an example of a mystical journal, not unlike Marie de l'Incarnation's *Relation of 1654*. Friar Michael intersperses comments and summaries, but the bulk of the text is his Latin rendering of Maria's Flemish original. Given that the text is mostly a day-to-day account of Maria's ecstasies, prayer states, and experiences of union with God, it is not easy to give it any order. Noting that Maria uses vocabulary taken from the final four mansions of Teresa of Avila's *Interior Castle*, Elisabeth Hense suggests a progression from the "prayer of quiet" (*ad profundam intimam quietam* in ed., 122; see Teresa's Fourth Mansion), through the "prayer of union" (*intimae coniunctionis, seu unionis mei spiritus cum diuino* in ed., 128; see Teresa's Fifth Mansion), to end in mystical marriage, that is, an "extraordinary and very great union with the Divinity, . . . in the quality of a very tender and loving bride" (*illa extraordinaria et praemagna unione cum Diuinitate . . . in qualitate tenerrimae et amantissimae sponsae* in ed., 152; see Teresa's Seventh Mansion). Maria certainly uses Teresian vocabulary to present her mystical experiences, and even once refers to "the interior castle of the soul,"[224] but it is hard to think that hers is just a version of Teresian mysticism.

Some of the characteristics of Maria's mysticism found in the Flemish material are also present in the Latin text. For example, Maria's sufferings of dereliction were not over early, because in July of 1673 she describes how she had to undergo the pains of hell by taking on herself the sins of the king of France so that they would not impede the progress of his army.[225] Second, the language of nothingness and annihilation found in the Flemish life is also present in the *Vita*. For example, in folio 48r she speaks of ordering the angels to help "the King and his soldiers . . . in promoting his business in Holland," noting that she does so with confidence and freedom of spirit despite the fact "I am still plunged in great disgrace and deeply sunk in my nothingness with annihilation and stupor [*in nihilo meo cum adnihilatione et stupore*]." In a manner similar to that found in Marguerite Porete,[226] Maria goes on to say that the deeper she descends into "the abyss of my unworthiness and nothingness," the greater the elevation she is given by God.[227] There is also some psychological analysis in the *Vita*, as when Maria speaks of the soul's three highest powers of memory, intellect, and will being united in God (f. 35v; ed., 154). She occasionally mentions the *fundus animae*, and once talks about how she receives prayer from God in the "passive intellect" (*intellectus passivus*; f. 40v; ed., 186). Her main interest, however, is in recounting what she directly experienced in her prayer campaign for the success of Louis XIV's war efforts.

Maria's descriptions of her mystical experiences seem to contain at least three main kinds of prayer, or union with God (terms that seem to be coterminus for her), although the vocabulary she uses is varied and one does not want to oversystematize her accounts. Maria distinguishes between "the spirit of passive prayer" (*spiritus passiuae orationis*) and "the spirit of love" (*spiritus amoris*), which "prays and speaks confidently with the Beloved" (f. 42v; ed. 194–95). The spirit of passive prayer, which can last for a long or short time, is without "thoughts, words, images, sights, or forms of things." In it the soul stands before

God "like a clear mirror" and notifies God in an essential way about its desires. God operates "that prayer . . . , because it flows at the same moment from God into the soul and reflows again from the soul into Him."[228] There is nothing of the self in this prayer. This seems to be the same prayer that Maria also refers to as "experiencing the sleep of love" (f. 30r, 31r; ed., 122-23, 128-29), or as "standing stretched out before God's face" (f. 31v, 32r; ed., 132-35, 136-39). On the other hand, there is another, more active form of prayer. She says that when "the spirit of love prays . . . something is mixed in of myself, and there acts of faith, hope and charity, etc., are tolerated, and thoughts and images according to the requirements of this prayer" (f. 42v; ed., 194-97). The prayer of the spirit of love, or Spirit of God, seems to include both a lower, more active phase, in which the soul "embraces all Christianity with a strange love and very tender affection" (f. 43r, 44v; ed., 198-99, 208-9), as well as a higher stage, where the love is directed with peace, quiet, and words of love to the Beloved alone. This seems to be the prayer that characterizes Maria's bridal union with Christ, what she calls "the prayer of the bride."[229]

Maria Petyt's accounts of union with God at times use language of deep, even indistinct, union. For example, in folio 41r-v she says, "It is amazing and hardly intelligible how I can say that I am one in God and how in the union I see God. . . . In the same way God gives the soul by grace what He is by nature, as long as this union lasts. It is one spirit with God, one operating, one understanding, one wanting, one loving. It does not know any difference or distance [*non nouit differentiam uel distantionem*] between me and mine, all is clearly one in that it knows and understands all."[230] A later text (f. 47v; ed., 222-25) speaks of how in aiding Louis XIV's army, "I perceived that the Divine Spirit connected and united with mine (for these two were then only one spirit and one being without difference or distinction) inclined and spread himself over that army." Although these texts use the language of union without distinction and difference, this union is operational; that is, it describes how Maria's working on behalf of Louis XIV is really God's action. In the spirit of Ruusbroec and the other masters of medieval mysticism from the Low Countries, Maria's teaching on deep union is a union of operation, of God taking over our knowing and loving, not some merging of essences.

Notes

1. For this sketch, I am using Marc R. Foster, *Catholic Germany from the Reformation to the Enlightenment* (New York: Palgrave Macmillan, 2007).

2. For a brief account of the Thirty Years' War, see Eire, *Reformations: The Early Modern World, 1450–1650*, 548–53.

3. For a survey of the history of the term and an argument for the Baroque as an international and supraconfessional cultural system of a recurrent nature, see Davidson, *Universal Baroque*, "Introduction" (1–24).

4. Two art-historical discussions are Peter Harbison, *Reflections on Baroque* (Chicago: University of Chicago Press, 2000); and Anthony Blunt, *Roman Baroque* (London: Pallas Athene Arts, 2001). With regard to Baroque literature, see part 1 of Harold B. Segel, *The Baroque Poem: A Comparative Survey* (New York: E. P. Dutton, 1974).

5. Foster, *Catholic Germany*, 4; on the religious dimensions, see 8–11, 86–87, 104–5, 176–77, and 182–83.

6. The best study of mysticism in seventeenth-century Germany is Bernard Gorceix, *Flambée et agonie: Mystiques du XVII siècle allemand* (Saint-Vincent-sur-Jabron: Éditions Présence, 1977). Félix Vernet, "Allemande (Spiritualité)," DS 1:314–51, is a listing of names rather than an analysis of developments.

7. In *Flambée et agonie*, Gorceix has discussions of a number of the Protestant mystics, including Daniel Czepko (1605–1660), Catherina Regina von Greiffenberg (1633–1694), Quirinus Kuhlmann (1651–1689), and Johann Georg Gichtel (1638–1710). These figures are little known in the English-speaking world, with the exception of the Austrian noblewoman von Greiffenberg, whose works have attracted feminist scholars; see, e.g., von Greiffenberg, *Meditations on the Incarnation, Passion, and the Death of Jesus Christ*, ed. and trans. Lynne Tatlock, Other Voice in Early Modern Europe (Chicago: University of Chicago Press, 2009).

8. The concentration on the Jesuits in this section does not mean that there were no contributions to mysticism from members of the other religious orders. A noted Capuchin mystical author was Victor Gelen, or Victor of Trier (ca. 1600–1669), whose *Summa practica theologiae mysticae* appeared in Latin in 1646 and was translated into German by the author in 1651. See Willibrord of Paris, "Gelen (Victor, Victor de Trèves), capuchin allemande, d. 1669," DS 6:179–81.

9. Guibert, *La spiritualité de la Compagnie de Jésus*, 321–30.

10. For a detailed account, see James Brodrick, *Saint Peter Canisius, S.J (1521–97)* (1935; repr., Baltimore: Carroll Press, 1960).

11. On Nicholas van Esch, see the chapter devoted to him in Titus Brandsma, *In Search of Living Water: Essays on the Mystical Heritage of the Netherlands*, Fiery Arrow Collection 10 (Leuven: Peeters, 2013), 125–51.

12. On this translation and Canisius's spirituality in general, see Brandsma, "The Spiritual Life of St. Peter Canisius," *In Search of Living Water*, 334–47.

13. Jos Andriessen, "Sandaeus (van der Sandt, Maximilien), jésuite, 1578–1656," DS 14:311–16.

14. The full title, in good seventeenth-century style, reveals his intent: *Pro theologia mystica clavis, elucidarium onomasticum vocabulorum et locutionum obscuriorum quibus doctores mystici tum veteres, tum recentiores, utuntur ad proprium suae disciplinae sensum paucis manifestandum*. I will use the modern reprint of this edition. The work often refers back to the 1627 *Theologia mystica* treatise.

15. On these two new types of literature, see Pierre Adnès, "Mystique. B. XVIe-XXe siècles," DS 10:1919-30.

16. For a sketch of these two works, see McGinn, *Spain*, 370-71. Sandaeus knew these books, as we can see from the *Clavis*, 150.

17. Certeau, *Mystic Fable: Volume One*, 75-76, 102, 108, 146, 170.

18. The following list is not exhaustive: Ignatius is cited in *Clavis*, 140, 301, and 353; Teresa in 28, 131, 150, 296; and John of the Cross in 18, 150, 288-89, and 296. Sandaeus was not friendly to women mystics; besides Teresa, the only other women cited are Gertrude the Great (312, 343), and Angela of Foligno.

19. *Clavis*, "Praeambula," cap. 1 (ed., 3).

20. *Clavis*, "Praeambula," cap. 3 (ed., 10). This chapter forms the center of the argument. To get a sense of Sandaeus's use of sources, it is worth noting that the four chapters of the Praeambula cite Blosius nine times; Bernard four times; Ruusbroec and Tauler three times each; Augustine, Gregory, and Bonaventure each twice; and a number of other mystics, including Teresa and John of the Cross, once.

21. Another Jesuit, Johannis Crombecius (Jean Van Crombeke), had attacked these terms in his 1613 *De studio perfectionis*. Sandaeus allows this terminology: see *inactio* (*Clavis*, ed., 245); *unio essentialis cum Deo* (*Clavis*, ed., 369). On this author, see Alexandre De Bil, "Crombecius (Van Crombeke, Jean), jésuite, 1558-1626," DS 2:2623-25.

22. Among these are *abyssus/abyssalis* (*Clavis*, ed., 33-36); *adhaesio* (*Clavis*, ed., 39-40); *caligo* (*Clavis*, ed., 116-19, with a number of later related terms about divine darkness); *cognitio dei per affirmationem et negationem* (*Clavis*, ed., 147-50); *desolatio mystica* (*Clavis*, ed., 161-63); *ecstasis*, as well as *excessus* (*Clavis*, ed., 190-93, 201-3); *indifferentia* (*Clavis*, ed., 245-47); *introverto* (*Clavis*, ed., 255-57); *iubilare* (*Clavis*, ed., 259-61); *loquela* (*Clavis*, ed., 266-68); *mors mystica* (*Clavis*, ed., 280-83); *otium* (*Clavis*, ed., 294-97); *pati divina* (*Clavis*, ed., 300-302); *resignatio* (*Clavis*, ed., 311-17); *superessentiale* (*Clavis*, ed., 339); *suspensio* (*Clavis*, ed., 339-40); *transformo/transformatio* (*Clavis*, ed., 354-56); and *visio* (*Clavis*, ed., 361-64).

23. For example: *amplexus, apis mystica, cella vinaria, ebrietas, esuries mystica, febris mystica, ferrum ignitum, gustus mysticus, languor, liber, nox* (using John of the Cross), *oculus simplex, osculum mysticum, sabbatum, scintilla, somnus, susurrium mysticum,* and the like.

24. *Clavis*, ed., 370. In the two entries under *unio* and *unitas* it is interesting to see the authorities Sandaeus uses. Harphius is cited nine times, and Ruusbroec four. Augustine is quoted twice, while other authorities are noted once (Ambrose, Bernard, Blosius, Dionysius, Tauler, and the *Theologia Germanica*).

25. *Clavis*, ed., 99. In the "Praeambula" (*Clavis*, ed., 9), Sandaeus says that *annihilatio* and other terms related to love are to be taken metaphorically (*per tropum*).

26. *Clavis*, ed., 102. Sandaeus's use of *inactio* here is significant. This is the Latin form of the Flemish *inwerken* found in Ruusbroec and Harphius. In his treatment of the word (*Clavis*, ed., 244-45) he insists that some human action continues even in the deepest forms of union, but that God is working these in us. The same teaching is also found in the entries *otium, pati divina,* and *quies* (see *Clavis*, ed., 294-95, 301, and 308).

27. Anton Arens, "Spee von Langenfeld (Frédéric), jésuite, 1591-1635," DS 14:1117-21; and Wilhelm Emrich, "Die Lyrik der katholischen Mystik: Friederich

Spee (1591–1635)," in Emrich, *Deutsche Literatur der Barockzeit* (Königstein: Athenäum, 1981), 99–106.

28. The title *Trutz-Nachtigall* is not easy to render in English; *Resisting-Nightingale* is my supposition. (My thanks to my colleague Hans-Josef Klauck for his consultation.) The edition used is Theo G. M. van Ooschot, ed., *Friedrich Spee. Trutz-Nachtigall* (Bern: Francke Verlag, 1985). There is no English version, and only a few of the shorter poems have been translated.

29. Emrich, *Deutsche Literatur der Barockzeit*, 99.

30. The best study is Gorceix, *Flambée et agonie*, chap. 3, "Première Partie: Le Jésuite rhénane" (99–125). See also Hans-Georg Pott, "Friedrich Spee und die Mystik," in Theo G. M. Oorschot, ed., *Friedrich Spee (1591–1635): Düsseldorfer Symposium zum 400. Geburtstag. Neue Ergebnisse der Spee-Forschung*, ed. Theo G. M. Oorschot (Bielefeld: Aisthesis Verlag, 1993), 30–50.

31. In *The Baroque Poem*, Segel includes 150 poems in original languages and translation, but none by Spee (although he is mentioned several times). Segel discusses the "thematic emphases" of Baroque poetry (96–98), as well as "Baroque Poetic Theory and Style" (101–29).

32. On the "echo-poems," see Alois M. Haas, "Friedrich von Spee—Geistliche Zeitvertreib," in Haas, *Sermo Mysticus: Studien zu Theologie und Sprache der deutschen Mystik*, Dokimion 4 (Freiburg, Switzerland: Universitätsverlag, 1979), 330–70.

33. The text of the thirty-four stanzas of No. 29 is in ed., 140–49. There is an analysis in Gorceix, *Flambée et agonie*, 121–23.

34. No. 25 (ed., 124–26), using the translation of George S. Schoolfield, *The German Lyric of the Baroque Period in English Translation* (Chapel Hill: University of North Carolina Press, 1961), 284–87.

35. Gorceix, *Flambée et agonie*, 102–8.

36. No. 3 (ed., 22–23). The translation is that of Schoolfield, *German Lyric of the Baroque Period*, 280–83.

37. No. 3: "O süssigkeit in schmertzen! / O schmerz in süssigkeit? / Ach bleibe doch im Hertzen / Bleib doch in Eigkeit" (ed., 22).

38. This becomes clear in stanza 7: "Ade zu tausent Jahren / O Welt zu guter nacht: / Ade lass mich nun fahren / Ich längst hab dich veracht. / In JESU lieb Ich lebe / Sag dir von Hertzen grund: / In lauter Frewd Ich schwebe / Wie sehr ich bin verwund" (ed., 23).

39. The starting place is the three-volume collection of Scheffler's works by Hans Ludwig Held, *Angelus Silesius, Sämtliche poetische Werke*, 3rd ed. (Munich: Carl Hanser, 1952). The first volume, *Die Geschichte seines Lebens und seiner Werke und Urkunden*, is crucial for its documentation about Scheffler's life. Among earlier studies, see Georg Ellinger, *Angelus Silesius: Ein Lebensbild* (Breslau: Korn, 1927). Hans Urs von Balthasar published a selection from the *Cherubinscher Wandersmann* and a study under the title *Angelus Silesius: Dich auftun wie die Rose* (Einsiedeln: Johannes Verlag, 1954). Useful introductions are Louise Gnädinger, "Angelus Silesius," in Harald Steinhagen and Benno von Wiese, eds., *Deutsche Dichter des 17. Jahrhunderts: Ihr Leben und Werk* (Berlin: Erich Schmidt, 1984), 553–75; and Alois M. Haas, "Christus ist Alles: Die Christusmystik des Angelus Silesius," in Haas, *Gottleiden–Gottlieben: Zur volkssprachlichen Mystik im Mittelalter* (Frankfurt am Main: Insel Verlag, 1989), 295–318. Further monographs and articles will be cited below.

40. Important treatments include Henri Plard, *La mystique d'Angelus Silesius* (Paris: Aubier, 1943); Jean Baruzi, *Création religieuse et pensée contemplative*, Les religions 8 (Paris: Aubier, 1951), part 2, Angelus Silesius (99–239); and Gorceix, *Flambée et agonie*, chap. 5, part 1 (233–75). There are a number of French translations of *Der Cherubinischer Wandersmann*.

41. The best work in English is the selection of epigrams (600 out of 1676) translated by Maria Shrady, *The Cherubinic Wanderer*, Classics of Western Spirituality (New York: Paulist Press, 1986), which contains a useful "Introduction" by Josef Schmidt (1–36). There are a number of other English versions, mostly partial, and often inadequate. There is no satisfactory monograph. Jeffrey L. Sammons, *Angelus Silesius*, Twayne's World Authors Series 25 (New York: Twayne, 1967) is a literary study, and Maria M. Böhm, *Angelus Silesius' "Cherubinischer Wandersmann": A Modern Reading with Selected Translations*, Renaissance and Baroque Studies and Texts 22 (New York: Peter Lang, 1997), treats Scheffler as a kind of "perennialist" mystic.

42. On Boehme, see McGinn, *Reformation*, 169–97.

43. On Scheffler's library, see Jean Orcibal, "Les sources étrangères du 'Cherubinischer Wandersmann' (1657) d'après la bibliothèque d'Angelus Silesius," *Revue de Littérature Comparée* 18 (1938): 494–506.

44. This edition, published in Vienna, bore the title *Johannis Angeli Silesii Sinn- und Schlussreime*. Books 1–2 appear to have been written ca. 1650–52, while books 3–5 are from around the time of his conversion in 1653. It was not until the second edition (Glatz, 1675) that Scheffler added the title *Der Cherubinischer Wandersmann*. Gottfried Arnold (1666–1714), the ecumenical Lutheran Pietist, reedited the work in 1701 and seems to have had much to do with keeping it alive for both Catholics and Protestants (who quietly forgot about Scheffler's anti-Protestantism).

45. *Heiliger Seelenlust* is edited in Held, *Sämtlicher poetische Werke*, 2:31–370. As Gorceix points out (*Flambée et agonie*, 244–49), this work has been rather neglected. Gorceix gives a brief analysis of the erotic mysticism of the work on 268–75, including some comparisons with Friedrich Spee. Josef Schmidt translates one of the poems from the *Heiliger Seelenlust* ("Introduction," in Shrady, *Angelus Silesius*, 20–22).

46. On Scheffler's vocation as doctor, priest, and poet, see Alois M. Haas, "Angelus Silesius—Arzt und Mystiker," in Haas, *Mystik im Kontext* (Munich: Wilhelm Fink Verlag, 2004), 388–404.

47. Jacques Le Brun sees Scheffler's life as a Catholic beginning with a positive Counter-Reformation stance and moving to one of a more negative Counter-Reformation view evident in his polemical works ("Les différentes faces de la Contre-Réforme: Angelus Silesius [Johannes Scheffler, 1624–1677]," in *Les deux réformes chrétiennes: Propagation et diffusion*, ed. Ilana Zinguer and Myriam Yardeni, Studies in the History of Christian Traditions 114 [Leiden: Brill, 2004], 354–68).

48. There have been many editions of the full form of *The Cherubic Pilgrim*. I will use that of Louise Gnädinger, *Cherubinischer Wandersmann oder geistreiche Sinn- und Schlussreime* (Zurich: Manesse Verlag, 1986), based on her larger critical edition of 1984. I will use the translations of Maria Shrady when adequate and make my own versions of those that have problems or ones she did not include. I will cite the text according to the formula CW with book and verse number (e.g.,

CW 1.30). I translate the titles (italicized) only when they add some clarification to the distichs. Because form and meaning are so closely tied in the CW, I will give the German originals.

49. On the *Pearl*, see McGinn, *Varieties*, 143–59.

50. From the "Vorrede" to the *Köstlichen Evangelischen Perle* as reprinted in Held, *Sämtliche poetische Werke*, 1:321–22.

51. For a list and discussion of these works, see Orcibal, "Les sources étrangères." There is a detailed study of Scheffler's relation to Sandaeus in M. Hildburgis Gies, *Eine lateinische Quelle zum "Cherubinischen Wandersmann" des Angelus Silesius*, Breslauer Studien zur historischen Theologie 12 (Breslau, 1929).

52. For a discussion, see Isabelle Raviolo, "Angelus Silesius," in *Encylopédie des mystiques rhénans d'Eckhart à Nicolas de Cues et leur réception*, ed. Marie-Anne Vannier (Paris: Éditions du Cerf, 2011), 94–100.

53. See the discussion above in chapter 1, 19.

54. Raviolo, "Angelus Silesius," 96.

55. Alois M. Haas, "Angelus Silesius: Die Welt, ein wunderschönes Nichts," in Haas, *Sermo Mysticus*, 378–91; quotation from 387.

56. On Czepko, see Gorceix, *Flambée et agonie*, chap. 2 (47–93); Alois M. Haas, "Daniel Czepko von Reigersfeld–Nosce te ipsum," in Haas, *Sermo Mysticus*, 371–77; and Annemarie Meier, *Daniel Czepko als geistlicher Dichter* (Bonn: Bouvier Verlag, 1975). For an edition, see Werner Milch, *Daniel von Czepko: Geistliche Schriften* (Darmstadt: Wissenschaftliche Buchgesellschaft, 1963).

57. Groups of distichs are scattered through the CW; e.g., 1.26–36 on death; 1.251–56 on being a child of God; 2.102–5 on the *Gottesgeburt*; 2.158–61 on the soul; 3.84–91 on the rose; 4.104–7 on death; 4.204–7 on the *Gottesgeburt*; 5.1–8 on the One; 5.90–95 on God and time; 5.241–46 on God as love; 6.129–34 again on the *Gottesgeburt*; 6.171–74 on God as the sea; 6.232–35 on the Trinity; and 6.240–43 and 253–59 on the wise man.

58. E.g., Schmidt, "Introduction," in Shrady, *Angelus Silesius*, 26: "*The Cherubinic Wanderer* is primarily a book of contemplative prayer exercising the soul in Ignatian conversion to become aware of the *de signatura rerum* [Boehme's term for the signification of things] in theological terms; the essence of things and truth is reached through poetic meditation."

59. Böhm, *Angelus Silesius' "Cherubinscher Wandersmann,"* 37. Böhm relies on Benno von Wiese, "Die Antithetik in den Alexandrinen des Angelus Silesius," *Euphorion* 29 (1929): 503–22.

60. CW 1.45 (ed., 43; my trans.). This is one of a number of distichs that seem to have been influenced by the famous formula from Eckhart's German Sermon 52 that the truly poor man "wants nothing, knows nothing, has nothing," which Scheffler could have found in many later sources, such as the *Evangelical Pearl*. For other such distichs, see CW 1.24, 2.14, 2.132, and 2.244.

61. Mariel Mazzocco, "Entre silence et vibrations sonores: La poésie mystique d'Angelus Silesius," *Rivista di storia e letteratura religiosa* 49 (2013): 443–56; quotation from 450.

62. Matthew Bagger, *The Uses of Paradox (Religion, Self-Transformation, and the Absurd)* (New York: Columbia University Press, 2007), xi. Bagger discusses a number of mystics (e.g., Dionysius, Nicholas of Cusa, John of the Cross), but not Angelus Silesius.

63. On Evagrius's aphoristic centuries, see McGinn, *Foundations*, 146.
64. Gorceix, *Flambée et agonie*, 250.
65. Harvey J. Egan, *An Anthology of Christian Mysticism* (Collegeville, MN: Liturgical Press, 1991), 501.
66. For an introduction and selection of texts, see Steven Chase, ed., *Angelic Spirituality: Medieval Perspectives on the Ways of Angels*, Classics of Western Spirituality (New York: Paulist Press, 2002).
67. Gorceix, *Flambée et agonie*, "Pan Cherubique" (249-66) and "Pan Seraphic" (266-75). Haas also stresses the complementarity of the CW and the HS and gives a short account of the latter ("Christus ist alles," 309-17).
68. CW 3.196: "Die Weisheit schauert Gott, die Liebe küsset ihn: / Ach, dass ich nicht voll Lieb und voller Weisheit bin!" (ed., 222; my trans.).
69. CW 1.183: "Was Freude muss doch sein, wenn Gott sich seine Braut / In seinem ewgen Wort durch seinen Geist vertraut!" CW 2.38: "Du magst Gott, wie du willst, für deinen Herrn erkennen: / Ich will ihm anders nichts als meinen Bräutigam nennen." CW 3.78: "Gott ist mein Salomon, ich seine Sulamith, / Wenn ich ihn herzlich lieb und er sich mir entbiet" (ed., 74, 109, 189; my trans.).
70. The following is a nonexhaustive list of the major couplets in the CW dealing with erotic union: 1.123, 1.183, 1.196, 1.260-62, 2.10, 2.14, 2.38, 2.93, 2.108, 3.51, 3.68, 3.78-79, 3.83, 3.121, 3.141, 3.149, 3.235, 4.40, 4.72, 4.88, 4.99, 4.138, 4.170-72, 4.175-76, 4.218, 5.180, 5.260, 5.269, 5.310, 5.340, 5.372, 6.9, 6.78, and 6.203.
71. Louise Gnädinger, "Die speculative Mystik im 'Cherubinischer Wandersmann' des Johannes Angelus Silesiius," *Studi Germanici* n.s. 4 (1966): 29-59, 144-90. "Das Engelthema" is presented in 144-70 (quotation from 168).
72. CW 3.165 (ed., 214; trans. Shrady, 79, adapted). For more on becoming all three orders, see CW 2.216, 4.108, and 5.215. Along with the angelization found in the tradition of the "Affective Dionysianism" of the Late Middle Ages, Scheffler may have been influenced by the way Bernard of Clairvaux talks about how the angels act in us in *De consideratione* V.5.12 (*Sancti Bernardi Opera* 3:476-77).
73. CW 1.3: "Weg, weg, ihr Seraphim, ihr könnt mich nicht erquicken! / Weg, weg, ihr Engel all und was an euch tut blicken! / Ich will nun eurer nicht: ich werfe mich allein / Ins ungeschaffne Meer der blossen Gottheit ein" (ed., 32; my trans.).
74. CW 3.203: "Wie gross sind wir gesehn! Die hohen Seraphim / Verdecken sich vor Gott: wir dürfen bloss zu ihm" (ed., 223; trans. Shrady, 81). CW 4.145: "Mensche, ich bin edeler als alle Seraphim, / Ich kann wohl sein, was sie, sie nie, was ich je bin" (ed., 274; trans. Shrady, 95). The more-than-angelic motif can also be found in CW 1.284, 2.44, 3.107, 3.114, 5.131, and 5.143.
75. CW 2.21: "Die Welt ist eitel Nichts, die Engel sind gemein: / Drum soll ich Gott und Mensch in Christo Jesu sein" (ed., 106; my trans.). See also 2.23 and 5.131.
76. John Tauler, Sermon 15, in Ferdinand Vetter, *Die Predigten Taulers* (Berlin: Weidmann, 1910; photomechanical reprint, 1968), 69.26-28.
77. CW 1.47: "Zeit ist wie Ewigkeit und Ewigkeit wie Zeit, / So du nur selber nicht machst einen Unterschied" (ed., 43; trans. Shrady, 41); see also 1.13: "Ich selbst bin Ewigkeit, wenn ich die Zeit verlasse / Und mich in Gott und Gott in mich zusammenfasse" (ed., 35). For more distichs on time and eternity, see, e.g., CW 1.188, 2.153, 4.135, and 5.23.

78. CW 5.127: "Die Seel, ein ewger Geist, ist über alle Zeit: / Sie lebt auch in der Welt schon in der Ewigkeit" (ed., 329; trans. Shrady, 110). On the relation of time and eternity in Scheffler, see Franz-Josef Schweitzer, "Zeit und Ewigkeit bei Angelus Silesius," in *Grundfragen christlicher Mystik: Wissenschaftliche Studientagung Theologia Mystica in Weingarten vom 7.–10. November 1985*, ed. Margot Schmidt and Dieter R. Bauer, Mystik in Geschichte und Gegenwart Abteilung 1.5 (Stuttgart-Bad Cannstatt: Frommann-Holzboog, 1987), 259-72.

79. The philosopher G. F. Leibniz (1636–1716) appears to have been the first to call Scheffler a pantheist. The accusation is still found today; see, e.g., Kołakowski, *Chrétiens sans église*, chap. 9. For an evaluation of the problems with Kołakowski's view of Scheffler as a pantheist, see Gorceix, *Flambée et agonie*, 262–63.

80. For an argument that all three aspects are part of Scheffler's identity as a Counter-Reformation mystic, see Le Brun, "Les différentes faces de la Contre-Réforme."

81. Examples of those who stress Scheffler as Christian mystic include Gnädinger, "Die speculative Mystik im 'Cherubinsicher Wandersmann'; and Haas, "Angelus Silesius: Die Welt, ein wunderschönes Nichts."

82. CW 1.8-11 (ed., 34; my trans.): 1:8: "Ich weiss, dass ohne mich Gott nicht ein Nu kann leben: / Werd ich zunicht, er muss von Not den Geist aufgeben." 1.9: "Dass Gott so selig ist und lebet ohn Verlangen, / Hat er sowohl von mir als ich von ihm empfangen." 1.10: "Ich bin so gross wie Gott, er ist als mich so klein, / Er kann nicht über mich, ich unter ihm nicht sein." 1.11: "Gott ist in mir das Feur und ich in ihm der Schein: / Sind wir einander nicht ganz inniglich gemein?"

83. Meister Eckhart, Pr. 52, in *Die deutschen und lateinischen Werke* (Stuttgart: Kohlhammer, 1936-), *Die deutschen Werke* 3:504.

84. CW 1.7: "Wo ist mein Aufenthalt? Wo ich und du nicht stehen. / Wo ist mein letztes End, in welches ich soll gehen? / Da, wo man keines findt. Wo soll ich denn nun hin? / Ich muss noch über Gott in eine Wüste ziehn" (ed., 33; trans. Shrady, 39, adjusted). The desert motif is not as strong in Scheffler as it is in Eckhart, but it does appear in several other couplets (see, e.g., CW 2.117, 2.175, and 5.316, which asserts, "Die Gottheit ist die Wüste; ed., 373).

85. CW 2.58: "Stirb oder leb in Gott! Du tust an beiden wohl, / Weil man Gott sterben muss und Gott auch leben soll" (ed., 115; my trans.).

86. CW 5.196: "Man kann den höchsten Gott mit allen Namen nennen; / Man kann ihm wiederum nicht einen zuerkennen" (ed., 346; my trans.). For other couplets on the impossibility of naming God, see 2.51, 5.14, and 5.197 (ed., 114, 328, 346).

87. CW 2.13: "Was ist die Jungfrauschaft? Frag, was die Gottheit sei! / Doch kennst du Lauterkeit, so kennst du alle zwei" (ed., 104; my trans.). CW 2.14 is similar: "Die Gottheit ist so nah der Jungfrauschaft verwandt, / Dass sie auch ohne die nicht Gottheit wird erkannt." CW 2.70 (ed., 118) defines *Lauterkeit* in an Eckhartian way: "Vollkommne Lauterkeit ist bild-, form-, liebelos: / Steht aller Eigenschaft, wie Gottes Wesen bloss." For some other texts on *Gottheit*, see CW 2.16, 4.127, and 5.298.

88. CW 3.168: "Die Gottheit ist ein Brunn! Aus ihr kommt alles her / Und lauft auch wieder hin: drum ist sie auch ein Meer" (ed., 215; my trans.). God as a fountain also appears in CW 1.55, 1.159, 1.179, and 5.216.

89. The sea/ocean image first appears in CW 1.3, where the poet speaks of

casting himself "ins ungeschaffne Meer der blossen Gottheit" (ed., 32). See also CW 4.135, 4.139, 4.156-57, and 5.338.

90. CW 6.174: "Viel Körnlein sind ein Brot, ein Meer viel Tröpfelein: / So sind auch unser viel in Gott ein einges Ein" (ed., 442; my trans.).

91. The use of the term *ein einiges Ein* to express the unity of God and the soul is found in CW 1.83, 1.285, 4.184, 5.6, 5.36, 5.321, and 5.347.

92. CW 1.81: "Bist du aus Gott geboren, so blühet Gott in dir, / Und seine Gottheit ist dein Saft und deine Zier" (ed., 52; my trans.). See also 1.90 (ed., 54).

93. CW 5.339: "*Die Gottheit Gründet Kein Geschöpf.* Wie tief die Gottheit sei, kann kein Geschöpf ergründen: / In ihren Abgrund muss auch Christi Seel verschwinden" (ed., 378; my trans.). *Abgrund* also appears in CW 1.68.

94. On *Grund* as a term for the divine nature, see CW 1.42: "Gott gründt sich ohne Grund und mist sich ohne Mass: / Bist du ein Geist mit ihm, Mensch, so verstehst du das" (ed., 42); see also CW 1.177 (*Grund* in the title), and 5.366. Scheffler uses *ergründen* in CW 1.6, 3.214, 4.22, and 5.339.

95. CW 5.29: "Ein Ungrund ist zwar Gott: doch wem er sich soll zeigen, / Der muss bis auf die Spitz der ewgen Berge steigen" (ed., 304; my trans.). On this text, see Baruzi, *Création religieuse,* 218.

96. CW 5.1: "Alls kommt aus Einem her und muss in Eines ein, / Wo es nicht will gezweit und in der Vielheit sein" (ed., 297; my trans.).

97. CW 5.6: "In Eins ist alles eins: kehrt zwei zurück hinein, / So ist es wesentlich mir ihm ein einges Ein" (ed., 298; trans. Shrady, 103).

98. CW 2.129: "Das Tier wird durch die Art, der Mensch durch den Verstand, / Der Engel durch das Schaun, durchs Wesen Gott bekannt" (ed., 132; my trans.). For other texts on the divine *Wesen,* see CW 2.70, and 2.125.

99. CW 2.145: "Was ist das Wesen Gotts? Fragst du mein Engigkeit? / Doch wisse, dass es ist ein Überwesenheit" (ed., 136; my trans.). In line with the Dionysian tradition, Silesius employs a number of other *über*-terms: *Übergottheit* (1.15), *Übernichts* (1.111), *Überheilig* (1.283 in title), *Überengelkeit* (2.44), *überlichte Licht* (4.23), *überschön* (5.189), and *Überunmöglichste* (6.153 in title).

100. CW 2.55: "Gott ist nur eigentlich: er lebt und liebet nicht, / Wie man von mir und dir und andern Dingen spricht" (ed., 115).

101. The group of CW 5.241-46 is in ed., 355-56. Quoted is 5.245: "Kein Nam ist, welcher Gott recht eigen wär: allein / Die Liebe heisst man ihn, so wert ist sie und fein" (my trans.). For more on God as love, see CW 1.70-71, 2.45, 3.37, 5.42 and 44. There is an extended treatment of the nature of love in general in CW 5.288-309.

102. CW 5.212: "Der Liebe Mittelpunkt ist Gott und auch ihr Kreis: / In ihm ruht sie, liebt alls in ihme gleicherweis" (ed., 350; my trans.); see also 3.28, and 3.148.

103. CW 1.199: "*Gott Ausser Kreatur.* Geh hin, wo du nicht kannst! Sieh, wo du siehest nicht! / Hör, wo nichts schallt und klingt: so bist du, wo Gott spricht" (ed., 77; trans. Shrady, 47, adapted). Compare this with John of the Cross, *Ascent of Mount Carmel* 1.13.

104. CW 2.153: "Was ist die Ewigkeit? Sie ist nicht dies, nicht das, / Nicht Nun, nicht ichts, nicht Nichts: sie ist, ich weiss nicht was" (ed., 137; trans. Shrady, 63). The fomula *nicht dies, nicht das* is reminiscent of Eckhart's view of God as "neither this, nor that" (i.e., nothing created).

105. CW 4.21: "*Der Unerkannte Gott*. Was Gott ist, weiss man nicht! Er is nicht Licht, nicht Geist, / Nicht Wonnigkeit, nicht Eins, nicht was man Gottheit heisst, / Nicht Weisheit, nicht Verstand, nicht Liebe, Wille, Güte, / Kein Ding, kein Unding auch, kein Wesen, kein Gemüte: / Er ist, was ich und du und keine Kreatur, / Eh wir geworden sind, was er ist, nie erfuhr" (ed., 241–42; my trans.).

106. CW 2.146: "*Gott ist Finsternis und Licht*. Gott ist ein lautrer Blitz und auch ein dunkles Nicht, / Das keine Kreatur beschaut mit ihrem Licht" (ed., 136; my trans.). For other texts on God as *nichts*, see 1.25, 1.111, and 1.200.

107. CW 3.199: "Die Allmacht halt die Welt, die Weisheit, die regiert, / Die Güte signet sie: wird hier nicht Gott gespürt?" (ed., 222; my trans.). See also 5.329. Another triad found in the tradition is the comparison of the Father to a fountain, the Son to the spring fed from the fountain, and the Holy Spirit to its flow (see 5.123; ed., 328). Also traditional is seeing the Holy Spirit as the kiss of the Father and the Son (6.238; ed. 456). For other texts on the Trinity, see 1.242, 3.215, 4.61, 5.241, 5.359, and 5.368.

108. CW 5.283: "Weil Gott dreieinig ist, so hat er Ruh und Lust: / Ruh kommt von Einheit her, Lust von der Dreiheit Brust" (ed., 365; my trans.). CW 4.166 (ed., 279) says that in God rest and activity are the same.

109. For example, CW 6.234: "Der Sohn erlöset uns, der Geist, der macht uns leben, / Des Vaters Allmacht wird uns die Vergottung geben" (ed., 455); see also 6.232–33 and 235.

110. CW 4.62: "Gott Vater is der Punkt; aus ihm fleisst Gott der Sohn, / Die Linie; Gott der Geist ist beider Fläch und Kron" (ed., 254; my trans.).

111. CW 1.257: "Dass Gott dreieinig ist, zeigt dir ein jedes Kraut, / Da Schewefel, Salz, Merkur in einem wird geschaut" (ed., 89; trans. Shrady, 50); see also 1.246. Boehme held that these three elements were the fundamental substances of the universe. Gnädinger in ed., 66n. 2, has a list of the distichs influenced by alchemical imagery.

112. CW 4.1 and 2: "Der ungewordne Gott wird mitten in der Zeit, / Was er nie ist gewest in aller Ewigkeit." "Das unerschaffne Licht wird ein erschaffenes Wesen, / Das sein Geschöpfe nur durch selbes kann genesen" (ed., 237; my trans.).

113. A series of couplets in CW 4.153–60 (ed., 276–78) explores how God is in all things.

114. CW 2.198: "*Gott Spielt mit dem Geschöpfe*. Dies alles ist ein Spiel, das sich die Gottheit macht: / Se hat die Kreatur um ihretwillen erdacht" (ed., 149; my trans.).

115. CW 5.91: "Da Gott der Welt erschuf, was schrieb man für ein Jahr? / Kein anders nicht, als das seins Umstands erstes war" (ed., 318; my trans.). See also 5.19 and 5.146.

116. CW 5.86: "Die Schöpfung ist ein Buch: wers weislich lessen kann, / Dem wird darin gar fein der Schöpfer kund getan" (ed., 317; my trans.).

117. Seeing man as *imago Trinitatis* is not a major theme in Silesius but is suggested in CW 1.148 (ed., 66).

118. CW 5.239–40: "Fragst du, warum mich Gott nach seinem Bildnis machte? / Ich sag, es war niemand, der ihm anders brachte." "Wann ist der Mensch zu Gott vollkommlich wiederbracht? / Wenn er das Muster ist, darnach ihn Gott gemacht" (ed., 355; my trans.). For more on the soul as *imago dei*, see CW 1.105, 1.272, 3.76, 3.109, and 4.58. On the soul coming forth from God and returning to him, see the series of distichs in CW 2.158–61 (ed., 138–39).

119. CW 1.108: "Die Rose, welche hier dein äusseres Auge sieht, / Die hat von Ewigkeit in Gott also geblüht" (ed., 58; trans. Shrady, 44). See also 1.107, 109–10.

120. CW 2.143: "In Gott ist alles Gott: ein einzigs Würmelein, / Das ist in Gott so viel, als tausend Gotte sein" (ed., 135; my trans.). See also 4.185.

121. CW 5.233: "*Wenn Der Mensch Gott Ist.* Eh als ich Ich noch war, da war ich Gott in Gott: / Darum kann ichs wieder sein, wenn ich nur mir bin tot" (ed., 354; my trans.). See also 5.259 and 5.332.

122. CW 1.5: "Ich weiss nicht, was ich bin, ich bin nicht, was ich weiss: / Ein Ding und nicht ein Ding, ein Stüpfchen und ein Kreis" (ed., 32; my trans.).

123. See Haas, "Die Welt—ein wunderschönes Nichts," 387–89, using such passages as CW 1.5, 1.46, 1.77, and 1.150.

124. CW 1.185: "Nicht du bist in dem Ort, der Ort, der ist in dir! / Wirfst du ihn aus, so steht die Ewigkeit schon hier" (ed., 74; my trans.). See also 1.187 and 2.71.

125. CW 1.190: "*Die Gleichheit.* Ich weiss nicht, was ich soll! Es ist mir alles ein: / Ort, Unort, Ewigkeit, Zeit, Nacht, Tag, Freud und Pein" (ed., 75; trans, Shrady 46, adapted).

126. CW 1.1: "Rein wie das feinste Gold, steif wie ein Felsenstein, / Ganz lauter wie Kristall soll dein Gemüte sein" (ed., 31; trans. Shrady, 39). The image of the soul as a crystal also is found in 1.6 and 3.242. Scheffler joins those mystics who make use of crystals and other gems as mystical symbols; see Mazzocco, *Le joyau de l'âme,* 139–53.

127. For example, CW 4.137: "Wer kann das Fünklein in seinem Feur erkennen? / Wer mich, wann ich in Gott, ob ich es sei, benennen?" (ed., 273). See also 5.349 and 5.569.

128. See CW 3.224: "Die Jungfrauschaft ist wert! Doch muss sie Mutter werden, / Sonst sie wie ein Plan von unbefruchter Erden" (ed., 227). See also 3.3 and 3.158. Eckhart's Pr. 2 analyzes the soul as both virgin and wife (*Die deutschen Werke,* 1:21–45).

129. CW 1.96: "Gott mag nicht ohne mich ein einzigs Würmlein machen! / Erhalt ichs nicht mit ihm, so muss es stracks zerkrachen" (ed., 55; my trans.).

130. CW 1.138: "Je mehr du dich aus dir kannst austun und entgiessen, / Je mehr muss Gott in dich seiner Gottheit fliessen" (ed., 65; my trans.).

131. CW 1.278: "Ich bin Gotts ander Er: in mir findt er allein, / Was ihm in Ewigkeit wird gleich und ähnlich sein" (ed., 93; my trans.). For other examples of divine-human reciprocity in book 1, see 1.8–11, 1.69, 1.73, 1.86, 1.100, 1.106, 1.133, 1.139, 1.167, 1.204, 1.212, 1.224, 1.259, 1.272, and 1.276–78.

132. CW 2.201: "Sag zwischen mir und Gott den eingen Unterschied? / Es ist mit einen Wort nichts als die Anderheit" (ed., 149; trans. Shrady, 66). For other such texts in book 2, see 2.125 and 2.180.

133. CW 3.202: "Gott wird von nichts verletzt, hat nie kein Leid empfunden: / Und doch kann meine Seel ihm gar das Herz verwunden" (ed., 223; my trans.). See also 3.80, 3.123, 3.135, and 3.146.

134. CW 5.48: "Zwei müsse es vollziehn: ich kanns nicht ohne Gott / Und Gott nicht ohne mich, dass ich entgeh dem Tod" (ed., 308; trans. Shrady, 106). See also 5.66 and 5.121.

135. CW 5.357: "Mensch, wenn dein Herz ein Tal, muss Gott sich drein ergiessen, / Und zwar so mildiglich, dass es muss überfliessen" (ed., 382; my trans.).

136. A point emphasized by Gorceix, *Flambée et agonie*, 251.

137. On Scheffler's view of Christ, see Haas, "Christus ist Alles," 295-319.

138. The closest Scheffler comes to this is in CW 5.325 (ed. 373), where he speaks about our sharing not only in being born in God but also in Christ's death, Resurrection, and Ascension.

139. CW 3.15: "Singt, singt, ihr Engel, singt! Mit hundertausend Zungen / Wird dieses werte Kind nicht würdiglich besungen. / Ach, möcht ich ohne Zung und ohne Stimme sein! / Ich weiss, ich sang ihm stracks das liebste Liedelein" (ed., 170; trans. Shrady, 72). For more on music, see 3.9 and 3.18.

140. CW 5.82: "Sag, wo die Liebe wird am liebsten gefunden? / Am Kreuz, wenn sie um des Geliebsten willn gebunden" (ed., 315; trans. Shrady, 108). In 5.159 we even find the Silesian picking up on the theme found in other mystics that Christ is still suffering and will be to the end of time. Book 2 also has couplets on the Passion (e.g., 2.11, 2.123, 2.167, etc.).

141. CW 1.121: "Willst du den Perlentau der edlen Gottheit fangen, / So must du unverrückt an seiner Menschheit hangen" (ed., 60; trans, Shrady, 45).

142. CW 1.155: "*Hier Muss Der Anfang Sein.* Mensch, willst du ewiglich beim Lämmlein Gottes stehn, / So must du schon allhier in seinen Tritten gehn" (ed., 67; my trans.); see also 2.23, 4.50, 5.223, etc. Connected with the imitation of Christ is the image of Christ as a book in which the meaning of life can be read (see 5.87 and 5.176-77).

143. CW 5.264: "Mensch, wenn dein Herz vor Gott wie Wachs ist weich und rein, / So drückt der heilge Geist das Bildnis Jesu drein" (ed., 360; my trans.).

144. CW 5.149: "Der Vielheit ist Gott Feind: drum zieht er uns so ein, / Dass alle Menschen solln in Christo Einer sein" (ed., 334; my trans.).

145. CW 5.155: "Der erst und letzte Mensch ist Christus selbst allein, / Weil all aus ihm entstehn, in ihm beschlossen sein" (ed., 336; my trans.). On Christ's universal role, see also 2.213 and 3.227.

146. CW 3.79 (ed., 190; my trans.), omitting the German here. CW 2.93 describes the Holy Spirit as the kiss of the Son in the marriage. At times there are some small groups of couplets on the sacred marriage (e.g., 4.175-77).

147. CW 4.88: "*Aus Dem Hohen Lied.* Der König führt die Braut in Keller selbst hinein, / Dass sie sich mag erwähln den allerbesten Wein. / So machts Gott auch mit dir, wenn du bist seine Braut: / Er hat nichts in sich selbst, das er dir nicht vertraut" (ed., 260; my trans.).

148. CW 2.14: "Die Seele, die nichts weiss, nichts will, nichts liebt, denns Ein, / Muss heute noch die Braut des ewgen Bräutgams sein" (ed., 104; my trans.).

149. CW 5.172: "Ich muss verwundert sein. Warum? Weil voller Wunden / Mein ewger Bräutigam, der Heiland, wird gefunden. / Was Nutzen bringt es dir? Es steher gar nicht fein, / Wenn Braut und Bräutigam einander ungleich sein" (ed., 385; my trans.).

150. CW 204: "Wen Gott zu seinem Sohn geboren hat auf Erden, / Der Mensch kann nimmermehr von Gott geschieden werden." CW 4.207: "Wer stets in Gotte bleibt, verliebt, gelassen ist, / Der Mensch wird allermeist für Gottes Sohn erkiest" (ed., 288-89; my trans.).

151. CW 6.134: "*Von Gott Geboren Werden ist Gänzlich Gott Sein.* Gott zeuget nichts als Gott: zeugt er dich seinen Sohn, / So wirst du Gott in Gott, Herr auf des Herren Thron" (ed., 433; my trans.). A similar message is found in 6.236 (ed.,

455): "Gotts Sohn ist Gott, mit Gott regiert auf einem Thron: / Nichts Höhers ist als ich, wenn ich bin dieser Sohn."

152. CW 1.61: "Wird Christus tausendmal zu Bethlehem geborn / Und nicht in dir: du bleibst noch ewiglich verlorn" (ed., 46; my trans.). See also 4.194.

153. CW 2.112: *"Aus und Ein. Gebären und Geborensein.* Wenn du in Wahrheit kannst aus Gott geboren sein / Und wieder Gott gebärn, so gehst du aus und ein" (ed., 128; my trans.).

154. CW 1.23: "Ich muss Maria sein und Gott aus mir gebären, / Soll er mich ewiglich der Seligkeit gewähren" (ed., 37; my trans.). The Mary theme also is found in 2.102, 2.104, 3.23, and 4.249. In 3.238 there is a description of the Nativity events as an allegory of the inner birth in the soul.

155. CW 2:228: *"Nur Eins Will Gott von Uns.* Ein einzigs Wort spricht Gott zu mir, zu dir, und allen: / Lieb! Tun wir das durch ihm, wir müssen ihm gefallen" (ed., 133; my trans.).

156. CW 3.191: "Wer Gott recht lieben will, der tuts ohn Mass und Ziel; / Er ist so süss und gut, man liebt ihn nie zuviel" (ed., 221; my trans.). CW 1.182 (ed., 74) says that the only service we should give to God is that of love.

157. CW 2.1: "Die Lieb ist ein Magnet, sie ziehet mich in Gott; / Und was noch grösser ist: sie reisset Gott in Tod" (ed., 101; my trans.). See also 6.118 and 6.245.

158. CW 1.16: "Wo Gott mich über Gott nicht sollte wollen bringen, / So will ich ihn dazu mit blosser Liebe zwingen" (ed., 35; trans. Shrady, 39). See also 3.59.

159. CW 5.200: "Mensch, was du liebst, in das wirst du verwandelt werden: / Gott wirst du, liebst du Gott, und Erde, liebst du Erden" (ed., 347; my trans.). The title says that this observation is taken from Augustine. Scheffler seems to have the bishop's *In Epistolam Ioannis ad Parthos* 2.4 in mind. CW 5.201: "Liebst du Gott über dich, den Nächsten wie dem Leben, / Was sonst ist, unter dir: so liebst du recht und eben" (ibid.; my trans.).

160. The third and longest of the couplet groups on love is in CW 5.288–30 (ed., 366–72). I have already referenced several of these.

161. CW 1.43: "Ich lieb ein einzig Ding und weiss nicht nicht, was es ist: / Und weil ich es night weiss, drum hab ich es erkiest" (ed., 43; trans. Shrady, 41).

162. CW 5.320: "Der nächste Weg zu Gott ist durch der Liebe Tür: / Der Weg der Wissenschaft bringt dich gar langsam für" (ed., 374; my trans.). See also 5.307.

163. CW 1.171: *"Gott Findet Man mit Nichtsuchen.* Gott ist nicht hier noch da: wer ihn begehrt zu finden, / Der lass sich Händ und Füss und Leib und Seele binden" (ed. 72; my trans.). Passivity to God's action also appears in 5.207: "Das allergrösste Werk, das du für Gott kannst tun, / Ist ohn ein einzigs Werk Gott leiden und Gott ruhn" (ed., 349).

164. CW 2.67: "Weil Abgeschiedenheit sich niemand macht gemein, / So muss sie ohne Sucht und eine Jungfrau sein" (ed., 117; my trans.).

165. CW 5.209: "Freund, wo dus wissen willst: das allerhöchste Leben / Ist abgeschieden sein und Gott stehn übergeben: (ed., 349; my trans.). See also 6.105, which does not, however, use the word *Abgeschiedenheit.*

166. CW 1.65: "Gott ist das ärmstes Ding, er steht ganz bloss und frei: / Drum sag ich recht und wohl, dass Armut göttlich sei" (ed., 47; my trans.).

167. CW 4.210: "Die Armut unsres Geists besteht in Innigkeit, / Da man sich aller Ding und seiner selbst verzeiht" (ed., 290; my trans.).

168. CW 2.140: "Nichts bringt dich über dich als die Vernichtigkeit: / Wer mehr vernichtigt ist, hat mehr Göttlichkeit" (ed., 135; my trans.).

169. CW 5.332: "Wenn ich in Gott vergeh, so komm ich wieder hin, / Wo ich von Ewigkeit vor mir gewesen hin" (ed. 377; my trans.).

170. A number of other distichs speak of abandoning or destroying the self without using the term *Vernichtigkeit*; see, e.g., CW 5.126 and 6.192.

171. For the history of *Gelassenheit*, see Ludwig Völker, "'Gelassenheit': Zur Entstehung des Wortes in der Sprache Meister Eckharts und seiner Überlieferung in der nacheckhartischen Mystik bis Jacob Böhme," in *'Getempert und Gemischet' für Wolfgang Mohr zum 65. Geburtstag*, ed. Franz Hundsnurscher and Ulrich Müller (Göppingen: Alfred Kümmerle, 1972), 281-312. This article, alas, does not include Silesius, nor does my essay "*Gelâzen/Gelâzenheit* from Eckhart to the Radical Reformers," *Meister-Eckhart-Jahrbuch* 13 (2019): 89–111.

172. CW 2.92: "*Die Geheimste Gelassenheit.* Gelassenheit fängt Gott: Gott aber selbst zu lassen, / Ist ein Gelassenheit, die wenig Menschen fassen" (ed., 122; my trans.).

173. CW 4.196: "Der Heilgen grösstes Werk und Arbeit auf der Erden / Ist Gott gelassen sein und ihm gemeiner werden" (ed., 287; my trans.). For other passages on releasing God, see CW 1.99, and 1.164.

174. CW 2.141: "Ein grundgelassner Mensch ist ewig frei und ein: / Kann auch ein Unterschied an ihm und Gotte sein?" (ed., 135; my trans.).

175. See, for example, CW 1.39, 2.133, 2.135-36, 2.144, 2.216, 4.191, 4.198, and 4.207.

176. For an introduction, see Alois M. Haas, "Im Schweigen Gott zur Sprache bringen—Gotteserfahrung der Mystik," in *Gott Denken und Bezeugen: Festschrift für Kardinal Walter Kasper zum 75. Geburtstag*, ed. George Augustin and Klaus Krämer (Freiburg: Herder, 2008), 317–55.

177. Mazzocco, "Entre silence et vibrations sonores."

178. CW 1.240: "*Das Stillschweigende Gebet.* Gott ist so über alls, dass man nichts sprechen kann: / Drum betest du ihn mit Schweigen besser an" (ed., 86; trans. Shrady, 49).

179. CW 1.19: "*Das Selige Stillschweigen.* Wie selig ist der Mensch, der weder will noch weiss, / Der Gott (versteh mich recht!) nicht gibet Lob noch Preis" (ed., 36; my trans.). See also 1.85, 1.299, 2.8, 2.68, 3.8, 3.15, 4.11, 5.129, 5.137, and 5.366.

180. CW 1.239: "*Gott Lobt Man in der Stille.* Meinst du, O armer Mensch, dass deines Munds Geschrei / Der rechte Lobgesang der stillen Gottheit sei?" (ed., 85; my trans.). See 1.294, which speaks of God as *ewge Stille*.

181. CW 2.19: "Geschäftig sein ist gut, viel besser aber beten; / Noch besser stumm und still vor Gott, den Herren, treten" (ed., 105; my trans.).

182. CW 4.173: "Der höchste Friede, den die Seele kann geniessen, / Ist sich aufs möglichst eins mit Gottes Willen wissen" (ed. 280; my trans); see also 3.156.

183. CW 4.181: "Die selge Seele weiss nichts mehr von Anderheit: / Sie ist ein Licht mit Gott und eine Herrlichkeit" (ed., 283; my trans.). CW 4.10: "Der Mensch hat eher nicht vollkomne Seligkeit, / Bis dass die Einheit hat verschluckt die Anderheit" (ed., 239; trans. Shrady, 87).

184. CW 2.224: "Wenn sich der Mensch entzieht der Mannigfaltigkeit / Und kehrt sich ein zu Gott, kommet er zur Einigkeit" (ed., 292; my trans.).

185. CW 2.178: "Nichts ist als ich und du: und wenn wir zwei nicht sein, / So ist Gott nicht mehr Gott und fällt der Himmel ein" (ed., 145; trans. Shrady, 65). CW 2.179: "Ach ja! Wär Ich im Du und Du im Ich ein Ein, / So möchte tausendmal de Himmel Himmel sein" (ed., 145; my trans.).

186. CW 6.175: "Mensch, du kannst dich mit Gott viel leichter eines sehn, / Als man ein Aug aufut: will nur, so ists geschehn!" (ed., 443; my trans.).

187. CW, "Errinerungs-Vorrede an den Leser" (ed., 10–12; my trans.).

188. Maria Shrady notes a comment Scheffler wrote in his edition of Sandaeus's *Clavis* under the entry "Transformatio/Deificatio": "(Spiritus cum Deo) unum efficitur, unus Spiritus, una anima, unum esse, una felicitas; alteritatem namque non recipit, Dionys. Carth. De vita solit. 1.2.cap 10" (Shrady, *Cherubinic Wanderer*, 98).

189. CW 1.216: "Gott ist mein Geist, mein Blut, mein Fleisch und mein Gebein: / Wie soll ich dann mit ihm nicht ganz durchgottet sein?" (ed., 81; my trans.).

190. CW 2.54: "Entbilde dich, mein Kind! So wirst du Gotte gleich / Und bist in stiller Ruh dir selbst dein Himmelreich" (ed., 114; my trans.). Also CW 2.59: "Wer ohn Empfinden liebt und ohn Erkennen kennt, / Der wird mit gutem Recht mehr Gott als Mensch genennt" (ed., 115; my trans.).

191. CW 2.163: "*Gott Wirkt Wie Das Feuer.* Das Feuer schmelzt und eint: sinkst du in Ursprung ein, / So muss dein Geist mit Gott in eins geschmelzer sein" (ed., 139; my trans.). The theme of fire and melting into God is found in the couplets where Silesius uses alchemical symbolism to describe the deification process; e.g., CW 1.102, 1.248, and 1.258.

192. CW 1.92: "Wer ist, als wär er nicht und wär er nie geworden, / Der ist (o Seligkeit!) zu lauter Gotte worden" (ed., 54; my trans.).

193. Eire, *Reformations*, "The Netherlands" (542–48; quotation from 546).

194. McGinn, *Varieties*, chap. 5., "A Mystical Renaissance in the Eastern Netherlands" (141–75). Other studies of this mystical movement can be found in Brandsma, *In Search of Living Water*, 125–86 ("Nicholas van Esch," "The Evangelical Pearl," and "Maria van Oisterwijk"); and the essays in Kees Schepers and Thom Mertens, eds., *1517–1545: The Northern Experience. Mysticism, Reform and Devotion between the Late Medieval and Early Modern Periods*, Ons Geestelijk Erf 87.1-2 (2016).

195. The best introduction to the period is Paul Mommaers, "Pays-Bas IV: Les XVIe et XVIIe siècles," DS 12:730–50.

196. "Jan Pelgrim Pullen (1550–1608)," in Brandsma, *In Search of Living Water*, 348–60; and Albert Ampe, "Pullen (Jean, Pelgrim), prêtre, vers 1520–1608," DS 12:2621-23.

197. An extract from the *Conversation*, which took place in November of 1587, can be found in Rik Van Nieuwenhove, Robert Faesen, and Helen Rolfson, eds., *Late Medieval Mysticism in the Low Countries*, Classics of Western Spirituality (New York: Paulist Press, 2008), 165–75. See Albert Ampe, "Nieuwlant (Claesinne van), béguine, vers 1540–1611," DS 11:344–45.

198. The point is noted by Mommaers, who provides a discussion of this work in "Pays-Bas IV: Les XVIe et XVIIe sieclès," DS 12:738–40. Along with its teaching on nothingness and attaining a superessential life, the text also emphasizes the Ruusbroecian notion that essential love demands both a loving ascent to God and a loving descent to activity in the world.

199. The most complete account of this mystical controversy is Jean Orcibal, *La rencontre du Carmel Thérésiene avec les mystiques du Nord* (Paris: Presses Universitaires de France, 1959), including many texts. For a summary, see Mommaers, "Le Pays-Bas IV: Les XVI e et XVIIe siècles," DS 12:735–38.

200. See the brief treatment in McGinn, *Spain*, 369, and the literature cited there.

201. On Tomás de Jesús, see McGinn, *Spain*, 371-76. The two treatises Tomás wrote against the Northern mystics were the *De variis erroribus spiritualium* of 1611 (see Orcibal, *La rencontre du Carmel*, 174-77), and the *Censura in libellum vulgo 'Theologia Germanica' sive Libellus Aureus nuncupatum* (*La rencontre du Carmel*, 178-224).

202. For a sketch of John's mystical teaching, see Mommaers, "Pays-Bas IV: Les XVI e et XVIIe siècles," DS 12:742-44.

203. The context within which Maria Petyt wrote is set out by Esther van de Vate, "Maria Petyt against the Background of the Political and Religious Situation in Flanders in the Seventeenth Century," in *Maria Petyt: A Carmelite Mystic in Wartime*, ed. Joseph Chalmers et al., Radboud Studies in Humanities 4 (Leiden: Brill, 2015), 22-51.

204. Albert Deblaere, S.J., wrote a dissertation on Maria Petyt in 1957, which was published as *De mystieke Schrijfster Maria Petyt (1623-1677)* (Gent: Secretarie der Academie, 1962). This contains a selection of her texts (256-390). Deblaere's 1979 essay on Maria has been reprinted: "Maria Petyt, écrivain et mystique flamande," in *Albert Deblaere, S. J. (1916-1994): Essays on Mystical Literature*, ed. Rob Faesen, Bibliotheca Ephemeridum theologicarum Lovaniensium 177 (Leuven: Leuven University Press, 2004), 223-90. There is an introduction in English (first written in Dutch in 1939) by Titus Brandsma, "Maria Petyt," *In Search of Living Water*, 361-73. See also Mommaers, "Pays-Bas IV: Les XVI e et XVIIe siècles," DS 12:746-49, and André Derville, "Petyt (Maria; Marie de Sainte-Thérèse), tertiaire du Carmel, 1623-1677," DS 12:1227-29. Important English essays can be found in Chalmers et al., *Maria Petyt, A Carmelite Mystic in Wartime*, which also includes the only one of her works available in English, a Latin text on the Dutch War of Louis XIV (see below).

205. For a survey of Maria's life, see Esther van de Vate, "Maria Petyt—A Short Biography," in Chalmers et al., *Maria Petyt, A Carmelite Mystic in Wartime*, 7-21.

206. Teresa'a *Interior Castle* was translated into Flemish in 1605. On the influence of Teresa on Maria, see Elisabeth Hense, "The Spirituality of Teresa of Avila and the Latin Manuscript about the Dutch War (folios 30r-49v)," in Chalmers et al., *Maria Petyt, A Carmelite Mystic in Wartime*, 352-65. More work is needed on the sources of Maria Petyt. We know that she read classic texts like Gertrude of Helfta, the *De imitatione Christi*, Hendrik Herp, and the *Evangelical Pearl*. Closer to her own time, she was influenced by Carmelite sources, especially Teresa, John of the Cross, Maria Maddelena de'Pazzi, and Jean de Saint-Samson.

207. Albert Deblaere, "Michel de Saint-Augustin," DS 10:1187-91.

208. Michel van Meerbeeck, "Daily Life at the Hermitage in Mechelen at the Time of Maria Petyt (1657-1677)," in Chalmers et al, *Maria Petyt, A Carmelite Mystic in Wartime*, 53-66.

209. This large work, published at Ghent in 1683-84, contains over 1,400 pages. The autobiography forms the first of the four parts. There is a modern photographical reprint of the work issued in 2002, as well as an edition of the autobiographical part by J. R. A. Merlier, *Het Leven van Maria Petyt (1623-1677)* (Zutphen: Thieme & Cie, 1976).

210. This text, the *Vita Venerabilis Matris Mariae a Sancta Theresia*, found in Rome, Carmelite Archives, Post. III, 70, ff. 30r-49v, has been edited and translated into English in Chalmers et al., *Maria Petyt, A Carmelite Mystic in Wartime*, 119-239.

211. Maria's rather surprising siding with Louis XIV is examined by Veronie Meeuwsen, "Maria Petyt's Support of the French King," in Chalmers et al., *Maria Petyt, A Carmelite Mystic in Wartime*, 240-51.

212. *Vita* f. 38r (ed., 168-70). In one place Maria herself seems disturbed by her visions and wonders if they are really *illuminationes supernaturales* or only the products of natural reason (f. 46r; ed., 214-17).

213. Among the unusual, though not unprecedented, aspects of the new *Vita*, are the at times extravagant claims Maria makes for her mystical authority. For example, on f. 47v she says that divine power flowed out both from her and from God over the French army, because "the Beloved has entrusted and given Holland to me" (ed., 224-25). Another disturbing text can be found in f. 39r (ed., 174-75), where God tells her she is his equal.

214. Brandsma, "Maria Petyt," 366-73. For Maria, as for many of the contemporary French mystics, the role of Mary, and especially the heart of Mary, was indispensable.

215. Brandsma, "Maria Petye," 372-73.

216. Some selections from Maria Petyt's and Michael of St. Augustine's writings on Mary can be found in Payne, *Carmelite Tradition*, 97-103; quotation from 98.

217. Mommaers, "Pays-Bas IV: Les XVIe et XVIIe siècles," DS 12:746.

218. Ibid., 747. Mommaers does not cite the location of this text from the *Life*.

219. Deblaere, "Itinéraire spirituel," in "Maria Petyt, écrivain et mystique flamande," 265-90.

220. Deblaere, "Itinéraire spirituel," 267-73. This introversion brings the soul to the level of "unity of spirit" (*eensaemheyt des gheests*) and "freedom of spirit."

221. Deblaere, "Itinéraire spirituel," 273-97; quotation from 278.

222. Deblaere, "Itinéraire spirituel," 279-86, citing texts from the *Life* (I:106-56).

223. Deblaere, "Itinéraire spirituel," 288-90, with the quotations from 288 and 289.

224. *Vita* f. 30v (ed., 126-27): ". . . nam spiritus solutus et liber ab omnibus et ab aliis rebus intactus se potest conseruare intus in castro animae." I will use the English version given with the *Vita*.

225. *Vita* f. 34r (ed., 146-49).

226 Marguerite Porete, *Le mirouer des simples ames*, ed. Romana Guarnieri and Paul Verdeyen (Turnhout: Brepols, 1986), e.g., chaps. 108 and 118 (292-94, 330-33).

227. *Vita* f. 48r (ed., 228-29). Other occurrences of annihilation language can be found in ed., 138 (*essentialis nihileitas*); ed., 150 (*ponit in nihilo meo*); ed., 162 (*talem orationem . . . annihilare*); and ed., 164 (*quasi annihilando*).

228. *Vita* f. 42r (ed., 192-93): ". . . quia actualiter fluunt ex Deo in animam, et iterum refluunt ex anima in ipsum."

229. On bridal union, see *Vita*, ff. 34v-35r (ed., 150-53); for the prayer of the bride, see f. 36v (ed., 162-65).

230. *Vita* f. 41rv (ed., 188-91).

Conclusion

As explained in the "Introduction," this volume brings to an end my treatment of an incredibly rich period in the history of Western mysticism, the era of early modernity (ca. 1500–1650/75). The sixteenth- and seventeenth-century explosion of publications by and about those we today call mystics produced a vast literature that would demand a lifetime to read. Hence, any general account, even about only some of the most important figures must, by its nature, be limited.

This final part of Volume VI comes under the heading of *The Persistence of Mysticism*, a title that occurred to me late in the book's gestation but that also fits the former two parts. The earlier iterations of Volume VI were confessional (*Mysticism in the Reformation*), and geographical-confessional (*Mysticism in the Golden Age of Spain*). Equally important, however, with chronology, confession, and geographical location, were the issues of content and theme. From the perspective of the argument that has been developed through the volumes of *The Presence of God*, the theme of mysticism as the special dialectical relation between the presence and absence of God in the lives of Christians has been a constant phenomenon. This volume has been written out of the conviction that, even in the tumultuous period 1500–1650/75, the great traditions of Christian mysticism were alive and well—that the past persisted, although in a changed historical context.

Along with the persistence of mysticism, this volume, and to some extent the previous two, have touched on many other important themes—some new, others old, but developed in new ways during this period. As we have seen, much attention has been given to the shifting nature of mystical discourse in the late sixteenth and the seventeenth centuries. This is not to say that close attention to the way in which mystics expressed their message was not important in the medieval period, but there seems to have been greater consciousness on the part of many mystics about the character of mystical writing in general, as well as about the peculiarities of the terms and modes of argumentation in mystical texts. The term "mysticism," used substantively to characterize a topic of investigation, emerged in the seventeenth century. Although the related term "science of the saints" was biblical in origin, one can say that it took on a different color in an age in which the mystics and their students often expressed an independent, sometimes even adversarial, approach to "scholastic theology." The term "mystical theology" continued to be used, but it too shifted in meaning, as those formerly called "contemplatives" began to be increasingly termed "mystics."

Another feature of the era was the dominance of affectivity over intellect in the mystical life. To be sure, mystics had always insisted that, since "God is love," it is love alone that can attain final union with God, but many of the major mystics of the Middle Ages had worked out nuanced views of how understanding and affectivity cooperated in the path to union. Even the "affective" Dionysianism of the Late Middle Ages paid attention to the role of knowing in preparing for the transition to the *apex affectus*, the summit of loving union. The early modern mystics did not, for the most part, totally neglect the role of intellect, but they tended to say less about it and often seem to have viewed reason, and perhaps even suprarational knowing, as a kind of danger in the mystical life. One sign of this, I believe, can be seen in the growing emphasis on "aspirations," that is, affective ejaculatory prayer, in the writings of many mystics, especially those found in this volume. To engage in contemplative prayer, even to attempt to attain a direct and intuitive knowledge of the divine nature if possible, seemed dangerous or misleading to some mystics. Better to pour the heart out before divine Love in fervent aspiration.

A third characteristic often appearing in this volume, and sometimes in the previous two, is the stress on annihilation as necessary for union. Annihilation language also featured in late medieval mysticism, but it takes on a surprising centrality in many of the figures presented here. Mystical annihilation was conceived of in many ways, beginning from forms of ascetical and moral stripping off of the sinful self to what I have called "hard" forms of annihilation that claim that, on some level at least, the created self and its operations need to be negated so that God alone can work in the soul. This is why I have suggested that the seventeenth century might be spoken of as "the Age of Annihilation." Closely allied with annihilation (how and in what ways is often difficult to say) was the growing concern with "pure love," once again scarcely a new theme, but one that exercised an increasing fascination on mystics, especially in France.

The list could go on, but one final issue that struck me as I reviewed this volume was the issue of ecstatic forms of consciousness. Many mystics, especially males, expressed suspicion with regard to such experiences, a caution that is evident throughout the history of Christian mysticism, because giving too much attention to the extraordinary impedes the true understanding of mysticism as a mode of life aimed essentially at more intensive and effective love of God and love of neighbor. Nonetheless, ecstatics abounded in the sixteenth and seventeenth centuries, especially among women, as so many Spanish, French, and Italian mystics demonstrate. Even mystics who were suspicious of ecstasy often had experiences of being taken outside themselves into inexpressible realms, moments of supra-consciousness that changed the course of their lives.

All in all, it is impossible to really "conclude" this volume and its predecessors, because the account given in these books does not end in 1650 or 1675, or even around 1700, when the mystical element underwent a crisis that, at least in Catholic Europe, marginalized it for two centuries or more. If, as I have argued from the outset of *The Presence of God*, the mystical element is part and parcel of Christianity, its demise would mean the end of something integral to Christian faith from the time of the gospel down to the present day. Although the permutations of mystical traditions have been many over the centuries, there is an underlying persistence that continues to surprise.

Bibliography

SECTION I. SOURCES

1. BARBE ACARIE (AVRILLOT) (1566–1618)

Texts

[Madame Acarie]. *Écrits spirituels.* Edited by Bernard Sesé. Carnets spirituels 30. Mesnil-sur-l'Estrée: Arfuyen, 2004.

2. ANONYMOUS: *THE EVANGELICAL PEARL* (ca. 1535)

Translation (French)

La perle évangelique–traduction française–(1602). Edited by Daniel Vidal. Grenoble: Éditions Jérôme Millon, 1997.

3. AUGUSTINE BAKER (1575–1641)

Texts

Holy Wisdom, or Directions for the Prayer of Contemplation . . . By the Ven. Father F. Augustin Baker. Methodically Digested by R. F. Serenus Cressy. London: Burns, Oates & Washbourne, 1876.
The Life and Death of Dame Gertrude More Edited from All the Known Manuscripts. Edited by Ben Wekking. Analecta Cartusiana 119.19. Salzburg: Institut für Anglistik und Amerikanistik, 2002.
Memorials of Father Augustine Baker and Other Documents Relating to the English Benedictines, vol. 33. Edited by Justin McCann and Hugh Connolly. London: Catholic Record Society, 1933.

The Life of Father Augustine Baker, O.S.B. (1575–1641) by Fr. Peter Salvin and Fr. Serenus Cressy. Edited by Justin McCann. London: Burns, Oates & Washbourne, 1933.
Secretum. Edited by John Clark. Analecta Cartusiana 119.7. Salzburg: Institut für Anglistik und Amerikanistik, 1997.
Directions for Contemplation: Book G. Edited by John Clark. Analecta Cartusiana 119.13. Salzburg: Institut für Anglistik und Amerikanistik, 2000.

Translations

The Inner Life and Writings of Dame Gertrude More. Revised and edited by Dom Benedict Weld-Blundell. Vol. 1. London: R. & T. Washbourne, 1910.
The Confessions of the Venerable Father Augustine Baker. Translated by Justin McCann. London: Burns, Oates & Washbourne, 1922.
The Cloud of Unknowing and Other Treatises by an English Mystic of the Fourteenth Century with a Commentary on the Cloud by Father Augustine Baker, O.S.B. Translated by Justin McCann. London: Burns, Oates & Washbourne, 1947.

4. CONSTANTIN DE BARBANSON (1582–1631)

Texts

Les secret sentiers de l'amour divin . . . . Cologne, 1623.

Translations

The Secret Paths of Divine Love by Father Constantine Barbanson. Abridged from the English version of Dom Anselm Touchet, O.S.B. Edited by Dom Justin McCann. London: Burns, Oates and Washbourne, 1928.

5. ROBERT BELLARMINE (1542–1621)

Texts

De Ascensione Mentis in Deum. Per Scalas Rerum Creatuarum. Opusculum Roberti Cardinalis Bellarmini. Cologne: C. ab Egmond, 1626.

Translations

Spiritual Writings. Translated and edited by John Patrick Donnelly and Roland J. Teske. Classics of Western Spirituality. New York: Paulist Press, 1989.

6. BENET OF CANFIELD (1562-1611)

Texts

[Benoît de Canfield]. *La Règle de Perfection. The Rule of Perfection.* Edited by Jean Orcibal. Paris: Presses Universitaires de France, 1982.

Translations

Emery, Kent, Jr. *Renaissance Dialectic and Renaissance Piety: Benet of Canfield's "Rule of Perfection." A Translation and Study.* Binghamton, NY: Medieval & Renaissance Texts & Studies, 1987.

7. ISABELLA CRISTINA BERINZAGA (1551-1624)

Per via di annichilazione: Un testo di Isabella Cristina Berinzaga redatto da Achille Gagliardi S.I. Edited by Mario Gioia. Aloisiana 25. Rome: Gregorian University Press, 1994.

8. BERNARD OF CLAIRVAUX (1090-1153)

Texts

Sancti Bernardi Opera. Edited by Jean Leclercq et al. 8 vols. Rome: Editiones Cistercienses, 1957-77.

9. PIERRE DE BÉRULLE (1575-1629)

Texts

Oeuvres complètes. Edited by Michel Dupuy. Translated by Auguste Piédagnel. 12 vols. Paris: Oratoire de Jésus/Éditions du Cerf, 1995-2005.
Oeuvres complètes de Cardinal de Bérulle: Reproduction de l'Édition Princeps (1644). 3 vols. Montsoult: Maison de l'Institution de Oratoire, 1960.
Opuscules de piété. 1644. Grenoble: Éditions Jérôme Millon, 1997.
Correspondance du Cardinal Pierre de Bérulle. Edited by Jean Dagens. 3 vols. Paris: Desclée de Brouwer; Louvain: Bureaux de la Revue, 1937-39.

Translations

Bérulle and the French School: Selected Writings. Edited by William M. Thompson. Translated by Lowell M. Glendon. Classics of Western Spirituality. New York: Paulist Press, 1989.

10. LOUIS DE BLOIS (BLOSIUS) (1506–1566)

Texts

[Ludovicus Blosius]. *Opera omnia.* Antwerp: Balthazar Moretus, 1632.
Manuale vitae spiritualis continens Ludovici Blosii Opera Spiritualia quaedam selecta. Edited by Carol Newsham. London: Thomas Richardson & Sons, 1859.

Translations

The Spiritual Works of Louis de Blois Abbot of Liesse. Edited by John Edward Bowden. London: Washbourne, 1876.
A Book of Spiritual Instruction (Institutio Spiritualis) by Ludovicus Blosius. Translated by Bertrand A. Wilberforce. London: n. p., 1900.
[Ludovicus Blosius]. *Comfort for the Faint-Hearted.* Translated by Father Jerome Bertram. London: Art & Book Co., 1902.

11. GIOVANNI BONA (1609–1674)

Texts

[D. Ioanne Bona]. *Via compendii ad Deum: Per motus anagogicos, & orationes iaculatorias. Liber Isagogicus ad mysticam theologiam.* Rome: Bernabò à Verme, 1657.
[Iohannis Cardinalis Bona]. *Opuscula Ascetica Selecta.* Freiburg-im-Breisgau: Herder, 1911.

12. JEAN-PIERRE CAMUS (1582–1652)

Texts

La théologie mystique. 1640. Grenoble: Éditions Jérôme Millon, 2003.

Translations

The Spirit of St. François de Sales by Jean Camus (Bishop of Belley). Translated by C. F. Kelley. New York: Harper & Brothers, 1952.

13. CATERINA DE'RICCI (1522–1590)

Texts

Collana Ricciana: Epistolario. Edited by Domenico Di Agresti. 5 vols. Florence: Leo S. Olschki, 1973–75.
Collana Ricciana: Fonti. Edited by Domenico Di Agresti. 9 vols. Florence: Leo S. Olschki, 1963–76.

Translations

Selected Letters. Edited by Domenico Di Agresti. Translated by Jennifer Petrei. Oxford: Dominican Sources, 1985.

14. JANE-FRANCES DE CHANTAL (1571–1641)

Texts

Sainte Jeanne-Françoise Frémyot de Chantal: Sa vie et ses oeuvres. 8 vols. Paris: E. Plon, 1874–79.

Translations

Saint Jane Frances Frémyot de Chantal: Her Exhortations, Conferences and Instructions. Westminster, MD: Newman Bookshop, 1947.

St. Francis de Sales: A Testimony by St. Chantal. Translated by Elisabeth Stopp. London: Faber & Faber, 1967.

15. CHARLES DE CONDREN (1588–1641)

Texts

Lettres du Père de Condren. Edited by P. Auvray and A. Jouffrey. Paris: Éditions du Cerf, 1943.

Translation

The Eternal Sacrifice. Translated by A. J. Montieth. London: Thomas Baker, 1906. Reprint, Classic Reprint Series. London: Forgotten Books, 2017.

16. RICHARD CRASHAW (1612/13–1649)

Texts

The English Poems of Richard Crashaw. Edited and with an Introduction by Richard Rambuss. Minneapolis: University of Minnesota Press, 2013.

17. JOHN EUDES (1601–1680)

Texts

Oeuvres complètes du Vénérable Jean Eudes. Edited by Joseph Dauphin and Charles Lebrun. 12 vols. Vannes: P. Lethielleux, 1905–11.

Translations

Bérulle and the French School: Selected Writings. Edited by William M. Thompson, 293–334. Classics of Western Spirituality. New York: Paulist Press, 1989.

The Life of Jesus in Christian Souls. Translated by Monsignor William J. Doheny. New York: Private Publication, 1981.

18. FRANCIS DE SALES (1567–1622)

Texts

Oeuvres de Saint François de Sales . . . Édition complète. 27 Vols. Annecy: J. Niérat et al., 1892–1964.

François de Sales et Jeanne de Chantal: Correspondance. Edited by David Laurent with an Introduction by Max Huot de Longchamp. Paris/Perpignan: Desclée de Brouwer, 2016.

Translations

Introduction to the Devout Life by St. Francis de Sales. Translated by John K. Ryan. Garden City, NY: Doubleday, 1955.

Treatise on the Love of God by St. Francis de Sales. Translated by Henry Benedict Mackey. Westminster, MD: Newman Press, 1953.

Treatise on the Love of God by St. Francis de Sales. Translated by John K. Ryan. 2 vols. Garden City, NY: Doubleday, 1963. Reprint, Rockford, IL: Tan Books, 1975.

A Selection of the Spiritual Letters of S. Francis de Sales. London: Rivingtons, 1871.

St. Francis de Sales. I: Letters to Persons in the World. Translated by Henry Benedict Mackey. London: Burns & Oates, n.d.

St. Francis de Sales: Letters to Persons in Religion. Translated by Henry Benedict Mackey. Westminster, MD: Newman Bookshop, 1943.

On the Preacher and Preaching: A Letter by Francis de Sales. Translated by John K. Ryan. Chicago: Regnery, 1964.

Francis de Sales, Jane de Chantal. *Letters of Spiritual Direction.* Edited by Wendy M. Wright and Joseph F. Powers. Translated by Péronne Marie Thibert. Classics of Western Spirituality. New York: Paulist Press, 1988.

The Mystical Explanation of the Canticle of Canticles, Composed by the Blessed Francis de Sales. Translated by Henry Benedict Mackey. London: Burns & Oates, 1908.

The Spiritual Conferences of St. Francis de Sales. Translated by Henry Benedict Mackey. London: Burns, Oates & Washbourne, 1906.

The Sermons of St. Francis de Sales on Prayer; The Sermons of St. Francis de Sales on Our Lady; The Sermons of St. Francis de Sales for Lent Given in 1622; The Sermons of St. Francis de Sales for Advent and Christmas. Translated by the Nuns of the Visitation. Rockford, IL: Tan Books, 1982–87.

19. ACHILLE GAGLIARDI (1538–1607)

Texts

Breve compendio di perfezione cristiana: Un testo di Achille Gagliardi S.I. Edited by Mario Gioia. Aloisiana 28. Rome: Gregorian University Press, 1996.

20. MARIA DOMITILLA GALUZZI (1595–1671)

Texts

Vita da lei narrata (1624). Edited by Olimpia Pelosi. Studi e Testi 6. Chapel Hill, NC: *Annali d'italianistica*, 2003.
Passione (Sororis M. Domitillae Capuccinae "Visioni pretese e abbastanza strane"). Edited by Paolo Fontana. In Fontana, *Santità femminile e Inquisizione*, 97–238. Rome: Libreria Editrice Vaticana, 2007.

21. CATHERINE GASCOIGNE (1600–1676)

Texts

Dame Catherine Gascoigne's Defense of Father Augustine Baker's Way of Prayer. In *English Convents in Exile, 1600–1800.* Volume 2, *Spirituality*, edited by Laurence Lux-Sterritt, 463–66. London: Pickering & Chatto, 2012.

22. PAOLO GIUSTINIANI (1476–1528)

Texts

Secretum Meum Mihi, o dell'amor di Dio: Ragionamenti sei. Frascati: Sacro Eremo Tuscolano, 1941.
Trattati, lettere e frammenti dai manoscritti dell'Archivio dei Camaldolesi di Monte Corona nell'Eremo di Frascati. 3 vols. Rome: Edizioni storia et letteratura, 1967–2012.

23. CLAUDE HOPIL (ca. 1580–1633)

Texts

Meditations sur le Cantique des Cantiques et Les douces extases de l'âme spirituelle. Geneva: Droz, 2000.

24. JEAN DE SAINT-SAMSON (1571–1636)

Texts

Oeuvres complètes. Edited by Hein Blommestijn. 10 vols. (3 published so far). Rome: Institutum Carmelitanum, 1992–.

Translations

Prayer, Aspiration and Contemplation from the Writings of John of St. Samson, O. Carm., Mystic and Charismatic. Edited and translated by Venard Poslusney. New York: Alba House, 1975.

25. LOUIS LALLEMANT (1588–1635)

Texts

Doctrine spirituelle. Edited by Dominique Salin. Paris: Desclée de Brouwer, 2011.

Translations

The Spiritual Teaching of Father Louis Lallemant of the Society of Jesus, Preceded by an Account of His Life by Father Champion, S.J. Edited by Alan G. McDougall. London: Burns, Oates & Washbourne, 1928.
The Spiritual Doctrine. Chestnut Hill, MA: Institute of Jesuit Sources, 2016.

26. LAWRENCE OF PARIS (1563–1631)

Texts

Le Palais d'amour divin de Jésus et de l'âme chrétienne . . . . Paris, 1602.

27. LAWRENCE OF THE RESURRECTION (1614–1691)

Texts

Écrits et entretiens sur la pratique de la présence de Dieu. Edited by Conrad De Meester. Epiphanie. Paris: Éditions du Cerf, 1996.

Translations

Writings and Conversations on the Practice of the Presence of God. Translated by Salvatore Sciurba. Washington, DC: ICS Publications, 1994.

28. MADELEINE DE SAINT-JOSEPH (1578–1637)

Texts

Une mystique du XVIIe siècle: soeur Catherine de Jésus. Edited by Jean-Baptiste Ériau. Paris: Desclée de Brouwer, 1929.
Lettres spirituelles. Edited by Pierre Serouet. Paris: Desclée de Brouwer, 1965.

Translations

Bérulle and the French School: Selected Writings. Edited by William M. Thompson, 191–214. Classics of Western Spirituality. New York: Paulist Press, 1989.

29. MARIE DE L'INCARNATION (MARIE GUYART) (1599–1672)

Texts

Écrits spirituels et historiques. Edited by Albert Jamet. 4 vols. Paris: Desclée de Brouwer, 1929–39.
Marie de l'Incarnation (1599–1672): Correspondance. Edited by Guy Oury. Solesme: Abbaye de Saint-Pierre, 1971.

Translations

Selected Writings. Edited and translated by Irene Mahoney. Sources of American Spirituality. New York: Paulist Press, 1989.
From Mother to Son: The Selected Letters of Marie de l'Incarnation to Claude Martin. Translated and with introduction and notes by Mary Dunn. Oxford: Oxford University Press, 2014.

30. MARIA MADDALENA DE'PAZZI (1566–1607)

Texts

Tutte le Opere di Santa Maria Maddalena de'Pazzi dai manoscritti originali. Edited by Bruno Nardini et al. 7 vols. Florence: Nardi, 1960–66.
Le parole dell'estasi. Edited by Giovanni Pozzi. Piccola Biblioteca 163. Milan: Adelphi, 1984.
"*Costretta della dolce verità scrivo.*" *L'Epistolario completo.* Edited by Chiara Vasciavero. Florence: Nerbini, 2007.

Translations

The Complete Works of Saint Mary Magdalene de'Pazzi, Carmelite and Mystic (1566–1607). Translated by Gabriel N. Pausback. 5 vols. Aylesford, IL: Carmelite Friars, 1969–75.

Selected Revelations. Translated with an introduction by Armando Maggi. Classics of Western Spirituality. New York: Paulist Press, 2000.

31. GERTRUDE MORE (1606–1633)

Texts

The Spiritual Exercises of the Most Vertuous and Religious D. Gertrude More . . . Confessiones Amantis. A Lovers Confession. Paris: Lewis de la Fosse, 1658. (This edition includes *Dame Gertrude's Apology* with separate pagination.) Facsimile reprint in *The Early Modern Englishwoman: A Facsimile Library of Essential Works*. General editors, Betty S. Travisky and Anne Lake Prescott. Series II. Printed Writings, 1641–1700: Part 4, Volume 3, edited by Arthur F. Marotti. Burlington VT: Ashgate, 2009.

Translation

The Inner Life and the Writings of Dame Gertrude More. Revised and edited by Dom Benedict Weld-Blundell. Vol. 2. London: R. & T. Washbourne, 1911.

32. JEAN-JACQUES OLIER (1608–1657)

Texts

Catéchisme chrétienne pour la vie intérieur et journée chrétienne. Edited by François Amiot. Paris: Le Rameau, 1954.

Lettres de M. Olier. Edited by É. Levesque. 2 vols. Paris: J. de Gigord, 1935.

L'âme cristal: Des attributs divins en nous. Edited by Mariel Mazzocco. Paris: Éditions du Seuil, 2008.

De la création du monde à la vie divine. Edited by Mariel Mazzocco. Paris: Éditions du Seuil, 2009.

Des anges: Fragrances divines et odeurs suaves. Edited by Mariel Mazzocco. Paris: Éditions du Seuil, 2011.

Tentations diaboliques et possession divine. Edited by Mariel Mazzocco. Paris: Honoré Champion, 2012.

Introduction à la vie et aux vertus chrétiennes. Edited by Mariel Mazzocco. Paris: Honoré Champion, 2016.

Translations

Bérulle and the French School: Selected Writings. Edited by William M. Thompson, 217–90. Classics of Western Spirituality. New York: Paulist Press, 1989.

33. BLAISE PASCAL (1623-1662)

Texts

Oeuvres complètes. Edited by Louis Lafuma. Paris: Éditions du Seuil, 1963.

Translations

Pensées. Translated by A. J. Krailsheimer. Baltimore, MD: Penguin Books, 1966.

34. MARIA PETYT (1623-1677)

Texts

Michael of Saint Augustine. *Het Leven vande Weerdighe Moeder Maria a Sta Teresia.* 2 vols. Ghent, 1683–84.
Het Leven van Maria Petyt (1623–1677). Edited by J. R. A. Merlier. Zutphen: Thieme, 1976.
Vita Venerabilis Matris Mariae a Sancta Theresia (Carmelite Archives, Post. III, 70, ff. 30r–49v). In *Maria Petyt: A Mystic in Wartime,* edited by Joseph Chalmers et al., 119–239. Radboud Studies in Humanities 4. Leiden: Brill, 2015.

35. CARDINAL RICHELIEU (ARMAND JEAN DU PLESSIS) (1585-1642)

Texts

Traité de la perfection chrétienne. Paris, 1646.

36. MAXIMILIAN SANDAEUS (VAN DER SANDT) (1578-1656)

Texts

Theologia mystica seu contemplatio divina religiosorum a calumniis vindicata. Mainz, 1627.
Pro theologia mystica clavis.... Cologne, 1640.

37. JOHANN SCHEFFLER (ANGELUS SILESIUS) (1624–1677)

Texts

Sämtliche poetische Werke. Edited by Hans Ludwig Held. 3rd ed. 3 vols. Munich: Carl Hanser, 1952.
Cherubinischer Wandersmann oder geistreiche Sinn- und Schlussreime. Edited by Louise Gnädinger. Zurich: Manesse Verlag, 1986.

Translation

The Cherubinic Wanderer. Translated by Maria Shrady. Classics of Western Spirituality. New York: Paulist Press, 1986.

38. LORENZO SCUPOLI (1530–1610)

Translations

Theatine Spirituality: Selected Writings. Edited and translated by William V. Hudon. Classics of Western Spirituality. New York: Paulist Press, 1996.

39. FRIEDRICH SPEE (1591–1635)

Texts

Trutz-Nachtigall. Edited by Theo G. M. van Ooschot. Bern: Francke Verlag, 1985.

40. JEAN-JOSEPH SURIN (1600–1665)

Texts

Questions importantes à la vie spirituelle: Sur l'amour de Dieu. Edited by Aloys Potter and Louis Mariès. Paris: Tequi, 1930.
Guide spirituel pour la perfection. Edited by Michel de Certeau. Paris: Desclée de Brouwer, 1963.
Triomphe de l'amour divin sur les puissances de l'Enfer en la possession de la Mère supérieure des Ursulines de Loudun, exorcisée par le Père Jean-Joseph Surin, de la Compagnie de Jésus; et, Science expérimentale des choses de l'autre vie. Collection Atopia. Grenoble: Éditions Jérôme Millon, 1990.
Correspondance. Edited by Michel de Certeau. Paris: Desclée de Brouwer, 1966.

Poésies spirituelles suivies des Contrats spirituels. Edited by Etienne Catta. Études de théologie et d'histoire de la spiritualité 15. Paris: Vrin, 1957.

Cantiques spirituels de l'Amour divin. Edited by Benedetta Papàsogli. Biblioteca della Rivista di storia e letteratura religiosa: Testi e documenti 16. Florence: Leo S. Olschki, 1996.

41. FRANÇOIS DU TREMBLAY (PERE JOSEPH) (1577-1638)

Texts

Introduction à la vie spirituelle par une facile méthode d'oraison . . . . Poitiers, 1616.

42. VINCENT DE PAUL (ca. 1580-1660)

Translations

Vincent de Paul and Louise de Marillac: Rules, Conferences, and Writings. Edited by Frances Ryan and John E. Rybolt. Classics of Western Spirituality. New York: Paulist Press, 1995.

SECTION II. SECONDARY WORKS

Adnès, Pierre. "Mariage spirituel." DS 10 (1980): 388-408.
———. "Mystique: B. XVIe-XXe siècles." DS 10 (1980): 1919-30.
Alberigo, Giuseppe. "From the Council of Trent to Tridentinism." In *From Trent to Vatican II: Historical and Theological Investigations*, edited by Raymond F. Bulman and Frederick J. Parella, 19-37. Oxford: Oxford University Press, 2006.
Allison, A. F. "Crashaw and St. François de Sales." *Review of English Studies* 24 (1948): 295-302.
Ampe, Albert. "Een kritisch onderzoek van de 'Institutiones Taulerianae.'" *Ons Geestelijke Erf* 40 (1966): 167-240.
———. "Nieuwlant (Claesinne van) béguine, vers 1540-1611," DS 11 (1981): 344-45.
———. "Pullen (Jean, Pelgrim) prêtre, vers 1520-1608." DS 12 (1984): 2621-23.
Ancilli, Ermanno. "Marie-Madeleine de Pazzi (sainte), carmélite, 1566-1607." DS 10 (1980): 576-88.
Andriessen, Jos. "Sandaeus (van der Sandt, Maximilien), jésuite, 1578-1656." DS 14 (1989): 311-16.

Arens, Anton. "Spee von Langerfeld (Frédéric), jésuite, 1591–1635." DS 14 (1989): 1117–21.

Armstrong, Christopher. "Augustine Baker and the Union of Nothing with Nothing." In *That Mysterious Man: Essays on Augustine Baker OSB, 1575–1641*, edited by Michael Woodward, 136–54. Abergavenny: Three Peaks Press, 2001.

Aveling, J. C. H. *The Handle and the Axe: The Catholic Recusants in England from Reformation to Emancipation.* London: Blond & Briggs, 1976.

Bachmann, Jakob. *La notion du temps dans la pensée de Pierre de Bérulle.* Winterthir: P. G. Keller, 1964.

Badir, Patricia. *The Maudlin Impression: English Literary Images of Mary Magdalene, 1550–1700.* Notre Dame, IN: University of Notre Dame Press, 2009.

Bagger, Matthew. *The Uses of Paradox (Religion, Self-Transformation, and the Absurd).* New York: Columbia University Press, 2007.

Balciunas, Vytautas. *La vocation universelle à la perfection chrétienne selon Saint François de Sales.* Annecy: Académie Salésienne, 1952.

Balthasar, Hans Urs von. *Angelus Silesius: Dich auftun wie die Rose.* Einsiedeln: Johannes Verlag, 1954.

———. *The Glory of the Lord: A Theological Aesthetics.* Volume 3: *Studies in Theological Styles. Lay Styles.* San Francisco: Ignatius Press, 1986.

———. *The Glory of the Lord: A Theological Aesthetics.* Volume 5: *The Realm of Metaphysics in the Modern Age.* San Francisco: Ignatius Press, 1991.

Barrett, John Douglas. "'Such a World of Books': Spiritual Reading in the Cambrai Treatises of Fr. Augustine Baker OSB." Ph.D. dissertation, Heythrop College (University of London), 2011.

Bartók, Tibor. "Louis Lallemant and his *Doctrine spirituelle*: Myths and Facts." In *A Companion to Jesuit Mysticism*, edited by Robert A. Maryks, 112–38. Brill's Companions to the Christian Tradition 78. Leiden: Brill, 2017.

Baruzi, Jean. *Création religieuse et pensée contemplative.* Les religions 8. Paris: Aubier, 1951.

Barzman, Karen-edis. "Cultural Production, Religious Devotion, and Subjectivity in Early Modern Italy: The Case Study of Maria Maddalena de'Pazzi." In *Women Mystic Writers,* ed. Dino S. Cervigni, 283–305. Annali d'italianistica, 13. Chapel Hill: University of North Carolina Press, 1995.

Bell, David. "A Doctrine of Ignorance: The Annihilation of Individuality in Christian and Muslim Mysticism." In *Benedictus: Studies in Honor of St Benedict of Nursia*, edited by E. Rozanne Elder, 30–52. Cistercian Studies Series 67. Kalamazoo: Cistercian Publications, 1981.

Bellemare, R. *La sens de la creature dans la doctrine de Bérulle.* Ottawa: Desclée de Brouwer, 1959.

Bellinger, Aidan. "Baker's Recusant & Benedictine Context." In *That*

Mysterious Man: Essays on Augustine Baker OSB, 1575-1641, edited by Michael Woodward, 42-56. Abergavenny: Three Peaks Press, 2001.

Benedict, Philip. "The Wars of Religion, 1562-1598." In *Renaissance and Reformation France*, edited by Mack P. Holt, 147-75. Short Oxford History of France. Oxford: Oxford University Press, 2002.

Benedictines of Stanbrook. *In a Great Tradition: Tribute to Dame Laurentia McLachlan, Abbess of Stanbrook by the Benedictines of Stanbrook*. New York: Harper & Brothers, 1956.

Bergamo, Mino. *L'anatomie de l'âme: De François de Sales à Fénelon*. Grenoble: Éditions Jérôme Millon, 1994.

———. *La science des saints: Le discours mystique au XVIIe siècle en France*. Grenoble: Éditions Jérôme Millon, 1992.

Bergin, Joseph. *Church, Society, and Religious Change in France, 1580-1730*. New Haven: Yale University Press, 2009.

———. *The Politics of Religion in Early Modern France*. New Haven: Yale University Press, 2014.

Bertonasco, Marc F. *Crashaw and the Baroque*. [Tuscaloosa]: University of Alabama Press, 1978.

Birrell, T. A. "English Catholic Mystics in Non-Catholic Circles I." *Downside Review* 94 (1976): 60-81.

———. *The Lives of Ange de Joyeuse and Benet Canfield*. New York: Sheed & Ward, 1959.

Blois, Georges de. *Louis de Blois: Un Bénédictin au xvi siècle*. Paris: Victor Palmé, 1875.

Blommestijn, Hein. "Aspiring as a Mystagogical Journey of Prayer." In *Seeking the Seeker: Explorations in the Discipline of Spirituality. A Festschrift for Kees Waaijman on the Occasion of His 65th Birthday*, edited by H. Blommestijn et al., 549-61. Leuven: Peeters, 2008.

Blunt, Anthony. "Gianlorenzo Bernini: Illusionism and Mysticism." *Art History* 1 (1978): 67-89.

———. *Roman Baroque*. London: Pallas Athene Arts, 2001.

Böhm, Maria M. *Angelus Silesius' "Cherubinischer Wandersmann": A Modern Reading with Selected Translations*. Renaissance and Baroque Studies and Texts 22. New York: Peter Lang, 1997.

Bord, André. "L'influence de Jean de la Croix sur François de Sales et Jeanne de Chantal." In *L'Unidivers Salésien: Saint François de Sales hier et aujourd'hui, Actes du Colloque international de Metz, 17-19 septembre 1992*, edited by Hélène Bordes and Jacques Hennequin, 51-64. Paris: Université de Metz, 1994.

Bossy, John. *The English Catholic Community 1570-1850*. New York: Oxford University Press, 1976.

Bottereau, Georges. "Lallemant (Louis), jésuite, 1588-1635." DS 9 (1976): 125-35.

Bowden, Caroline, general ed. *English Convents in Exile, 1600–1800*. 6 vols. London: Pickering & Chatto, 2012.
Brandsma, Titus. *In Search of Living Water: Essays on the Mystical Heritage of the Netherlands*. Fiery Arrow Collection 10. Leuven: Peeters, 2013.
Brenninger, Johannes. "Chéron (Jean)." DS 2.1 (1953): 821–22.
Breton, Stanislas. *Deux mystiques de l'excès: J.-J. Surin et Maître Eckhart*. Cogitatio fidei 135. Paris: Éditions du Cerf, 1985.
Brodeur, Raymond, ed. *Femme, mystique et missionnaire: Marie Guyart de l'Incarnation*. Quebec: Les Presses de l'Université de Laval, 2001.
Brodrick, James. *Robert Bellarmine, Saint and Scholar*. Westminster, MD: Newman Press, 1961.
———. *Saint Peter Canisius, S.J. (1521–97)*. 1935. Reprint, Baltimore: Carroll Press, 1960.
Brown, Judith. *The Life of a Lesbian Nun in Renaissance Italy*. Oxford: Oxford University Press, 1986.
Bruneau, Marie-Florine. *Women Mystics Confront the Modern World: Marie de l'Incarnation (1599–1672) and Madame Guyon (1648–1717)*. SUNY Series in Western Esoteric Traditions. Albany: State University of New York Press, 1998.
Fr. Bruno de Jésus-Marie (O.C.D.). *Le Belle Acarie, bienheureuse Marie de l'Incarnation*. Paris, 1942.
Buckley, Michael J. "Seventeenth-Century French Spirituality: Three Figures." In *Christian Spirituality: Post-Reformation and Modern*, edited by Louis Dupré and Don E. Saliers, 28–68. World Spirituality 18. New York: Crossroad, 1989.
Burnaby, John. *Amor Dei: A Study of the Religion of St. Augustine*. London: Hodder & Stoughton, 1938.
Bush, Douglas. *English Literature in the Earlier Seventeenth Century, 1600–1660*. Oxford: Oxford University Press, 1962.
Butler, Cuthbert. *Western Mysticism: The Teaching of SS. Augustine, Gregory, and Bernard on Contemplation and the Contemplative Life*. New York: E. P. Dutton, 1923.
Cadoux, Richard. *Bérulle et la question de l'homme: Servitude et liberté*. Paris: Éditions du Cerf, 2005.
Cai, Raffaele. "Catherine de Ricci (Sainte)." DS 2.1 (1953): 326–27.
Calvet, Jean. *La littérature religieuse de François de Sales à Fénelon*. Histoire de la littérature française 5. Paris: Duca, 1956.
Camilleri, Charlò. "To Be Is to Gaze and Be Gazed At: Vision in Maria Maddalena de'Pazzi's Mysticism." *Studies in Spirituality* 19 (2009): 35–46.
Canivez, J.-M. "Bona (Jean)." DS 1 (1937): 1762–66.
Carraud, Vincent. "De l'état de néant à l'état anéanti: Le système du néant de Bérulle." *Cahiers de Philosophie de l'Université de Caen* 43 (2007): 211–47.

Catena, Carmelo C. *Santa Maria Maddalena de'Pazzi carmelitana: Orientamenti spirituali ed ambiente in cui visse*. Rome: Institutum Carmelitanum, 1966.

Cavallera, Ferdinand. "Spiritualité en France au XVII siècle: Reforme de la Nomenclature." *Revue d'ascétique et de mystique* 29 (1953): 58-64.

Certeau, Michel de. "Jean-Joseph Surin." In *Spirituality through the Centuries: Ascetics and Mystics of the Western Church*, edited by James Walsh, 293-342. New York: P. J. Kenedy & Sons, 1964.

———. "Jean-Joseph Surin, interprète de Saint Jean de la Croix." *Revue d'ascétique et de mystique* 46 (1970): 45-70.

———. *The Mystic Fable. Volume One*. Chicago: University of Chicago Press, 1992.

———. *The Mystic Fable. Volume Two*. Chicago: University of Chicago Press, 2015.

———. "'Mystique' au XVIIe siècle: Le problème de langage 'mystique.'" In *L'Homme devant Dieu: Mélanges offerts au Père Henri de Lubac*, 2:267-91. 3 vols. Paris: Aubier, 1963.

———. "Les oeuvres de Surin." *Revue de ascétique et de mystique* 40 (1964): 443-76; 41 (1965): 55-78.

———. *The Possession at Loudun*. Chicago: University of Chicago Press, 1996.

———. "La Spiritualité moderne." *Revue d'ascétique et de mystique* 44 (1968): 33-42.

———. "Surin's Melancholy." In Certeau, *Heterologies: Discourse on the Other*, 101-15. Minneapolis: University of Minnesota Press, 1986.

Cervigni, Dino S., ed. *Women Mystic Writers*. Annali d'italianistica 13. Chapel Hill: University of North Carolina Press, 1995.

Chaillot, Gilles. "Jean-Jacques Olier: Lecture de Denys L'Aréopagite." *Bulletin de Saint-Sulpice. Jean-Jacques Olier (1608-1657)* 14 (1988): 48-88.

Chaix, Gérald. *Réforme et contre-réforme catholiques: Recherche sur la Chartreuse de Cologne au XVIe siècle*. 3 vols. Analecta Cartusiana 80. Salzburg: Universität Salzburg, 1981.

Chalmers, Joseph, et al., eds. *Maria Petyt: A Carmelite Mystic in Wartime*. Radboud Studies in Humanities 4. Leiden: Brill, 2015.

Charmot, F. *Ignatius of Loyola and Francis de Sales: Two Masters–One Spirituality*. St. Louis and London: B. Herder, 1966.

Chase, Steven, ed. *Angelic Spirituality: Medieval Perspectives on the Ways of Angels*. Classics of Western Spirituality. New York: Paulist Press, 2002.

Chorpenning, Joseph F. "*Lectio Divina* and Francis de Sales's Picturing of the Interconnection of Divine and Human Hearts." In *Imago Exegetica: Visual Images as Exegetical Instruments, 1400-1700*, edited by Walter S. Mellon, James Clifton, and Michael Weemans, 449-77. Intersections 33. Leiden: Brill, 2014.

Cirillo, A. R. "Crashaw's 'Epiphany Hymn': The Dawn of Christian Time." *Studies in Philology* 67 (1972): 67–88.

Clark, John P. H. "Augustine Baker, O.S.B.: Towards a Re-Assessment." *Studies in Spirituality* 14 (2004): 209–24.

———. "Augustine Baker's *Secretum*: Sources and Affinities." In *That Mysterious Man: Essays on Augustine Baker OSB, 1575–1641*, edited by Michael Woodward, 123–35. Abergavenny: Three Peaks Press, 2001.

———. "Towards a Chronology of Father Augustine Baker's Writings." In *Dom Augustine Baker (1575–1641)*, edited by Geoffrey Scott, 111–32. Leominster: Gracewing, 2011.

Clooney, Francis X. *Beyond Compare: St. Francis de Sales and Śrī Vedānta Deśika on Loving Surrender to God.* Washington, DC: Georgetown University Press, 2008.

Cochois, Paul. *Bérulle et l'École française.* Bourges: Éditions du Seuil, 1963.

———. "Bérulle et le Pseudo-Denys." *Revue d'histoire des religions* 159 (1961): 173–204.

———. "Bérulle, hiérarque dionysien." *Revue d'ascétique et de mystique* 37 (1961): 314–53; 38 (1962): 354–75.

Cochrane, Eric. *Italy, 1530–1630.* London: Longman, 1988.

Cognet, Louis. *Introduction aux mystiques rhéno-flamands.* Paris: Desclée de Brouwer, 1968.

———. "The Leadership Position of France." Part 1 in *The Church in the Age of Absolutism and Enlightenment*, edited by Wolfgang Müller et al., 3–106. History of the Church 6. New York: Crossroad, 1981.

———. *Post-Reformation Spirituality.* New York: Hawthorn, 1959.

———. *La spiritualité moderne.* Volume 1: *L'essor: 1500–1650.* Histoire de la spiritualité chrétienne 3. Paris: Aubier, 1966.

Cousins, Anthony D. *The Catholic Religious Poets from Southwell to Crashaw. A Critical History.* Westminster, MD: Christian Classics, 1991.

Cramer, Anselm. "Baker's Editors: Cressy to McCann." In *That Mysterious Man: Essays on Augustine Baker OSB, 1575–1641*, edited by Michael Woodward, 245–59. Abergavenny: Three Peaks Press, 2001.

Cunnar, Eugene R. "Opening the Religious Lyric: Crashaw's Ritual, Liminal, and Visual Wounds." In *New Perspectives on the Seventeenth-Century English Religious Lyric*, edited by John R. Roberts, 237–67. Columbia: University of Missouri Press, 1994.

Cunningham, Agnes. "Women in the French School: Some No Longer Hidden Faces." In *L'École française aujourd'hui: The French School Today. Bulletin de Saint-Sulpice* 22 (1996): 119–37.

Cuthbert, Father, O.S.F.C. *The Capuchins: A Contribution to the History of the Counter-Reformation.* 2 vols. London: Sheed & Ward, 1928.

Daeschler, R. "Amour-Propre." DS 1 (1937): 533–44.

———. "Anéantissement." DS 1 (1937): 560–65.

Dagens, Jean. *Bérulle et les origines de la restauration catholique (1575–1611)*. Bruges: Desclée de Brouwer, 1962.

———. *Bibliographie chronologique de la littérature de spiritualité et des sources (1501–1610)*. Paris: Desclée de Brouwer, 1952.

Dailey, Thomas F. "A Song of Prayer: Reading the Canticle of Canticles with St. Francis de Sales." *Studia Mystica* 15.4 (1992): 65–82.

d'Angers, Julien-Eymard. "Les degrees de perfection d'après saint François de Sales." *Revue d'ascétique et de mystique* 44 (1968): 11–31.

———. "L'exemplarisme bérullien." *Revue des sciences religieuses* 31 (1957): 122–32.

———. *L'humanisme chrétien au XVIIe siècle: St. François de Sales et Yves de Paris*. The Hague: Martinus Nijhoff, 1970.

Daniels, Antoine. *Les rapports entre Saint François de Sales et Les Pays-Bas 1550–1700*. Nijmegen: Centrale Drukkerij, 1932.

Davidson, Peter. *The Universal Baroque*. Manchester: Manchester University Press, 2007.

Davis, Natalie Zemon. "Marie de l'Incarnation: New Worlds." In Davis, *Women on the Margins: Three Seventeenth-Century Lives*, 63–139. Cambridge, MA: Harvard University Press, 1995.

De Bil, Alexandre. "Crombecius (Van Crombeke, Jean), jésuite, 1558–1626." DS 2.2 (1953): 2623–25.

Deblaere, Albert. *De mystieke Schrijfster Maria Petyt (1623–1677)*. Gent: Secretarie der Academie, 1962.

———. "Essentiel (Superessentiel, suressentiel)." DS 4.2 (1961): 1346–66.

———. "Maria Petyt, écrivain et mystique flamande." In *Albert Deblaere, S. J. (1916–1994): Essays in Mystical Literature*, edited by Rob Faesen, 223–90. Leuven: Leuven University Press, 2004.

———. "Michel de Saint-Augustin." DS 10 (1980): 1187–91.

Derville, André. "Homme intérieur. 4: Le 17e siècle français." DS 7.1 (1969): 669–74.

———. "Petyt (Maria, Marie de Sainte-Thérèse), tertiare du Carmel." DS 12 (1984): 1227–29.

Devaux, Augustine. "Surius (Sauer, Laurent)." DS 14 (1988): 1325–29.

Deville, Raymond. *The French School of Spirituality: An Introduction and Reader*. Pittsburgh: Duquesne University Press, 1994.

Devos, Roger. "Jeanne-Françoise de Chantal (sainte)." DS 8 (1974): 859–69.

Diefendorf, Barbara. "Contradictions of the Century of Saints: Aristocratic Patronage and the Convents of Counter-Reformation Paris." *French Historical Studies* 24.3 (2001): 469–99.

———. *From Penitence to Charity: Pious Women and the Catholic Reformation in Paris*. Oxford: Oxford University Press, 2004.

———. "The Religious Wars in France." In *A Companion to the Reformation World*, edited by R. Po-chia Hsia, 150–68. Malden, MA: Blackwell, 2004.

Dijk, Willibrord Christian van. "Richelieu (Armand Jean du Plessis), cardinal, 1585-1642." DS 13 (1987): 656-59.
Dodin, André. "Duval (André), théologien française, 1564-1638." DS 3 (1957): 1857 -62.
Donlan, Thomas A. "Oasis of Gentleness in a Desert of Militancy: François de Sales's Contribution to French Catholicism." In *Surrender to Christ for Mission: French Spiritual Traditions*, edited by Philip Sheldrake, 90-108. Collegeville, MN: Liturgical Press, 2018.
Dubois-Quinard, Madeleine. "Laurent de Paris, capuchin, d. 1631." DS 9 (1976): 406-15.
———. *Laurent de Paris: Une doctrine du pur amour*. Rome: Institute for Capuchin Studies, 1959.
———. "L'humanisme mystique de Laurent de Paris: L' anéantissement de l'âme." *Études Franciscaines* n.s. 14 (1964): 31-57.
Dunn, Mary. *The Cruelest of Mothers: Marie de l'Incarnation, Motherhood, and Christian Tradition*. New York: Fordham University Press, 2016.
Dupré, Louis. "Jansenism and Quietism." In *Christian Spirituality: Post-Reformation and Modern*, edited by Louis Dupré and Don E. Saliers, 121-42. World Spirituality 18. New York: Crossroad, 1989.
Dupuy, Michel. *Bérulle: Une spiritualité de l'adoration*. Tournai: Desclée, 1964.
———. *Le Christ de Bérulle*. Paris: Desclée, 2001.
———. "Intérieur de Jésus." DS 7.2 (1971): 1870-77.
———. "Introversion." DS 7.2 (1971): 1904-18.
———. *Pierre de Bérulle*. Paris: Bloud & Gay, 1964.
———. *Se laisser à l'esprit: L'itinéraire spirituel de Jean-Jacques Olier*. Paris: Éditions du Cerf, 1982.
———. "Surin (Jean-Joseph), jésuite, 1600-1665." DS 14 (1990): 1311-25.
Dutton, Elisabeth, and Victoria Van Hyning. "Augustine Baker and the Mystical Canon." In *Dom Augustine Baker (1575-1641)*, edited by Geoffrey Scott, 85 -110. Leominster: Gracewing, 2011.
Duval, André. *La vie admirable de la bienheureuse soeur Marie de l'Incarnation, religieuse converse en l'ordre de Notre-Dame du Carmel et fondatrice de cet ordre en France, appelée dans le monde Mademoiselle Acarie*. Paris, 1621.
Egan, Harvey J. *An Anthology of Christian Mysticism*. Collegeville, MN: Liturgical Press, 1991.
Eire, Carlos M. N. *Reformations: The Early Modern World, 1450-1650*. New Haven: Yale University Press, 2016.
Eliot, T. S. *The Varieties of Metaphysical Poetry by T. S. Eliot*. Edited by Ronald Schuchard. San Diego: Harcourt Brace & Company, 1993.
Ellinger, Georg. *Angelus Silesius: Ein Lebensbild*. Breslau: Korn, 1927.
Emrich, Wilhelm. *Deutsche Literatur der Barockzeit*. Königstein: Athenäum, 1981.
Eulogio de la Vierge du Carmel et al. "Denys L'Aréopagite: En Occident. E. 17e et 18e siècles." DS 3 (1957): 410-29.

Faesen, Rob. "Achille Gagliardi and the Northern Mystics." In *A Companion to Jesuit Mysticism*, edited by Robert A. Maryks, 82–111. Leiden: Brill, 2017.

———. "A French Mystic's Perspective on the Crisis of Mysticism: Jean-Joseph Surin (1600–1665)." In *Mysticism in the French Tradition: Eruptions from France*, edited by Louise Nelstrop and Bradley B. Onishi, 149–67. Contemporary Theological Explorations in Christian Mysticism. Burlington, VT: Ashgate, 2015.

Febvre, Lucien. "The Origins of the French Reformation: A Badly-Put Question?" In *A New Kind of History: From the Writings of Lucien Febvre*, edited by Peter Burke, 44–107. New York: Harper & Row, 1973.

Ferrari, Anne. *Figures de la contemplation: La "rhétorique divine" de Pierre de Bérulle*. Paris: Éditions du Cerf, 1997.

Fletcher, F. T. H. *Pascal and the Mystical Tradition*. Oxford: Blackwell, 1954.

Fontana, Paolo. *Santità femminile e Inquisizione: La "Passione" di Suor Domitilla Galluzzi (1595–1671)*. Fontes Archivi Sancti Officii Romani 3. Rome: Libreria Editrice Vaticana, 2007.

Freeman, Laurence. "Baker and the Contemplative Ideal." In *That Mysterious Man: Essays on Augustine Baker OSB, 1575–1641*, edited by Michael Woodward, 191–201. Abergavenny: Three Peaks Press, 2001.

Foster, Marc R. *Catholic Germany from the Reformation to the Enlightenment*. New York: Palgrave Macmillan, 2007.

Gaffney, James. *Augustine Baker's Inner Light: A Study in English Recusant Spirituality*. Scranton, PA: University of Scranton, 1989.

Gies, M. Hildburgis. *Eine lateinische Quelle zum "Cherubinischen Wandersmann" des Angelus Silesius*. Breslauer Studien zur historischen Theologie 12. Breslau: Müller & Seiffert, 1929.

Gilson, Etienne. *La liberté chez Descartes et la théologie*. Paris: Alcan, 1913.

Girolamo, Luca M. di. *Santa Maria Maddalena de'Pazzi: Esistenza e teologia a confronto*. Rome: Edizioni Carmelitane, 2010.

Gnädinger, Louise. "Angelus Silesius." In *Deutscher Dichter des 17. Jahrhunderts: Ihr Leben und Werk*, edited by Harald Steinhagen and Benno von Wiese, 553–75. Berlin: Erich Schmidt, 1984.

———. "Die spekulative Mystik im 'Cherubinischen Wandersmann' des Johannes Angelus Silesius." *Studi Germanici* n.s. 4 (1966): 29–59, 144–90.

Goetz, Joseph, et al. "Extase." DS 4.2 (1961): 2045–2189.

Goffi, Tullo, and Pietro Zovatto, *La spiritualità del settecento: Crisi di identità e nuovi percorsi (1650–1800)*. Storia della spiritualità (Bologna, Italy) 6. Bologna: Edizioni Dehoniane, 1990.

Gorceix, Bernard. *Flambée et agonie: Mystiques du XVIIe siècle allemand*. Saint-Vincent-sur-Jabron: Éditions Présence, 1977.

Gorday, Peter J. *Pure Love, Pure Poetry, Pure Prayer: The Life and Work of Henri Bremond*. Eugene, OR: Wipf & Stock, 2018.

Gouhier, Alain. "Néant." DS 11 (1982): 64-80.
Goujon, Patrick. *Prendre part à l'intransmissible: La communication spirituel à travers la correspondance de Jean-Joseph Surin.* Grenoble: Éditions Jérôme Millon, 2008.
Greiffenberg, Catharina Regina von. *Meditations on the Incarnation, Passion, and Death of Jesus Christ.* Edited and translated by Lynne Tatlock. The Other Voice in Early Modern Europe. Chicago: University of Chicago Press, 2009.
Gueullette, Jean-Marie. *Eckhart en France: La lecture des "Institutions spirituelles" attribuées à Tauler, 1548-1699.* Grenoble: Éditions Jérôme Millon, 2012.
———. "L'usage périlleux de la notion d'école de la spiritualité." In *Les écoles de pensée religieuse à l'époque moderne: Actes de la Journée d'Études de Lyon (14 janvier 2006)*, edited by Yves Krumenacker and Laurent Thirouin, 185-201. Chrétiens et sociétés: Documents et mémoires 5. Lyon: Université Jean Moulin, 2006.
Guibert, Joseph de. *La spiritualité de la Compagnie de Jésus: Esquisse historique.* Bibliotheca Instituti Historici S.I. 4. Rome: Institutum Historicum S.I., 1953.
Guilday, Peter. *The English Catholic Refugees on the Continent, 1558-1795.* Volume 1: *The English Colleges and Convents in the Catholic Low Countries, 1558-1795.* London and New York: Longman, Green, 1914.
Haas, Alois M. "Angelus Silesius: Die Welt, ein wunderschönes Nichts." In Haas, *Sermo mysticus: Studien zu Theologie und Sprache in der deutschen Mystik*, 378-91. Freiburg, Switzerland: Universitätsverlag, 1979.
———. "Angelus Silesius—Artz und Mystiker." In Haas, *Mystik im Kontext*, 388-404. Munich: Wilhelm Fink Verlag, 2004.
———. "Christus ist Alles: Die Christusmystik des Angelus Silesius." In Haas, *Gottleiden-Gottlieben: Zur volksprachlichen Mystik im Mittelalter*, 295-318. Frankfurt-am-Main: Insel Verlag, 1989.
———. "Daniel Czepko von Reigersfeld—Nosce te ipsum." In Haas, *Sermo mysticus: Studien zu Theologie und Sprache in der deutschen Mystik*, 371-77. Freiburg, Switzerland: Universitätsverlag, 1979.
———. "Friedrich von Spee—Geistliche Zeitvertreib." In Haas, *Sermo mysticus: Studien zu Theologie und Sprache in der deutschen Mystik*, 330-70. Freiburg, Switzerland: Universitätsverlag, 1979.
———. "Im Schweigen Gott zur Sprache bringen—Gotteserfahrung in der Mystik." In *Gott Denken und Bezeugen: Festschrift für Kardinal Walter Kasper zum 75. Geburtstag*, edited by George Augustin and Klaus Krämer, 317-55. Freiburg: Herder, 2008.
———. "Mors mystica—Ein mystologisches Motiv." In Haas, *Sermo mysticus: Studien zu Theologie und Sprache in der deutschen Mystik*, 392-480. Freiburg, Switzerland: Universitätsverlag, 1979.
Habert, Germain. *La Vie du Cardinal de Bérulle.* Paris, 1646.

Hamon, Auguste. "Coeur (Sacré)." DS 3 (1957): 1023–46.
Harbison, Peter. *Reflections on Baroque*. Chicago: University of Chicago Press, 2000.
Hense, Elisabeth, and Edeltraud Klueting. *Die dunkle Stille: Das Epithalamium von Jean de Saint-Samson als spirituelles Dokumentationstheater*. St. Ottilien: EOS Verlag, 2012.
———. "The Spirituality of Teresa of Avila and the Latin Manuscript about the Dutch War (folios 303r–49v)." In *Maria Petyt: A Mystic in Wartime*, edited by Joseph Chalmers et al., 352–65. Radboud Studies in Humanities 4. Leiden: Brill, 2015.
Houdard, Sophie. *Les invasions mystiques: Spiritualités, hétérodoxies et censures au début de l'époque moderne*. Paris: Belles Lettres, 2008.
Howells, Edward. "From Late Medieval to Early Modern: Assessing the Mystical Theology of Pierre de Bérulle." In *Mysticism in the French Tradition: Eruptions from France*, edited by Louise Nelstrop and Bradley B. Onishi, 169–83. Contemporary Theological Explorations in Christian Mysticism. Burlington, VT: Ashgate, 2015.
———. "Relationality and Difference in the Mysticism of Pierre de Bérulle." *Harvard Theological Review* 102 (2009): 225–43.
Hudon, William V. "The Papacy in the Age of Reform, 1513–1644." In *Early Modern Catholicism: Essays in Honor of John W. O'Malley, S.J.*, edited by Kathleen M. Comerford and Hilmar M. Pabel, 46–66. Toronto: University of Toronto Press, 2001.
Huijben, Jacques. "Aux sources de la spiritualité française du XVIIe siècle." *Supplement à la Vie Spirituelle* 25 (1930): [113–39]; 26 (1931): [17–46], [75–111]; 27 (1931): [94–122].
Huxley, Aldous. *Grey Eminence*. New York and London: Harper & Brothers, 1941.
Iparraguirre, Ignacio, and André Derville. "Gagliardi, Achille." DS 6 (1967): 54–64.
Jacqueline, Bernard. "L'Influence de S. Bernard au XVIIe siècle." *Collectanea Cisterciensia* 42 (1980): 22–35.
Janssen, Canisius (P.W.). *Les origines de la réforme des carmes en Frances en XVIIe siècle*. The Hague: Martinus Nijhoff, 1963.
Juardo, Manuel Ruiz. "Loarte (Gaspard), jésuite (1498–1578)." DS 9 (1976): 949–52.
Kelley, C. F. *The Spirit of Love Based on the Teaching of St. Francis de Sales*. New York: Harper & Brothers, 1951.
Kleinman, Ruth. *Saint François de Sales and the Protestants*. Geneva: Droz, 1962.
Knowles, David. *The English Mystical Tradition*. London: Burns, Oates & Washbourne, 1961.
Knox, Ronald Arbuthnott. *Enthusiasm: A Chapter in the History of Religion*. Oxford: Oxford University Press, 1950.

———. *Literary Distractions.* London and New York: Sheed & Ward, 1958.
Koehler, Théodore. "Servitude (Saint Esclavage)." DS 14 (1989): 730–45.
Kołakowski, Leszek. *Chrétiens sans église: La conscience religieuse et le lien confessionnel au XVIIe siècle.* Bibliothèque de philosophie. Paris: Éditions Gallimard, 1987.
———. *God Owes Us Nothing.* Chicago: University of Chicago Press, 1995.
Koster, Dirk. *Francis de Sales.* AZ Norden, The Netherlands: Bert Post, 2000.
Krumenacker, Yves. *L'école française de spiritualité: Des mystiques, des fondateurs, des courants er leurs interprètes.* Histoire. Paris: Éditions du Cerf, 1999.
Kuchar, Gary. "A Greek in the Temple: Pseudo-Dionysius and Negative Theology in Richard Crashaw's 'Hymn in the Glorious Epiphany.'" *Studies in Philology* 108 (2011): 261–98.
Lajeunie, E.-M. *Saint François de Sales: L'homme, la pensée, l'action.* 2 vols. Paris: Guy Victor, 1964.
Langelaan, James S. "Man, the Image and Likeness of God: Nature and Supernature according to St. Francis de Sales." *Downside Review* 95 (1977): 35–48.
Latz, Dorothy L. "The Mystical Poetry of Dame Gertrude More." *Mystics Quarterly* 16 (1990): 66–82.
Lawes, Richard. "Can Modern Psychology Help Us Understand Baker's *Secretum Sive Mysticum*?" In *That Mysterious Man: Essays on Augustine Baker OSB, 1575–1641*, edited by Michael Woodward, 211–33. Abergavenny: Three Peaks Press, 2001.
Le Brun, Jacques. "Le Dieu des mystiques au XVIIe S." In *Dieu au XVIIe siècle: Crises et renouvellements du discourse*, edited by Henri Laux and Dominique Salin, 265–76. Paris: Éditions Facultés Jésuites de Paris, 2002.
———. "Les différentes faces de la Contre-Réforme: Angelus Silesius (Johannes Scheffler, 1624–1677)." In *Les deux réformes chrétiennes: Propagation et diffusion*, edited by Ilana Zinguer and Myriam Yardeni, 354–68. Studies in the History of Christian Traditions 114. Leiden: Brill, 2004.
———. "France. VI: Le Grand Siècle de la spiritualité française et ses lendemains." DS 5 (1964): 917–53.
———. "Humanisme et spiritualité. VII: L'Humanisme dévot." DS 7.1 (1969): 1028–33.
———. *La pur amour de Platon à Lacan.* Paris: Éditions du Seuil, 2001.
———. *Soeur et amante: Les biographies spirituelles feminins du XVIIe siècle.* Geneva: Droz, 2013.
Leclercq, Jean. *Alone with God: A Guide to the Hermit Way of Life, Based on the Teachings of Blessed Paul Giustiniani.* London: Hodder & Stoughton, 1961.

———. "Giustiniani (Paul), camaldule, 1476–1528." DS 6 (1967): 414–17.
———. *Un humaniste eremite: Le bienheureux Paul Giustiniani (1476–1528)*. Rome: Edizione Camaldoli, 1951.
Lécuyer, Jean. "Docilité au Saint-Esprit." DS 3 (1967): 1471–97.
Leonard, Amy. "Female Religious Orders." In *A Companion to the Reformation World*, edited by R. Po-chia Hsia, 237–54. Malden, MA: Blackwell, 2004.
Leonardi, Claudio. "La santità delle donne." In *Scrittrici mistiche italiane*, edited by Giovanni Pozzi and Claudio Leonardi, 43–57. Genoa: Marietti, 1988.
Levi, Anthony. *French Moralists: The Theory of the Passions, 1585 to 1649*. Oxford: Clarendon Press, 1964.
Liebowitz, Ruth P. "Virgins in the Service of Christ: The Dispute over an Active Apostolate for Women during the Counter-Reformation." In *Women of Spirit: Female Leadership in Jewish and Christian Traditions*, edited by Rosemary Ruether and Eleanor McLaughlin, 131–52. New York: Simon & Schuster, 1977.
Lierheimer, Linda. "Preaching or Teaching? Defining the Ursuline Mission in Seventeenth-Century France." In *Women Preachers and Prophets through Two Millennia of Christianity*, edited by Beverly Mayne Kienzle and Pamela J. Walker, 212–26. Berkeley: University of California Press, 1998.
Liuima, Antanas. *Aux sources du Traité de l'Amour de Dieu de Saint François de Sales*. 2 vols. Collectanea spiritualia. Rome: Librairie Editrice de l'Université Gregorienne, 1959–60.
Loarte, Gaspar. *Instrutione et avertimenti per meditare la passione di Cristo nostro redentore, con alcune meditationi intorno ad esse*. Rome, 1571.
Lollini, Massimo. "Scrittura obbediente e mistica tridentina in Veronica Giuliani." In *Women Mystic Writers*, ed. Dino S. Cervigni, 351–69. Annali d'italianistica 13. Chapel Hill: University of North Carolina Press, 1995.
Low, Anthony. *Augustine Baker*. New York: Twayne, 1970.
———. "Richard Crashaw." In *The Cambridge Companion to English Poetry: Donne to Marvell*, edited by Thomas N. Corns, 242–55. Cambridge: Cambridge University Press, 1993.
Lunn, David. *The English Benedictines, 1540–1688: From Reformation to Revolution*. New York: Barnes & Noble, 1980.
———. "Father Augustine Baker (1575–1641) and the English Mystical Tradition." *Journal of Ecclesiastical History* 26 (1975): 267–77.
Lux-Sterritt, Laurence, ed. *English Convents in Exile, 1600–1800*. Volume 2, *Spirituality*. London: Pickering & Chatto, 2012.
———. *English Benedictine Nuns in Exile in the Seventeenth Century: Living Spirituality*. Manchester: Manchester University Press, 2017.
Lynn, Mary Loyola, and Mary Grace Flynn. *Index to the Writings of Saint*

Francis de Sales. Philadelphia: Visitation Monasteries in the United States, 1968.

MacGregor, Kirk R. *Luis de Molina: The Life and Theology of the Founder of Middle Knowledge.* Grand Rapids: Zondervan, 2015.

Maggi, Armando. *Uttering the Word: The Mystical Performances of Maria Maddalena de'Pazzi, A Renaissance Visionary.* Albany: State University of New York Press, 1998.

———. "The Voice and the Silences of Maria Maddalena de'Pazzi." In *Women Mystic Writers,* ed. Dino S. Cervigni, 257–81. Annali d'italianistica 13. Chapel Hill: University of North Carolina Press, 1995.

Mahnke, Dietrich. *Unendliche Sphäre und Allmittelpunkt.* Halle: Niemeyer, 1937.

Mali, Anya. "L'état de victime et le 'petit discourse' mystique." In *Femme mystique et missionaire: Marie Guyart de l'Incarnation,* edited by Raymond Brodeur, 211-20. Quebec: Les Presses de l'Université de Laval, 2001.

———. *Mystic in the New World: Marie de l'Incarnation (1599–1672).* Studies in the History of Christian Thought 72. Leiden: Brill, 1996.

Manzoni, Giuseppe. "Victimale (Spiritualité)." DS 16 (1992): 531–45.

Marcocchi, Massimo, ed. *Spiritualità et vita religiosa tra Cinquecento e Novecento.* Brescia: Morcelliana, 2005.

Marie-Thérèse de Saint-Joseph. "Marie de l'Incarnation (bienheureuse)." DS 10 (1980): 486–87.

Marín, Juan Miguel. "Annihilation and Deification in Beguine Theology and Marguerite Porete's *Mirror of Simple Souls.*" *Harvard Theological Review* 103 (2010): 89 –109.

———. "A Beguine's Spectre: Marguerite Porete [d. 1310], Achille Gagliardi [d. 1607] and Their Collaboration across Time." *The Way* 51.3 (2012): 93 –110.

Marion, Jean-Luc. "The Idea of God." In *The Cambridge History of Seventeenth-Century Philosophy,* edited by Daniel Garber and Michael Ayers, 1:265–304. Cambridge: Cambridge University Press, 1998.

Maritain, Jacques. "Apropos of the French School." *Revue Thomiste* 71 (1971): 463 –79.

Marotti, Arthur F. "Saintly Idiocy and Contemplative Empowerment: The Example of Dame Gertrude More." In *Mysticism and Reform, 1400–1750,* edited by Sara S. Poor and Nigel Smith, 151-76. ReFormations: Medieval and Early Modern. Notre Dame, IN: University of Notre Dame Press, 2015.

Martz, Louis L. *The Poetry of Meditation: A Study of English Religious Literature of the Seventeenth Century.* New Haven: Yale University Press, 1954.

———. *The Wit of Love.* Notre Dame, IN: University of Notre Dame Press, 1969.

Marxer, François. "L'École Française: Le théologie entre éblouissement théocentrique et faille Christologique." In Bremond, *Histoire*, 1:875-905.

Maryks, Robert A., ed. *A Companion to Jesuit Mystcism*. Brill's Companions to the Christian Tradition 78. Leiden: Brill, 2017.

Matter, E. Ann. "The Commentary on the Rule of Clare of Assisi by Maria Domitilla Galluzzi." In *Creative Women in Medieval and Early Modern Italy: A Religious and Artistic Renaissance*, edited by E. Ann Matter and John Coakley, 201-11. Philadelphia: University of Pennsylvania Press, 1994.

———. "Interior Maps of an Eternal External: The Spiritual Rhetoric of Maria Domitilla Galluzzi d'Acqui." In *Maps of Flesh and Light: The Religious Experience of Medieval Women Mystics*, edited by Ulrike Wiethaus, 60-73. Syracuse, NY: Syracuse University Press, 1993.

———. "The Personal and the Paradigm: The Book of Maria Domitilla Galluzzi." In *The Crannied Wall: Women, Religion, and the Arts in Early Modern Europe*, edited by Craig A. Monson, 87-103. Ann Arbor: University of Michigan Press, 1992.

Mazzocco, Mariel. "Entre silence et vibrations sonores: La poésie mystique d'Angelus Silesius." *Rivista di storia e letteratura religiosa* 49 (2013): 443-56.

———. *Le joyau de l'âme: Diamants et autre gemmes mystiques*. Paris: Albin Michel, 2019.

———. "Les 'petits mots' d'un aventurier mystique," and "Vocabulaire mystique de Jean-Jacques Olier." In *Jean-Jacques Olier: Tentations diaboliques et possession divin*, edited by Mariel Mazzocco, 135-280. Paris: Honoré Champion, 2012.

———. "Perdersi per ritrovarsi: L'avventura del desiderio nella letteratura mistica." *Rivista di storia e letteratura religiosa* 48 (2012): 65-98.

———. "Les sources mystiques de Jean-Jacques Olier." *Bulletin de Saint-Sulpice: Jean-Jacques Olier (1608-1657). Hier et Aujourd'hui* 34 (2008): 103-16.

———. "'Suressential': Aux sources d'un langage mystique." *Revue de l'histoire des religions* 4 (2013): 609-27.

Mazzoni, Cristina. "Bibliographical Essay." In *Women Mystic Writers*, ed. Dino S. Cervigni, 401-35. Annali d'italianistica 13. Chapel Hill: University of North Carolina Press, 1995.

Mazzonis, Querciolo. *Spirituality, Gender, and the Self in Renaissance Italy: Angela Merici and the Company of St. Ursula (1474-1540)*. Washington, DC: Catholic University of America Press, 2007.

McCann, Justin. "Father Baker's Tercentenary." *Downside Review* 79 (1941): 355-71.

McCosker, Philip. "The Christology of Pierre de Bérulle." *Downside Review* 124 (2006): 111-34.

McDonnell, Eunan. *The Concept of Freedom in the Writings of Francis de Sales.* Bern: Peter Lang, 2009.

McGinn, Bernard. "'Evil-Sounding, Rash, and Suspect of Heresy': Tensions between Mysticism and Magisterium in the History of the Church." *Catholic Historical Review* 90 (2004): 193–212.

———. *"Gelâzen/Gelâzenheit* from Eckhart to the Radical Reformers." *Meister-Eckhart-Jahrbuch* 13 (2019): 89–111.

———. "The Language of Inner Experience in Christian Mysticism." *Spiritus* 1 (2001): 156–71.

———. *Meister Eckhart Teacher and Preacher.* Classics of Western Spirituality. New York: Paulist Press, 1986.

———. "A Sixteenth-Century Mystical Renaissance in the Eastern Netherlands." In *1517–1545: The Northern Experience. Mysticism, Reform and Devotion between the Late Medieval and the Early Modern Periods*, edited by Kees Schepers and Thom Mertens, 28–59. *Ons Geestelijk Erf* 87 (2016).

———. "Suffering, Dereliction, and Affliction in Christian Mysticism." In *Suffering and the Christian Life*, edited by Karen Kilby and Rachel Davies, 55 –70. London: T&T Clark, 2019.

McGrath-Merkle, Clare. *Bérulle's Spiritual Theology of the Priesthood: A Study in Speculative Mysticism and Applied Metaphysics.* New York: Peter Lang, 2018.

Meeuwsen, Veronie. "Maria Petyet's Support for the French King." In *Maria Petyt: A Mystic in Wartime*, edited by Joseph Chalmers et al., 240–55. Radboud Studies in Humanities 4. Leiden: Brill, 2015.

Meier, Annemarie. *Daniel Czepko als geistlicher Dichter.* Studien zur Germanistik, Anglistik, und Komparatistik 33. Bonn: Bouvier, 1975.

Merton, Thomas. "Self-Knowledge in Gertrude More and Augustine Baker." In Merton, *Mystics and Zen Masters*, 154–77. New York: Dell, 1961.

Michel. Suzanne-P. "Epithalme." DS 4.1 (1960): 907–9.

———. "Jean de Saint-Samson, mystique carme, 1571–1636." DS 8 (1974): 703–10.

Michon, Hélène. "Le Coeur dans la tradition augustinienne." In *Augustin au XVIIe siècle*, edited by Laurence Devillairs, 203–20. Florence: Leo S. Olschki, 2007.

———. *Saint François de Sales: Une nouvelle mystique.* Paris: Éditions du Cerf, 2008.

Milcent, Paul. "Jean Eudes (saint)." DS 8 (1974): 488–501.

Milch, Werner. *Daniel von Czepko: Geistliche Schriften.* Darmstadt: Wissenschaftliche Buchgesellschaft, 1963.

Molien, Auguste. "Bérulle (Cardinal Pierre de)." DS 1 (1937): 1539–81.

———. "Condren (Charles de)." DS 3 (1957): 1373–88.

Mommaers, Paul. "Benoît de Canfield: Sa terminologie 'essentielle.'" *Revue d'histoire de spiritualité* 47 (1971): 421–54; 48 (1972): 37–68.

———. "Benoît de Canfield et ses sources flamandes." *Revue d'histoire de spiritualité* 48 (1972): 401–34; 49 (1973): 37–66.

———. "Pays-Bas. IV: Les XVIe et XVIIe siècles." DS 12 (1984): 730–50.

Morello, Giovanni, ed. *Visioni ed estasi: Capolavori dell'arte europea tra Seicento e Settecento*. Milan: Skira, 2003.

Morgain, Stéphane-Marie. *Pierre de Bérulle et les Carmélites de France*. Paris: Éditions du Cerf, 1995.

———. *La théologie politique de Pierre de Bérulle (1598–1629)*. Collection "La France au fil des siècles." Paris: Publisud, 2001.

Morkovsky, Mary Christine. "Women and the French School of Spirituality." In *Surrender to Christ for Mission: French Spiritual Traditions*, edited by Philip Sheldrake, 109–26. Collegeville, MN: Liturgical Press, 2018.

Mueller, Janel. "Women among the Metaphysicals: A Case, Mostly, of Being Donne for." *Modern Philology* 87 (1989): 142–58.

Mursell, Gordon. "'On Being Loved': The Assurance of Divine Love in the Works of Augustine Baker." In *Dom Augustine Baker (1575–1641)*, edited by Geoffrey Scott, 65–83. Leominster: Gracewing, 2011.

Nadeau-Lacour, Thérèse. *Marie Guyart de l'Incarnation: Une femme mystique au coeur de l'histoire*. Paris: Artège, 2015.

Nant, Candide de. "Constantin de Barbanson." DS 2.2 (1953): 1634–41.

Nédoncelle, Maurice. "Intériorité. II: Intériorité et vie spirituelle." DS 7.2 (1971): 1889–1903.

Neill, Kerby. "Structure and Symbol in Crashaw's *Hymn to the Nativity*." *Publications of the Modern Language Association of America* 63 (1948): 101–13.

Nelstrop, Louise, and Bradley B. Onishi, eds. *Mysticism in the French Tradition: Eruptions from France*. Contemporary Theological Explorations in Christian Mysticism. Burlington, VT: Ashgate, 2015.

Newman, Barbara. "Annihilation and Authorship: Three Women Mystics of the 1290s." *Speculum* 91 (2013): 591–630.

Norman, Marion. "Dame Gertrude More and the English Mystical Tradition." *Recusant History* 15 (1979): 192–211.

Noye, Irénée. "Jésus (Nom de)." DS 8 (1974): 1109–26.

Noye, Irénée, and Michel Dupuy. "Olier (Jean-Jacques)." DS 11 (1982): 737–51.

Occhialini, U., et al., eds. *L'estasi*. Vatican City: Libreria Editrice Vaticana, 2003.

O'Malley, John W. *Trent: What Happened at the Council*. Cambridge, MA: Belknap Press of Harvard University Press, 2013.

Orcibal, Jean. *Le Cardinal de Bérulle: Évolution d'une spiritualité*. Paris: Éditions du Cerf, 1965.

———. "Divinisation. V: Au 17e siècle." DS 3 (1957): 1445–52.

———. *La rencontre du Carmel Thérésienne avec les mystiques du Nord.* Paris: Presses Universitaires de France, 1959.

———. "Les sources étrangères du 'Cherubinischer Wandersmann (1657)' d'après la bibliothèque d'Angelus Silesius." *Revue de Littérature Comparée* 18 (1938): 494–506.

Oorschot, Theo G. M., ed. *Friedrich Spee (1591–1635): Düsseldorfer Symposium zum 400. Geburtstag. Neue Ergebnisse der Spee-Forschung.* Bielefeld: Aisthesis Verlag, 1993.

O'Reilly, Terence. "The Mystical Theology of Saint Francis de Sales in the *Traité de l'amour de Dieu*." In *Mysticism in the French Tradition: Eruptions from France*, edited by Louise Nelstrop and Bradley B. Onishi, 207–20. Contemporary Theological Explorations in Christian Mysticism. Burlington, VT: Ashgate, 2015.

Oury, Guy. *Marie de l'Incarnation.* 2 vols. Solesmes: Abbaye de Saint-Pierre, 1973.

———. "Marie de l'Incarnation." DS 10 (1980): 487–507.

———. "Mystique de l'immanence et mystique nuptiale." In *Femme mystique et missionnaire: Marie Guyart de l'Incarnation*, edited by Raymond Brodeur, 157–67. Quebec: Les Presses de l'Université de Laval, 2001.

Papàsogli, Benedetta. *Gli Spirituali Italiani e Il "Grand Siècle.* Rome: Edizioni di Storia e Letteratura, 1983.

Payne, Steven. *The Carmelite Tradition.* Spirituality in History. Collegeville, MN: Liturgical Press, 2011.

Pelosi, Olimpia. "Tra *eros* e *caritas*: Le 'pene d'amore' di Maria Domitilla Galluzzi." In *Women Mystic Writers,* ed. Dino S. Cervigni, 307–32. Annali d'italianistica 13. Chapel Hill: University of North Carolina Press, 1995.

Peltier, Henri. *Histoire du Carmel.* Paris: Éditions du Seuil, 1958.

Petersson, Robert T. *The Art of Ecstasy: Teresa, Bernini, and Crashaw.* New York: Athenaeum, 1970.

Petrocchi, Massimo. *L'estasi nelle Mistiche Italiane della Riforma Cattolica.* Naples: Libreria Scientifica Editrice, 1958.

———. "Italie. IV: Période Moderne (16e–18e siècles). A. Le 17e siècle." DS 7.1 (1971): 2252–58.

———. *Storia della spiritualità italiana.* Turin: Società Editrice Internazionale, 1996.

Piron, Sylvain. "Adnichilatio." In *Mots médiévaux offerts à Reudi Imbach*, edited by I. Atucha et al., 23–33. Oporto, Portugal: Féderation Internationale des Instituts d'Études Médiévales, 2011.

Pitaud, Bernard. *Jean-Jacques Olier (1608–1657).* Brussels: Lessius, 2017.

Plard, Henri. *La mystique d'Angelus Silesius.* Paris: Aubier, 1943.

Pobladura, Melchiorre da. "Cappucini." In *Dizionario degli Istituti di Perfezione*, edited by Guerrino Pelliccia and Giancarlo Rocca, 2:203–52. 10 vols. Rome: Edizioni Paoline, 1973–2003.

Poli, Tullio. *Punta suprema dell'anima: Virtù teologali preghiera semplice e adesione alla voluntà divina secondo S. Francesco di Sales*. Analecta Gregoriana B.76. Rome: Gregorian University Press, 1982.

Pott, Hans-Georg. "Friedrich Spee und die Mystik." In *Friedrich Spee (1591-1635): Düsseldorfer Symposium zum 400. Geburtstag. Neue Ergebnisse der Spee-Forschung*, edited by Theo G. M. Oorschot, 30-50. Bielefeld: Aisthesis Verlag, 1993.

Pottier, Aloys, and Michel-Jean Picard. "Coton (Pierre), jésuite (1564-1626)." DS 2.2 (1953): 2422-32.

Pouillard, C. *Le Père Condren: Le mystique de l'Oratoire*. Paris: FAC, 1994.

Pourret, Pierre. *La Spiritualité Chrétienne*, Volume 3, *Les Temps Modernes*. Paris: Gabalda, 1927.

Power, Edmund. "The Spirituality of *Sancta Sophia*." In *Dom Augustine Baker (1575-1641)*, edited by Geoffrey Scott, 1-18. Leominster: Gracewing, 2011.

Power, Joseph F. "Entre l'une et l'autre volonté divine." In *L'Unidivers salésien: Saint François de Sales hier et aujourd'hui*, edited by Hélène Bordes and Jacques Hennequin, 265-75. Paris: Université de Metz, 1994.

Pozzi, Giovanni, and Claudio Leonardi, eds. *Scrittrici mistiche italiane*. Genoa: Marietti, 1988.

Praz, Mario. *The Flaming Heart*. Garden City, NY: Doubleday Anchor, 1958.

Preckler, Fernando Guillén. *"État" chez le cardinal de Bérulle: Théologie et spiritualité des "états" bérulliens*. Analecta Gregoriana 197. Rome: Gregorian University Press, 1974.

Puniet, P. de. "Blois (Louis de) ou Blosius." DS 1 (1937): 1730-38.

Rapley, Elizabeth. *The Dévotes: Women and Church in Seventeenth-Century France*. Montreal and Kingston: McGill-Queens University Press, 1990.

Ravier, André. *Francis de Sales: Sage and Saint*. San Francisco: Ignatius Press, 1988.

Raviolo, Isabelle. "Angelus Silesius." In *Encyclopédie des mystiques rhénans: D'Eckhart à Nicolas de Cues et leur réception*, edited by Marie-Anne Vannier, 94-100. Paris: Éditions du Cerf, 2011.

Rayez, André. "Gaultier (René), tradeucteur." DS 6 (1967): 144-47.

———. "Indifference." DS 7.2 (1971): 1688-1708.

Regazzoni, Mauro. "Capitolo 27: Il 'Vissuto' Mistico." In *Storia della spiritualità italiana*, edited by Pietro Zovatto, 399-423. Rome: Città Nuova, 2002.

Rhodes, J. T. "Blosius and Baker." In *Dom Augustine Baker, 1575-1641*, edited by Geoffrey Scott, 133-52. Leominster: Gracewing, 2011.

Riccardi, Antonio. "The Mystic Humanism of Maria Maddalena de'Pazzi." In *Creative Women in Medieval and Early Modern Italy: A Religious and*

Artistic Renaissance, edited by E. Ann Matter and John Coakley, 212–36. Philadelphia: University of Pennsylvania Press, 1994.

Rivet, Mother Mary Majella. *The Influence of the Spanish Mystics on the Works of Saint Francis de Sales.* Washington, DC: Catholic University of America, 1941.

Robinson, Joanne Maguire. *Nobility and Annihilation in Marguerite Porete's "Mirror of Simple Souls."* SUNY Series in Western Esoteric Traditions. Albany: State University of New York Press, 2001.

Salin, Dominique. "'L'invasion mystique' en France au XVIIe S." In *Dieu au XVIIe siècle: Crises et renouvellements du discours*, edited by Henri Laux and Dominique Salin, 241–66. Paris: Facultés Jésuites de Paris, 2002.

Sammons, Jeffrey L. *Angelus Silesius.* Twayne's World Authors Series 25. New York: Twayne, 1967.

Sanson, Henri. *St. Jean de la Croix entre Bossuet et Fénelon: Contribution à l'étude de la querelle du Pur Amour.* Paris: Presses Universitaires de France, 1953.

Saudreau, Auguste. *Mystical Prayer according to St. Jane de Chantal.* London: Sheed & Ward, 1929.

Scaduto, Mario. "Italie. IV: Période Moderne (16e–18e siècles). A. Le 16e siècle." DS 7.1 (1971): 2236–52.

Sceaux, Raoul de, and André Rayez. "Joseph de Paris, capuchin, 1588–1638." DS 8 (1974): 1372–88.

Schepers, Kees, and Thom Mertens, eds. *1517–1545: The Northern Experience. Mysticism, Reform and Devotion between the Late Medieval and Early Modern Periods. Ons Geestelijk Erf* 87.1–2 (2016).

Schmidt, Josef. "Introduction." In Angelus Silesius, *The Cherubinic Wanderer.* Translated by Maria Shrady, 1–36. Classics of Western Spirituality. New York: Paulist Press, 1986.

Scholem, Gershom. "Mysticism and Society." *Diogenes* 58 (1967): 1–24.

Schoolfield, George S. *The German Lyric of the Baroque Period in English Translation.* Chapel Hill: University of North Carolina Press, 1961.

Schweitzer, Franz-Josef. "Zeit und Ewigkeit bei Angelus Silesius." In *Grundfragen christlicher Mystik: Wissenschaftliche Studientagung Theologia Mystica in Weingarten vom 7.–10. November 1985*, edited by Margot Schmidt and Dieter R. Bauer, 259–72. Mystik in Geschichte und Gegenwart Abteilung 1.5. Stuttgart-Bad Cannstatt: Frommann-Holzboog, 1987.

Scicluna, Ivan. "*L'Epithalme* of Jean de Saint-Samson (1571–1636)." *Studies in Spirituality* 18 (2008): 289–311.

Scott, Geoffrey, ed. *Dom Augustine Baker (1575–1641).* Leominster: Gracewing, 2011.

Secondin, Bruno. *Santa Maria Maddalena de'Pazzi: Esperienza e dottrina.* Rome: Institutum Carmelitanum, 1974.

Segel, Harold B. *The Baroque Poem: A Comparative Survey.* New York: E. P. Dutton, 1974.

Serouet, Pierre. "François de Sales (saint)." DS 5 (1964): 1057–97.

———. "Madeleine de Saint-Joseph." DS 10 (1980): 57–60.

Sheppard, Lancelot C. *Barbe Acarie, Wife and Mystic.* New York: David McKay, 1953.

Sluhovsky, Moshe. *Believe Not Every Spirit: Possession, Mysticism, and Discernment in Early Modern Catholicism.* Chicago: University of Chicago Press, 2007.

———. "Mysticism as an Existential Crisis: Jean-Joseph Surin." In *A Companion to Jesuit Mysticism*, edited by Robert A. Maryks, 139–65. Leiden: Brill, 2017.

Spearritt, Placid. "The Survival of Medieval Spirituality among the Exiled Black Monks." In *That Mysterious Man: Essays on Augustine Baker OSB, 1575-1641*, edited by Michael Woodward, 19–41. Abergavenny: Three Peaks Press, 2001.

Stefanotti, Robert. *"The Holy Sepulchre Canticle" of John of St. Samson (1571–1636): A Synecdochical Study of His Spiritual Imagery, Language and Style.* Rome: Gregorian University Dissertation, 1991.

Steuert, Dom Hilary. "A Study of Recusant Prose: Dom Serenus Cressy, 1605-74." *Downside Review* 66 (1947/48): 165–78, 287–301.

Stopp, Elisabeth. *Hidden in God: Essays and Talks on St. Jane Frances de Chantal.* Philadelphia: St. Joseph's University Press, 1999.

———. *Madame de Chantal: Portrait of a Saint.* Westminster, MD: Newman Press, 1963.

———. "Saint Francis de Sales: Attitudes to Friendship." *Downside Review* 113 (1995): 175–92.

Stroppa, Sabrina. "L'annichilazione e la censura: Isabella Berinzaga e Achille Gagliardi." *Rivista di storia et letteratura religiosa* 32 (1996): 617–25.

———. *Sic arescit: Letteratura mistica del Seicento italiano.* Biblioteca della Rivista di storia e letteratura religiosa: Studi 8. Florence: Leo S. Olschki, 1998.

Tedeschi, John. *The Prosecution of Heresy: Collected Studies on the Inquisition in Early Modern Italy.* Binghamton, NY: Medieval and Renaissance Texts and Studies, 1991.

Temple, Liam Peter. *Mysticism in Early Modern England.* Studies in Modern British Religious History 38. Woodbridge: Boydell Press, 2019.

Terestchenko, Michel. *Amour et désespoir de François de Sales à Fénelon.* Paris: Éditions du Seuil, 2000.

Thayer, David. *"Kenosis* and *Anéantissement*: The Abnegations of Christ as the Key to Christian Identity—Some Lessons from the French School." *Bulletin de Saint-Sulpice.* Christology. Actualité—Enseignement. *Teaching Christology* 27 (2001): 192–207.

———. "*Néants capables de Dieu: Anéantissement*, Freedom and Individuation in the Anthropology of the French School." *Bulletin de Saint-Sulpice. L'École Française Aujourd'hui. The French School Today* 22 (1996): 94-107.

Thompson, William M. "The Christic Universe of Pierre de Bérulle and the French School." *American Benedictine Review* 29 (1978): 320-47.

———. "Olier's 'La Journée Chrétienne' as a Guide for Today's Theology." *Bulletin de Saint-Sulpice. Jean-Jacques Olier (1608-1657)* 14 (1988): 113-27.

———. "Women in the French School: Some No Longer Hidden Faces." *L'École française aujourd'hui. The French School Today. Bulletin of Saint-Sulpice* 22 (1996): 119-37.

Thurston, Herbert. *The Physical Phenomena of Mysticism*. Chicago: Henry Regnery, 1952.

———. *Surprising Mystics*. Chicago: Henry Regnery, 1955.

Toczysky, Suzanne. "'Blessed the Breasts at Which You Nursed': Mother-Child Intimacy in St. Francis de Sales' *Treatise on the Love of God*." *Spiritus* 15 (2005): 191-213.

Tracy, David. "The Catholic Imagination: The Example of Michelangelo." In *Heavenly Bodies: Fashion and the Catholic Imagination*, edited by Andrew Bolton, 10-16. New York: Metropolitan Museum of Art, 2018.

Trosa, Dionisia. *Prolegomeni alla spiritualità di S. Caterina di Ricci*. Florence: Leo S. Olschki, 1975.

Tyler, Peter. "Mystical Writing as *Theologia Mystica*." In *Dom Augustine Baker OSB (1575-1641)*, edited by Geoffrey Scott, 51-63. Leominster: Gracewing, 2011.

van de Vate, Esther. "Maria Petyt—A Short Biography." In *Maria Petyt: A Carmelite in Wartime*, edited by Joseph Chalmers et al., 7-21. Radboud Studies in Humanities 4. Leiden: Brill, 2015.

Van Meerbeeck, Michel. "Daily Life in the Hermitage in Mechelen at the Time of Maria Petyt (1657-1677)." In *Maria Petyt: A Carmelite Mystic in Wartime*, edited by Joseph Chalmers et al., 53-66. Radboud Studies in Humanities 4. Leiden: Brill, 2015.

Van Nieuwenhove, Rik, Robert Faesen, and Helen Rolfson, eds., *Late Medieval Mysticism in the Low Countries*. Classics of Western Spirituality. New York: Paulist Press, 2008.

Van Schoote, Jean-Pierre. "Inaction." DS 7.1 (1971): 1630-39.

———. "Le Perle Évangélique." *Revue de ascétique et de mystique* 37 (1961): 79-92, 291-313.

———. "Les traducteurs français des mystiques rhéno-flamandes et leur contribution à l'élaboration de la langue devote à l'aube de XVIIe siècle." *Revue d'ascétique et de mystique* 39 (1963): 319-37.

Vansteenberghe, E. "Aspirations." DS 1 (1937): 1018-25.

Varden, Erik. *Redeeming Freedom: The Principle of Servitude in Bérulle.* Studia Anselmiana 152. Rome: Pontificio Ateneo S. Anselmo, 2011.

Vasta, Marlena Modica. "Mystical Writing." In *Women and Faith: Catholic Religious Life in Italy from Late Antiquity to the Present,* edited by Lucetta Scaraffia and Gabriella Zarri, 205-18. Cambridge, MA: Harvard University Press, 1999.

Veghel, Optat de. *Benoît de Canfield (1561-1610): Sa vie, sa doctrine et son influence.* Bibliotheca Seraphico-Capuccina, Sectio Historica 11. Rome: Institutum Historicum Ord. Fr. Min. Cap., 1949.

Vermeylen, Alphonse. *Sainte Thérèse en France au XVIIe Siècle, 1600-1660.* Louvain: Publications Universitaires de Louvain, 1958.

Vernet, Félix. "Allemande (Spiritualité)." DS 1 (1937): 314-51.

Vetö, Miklos. "La Christo-logique de Bérulle." In *Pierre de Bérulle: Opuscules de pieté,* 7-136. Grenoble: Éditions Jérôme Millon, 1997.

Vidal, Daniel. "Le coup terrible du néant." In *La perle évangélique – traduction français (1602),* 9-170. Grenoble: Éditions Jérôme Millon, 1997.

———. *Critique de la raison mystique: Benoît de Canfield. Possession et dépossession au XVIIe siècle.* Grenoble: Éditions Jérôme Millon, 1990.

Viller, Marcel. "Autour de 'l'Abregé de la perfection': L'influence." *Revue d'ascétique et de mystique* 13 (1932): 34-59, 257-93.

———. "Beaucousin (Richard)." DS 1 (1937): 1314-15.

Völker, Ludwig. "'Gelassenheit': Zur Entstehung des Wortes in der Sprache Meister Eckharts und seiner Überlieferung in der nacheckhartischen Mystik bis Jacob Böhme." In *'Getempert und Gemischet': Für Wolfgang Mohr zum 65. Geburtstag von seiner Tübinger Schülern,* edited by Franz Hundsnurscher and Ulrich Müller, 281-312. Göppingen: Alfred Kümmerle, 1972.

Vos, Lambert (Henri). *Louis de Blois, Abbé de Liessies (1506-1566): Recherches bibliographiques sur son oeuvre.* Turnhout: Brepols, 1992.

Vuarnet, Jean-Noël. *Extases féminines.* Paris: Arthaud, 1980.

Warren, Austin. *Richard Crashaw: A Study in Baroque Sensibility.* Ann Arbor: University of Michigan Press, 1939.

Watkin, E. I. *Poets and Mystics.* London and New York: Sheed & Ward, 1953.

Wekking, Ben. "Baker's Biography of Dame Gertrude More." In *That Mysterious Man: Essays on Augustine Baker OSB, 1575-1641,* edited by Michael Woodward, 155-73. Abergavenny: Three Peaks Press, 2001.

Wiese, Benno von. "Die Antithetik in den Alexandrinen des Angelus Silesius." *Euphorion* 29 (1929): 503-22.

Willibrord of Paris. "Gelen (Victor, Victor de Trèves), capuchin allemande, d. 1669." DS 6 (1967): 179-81.

Woodgate, A. *Charles de Condren.* London: Browne & Nolan, n.d.

Woodward, Michael, "Bakerdata: An Annotated Bibliography of Published Texts and Secondary Sources." In *That Mysterious Man: Essays* on *Augustine Baker OSB, 1575–1641*, edited by Michael Woodward, 260–72. Abergavenny: Three Peaks Press, 2001.

———, ed. *That Mysterious Man: Essays on Augustine Baker OSB, 1575–1641*. Abergavenny: Three Peaks Press, 2001.

Wright, Wendy M. *Bond of Perfection. Jeanne de Chantal and Françcois de Sales*. New York: Paulist Press, 1985.

———. "Captured Yet Free: The Rich Symbolism of the Heart in French Spirituality." In *Surrender to Christ for Mission: French Spiritual Traditions*, edited by Philip Sheldrake, 71–89. Collegeville, MN: Liturgical Press, 2018.

———. *Heart Speaks to Heart: The Salesian Tradition*. Traditions of Christian Spirituality. Maryknoll, NY: Orbis Books, 2004.

———. "Seventeenth-Century French Mysticism." In *The Wiley-Blackwell Companion to Christian Mysticism*, edited by Julia Lamm, 437–51. Malden, MA: Wiley-Blackwell, 2013.

Young, R. V. *Richard Crashaw and the Spanish Golden Age*. New Haven: Yale University Press, 1978.

Zovatto, Pietro, ed. *Storia della spiritualità italiana*. Rome: Città Nuova, 2002.

Index of Scripture References

Old Testament

Genesis
1:2	199
1:26	110, 113
1:26-27	204
2:24	64
3:15	202

Exodus
3:2-6	323
24:14	151
25:40	72

Deuteronomy
5:9	151
6:5	453

Ruth
1:16	323

Hosea
2:14	65

Psalms
2:7	215
38:6	211
40	382
41:4	379
44:2	448
52:4	446
72:22	452
81:6	420
98:1	301
118:38	379
119:16	324
131:12	65

Song of Songs
1:1	118, 127, 288, 299, 315
1:4	320
1:15	299
2:4	393, 499, 501
2:5	304, 379
2:12	379
2:16	129
3:1	299
3:4	132, 299
3:6	161
4:7	302
4:9	135, 497, 499
5:1	132
5:2	379
6:7-8	149-50
7:10	150
8:4	320

Isaiah
7:9	152
24:16	356, 452
45:15	327
49:2	60
58:10	293
63:3	393

Jeremiah
2:13	151
11:13	324

New Testament

Matthew
5:3-12	153
6:10	142
10:37	312
11:28-30	96
16:24	26
22:23	150
22:37	453
22:39	453
26:38	329
27:46	144, 225, 324
28:20	235
28:30	236

Mark
1:13	216

Luke
1:35	220, 434
1:38	219
7:36-50	233
7:47	233-34
10	226
22:42	56, 426, 428
22:43	147
23:46	147

John
1:14	440
3:16	224
4:23	436
10:9	240
10:38	232
13:7	444
14:10	228
14:28–29	225
15:5	224
15:15	439
16:7	377
16:15	200
17:2	449
17:3	229, 324
17:5	217, 439
17:20–23	231
17:21	231
17:21–23	197
17:22–23	232, 248, 288
17:25	323
19:26–27	221
19:30	445
20:11–18	233
20:17	323

Acts
9:15	211
17:28	298

Romans
5:5	223
8:3	210, 216
8:14	223
8:35	454
9:3	28
9:5	285, 478

1 Corinthians
2:2	192
2:6	58
3:2	62
3:17	287
6:17	42, 161, 183, 210, 231, 236, 247, 288, 331
13:13	501
15:28	252, 453

2 Corinthians
3:17	158
5:14	139
12:4	414

Galatians
2:19	226
2:20	147, 210, 428, 447, 453
2:21	163
5:22	153

Ephesians
3:18	310
5:30	245

Philippians
2:7	27, 207, 209
2:8	135

Colossians
1:16	115
3:1–2	217
3:14	95

Hebrews
9:10	237
9:11–28	237

James
1:7	238, 455

1 John
4:8	224, 493
4:16	453

1 Timothy
2:5	447

Revelation
20	443

Index of Names

Aaron, 120
Abraham, Patriarch, 119, 144, 154, 323
Abraham von Franckenberg, 482
Acarie, Barbe (Marie de l'Incarnation), Blessed, 11-12, 20, 22-23, 36, 43-49, 51-52, 94, 185, 187, 189, 240-41, 274, 294
Acarie, Pierre, 43-44
Adam, 93, 99, 112, 114, 115, 201-2, 208, 211, 216, 358
Adolphus, Gustavus, King of Sweden, 472
Alacoque, Margaret Mary, Saint, 244
Alexander VII, Pope, 100, 454
Alfonso of Madrid, 54
Alvarez, Balthasar, SJ, 274, 288, 416
Alvarez de Paz, 288
Amelote, Denis, 241-44
Ana de Jesus, 11, 187
Ana de San Bartolome 11, 187
Anacreon, 481
André, Archbishop of Bruges, 101
Angela of Foligno, Saint, 17, 44, 109, 143, 292
Angélique de Saint-Jean, 322
Annas, 444
Aquaviva, Claudio, SJ, 274, 290, 415-17
Aristotle, 103, 120, 290
Arnauld, Angelique, 100
Arnauld Family: Angélique, Agnès, Antoine, 322-24

Augustine, Bishop of Hippo, Saint, 16, 27, 38, 43, 50, 53, 92, 109, 114, 116-17, 119-21, 145, 152, 184, 198-99, 208, 229, 247, 282, 287, 296, 321, 323, 437, 441-42, 447-48, 475, 484, 498, 510
Avellino, Andrea, 412

Bagger, Matthew, 486
Baker, Augustine (David), 350-80, 383, 455
Baker, Richard, 350
Balthasar, Hans Urs von, 156, 181, 485
Bañez, Domingo, 93
Barbanson, Constantin, de, 75-76, 356, 475, 509
Barlow, Rudisind, 354
Barrett, John, 355
Bascio, Matteo da, 10, 410
Basil, Saint, 126, 160
Beatrice Avite, Sister, 433
Beaucousin, Richard, 45, 47, 94, 185
Beaufort, Joseph de, 306-8
Beaumont, Joseph, 381
Behemoth, 284
Bellarmine, Robert, SJ, Saint, 189, 289, 413-14, 417
Benet of Canfield (William Fitch), 17, 22, 26-27, 36, 44-45, 50-74, 94, 107, 135, 182, 185, 287, 350, 364, 508-10
Bergamo, Mino, 23, 24, 102, 118-20

573

Berinzaga, Isabella Cristina, 17, 20, 185, 414–423, 427, 508
Bernard of Clairvaux, Saint, 14, 16, 26–28, 53, 109, 114, 121, 126, 154, 184, 229, 288, 296, 385, 452, 475, 484, 501
Bernardino de Laredo, 19
Bernini, Gian Lorenzo, 391–92, 411
Bertonasco, Marc F., 384
Bérulle, Claude de, 184
Bérulle, Pierre de, Cardinal, 9, 11–12, 17–18, 21–22, 26–27, 46–48, 94, 96, 100, 135, 181–253, 273–74, 279, 294, 298, 310, 322, 365, 384, 391, 417–18, 438, 478, 498
Binet, Etienne, SJ, 48, 417
Blomeveen, Peter, 18, 478
Blommestijn, Hein, 297
Blosius, Ludovicus, (Louis de Blois), 36–43, 288, 349–50, 356, 475, 483–84
Boehme, Jacob, 482–84, 492, 494
Böhm, Maria M., 486
Bona, Giovanni, Cardinal, 434, 454–58
Bonaventure, Saint, 17, 53, 72–73, 109, 122, 126, 182, 184, 192, 197–98, 288, 290, 368, 413–14, 475, 483, 487
Borgia, Francis, SJ, 290
Borri, Giuseppe Francesco, 433
Borromeo, Charles, Saint, 94, 154, 412, 415, 430–31, 451
Borromeo, Frederico, 430
Bossuet, Jacques-Bénigne, 27
Brandsma, Titus, 511–12
Bremond, Henri, 8, 14, 20–22, 27–28, 43, 49–50, 90, 124, 181–82, 192, 214, 242–43, 273, 276, 283, 285, 308–9
Breton, Stanislas, 282
Brossier, Marthe, 52, 185
Brousse, Jacques, 50–51
Brûlart, Madame, 125
Bruneau, Marie-Florine, 313
Burgoing, François, 244

Caiaphas, 444
Calvin, John, 4, 36, 91, 158
Camus, Jean-Pierre, Bishop of Belley, 21, 124–25, 129, 156
Canisius, Peter, SJ, Saint, (Peter Kanis), 19, 472–74
Careri, Giovanni, 473
Carraud, Vincent, 182
Carre, Thomas (Miles Pinkney), 381
Cassian, John, Saint, 369, 452
Castellio, Sebastian, 19
Caterina de'Ricci, O.P., Saint, 431–32, 439
Catherine de'Medici, 4–5
Catherine of Bologna, Saint, 17
Catherine of Genoa, Saint, 17, 20, 22, 26, 54, 109, 136, 151, 210, 247, 295, 409
Catherine of Jesus, 240
Catherine of Siena, Saint, 17, 20, 109, 129, 247, 309, 430–31, 434, 437, 446–48
Celse-Bénigne de Chantal, 97
Certeau, Michel de, 24–25, 283, 285, 288, 474
Chantal, Christophe, Baron de, 95
Charles I, King of England, 190, 233, 381
Charles V, Emperor, 4, 37, 409, 507
Charles IX, King of France, 4–5
Charles-Emmanuel I, Duke of Savoy, 93
Charlotte de Hardy de Sancy, 46
Châtel, Jean, 274
Chéron, Jean, 286–87, 289–90, 292
Chrysostom, John, Saint, 126
Claesinne van Nieuwlants, 508
Claire d'Abra de Raconis, 46
Clare of Assisi, Saint, 157, 433–34
Clark, J. P. H., 355
Claude de Granier, Bishop, 93–94
Clement VII, Pope, 409
Clement VIII, Pope, 93, 414, 417
Clement IX, Pope, 454
Cochois, Paul, 191, 238
Cognet, Louis, 17, 21–22, 52, 239–40, 243
Condren, Charles de, 187, 241–43, 245
Copernicus, Nicolaus, 192, 212
Cortona, Margaret of, Saint, 443

Coton, Pierre, SJ, 10, 45, 274
Courtade, François, 21
Cousins, Anthony D., 385
Cowley, Abraham, 396
Crashaw, Richard, 380–96
Crashaw, William, 381
Cressy, Serenus, 355, 357–58, 361, 365
Croce, Benedetto, 473
Czepko, Daniel, 485

Dagens, Jean, 184–85, 232
Deblaere, Albert, SJ, 512–13
Denis de la Mère de Dieu, 189–90
Denis de Marquement, Bishop, 98
Denis the Carthusian, 288, 484
Deschamps Brothers, 323
Diefendorf, Barbara, 45
Diego de Jesús, 474
Dionysius (St Denis or Denys), 16–17, 22, 25, 48, 53, 55, 58, 63, 109, 112, 122, 151, 156, 184, 188, 194, 198–99, 237–38, 247–48, 282, 285, 288, 290, 310, 388–89, 475, 477, 487, 493
Dominic de St Albert, 11
Donatien de Saint-Nicholas, 295
Donne, John, 382
Drexel, Jerome, 473
Dubois-Quinard, Madeleine, 74–75
Duke of Alba, 507
Duke of Parma, 507
Duns Scotus, 111, 206
Dupuy, Michel, 227
Duval, André, 43, 46–48, 187, 189

Eck, John, 38
Eckhart, Meister, 19, 26, 38–40, 42, 54, 66, 121, 198, 203, 249–51, 304, 439, 484–85, 489, 491–97, 500–503, 506
Egan, Harvey J., 487
Eire, Carlos, 507
Eliot, T. S., 382
Elisabeth of Schönau, Saint, 17
Emery, Kent, 53–54
Emrich, Wilhelm, 479
Eriugena, John Scottus, 494
Esther van de Vate, 510
Eudes, John, Saint, 12, 187, 243–45

Eugenio d'Ors, 473
Eve, 99

Farel, William, 4, 36
Favre, Antoine, 93
Fénelon, François, 14, 25, 27, 305–7
Ferdinand II, King, 472
Ferdinand III, King, 472
Ficino, Marsilio, 16, 54
Fitch, William. *See* Benet of Canfield
Fontana, Paolo, 433, 435
Fortunatus, Venantius, 390
Foster, Marc, 473
Francis de Boisy, 91–92
Francis de Sales, Saint, 13–14, 17, 21, 23–24, 27, 39–40, 46, 48, 50, 55, 69, 75, 89–163, 185, 191–92, 197, 208, 225, 240, 243, 245, 247, 273–74, 285, 287–88, 312, 314, 329, 381, 384, 413–14, 457
Francis of Assisi, Saint, 10, 72–73, 129, 136, 144, 157, 289, 435, 487
Francis I, King of France, 4
Francis II, King of France, 4
Francis Xavier, Saint, 134, 290
Francisco de Osuna, 19
Freeman, Lawrence, 369
Frémyot, André, Archbishop of Bourges, 158–59

Gabriel, Angel, 227
Gaffney, James, 359
Gagliardi, Achille, SJ, 20, 26, 54, 185, 204, 247, 249, 414–29, 437, 458, 508
Galileo Galilei, 411
Gallemant, Jacques, 46–47, 187, 189
Gallus, Thomas, 17, 368, 487
Galluzzi, Maria Domitilla, O.F.M. Cap, 432–36
Gascoine, Dame Catherine, 353
Gaston d'Orleans, 242
Gaston de Renty, 23
Gelen, Victor, 483
Génébrard, Gilbert, 91
Gerson, Jean, 14, 42, 109, 247, 287–88, 290, 475
Gertrude of Hackeborn, Saint, 483
Gertrude of Helfta, Saint, 17

Gertrude the Great, Saint, 18, 38, 109
Gioia, Mario, 414–15, 423
Giustiniani, Paolo (Tommaso), Blessed, 410, 452–54, 458
Gnädinger, Louise, 488
Gorceix, Bernard, 481, 486–487
Gorday, Peter, 14, 27
Goulu, Jean de Saint François, 16
Gracián, Jéronimo, 62, 508
Gregory XIII, Pope, 188, 410
Gregory of Nyssa, Saint, 129
Gregory the Great, Pope and Saint, 38, 152, 229, 278, 475
Gualtier, René, 20, 23, 46
Gueullette, Jean-Marie, 19, 54
Guibert, Joseph de, 274, 473
Guise, Duke of, 5

Haas, Alois M., 484–85
Hadewijch of Antwerp, 302
Harbison, Robert, 473
Harphius. *See* Herp, Hendrik
Haye, George de la, 312, 317
Henrietta Maria, Queen of England, 190–91, 233, 235, 381
Henry, Duke of Guise, 5–6
Henry III, King of France, 5–6
Henry IV, King of France, (Henry of Navarre), 5–6, 8, 10, 43–46, 52, 74, 185, 190, 274
Hense, Elisabeth, 511, 513
Herbert, George, 382
Herman, Nicholas. *See* Lawrence of the Resurrection
Hermes Trismegistus, 198
Herp, Hendrik (Harphius), 17–18, 26, 39–40, 53, 55, 75, 109, 156, 185, 247, 288, 295–97, 299–300, 349, 352, 367, 416, 475–78, 484, 509, 513
Hildegard of Bingen, Saint, 17
Hilton, Walter, 54, 349
Horgan, Maurya, xv
Howells, Edward, 199–200, 207, 229–30
Hugh of Balma, 483
Hugh of Saint-Victor, 17
Huijben, Jacques, 16–17, 20
Hull, Francis, 353

Hulst, M., 21
Huxley, Aldous, 76

Ignatius Loyola, SJ, Saint, 10, 15, 37, 58, 104, 144, 155, 234, 273–74, 276, 285, 290, 314, 361, 410, 416, 472, 475
Innocent X, Pope, 322
Innocent XII, Pope, 25
Irenaeus of Lyons, Saint, 182
Isaac, Patriarch, 144, 154, 323
Isaiah, 196

Jacapone de Todi, 390
Jacob, Patriarch, 119, 323
Jan van Leeuwen, 292
Jane de Chantal, Saint, 14, 21, 23, 90–100, 107, 121, 125, 143, 156–63, 312, 414
Jane de Sales, Sister of Francis, 96
Jansen, Cornelius, Bishop, 321–22, 411
Jean de Bernières-Lovigny, 23
Jean de Quintanadoine de Brétigny, 19, 46–47
Jean de Saint-Samson, 11, 22, 294–304
Jean Desmarets de Saint-Sorlin, 77
Jeanne des Anges, 283–84
Job, 143
John of Avila, Saint, 144
John of Damascus, Saint, 126, 364
John of the Cross, Saint, 15, 20, 24–25, 46, 54, 71, 76, 109, 121, 134, 146, 155, 157, 162, 232, 247, 249, 286, 288, 291–93, 295, 298, 302, 305, 307, 319, 349–50, 356, 369, 417, 474–75, 480, 483, 493, 509
John the Apostle, 146, 433
John the Evangelist of Bois-le-Duc, 509
Jones, Leander, 352
Jordaens, Willem, 17
Joseph, Saint, 160, 284
Joseph de Jésus, 295
Joseph of Cupertino, Saint, 429, 451
Juan de Jesús-Maria, 288
Judas, 443
Julian of Norwich, Saint, 54, 349

Kalkbrenner, Gerard, 18

Index of Names

Kanis, Peter. *See* Canisius, Peter
Knowles, David, 356–57, 359, 369
Knox, Ronald, xiv
Kobelski, Paul, xv
Krumenacker, Yves, 22, 239
Kuchar, Gary, 384, 388

Lalemant, Jerome, 313
Lallemant, Louis, SJ, 273, 275–83, 285–86
Landspergius, Johannes, 351
Lawrence of Brindisi, Saint, 51
Lawrence of Paris, 74–75, 509
Lawrence of the Resurrection (Nicholas Herman), 273, 294, 304–8
Lazarus, 234
Le Brun, Jacques, 21, 27, 239
Lefèvre d'Étaples, Jacques, 17
Leo X, Pope, 409
Leonardi, Claudio, 430
Lessius, Leonard, 189, 289–90
Liuima, Antanas, 110
Loarte, Gaspar, SJ, 437
Loher, Dirk, 18
Louis IX, King of France, Saint, 154
Louis XIII, King of France, 6, 100, 190, 242
Louis XIV, King of France, 6–8, 411, 507–8, 510, 514–15
Louis de Blois. *See* Blosius, Ludovicus
Louis de la Puente, 20
Louis de la Rivière, 45
Louis of Guise, Cardinal, 6
Low, Anthony, 383
Luca, Giuseppe de, 411
Luis de Granada, 20, 295, 297
Luis de la Puente (DuPont), 274, 484
Luis de Léon, 15
Luis de Molina, SJ, 92, 322
Louise de Charmoisy, 99, 103
Louise de Marillac, Saint, 13
Luther, Martin, 19, 38, 91

Madame Guyon, Jeanne, 23, 25, 135, 252, 309
Madeleine de St. Joseph, 240–41
Maggi, Armando, 438, 442, 447
Main, John, 369

Malaval, François, 22–23
Marguerite de Gondi, 46
Marguerite (Margot) of Valois, 5
Maria Domitilla Galluzzi, O.F. M., Cap., 432–36
Maria Maddalena de'Pazzi, O. Carm., Saint, 430–31, 436–51
Maria of St. Teresa. *See* Petyt, Maria
Marie de l'Incarnation (Marie Martin née Guyart), Saint, 13, 23, 27, 273, 308–21, 513
Marie de l'Incarnation (Barbe Acarie). *See* Acarie, Barbe
Marie de'Medici, 6
Marie des Vallées, 243
Marie de Tudert, 46
Marina de Escobar, 484
Martha and Mary, friends of Jesus, 58, 76, 138, 226, 240
Martin, Claude, 309–10, 312–15, 318, 321
Martino, Leander de Saint, 361
Martz, Louis, 385, 394
Marxer, François, 22
Mary, Mother of Jesus (Blessed Virgin), 24, 47, 60, 94, 129, 139, 146, 160, 188–89, 196, 199, 202, 215–16, 218–22, 226–28, 232, 234, 238, 244–45, 279, 317, 319–20, 383, 387, 390, 418, 437, 442, 444, 448–50, 500–501, 511
Mary Magdalene, Saint, 191, 193, 226, 232–35, 238, 384, 391
Matter, E. Ann, 430
Mazarin, Cardinal, 6, 10, 472
Mazzocco, Mariel, 486, 504
McCann, Justin, 355
McGinn, Patricia Ferris, xv
Mechthild of Hackeborn, Saint, 17, 18, 109, 483
Mercurian, Everard, SJ, 274, 289–90, 415–16
Merici, Angela, Saint, 12, 97
Merton, Thomas, 356
Michael of St. Augustine, 510–13
Michelangelo Buonarotti, 409
Michel de Marillac, 23, 46
Michon, Hélèn, 102, 110

Milcent, Paul, 244
Molien, Auguste, 191, 204
Molinos, Miguel, xiv, 418
Mommaers, Paul, SJ, 512
Morales, Sebastiano, 415
More, Dame Gertrude, 353, 356, 358, 374–80
Morice, Jacques, 18
Moses, 220, 323, 458
Myers, Chris, xv

Neri, Philip, Saint, 12, 47, 96, 134, 188, 409, 431, 451
Nicolás de Jesús-María, 474, 484
Nicholas of Cusa, 54, 212, 494
Nicholas van Esch, 474
Nimrod, Count Sylvius of Würtemberg-Oels, 482

Olier, Jean-Jacques, 12, 27, 135, 187, 245–53, 322, 496
O'Malley, John, 410
Opitz, Martin, 479
Optat de Veghel, 54
Orcibal, Jean, 53
Origen, 229, 475
Orpheus, 198
Oury, Guy, 310

Pallotta, Cardinal, 381
Pascal, Blaise, 273, 321–32
Paul, Apostle, 94, 115, 136, 139, 158, 163, 210, 220, 245, 478
Paul III, Pope, 10, 37, 410, 430
Paul IV, Pope, 410, 430
Paul V, Pope, 93, 431
Pelagia, Saint, 433
Pelagini, 433
Peltrie, Madame de la, 318
Percy, Dame Mary, 417
Père Joseph de Paris, François Leclerc du Tremblay (the Grey Eminence), 76
Péronne-Marie de Châtel, Mother, 159
Peter, Apostle, 94
Peter de Alcántara, 20, 72, 290
Petersson, Robert T., 391
Petrarch, 481

Petyt, Maria (Maria of St. Teresa), 507, 509–15
Philip II, King of Spain, 4–5, 507
Philip III, King of Spain, 507
Philothea, 103–7, 122–23, 154
Pico della Mirandola, 192, 475
Pierre de Ronsard, 295
Pietro de Ribandeneyra, SJ, 20
Pilate, 330, 443–44
Pinkney, Miles. *See* Carre, Thomas
Pius IV, Pope, 410
Pius V, Pope, 410–11
Pius IX, Pope, 100
Plato, 27, 136
Poiret, Pierre, 307, 418
Poli, Tullio, 121–22
Ponticus, Evagrius, 486
Porete, Marguerite, 14, 26–27, 65, 427, 453, 514
Portoghesi, Paolo, 473
Possevino, Antonio, SJ, 92
Power, Edmund, 365
Pozzi, Giovanni, 438
Praz, Mario, 391, 473
Preckler, Fernando Guillen, 214, 218
Prichard, Leander, 354
Pseudo-Tauler, 26, 43, 295, 349, 416, 437, 483
Puccini, Vincenzo, 437

Rambuss, Richard, 380, 385
Ramus, Peter, 52
Rancé, Armand Jean de, 10
Ravier, André, 101
Raviolo, Isabelle, 484
Raymond of Capua, Saint, 20
Raymond of Saint Bernard, 310, 317
Revol, Antoine, Bishop, 295
Richard of Saint-Victor, 17, 53, 60, 137–38, 279–82
Richelieu, Cardinal, Armand-Jean du Plessis, 6–10, 76–77, 100, 190–91, 284, 472
Rigoleuc, Jean, SJ, 275
Rodriguez, Alonso, 274
Rolle, Richard, 299, 349
Romuald, Saint, 452
Ruusbroec, Jan van, 17–18, 26, 38–42,

53, 55, 68, 73, 156, 247, 278, 288, 295, 300, 416, 475-77, 483-84, 494, 508-9, 513, 515

Saint-Cyran, abbé, Duvergier de Hauranne, 322-23
Salin, Dominique, 24, 275, 277, 279-80
Sandaeus (van der Sandt), Maximilian, 474-79, 483-84, 504
Sauer, Laurent (Laurentius Surius), 18-19, 38, 40, 53
Savonarola, Girolamo, 431, 483
Scheffler, Johannes, (Angelus Silesius), 481-507, 509
Schmidt, Joseph, 485
Scholem, Gershom, 15
Scicluna, Ivan, 299
Scupoli, Lorenzo, 20, 54, 92, 412
Segel, Harold B., 479
Seripando, Girolamo, 410
Silesius, Angelus. *See* Scheffler, Johannes
Sixtus V, Pope, 410
Solomon, King, 119, 488, 498
Spee, Friedrich von Langenfeld, SJ, 479-81
Stagel, Elizabeth, 157
Stroppa, Sabrina, 455
Suarez, Francisco, SJ, 289, 292
Surin, Jean-Joseph, SJ, 273, 275, 282-93, 305
Surius, Laurentius. *See* Sauer, Laurent
Suso, Henry, Blessed, 18, 38-40, 54, 157, 289, 416, 475, 484, 500
Sweeney, Norbert, 355

Tapié, Victor, 473
Tauler, John, 18-19, 38-40, 54, 76, 109, 156, 247, 252, 283, 288, 302, 349, 352, 367, 437, 456, 474-77, 483-84, 489, 492, 496-97, 505-6, 509
Teresa of Avila, Saint, 10-12, 15, 19-20, 24-25, 44, 46-47, 54, 62, 66, 73, 108-9, 121, 126, 130, 132-38, 155-57, 162, 187, 232, 247, 274, 281-82, 286-93, 295, 305, 307,
310-11, 313-14, 349-350, 356, 361, 364, 369, 381, 384, 391-94, 411, 416-17, 435, 475, 508-10, 513-14
Teresa of Calcutta, Saint, 144
Teyssonier, Marie de Valence, 45
Thérèse de Lisieux, Saint, 317
Thibault, Philippe, 294
Thiene, Gaetano de, Saint, 412
Thomas à Kempis, 295
Thomas Aquinas, Saint, 185, 199, 206, 277, 390
Thompson-Uberuaga, William, 181, 184, 244
Tomás de Jesús, 288, 293, 484, 509
Traherne, Thomas, 380
Traversari, Ambrogio, 16
Tronson, Louis, 246

Urban VIII, Pope, 181, 190-91, 411
Ursula, Saint, 12

Van Es, Nicholas, 18
Van Wevele, Godeverd, 19
Vaughn, Henry, 388
Vervoort, Frans, 295
Vetö, Miklos, 197, 232
Vincent de Paul, Saint, 9, 13, 100, 187, 239, 245, 322
Virgil, 481
Vitelleschi, Muzio, SJ, 275, 283, 285

Warren, Austin, 388, 390-91
Watkin, E. I., 357, 380
Weigel, Valentin, 483
Wekking, Ben, 356
Weld-Blundel, Benedict, 356
William of Ockham, 495
William of St. Thierry, 121, 452, 484
Wiseman, Nicholas, Cardinal, 38
Wölfflin, Heinrich, 473
Wright, Wendy M, 95, 99, 157

Yeats, William Butler, xv
Young, R. V., 383, 395

Zwingli, Ulrich 4

Index of Subjects

Abandonment, 41, 139, 144, 146, 158, 235, 251, 279, 288, 298, 311–14, 324, 372, 440, 512
Abasement, 182, 186, 190, 197, 206–10, 215–16, 218–19, 221, 225, 231, 234, 249, 426. *See also* Annihilation
Abnegation, 26, 45, 57, 61, 207, 251, 291, 424
Absence of God, 371, 379, 436, 438. *See also* Presence
Absolutism, xiii–iv, 3, 7, 184
Absorption. *See* Ecstasy and Rapture
Abstract School of Mysticism, 21–22, 63
Abstraction, 58, 62–63, 229, 290, 360, 362–63, 365, 375–76, 454, 476, 512
Abyss, 40–42, 65, 67, 194, 232, 242, 251, 302, 310, 312, 319, 328, 419, 429, 434, 439, 451, 456
Act of Supremacy, 347
Action. *See* Contemplation and Action
Acts, Direct and Reflex, 133, 145, 427
Adhesion and Inhesion, 58, 122, 137, 182–83, 193, 210, 222–26, 229, 231, 236, 240, 243, 324, 371, 375, 475, 498
Admiration, 59–60, 137, 139, 198, 218, 224, 227, 413, 429, 458
Adoration, 140, 181, 183, 189, 197, 202, 204, 212, 214–18, 227–29, 231–32, 236, 238, 241–45, 248, 308, 310–11, 366, 390
Affections, 73, 104, 115, 117–18, 131, 135, 138, 141, 148–49, 151, 159, 227, 279, 296, 331, 366, 368, 376–77, 379, 457, 478, 515
Affectivity, 28, 65, 122–23, 131, 244, 282, 291, 358, 382–84, 435, 480, 533. *See also* Love
Affliction. *See* Dereliction, Desolation, Affliction
Allegory, 102, 289
Alumbrados, xiv, 15, 353, 360
Analogy, 102–3
Anagogy, 454–55, 457
Angels, 50, 112, 193, 201, 212, 219, 222, 226, 233, 237–38, 246, 284, 315, 367, 387, 392–94, 418, 446, 487–89, 506–7, 514. Guardian angels, 160, 312
Annihilation, 17, 22, 26–27, 41–42, 45, 49, 62, 65–66, 73, 75, 134–35, 147, 160, 162, 182, 185–86, 189–90, 194, 206–12, 216–19, 221, 224–25, 229, 239–41, 243, 245, 247–53, 275, 277, 279, 311–12, 318–19, 363, 367, 395, 416, 418–29, 431, 438, 453–54, 456, 478, 490, 503, 508–10, 512–14, 533–34. Exinanition, 27, 182, 190, 206, 209, 211, 226. Passive and Active Annihilation, 51–52, 61, 67–71
Annunciation, 219, 221, 309, 442
Anthropology (General), 39–40, 68, 110, 113–23, 127–28,

580

Index of Subjects 581

132-34, 137, 145, 155, 158, 203-4, 211, 217, 250-51, 282, 297, 302, 308, 316, 320, 325-32, 358, 367, 370-71, 425-26, 456, 478, 489, 495-96, 512. Intellect and Will, 367-71, 422, 425, 428, 456, 478, 496, 514, 533. *See also* Love and Knowledge. Three Powers of Soul (Memory, Understanding, Will), 39, 58, 117, 122, 133-34, 147, 162, 320, 358, 376, 514. *See also Apex mentis*; Center of the Soul; Image of God

Apex mentis/affectus (Summit, Supreme Point of Soul), 49-50, 53, 69, 108-9, 119-22, 127, 136, 143, 146-47, 153, 162, 204, 244, 307, 358, 367-68, 371, 377, 428, 456, 477, 535. Dungeon of Spirit, 143, 288. *See also* Center of the Soul

Appetites, 112, 117-19, 144

Apocalypticism, 6, 8, 409

Apophatic Theology, 49, 108, 120, 194, 248, 282, 297, 308, 310, 384, 388-89, 442-43, 455, 493-94. *See also* Ineffability, and Nothingness

Apostolic Life and Service, xiv, 12-13, 44-45, 96-97, 188, 227-28, 232, 234, 238, 246, 274, 276, 281, 292, 313, 317, 321, 409, 415, 479

Aridity. *See* Dereliction, Desolation, Affliction

Ascension of Christ, 217, 219, 225, 230, 235, 445, 448-50

Ascent of the Soul, 108, 128, 130-39, 148, 364, 381, 391, 413-14, 425, 450, 487

Asceticism, 38, 41, 51, 246-47, 251, 285-86, 289, 324-25, 362, 395, 412, 452, 454, 511, 533

Aspirations and Ejaculations, 41, 58-59, 137, 154, 296-98, 306, 351, 357, 365-70, 383, 455-58, 533. *See also* Prayer

Assumption of the Virgin, 219, 384, 391, 450

Audition. *See* Locution

Augustinian Order, 410

Augustinianism, 114, 145, 152, 184, 208, 247, 282, 321-24, 441-42, 498

Authority, 3, 95, 107, 193, 198, 236, 274, 326, 350, 360, 364, 374, 411, 455, 475

Bakerism, 349, 354-55, 374-75

Baroque, 50, 191, 365, 380, 382-83, 389, 391, 394, 411, 472-73, 479-81, 485, 490, 506

Beatitude, 105, 200, 286, 310, 312, 325, 327, 446, 478, 500-501, 503-6

Beauty, 112-13, 117, 120, 131, 138, 145, 203, 252, 300, 302, 310, 362, 371, 388-89, 391, 419

Being (*ens/esse*), 67, 195, 199-201, 206-7, 210, 213, 219, 224, 238, 242-43, 288, 293, 299, 301, 310, 332, 367, 372, 438-39, 449, 478, 492-93, 505, 511, 513. *See also* Existence

Benedictine Order, 11, 32-39, 44, 313, 348-51, 353-54, 361, 372-80

Benevolence. *See* Love

Betrothal, Mystical (*See* Marriage, Mystical)

Bible, 25, 57, 93, 102, 109-10, 119-20, 126, 278, 323-24, 328, 348, 433, 441, 504. *See also* Song of Songs

Birth of the Word/ Jesus in the Soul, 42, 95, 215, 280, 432, 484, 492, 500-501. Three Births of the Word, 196, 205, 219-20

Bishop, Office of, 8-10, 13, 93-94, 153, 188, 349, 412

Blood of Christ, 280, 309-10, 314, 329, 383, 385-87, 390, 434-35, 439-41, 447-49, 499. *See also* Passion

Body, 58, 67, 133, 203, 217, 246, 317, 326, 328, 352, 362, 376, 390, 424, 435. *See also* Anthropology

Bourbon, House of, 4

Bridal Mysticism. *See* Mystical Marriage

Call (Divine), 359-61, 375-76, 378. *See also* Inspirations

Camaldolese Order, 410

Capuchin Order, 10, 51-52, 74-77, 185, 410, 432-36, 509

Caritas. See Love; Theological virtues

Carmelite Order, 10–11, 44–48, 187, 189, 240, 286, 293–95, 305, 391, 393, 436, 508–15
Carthusian Order, 18–20, 38, 45, 47–48, 474
Catholic Reform. *See* Reform
Center and Depth (*fundus, fond*) of the Soul, 75–76, 204, 250–51, 281, 292–93, 302, 318–20, 358, 369, 371, 377, 386, 476, 493, 512, 514. *See also Apex mentis*
Certainty, Religious, 282, 323, 327, 458
Chalcedon, Council of, 205
Chastity, 105, 138, 314, 499
Christ and Christology, 22, 56, 71–73, 104, 114–15, 121, 130, 139, 144, 147, 151, 188–90, 195, 197–98, 200, 206, 223–26, 303, 314–15, 330–31, 365, 386–90, 395, 414, 426, 428, 441, 443, 488, 498–501, 506, 512. Absolute Predestination of Christ, 111–12, 206. Christocentricism, 25–26, 41, 45, 181–82, 184–86, 190–91, 218, 240, 384, 423. Humanity of Christ, 22, 26, 49, 65, 72, 187, 205, 237, 240, 280, 364–65, 377, 418, 441, 498. Hypostatic Union, 205, 211, 213, 215, 218, 231–32, 311, 315, 477
Church and Ecclesiology, 10, 124, 141–42, 190, 237–38, 248, 303, 408, 432–33. *See also* Mystical Body
Cistercian Order, 10–11, 100, 310, 322, 452, 454
Coincidence of Opposites, 52, 60, 66, 71, 328, 388. Law of Opposites, 208, 215
Commandments, 140–41, 147–49, 227
Commendam System, 9–10
Communication, 112, 118, 121–22, 127–28, 161, 196–97, 214, 223, 230, 232, 236, 238, 248, 252, 283, 287, 292–93, 328, 330, 368, 438–41, 451
Compassion, 90–92, 129, 135, 146, 221, 390, 423
Complaceny. *See* Love
Concordats, 3–4

Confession, 104–5, 288, 324, 332, 377–78. *See also* Penance
Confraternities, 6, 9, 409
Conscience, 161, 277
Consciousness (Mystical), 48, 139, 143, 296, 300, 513
Consolation, 72, 106, 108, 143, 146, 162, 204, 232–33, 247, 279, 307, 318, 425. *See also* Delights
Contemplation, 38, 58–61, 63, 126, 130–33, 151, 156, 198, 217, 227–30, 236, 244, 274, 280–82, 296–97, 301, 328, 350–51, 353–54, 357–61, 366–72, 377, 416, 420–22, 448, 452, 455, 457–58, 475–76, 488, 502, 512. Active and Passive Contemplation, 350–52, 354, 356, 363, 366–77, 456. Acquired and Infused Contemplation, 287, 366. Contemplation and Action, 12–13, 55–74, 76, 138–39, 154, 191, 226–27, 229, 240, 245–46, 276, 278, 312–13, 316–17, 361, 425, 457
Contrition, 104
Conversion, 36, 50–51, 91, 127–28, 136, 233–34, 276–77, 309–10, 313, 319, 321, 323, 330, 350, 373, 375, 381–82, 389, 391, 394, 426, 452, 478, 482, 486, 490, 507
Cooperation with Grace, 116, 122, 128–29, 136–37, 158, 210, 223, 279. *See also* Grace
Co-Redemption, 450
Counsels, 140–41, 147, 361
Counter-Reformation, xiii, 10, 55, 74, 322, 357, 411, 472, 482
Creation and Creature, 26, 66, 71, 132, 183, 195, 197–203, 207–8, 211, 213, 217, 223, 226, 241–42, 246, 250–51, 301, 326, 389, 413, 418, 424, 439, 450–51, 480, 484, 491, 494–97, 501, 505, 533
Cross and Theology of Cross, 48, 51, 73, 98, 108–9, 135, 155, 209, 213, 216–17, 221, 225, 230, 234, 241, 248–49, 321, 324, 329–31, 365, 371, 379, 387, 390, 423, 425, 430, 432–33, 435, 445, 498. *See also* Blood of Christ; Passion

Dark Night, 146, 245, 293, 318, 426, 510
Daughters of Charity/Ladies of Charity, 13
De Auxiliis Controversy, 93, 411
Deification, 70, 132, 194, 197, 216, 223, 228-30, 232, 236, 245, 247, 252, 282, 303, 331, 363, 420, 424-26, 428-29, 456, 476-77, 504-8, 515
Delight, 96, 106, 118, 122, 129-30, 132, 158, 272, 300-302, 306, 379, 395, 425, 493, 500
Denudation, 63, 65, 376. *See also* Nakedness
Depth (*fond/fundus*) of the Soul. *See* Center of the Soul
Dereliction, Desolation, Affliction, 41, 75, 135, 142-44, 146-47, 162, 281, 291-92, 304-5, 310-11, 314-15, 318, 351, 357, 359, 362, 371, 437, 513-14. *See also* Suffering
Desire. *See* Love.
Detachment, 96, 99, 245, 291, 448, 450, 497, 502-3. *See also* Releasement
Devil, 50, 52, 96, 138-39, 185-86, 190, 193, 215, 240, 243, 278, 283-84, 290-91, 317-18, 395, 412-13, 430, 435, 437, 442, 445, 448
Dévots, 8, 12, 23, 45-46
Devotion and Devout Life, 104-7, 110, 115, 123-24, 126, 131, 138, 144, 152, 154, 184, 186, 191, 197, 205, 219, 228, 233, 244, 246, 275, 279, 282, 329, 365, 381, 383, 431, 434, 481, 490, 498
Dialectic, 15, 221, 326, 388-89
Dionysianism, 16-17, 22, 25, 48, 55, 112, 151, 156, 184, 194, 198-99, 237-38, 247-48, 250, 282, 285, 290, 372, 388-89, 455, 476, 487. Affective Dionysianism, 53, 58-59, 63, 122, 368, 487, 533
Direction, Spiritual, 45-46, 90, 95-100, 142, 145, 153, 157, 185, 242, 246, 294, 305, 315, 317, 349, 351-54, 357-58, 375, 378, 415, 508, 510-11
Discernment of Spirits (*discretio spirituum*), 44, 277-78, 281, 285, 290-91, 370, 430, 454

Discourse, Mystical. *See* Language, Mystical.
Divestment and Dispossession, 57, 419, 424-25, 427, 429
Divinization. *See* Deification
Doceur, 102, 158
Docta ignorantia, 456
Dominican Order, 93, 411, 431-32, 436

Ecstasy and Rapture, 43-44, 46, 48-51, 76, 97, 105, 108, 134-35, 137-40, 142, 151, 183, 221, 232, 278, 281-82, 290-92, 296, 299, 303, 307, 311-12, 314, 320, 351, 370, 374, 380, 391-92, 394, 411, 422, 424-25, 428-30, 431-33, 436-43, 446, 448, 450, 455-56, 458, 513, 534. *See also* Suspension
Edict of Nantes, 6-7, 52, 74, 185
Education, 8, 10, 12, 91, 274, 306, 349, 381, 472, 482, 509
Eighty Years' War, 507-8
Ein einges Ein (Simple One), 484, 492, 504
Election, 104, 186
Elevation, 59, 61, 75, 183, 191, 208, 215, 219, 229, 235, 298, 310, 368, 515
Emanation. *See* Flow/Flowing
Enjoyment. *See* Beatitude; Joy
Enlightenment. *See* Illumination
Epektasis, 129, 135, 293
Epiphany, 385, 388-89
Erotic Language. *See* Mystical Marriage; Sexuality and Sexual Language
Essence, 42, 187, 194, 196, 205, 211, 214, 247, 293, 304, 351, 419-20, 424, 456, 515. *See also* Being
Estrangement. *See* Dereliction, Desolation, Affliction
Eternity, 200, 212, 215, 310, 319, 324, 387, 489, 492-97, 500, 505
Eucharist, Sacrament of, 41, 49-50, 128, 132, 162, 195-97, 215, 230, 235-37, 239, 241, 280, 287-88, 303, 311-12, 322-23, 390, 413, 434, 448

Evil, 145, 202, 327, 330. *See also* Sin
Examination of Conscience, 288, 349, 376
Exemplar, 40, 182, 196, 214, 232, 236, 242, 384. *See also* Ideas (Divine)
Existence in God (Virtual Pre-existence), 26, 40, 439–40, 449, 484, 495–96, 503, 506
Experience (Mystical), 24–25, 44, 48, 59, 156, 159, 186, 232, 277, 285, 289–90, 293, 295, 299, 309–12, 314–17, 320–21, 323–24, 330, 332, 349–53, 357, 375, 414–15, 422, 433, 441, 452, 513–14, 534

Faith, 68–72, 91, 103, 119–20, 127–28, 146, 160–61, 193, 195, 209, 217, 230, 239, 247, 249–50, 252, 276, 278–79, 287, 293, 307, 319, 323, 327–28, 364, 366–67, 369–72, 377, 420, 422, 458, 511, 534
Fall of Humanity, 114–15, 158, 201–2, 208, 242, 326, 358, 360
Father (God the), 138, 146, 198, 216, 220, 238, 329–30, 439, 442, 444, 447, 449, 499
Fear, 57, 92, 153
Fecundity, 196, 199, 213, 215, 301–2
Felicity. *See* Beatitude
Flow and Flowing (*fluxus, flus*), 41–42, 63–64, 120, 134–35, 151, 197–98, 201–3, 209, 299, 301–2, 363, 491–92, 497, 515
France, Kingdom of, 3–7, 9, 76–77, 190, 274, 284, 409, 411, 472
Franciscan Order, 50, 73, 487. *See also* Capuchin Order
Freedom (and Free will), 16, 28, 56, 71, 91–93, 112, 114–15, 132, 141, 154, 158, 161, 201, 210, 232, 244, 249, 289, 321–22, 324, 411, 438. Freedom of Spirit (*libertas spiritus*), 96, 116, 158–59, 249, 275, 279, 359–60, 365, 379
French School of Mysticism, 20–22, 239
Friend of God, 113, 128, 149, 151, 293, 298, 362, 420–21

Friendship, Spiritual, 95–99, 107, 118, 156–57, 159, 233, 240, 415

Gallicanism, 3, 7
God, Nature of, 40, 42, 55, 62–71, 92–93, 111–13, 126–27, 161, 187, 194–201, 250, 280, 285, 300–301, 310–11, 323–24, 327–28, 351, 364, 367–68, 376–77, 413–14, 419, 438–41, 453–54, 488, 491–94, 503. God/Godhead Distinction, 301, 484, 488, 491–93, 497, 499, 504–5. Theocentric Mysticism, 181–82, 185, 190–92, 195, 240, 242
Good and Goodness, 49, 90, 92, 102, 112–15, 117–18, 120, 127–29, 131, 136, 138, 140, 142, 148–49, 151, 153–54, 201–2, 208, 217, 224, 238, 246, 288, 292, 309–10, 320, 324, 327, 330, 332, 362, 367, 385, 390, 422, 424, 435, 440, 448, 456, 501
Gospel, 140, 323–24, 534
Grace, 41, 48, 55, 75, 92–93, 95, 98, 103, 105, 109, 115–16, 123, 141, 151–52, 156, 158, 161, 181, 185, 188, 193, 201, 203, 207–12, 215, 217–18, 220, 222–24, 226, 228–29, 231, 233–36, 238, 243, 245, 278–80, 287–90, 292–93, 307–8, 319, 321–25, 328, 331, 358–59, 366, 368, 372, 411, 415, 417–19, 424, 451, 477–78, 487, 505, 512, 515. Overflow of Grace into Senses, 377
Grandeur, 191, 194, 203, 206, 208–9, 216, 224, 312, 512
Ground (*grunt*) of the Soul. *See* Center of the Soul
Guise, House of, 4–5

Habit, 281–82, 292, 368
Handbooks, Spiritual, 38, 52, 55, 75, 105, 243, 274, 285–86, 430, 437, 454
Happiness. *See* Beatitude
Hapsburg, House of, 4, 6–7, 190, 409, 471–72, 482, 507, 510
Heart, 24, 89, 96–97, 106, 110, 113–14, 118, 121–23, 125, 130, 140, 142–43, 147, 149, 152–53, 155, 158–59, 160,

Index of Subjects 585

183, 213, 216, 221, 244-45, 276-77, 286, 293, 305, 311, 314-15, 326-27, 378-80, 385-87, 392, 394-95, 419, 437, 441, 448, 481, 488, 497, 499.
Exchange of Hearts, 311, 315, 437
Heaven, 41, 91, 133, 144, 162, 194-212, 214, 218, 220, 224-25, 229, 233-34, 303, 307, 363, 385, 387, 391, 393, 396, 422, 426, 451, 489, 505
Hell, 144, 201, 208, 284-85, 292-93, 305, 307, 318-19, 384, 514
Heresy, 91, 93, 322, 348, 353, 430, 497, 505
Hermit Life (Anchorite), 142, 354, 452, 454, 510
Hiddenness of God. *See* Apophatic Theology
Hierarchy, 25, 188, 212, 222, 233, 235, 237-38, 247, 487. *See also* Dionysianism
Holy League (Catholic League), 5-6, 8, 10, 43-44, 52, 74, 185, 274
Holy Office, 411
Holy Roman Empire, 3, 408, 471-72
Holy Spirit, 49, 152-53, 161, 199, 215, 220, 223, 231, 238, 243-44, 248-49, 275-78, 280, 285, 287, 296-98, 320, 349, 358-60, 366, 369-70, 375, 445, 478, 488, 499, 515. Seven Gifts of the Holy Spirit, 152-53, 278, 290, 458
Huguenots, 4-7, 46, 74, 185
Humanism, 54, 74, 90-91, 192, 203, 452, 479. Devout Humanism, 90
Humility, 47, 49, 60, 98, 105, 124, 142, 158, 214-15, 218-19, 227-28, 248-49, 279, 290-91, 315, 325, 362, 365, 371, 418-19, 427, 432, 487, 513

Ideas (Divine), 40, 196, 450, 495
Idleness. *See* Quiet/Quietism
Illapsum, 252, 476
Illumination, 49-50, 59, 65, 68, 94, 119-20, 138, 142, 187, 241, 275, 277-79, 281-82, 304, 310, 312, 316, 359, 361, 418-21, 439, 452, 490. *See also* Light

Illuminism, 353, 359-60
Image of God (*imago dei*), 39-40, 110, 112, 114, 150, 203-4, 228, 414, 495, 497. *See also* Anthropology.
Image, 62, 64-65, 67-68, 72, 185, 360, 365-70, 376-77, 383, 389, 391, 393, 506, 514
Imagination, 41, 147, 160, 230, 282, 292, 306, 311, 317, 328, 353, 364-65, 417
Imitation of Christ, 57-58, 143, 148, 190, 210, 216-17, 222-23, 226, 231, 241, 248, 280, 321, 329, 379, 427, 430, 445, 457, 498-99, 511-12. *See also* Christ and Christology
Incarnation, 112, 181-82, 188, 195-97, 199, 202, 206-7, 211-18, 220-21, 224, 226-27, 233, 236, 243, 279, 301, 311, 385, 447, 498, 506. *See also* Christ and Christology
Inclination, 114-17, 119, 127, 138, 140, 293, 358. *See also* Propensities
Incomprehensibuluty. *See* Ineffability
Index of Forbidden Books, 36, 66, 418
Indifference (Holy), 89, 98-99, 116, 122, 134, 140, 143-48, 155, 158, 279, 291, 307, 360, 424-25
Indwelling, 183, 196, 287, 371-72
Inebriation (Mystical), 132, 390, 393
Ineffability, 55, 67, 195-97, 205, 297, 299-301, 315, 324, 367, 369-70, 385, 419, 440, 453, 455, 476, 487, 491
Infinity, 23-24, 58, 112-13, 181, 183, 201, 209, 212-13, 242, 245, 252, 293, 296, 301-3, 310, 328, 332, 367, 372, 377, 440, 442, 498
Inquisition, 7. Roman Inquisition, 417, 430, 433. Spanish Inquisition, xiv, 15
Inspirations, 108, 119, 138, 141-42, 147, 161, 228, 235, 278, 353, 357, 359-62
Institutiones spirituales (Pseudo-Tauler), 18-19, 38, 43, 54, 295, 416, 437, 475, 484
Intellect. *See* Anthropology; Knowledge

Intention, 56–57, 60, 71, 105, 112, 140, 154, 276, 289, 292, 359–60, 362, 364, 375, 426

Interiority (Prayer and Practice), xiv, 23–24, 53, 59, 61, 123, 161, 214, 218, 227, 244, 274, 276, 278–79, 286–87, 306, 357, 372, 395, 416, 503

Introspection, Interiorization, Introversion, 23–24, 27–28, 375–76, 512

Inworking (*inactio*), 60, 62, 370, 476, 478

Itinerary (Mystical), 53–55, 124–25, 149–50, 276, 285–86, 296, 313–14, 497–98. Threefold Itinerary (beginners, advanced, perfect/ purgation, illumination, union), 61, 77, 280, 314, 357, 364, 366, 418, 454

Jansenism, 3, 16, 28, 93, 100, 114, 158, 244, 288, 321–26, 331, 510

Jesuit Order, 8, 10, 19–20, 37, 45, 93, 184, 186, 273–77, 283, 285, 290, 322–24, 349, 374–76, 378, 410–11, 414–29, 436, 472–81, 490

Joy, 214, 218, 225, 242, 287, 304, 312, 323, 364, 379, 392, 395, 423, 447, 500. *See also* Delight

Judaism, 213, 323

Justice, 140, 142, 319, 483

Justification. *See* Salvation

Kingdom of God/Christ, 243, 245, 312, 506, 509

Knowledge, 59, 66, 75, 112, 119–21, 138, 192–93, 198, 203, 229, 249, 278, 281, 287, 291, 294, 312, 326–27, 362, 368, 372, 384, 419, 422–23, 425, 475, 487, 489, 533. *See also* Love and Knowledge

Laity, 11, 23, 44, 98, 102, 283, 288, 305, 410, 412

Language (Mystical), 24–25, 101–2, 251, 288–90, 299, 388–89, 394–95, 436–43, 453, 474–79, 532–33

Law, 59, 322–23, 389

Liberty. *See* Freedom

Light, 68–69, 315, 320, 353, 369–71, 376, 386–89, 393–94, 419, 421, 424–25, 438, 506

Liquefaction, 363, 393, 422, 506

Liturgy, 188, 213, 245, 294, 347–48, 378, 381, 384, 390–91, 433, 440–41, 454

Locutions (Mystical), 290, 359, 395

Love and Desire, 49–51, 63–64, 74–75, 89–90, 105, 107–11, 113–18, 123–24, 126, 128–29, 135–36, 145–46, 148–51, 153–55, 194, 199, 209–10, 221, 224–26, 232–35, 238, 241, 245, 251, 253, 277, 279, 281, 288, 293, 296–99, 302–4, 308, 315, 325, 330–31, 362, 371, 377, 379, 384, 386, 391–94, 415, 420–22, 424–26, 432, 439, 443, 451–52, 453–54, 476–77, 480–81, 492–93, 501–2, 515, 533–43. Affective and Effective Love, 108, 152, 279 (= Love of Conformity and Love of Submission, 130, 140–48). Love and Knowledge, 41, 131, 193–94, 298, 316, 329, 367, 487, 502, 533. Love of Complacency and Love of Benevolence, 107, 113, 126–30. Working and Enjoying Love, 64, 68, 70. Pure Love, 27–28, 45, 75, 99, 115, 124, 151, 285, 315, 319, 321, 427, 454, 534. *Ludus amoris* (Game of Love), 296, 300, 304. Uniting and Separating Love, 224–26. Love of Desire and Love of Friendship, 362. *Ordo caritatis* (Ordering of Love), 362, 501

Lutheranism, xiii, 37, 347, 472, 482

Lucifer. *See* Devil

Marriage (Mystical), 64, 138, 149, 161, 282, 288, 291–93, 298–309, 311, 315–16, 391–92, 431, 435–36, 445–48, 450, 484, 498–501, 512, 514

Mary and Mariology, 60, 91–92, 94, 129, 139, 146, 150, 188, 196, 215–16, 218–22, 226, 279, 317, 319–20, 383, 387, 393, 418, 442, 444–45, 450, 500–501, 511–12

Mary Magdalene, 226, 232–35, 391

Martyrdom, 138, 158–60, 311, 349, 374, 386, 391–92, 394, 423, 427, 511
Mediator and Mediating, 181–82, 237, 239, 328, 419, 425
Meditation, 41, 58, 61, 75, 104–6, 125, 130–33, 159–61, 191, 219, 233–34, 237, 244, 246, 274, 280, 297, 314, 328–29, 349, 351, 353–54, 357, 364–65, 368, 375, 378, 383, 385, 390, 418, 420, 433, 437, 442, 444, 480, 485. *See also* Prayer
Melancholy, 124, 153, 284, 293
Merit, 56, 116, 286, 292, 359–60, 427
Microcosm, 113, 198, 203, 328. *See also* Anthropology
Miracle, 203, 234, 284, 326, 328, 387, 415, 441, 445
Missions, 8–9, 91, 93, 233, 239, 243–44, 246, 283, 313, 318, 349, 354
Monarchy, 112–13, 117, 348
Monophysitism, 190, 205
Mors mystica (Mystical Death), 139, 146–47, 252, 282, 303–4, 311, 316, 363, 392, 394–95, 457
Mortification, 57–58, 159, 161, 211, 247, 279, 290, 298, 315, 357, 360, 362, 365, 371, 373, 375–76
Music and Musical Instruments, 382, 419, 480, 498
Mysticism (Concept of), xiii-xv, 8, 10, 14–28, 197, 236, 246, 273, 275, 295, 308, 356–57, 363, 373, 429, 433, 474–79, 508, 532–34. *See also* Consciousness (Mystical)
Mystical Body of Christ, 72, 221, 245, 330–31, 499
Mystical Theology (*theologia mystica*), 25, 62, 76, 102, 106–7, 126–27, 130, 156, 194, 289, 297, 363, 454–57, 475–76, 533

Nakedness (Mystical), 41, 64, 98–99, 148, 249–51, 303, 390, 428
Name of Jesus, 385–86, 440, 481, 489
Nativity of Christ, 215, 385–87, 434, 437, 440, 498
Negation. *See* Apophatic Theology
Neoplatonism, 54, 75, 197, 212, 456

Nestorianism, 190, 205
Nobility of the Robe, 23, 95, 184
Northern European Medieval Mysticism, 16–19, 22, 38, 42–43, 53–54, 75, 109, 120–21, 185, 215, 247, 250, 295, 300, 349, 416, 448, 474–75, 484, 490, 492, 502, 506, 509
Nothingness, 60, 65–66, 69–70, 182, 188, 200, 202–3, 207–11, 213, 221–22, 241–43, 247–49, 279, 296, 312, 315, 329, 362, 372, 418–22, 425–26, 428, 434, 438, 450–51, 452–53, 489, 494, 499, 506, 512–14. *See also* Annihilation

Obedience, 96–97, 105, 141–42, 158, 206, 278, 325, 329, 361, 375–76, 378–79, 427, 432, 434
One (God as), 300–301, 488, 492–93. *See also* Ein einges Ein
Oratory, Congregation of, 12, 44, 96–97, 187–88, 213, 228, 238–39, 241–44, 409
Orthodoxy, 15, 205

Pantheism, 489–90, 494, 496
Papacy and Popes, 3, 7–8, 322, 325, 347–48, 408–11, 416–17, 430, 454
Paradise. *See* Heaven
Participation, 200, 209–10, 223, 225, 230, 247, 249, 253, 284, 331, 372, 419–20, 422, 424, 439, 449
Passion of Christ, 41, 49, 54, 56–58, 62, 65, 67, 71–73, 129, 135, 146, 151, 155, 215–16, 226, 277, 329, 364–65, 384, 389–90, 415, 423, 431, 433, 435, 442–45, 498, 526. *See also* Cross
Passions and Emotions, 117–18, 319, 331, 357, 360, 362, 412, 475
Passivity, 48, 59, 61–64, 66–67, 76, 148, 156, 162, 214, 238, 251–52, 296, 369–70, 393, 420, 427–28, 455–56, 512. *See also* Quiet/Quietism
Patience, 358–60, 365, 377
Peace, 360, 362, 464, 480, 504
Peace of Augsburg, 471
Penance, Acts of, 145, 159, 233, 315, 389, 412, 430, 435

Perfection, 53, 67, 69, 72, 75, 95, 113–14, 124–25, 128, 131, 141, 148–49, 237–38, 243, 247, 250, 276, 278, 281, 285, 289, 291, 293, 359, 371, 417, 424, 426, 457, 474, 511
Philosophy, 66, 152, 192, 224, 323, 325–26, 367, 478
Piety, 57, 191, 309, 325, 382, 434, 482
Platonism, 196
Pneumatology. *See* Holy Spirit
Poetry (Mystical), 285, 295, 298, 378, 380–96, 479–81, 484–87
Possession, Diabolical. *See* Devil
Poverty, 105, 248–49, 279, 294, 320, 330, 439, 502–3
Prayer (General), 59, 95, 97, 101, 104, 108, 122–23, 125–27, 130–39, 145, 157, 160–63, 217, 238, 242, 250–51, 275, 280–82, 288, 291–92, 314, 354, 362, 364–72, 373, 375–76, 413, 476, 504, 511–15. Affective Prayer, 364, 376. Mental Prayer, 125, 294, 351, 364. Prayer of Forced Acts of the Will, 357, 365–66, 368–69. Prayer of the Heart, 160. Prayer of Quiet or Repose, 108, 133–34, 149, 512–13. Prayer of Presence of God, 291. Prayer of Silence, 274, 281, 291, 504. Prayer of Simple Regard, 157, 159, 162, 244, 281. Prayer of Recollection, 19, 108, 132–33, 149, 291, 314. Prayer of Union, 108, 134, 136, 231, 292, 297, 513
Pre-Quietism, xv, 51
Preaching, 93–95, 101, 110, 142, 153, 232, 284, 484
Predestination, 50, 91–92, 116, 158, 321–22, 326–27, 384
Presence of God (and Christ), 48–49, 65, 69, 75, 122, 132–34, 136, 160–63, 183, 230, 233, 235, 239, 280–81, 286–88, 300, 305–8, 379, 421–22, 436, 458, 532. *See also* Consciousness (Mystical)
Pride, 210, 326, 331, 425
Priesthood, 235–39, 242–43, 248, 412
Principle, 198, 213, 231, 253, 276, 301–2, 325, 363, 425

Probabilism, 322
Propensities, 358, 375–76
Prophecy, 201, 292, 430–31, 433, 510
Protestantism, 4–7, 18, 74, 90–91, 93, 187, 219, 278, 283, 305, 321, 347–48, 381–82, 410–13, 418, 420, 471, 473, 482–83, 485, 490, 507, 509–11.
Providence, 89, 111–13, 115, 147, 154, 198, 202, 208, 212, 314, 424
Pure Love. *See* Love
Purgation, 104, 315, 319–20, 369, 387, 418, 423, 512
Purgatory, 292–93, 319
Purity, 277, 314, 320, 365, 439–40, 448–49, 450–51, 502

Quakers, 15, 360–61
Quiet/Quietude, 76–77, 151, 291, 427
Quietism, xiv–xv, 3, 7, 15, 28, 37, 66–67, 69, 106, 144, 151, 295, 305, 307, 321, 412, 420, 454

Rapture. *See* Ecstasy and Rapture
Reading (Spiritual), 285–89, 294, 310, 351, 358–59, 372, 412, 483–84
Reason, 69, 72, 118–20, 192–93, 233, 277, 287, 297, 325–27
Reciprocity of God and Human, 128–29, 136, 490–97
Recollection, 41, 122, 161, 276–77, 286–87, 291, 306, 360. *See also* Prayer
Rectitude, Rule of, 52–53, 56
Recusants, xiv, 347–49, 373–74
Redemption. *See* Salvation
Reduction, 52, 71, 135
Reform, Catholic, 8–13, 18, 36–37, 44, 90, 94–96, 183, 187, 409–10, 416, 431
Reformation, xiii, 3, 7, 19, 37, 408–9, 458
Relation, 113, 182, 199–201, 206, 208, 210, 218, 220, 229–30, 237, 244, 429, 440, 495
Releasement, 251, 448, 451, 497, 503
Remembrance, 68–71, 369
Renaissance, 52, 101, 153, 409, 413, 473, 485
Renunciation. *See* Abandonment

Repentence, 145, 391. *See also* Penance
Resignation, 61, 92, 120, 143-158, 366, 377, 513. *Resignatio ad infernum*, or the Impossible Supposition, 28, 144, 285, 478-79
Resurrection of Jesus, 148, 213, 215, 217-18, 225, 234, 248, 499
Revelations, 76, 246, 313, 324, 438, 440-42, 445, 448, 451
Rhetoric, 52, 101, 184, 233, 414, 485

Sacraments, 104-5, 125, 128, 228, 236, 276, 412
Sacrifice, 241-43, 248-49
Saint Bartholomew's Day Massacre, 5
Salvation, 25, 91-92, 110, 112, 115, 144-45, 151, 154, 158, 185, 192, 228, 235, 237, 243, 249, 305, 326-29, 331, 412, 425, 435, 444-45, 494, 500. Salvation History, 201-3, 211-13, 325, 499
Satan. *See* Devil
Scholasticism, 25, 39, 76, 101, 103-4, 115-16, 153, 289-90, 358, 367, 429, 452, 455-56, 475-76, 533
School of Love, 193-94, 234
Science of the Saints, 25, 110, 161, 192-93, 277, 297, 533
Self-knowledge, 115, 198, 296, 326, 328, 421
Semi-Pelagian, 116
Seminaries, 8, 12, 244-45, 412
Servitude, 47, 183, 188, 214, 218, 222. Vow of Servitude, 188-90, 205, 208, 222, 240, 245
Sexuality and Sexual Language, 60, 64, 288, 383, 394-95, 499-500
Silence and Stillness, 59, 154, 161, 195, 294, 328, 362, 417, 433, 438, 444, 503-4, 512
Simplicity, 49, 62, 162, 227, 289, 308, 360, 375-76
Sin, 41, 67, 92, 103-4, 106, 114-15, 142, 145, 149, 206-11, 216, 225, 241, 249, 279, 296, 302, 309, 319, 323-24, 328-31, 394, 420-21, 426, 439, 446, 453, 533
Sleep of the Faculties. *See* Suspension

Solitude, 65, 122, 357, 360-61, 379, 456
Son (God the), 112, 161, 193, 196, 198, 201, 216, 218, 222, 231, 237, 242, 244, 320, 432, 488, 498. *See also* Christ and Christology; Word
Song of Songs, 57, 60, 64, 91, 101, 107, 129, 149-50, 161, 298-99, 311, 313, 315, 379, 446, 481, 488, 499. *See also* Bible
Soul. *See* Anthropology
Spiritual Exercises and Practices (General), 48, 56-57, 63, 104-6, 148, 154, 208, 287, 306, 322, 361, 365, 423. Ignatian *Spiritual Exercises*, 58, 104, 186, 418
Spirituality, 188, 219, 222, 232, 247, 274, 276, 278, 349, 374, 411-13. Spiritual Combat, 20, 412-13
States (*états*) of Jesus, 26, 183, 199, 204-5, 210-11, 213-15, 217-19, 236, 238, 240, 243, 279, 498. State and Action, 214-15, 224
Stigmata, 44, 136, 435, 437
Subsistence, 189, 196, 200, 202-3, 205, 207, 210, 220, 224, 230, 236. *See also* Incarnation
Suffering, 58, 72-73, 129, 209, 279, 284, 288, 292-93, 296, 315, 320, 371, 376, 390, 423, 426, 431-32, 435, 444-45, 512. *See also* Dereliction, Desololation, Affliction
Sulpician Congregation, 21, 246
Summit of the Soul. *See Apex mentis*
Supereminent, 55, 61, 63, 67, 69, 71-73, 107, 250, 299-300, 377, 477, 509
Superessential, 17, 26, 39-40, 55, 238, 250, 299-300, 456, 508, 512
Supernatural, 63, 68, 115, 152-53, 287, 289-90, 327, 353, 370, 374, 388, 419
Supposit, 303. *See also* Anthropology
Suspension of the Faculties, 133, 137, 232, 282, 297, 320. *See also* Ecstasy and Rapture
Sweetness, 102, 112-13, 115, 128, 132, 138, 145, 147, 152, 162, 277, 304, 316, 380, 388, 392, 394-95, 435, 501. *See also Doceur*

Symbols (Mystical). General, 476–77. Particular: (1) Bed (Song of Songs 1:15), 299. (2) Bee, 102, 131, 386. (3) Book, 483, 495. (4) Castle, 289, 514. (5) Circle and Point, 493, 502. (6) Cloud and Darkness, 193, 351, 369, 371. (7) Crystal, 250, 496. (8) Desert, 491. (9) Embrace (Song of Songs 2:6), 209, 301, 303–4. (10) Flower, 102. (11) Fountain, 491. (12) Heated Iron, 483. (13) Kiss of Mouth (Song of Songs 1:1), 118, 127, 288, 299, 315, 394. (14) Log and Fire, 252. (15) Mirror, 422, 432, 443, 447, 511, 515. (16) Mother and Baby, 129, 133, 136, 147. (17) Ocean/Sea, 40, 56, 163, 194, 232, 247, 288, 297, 310, 314, 367, 377–78, 492, 504. (18) Sphere, 197–98. (19) Statue, 134. (20) Sun, 55–56, 58, 61, 193, 212, 227, 386, 422. (21) Tree, 136. (22) Whale, 377. (23) Wine and Wine-Cellar (Song of Songs 2:4), 499. (24) Wound of Love (Song of Songs 4:9), 60, 135–36, 159, 216, 232, 311, 379, 386, 390, 392–94, 481, 497, 499–500. *See also* Transverberation

Synderesis, 121. *See also* Anthropology

Taste, 59–60, 65, 282, 293, 372, 422
Tears, 323, 390–91, 457
Temptation, 41, 50, 96, 105–6, 121, 157, 215, 284, 319, 426–27
Theatine Order, 20, 409, 412
Theological Virtues (Faith, Hope, Charity), 75, 107, 117, 120, 122, 127–28, 146, 152, 161, 307, 370, 425, 456, 479, 501, 515
Thirty Years' War, 6, 8, 190, 305, 411, 472, 479, 507
Thomism, 120, 185, 206, 278
Touches (Mystical), 48, 60, 134, 161, 293, 311, 316, 512
Transfiguration, 217
Transformation (Mystical), 41, 59, 64, 122, 140, 232, 250, 252, 297, 304, 363, 387, 394, 422, 424–25, 426, 435, 453, 485, 501. *See also* Deification
Translations (Role of), 16–20, 38, 45–47, 103, 274, 356, 374, 417
Transverberation, 135–36, 392, 394–95. *See also* Symbols. Wound of Love
Treaty of Westphalia, 472, 507
Trent (Council) and Post-Tridentine Catholicism, xiii, 3, 7–8, 12–13, 98, 190, 219, 238, 244, 410–12, 430, 472
Trinity, 40, 42, 49, 94, 112, 153, 181–82, 188, 194–202, 208, 213–14, 219–20, 228, 230–31, 244, 252, 283, 287, 293, 301, 310, 312–13, 315–16, 331, 420, 439–40, 446–48, 450, 456, 477, 480, 494, 511. Divine Persons, 195, 198–200, 213, 315
Truth, 119, 193, 208, 210, 299, 306, 326–27, 331, 366–67, 458

Understanding. *See* Knowledge
Universe (Uni-diverse), 110–11, 148, 198, 301, 328, 388, 414
Union (Mystical), 22, 26, 28, 39–42, 45, 55, 61, 64–65, 68, 70, 72, 74, 90, 96, 107–8, 114, 118, 121–23, 127–28, 136–39, 147–53, 155, 158–59, 161–63, 182–83, 185, 194, 197, 214, 225, 229–32, 235, 244–45, 247, 250, 276, 280, 282–83, 291–93, 296–300, 302–8, 310–13, 316, 318–19, 321, 330–32, 356, 361, 363–64, 367–72, 375–79, 418–25, 428, 435, 440, 448–49, 455–56, 458, 477, 487–89, 504–8, 511, 513–14. Active and Passive Union, 363. Essential Union, 476–77, 508. Union without Distinction or Difference, 42, 247, 250–52, 300, 302–4, 422, 477, 484, 503–5, 515. Hypostatic Union. *See* Christ and Christology
Unity, 194–95, 198, 205, 213, 231, 236, 360, 367, 477. *See also* One (God as)
Unknowing. *See* Apophatic Theology, *Docta ignorantia*, Ineffability
Ursuline Order, 12–13, 44, 97, 308–14, 316–17

Valois, House of, 4
Victim (State of), 237, 241–43, 245, 248, 318, 320–21, 392
Victorines, 16–17
Virginity, 450, 491, 500, 502
Virtue, 57–58, 70, 75, 102, 105, 109, 123, 125, 138, 144, 148, 152–53, 156, 158–60, 162, 245, 247–49, 276, 288, 291, 296, 306, 359, 362, 365, 413, 419–20, 425–26, 428, 450, 479, 483. Little Virtues, 96, 105, 129, 154, 158. *See also* Theological Virtues
Vision and Visions, 47–48, 63, 94, 247, 282, 284, 290, 299, 309, 351, 359, 370, 430, 432–34, 510, 512. Beatific Vision, 220–21, 312–13, 315, 317, 363, 436
Visitandine Order, 13, 95–99, 101, 107, 156–60, 244
Vows, 96–98, 189, 218, 245, 294, 315, 392

Wars of Religion, xiv, 4–7, 9, 37, 44, 184, 187, 273–74, 308, 408
Western Mysticism, xiv, 349, 374–75, 485, 532

Will of God, 26, 53–74, 108, 140–48, 206, 319, 329, 366, 424, 427–28, 504. Essential Will, 53, 62–71. Signified, or Expressed Will and Will of Good Pleasure, 108, 140–48, 158, 278. Universal Salvific Will, 28, 92–93, 108, 112, 116, 141, 158
Wisdom, 49, 74, 142, 153, 162, 278, 296, 326, 389, 483, 487–88, 493, 495, 502
Witch Craze, 479
Women (Role of), 13, 17, 23, 97–99, 109, 240, 299, 308–9, 353–54, 412, 414–23, 429–31
Word of God (i.e., Son), 182, 198, 202, 301, 310, 316, 319, 365, 387, 436, 438–40, 442, 446–48, 451, 506. *See also* Christ and Christology
Works and Working (Divine and Human), 70, 352, 362, 372, 478, 515
Wound of Love. *See* Symbols. Wound of Love

Zeal, 12, 150–51, 228, 327

www.ingramcontent.com/pod-product-compliance
Lightning Source LLC
Chambersburg PA
CBHW030102010526
44116CB00005B/57